STEPHEN KING:
UNCOLLECTED, UNPUBLISHED

REVISED AND EXPANDED
FOURTH EDITION

By

ROCKY WOOD

Overlook Connection Press

- 2012 -

Stephen King: Uncollected, Unpublished
Revised & Expanded Fourth Edition

© 2012, Rocky Wood

'Dino' and Chapter 71 from 'Sword in the Darkness', by Stephen King are both copyright, Stephen King, and are printed with permission.

Dust Jacket illustration © 2012 by Erik Wilson

This edition is published and © 2012 by
Overlook Connection Press
PO Box 1934
Hiram, Georgia 30141

www.overlookconnection.com
overlookcn@aol.com

First Hard Cover Edition
ISBN-13: 978-1-892950-59-8

First Trade Paperback edition
ISBN-13: 978-1-892950-96-3

This book is a work of non-fiction, with fiction excerpts. All rights reserved. No part of this book may be reproduced or transmitted in any form or by any means, electronic or mechanical, without the written permission of the Publisher, Overlook Connection Press.

TABLE OF CONTENTS

Introduction	9
Linking Stephen King's Realities	23
The Lost and Hidden Works	51
Variations and Versions in King's Fiction	67
The Uncollected, and The Unpublished	85
The Aftermath	85
American Vampire	90
An Evening at God's	93
Before the Play	94
The Blue Air Compressor	99
But Only Darkness Loves Me and I Hate Mondays	101
The Cannibals	103
Cat's Eye and General	106
Charlie	110
Children of the Corn – Unproduced Screenplay	113
Chinga and Molly	117
Comb Dump	125
The Crate	128
Creepshow Screenplay	132
Cujo - Unproduced Screenplay	140
Dave's Rag: Jumper and Rush Call	143
The Dead Zone - Unproduced Screenplay	145
Desperation - Screenplay	150
Dolan's Cadillac – Unproduced Screenplay	153
The Drum Stories	155
The Dune	160
For the Birds	162
The Furnace	162
George D X McArdle	163
The Glass Floor	169
Golden Years	172
Heroes for Hope Starring the X-Men	176
Herman Wouk is Still Alive	178
I Was A Teenage Grave Robber / In A Half-World of Terror	179

Jhonathan and the Witchs	184
Keyholes	185
The Killer	187
The King Family and the Wicked Witch	189
The Leprechaun	193
The Little Green God of Agony	195
Man With A Belly	197
Maximum Overdrive	199
Mile 81	203
Mobius	206
Morality	207
The New Lieutenant's Rap	208
The Night of the Tiger	212
Night Shift - Unproduced Screenplay	215
The Old Dude's Ticker	221
People, Places and Things	225
Pet Sematary Screenplay	231
The Plant	234
The Poems	240
'Dino' by Stephen King	250
Premium Harmony	252
The Reploids	253
Rose Red Screenplay	258
The Shining Screenplays	263
The Shotgunners	269
Skybar	272
Slade	273
Sleepwalkers	278
Something Wicked This Way Comes	283
Sorry, Right Number – The Shooting Script	286
Squad D	288
The Stand Screenplays	292
The Star Invaders	299
Stories from Journals	302
Stories Swallowed by Monsters	311
Sword in the Darkness	327
Chapter 71 of 'Sword in the Darkness' by Stephen King	336
Throttle	355

Untitled (The Huffman Story)	359
Untitled Screenplay (Radio Station)	364
Ur	366
Weeds	369
Wimsey	372
End Notes	377
Appendix: The Works of Stephen King	383
Acknowledgements and About the Author	395

INTRODUCTION

Stephen King has published over 200 works of fiction (*this is made up of 42 published novels, 109 collected short works of fiction and 54 uncollected short works of fiction*), many of those in a number of versions. Research shows there are at least another 54 pieces of King's fiction that have *not* been published - of these many may be accessed by researchers, either in King's papers held at his alma mater, the University of Maine at Orono, or through other means.

Yet, most King fans are unaware that some King fiction has been published, but not collected in a mainstream King volume such as *Night Shift*. There are 54 'uncollected' works, some of which were only discovered in recent years. For instance, research for this very book uncovered a previously unknown poem, published nearly two decades ago!

This book concentrates on these two categories – 54 *unpublished*[1] and 54 *uncollected* works of fiction. These 108 novels, shorter works of fiction, screenplays and poems are combined in the 71 sub-chapters following the initial four major chapters, which cover King's Realities, the Lost and Hidden Works, and the Variations and Versions in his fiction. A previously unpublished and lengthy chapter from a King novel, and a poem that has only appeared once before, are also included.

The general King readership can easily access over 150 individual Works of Fiction, in some 42 published novels[2], with 109 shorter works compiled in his nine collections[3].

It is at that point that the average reader will find it much harder to access the next level of works - those published but *not* appearing in a King collection, many appearing in obscure magazines, limited editions, anthologies or exclusively as eBooks[4]. With time (and often money) these items can be found, and read.

Next there are the three levels of *unpublished* works. The first circulate within the King community in photocopied or electronic form. The second level includes those in the Stephen Edwin King papers, which have been deposited at the Special Collections Unit of the Raymond H Fogler Library of the University of Maine in Orono. The public may read most of these papers, including some unpublished works. However, the most important, including early novel length manuscripts, require written permission from Stephen King before the staff may provide access. King kindly provided that permission to the author of this book.

The third level of unpublished works cannot be accessed at all. Many of them are unknown in any detail outside King's closest inner circle. A detailed discussion of these, the most closeted of King's works, see Chapter 3, *The Lost and Hidden Works*.

Among the works reviewed in this book are those well known to King fans (*The Glass Floor*) and those previously unknown (*Dino*). There are poems and screenplays - some of the screenplays are original concepts (*Sleepwalkers*), one adapts the work of another author (Bradbury's *Something Wicked This Way Comes*) and others adapt King's own work. Many have been produced for the screen.

A number of novels are also reviewed, including *Sword in the Darkness*. There are also quite a number of incomplete works, ranging from novels (*George D X McArdle*) to screenplays (one about a haunted radio station) and short stories (*Comb Dump, Keyholes*).

Research for this book resulted in the 'rediscovery' of two works previously unknown in the King community. One, a screenplay intended for *The X-Files* and titled *Molly*, was kindly provided to the author by a super-collector, Chris Cavalier and is reviewed in the chapter *Chinga and Molly*. The second was a poem, *Dino*. Amazingly, this poem was published in an obscure university literary magazine in 1994 but had been missed by all King researchers before its appearance on eBay in March 2004. The story behind its rediscovery appears in *The Poems* chapter.

In many ways it was the very mass of King's output that drove the need for this book. Starting from scratch it can take quite some time just to compile an accurate list of all King's fiction. Even working from such a list[5] it will take collectors and experts years to access a copy of each available work.

In total there are at least 274 separately identifiable King story-lines, including other fictional works such as poems and screenplays. When all the differing versions, variations and titles of these works are taken into account there are about 387 different variants!

King is famed (and sometimes brick-batted) for the sheer volume of words he produces. Many novels are in the high hundreds of pages, with three exceeding 900, epics in their own right. One mythology (*The Dark Tower*) is barely contained in seven novels, two novellas, a raft of related tales and a series of *Marvel* comic extensions.

The volume, breadth and quality of King's work, along with its exposure through screen presentations on film and television has created enormous interest in his fiction, from simple fans of his story telling to students reading entertaining stories as they learn the art of creative writing, to researchers and academics.

This review is not meant to be any form of biography or criticism. King's background and life *are* central to his fiction, with many works being disguised autobiography, but the intention here is to provide information about King's obscure works, not his life. There are a number of quality books and articles in the area of biography and literary criticism to which the reader may refer.

The key to understanding the King phenomenon however, is not the vast magnitude of his output, or even its quality but, in fact, the emotional impact he has upon his readers and viewers.

Describing the joy that Stephen King brings his 'consumers' (King's stories are consumed by the users of most major media, not just the written ones) is both simple and complex. At its core is a powerful or entertaining story, well written by a master craftsman. Surrounding the core is a series of layers that are either unique or are uniquely combined in the one entertainment phenomenon.

King is at once an innovator while being deeply grounded in the traditions of his chosen genres as well as literature in general. He is both a modern man and a self-confessed 'hick', living in a semi-rural backwater State (admittedly a delightful one), eschewing the normal 'rewards' of celebrity, including the obligatory lifestyle in Hollywood or New York.

As an innovator, King was the first major author to release a significant story on the Internet (*Riding the Bullet*), the result of which was the near melting-down of servers worldwide. He was the also first major author to serialize a significant story on the Internet (*The Plant*), even using a relatively successful 'honor' system for payment. He also reinvented the serial novel (*The Green Mile*) and has both written original works and adapted his own for the screen.

He has an astounding ability to tell a tale, describe a scene in glorious detail and deliver a fully formed character. He takes us into the minds and motivations of characters (especially children). When he chose to do this with women (*Dolores Claiborne*, *Rose Madder* and *Gerald's Game*) King proved the breadth of his skill. Even Cujo's thought processes were laid out for the reader.

King's work appeals to young and old, male and female and to people of very diverse cultural backgrounds, this despite the very American nature of his writing. An adult King reader, perhaps wary of some themes, can ease a younger person into the body of work through such stories as *Eyes of the Dragon*, *The Girl Who Loved Tom Gordon* or *The Body*. If horror gives you nightmares read his fantasy, if fantasy bores you there are many mainstream stories of power (*The New Yorker* short stories, *Hearts in Atlantis*). If science fiction appeals to you King even offers a number of stories in that genre, although they are often not his strongest.

For reasons perhaps of snobbery King's prolific nature is used by some as a weapon of criticism against his overall body of work and his position in the literary firmament. Yet, one of the advantages of this great selection of tales is surely that it contains something for any reader, except perhaps those who proclaim only dense and unreadable works to be 'worthy'.

Apart from creating his own mythologies King has never been afraid to dive into the roots of horror and fantasy fiction to deliver vampires, werewolves, haunted houses and to otherwise add to the well-trodden themes of the genres. Equally, he has been willing to merge other mythologies into his work (Oz in *The Dark Tower* Cycle, for example) or to add to those created by others. For instance, he has created Sherlock Holmes, Cthulhu Mythos and (unpublished) Wimsey stories.

King ranges easily from the unique story (*The Green Mile*) to the effective reworking of an older theme (*'Salem's Lot*) and back to his own more original late 20th Century technophobia (*Trucks*). In fact, in October 2005 King said, 'I just like telling stories. And if there's one message that comes up again and again, it's "Love conquers Fear". And if there's one concern that comes up again and again, it's "Don't trust the technology – it may not be your friend."'[6]

Horror literature is replete with haunted houses but King gave us not only the world's most famous haunted hotel, a haunted car, a haunted hospital and even a haunted laundry machine! Within hotels we have suffered haunted rooms (*1408*) and even the most effective haunted bathtub imaginable.

Of course King is vitally at home with F-E-A-R, both the real and the imaginary. The sheer brilliance of *Autopsy Room Four* is not that it could happen (and it *could*) but the terrible fear the reader has of imagining him or herself in that very situation. Could you retain *your* sanity looking at the deadlights? Would you want to be a young child home alone with Gramma? Certain scenes in *'Salem's Lot* are among the most terrifying in fiction and Paul Sheldon's realization in *Misery* that Annie Wilkes' intends to hobble him is one of the scariest King has ever put to paper. On a simpler scale little Tad Trenton's all too familiar fear in *The Monster in the Closet* scenes of *Cujo* recalls our own childhood with intense accuracy. Another little boy was left catatonic as a result of his visit to Room 217 - many readers found the description of that encounter almost unbearable.

If there is a core theme in King's Work, it is that of Good versus Evil, the Dark Side (or 'the Red') versus the White. Sometimes this is portrayed in religious terms (*The Stand, 'Salem's Lot, Desperation*) but often more simply as that of good men and women (Roland and his ka-tet) *standing* against the powers of evil, often unsuccessfully. All too often, as in the 'real' world, good men die, good women are beaten down and good causes lost. King does not resile from the truth of a story where it is clear that there is no happy ending.

King says this about the matter in *An Evening With Stephen King*[7]: 'In *Cujo* and *Storm of the Century* ... I tried to express the belief that sometimes good people do not win. Sometimes good people die. Sometimes good people are corrupted ... Last but not least I have expressed in several books my belief in some insensate force – not necessarily God – I'm not sure I believe in that in a personal way, but in the sort of way that William Wordsworth talked about and then later in his prose, John Steinbeck, when they talked about an oversoul. In my books, I've called that "the coming of the white."'

And this, in *Straight Up Midnight: An Introductory Note*, in *Four Past Midnight*: 'I still believe in the resilience of the human heart and the essential validity of love; I still believe that connections between people can be made ... I still believe, I suppose, in the coming of the White and in finding a place to make a stand ... and defending that place to the death. They are old-fashioned concerns and beliefs, but I would be a liar if I did not admit I still own them. And that they still own me.'

Yet, the everyman individual often rises up in a King story and ultimately wins through, often at great cost. As an example, Johnny Smith with his oh-so anonymous surname is able to defeat a potential megalomaniac but loses his life in *The Dead Zone*. Stu Redman, the only survivor of four men sent to confront Flagg *also* carries a splendidly resonant surname. John Coffey was unable to save two little girls but did save a small mouse and a woman's life before being cruelly taken from this world (King acknowledges in *On Writing* the deliberate choice of John's initials, 'after the most famous innocent man of all time'). LT de Witt, Martha Rosewall and Darlene Pullen somehow won little victories of their own. Dolores Claiborne, Rose McClendon and Jessie Burlingame were all able to battle and defeat spousal or sexual abuse. The Loser's Club *stood* against Pennywise twice; and Gary Jones was able to defeat an alien invasion through the powers of his mind.

It is often when describing basic human horrors that King is at his most effective. Whether it is spousal abuse (*Rose Madder*, *Dolores Claiborne*); blackmail (*Apt Pupil*); sexual predation (*Gerald's Game*); suicide and despair (*All That You Love Will Be Carried Away*, *The Last Rung on the Ladder*); false imprisonment (*Rita Hayworth and Shawshank Redemption*); or approaching death (*The Woman in the Room*), King brings the depravity of certain events and the very human responses to them directly home.

Sometimes the story appears to be for story's sake (*My Pretty Pony*, the original version of *Blind Willie*, *The Death of Jack Hamilton*, *Hearts in Atlantis*, *It Grows On You*). On the other hand King has said if he cannot scare the reader he is not above the gross-out. He used zombies and worms in *Home Delivery*, the self-amputating *Survivor Type*, a creature sucking its victim through the boards of *The Raft* and pie disgorging in *The Revenge of Lardass Hogan* to make this point.

King's characterizations and ability to get the reader to empathize with the heroes (Stu Redman, Nick Andros, Dolores Claiborne, Rose Daniels/McClendon, Danny Torrance, the Losers Club); the victims (Tad Trenton, The Trashcan Man, Sara Tidwell, Mr Jingles, Louis Creed); and even many of the apparent villains (Cujo, Sara Tidwell again) are superb.

At times King ties us so deeply to a character that the reader also suffers the loss when they die (King has often pointed out that *he* does not kill characters, the *story* does). Mattie Devore in *Bag of Bones*, Susan Norton of *'Salem's Lot*, Tad Trenton in *Cujo*, Nick Andros in *The Stand*, Susan Delgado (*The Dark Tower IV: Wizard and Glass*), Henry Leyden of *Black House*, Wolf in *The Talisman*, Duddits Cavell in *Dreamcatcher*, and Eddie Dean, Jake Chambers and Oy of *The Dark Tower* serve as tear-inducing examples.

King's shorter works often provide his most haunting, memorable or unique characters. Think Gary and his tormentor in *The Man in the Black Suit*; Gary Paulson in *It Grows On You*; the eponymous Mrs. Todd; Stella Godlin of *The Reach*; the maître d' at the Gotham Café; or Jordy Verrill's lonesome death in *Weeds*.

It is also the lesser characters in novels that are sometimes among the most memorable. Duddits Cavell in *Dreamcatcher*, Mr Jingles or indeed Delacroix in *The Green Mile*, Rhea of the Coos (*The Dark Tower IV: Wizard and Glass*), The Trashcan Man and Tom Cullen (*The Stand*) are all unique creations and stand in one's memory long after the story is laid aside.

The ranks of the villains King has created are either original (Pennywise/It, Andre Linoge, the Overlook Hotel, Randall Flagg, the Crimson King) or at least provide a powerful addition to the ranks of the derivative villain (Leland Gaunt, Kurt Barlow, Max Devore, Charles Burnside, Sunlight Gardener). Few if any could be described as single dimensional or lacking in, if you will excuse the pun, character.

Of course, there are also those we can pretty much have outright dislike for – Percy Wetmore (*The Green Mile*), Ace Merrill (*The Body*, *Nona* and *Needful Things*), Pop Merrill (*The Sun Dog*), Joe St George, Sr. (*Dolores Claiborne*) and Roland LeBay (*Christine*) are all nasty examples of humanity but at the same time all too believable. Where a reader may not *really* believe a vampire, werewolf or supernatural monster exists, it is easy to accept the existence of these human monsters. We probably all know one or two ourselves.

In review it is astounding how many of King's characters are original and memorable and time is likely to show that many will join the ranks of the legendary fictional characters created by Twain, Dickens, Hugo, Stevenson, Tolkien or Shakespeare. Among those that may achieve such longevity are Roland Deschain, Randall Flagg, Jack Torrance, John Coffey and Carrie White.

King's ability to create an entire World (Roland's, for instance, or The Territories) or the magnificently painted lives of small towns and cities (Derry, Castle Rock, Jerusalem's Lot) and their residents is close to legendary.

Castle Rock is so comfortable to King readers that it feels like pulling on an old jumper when we delve back into its doings. Derry, a larger town, is less comfortable but it takes only a few words early in *Dreamcatcher* to bring it back into focus for seasoned readers. As the years went by we learnt more of

Roland's World, a creation that rivals that of Tolkien's Middle Earth. The Territories were well sketched in *The Talisman* and we received another glance at the end of *Black House*. Undoubtedly, when King and Straub choose to complete the story of Jack Sawyer, we will receive a much deeper description of that strange agrarian realm.

Stephen King's Maine is now legend. Apart from Castle Rock and Derry dozens of small towns have grabbed our imaginations or stirred our nightmares. Jerusalem's Lot is synonymous with the modern American vampire. Maine has a huge number of islands and a lengthy coastline and King has used these to effect in creating Little Tall Island, Goat Island and Gennesault Island, among others. Harlow is well developed as Castle Rock's neighbor; Willow visited but once by readers and the Grahams alike; the Lakes District – Dark Score, Kashwakamak, Long Lake; Gates Falls, the history of which King has been revealing to us as long as any town; Haven, destroyed by forces both external and internal; Chamberlain, the site of the Black Prom; and scores of others both real and imagined – Ogunquit, Tarker's Mills, Lewiston/Auburn, Bridgton, Pownal, Chester's Mill, Ludlow (and its dangerous road) and the wilds of the Jefferson Tract, have all taken their place in the myth that is Stephen King's Maine.

But it is not simply the geography of Maine that King paints so superbly. The people, the lifestyle, the self-reliant and closely held Yankee culture, and the community all shine through. The benefits and of course the downsides of small-town, rural and hard scrabble areas of Maine life are delivered to the reader, warts and all in story after story. It is this grounding in absolute reality that is one of the great attractors of King's fiction and will be one of the keys to its standing the test of time, with a readership for many decades to come.

It takes a lot of skill, dedication and not a little respect for both the geographies King creates and his readers, for him to deliver on the promise of creating a full-blown town or world. In many ways it would have been easier for King to set each story in a new town or anonymous locations without having to concern himself with relevant back-story. It is telling, perhaps, that the key locations (in our world at least) that recur are in Maine. That same feeling of *connection* between the author and his geographical subject only really seems to occur otherwise in the case of Roland's World or Colorado (*The Stand, Misery, The Shining, Before the Play*). While other locations are generally well described the depth and instant familiarity seem to be missing.

That is not to say that some memorable towns have not been created outside Maine – Desperation, Nevada; Rock and Roll Heaven, Oregon; many of the devastated small towns of *The Stand* such as Arnette and Shoyo; and Gatlin, Nebraska. But few seem to reach the level of 'reality' that marks King's Maine creations.

King often despairs of the lack of interest in the skills and art of fiction writing that exists today. The media is only interested in surface matters (*where do you get your ideas?*) and rarely is this prominent exponent of his art asked how his skills developed and how he views the practice of creative writing. Fortunately, he has provided a number of dissertations on the matter in articles, interviews and in two non-fiction books, *On Writing* and *Danse Macabre*. Those interested should take the time to discover these contributions, which go a long way to explaining why King is so successful. Apart from brilliant story ideas and the ability to create characters and backgrounds to suit them, King is a *craftsman*, dedicated, as are all good craftsmen, to delivering the best product he can.

Let's look then at King's skills inside the two major delivery methods – the written word and the world of film and television.

The Literary Arts

Unlike many authors King seems at home in virtually all forms of writing. While he has indulged in relatively little poetry, his efforts there are judged well by those who understand the form. His short stories range from the bizarre (*Battleground*) to the sublime (*That Feeling, You Can Only Say What It Is In French*). The relatively unusual form of the novella is well represented in King's credits; think of *The Mist* or *The Body*. Of course, King certainly knows how to write a novel, some of truly epic length (*It, The Stand*) and has also been able to create a highly successful and satisfying series (*The Dark Tower* Cycle) as well as the most successful serialized novel of modern times (*The Green Mile*), which once held six of the ten top positions on best-seller lists!

He has been equally successful with screenplays. Although they are of mixed quality, the motivation and timing of each should be taken into account. Balance for instance the schlock of *Maximum Overdrive* (which appears to have achieved pretty much exactly what King intended) with *Storm of the Century*, a very powerful and disturbing tale.

As the years have passed King has progressed in literary opinion and has begun to receive at least some acknowledgement for the high quality of his writing as well as the sheer power of his stories. Even the august magazine *The New Yorker* regularly publishes his tales. Until recently awards came mainly from within the Horror, Science Fiction and Fantasy literary communities. Recognition from one's own peers is likely to have brought King a certain degree of satisfaction, considering his early roots as a hard-core fan and consumer of these genres.

The Bram Stoker Awards have been awarded since 1987 by members of the Horror Writers Association. King has won Best Novel for *Misery* (in a tie with McCammon's epic, *Swan Song*), *The Green Mile*, *Bag of Bones*, *Lisey's Story* and *Duma Key*; Best Fiction Collection for *Four Past Midnight*, *Full Dark, No Stars* and *Just After Sunset*; Best Long Fiction for *Lunch at the Gotham Café*;

and Best Non-Fiction for *On Writing*. Through 2010 he has been nominated a further 18 times. In 2003 he received the HWA's Lifetime Achievement Award.

The World Fantasy Awards are nominated by members of the World Fantasy Convention and selected by a panel of judges to acknowledge excellence in fantasy writing and art. King has won the Convention Award and the Short Fiction Award, for *The Man in the Black Suit*. In 2007 King received the Grand Master Award from the Mystery Writers of America. The Grand Master Award recognizes important contributions to the mystery genre over time, as well as a significant output of consistently high quality.

The British Fantasy Society has awarded King the August Derleth Award for Best Novel in 1983 (*Cujo*), 1987 (*It*), 1999 (*Bag of Bones*) and 2005 (*The Dark Tower*); Best Short Story for *The Breathing Method* in 1983; and a Special Award in 1981.

Stepping outside genre to more mainstream awards King (and O'Nan) won a Quill Award in 2005 for *Faithful* and King was nominated for *Cell* in the 2006 Awards. The O. Henry Awards are an annual collection of the year's best stories published in American and Canadian magazines and written by American or Canadian authors. King won first prize (in other words judged to have been the *best* story written by a North American and published in a North American magazine) in 1996 for *The Man in the Black Suit*. In doing so he joined William Faulkner, Irwin Shaw, Truman Capote, John Cheever, John Updike, Joyce Carol Oates, Bernard Malamud, Saul Bellow and Alice Walker as winners of the year's best stand-alone story.

Even greater recognition was accorded King in September 2003, when the National Book Foundation announced it would award him its 2003 Medal for Distinguished Contribution to American Letters at the National Book Awards Ceremony and Benefit Dinner on 19 November that year. The Medal was presented to King, who then delivered the keynote address to some 1000 authors, editors, publishers and friends of the book industry. Previous recipients of the Medal include Saul Bellow, Studs Terkel, John Updike, Ray Bradbury, Arthur Miller and Philip Roth.

In giving the award the Foundation said, "Stephen King's writing is securely rooted in the great American tradition that glorifies spirit-of-place and the abiding power of narrative. He crafts stylish, mind-bending page-turners that contain profound moral truths - some beautiful, some harrowing - about our inner lives. This Award commemorates Mr. King's well-earned place of distinction in the wide world of readers and booklovers of all ages." King stated, "This is probably the most exciting thing to happen to me in my career as a writer since the sale of my first book in 1973." Amusingly enough, King and John Grisham once purchased their own tickets to the annual National Book Awards presentation by the Foundation, King telling *The New York Times* somewhat tongue-in-cheek, "…that was the only way we were going to get in the door."

There is no doubt King has been responsible for a revival in reading generally and is actually responsible for many teenagers and young people taking up reading as a pleasure for the first time in their lives.

It is known that King is somewhat uncomfortable about being compared with other writers but it is also true that, as the years have passed, more and more critics, academics and others have found themselves drawn to pass comment upon King's position in the pantheon.

King's output will stand the test of time as both popular fiction and as the subject of academic study. Courses teach King works across the high schools and colleges of America. Teachers and professors have come to the understanding that they can offer King stories that not only help teach the art of creative writing but actually engage their students.

King has become the Dickens of our times – popular with readers, although initially unpopular with certain critics. As time passed many of Dickens' works became the standard fare of entertainment. Characters such as Scrooge, Nicholas Nickleby and Oliver Twist, and stories such as *A Tale of Two Cities* and *Great Expectations* are now embedded in our culture. Dickens, as does King, expressed the characteristic concerns of his time.

There is also much of the Mark Twain about Stephen King. Twain was a master of writing characters who were young and creating new twists on old themes. He helped bring a new 'American' style of writing to English literature. His body of work is now standard study throughout the American education system. King has all these attributes, being the most visible and popular of writers delivering the mainstream American culture of the last forty years.

Nathaniel Hawthorne, whose portrayals of New England are still among the richest ever written, was also prominent in establishing a truly American literary voice. There is no doubt King has continued Hawthorne's tradition. With his roots clearly in the American horror tradition, King stands well beside predecessors such as Shirley Jackson, H P Lovecraft (another New Englander who expressed well the topography and culture of the area, and was the creator of an imaginary town, Arkham) and Edgar Allen Poe (about whom no more need be said).

Perhaps Dr. Michael Collings, noted King critic and former Professor of English at Pepperdine University in California, writing in Spignesi's *The Essential Stephen King*, put it the most succinctly: 'William Shakespeare was the Stephen King of his generation.'

When King critics and observers such as Winter, Blue, Spignesi, Collings and Beahm, among others, offered similar views a quarter century ago they were *not* welcomed by the mainstream of literary critics or academia. Today, there are still those who resist but they are in the minority and tend to lack credibility. It will be interesting to see an assessment in another quarter century but it does not take one of the balls from the Wizard's Rainbow to predict that King will become codified as one of the great American writers.

The Visual Arts

King's stories have been adapted to the big and small screen in near record numbers, with varying degrees of success. For every *Carrie* or *The Green Mile* there has been an unfortunate *Sometimes They Come Back* or *Dreamcatcher*. However, film and television are arguably *the* key influencers of world culture and have been for a half-century or more. This has exposed King's work to every corner of the earth. Along with the Americanization of world culture one could argue a lesser but still influential King-ization (the man himself would surely be horrified by the very concept).

Almost any Western adult will have heard of a girl called Carrie. Anyone interested in movies will have seen, or been exposed to opinion of, Kubrick's *The Shining*. The name of one dog, Cujo, now needs no explanation. *The Shawshank Redemption* is one of the most widely loved movies of all time. *Stand by Me* is regarded as one of the leading 'coming of age' stories ever made. *The Green Mile* brought audiences to tears wherever it was shown. King television series and mini-series such as *The Dead Zone*, *The Stand*, *Storm of the Century* and *Rose Red* were prime-time successes not just in the United States but wherever they are shown.

King adaptations have served for some powerful performances (think of Ian McKellen in *Apt Pupil*, Jack Nicholson in *The Shining*, Kathy Bates in *Misery*) and there is a rapidly evolving shortage of actors and actresses who have not, in fact, appeared in a King movie, television production or read an audiobook. Despite the snobbery aimed at horror, science fiction and fantasy (finally shattered in 2004 by Peter Jackson's *The Lord of the Rings: The Return of the King*) even the Academy of Motion Picture Arts and Sciences has had to deliver Oscars to productions of King's work. Today, King movies and mini-series fill the world's DVD shops.

King as a World Phenomenon

One should not make the mistake of thinking of King as a purely North American phenomenon (his sales in the UK or Australia on a per capita basis are just as impressive) or even as limited to the English language. His books have been translated into dozens of languages and there are huge fan bases in countries such as Germany, Italy, France and Holland. As economic and literary freedoms have reached Eastern Europe so have King books, with a growing fan base and publications in the local languages of the former Soviet bloc. *Riding the Bullet* was first published in text form in Japan, where King books and movies have an enormous following. Similarly, King has had widespread influence in Latin America, South Africa, India and South-East Asia. Perhaps only China and the Arab world have resisted the wave, but for how long?

King is not just a successful writer but is also a truly global multi-media phenomenon, with massive exposure on television, film, the internet, audio books, even the stage and computer games.

There appear to be a multitude of reasons for this but it appears the unique mix of our times and King's style has resulted in the massive popularity of all things King. The horror, science fiction and fantasy genres have existed in modern form for two centuries, at varying levels of popular acceptance and success. There is no doubt however, that the surge in popularity for horror (and King appeared on the scene just as horror was returning to the fore in the early 1970s), science fiction (again, a comeback of SF can be traced solidly to the mid-1970s) and even fantasy (more recently moving out of obscurity and again confirmed as part of mainstream culture by Jackson's brilliant interpretations of *The Lord of the Rings* saga) has never reached a higher level than the last quarter of the 20th century and the early 21st.

This allowed King's works to move easily from 'genre' into the mainstream. A few continued to try to peg him as a horror writer, as some badge of disgrace, but as King proved he was capable of more than one genre, so did the common opinion move quickly to a higher level of respect for that very style of fiction.

In the same 35-year period there has been an explosion in the need for entertainment software. Technology advanced rapidly, allowing more channels on cable and satellite television, the video rental industry appeared and boomed, the internet exploded from literally nowhere in the early 1990s, and DVDs as a method of delivery came to the fore in the very late 1990s.

Ironically, as every year doomsayers predicted the death of the book, that form, magazines and reading each proved resilient. Governments everywhere were in deregulation mode, selling their telecommunication companies, allowing more television and radio stations and introducing Pay-TV into Europe, Asia and specific countries, such as the UK (late 1980s) and Australia (mid 1990s). Major producers of entertainment software such as Disney and News Corporation (owners of FOX) suddenly realized there was more money to be made by selling a video (and later, DVD) than there was in a movie ticket, or television advertising revenues. 'Blockbusters' began to run only a few weeks in movie theatres before moving to multiple lucrative avenues of distribution – video and DVD rental, Pay-TV, video and DVD sales, and Free-To-Air television. All this was both the cause and a symptom of the splintering of the media. By 2000 'mass media' was already a contradiction in terms, as the consumer had a choice of dozens, if not hundreds of TV channels, thousands of magazines, multiple local movie screens, tens of thousands of videos and DVDs and literally hundreds of thousands of book titles, along with millions of web sites, all at the click of a mouse or remote control.

This combination of surging technology, deregulation, the change in marketing tactics by entertainment software 'manufacturers' and the splintering of the media has had two major results – freedom of choice for the consumer, and an unprecedented demand for new product.

King sat at the epicenter of this change. Here was a man who was capable of, and interested in, creating large volumes of entertainment product. Here was a man in touch with cultural trends (brand names, popular and sub-culture music themes and other cultural iconography abound in King's works). And here was a need. The perfect marriage was consummated, with King creating the raw material in droves and the publishing and filmed entertainment worlds providing it to the consumer in unprecedented quantities.

Today, anyone can easily find a King movie or mini-series on a television channel near him. Anyone can find a King movie on the big screen or dozens of them at her local video store. We can all find all his mainstream books still in print at the local bookstore or on-line seller, at the library or second hand bookshop. Those who prefer the audiobook will find the majority of his works available in that form. The user of the internet will find hundreds of websites and chatrooms dedicated to the world of King. Bands perform songs based on King material. With the general exception of the live stage and the musical it is hard to think of an entertainment mode that has evaded King's successful reach.

It is the combination of King's brilliance as a storyteller with his strong willingness to experiment with new modes of delivery and the fundamental change in the entertainment market that has resulted in the sheer size and impact of the phenomenon that is King.

The Proof

As any hard core King fan knows there are those who 'refuse' to read King (one often wonders if some of these people are actually readers at all), writing him off as 'that horror writer' or similar put-downs. Try surprising these doubters with the simple riposte, *Did you enjoy The Shawshank Redemption?* For the vast majority of moviegoers the answer is *Yes*. How about *The Green Mile and Stand by Me?* Almost always *yes* again. Try informing the doubter that these are King stories, and highly accurate to the book versions. Jam in a bit of *The Shining* for the serious movie snob (the ones for whom Kubrick could do no wrong) and the doubter will be on the way to conversion, or is at least may be left muttering, inanely.

In Conclusion

This book's value lies firmly in providing King's 'Constant Readers'[8] with the latest information about 107 King works of fiction that they may not know of and, in the case of most pieces, have not read. These works of prose, poems and screenplays represent a significant portion of the King's output and a study of them contributes immensely to understanding how an obscure, hardscrabble Maine schoolteacher, with no more than talent, craftsmanship, dreams and determination, became the most popular storyteller of his time.

What is the Joy of Stephen King? Should the man answer the question himself but two words should suffice – 'The Story'.

Let the telling begin...

Recommended Resources and Further Reading

(1) *On Writing*, Stephen King, Scribner, 2000
(2) *Danse Macabre*, Stephen King, Everest House, 1981
(3) *Light Behind the Shadow Trapped Within the Words* in *Horror Plum'd*, Michael Collings, Overlook Connection Press, 2002
(4) *I Am a Hick, and This Is Where I Feel at Home* by Elaine Landa, in *Feast of Fear*, Ed: Tim Underwood and Chuck Miller, Carroll & Graf, 1989
(5) *Prelude: An Anecdote to Illustrate How Stephen King's Fans Feel About His Work*, in *The Essential Stephen King*, Stephen J Spignesi, GB Books, 2001
(6) *In the Matter of Stephen King* by Tyson Blue in *The Essential Stephen King*, Stephen J Spignesi, GB Books, 2001
(7) *The Complete Guide to the Works of Stephen King*, Rocky Wood, David Rawsthorne and Norma Blackburn, Kanrock Partners, 2004
(8) *The Lost Works of Stephen King*, Stephen Spignesi, Birch Lane Press, 1998
(9) *The Unseen King*, Tyson Blue, Starmont House, 1989
(10) *The Stephen King Illustrated Companion*, Bev Vincent, Fall River Press, 2009
(11) *Stephen King: A Primary Bibliography of the World's Most Popular Author*, Justin Brooks, Cemetery Dance Publications, 2008
(12) *Stephen King: The Non-Fiction*, Rocky Wood and Justin Brooks, Cemetery Dance Publications, 2009
(13) *Stephen King: A Literary Companion*, Rocky Wood, McFarland, 2011

LINKING STEPHEN KING'S REALITIES

From his earliest writings Stephen King has been engaged in the process of establishing various groupings, or 'Realities' in which his work can be placed; and in developing stories and story-lines within them.

It is now clear that King planned one of these Realities (that relating to the mythology of Roland Deschain's travels toward the Dark Tower) from a time even before the day he typed the first words of *The Gunslinger*. He then 'simply' continued to develop that Reality in the following decades! Another Reality, which is based in Maine, seems to have appeared naturally, as a series of King's stories began congregating in the remote, beautiful part of America that happened to be King's home State.

In fact, to any but the casual reader, it quickly becomes clear that all King's works of fiction can be grouped into particular Realities. Arbitrary though any classification system may be the authors of *The Complete Guide to the Works of Stephen King*[9] developed their own using five great, sweeping Realities, placing each of King's Works of Fiction in one or more of them. The author of this book was one of those who developed those Realities, which we will now review.

All King fiction, screenplays and poetry, published or unpublished, and poetry are included in this survey.

The five Realities are:

- The Dark Tower
- Maine Street Horror
- The Stand
- America Under Siege
- New Worlds

The Dark Tower

This Reality is officially recognized by King. A list of all King's novels and collections included in *The Dark Tower V: Wolves of the Calla* first featured the highlighting of tales that, in King's opinion, are connected to the Dark Tower mythology.

The author relates something of the origins of the Dark Tower Cycle in his introduction to the Revised Edition of *The Gunslinger - On Being Nineteen (and a Few Other Things)*. From as early as his reading of J.R.R. Tolkien's classic, *The Lord of the Rings* in 1966 and 1967 King had determined to write something as sweeping, 'but I wanted to write my own kind of story.'

'Then (in 1970), in an almost completely empty movie theater ... I saw a film directed by Sergio Leone. It was called *The Good, The Bad and the Ugly*, and before the film was half over, I realized what I wanted to write was a novel that contained Tolkien's sense of quest and magic but set against Leone's almost absurdly majestic Western backdrop ... And, in my enthusiasm ... I wanted to write not just a *long* book, but *the longest popular novel in history*. I did not succeed in doing that, but I feel I had a decent rip; *The Dark Tower*, volumes one through seven, really comprise a single tale...'

The first appearance of a Dark Tower story was of *The Gunslinger* in *The Magazine of Fantasy and Science Fiction* for October 1978. However, King had been working on his magnum opus since 1970, taking Robert Browning's 1855 epic poem *Childe Roland To The Dark Tower Came* as his inspiration. The various parts[10] that would become the first novel set in this Reality, *The Dark Tower: The Gunslinger*, each initially appeared in *The Magazine of Fantasy and Science Fiction*, before being combined into the novel, first published in 1982. A mass-market edition of *The Dark Tower: The Gunslinger* was not published until 1988 and it was only from that point that King's wider fan base *may* have begun to appreciate the importance of this Reality to his overall fictional output.

King slowly added to what 'The Dark Tower Cycle' with these novels: *The Dark Tower II: The Drawing of the Three* (1987); *The Dark Tower III: The Wastelands* (1991); *The Dark Tower IV: Wizard and Glass* (1996); *The Dark Tower V: Wolves of the Calla* (2003); *The Dark Tower VI: Song of Susannah* (2004); and *The Dark Tower VII: The Dark Tower* (2004).

As time passed, King also published *The Bear*[11] (1990), an 'excerpt' from *The Dark Tower III: The Wastelands*, although it was heavily revised before being included in the novel. He also released a Dark Tower novelette, *The Little Sisters of Eluria* (1998); and began to refer explicitly to Dark Tower mythology in his mainstream stories. The major references there were in *Insomnia* (1994), *Low Men in Yellow Coats* (1999), *Heavenly Shades of Night Are Falling* (1999) and *Black House* (2001). He also provided a lifeline for Dark Tower junkies by giving them a free, on-line taste of *Wolves of the Calla* in an excerpt, *Calla Bryn Sturgis*, published on his web-site in August 2001 and later revised for inclusion in the novel; and allowed the publication of the short story, *The Tale of Gray Dick* (February 2003), excerpted from the same novel, although that too was revised for the novel's appearance.

Then, in June 2003, King published a Revised and Expanded edition of the Cycle's first novel, *The Gunslinger*. He explains the reasoning for the rewrite in his *Foreword* to the Revised Edition, '...although each book of the Tower series was revised as a separate entity, I never really looked at the work as a whole until I'd finished Volume Seven, *The Dark Tower*. When I looked at the first volume ... three obvious truths presented themselves. The first was that *The Gunslinger* was written by a very young man, and had all the problems of a very young man's book. The second was that it contained a great many errors and false starts, particularly in the light of the volumes that followed. The third was that *The Gunslinger* did not even *sound* like the later books – it was, frankly, rather difficult to read. All too often I heard myself apologizing for it, and telling people that if they persevered, they would find the story really found its voice in *The Drawing of the Three*.'

In October 2005 King and Marvel Comics announced the Dark Tower mythos would be extended with the publication of an initial six comic arc (to be collected in a hardcover edition). A series of arcs were published from 2007 and can be also purchased in collected hardback editions. Readers should note the original comic 'arcs', while collected in the hardcover graphic novels, contain a lot of background material about the Dark Tower Universe that are *not* included in those collections. This background is described by King's former research assistant and writer of the comic series, Robin Furth. The comics and graphic novels may be purchased from specialist stores or on the internet without difficulty.

The series released or announced to date (in reading order) are:

The Dark Tower: Gunslinger Born; *The Dark Tower: The Long Road Home*; *The Dark Tower: Treachery*; *The Dark Tower: The Sorcerer* (one-shot comic, not collected); *The Dark Tower: Fall of Gilead*; *The Dark Tower: The Battle of Jericho Hill*; *The Dark Tower: The Gunslinger – The Journey Begins*; *The Dark Tower: The Little Sisters of Eluria*; and *The Dark Tower: The Battle of Tull*. While *The Dark Tower: Sheemie's Tale* (a one-shot) was announced, there is no sign of it actually being published at the time of writing.

King's first story with strong Dark Tower connections in five years appeared in 2009, when *Ur* was first published, as a download for Amazon's Kindle 2 e-reader. While it has yet to see a print publication the audio book was released on 16 February 2010 (King hand-picked the narrator, Holter Graham). This uncollected story is the subject of a chapter later in this volume.

In 2012 he will publish an extension to the mythos, with a novella that falls mid-stream in the narrative, *The Wind Through Keyhole*.

Most Dark Tower experts also link *Eyes of the Dragon* (first published as a Limited Edition in 1984 and heavily revised for mass-market release in 1987) to the Dark Tower Cycle. The following then, is a full list of Dark Tower stories.

Primary Setting:

The Bear
Calla Bryn Sturgis
The Dark Tower: The Gunslinger
The Dark Tower II: The Drawing of the Three
The Dark Tower III: The Wastelands
The Dark Tower IV: Wizard and Glass
The Dark Tower V: Wolves of the Calla
The Dark Tower VI: Song of Susannah
The Dark Tower VII: The Dark Tower
The Little Sisters of Eluria
The Wind Through the Keyhole
The Tale of Gray Dick

Other Stories of Dark Tower Importance:

Bag of Bones
Black House
Desperation
11/22/63
Everything's Eventual
Eyes of the Dragon
From a Buick 8
Heavenly Shades of Night Are Falling
Insomnia
It
Low Men in Yellow Coats
The Mist
The Regulators
The Reploids
Rose Madder
'Salem's Lot
The Stand
The Talisman
Under the Weather
UR

As indicated *The Bear, Calla Bryn Sturgis* and *The Tale of Gray Dick* all initially appeared in significantly different form from that in the novel from which they were excerpted. For more detail see the *Stories Swallowed by Monsters* chapter.

Notes related to post-*The Dark Tower VII* stories with clear Dark Tower references follow.

In *UR* one of the creatures that visit Wesley Smith is described as 'in the yellow coat' (both wear 'long mustard-colored coats'). They are described in a manner that leaves no doubt they are the same type of creature that hunted Ted Brautigan in *Low Men in Yellow Coats* and that appear in *The Dark Tower V: Wolves of the Calla, The Dark Tower VI: Song of Susannah, The Dark Tower VII: The Dark Tower and Heavenly Shades of Night Are Falling*. As examples, their faces 'kept changing and what lay just beneath the skin was reptilian. Or birdlike. Or both'; and 'On their lapels, where lawmen would have worn badges, both wore buttons bearing a red eye.' They specifically reference 'The Tower' and 'The rose', as well as 'this level of the Tower.'

King's 2011 short story, *Under the Weather*, collected in the paperback editions of *Full Dark, No Stars*, references Nozz-A-La, a drink which only appears in the Dark Tower and Kingdom Hospital versions of Earth (both of these have been established to be *not* the same Earth reality as the one in which *we* live). King's 2011 novel *11/22/63* includes some obscure Dark Tower connections (such as a Takuro Spirit car).

Dark Tower tales are primarily set in that Reality but there is also a deep and abiding linkage with our world (and, due to the nature of the Tower itself, all other Universes and Realities). There is a very important location off-World to Roland's - a sometime vacant lot at the corner of 2nd Avenue and 46th Street in New York City (in this Reality, each New York City can seem slightly different from the one we know). And, significant events occur in the state of ... Maine!

The Dark Tower Cycle is set in an alternate reality, Roland Deschain's world. Roland is the last of the Gunslingers, a knight/warrior of sorts. Many years ago he embarked on a quest to find the Dark Tower and save it from destruction.

The geography of Roland's world is somewhat obscure but some towns have featured strongly in his life, including the now lifeless Eluria (in Mid-World) and Tull; the urban jungle of Lud; Hambry in the Barony of Mejis (where he found and lost the love of his life); and Calla Bryn Sturgis (in End-World). Roland hails from Gilead, in New Canaan, a city-state that had gone out of existence 1000 years before he arrived in Calla Bryn Sturgis. In the Calla, Roland and his small band of followers met Pere Callahan, who had once lived in the town of Jerusalem's Lot, in a wholly different world.

The Dark Tower itself is in End-World, a geographical location from which

Jack Sawyer and Tyler Marshall rescued hundreds of kidnapped children, returning them to our world (*Black House*). Ted Brautigan and other 'Breakers', toiling under the slavery of the Crimson King, were reluctantly hard at work there, trying to break the Beams that secure all Universes and Realities to the Dark Tower.

In her Concordance to the Dark Tower[12] Robin Furth defines the Dark Tower itself as, '…a looming gray-black edifice which is simultaneously the center of all universes and the linchpin of the time/space continuum. All worlds and all realities are contained within its many levels … The line of Eld, of which Roland is the last, is sworn to protect the Tower. Yet a terrible illness affects this structure, one that is often compared to cancer … The Tower is held together by a network of magical magnetic forces-rays, known as Beams … the Beams, Portals and mechanical Guardians are breaking down. If the weakening Beams collapse and the Tower falls, all creation will blink out of existence.'

King's original inspiration, *Childe Roland To The Dark Tower Came* is reproduced as an Appendix to this chapter.

Maine Street Horror

The most comfortable setting for a King story is his home state of Maine, in the beautiful New England region of the northeastern United States. King's deep love of the land, lakes, sea, islands, people and culture of Maine is a keynote to his body of work. Maine Street Horror Reality stories are largely set in the state of Maine and exist in our world's physical existence and (mostly) in our timeline.

In addition to using real towns and cities such as Pownal, Bridgton, Portland, Bangor, Brewer, Durham (King's later childhood was spent there), Augusta, Mechanic Falls, Fryeburg, Old Orchard Beach or Lewiston/Auburn, King took early to creating a fictional Maine. This Maine is so well portrayed that a visitor to the State can almost expect to turn the corner of some country road and actually find one of the towns King has created.

From a Constant Reader's point of view the favorite fictional town is likely to be either Castle Rock or Derry. Among other fictional creations are the Rock's neighbor, Harlow; the vampire-infested Jerusalem's Lot; Haven, past home of *The Tommyknockers*; Ludlow and its deadly Route 15; Little Tall Island, where Dolores Claiborne lived and which suffered the *Storm of the Century*; the zombie-targeted Gennesault Island; Goat Island and its nearby Reach; Blainesville; Johnny Smith's Cleaves Mills; Carietta White's Chamberlain; Gates Falls (with its ubiquitous mill); Huffman; Willow, with its *Rainy Season*; Chester's Mill; Weathersfield; the Jefferson Tract, recently visited by aliens; Tarker's Mills, once home to a werewolf; the haunted TR90 and Dark Score Lake; Motton and Kashwakamak.

The sheer breadth and depth of these towns and their residents, cut wholly from the cloth by King, is testament to his descriptive powers. To the reader, most of these towns feel so real it can be a shock (if a comforting one, at times) to discover they do not, in fact, actually exist.

Many stories involve Stephen and Tabitha King's alma mater, the University of Maine at Orono ('UMO') and dozens of King's characters attended it or one of the other UMaine campuses. Among these are Jo Arlen and Mike Noonan (*Bag of Bones*); Pete Riley, Carol Gerber and Stokely Jones (*Hearts in Atlantis*); Stephanie Stepanek and David Drayton (*The Mist*); Amy Lauder (*The Stand*); Michael Anderson (*Storm of the Century*); Joe St George, Jr. (*Dolores Claiborne*); Gordon Lachance (*The Body*); John Smith and Sarah Bracknell (*The Dead Zone*); Victor Pascow (*Pet Sematary*); Alan Parker (*Riding the Bullet*); and young Gary (*The Man in the Black Suit*). Among those teaching at the University was Thad Beaumont (*The Dark Half*); and Dr. Louis Creed worked in the infirmary there before losing his family and his mind (*Pet Sematary*). Jim Gardener was once a poet in residence (*The Tommyknockers*).

A less happy place for the characters to visit has been Shawshank Prison, host to Red and Andy Dufresne (*Rita Hayworth and Shawshank Redemption*); George Footman (*Bag of Bones*); Richard Macklin (*It*); Nat Copeland (*Needful Things*); and Ace Merrill (*The Sun Dog*), among others. Those with mental health problems were more likely to end up at Juniper Hill, near Augusta. Among inmates there have been Raymond Joubert (*Gerald's Game*); Henry Bowers (*It*); Nettie Cobb and Bill Keeton (*Needful Things*).

One should take care hitch-hiking the highways and back roads of Maine but while doing so one just might catch a passing view of Ophelia Todd (*Mrs. Todd's Shortcut*) or George Staub (*Riding the Bullet*).

Castle Rock is probably the most famous of King's fictional towns. He has sketched its history and the doings of its denizens since its initial appearance in *The Dead Zone* (published in 1979). 'The Rock' has been the site of many strange and mysterious events, including the Castle Rock Strangler murders (1970 to 1975); killings by a rabid dog in *Cujo* (1980); the destruction of much of the downtown by explosives in *Needful Things* (1991); and a series of lesser, more human, but often tragic events. Castle Rock is the County seat of Maine's smallest county, Castle County and last featured prominently in *Bag of Bones*, *Premium Harmony* and *Under the Dome*.

Among interesting parts of Castle Rock are Castle Falls, the Castle River, the GS&WM railroad trestle, Castle Heights (near the bridge to neighboring Harlow), Castle Hill (on which Red's wife crashed, leading to his imprisonment in Shawshank), Castle Lake, the Castle Stream, the Bandstand and Town Common, Southwest Bend, Castle View and the Homeland Cemetery (George Stark was 'buried' there in *The Dark Half*). Out on Town Road #3 one might find the old Camber place (*Cujo*) or one might drive down Maple Sugar Road to the

Birches Cemetery (*Gramma*), or one could cruise the Black Henry Road past George McCutcheon's old Cresswell truck sitting in Otto Schenck's meadow (*Uncle Otto's Truck*).

Around 1900 Sara Tidwell and Jared Devore may have walked the town's streets (*Bag of Bones*) and, in the summer of 1914, the Devil may have visited the banks of Castle Stream (*The Man in the Black Suit*). In 1960 four young boys set out from Castle Rock in search of a body and discovered much more (*The Body*). A teenager who harassed them at the time would be responsible for much of the devastation of the town three decades later (*Needful Things*). A creature that emerged from a Polaroid camera killed the same man's uncle. (*The Sun Dog*). An inadvertent psychic attended the town at the behest of Sheriff George Bannerman and flushed out local deputy, Frank Dodd, a serial killer (*The Dead Zone*); but, not five years later, a rabid dog killed Bannerman (*Cujo*). The Beaumonts had a home near town that was visited by Thad Beaumont's alter ego and burned down in a subsequent fire (*The Dark Half*).

The Sheriffs of Castle Rock make many appearances across the stories in this Reality, from the late Bannerman to the more fortunate (if somewhat traumatized) Alan Pangborn, to the Barney Fife-like Norris Ridgewick.

The following are the important Castle Rock stories. We suggest readers follow the order of publication in reading them to achieve the full benefit of discovering Castle Rock and its history.

- *The Dead Zone* (1979)
- *Cujo* (1981)
- *The Body* (1982)
- *Uncle Otto's Truck* (1983, collected in *Skeleton Crew*, 1985)
- *Gramma* (1984, collected in *Skeleton Crew*, 1985)
- *Mrs. Todd's Shortcut* (1984, collected in *Skeleton Crew*, 1985)
- *Nona* (first published as a Castle Rock story in 1985)
- *The Dark Half* (1989)
- *The Sun Dog* (1990)
- *Needful Things* (1991)
- *It Grows On You* (first published as a Castle Rock story in 1993)
- *The Man in the Black Suit* (1994, collected in *Everything's Eventual*, 2002)
- *Bag of Bones* (1998)
- *Premium Harmony* (2009)

Derry, a town near Bangor has an even more troubled past than Castle Rock. Derry was first mentioned in *The Bird and the Album* (published in 1981 and reviewed in another chapter of this book, *Stories Swallowed by Monsters*). In 1741 the town's entire population disappeared without trace; and 67 people died when the water tower collapsed in 1985. Derry appears to suffer a form of collective memory loss, considering the rampage against its children by a monster, often masquerading as a clown, every quarter century or so, most recently in 1957/58 and 1984/85 (*It*). During the interludes between Pennywise/It's appearances Derry has also been the site of a political killing in *Insomnia* (1993) and individual human tragedy. As recently as 2001 there was further evidence that Pennywise, the clown/monster survives (*Dreamcatcher*).

Among residents of note over the years were Ralph Roberts (*Insomnia*); Mike and Johanna Arlen Noonan (*Bag of Bones*): Richard Kinnell (*The Road Virus Heads North*); Morton Rainey of *Secret Window, Secret Garden* (Noonan, Kinnell and Rainey were all successful writers); Henry Devlin, Gary Jones, Joe Clarendon, Pete Moore and Duddits Cavell (*Dreamcatcher*); and a group who called themselves 'the Loser's Club' (*It*).

Interesting geographical features of the town include The Barrens, The Standpipe and the Kissing Bridge (the latter two were destroyed in 1985). Cruising Up-Mile Hill one will pass a Rite-Aid, outside which Jo Noonan died one hot August day in 1994; and perhaps come to Secondhand Rose, Secondhand Clothes (*Insomnia*). One would pass the old Tracker Brothers depot (*It, Dreamcatcher*) if driving Kansas Street or the site of the old Rainey home and, if the road is followed far enough out of town, one would reach Richard Kinnell's house, perhaps to see a Trans Am parked outside. When cruising Neibolt Street avoid number 29. However, the Derry Home Hospital does have an excellent reputation. And, never, *never* go into the sewers!

The following are the important Derry stories. Again, we suggest readers follow the order of publication in reading them to achieve the full benefit of discovering Derry and its history.

- *The Bird and the Album* (1981, revised and later included in *It*)
- *It* (1986)
- *Secret Window, Secret Garden* (1990)
- *Insomnia* (1994)
- *Autopsy Room Four* (1997, collected in *Everything's Eventual*, 2002)
- *Bag of Bones* (1998)
- *Dreamcatcher* (2001)

Jerusalem's Lot, Maine, having been the earlier site of devil-worship and the disappearance of its entire populace in 1789, was taken over by a colony of vampires and effectively abandoned again by the living in 1975. Despite the town's destruction by fire in 1976 vampires were known to be in the area as late as 1977. Jerusalem's Lot's history may be read and discovered in the following order: *Jerusalem's Lot, 'Salem's Lot, One for the Road* and parts of *The Dark Tower V: Wolves of the Calla*.

One of the later Maine Street Horror tales was the outstanding TV series, *Kingdom Hospital*, set at the Kingdom Hospital in Lewiston (although probably not in *our* reality).

The following is a full list of the works that are part the Maine Street Horror Reality. The list includes unpublished works. Each is listed with their primary geographical settings.

Story:	Primary Settings:
Autopsy Room Four	Derry
Bag of Bones	Dark Score Lake/TR90/Derry/Castle Rock
The Bird and the Album	Derry
Blaze	Cumberland County
The Blue Air Compressor	Shore Road
The Body	Castle Rock
But Only Darkness Loves Me	Ledge Cove
Carrie	Chamberlain
Chinga	(Unnamed Town)
The Colorado Kid	Moose-Lookit Island
Comb Dump	Augusta
Cujo and its Unproduced Screenplay	Castle Rock
Cycle of the Werewolf	Tarker's Mills
The Dark Half	Castle Rock/Ludlow
The Dark Tower V: Wolves of the Calla	Jerusalem's Lot/East Stoneham
The Dark Tower VI: Song of Susannah	East Stoneham/Bridgton
The Dark Tower VII: The Dark Tower	East Stoneham/Lovell
The Dead Zone and its Unproduced Screenplay	Castle Rock/Cleaves Mills/Pownal
Do the Dead Sing?	Goat Island
Dolores Claiborne	Little Tall Island
Dreamcatcher	The Jefferson Tract/Derry
11/22/63	Lisbon Falls; Derry
The Fifth Quarter	Carmen's Folly
Gerald's Game	Kashwakamak Lake/Dark Score Lake
The Girl Who Loved Tom Gordon	The Backwoods
Gramma	Castle View

Graveyard Shift	Gates Falls
Gray Matter	Near Bangor
Hearts in Atlantis	The University of Maine
Herman Wouk is Still Alive	Interstate-95
Home Delivery	Gennesault Island
I Know What You Need	(Various)
Insomnia	Derry
It	Derry
It Grows On You (*Marshroots*/ *Weird Tales* and *Whispers* versions)	Harlow
It Grows On You (*Nightmares & Dreamscapes* version)	Castle Rock
Jerusalem's Lot	Jerusalem's Lot
Kingdom Hospital	Lewiston
The King Family and the Wicked Witch	Bridgton
The Langoliers	Bangor
The Leprechaun	(Owen King's home)
The Lonesome Death of Jordy Verrill	Near Castle Rock
The Long Walk	(On the Road)
The Man in the Black Suit	Castle Stream/Motton
Mile 81	Mile 81 Rest Stop, near Auburn
The Mist	Bridgton
Molly	Ammas Beach
The Monkey	Casco
The Monster in the Closet	(Tad Trenton's bedroom)
Movie Show	Harlow/Lewiston
Mrs. Todd's Shortcut	Castle Rock and roads to Bangor
Needful Things	Castle Rock
Night Shift (Unproduced Screenplay)	Weathersfield
Nona (*Shadows*)	Blainesville
Nona (*Skeleton Crew*)	Castle Rock
One for the Road	Falmouth, near Jerusalem's Lot
Pet Sematary	Ludlow
Premium Harmony	Castle Rock
Rage	Placerville
Rainy Season	Willow
The Reach	Goat Island
The Revelations of 'Becka Paulson	Haven
The Revenge of Lardass Hogan	Gates Falls
Riding the Bullet	Gates Falls/Harlow

Rita Hayworth and Shawshank Redemption	Shawshank Prison
The Road Virus Heads North	Wells/Derry
'Salem's Lot	Jerusalem's Lot
Secret Window, Secret Garden	Derry/Tashmore Glen
Silver Bullet	Tarker's Mills
Squad D	Castle Rock
Storm of the Century	Little Tall Island
Strawberry Spring (*Ubris* version)	Wiscassett College
Stud City	Auburn/Lewiston
Suffer the Little Children (*Nightmares & Dreamscapes* version)	Summer Street School
The Sun Dog	Castle Rock
Sword in the Darkness	Gates Falls
Thinner	Bangor/Boothbay Harbor
The Tommyknockers	Haven
Uncle Otto's Truck	Castle Rock
Under the Dome	Chester's Mill
Untitled (*The Huffman Story*)	Huffman
Untitled Screenplay (Radio Station)	WOKY, Western Maine
The Woman in the Room	Central Maine Hospital

The Stand

Stories in The Stand Reality relate to the fundamental change to our world following a devastating superflu epidemic. As many Maine Street Horror, America Under Siege and even Dark Tower events in our world occur after the varying superflu strike dates (1980 in the original version; 1985 in certain paperback editions of the original version and King's unproduced movie script; or 1990 in the *Complete and Uncut* version) it follows that The Stand Reality is in fact an alternate reality/timeline to that in which we exist.

Apart from the variations of *The Stand* itself, the *Night Surf* stories are part of this Reality, linked as they are by the same epidemic, Captain Trips. In *The Dark Tower IV: Wizard and Glass* Roland and his ka-tet (King defines this term as 'those bound by destiny'[13]), along with Flagg, briefly visit another world, strangely like ours but clearly *not* our reality, which has also been devastated by Captain Trips.

The Stand Reality crosses America with large cities (New York) and small towns (Ogunquit, Arnette, Stovington, May, Pratt, Hemingford Home, Woodsville) equally devastated. Survivors are drawn to the 'dark side' (if readers will excuse the reference to a very different mythology) in Las Vegas or to the side (literally) of a religious, old black woman in Boulder.

One hopes King will one day revisit this Reality, if for no reason other than to bring Constant Readers up-to-date with the doings in Maine of our friends, Stu Redman and Fran Goldsmith and their son, Peter.

The following is a full list of the works that fall within The Stand Reality. The list includes unpublished works.

Primary Setting:

Night Surf
The Stand (Original, Uncut, Unproduced Movie Screenplay and Mini-Series Screenplay)

Secondary Setting:

The Dark Tower IV: Wizard and Glass

America Under Siege

Unfortunately, living outside the state of Maine is not enough for characters to avoid the depredations of King and his fertile imagination. King stories are in fact set all over America and also, rarely, in overseas locations (for instance, England in the case of *Crouch End* and *Wimsey*; an unnamed South American country for *In the Deathroom*; and a deserted island, possibly in the Caribbean, for *Survivor Type*). Perhaps the most significant overseas country for both setting and impact upon characters and events is Vietnam (see in particular the latter four stories in the *Hearts in Atlantis* collection; *Squad D*, *Autopsy Room Four*, *The Old Dude's Ticker*, *Children of the Corn*, *The Dead Zone*, *The Dark Tower II: The Drawing of the Three*, *Desperation*, *Firestarter*, and *'Salem's Lot*).

The America Under Siege Reality works are linked by their common location in our world's version of the United States (or with US citizens as characters) and in our 'normal' timeline. When a story deviates into a timeline in which the world as we know it fundamentally changes (for instance, *The Stand* or *The End of the Whole Mess*) it is classified in a more relevant Reality.

Many America Under Siege Reality stories are very much from the mainstream (*All That You Love Will Be Carried Away*, *Rest Stop* or *That Feeling, You Can Only Say What It Is In French*) and include many of King's rare but powerful crime genre stories.

New York, a large and often faceless city is cover for mayhem (*The Ten O'Clock People*, *Lunch at the Gotham Café*), mystery (*The Breathing Method*, *The Man Who Would Not Shake Hands*), murder (*The Man Who Loved Flowers*, *The Plant*, *Sneakers*), penance (*Blind Willie*) and, rarely, positive results (*Dedication*).

Large cities such as Boston (*Cell*), Los Angeles (*The Talisman*), Las Vegas (*Dolan's Cadillac*), Seattle (*Rose Red*) and even imaginary urban areas such as Harding (*The Running Man* and *Sword in the Darkness*) play host to King stories.

But it is small-towns and semi-rural locations that most quickly come to mind when considering King's assault on America through supernatural means (*Children of the Corn*) or the simple horrors of everyday life (*All That You Love Will Be Carried Away*). Isolated towns and residences such as Gatlin, deep in the cornfields of Nebraska and close to Hemingford Home; or Travis, Indiana (*Sleepwalkers*) serve as wonderful backdrops for the doings of supernatural creatures (*Black House*) or the very human horrors that occur at the Wilkes' farm (*Misery*).

It is not possible to sit easy while thinking of Junction City, Iowa (*The Library Policeman* and future home of *Needful Things*' Leland Gaunt); or of Desperation, Nevada. Children should avoid Oatley, New York (*The Talisman*), although Arcadia Beach, New Hampshire might serve for a summer holiday. If seeking to attend a concert one should cross Rock and Roll Heaven, Oregon (*You Know They've Got a Hell of a Band*) from any list; and the flashing lights from a particular shed in Statler, Pennsylvania should also be avoided (*From a Buick 8*).

Thinking of a quiet retirement? Then avoid French Landing, Wisconsin (*Black House*). Wanting to live safe from The Shop? Forget Lakeland, Ohio (*Firestarter*) or Falco Plains, New York (*Golden Years*). Want to avoid killer cars? Then Libertyville, Pennsylvania (*Christine*) is not for you.

One town, however, appears to have fewer dangers. In response to the inane question of where he gets his ideas, King has often stated they come from a shop in Utica. Utica appears often and was the crossover point for Clyde Umney (*Umney's Last Case*). Bobbi Anderson (*The Tommyknockers*) grew up there and Alan Pangborn, later Sheriff of Castle Rock, was once a policeman in the town.

Sometimes it is not towns but other locations that are best avoided. For instance, Cold Mountain Penitentiary (*The Green Mile*) and the Overlook Hotel (*The Shining*) have ended many a life.

The following is a full list of the works defined as part of the America Under Siege Reality. It includes unpublished works.

11/22/63
1408
1922
All That You Love Will Be Carried Away
American Vampire
Apt Pupil
The Ballad of the Flexible Bullet
Battleground
Before the Play

Big Driver
Big Wheels
Black House
Blind Willie
Blockade Billy
The Boogeyman
The Breathing Method
Brooklyn August
Cain Rose Up
The Cannibals
The Cat From Hell
Cat's Eye
Chattery Teeth
Children of the Corn and its Unproduced Screenplay
Christine
Code Name: Mousetrap
The Crate
The Dark Man
The Dead Zone and its Unproduced Screenplay
The Death of Jack Hamilton
Dedication (Both Versions)
Desperation and the Screenplay
Dino
Dolan's Cadillac and its Unproduced Screenplay
Donovan's Brain
The Dune
The Evaluation
Everything's Eventual
Fair Extension
Father's Day
Firestarter
From a Buick 8
The Furnace
General
Ghost Brothers of Darkland County
George D X McArdle
The Glass Floor
Golden Years
A Good Marriage
The Green Mile
The Hardcase Speaks

Harrison State Park '68
Harvey's Dream
Heavenly Shades of Night Are Falling
Here There Be Tygers
The Hotel at the End of the Road
The House on Maple Street
I Hate Mondays
I Was A Teenage Grave-Robber (aka, *In A Half-World of Terror*)
In the Deathroom
Jumper
Keyholes
L.T.'s Theory of Pets
The Last Rung on the Ladder
The Lawnmower Man
The Ledge
The Library Policeman
Lisey and the Madman
The Little Green God of Agony
Low Men in Yellow Coats
Luckey Quarter
Lunch at the Gotham Café
The Man Who Loved Flowers
The Man Who Would Not Shake Hands
Man With a Belly
The Mangler
Memory
Misery
Mobius
Morning Deliveries (Milkman #1)
Mostly Old Men
The Moving Finger
My Pretty Pony
Never Look Behind You
The New Lieutenant's Rap
The Night Flier
The Night of the Tiger
The Old Dude's Ticker
Paranoid: A Chant
The Plant
Popsy
The Pulse
Quitter's Inc.

The Raft
The Reaper's Image
The Regulators
The Reploids
Rest Stop
Roadwork
Rose Madder
Rose Red
The Running Man
Rush Call
The Shining (All Versions)
The Shotgunners
Silence
Skybar
Slade
Sleepwalkers
Sneakers
Something To Tide You Over
Something Wicked This Way Comes
Sometimes They Come Back
Sorry, Right Number
Stationary Bike
The Stranger
Strawberry Spring (*Night Shift* version)
Suffer the Little Children (*Cavalier* version)
Survivor Type
Sword in the Darkness
The Ten O'Clock People
That Feeling, You Can Only Say What It Is In French
They're Creeping Up On You
The Thing at the Bottom of the Well
The Things They Left Behind
Thinner
Trucks
Umney's Last Case
Under the Weather
Untitled (*Chip Coombs*)
Untitled (*She Has Gone to Sleep While ...*)
The Wedding Gig
Weeds
Why We're In Vietnam
You Know They Got a Hell of a Band

New Worlds

From time to time King has taken readers on trips to New Worlds of Science Fiction or Fantasy. Sometimes these rides are ultimately uplifting, but some are terminal. As a result certain stories are classified as being part of the New Worlds Reality, in whole or part.

Once these New Worlds are exposed there is often no return (for example Trooper Ennis Rafferty of *From a Buick 8*; or Norman Daniels, who got too close a look at Rose Madder's land). Sometimes characters return but with more than they bargained for (*I Am the Doorway, Mobius* or *The Jaunt*). Others are saved from a messy end (*Beachworld*) and others are not (*Beachworld* again, or *Charlie*).

In some cases our world takes a permanent turn for the worse, through scientific arrogance (*The End of the Whole Mess*); or nuclear war (*The Aftermath*). If The Stand mythology did not have its own, separate Reality, those stories would qualify for the New Worlds Reality.

In yet other cases parallel dimensions or realities impinge upon ours. We know from the Dark Tower Reality that there are places where the walls between realities are 'thin', and this is proven to be the case in a section of London (*Crouch End*) and on Poplar Street in Wentworth, Ohio (*The Regulators*). *Kingdom Hospital* is set in a reality close to but not, our own (in that reality the New England Robins, not the Boston Red Sox, lost a World Series on an error!)

Some alternate worlds appear charming but danger can present itself. *Eyes of the Dragon* is set in Delain, interestingly the same town from which James and John Norman (*The Little Sisters of Eluria*) hailed. Flagg was rumored to come from Garlan (*Eyes of the Dragon*). In the Dark Tower Cycle John Farson began his evil ways in that very same Mid-World kingdom. The Old Star can be seen from Delain as well as from Roland's world. It remains uncertain as to whether these lands are fully part of The Dark Tower Reality, or are simply linked.

The same uncertainty presents itself in relation to The Territories (*The Talisman* and *Black House*), an agrarian monarchy that uses magic as a replacement for science. Jack Sawyer discovered The Territories, a world achingly close to ours, when not yet a teenager and set out across it, and America, on a great quest. He returned there, near death, as a middle-aged man. It is to be hoped that King and Peter Straub will complete a trilogy of Sawyer stories as the last would likely be set, as Straub has indicated, in the Territories, with its twinners and wondrous creatures.

The following is a full list of the works defined as part of the New Worlds Reality. The list includes unpublished material.

The Aftermath
An Evening at God's
Beachworld
The Beggar and the Diamond
Black House
Blockade Billy
Cell
Charlie
Crouch End
The Cursed Expedition
The End of the Whole Mess
Eyes of the Dragon
For Owen
For the Birds
The 43rd Dream
Heroes for Hope
Home Delivery
I Am the Doorway
I've Got to Get Away
The Jaunt
Jerusalem's Lot
Jhonathan and the Witchs
The Killer
Kingdom Hospital
Maximum Overdrive
The Mist
Mobius
Muffe
The Other Side of the Fog
The Pulse
The Star Invaders
The Talisman
The Word Processor
Word Processor of the Gods
You Know They Got a Hell of a Band

Unclassified

It is impossible to classify four works, two poems and two stories set in England (a sort of England Under Siege Reality). The English stories are *The Doctor's Case*, in which Dr. Holmes solves a murder; and *Wimsey*, the beginning of an aborted detective novel (see the chapter later in this book).

The two poems, *In the Key Chords of Dawn* and *Woman With Child* also defy the classification system. They are also discussed in 'The Poems' chapter.

Conclusion

Perhaps the most important conclusion to be had from this discussion is that it is possible to link all the Realities!

For instance, *The Stand* is linked by Hemingford Home, Nebraska to *Children of the Corn* and *It* (America Under Siege stories); and through Flagg to both the Dark Tower and New Worlds. *The Stand* also has strong links to Maine towns that also feature in the Maine Street Horror tales.

A number of geographical locations (both real and imaginary) stand astride a number of Realities, for instance Topeka in The Stand Reality appears in New Worlds via *The Running Man* and in The Dark Tower Reality via *The Dark Tower IV: Wizard and Glass*. Stovington, Vermont appears in America Under Siege's *The Shining*, and in The Stand Reality. Indeed, there are hundreds of such links.

Characters also cross Realities. A certain Randall Flagg is the primary candidate, appearing in the Dark Tower, New Worlds (*Eyes of the Dragon*) and The Stand Realities. Father/Pere Callahan has transited from Maine Street Horror to The Dark Tower; and Ted Brautigan has managed appearances in both the Dark Tower and America Under Siege Realities. Jack Sawyer, who once lived in the America Under Siege Reality and was but a visitor to the New World of the Territories, is now a permanent resident there.

If it is possible that all Worlds are contained within an atom in a blade of purple grass, as has been posited in the Dark Tower Reality; then it is equally possible for all these Realities to be contained in the mind of a single writer.

The wonders that remain are the as yet untold tales that will flow from the pen/keyboard of the White King.

APPENDIX: CHILDE ROLAND TO THE DARK TOWER CAME (1855)

By Robert Browning (1812-1889)

I
My first thought was, he lied in every word,
That hoary cripple, with malicious eye
Askance to watch the workings of his lie
On mine, and mouth scarce able to afford
Suppression of the glee, that pursed and scored
Its edge, at one more victim gained thereby.

II
What else should he be set for, with his staff?
What, save to waylay with his lies, ensnare
All travellers who might find him posted there,
And ask the road? I guessed what skull-like laugh
Would break, what crutch 'gin write my epitaph
For pastime in the dusty thoroughfare.

III
If at his counsel I should turn aside
Into that ominous tract which, all agree,
Hides the Dark Tower. Yet acquiescingly
I did turn as he pointed, neither pride
Now hope rekindling at the end descried,
So much as gladness that some end might be.

IV
For, what with my whole world-wide wandering,
What with my search drawn out through years, my hope
Dwindled into a ghost not fit to cope
With that obstreperous joy success would bring,
I hardly tried now to rebuke the spring
My heart made, finding failure in its scope.

V

As when a sick man very near to death
Seems dead indeed, and feels begin and end
The tears and takes the farewell of each friend,
And hears one bit the other go, draw breath
Freelier outside, ('since all is o'er,' he saith
And the blow fallen no grieving can amend;')

VI

When some discuss if near the other graves
be room enough for this, and when a day
Suits best for carrying the corpse away,
With care about the banners, scarves and staves
And still the man hears all, and only craves
He may not shame such tender love and stay.

VII

Thus, I had so long suffered in this quest,
Heard failure prophesied so oft, been writ
So many times among 'The Band' to wit,
The knights who to the Dark Tower's search addressed
Their steps - that just to fail as they, seemed best,
And all the doubt was now - should I be fit?

VIII

So, quiet as despair I turned from him,
That hateful cripple, out of his highway
Into the path he pointed. All the day
Had been a dreary one at best, and dim
Was settling to its close, yet shot one grim
Red leer to see the plain catch its estray.

IX

For mark! No sooner was I fairly found
Pledged to the plain, after a pace or two,
Than, pausing to throw backwards a last view
O'er the safe road, 'twas gone; grey plain all round;
Nothing but plain to the horizon's bound.
I might go on, naught else remained to do.

X
So on I went. I think I never saw
Such starved ignoble nature; nothing throve:
For flowers - as well expect a cedar grove!
But cockle, spurge, according to their law
Might propagate their kind with none to awe,
You'd think; a burr had been a treasure trove.

XI
No! penury, inertness and grimace,
In some strange sort, were the land's portion. 'See
'Or shut your eyes,' said Nature peevishly,
'It nothing skills: I cannot help my case:
''Tis the Last Judgement's fire must cure this place
'Calcine its clods and set my prisoners free.'

XII
If there pushed any ragged thistle-stalk
Above its mates, the head was chopped, the bents
Were jealous else. What made those holes and rents
In the dock's harsh swarth leaves, bruised as to baulk
All hope of greenness? Tis a brute must walk
Pashing their life out, with a brute's intents.

XIII
As for the grass, it grew as scant as hair
In leprosy; thin dry blades pricked the mud
Which underneath looked kneaded up with blood.
One stiff blind horse, his every bone a-stare,
Stood stupified, however he came there:
Thrust out past service from the devil's stud!

XIV
Alive? he might be dead for aught I knew,
With that red gaunt and colloped neck a-strain.
And shut eyes underneath the rusty mane;
Seldom went such grotesqueness with such woe;
I never saw a brute I hated so;
He must be wicked to deserve such pain.

XV

I shut my eyes and turned them on my heart,
As a man calls for wine before he fights,
I asked one draught of earlier, happier sights,
Ere fitly I could hope to play my part.
Think first, fight afterwards, the soldier's art:
One taste of the old time sets all to rights.

XVI

Not it! I fancied Cuthbert's reddening face
Beneath its garniture of curly gold,
Dear fellow, till I almost felt him fold
An arm to mine to fix me to the place,
The way he used. Alas, one night's disgrace!
Out went my heart's new fire and left it cold.

XVII

Giles then, the soul of honour - there he stands
Frank as ten years ago when knighted first,
What honest man should dare (he said) he durst.
Good - but the scene shifts - faugh! what hangman hands
Pin to his breast a parchment? His own bands
Read it. Poor traitor, spit upon and curst!

XVIII

Better this present than a past like that:
Back therefore to my darkening path again!
No sound, no sight as far as eye could strain.
Will the night send a howlet or a bat?
I asked: when something on the dismal flat
Came to arrest my thoughts and change their train.

XIX

A sudden little river crossed my path
As unexpected as a serpent comes.
No sluggish tide congenial to the glooms;
This, as it frothed by, might have been a bath
For the fiend's glowing hoof - to see the wrath
Of its black eddy bespate with flakes and spumes.

XX
So petty yet so spiteful! All along,
Low scrubby alders kneeled down over it;
Drenched willows flung them headlong in a fit
Of mute despair, a suicidal throng:
The river which had done them all the wrong,
Whate'er that was, rolled by, deterred no whit.

XXI
Which, while I forded - good saints, how I feared
To set my foot upon a dead man's cheek,
Each step, of feel the spear I thrust to seek
For hollows, tangled in his hair or beard!
- It may have been a water-rat I speared,
But, ugh! it sounded like a baby's shriek.

XXII
Glad was I when I reached the other bank.
Now for a better country. Vain presage!
Who were the strugglers, what war did they wage,
Whose savage trample thus could pad the dank
soil to a plash? Toads in a poisoned tank
Or wild cats in a red-hot iron cage -

XXIII
The fight must so have seemed in that fell cirque,
What penned them there, with all the plain to choose?
No footprint leading to that horrid mews,
None out of it. Mad brewage set to work
Their brains, no doubt, like galley-slaves the Turk
Pits for his pastime, Christians against Jews.

XXIV
And more than that - a furlong on - why, there!
What bad use was that engine for, that wheel,
Or brake, not wheel - that harrow fit to reel
Men's bodies out like silk? With all the air
Of Tophet's tool, on earth left unaware
Or brought to sharpen its rusty teeth of steel.

XXV

Then came a bit of stubbed ground, once a wood,
Next a marsh it would seem, and now mere earth
Desperate and done with; (so a fool finds mirth,
Makes a thing and then mars it, till his mood
Changes and off he goes!) within a rood -
Bog, clay and rubble, sand, and stark black dearth.

XXVI

Now blotches rankling, coloured gay and grim,
Now patches where some leanness of the soil's
Broke into moss, or substances like boils;
Then came some palsied oak, a cleft in him
Like a distorted mouth that splits its rim
Gaping at death, and dies while it recoils.

XXVII

And just as far as ever from the end!
Naught in the distance but the evening, naught
To point my footstep further! At the thought,
A great black bird, Apollyon's bosom friend,
Sailed past, not best his wide wing dragon-penned
That brushed my cap - perchance the guide I sought.

XXVIII

For, looking up, aware I somehow grew,
'Spite of the dusk, the plain had given place
All round to mountains - with such name to grace
Mere ugly heights and heaps now stolen in view.
How thus they had surprised me - solve it, you!
How to get from them was no clearer case.

XXIX

Yet half I seemed to recognise some trick
Of mischief happened to me, God knows when -
In a bad dream perhaps. Here ended, then
Progress this way. When, in the very nick
Of giving up, one time more, came a click
As when a trap shuts - you're inside the den.

XXX
Burningly it came on me all at once,
This was the place! those two hills on the right,
Crouched like two bulls locked horn in horn in fight;
While to the left a tall scalped mountain ... Dunce,
Dotard, a-dozing at the very nonce,
After a life spent training for the sight!

XXXI
What in the midst lay but the Tower itself?
The round squat turret, blind as the fool's heart,
Built of brown stone, without a counterpart
In the whole world. The tempest's mocking elf
Points to the shipman thus the unseen shelf
He strikes on, only when the timbers start.

XXXII
Not see? because of night perhaps? - why day
Came back again for that! before it left
The dying sunset kindled through a cleft:
The hills, like giants at a hunting, lay,
Chin upon hand, to see the game at bay, -
'Now stab and end the creature - to the heft!'

XXXIII
Not hear? When noise was everywhere! it tolled
Increasing like a bell. Names in my ears
Of all the lost adventurers, my peers -
How such a one was strong, and such was bold,
And such was fortunate, yet each of old
Lost, lost! one moment knelled the woe of years.

XXXIV
There they stood, ranged along the hillsides, met
To view the last of me, a living frame
For one more picture! In a sheet of flame
I saw them and I knew them all. And yet
Dauntless the slug-horn to my lips I set,
And blew.

THE LOST AND HIDDEN WORKS

King is prolific but has largely been careful to only release works he was comfortable with at a particular stage of his career. As a result, there are now more than two dozen known works of fiction that have never seen the light of day.

Who knows what lies in the filing cabinets of publishers, the attics of Maine and New England or other nooks and crannies? What we do know is that King himself has a treasure-trove of material. The questions of whether any will be published or whether some or all will ever be deposited with the Stephen Edwin King papers at the Special Collections Unit of the Raymond H Fogler Library of the University of Maine at Orono are for him to answer. It is to be hoped, for the sake of future researchers, that these items will one day find themselves in a protected place, even if access is heavily restricted.

This chapter reviews the works of fiction that have never been seen by researchers and King experts, let alone fans. They have either been lost or King has held them so closely that they have not been read by anyone outside his inner circle. The search for 'lost' King work will continue unabated for decades. King himself still seeks the lost manuscript *of The Float*. The works covered here have either been completely lost; or it is known King holds them. Stories only 'rumoured' to have been written or to exist are not surveyed.

An excellent Chapter on the subject of the unwritten tales, *The Almost Stories*, appears in Spignesi's *The Lost Work of Stephen King*[14]. King tells of one story too scary for him to even write in his *Introduction* to Michel Houellebecq's *H.P. Lovecraft: Against the World, Against Life*[15]. The story, which was to have been titled *Lovecraft's Pillow*, would have dealt with that fantastical writer's dreams and possibly his death.

In a TV interview with Stanford ('Sandy') Phippen on the Maine Public Broadcasting Network[16] King revealed he has written hundreds of poems - Sanford Phipps (interviewer): 'Aren't there more poems? There was something about fifty poems … will there be an anthology of Stephen King poetry?' King: 'Oh gosh, there's probably … there's probably 500, 600 poems that I have in different places. I love poetry and I've written a bunch of them but it's not very good." In fact only fifteen have been published as of late 2011.

The Accident was a one-act play written by King in 1969 but not seen since[17]. King revealed the following information to the author of this book: 'It was a one-acter I wrote for a play award given by the U of Maine English Department. There was a small stipend, so I wrote this little play that was actually set in the Kennebec Fruit[18] (by another name). As I recall, the idea was this: the two most popular students in a small-town high school have died in a road accident. While the whole town goes to the funeral, these two loveable losers (one a boy, the other a girl) discuss how fucked-up the world is and make jokes. By the end, they're necking like crazy, laughing, and saying things like "Thank God they didn't suffer." The only exchange I remember is this:

BOY: They're in a better place now.
GIRL: Yes. Pennsylvania.

Anyway, I won the prize. $40, which I promptly blew on beer, cigarettes, and Big Macs.'[19]

After the Play was an epilogue to *The Shining* but was merged into the novel. King has stated the full version is lost. There is a separate chapter in this volume describing *Before the Play*, the prologue to *The Shining*.

Asylum. The 6 February 2001 edition of *Variety* magazine reported King had written an adaptation of Patrick McGrath's novel *Asylum* for Paramount Pictures, only the second known time he has tackled a work other than his own for the screen. According to Justin Brooks, "the original adaptation was written by Chris Baylis, with other rewrites penned by Patrick Marber. King's involvement started as a script polish for the film's director, Jonathan Demme, but King eventually rewrote the screenplay from scratch." In 2011 King, in correspondence with the author of this book, confirmed he did indeed write an entirely new screenplay[20]. It was probably written about late 2000/early 2001. The movie was released in the US in September 2005, using a screenplay by Patrick Marber and Balis.

The Blob. In 1965 a fanzine, *Comics Review* issue #3 carried the third part in a serialization of King's *I Was A Teenage Grave Robber*. The Table of Contents page included this: 'COMING ATTRACTIONS / In future issues, we hope to have more work by STEVE KING, possibly THE BLOB, based on the movie.' There is no separate evidence that King ever novelized this movie but it would have been in keeping with his behavior in practicing writing around this time. The magazine's editor, Mike Garrett, had this recollection when queried in 2008: 'I don't recall ever reading King's version of THE BLOB. I did read at least two or three other King manuscripts, but I have no recollection of them specifically.'[21] More detail appears in the separate Chapter, *I Was A Teenage Grave Robber*.

Douglas Winter quotes King as saying:[22] 'I had a bad year in 1976 – it was a very depressing time ... for a time, I worked on something called *The Corner*; it didn't turn out.' King had this to say about it to the author of this book[23]:

'Can't remember much, except it was about a young man who runs a convenience store in the inner city. I think he was going to face off first against druggies and then against some sort of Mr. Big crime boss. It would undoubtedly have been a Bachman.'

People, Places and Things was a collection of eighteen short stories self-published by King and his friend Chris Chesley under the name of the Triad Publishing Company. First published in 1960, it was reprinted in 1963. Chesley was one of King's close childhood friends growing up in Durham, Maine. Unfortunately, two of the King stories listed in the Table of Contents have been lost – no known copies of *The Dimension Warp* and *I'm Falling* exist.

King has this to say about *The Float* in the *Notes* to *Skeleton Crew*, 'I wrote this story (*The Raft*) in 1968 as 'The Float'. In late 1969 I sold it to *Adam* which paid not on acceptance only on publication...' (While King received the check, for $250, he never saw the magazine and never has). 'Somewhere along the way I lost the original manuscript too.'

Ghosts is a 1997 short musical horror film starring Michael Jackson in various roles. King is credited for the idea and 'story'. The screenplay is credited as by Mick Garris, Michael Jackson and Stan Winston.

The Ghost Brothers of Darkland County is a collaboration between John Mellencamp and Stephen King. This is the latest official information at time of writing: "John Mellencamp has virtually completed recording and 'assembling' *The Ghost Brothers of Darkland County* musical theater collaboration with Stephen King. John and King have edited the initial three-hour program down to two hours and 10 minutes - with a bit more editing still to come before producer T-Bone Burnett completes the tracks. When finished, the recording will be available in a novel book package containing the full text, two discs featuring the entire production of the spoken word script and songs performed by the cast, and a third CD of the songs only. The story involves domestic turmoil, and is played by a stellar cast led by Kris Kristofferson, in the role of Joe, the father, and Elvis Costello, as the satanic character The Shape. Rosanne Cash plays Monique, the mother, with the sons enacted by Will Daily (Frank), Dave Alvin (Jack), Alvin's real-life brother Phil Alvin (Andy) and John (Drake). Sheryl Crow stars as Jenna and Neko Case is Anna, with boxing legend Joe Frazier playing caretaker Dan Coker and Stephen King himself in the role of Uncle Steve. The narrator is "24" star Glenn Morshower. John stressed that the three-disc package is not a traditional audio book, but offers an experience more akin to listening to an old radio show with music; he further emphasized the challenge inherent in making such a project work." At the time of writing it was still intended to publish the 'book'. The show premiered at the Alliance Theatre in Atlanta, Georgia, in April 2012.

The Alliance Theatre's website promoted the musical in this manner: 'In keeping with the Alliance's tradition of producing new American musicals, the company will produce the world premiere of *Ghost Brothers of Darkland County*, a chilling new musical with music and lyrics by John Mellencamp and book by Stephen King, as the closing show of the Alliance Stage Series season set for spring, 2012. One of the world's most popular authors and one of America's most honored musicians have created a riveting Southern gothic musical fraught with mystery, tragedy, and ghosts of the past, along with a roots and blues-tinged score that is sure to leave audiences asking for more. Alliance Artistic Director Susan V. Booth directs, with musical direction provided by legendary producer T Bone Burnett. In the tiny town of Lake Belle Reve, Mississippi in 1957, a terrible tragedy took the lives of two brothers and a beautiful young girl. During the next forty years, the events of that night became the stuff of local legend. But *legend* is often just another word for lie. Joe McCandless knows what really happened; he saw it all. The question is whether or not he can bring himself to tell the truth in time to save his own troubled sons, and whether the ghosts left behind by an act of violence will help him – or tear the McCandless family apart forever.'

King relates the history of *Happy Stamps* ('My first really original story idea …') in sections 14 – 16 of the *C.V.* section of *On Writing*. 'The hero of my story was your classic Poor Schmuck, a guy named Roger who had done jail time twice for counterfeiting money — one more bust would make him a three-time loser. Instead of money, he began to counterfeit Happy Stamps . . . except, he discovered, the design of Happy Stamps was so moronically simple that he wasn't really counterfeiting at all; he was creating reams of the actual article.' Roger and his mother decide to send in enough stamps to buy an entire house. 'Roger discovers, however, that although the *stamps* are perfect, the *glue* is defective. If you lap the stamps and stick them in the book they're fine, but if you send them through a mechanical licker, the pink Happy Stamps turn blue.' As a result, Roger is left with the task of licking *millions* of stamps. King concludes: 'There were things wrong with this story (the biggest hole was probably Roger's failure simply to start over with different glue), but it was cute, it was fairly original, and I knew I had done some pretty good writing. After a long time spent studying the markets in my beat-up *Writer's Digest,* I sent "Happy Stamps" off to *Alfred Hitchcock's Mystery Magazine*. It came back three weeks later with a form rejection slip attached. This slip bore Alfred Hitchcock's unmistakable profile in red ink and wished me good luck with my story. At the bottom was an unsigned jotted message, the only personal response I got from *AHMM* over eight years of periodic submissions. "Don't staple manuscripts," the postscript read. "Loose pages plus paperclip equal correct way to submit copy." This was pretty cold advice, I thought, but useful in its way. I have never stapled a manuscript since.'

During the Q&A session after a presentation at George Mason University on 23 September 2011 King said: "God, there's a wonderful, half-finished novel called – get ready for this, this is really purple – the novel is called *Hatchet Head*. It was about a teenage boy who's doing a term paper on capital punishment and this one particular inmate who has been executed, and then after he's been executed he starts writing this kid letters and saying, "I'm coming to see you." And murders along the way with the same MO but I couldn't figure it out, so ... I got about a hundred and fifty pages and stopped." When questioned about the novel a week later King replied, "It's actually quite recent, certainly post-accident. Probably 2004. It was a blind alley."[24]

In a non-fiction piece on *Low Men in Yellow Coats* published in 2009's *Stephen King Goes to the Movies*, King has this to say: '... the fact is that "Low Men" is only part of a loosely constructed novel, which still isn't really done ("The House on Benefit Street," the story of what happened to Bobby's childhood girlfriend, Carol, remains to be written.' Further information appeared on King's official message board: "The following question was raised, 'I read the intro of "Low men in yellow coats" present in "Stephen King goes to the Movies" and it mentions one chapter King didn't write yet for Hearts in Atlantis. It's called "The house on Benefit Street" and it's the story of what happened to Carol (Bobby childhood's girlfriend). Any news about this? Does King plan to write it?'" The Moderator, who is King's personal assistant, responded as follows, 'Steve got the idea to do this 2 or 3 years ago, I think. He had asked me to get the audio versions of Hearts in Atlantis to listen to while he drove to Florida to get him back in the groove and then planned to begin writing it when he arrived. I don't know what happened between November and January, but he started writing another project instead. I'd asked him recently if he still planned to write it but he wasn't sure if he would as he has other projects ... he's working on that are taking priority.'

King began *The House on Value Street*, a novel inspired by Patty Hearst's kidnapping, while living in Boulder in the late summer of 1974. It did not work and he abandoned it after six weeks. What happened to the manuscript is unknown. King gives some detail of the work in *Danse Macabre*:[25] 'It was going to be a *roman à clef* about the kidnapping of Patty Hearst, her brainwashing ... her participation in the bank robbery, the shootout at the SLA hideout in Los Angeles – in my book, the hideout was on Value Street, natch – the fugitive run across the country, the whole ball of wax. It seemed to me to be a highly potent subject, and while I was aware that lots of non-fiction books were sure to be written on the subject, it seemed to me that only a novel might really succeed in explaining all the contradictions... I gathered my research materials ... and then I attacked the novel. I attacked it from one side and nothing happened. I tried it from another side and felt it was going pretty well until I discovered all my characters sounded as if they had just stepped whole and sweaty from the dance marathon in Horace McCoy's *They Shoot Horses, Don't They?* I tried it *in media res*. I tried to imagine it as a stage play, a trick that sometimes works for me when I'm badly stuck. It didn't work this time.'

Kingdom Hospital was a milestone in King's career. His second attempt at series television, it ran over 15 hours in 2004. According to the ABC website, *Stephen King's Kingdom Hospital* was 'the haunting new drama series created directly for television by the award-winning, bestselling master of horror. Using Lars Von Trier's Danish miniseries *Riget* (a.k.a. *The Kingdom*) as a point of inspiration, King tells the terrifying story of The Kingdom, a hospital with a bizarre population that includes a nearly blind security guard, a nurse who regularly faints at the sight of blood and a paraplegic artist whose recovery is a step beyond miraculous. When patients and staff hear the tortured voice of a little girl crying through the halls, they are dismissive of any suggestion of mysticism or unseen powers ... but at their own peril.'

The Sony TV website told us, 'Kingdom Hospital stands as a supposed shimmering example of modern medicine, but its doctors and patients have begun to collide with lurking supernatural forces which reveal its troubled history. Built upon the site of a great fire, which killed many children over 100 years ago, the hospital still hosts remnant spirits of the unsettled dead.' King used his own near death experience as the inspiration for the character of Peter Rickman. In the last episode, he gave cameo appearances as Johnny B Good and a lawyer on TV in addition to the audio cameo as the AA sponsor on the telephone in episode six.

To date, copies of the telescript for all nine episodes King wrote or co-wrote have yet to surface.

The first two-hour episode was shown 3 March 2004 and garnered over 14 million viewers, the best new series launch on ABC-TV for over 2 ½ years, although ratings rapidly declined for later episodes. The network unforgivably split the series, with a two-month gap between the ninth and tenth episodes. Ironically, perhaps the finest episode in the series was King's sad, compelling and redemptive take on events following an alternate reality 1987 World Series, *Butterfingers*, the last shown before the enforced break.

King and Richard Dooling wrote the teleplays. One episode, in the first known collaboration with her husband, was based on a storyline by Tabitha King. The overall story was original to King, using characters by Lars van Trier. Craig R Baxley directed, as he had *Rose Red*, *The Diary of Ellen Rimbauer* and *Storm of the Century*. Ed Begley Jr. played Dr. Jesse James; Andrew McCarthy appeared as Dr. Hook; Jack Coleman as Peter Rickman; Diane Ladd as Mrs. Druse; and Bruce Davison played Dr. Stegman. The DVD was released in late 2004.

In a column titled *A Kingdom That Didn't Come* in *Entertainment Weekly* for 9 July 2004 King explains why he thinks the series flopped in the ratings. Importantly, he states, 'As late as March Rick [*Dooling*] and I delivered a season 2 "bible" which the Alphabet net bought, paid for and eagerly received.' Unfortunately there are no plans to produce that second series.

The episodes and writers were: *Thy Kingdom Come* (Stephen King); *Death's Kingdom* (King); *Goodbye Kiss* (King); *The West Side of Midnight* (King); *Hook's Kingdom* (King and Richard Dooling); *The Young and the Headless* (Dooling); *Black Noise* (Dooling); *Heartless* (Dooling); *Butterfingers* (King); *The Passion of Jimmy Criss* (Stephen King, based on a storyline by Tabitha King); *Seizure Day* (Dooling); *Shoulda Stood in Bed* (King); *Finale* (King). *The Passion of Jimmy Criss* was retitled *On the Third Day* for the DVD release, perhaps as a result of the runaway success of Mel Gibson's *The Passion of the Christ*.

There were many subtle, and none too subtle links, from *Kingdom Hospital* to King's other fiction and the series itself is mentioned in *The Dark Tower VI: Song of Susannah*.

On 25 March 1982 King gave a speech at the University of Dayton in which he said: "I can remember getting the idea for a story in the Stapleton International Airport, which is in Denver. And I got it because my wife had to go the bathroom. We were going to catch a plane and we were walking down the concourse and she said, "I've gotta go" and I said, "Go" and she went, and I'm standing outside and suddenly I notice that I'm not alone outside this room. I realized I wasn't alone. There were about five guys all standing out there with their hands in their pockets and they always look the same way outside the ladies' room. They're just..."well, I'm here of course, outside the ladies' room and that's what I'm doing right now" and it suddenly occurred to me, there's an old joke about the one place where Superman can't go and I thought, "This is it. It's off limits for half of the human race." They never see the inside of a ladies' room unless they're weird I suppose or something and suddenly I thought of this story and I sat and I wrote it."

"And what really fascinated me about this story was this sort of chain of command idea that came into it. The story begins with a man and his wife who are going to catch a plane...our situation, and the woman says, "I've gotta go" and the guy says, "Go" and he stands outside and as he's waiting, another guy comes along with his girlfriend and she says that she has to go and she goes in and the two of them are standing out there. And the first guy's (the hero's) plane is called and his wife doesn't come and then it's final boarding call for this plane and he's looking at the door and he can't quite go in but she's not coming out. And the second guy's girlfriend is not coming out. Meanwhile, a business-type and his wife has come along and she hasn't come out and there are three guys standing around out there and he's missed his plane, he's getting his worried, he doesn't know what to do. I mean, it's the ladies' room, right? It isn't like, you know, Hydra, the three-headed monster. It's just the ladies' room."

"So, two salesmen come along, who are quite inebriated and they're obviously with women who are not their wives and they go in and the two ladies don't come out and finally one of the fellas, quite drunk says, "I'm not gonna put up with this. I'm gonna go in and see what's going on." So, he goes in and you know those pneumatic door closer things that they have there. Well, the door is sliding shut after he goes in and just before it slips home into its socket, they hear this traveling salesman begin to scream. You know, he's screaming his lungs out and they're all standing around looking at each other like this and so, one of them says, "Alright, let's get one of the lady security guards." So, one of them goes up to…and now they're real scared, you know and they go up to the place where they check you through and they have the little beeper and everything and they get one of the women security guards who's laughing at them, but she comes back down and she goes in and of course doesn't she doesn't come out, okay."

"So at this point they get the head of security who goes in with a gun, you know and he doesn't come out. And I really got to love that story because I could see it building up to the head of the airport, you know? After the head of the airport, you know, the mayor, the state police, the Governor. Finally, the President all over this ladies' room, but I couldn't figure out what was in there, so I just quit it. But, it was fun, you know, working on that story was a lot of fun."

King also talked about the story during an appearance on the *Late Night With Conan O'Brien* TV show on May 5, 1995: "I had an idea one time for a story about the ladies room at Stapleton Airport in Denver, Colorado. I know, but the way … see what happens is David Copperfield makes the whole thing disappear. No, actually what the story was gonna be is this guy and his wife are on their way to their plane and the woman says, "Hon, I gotta use the ladies room." "Okay, but remember – five minutes, we've gotta be to the gate." She goes in and she doesn't come out, and the guys just standing out there, 'cause everybody, every guy's been in this position at one time or another where you're … it's the one place even Superman can't go, right? So, there you are and so, and everybody is strange to everybody else in this airport. So another guy comes up and his wife goes in and then there's two guys standing out there and one of them says, "I'm gonna be late for my plane." And the other guy says, "Yeah." Soon, there's a third guy and then a fourth, finally one guy says, "Well, screw it, I'm gonna go in and get her," and he goes in and just as the thing slides closed on that pneumatic door closer you hear screams from inside, you know. I thought, "Whoa! This is good, I like this." So, they go and get the security people, right? And they go inside, and they don't come out. So, pretty soon you get the state militia, you get the FBI, you get the Governor involved, you get the Army, the rest of it. But I could never figure out what the hell was going on in there, so …"

When asked about the story in 2011 King responded, "Yeah, that was called *The Ladies Room*. Not very PC, I know, but that was an earlier time. Everything I had to say about it you've got. It was a great idea, but it just never turned out. *Mile 81* is close to it in structure."[26]

Land of 1,000,000 Years Ago was advertised in *Dave's Rag* as '…the new

King story!!!!'. It is assumed this was written, or was to be written, by young Stephen (only eleven at the time). The advertisement read: ' "Land of 1,000,000 Years Ago." Exciting story of 21 people prisoners on an island that should have been extinct 1,000,000 years ago. Order through this newspaper.' The same edition of the newspaper (Summer 1959) advertises a 'New Book by Steve King!', *Thirty-One of the Classics*. The text of that advertisement, 'Read "Kidnapped", "Tom Sawyer", and *many* others!!! If you order in three weeks, only 30c. Contact Steve King %Dave's Rag' (*sic*)'. *Dave's Rag* itself was a newspaper self-published by Steve King's brother, Dave. King relates much of its history in *On Writing* and two King stories from the newspaper, *Jumper* and *Rush Call* are reviewed in a separate chapter of this book.

According to a 1986 article in *Time* magazine King was working on '*Livre Noir*, a detective story in French, "the language that turns dirt into romance." The quote is presumably from what the article called 'the indisputable King of horror' himself. The story also revealed King, promoting *It* at the time, had 'plans to study French in order to finish' the story, indicating it had at least been started. In the opinion of this author, the whole thing smacks of a casual joke on King's part; and King has never once mentioned the book or supported the claim since.

Milkman was an aborted novel, from which two segments, *Morning Deliveries (Milkman #1)* and *Big Wheels (Milkman #2)*, were re-written and published as short stories. *Big Wheels* was first published in a 1980 anthology, *New Terrors 2* before King completely re-wrote it for an appearance in *Skeleton Crew*.

Mr. Rabbit Trick may be the first story King ever wrote. According to an article by Martyn Palmer in *The Times* magazine (re-published in *The Australian Women's Weekly* magazine for January 2004) King '…first started writing as a seven-year-old, when he presented his mother with a short story called *Mr Rabbit Trick*, about magic animals.' As the article resulted from an interview King gave in Los Angeles to promote *The Dark Tower V: Wolves of the Calla* we can presume King revealed this information. King also refers to what is almost certainly the same story in part 8 of the 'C.V.' section of *On Writing*, in which he notes he wrote four or five Mr Rabbit Trick stories. He sold four of them to his mother for a quarter a piece, "That was the first buck I made in this business."

In April 2005 it was revealed that King had co-written a script for a sequel to the movie, *The Night Flier*, based on his short story of the same name. Producer Richard P Rubinstein told *Fangoria* magazine, "Mark Pavia, director of the original, came to me with a screenplay for the sequel," the producer reports. "I don't usually like sequels, but I thought the script was good and gave it to Stephen to see what he thought." Not only did King enjoy the screenplay, he decided to get directly involved. "I thought the script would sit on his shelf for a while," Rubinstein says, "but suddenly, Steve came to me with a corrected and rewritten screenplay by himself. When I told Mark, I thought he was going to have a heart attack. There were some things he would miss from his original version, but now he had an improved one co-written by Stephen King himself!"

King's office confirmed he had indeed written an updated draft while in Florida during the winter of 2004-5. The current title for the unproduced movie is *The Night Flier 2*.

Old Chief Woodenhead – see *Pinfall* below.

On the Island is a novel King wrote in the period from 1985-90. In an interview with Tim Adams for *The Guardian* (UK) and published in September 2000, King said the following of the novel, "I started a book … about 15 years ago. It was called *On the Island*, and it was about rich people who talked these street kids into going to an island and being hunted, with paintballs. And they get there and they find these guys are actually shooting live rounds, and in my story there were two or three who escaped and waited for these rich guys to come back. I've got it on a shelf somewhere." Previous editions of this book revealed that a 209 page manuscript was held in a box in King's office. In July 2011 King told the author of this book he also retains 160 pages of manuscript, "all hand-written, in a big ledger book"[27].

Pinfall was a screenplay segment for the movie, *Creepshow 2*. King confirmed he wrote a 'synopsis' for it, as well as for the *Old Chief Woodenhead* section of the same movie; and confirmed he did not write either screenplay segment.[28]

King wrote *The Pit and the Pendulum*, which he and Chris Chesley sold copies of at Durham's elementary school. It 'novelized' the 1961 movie of the same name. All trace of the story has been lost. King tells its story ('…turned out to be my first best-seller') in section 18 of the *C.V.* part of *On Writing*. King's entertaining re-telling of the whole incident, in which he also reveals selling copies of another story, *The Invasion of the Star-Creatures* that summer, is highly recommended. Concluding his retelling of the incident King says, 'Miss Hisler told me I would have to give everyone's money back. I did so with no argument, even to those kids (and there were quite a few, I'm happy to say) who insisted on keeping their copies of V.I.B. #1. I ended up losing money on the deal after all, but when summer vacation came I printed four dozen copies of a new story, an original called *The Invasion of the Star-Creatures*[29], and sold all but four or five.'

Note that some kids 'insisted on keeping their copies' of this story. Unlikely though it may seem, is it possible a copy will turn up one day when one of King's ex-schoolmates cleans out an old box of keepsakes?

King had previously related the history *The Pit and the Pendulum* in Douglas Winter's *The Art of Darkness*:[30] 'One day I went to Brunswick to see the American International Film of *The Pit and the Pendulum* with Vincent Price, and I was very impressed by it – very, very scared. And when I went home, I got a bunch of stencils, and I wrote a novelization of the movie, with chapters and everything – although it was only twelve pages long. I bought a ream of typewriter paper, and I bought a stapler and some staples, and I printed, on Dave's machine, about two hundred and fifty copies of this book. I slugged in a price of a dime on them, and when I took them to school, I was just flabbergasted. In three days, I sold something like seventy of these things. And all of a sudden, I was in the black – it was like a license to steal. That was my first experience with bestsellerdom. But they shut me down. They took me to the principal's office and told me to stop, although there didn't seem to be any real reason. My aunt[31] taught in that school, and it was just not seemly; it wasn't right. So I had to quit.'

According to Chris Chesley, there was another such story, although he does provide the title. Chesley told Beahm[32], 'In another story, King playfully wove fact and fiction, using the real names of fellow students in a fictional hostage situation. "It was all of twenty pages," recalled Chesley, "and it was a story where he used real kids who had taken over the grammar school. Of course, the people that were in the story read the story; because of things like that, King was lionized. He could take real people and set them into this setting where we were heroes. In this story, we died fighting the National Guard. The kids he liked best 'died' last; so naturally, we were all wondering when we were going to 'die'."'

In his introduction to *The Old Dude's Ticker*, King mentions he wrote two pastiches[33] about 1971-1972. 'The first was a modern day revision of Nikolai Gogol's story, "The Ring" (my version was called "The Spear", I think)'. That one is lost. The other story was, of course, *The Old Dude's Ticker*, which is the subject of a chapter of this book.

In 2011 King revealed to the author of this book that he had abandoned a novel titled *The Reploids* in the mid-1980s after forty pages of manuscript. This was the first time the King community was aware that the short story of the same name actually came from a busted novel. A detailed Chapter about *The Reploids* short story appears later in this volume.

According to a piece King wrote in *The Boston Globe*[34] in appreciation of Stephen Jay Gould, the pre-eminent American paleontologist, evolutionary biologist, and historian of science, King wrote a "vernacular version of the Book of Genesis" and sent it to Gould. While the newspaper article reported the title was *The Street Kid's Genesis*, in correspondence with the author of this book, King said: 'It was actually called *The Street Kid's Bible*. I had this crazy idea of translating the whole Bible into a kind of hip-hop thing. Not black, just slang. I know it sounds just wrong, but part of being a good writer is giving all sorts of nutty ideas a test drive. As I recall, I got through the Garden of Eden ("Snake says, 'Why should *you* always be second best, honey?'") and then gave up.'[35]

Training Exercises is an unproduced film treatment. According to the *Castle Rock* newsletter for May 1986: 'Training Exercises is a treatment developed by

Stephen King. It concerns a number of elderly WWII and Korean warhorses who own their own Pacific Island and trick young kids into coming each year to participate in a harmless "training exercise." The hero is a kid of 18 or so, a down-and-out and would-be actor from L.A., who answers an ad and becomes part of this year's Training Exercise. Except it all turns out to be real, with blood, bullets and death. These old guys have been slaughtering people for years.'

Interestingly, King plugged *Battle Royale* by Koushun Takami in his *Entertainment Weekly* column for 12 August 2005. King's short take on the novel: 'Forty-two Japanese high school kids who think they're going on a class trip are instead dropped on an island, issued weapons ranging from machine guns to kitchen forks, and forced to fight it out until only one is left alive. *Royale* bears some resemblance to Richard Bachman's *The Long Walk*.'

In *Stephen King Collectibles: An Illustrated Price Guide* [36] author George Beahm writes of an *Untitled* work not referenced anywhere else in published King research: '…I know of an unpublished story in short manuscript form, inscribed to the mother of one of King's childhood friends from Durham …'. It is unclear whether this is an otherwise unknown story, or a simply a manuscript of an unpublished short story noted elsewhere in this chapter.

Untitled: King once said he tried to write an erotic novel in 1968, while studying at the University of Maine. He wrote about forty pages and 'while writing a scene in which gorgeous twin sisters are making love in a birdbath, I collapsed in shrieks of laughter and banished the project into the oilstove.'

When asked about it by the author of this book he responded: 'No, I really did try. I used to get *Writer's Digest* back then (when I could afford it), and read a piece saying one of the better porno/erotica houses—I think it was Olympia Press—would pay up to $4,000 for novels of x word length...maybe 40,000 to 60,000. I thought to myself, "Holy shit, I could pay a year's tuition and not have to spend my summer sweating my guts out at the mill." I even had how many words I'd need to do per night to finish in a month figured out … I just couldn't. It was too ludicrous.'

Untitled: King told Douglas Winter this in an interview: 'I can remember the first real horror story that I wrote. I was about seven years old, and I had internalized the idea from the movies that, when everything looked blackest, the scientists would come up with some off-the-wall solution that would take care of things. I wrote about this big dinosaur that was really ripping ass all over everything, and finally one guy said, "Wait, I have a theory – the old dinosaurs used to be allergic to leather." So they went out and threw leather boots and leather shoes and leather vests at it, and it went away.'[37]

Untitled: The *Lisbon Monthly* for November 1986 carried an article titled *Stephen King: "Lisbon High's Most Celebrated Alumnus"*. In this article Ambra Watkins reports King 'also wrote a successful script for Class Day about Batman and Robin.' More detail appears in the 1967 Lisbon High School

Yearbook which reports, 'Two members of the Drum staff decided to write their own little skit for class night based on the television program, "Batman" ... Danny Emond and Steve King began writing their comic tale ... After finishing the script, the (senior class) committee approved the writing, made minor changes and began to put it together for the stage. Steve and Danny took the leading roles of Batman and Robin. The plot concerned a possible attack on Lisbon High which was to be prevented by the daring duo ... When Batman and Robin were needed, the two appeared on a tricycle down the middle of the gymnasium.' A photo from the yearbook shows King played Robin in the skit, performed on the evening of 7 June 1966. The class graduated the following day.

Untitled: In *Practicing the (Almost) Lost Art*, his introduction to *Everything's Eventual*, King notes he attempted to write a radio play 'sort of like the ones I used to listen to with my grandfather when I was growing up (and he was growing old) in Durham, Maine. A Halloween play, by God! It was intended in the style of Orson Welles' infamous Halloween radio adaptation of H G Wells' *The War of the Worlds*. There would be a broadcast from a Bangor station he owned, purporting to be direct from a UFO landing in Bangor (and the concept could be syndicated to cities and towns across America). 'So what happened? I couldn't do it, that's what happened. I tried and I tried, and everything I wrote came out sounding like narration ...Not a play...but something more like a book on tape...It was busted and I didn't know how to fix it.'

King says of this concept: 'That actually did get done...as a 2-minute station promo! It's long lost now, of course, but it scared the shit out of people.'[38]

Untitled: In February 2007, author Stephen R. Donaldson reported on his official website: 'Incidentally (for you trivia buffs), he [King] and I once collaborated—with quite a few other writers—on what I think of as a 'gag' story. It was so long ago that I've forgotten most of the details. But the purpose of the exercise was to raise money for a charity at an sf/f convention. Without any prior discussion, each writer in turn wrote for 30-45 minutes, then folded the paper so that only the last sentence was visible. With only that last sentence for 'context,' the next writer attempted to continue the 'story.' I had to go on from King's last sentence. The result, as I recall, was hysterically surreal.' Donaldson recalls this was around 1980. It seems likely that the finished result was later auctioned but no trace of it has ever surfaced.

Untitled: King told www.TIME.com the following in November 2009[39]: '(*The Tommyknockers*) was another case of a book I tried to write a long time ago. I had the idea of the guy stumbling over the flying saucer when I was a senior in college. I had 15 or 20 pages and I just stopped. I don't remember why. I think it was probably like *Under the Dome*. The canvas was just too big. And so I quit. The pages went God knows where. Years later the idea recurred and I just got swept up by the concept.' When checking with King in August

2011 during research for the latest edition of this book he was able to confirm this 'lost' manuscript was indeed an early draft of the later novel, 'It had no title, but it really WAS *The Tommyknockers*.'[40]

Untitled: King told the Associated Press this in 1979: 'For example, I'm working on a story now about a guy who goes to his small town's restaurant every afternoon for coffee. One day he goes in and a different waitress takes his order. When he asks about the other waitress, the new one denies there ever was such as person. That's a frightening situation. How does a person cope?'[41] In research for this book King recalled attempting the tale.[42]

Untitled: In 1989, King said in a public speech, 'A few years ago, I did try very hard to write a western, because it's a form I like. I wrote about 160 pages and the only scene that really had any power was when this old guy got drunk outside this farmhouse and fell into the pigsty, and the pigs ate him. That one scene has some real drive and punch. This is what turned on my lights, for reasons I don't understand.[43]' In research for this book King was asked if this was the same busted novel as *George D X McArdle* (see the separate chapter) and replied that they were two separate western novels[44]. No more is known about this particular untitled work.

Verona Beach was a piece of fiction King worked on in college. It apparently became the basis of *The Talisman*.

Sometime in the school year of 1963-64 King edited a satirical take-off of the high school newspaper he later edited, *The Drum* (two stories from that newspaper, *Code Name: Mousetrap* and *The 43rd Dream* are subject of a separate chapter of this book). The satire was titled *The Village Vomit*, King tells its sordid story in section 19 of the *C.V.* part of *On Writing*. In part he says, 'One night - sick to death of Class Reports, Cheerleading Updates, and some lamebrain's efforts to write a school poem - I created a satiric high school newspaper of my own when I should have been captioning photographs for *The Drum*. What resulted was a four-sheet which I called *The Village Vomit*. The boxed motto in the upper lefthand corner was not "All the News That's Fit to Print" but "All the Shit That Will Stick." That piece of dimwit humor got me into the only real trouble of my high school career.' No known copies of *The Village Vomit*, which included a number of articles, exist.

Douglas Winter quotes King in *Stephen King: The Art of Darkness*[45] as saying: 'I had a bad year in 1976 – it was a very depressing time. I started a book called *Welcome to Clearwater*, but it was busted.'

What Tricks Your Eye was King's first attempt at the story that would become *The Green Mile*. He tells its story in the *Introduction* to the combined volume of that originally serialized novel. King developed the tale in 1992 or 1993. It has never been released in any form and it is now very unlikely that it will. The best we can hope for is that it will be deposited at the Fogler Library. In the story a man on death row develops an interest in magic tricks. Luke Coffey was a large black man awaiting his punishment at Evans Notch in 1932. As the date of his execution drew near he developed an interest in sleight-of-hand magic tricks and, as a result, was able to disappear from the prison. His story is told from the perspective of an old trusty who sold cigarettes and novelties from his cart.

Updates from previous editions: As suspected King has confirmed he never worked on a screenplay for *Carrion Comfort*[46]. Previous editions indicated King had written a screenplay version of *Poltergeist* but it has since been clarified: 'I was going to write the script for *Poltergeist*. We had agreed to everything, but then I was on vacation and out of the country and my agent screwed up the deal.'[47] Previous editions indicated King had been working on a novel titled *The Doors* but it has since been discovered that the original source material, an auction listing for one of his famous ledgers, reported the matter incorrectly. The section titled 'The Doors' was in fact part of King's notes for *The Drawing of the Three*, part of which appeared in the same ledger. Of course, Roland Deschain's 'drawing' of people from Keystone Earth to All-World through 'Doors' is a major storyline in that novel.[48]

Further note: there has been speculation King once wrote a sixties rock-'n'roll novel titled *The Pretenders*. The author himself has specifically denied writing any such novel, by that or any other title[49].

VARIATIONS AND VERSIONS IN KING'S FICTION

There has been little discussion over the years of King's penchant for revising his fiction and this is quite surprising. The fact there are almost as many King works of fiction that have been revised for re-publication as those that have not should have led to further discussion and interest than has been accorded.

Most authors publish a story once and that first (and only) version becomes the standard form of the work no matter how often it is reprinted or wherever it is republished.

In this matter King, as is often the case, is different. It is possible that no King work is ever truly 'finished'. He often publishes a short story in a magazine and later reworks it for publication in one of his collections, such as *Night Shift* or even to include as parts of a novel.

These revisions range from relatively minor wording changes (for example, *Battleground*) to more significant rewrites (*Children of the Corn*), to total rewrites which will often include major character name changes and the transfer of a story-line to entire new towns or timelines (*It Grows on You* or *Nona*). Even novel-length works such as *Eyes of the Dragon* have been revised.

If a collector were to obtain each publication of every story it would be necessary to benchmark it against other publications. The next problem is determining whether changes are simply 'Variations' (minor updates) or represent a whole new 'Version' of the story.

The rule of thumb used for this publication is that where a work has been published and a later publication includes relatively minor variations (small text changes, no significant changes in Characters or Plot), these are classified as a 'Variation'. In those cases there is only one substantive 'Version' of that work. However, where the later publication includes relatively significant changes in Plot, Character, Location and so on, or a very significant rewrite of the text, that later work is a new 'Version' of the tale.

Novels

To date, King has revised four novels; allowed 'deleted scenes' to be published from one; marginally revised material for another; and added a fictional *Foreword* to certain editions of yet another.

An entirely fictional *Foreword to Paperback Edition* appears in certain Signet (US) mass market paperback editions of *Dolores Claiborne*, the first of which appeared in December 1993, the same year as the first edition hardback was published. It is noteworthy that this addition has never appeared in a UK-rights paperback.

King's own imprint, Philtrum Press first published *Eyes of the Dragon* in 1984, in a Limited Edition of 1250. The mass-market edition, published in 1987, contains important differences in the text, including character changes. An entire chapter from the Limited was not included in the mass-market edition. The original title of the manuscript was *The Napkins*, which refers to Peter's method of escape. King first wrote the story for his daughter, Naomi and relates this motivation in a short non-fiction piece, *Why I Wrote the Eyes of the Dragon*, which appeared in the *Castle Rock* newsletter for February 1987. The differences between the two publications clearly show that they are quite separate versions of the same tale.

The Green Mile is one of the best loved of King's tales, by both readers and moviegoers in general. This is partly due to it being one of the best screen adaptations of a King story and *that* is almost entirely down to Frank Darabont, who wrote the screenplay and directed. *The Green Mile* was King's first complete serialized novel. Published each month from March until August 1996, it was later re-published in omnibus (1996) and hardback (2000) editions with minor updates, largely relating to certain errors. King had this to say in the combined edition, 'I did change the moment where Percy Wetmore, bound in a straightjacket, raises one hand to wipe the sweat from his face'. The original Book Six, *Coffey on the Mile*, read: 'I reached up, grabbed the end of the runner he'd worked loose, and gave it a hard yank. It made a loud peeling sound. Brutal winced. Percy yipped with pain and began rubbing his lips. He tried to speak, realized he couldn't do it with a hand over his mouth, and lowered it.' The combined edition reads: 'I reached up, grabbed the end of the runner he'd worked loose, and gave it a hard yank. It made a loud peeling sound. Brutal winced. Percy yipped with pain and his eyes watered.'

In the earlier chapter detailing King's Realities it was noted that in 2003 he released a revised and expanded version of the first Dark Tower novel, *The Gunslinger*. In that case King's major reasons for revision related to bringing the first volume of a seven volume epic into line with the mythology of the subsequent volumes; and to fixing the writing problems suffered by the young man who wrote the novels' five parts over the period from 1970 to its initial publication as a Limited Edition in 1982.

The parts that made up the novel were first published in *The Magazine of Fantasy and Science Fiction* during 1978, 1980 and 1981. There are notable differences between the original publications in the magazine and the subsequent Limited Edition published by Grant (1982), republished as a mass-market version by NAL (1988). While some of the at least 98 changes were apparently to improve the writing or to fix errors, others are substantive. Compare for instance Roland saying, 'I trained David. I friended him' in *The Slow Mutants* to 'I never trained David. I friended him' in the original novel.

So, there are actually *three* versions of *The Gunslinger* – the combination of the five short stories, the 'original' novel and the 'revised and expanded' novel!

Editions of *Cell* released in January and February 2006 carried 'an excerpt – in the author's hand' of *Lisey's Story*, from 'Part One: Bool Hunt / Chapter One: Lisey and Amanda (Everything the Same)'. This 'excerpt' was slightly revised in the final edition of the novel (see also the note about revision of the *Lisey and the Madman* below).

In 2004 Centipede Press published a deluxe edition of *'Salem's Lot*, which also included forty-nine pages of 'Deleted Scenes' from the original manuscript. These scenes were included in a separate section after the original version, making the examination of the excised material a simple matter. The signed Limited was of 425 copies; an unsigned edition was released in 2005. The book also included *Jerusalem's Lot* and *One for the Road*, as well as King's 1999 *Introduction* to the Signet/Pocket edition of *'Salem's Lot*, published in this instance as the *Afterword*. A trade version was published in November 2005.

Three key changes from the first draft of the novel to the final version are of interest. The town infested by vampires was not Jerusalem's Lot, but Momson (Momson, Vermont appears separately in the final version; but Momson, Maine appears in certain of the 'Deleted Scenes'); the head vampire's name was Sarlinov, not Barlow; and Father Callahan killed himself with a knife when confronted by Sarlinov (King took some form of pity on the Father in the published novel, allowing him to leave town by bus after losing his faith and, therefore, also allowing his appearance nearly three decades later in another town under threat, Calla Bryn Sturgis of *Wolves of the Calla*).

Regarded by many as King's masterpiece, *The Stand* was first published in 1978, although it had been severely edited for length by King's publishers. Subsequent paperback editions used the original hardcover text for a period. The timeline of the events in this first version is 1980. US paperback editions of this original edition moved to a new timeline of 1985. The Signet edition of January 1980 was the first of these editions. In it King provides an *Author's Note*, which concludes 'minor revisions have been made for this Signet edition of this novel'. Most, if not all, overseas paperback editions used the original hardcover text until The *Complete and Uncut* edition was released. Books carrying this 1985 timeline form the *second* version of the tale.

In 1990 King arranged for the republication of the book as he had originally intended, in a *Complete and Uncut* edition, with a 1990 timeline; and this forms the *third* version. In addition to restoring most of the material cut from the original novel that version also included new material. King also penned two screenplay adaptations, an unproduced movie script and the produced mini-series script. These form the *fourth* and *fifth* versions of the tale! The two scripts are discussed in considerable detail in a later chapter.

Short Stories/Novellas/Screenplays

The major area for King's revisions is of his short stories and novellas. This partly resulted from his updating of his *earliest* stories for collection in his mass market books; and partly from appears to be a form of perfectionism – it seems Big Steve is never finished with a story and simply cannot resist a chance to make it better, or to change it to reflect his mood or the point in his career (for instance, a number of stories were converted into Castle Rock tales on revision).

King has also adapted many of his stories for the screen. Some of these scripts were produced, others were not, but each resulted in a slightly different story from that adapted. So, here is a rather lengthy tour of Stephen King's list of revised tales.

1408 was originally published in the audio book *Blood and Smoke* (1999). Its first text appearance was in *Everything's Eventual* (2002). That publication contained a number of differences from the original audio version. They were relatively minor (for instance, one changed the name of a song and the other changed a name mentioned by Mike Enslin) and did not constitute a new version of the story.

All That You Love Will Be Carried Away was originally published in *The New Yorker* magazine for 29 January 2001. It was republished in *Everything's Eventual* with minor variations (for example, the town of Hackberry Chalk, Texas became Hackberry, Texas).

The Ballad of the Flexible Bullet was first published in *The Magazine of Fantasy and Science Fiction* for June 1984. King made minor revisions for its inclusion in *Skeleton Crew* the following year, including the correction of an error (in the magazine version Henry Wilson cut the power cable to his car radio but still managed to listen to it during the trip!)

Battleground was originally published in *Cavalier* for September 1972. For its publication in *Night Shift* (1978) there were very minor wording revisions. A new version of the story was included in the unproduced *Night Shift* screenplay.

Beachworld originally appeared in *Weird Tales* for Fall 1984 and was republished in *Skeleton Crew* the following year with minor wording variations and the deletion of a character ("Send Chang down. One of these boys is badly dehydrated.")

The short story *The Bear* forms part of *The Dark Tower III: The Wastelands*. It was originally published in *The Magazine of Fantasy and Science Fiction* for December 1990. When included in *The Wastelands* (1991) the story was significantly different from the earlier version (see the later chapter in this book, *Stories Swallowed by Monsters* for more detail).

Before the Play is the prologue deleted from *The Shining*. It was first published in *Whispers* magazine, #17/18 in August 1982. Two sections were deleted for a republication in the *TV Guide* issue for 26 April to 2 May 1997, which coincided with the debut of the mini-series version of *The Shining* that week. Full detail of the history of this tale and the changes appear in a later chapter. The two publications are really one version, with the second an 'abridged' form.

Two parts of *The Dark Tower IV: Wizard and Glass* were initially published in 1996 in a free giveaway paperback that accompanied some copies of *Desperation* and *The Regulators*. They were *Beneath the Demon Moon* and *The Falls of the Hounds*. There were numerous variations in the text between the booklet and the subsequent novel.

Big Wheels - A Tale of the Laundry Game (Milkman #2) is a story King developed from an aborted novel, *The Milkman*. It first appeared in an anthology, *New Terrors 2* in 1980. King so substantially revised the story for its appearance in *Skeleton Crew* in 1985 that the two appearances are totally different versions of the tale.

The Bird and the Album was first published in *A Fantasy Reader: The Seventh World Fantasy Convention Program Book* on 30 October 1981. This short tale was published five years before it was included as part of the novel *It*. King substantially rewrote the piece for its inclusion in the novel. Full details of the story's history and changes appear in a later chapter, *Stories Swallowed by Monsters*.

Blind Willie exists in three forms. First published in *Antaeus* for Autumn 1994, that version of the tale was republished in *Six Stories* (a Limited Edition collection issued by King's own Philtrum Press imprint in 1997, but never released as a mass-market publication) with quite a number of minor revisions, including changing the name of a celebrity mentioned in passing (from O.J. Simpson to Michael Jackson!); and changing the first name of Willie Teale's fake wife.

King then completely rewrote *Blind Willie* for its appearance in *Hearts in Atlantis*, to make the characters part of the storyline of that collection. Bill Teale became Bill Shearman (one of the boys who beat up Carol Gerber in *Low Men in Yellow Coats*) and, instead of 'Blind Willie' Teale, Shearman posed as 'Blind Willie' Garfield (he still had Bobby Garfield's glove, which he used when begging). As a result there are two clear versions of the tale – the *Antaeus* version and the *Hearts in Atlantis* version.

The Blue Air Compressor (subject of a later chapter) is one of the earliest of King's published works. It originally appeared in *Onan* magazine for January 1971; and was republished with relatively minor amendments in *Heavy Metal* magazine for July 1981. Some of the variations appear to be correction of typesetting errors in *Onan*. Others are editing and style changes. Two sections were deleted from the *Heavy Metal* version (one reads, 'It is desperately important that the reader be made cognizant of these facts'; the other effectively corrects what King regarded as a minor error).

The Boogeyman was first published in *Cavalier* for March 1973 and was reprinted in *Gent* for December 1975. There were extremely minor revisions for its subsequent appearance in *Night Shift* (1978).

Cain Rose Up was first published in the Spring 1968 edition of the University of Maine literary magazine, *Ubris*. Considering King was a college student at that time it is not surprising he choose to completely rewrite the story for its appearance in *Skeleton Crew* 17 years later. One character name was changed and the original text is almost unrecognizable in places. The extra maturity in King's writing shows between what are clearly versions of the story.

Calla Bryn Sturgis was first released on King's official website, www.stephenking.com on 21 August 2001. Readers were told it was the Prologue to the upcoming novel, *The Dark Tower V: Wolves of the Calla* but hints were provided that this would not be its final form in the book. In fact, so as not to give away certain events in the novel, there had been some careful editing and changes. The story was delivered in such substantially different form as the Prologue, *Roont* when the novel was published in 2003 that there is no doubt the short story is a version of the tale. More detail appears in a later chapter, *Stories Swallowed by Monsters*.

The *Cat's Eye* screenplay (1984) is reviewed in a later chapter. It contains a wrap-around section (published in a radically different form as *General* in the 1997 anthology *Screamplays*); as well as versions of *The Ledge* (originally published in *Penthouse* for July 1976 and revised for inclusion in 1978's *Night Shift*), and *Quitter's, Inc.* (an original story for the *Night Shift* collection), both involving fairly significant changes to the original short stories.

Chattery Teeth has appeared in two distinct versions. The first was published in *Cemetery Dance* magazine for Fall, 1992; it was significantly revised for *Nightmares and Dreamscapes* (1993).

Three versions of *Children of the Corn* exist. These are the original short story, published in *Penthouse* for March 1977; its republication in *Night Shift* (1978); and an unproduced screenplay written by King (c.1978). The *Night Shift* version contains a number of changes; many of them are cosmetic but a number are specifically factual, meaning that each form, including the screenplay, are separate versions. The factual changes from the short stories to the screenplay are extensive and these are discussed in a later chapter, dealing with that script.

The Crate also exists in three versions. It was originally published in *Gallery* magazine for July 1979. King revised the story for inclusion in his *Creepshow* screenplay (also 1979) and there was further alteration for its appearance in the graphic novel *Creepshow* (1982). *The Crate* is described in a later chapter.

King's screenplay for *Creepshow* (subject of a later chapter) contains versions of five stories. Each story also appeared in the Graphic Novel *Creepshow*, in each case somewhat revised from the original screenplay. The stories are: *Father's Day* (the only versions of the story are the screenplay and the Graphic Novel); *The Lonesome Death of Jordy Verrill* (known as *Weeds* in its text format published in two early men's magazines); *The Crate* (as noted, it appeared in the screenplay, the Graphic Novel and *Gallery* magazine for July 1979, plus reprints of that version in anthologies); *Something to Tide You Over* (the only versions of this story are the screenplay and the Graphic Novel); and *They're Creeping Up on You* (again, the only versions of the story are the screenplay and the Graphic Novel).

Crouch End first appeared in an anthology of Lovecraftian stories, *New Tales of the Cthulhu Mythos* in 1980. It was heavily revised for its later inclusion in *Nightmares and Dreamscapes* (1993). In the earlier version there is mention of a husband who went out for a pack of fags (English slang for cigarettes) and never came back. That is just how King's father left his family.

King wrote screenplay versions of his novel *Cujo* and *The Dead Zone* but neither was produced. The events in both scripts differ radically from the novels. Both screenplays are covered in later chapters. He also wrote a screenplay adaptation of *Cycle of the Werewolf*, which was produced as *Silver Bullet*, more of which below.

Dedication first appeared when King biographer Douglas E Winter edited an anthology, *Night Visions 5*, released in a Limited Edition and a trade hardback in 1988. The anthology actually included three King stories, the most ever released in one volume outside one of King's own collections. They were *The Reploids*, *Dedication* and *Sneakers*. Gollancz of the United Kingdom published the anthology in 1989 under the title, *Dark Visions: All Original Stories*. Berkley Books finally released the anthology in the US as a mass-market paperback in 1990 under yet another title, *The Skin Trade*. King completely rewrote *Dedication* for its appearance in *Nightmares and Dreamscapes*. They are clearly two different versions of the same tale.

Another King screenplay is his adaptation of *Desperation*. Again, the storyline was changed enough to justify calling this script a version. More detail is provided in the later chapter.

Do the Dead Sing? is one of the few King stories for which the title was changed when republished. It originally appeared in *Yankee* magazine for November 1981. King so substantially revised it for its inclusion in *Skeleton Crew* under the title, *The Reach* that the two are clearly separate versions of the tale. A major change was the use of the term 'Do You Love?' in *Skeleton Crew*.

Dolan's Cadillac was first published serially in the *Castle Rock* newsletter over five issues from February to June 1985. King substantially revised it for publication as a Limited Edition from Lord John Press (1989) and included that version in *Nightmares and Dreamscapes* (1993). He also began a screenplay, which is the subject of a later chapter.

The End of the Whole Mess first appeared in *Omni* magazine for October 1986. King substantially rewrote it for *Nightmares and Dreamscapes*. As well as significant text changes a number of facts, characters and even timelines changed in the new version.

Everything's Eventual was initially published *in The Magazine of Fantasy and Science Fiction* for October 1997. Uniquely, it was reappeared in text form as part of the computer game, *F13*[50] in January 1999 and then in the *Everything's Eventual* collection of fourteen King stories released in 2002. There are a number of variations between the different forms of publication but not enough to represent anything more than variations within the one tale. There are some variations in characters and of one date (William Unger was asked to run for the US Senate four years later in the collected story).

The story *Father's Day* appears only in the graphic novel, *Creepshow* (1982) and the 1979 screenplay for the movie of the same name (reviewed in a later chapter). As a result of the publishing format there are differences between the two versions.

The Fifth Quarter is another story that exists in three distinct versions, one of those not published under King's name. The crime tale was first published in *Cavalier* magazine for April 1972, under the pseudonym John Swithen. Other than Richard Bachman, Swithen is the only other pseudonym for King; and *The Fifth Quarter* is the only story for which the Swithen pseudonym was used. Interestingly, according to Bachman's 'death notice' in the *Castle Rock* newsletter for May 1985, Swithen was Bachman's half-brother! *The Fifth Quarter* was republished in a new version and under King's name in *The Twilight Zone Magazine* for February 1986 and in a yet another version in *Nightmares & Dreamscapes* (1993). In the latter versions John Swithen is mentioned, as a folksinger and writer.

The screenplays of *General* and the wrap-around parts of the *Cat's Eye* script generally represent the same story but with significant enough textual differences for them to be declared as separate versions of the one story. The only form of publication of *General* was in a 1997 anthology of horror scripts, *Screamplays*, edited by Richard Chizmar.

The Glass Floor was King's first professional sale but has never been included in one of his collections. The subject of a later chapter, it first appeared in *Startling Mystery Stories* magazine for Fall 1967. King allowed it to be reprinted in the Fall 1990 issue of *Weird Tales*. As to the revision for *Weird Tales*, King says in a foreword to the story: 'Darrell Schweitzer, the editor of *Weird Tales®*, invited me to make changes if I wanted to, but I decided that would probably be a bad idea. Except for two or three word-changes and the addition of a paragraph break (which was probably a typographical error in the first place), I've left the tale just as it was. If I really *did* start making changes, the result would be an entirely new story.'

Gramma was originally published in *Weirdbook* magazine for Spring 1984; and was substantially revised for its publication in *Skeleton Crew* the following year. King corrected an error in that second version. On Page 6 of Weirdbook we read: '...after Gramma and Granpa had gotten married, way back in 1914 ...' However, according to the implied timeline (the story is set in October 1980, Gramma was 83 and Granpa was three to four years younger than her) this means Granpa was born in 1900 or 1901 and would be 13 or 14 when he married, which is most unlikely. King deleted the reference to the marriage date in *Skeleton Crew*.

Here There Be Tygers was one of the first stories King published, appearing in *Ubris* magazine for Spring 1968. It was marginally revised for its inclusion in *Skeleton Crew* in 1985. There were some minor changes in character details and a small, new section was added to the later publication but these are not significant enough for the two forms to be regarded as anything other than variations.

Home Delivery, a zombie tale, was first published in an anthology, *The Book of the Dead* in 1989. King substantially rewrote the story for *Nightmares and Dreamscapes* (1993). These two forms therefore represent different versions.

I Know What You Need was first published in *Cosmopolitan* magazine for September 1976. It was republished with minor changes and the correction of an error in *Night Shift* (1978). In the *Cosmopolitan* version Ed Hamner reappears in Liz Rogan's life no earlier than the October following Tony Lombard's death: 'A week passed, then two, then it was October.' On page 274 Alice says: 'He even knew the right psychological moment to step back into your life last September.' This error was corrected in the *Night Shift* version with Alice referring to October. The changes in total are minor. King also adapted this story for his unproduced *Night Shift* screenplay, covered in a later chapter.

I Was a Teenage Grave Robber first appeared in partial form in a mimeographed 'fanzine', *Comics Review* over three issues in 1965 (the fourth and final part never appeared but subscribers were sent printed pages of the concluding material). It was republished with considerable textual differences (but little change to the story-line) in another fanzine, *Stories of Suspense* the following year with a new title, *In A Half-World of Terror*. The tale is reviewed in a later chapter.

I've Got to Get Away was a story in *People, Places and Things*, a collection of eighteen short stories self-published by Stephen King and his friend Chris Chesley as the 'Triad Publishing Company' in 1960, and reprinted in 1963. *The Killer*, published in *Famous Monsters Of Filmland*, #202 for Spring 1994, is an apparent re-write of *I've Got to Get Away*. Both stories are subject of later chapters.

Another story with a very interesting publishing history is *In the Deathroom*. Its first two appearances were not in traditional mass-market books. The story was first released in the audiobook, *Blood and Smoke* (1999) and did not see print until its inclusion in a Book of the Month Club only publication, *Secret Windows: Essays and Fiction of the Craft of Writing* in 2000. Its first mass-market publication was in *Everything's Eventual* (2002). There were minor variations with each form of publication but not enough for any of the forms to be regarded as a separate version.

It Grows on You exists in three versions, one of those including further variations. The first publication of the story was in *Marshroots* for Fall, 1973. That version was republished in *Weird Tales* for Summer, 1991 with minor variations (it is interesting that King amended the *first* version of the tale *after* the second version had been published). There was a significant revision of the story for its publication in *Whispers* #17/18 for July 1982 and this represents the second version. A very major revision for its inclusion in *Nightmares and Dreamscapes* (1993) represents the third version. Importantly, in that last version *It Grows on You* becomes a Castle Rock story, earlier versions having been set in Harlow. An error was also corrected in this version. King has this to say about the revisions, prior to *Nightmares and Dreamscapes*, writing in 1982[51]: ' "It Grows On You" was originally written in 1973, rewritten in 1975 for publication in a small-circulation literature magazine called *Marshroots*. I've rewritten it for a third time for its real debut, here in *Whispers*. It's one of the few stories from that period that I really love …'

The science fiction tale *The Jaunt* was originally published in *The Twilight Zone Magazine* for June 1981. In the *Notes* to *Skeleton Crew* King says, 'This was originally for *Omni,* which quite rightly rejected it because the science was so wonky. It was Ben Bova's idea to have the colonists in the story mining for water, and I have incorporated that in this version.' The *Skeleton Crew* version was published in 1985. As King himself noted, these two forms of publication are different versions.

Jumper was originally published in a neighborhood newspaper put out by King's older brother David, over three parts in the winter of 1959-60, technically making it and *Rush Call* the earliest published of King's works. It was republished in *Secret Windows: Essays and Fiction on the Craft of Writing* in 2000. According to the editors, 'The stories are transcribed without the benefit of copyediting. Only the spelling has been corrected.'

L T's Theory of Pets was first published in the Limited Edition collection, *Six Stories* in 1997. It was republished in *Everything's Eventual* (2002) with what appear to be two corrections of typographical errors but no other changes.

The Lawnmower Man appears in two versions, with one of those versions varying from one publication to the other. It was first published in *Cavalier* magazine for May 1975 and was republished in *Night Shift* (1978) with minor variations. A separate version appeared as a comic in Marvel Magazine Group's *Bizarre Adventures*, Volume 1, Number 29 for October 1981.

Penthouse magazine for July 1976 carried the first appearance of *The Ledge*. There were six very minor updates for its inclusion in *Night Shift* (1978). King also adapted the story in the *Cat's Eye* screenplay.

A chapter of the *Lisey's Story* was first published in an anthology, *McSweeney's Enchanted Chamber of Astonishing Stories*, edited by Michael Chabon and released in November 2004, as *Lisey and the Madman*. This section was heavily revised for the final novel (see also the note about revision of the novel above).

The only true stand-alone Dark Tower short fiction piece is *The Little Sisters of Eluria*. It was originally published in an anthology, *Legends: Short Novels by the Masters of Modern Fantasy* in 1998. For inclusion in the 2002 collection *Everything's Eventual* there were very minor revisions. Many of these were of style but there were a few of substance.

The Lonesome Death of Jordy Verrill is the title used in the graphic novel *Creepshow* for the story originally published as *Weeds* in *Cavalier* magazine for May 1976 and reprinted in *Nugget* magazine for April 1979. There are effectively three versions of this tale, when the screenplay for the *Creepshow* movie is taken into account.

Low Men in Yellow Coats is the Dark Tower related story that begins the collection *Hearts in Atlantis*. An excerpt from the story was published in *Family Circle* for 3 August 1999. There are three very minor wording variations between the two publications.

An intriguing little tale, *The Luckey Quarter* appears in two distinct versions. It was first published in a national newspaper, *USA Weekend* for 30 June to 2 July 1995. King then significantly revised the story for its publication in the Limited *Six Stories* (1997). That version was reprinted in the mass-market collection, *Everything's Eventual* in 2002.

The darkly amusing story, *Lunch at the Gotham Café*, also has an interesting publishing history. It first appeared in an anthology, *Dark Love* in 1995 and won the Long Fiction Bram Stoker Award for 1995 from the Horror Writers Association. King then significantly revised the tale for its appearance in the Limited Edition, *Six Stories* in 1997. The first time the tale was practically available in mass-market form was as part of the audio book, *Blood and Smoke*, released in 1999, using the *Six Stories* version. The first mass-market text release was in the *Everything's Eventual* collection in 2002. That publication included minor variations to the *Six Stories* version.

King won the 1996 O. Henry Award for Best American Short Story and the 1994 World Fantasy Award for Best Short Fiction for *The Man in the Black Suit*. It was originally published in *The New Yorker* magazine for 31 October 1994 and republished with numerous minor revisions in *Six Stories* (1997). It was collected in *Everything's Eventual* in 2002 and for that publication King made further minor revisions. As the revisions are indeed minor (for instance, there is a change of the year in which Gary wrote his story down in his diary) each form is nothing more than a variation.

The Man Who Loved Flowers was originally published in *Gallery* magazine for August 1977. When republished in *Night Shift* the following year there were five almost insignificant changes, four in style and one of substance, but barely that (the word 'yoe' was changed to 'yowl'!)

The *Man Who Would Not Shake Hands* was first published in a 1981 anthology, *Shadows 4*. It was significantly revised, most of the changes relating to King's updating of the story to link it with *The Breathing Method* as a 'Club' story, for its publication in *Skeleton Crew* four years later. The original version also appears in *The Best of Shadows*, published after *Skeleton Crew*, in 1989. These are clearly two different versions of the same tale.

A story inspired by King's work in an industrial laundry, *The Mangler* was originally published in *Cavalier* for December 1972. King rewrote it for *Night Shift* (1978). However, as few facts change (Hunton's friend Mack Jackson becomes Mark, for instance) the two forms are variations, not versions.

Memory, a moving short story, first appeared in *Tin House* magazine for Summer 2006 and, in 2007, in the hardcover first edition of *Blaze*. It was revised for inclusion in the novel, *Duma Key*.

One of King's novellas, *The Mist* was first published in a 1980 anthology, *Dark Forces*, edited by King's agent at the time, Kirby McCauley. King substantially rewrote it for *Skeleton Crew* (1985). In the *Notes* to that collection he says, 'I never liked it much until the rewrite ...' The two forms, while using the same characters, show substantial changes in storyline and must be considered as totally separate versions.

The Monkey was originally published in *Gallery* magazine for November 1980. King so significantly rewrote the story for its inclusion in *Skeleton Crew* in 1985 that they are clearly separate versions.

The Monster in the Closet was promoted as an 'excerpt' from the novel *Cujo* when it appeared in the *Ladies Home Journal* for October 1981. However, the form of the story was *not* a direct excerpt, as it spanned a number of sections of the novel and there are some minor changes, as well as material added. More detail is included in the *Stories Swallowed by Monsters* chapter later in this book.

Another story to appear first in *The Magazine of Fantasy and Science Fiction* was *The Moving Finger*, in the December 1990 edition. It was so significantly revised *Nightmares and Dreamscapes* (1993) as to represent two quite different versions of the same tale.

A tale inspired by one of Tabitha King's habits, *Mrs. Todd's Shortcut* was first published in *Redbook* for May 1984. The story was updated with minor variations for *Skeleton Crew* (1985) but these were not significant enough to warrant a second version being declared. In the *Notes* to *Skeleton Crew* King describes the genesis of this story, 'My wife is the real Mrs. Todd; the woman really *is* mad for a shortcut, and much of the one in this story really exists. She found it too. And Tabby really *does* seem to get younger sometimes…'

The Whitney Museum originally published *My Pretty Pony* in 1988 as a Limited Edition. In October of that year it was released in a Limited Trade Hardback. King so substantially revised the tale for its inclusion in *Nightmares and Dreamscapes* in 1993 as to leave no doubt these are two separate versions of the same tale.

The New Lieutenant's Rap has a unique history. Printed as a chapbook under King's Philtrum Press imprint, the entire text is in King's handwriting. It was provided to guests at a New York City party to celebrate King's 25th anniversary in book publishing in April 1999. Marsha DeFilippo, King's secretary, confirmed to the author of this book that copies were left at the party by guests who did not know what they were leaving behind! The story has never been published in the mass market and most likely will not be. Differing substantially from *Why We're In Vietnam*, which appeared in *Hearts in Atlantis* later that year, it is effectively an earlier version of that story. *The New Lieutenant's Rap* is reviewed in a later chapter.

A vampire tale, *The Night Flier* was originally published in an anthology, *Prime Evil: New Stories by the Masters of Modern Horror*, in a Donald M Grant Limited Edition (April 1988) and a mass market hardback issued by NAL (June 1988). King significantly revised the story for *Nightmares and Dreamscapes* (1993) and they are clearly separate versions. For instance, in the earlier version King mentions himself, Johnny Smith and Jerusalem's Lot but deleted these very important references from the collected version.

King wrote a screenplay titled *Night Shift* that was never produced and is the subject of a later chapter in this book. The script included revised versions of *Strawberry Spring*, *I Know What You Need* and *Battleground*.

Night Surf is one of King's earliest published stories and forms a prototype for his later masterpiece, *The Stand*. It was first published in the literary magazine, *Ubris* for Spring 1969 and contained King's first use of the term 'Captain Trips' to describe a worldwide superflu epidemic. He substantially revised the tale for its appearance in *Cavalier* for August 1974 and further minor revisions were made for *Night Shift* (1978). As a result there are two versions, the original *Ubris* and the revised *Cavalier/Night Shift*.

The atmospheric tale *Nona* was originally published in the 1978 anthology, *Shadows* and was substantially revised for *Skeleton Crew* (1985). In the latter version it became a Castle Rock story while in the earlier it had been set in

Blainesville, Maine, a town with the same geography as Castle Rock! Of perhaps most interest is that the original Ace Carmody (who dies in a car crash) becomes the infamous Castle Rock character Ace Merrill (he does not die in this tale) in the *Skeleton Crew* version. An error in the *Shadows* version was also corrected in the later publication.

The short sequel to *'Salem's Lot*, *One for the Road*, was first published in *Maine* magazine for March/April 1977. King made very minor revisions before republishing it in *Night Shift* the following year, but these are no more than variations. It was later republished in an anthology, *Vampire Omnibus* (1995). There were very minor revisions (style only) in that publication but, almost uniquely, the story appeared under the title *Return to 'Salem's Lot*.

King's 1986 screenplay for the movie version of *Pet Sematary* is remarkably faithful to the novel but does include a number of factual changes in the storyline. The screenplay is certainly a version of the story and is covered in considerable detail in a later chapter.

King originally provided *The Plant* as a Christmas gift to a limited number of people in 1982, 1983 and 1985. Published by his imprint, Philtrum Press as a serialized novel, he stopped writing the story after the 1985 episode. To worldwide publicity King returned to the tale in 2000, updating the storyline and releasing it again as a serialized novel on the internet through his official website, www.stephenking.com. After six parts, *The Plant* folded its leaves once more, with the story once again unfinished. The history of this unusual publishing venture is detailed in a later chapter.

Another vampire tale, *Popsy* first appeared in an anthology, *Masques II* in 1987. King made a significant number of textual changes, but changed few 'facts' for *Nightmares and Dreamscapes* (1993). Among the changes was the correction of an error. In the *Masques* version Sheridan handcuffs Popsy's grandson: 'Sheridan clamped the other cuff on the arm of the seat and then fell back into his own...' But, in the *Nightmares and Dreamscapes* version: 'Sheridan locked the other cuff onto the strut and then fell back into his own seat ... ' This was originally an error in that the handcuff was actually secured to a specially welded strut in the van. As so much text was changed each appearance should be treated as a separate version. In the *Notes* to *Nightmares and Dreamscapes* King states that he 'rather thinks' that Popsy is also the eponymous character in *The Night Flier*.

Quitters, Inc., a tale describing a rather radical quit smoking program, was one of the few stories in the 1978 *Night Shift* collection that had not previously been published. King adapted it for inclusion in the *Cat's Eye* screenplay, changing many details.

The Raft was first published in *Gallery* magazine for November 1982, included as a pullout booklet. It was republished in *Skeleton Crew* in 1985 with a number of minor changes. These included the introduction of the term, 'Do

You Love?' and the correction of three minor errors. However, the two publications are simply variations of the same story.

The only story set in Willow, Maine, *Rainy Season* was originally published in *Midnight Graffiti* magazine for Spring of 1989. King substantially revised it for *Nightmares and Dreamscapes* (1993), creating a second version of the tale.

The Reach is one of the few King stories for which the title was changed. As mentioned earlier, it was originally published as *Do the Dead Sing?* in *Yankee* magazine for November 1981. He then substantially revised the story and included it in *Skeleton Crew* under the new title.

The Reaper's Image was King's second professional sale, for which he received $35, and appeared in *Startling Mystery Stories* for Spring 1969. He made minor revisions for its appearance sixteen years later in *Skeleton Crew*. The only known reprints of the original variation are in anthologies edited by R Chetwynd-Hayes and Stephen Jones[52]. The two appearances are no more than variations.

Part of *Pet Sematary* was published in the *Satyricon II Program Book* in 1983[53]. This excerpt was titled *The Return of Timmy Baterman*. There are very minor variations between the short story and the final book but these have no impact on the characters.

The Revelations of 'Becka Paulson was first published in *Rolling Stone* magazine for 19 July and 2 August 1984. King substantially revised it to form part of the novel *The Tommyknockers* in 1987. In its original form it also appears in the Limited Edition only of *Skeleton Crew* (1985) and was republished in a 1991 anthology, *I Shudder at Your Touch*. The tale is covered in detail in the later chapter, *Stories Swallowed by Monsters*.

The Revenge of Lardass Hogan is also described in the *Stories Swallowed by Monsters* chapter. It was originally published in *Maine Review* magazine. King updated it and included in his 1982 novella, *The Body* as a Gordie Lachance story. There are considerable differences between the two versions.

The Road Virus Heads North was first published in an anthology, *999* in 1999 and was revised for publication in the collection, *Everything's Eventual* in 2002. Although the revisions were relatively minor, as character names were changed each publication deserves the status of a version.

Rush Call, like *Jumper*, was originally published in a neighbourhood newspaper put out by King's older brother David, over three parts in the winter of 1959-60, technically making them the earliest published of King's works. They were both republished in *Secret Windows: Essays and Fiction on the Craft of Writing* in 2000. According to the editors, 'The stories are transcribed without the benefit of copyediting. Only the spelling has been corrected.'

King has twice adapted his classic novel *The Shining*. The unproduced movie screenplay and the mini-series screenplay, which was produced, are covered in a later chapter. The various revisions King made to the particular storyline and mythology of this tale are also detailed in that chapter.

Silver Bullet is King's screenplay version of the short novel, *Cycle of the Werewolf*. In November 1985 Signet published a tie-in book to the movie. That edition carried *Cycle of the Werewolf*, the original shooting script for the film and a new Foreword by King. As the published screenplay was King's final shooting script, it differed from the release print of the film.

Sneakers first appeared in the anthology, *Night Visions 5*, mentioned earlier in regard to the short story, *Dedication*. Gollancz of the United Kingdom published the anthology in 1989 under the title, *Dark Visions: All Original Stories*. Berkley Books finally released the anthology in the US as a mass-market paperback in 1990 under yet another title, *The Skin Trade*. King completely rewrote *Sneakers* for *Nightmares and Dreamscapes* (1993). For instance, in the original the killer is unknown but in the collected version the ghost reveals to John Tell that Paul Jannings had killed him. The two forms are clearly two different versions of the same tale.

Something To Tide You Over appears in the 1982 graphic novel, *Creepshow* and, in a slightly different version, as part of the screenplay for the movie of the same name.

Sometimes They Come Back was originally published in *Cavalier* magazine for March 1974. Very minor variations made to the text for its inclusion in *Night Shift* (1978).

The 'Final Shooting Script' of *Sorry, Right Number* is held in a box at the Special Collections Unit of the Raymond H Fogler Library at the University of Maine, Orono. Dated July 11, 1986, it is significantly different from the *Nightmares and Dreamscapes* version published in 1993. King gives the background to the screenplay in the *Notes* to that collection. In them he confirms that the *Nightmares and Dreamscapes* version was written first and the shooting script later to fit budgetary requirements. There are key factual differences between the two scripts, reviewed in a later chapter.

The serial killer short story *Strawberry Spring* was originally published in *Ubris* magazine for Fall 1968. King substantially rewrote the tale for its publication in *Cavalier* for November 1975 (reprinted in *Gent* for February 1977). The later version was collected in *Night Shift* (1978). In a third version King adapted the story for his unproduced *Night Shift* screenplay, which is detailed in a later chapter, which includes the key differences between each version of *Strawberry Spring*.

Stud City was also published in *Ubris*, for Fall 1969. King heavily revised it and included it as a story written by Gordie Lachance in the 1982 *Different Seasons* novella *The Body*. The original version is dealt with in a later chapter, *Stories Swallowed by Monsters*.

Suffer the Little Children was first published in *Cavalier* for February 1972. It was reprinted in that form in a number of anthologies before King significantly revised the story for 1993's *Nightmares and Dreamscapes*. Perhaps the key difference between the two versions is that in the latter the story is set in Maine, while in the earlier the location is unclear.

Survivor Type, a tale of self-cannibalism, was first published in *Terrors*, an anthology published by Playboy Press in 1982. King made minor revisions for its appearance in *Skeleton Crew* (1985).

The Tale of Gray Dick is a version of the chapter of the same name in *The Dark Tower V: Wolves of the Calla*, published in November 2003. The stand-alone short story was first published in the magazine, *Timothy McSweeney's Quarterly Concern* on 25 February 2003; and in an anthology, *McSweeney's Mammoth Treasury of Thrilling Tales* the following month. Prior to the release of the novel informed sources advised that there were variations between this publication and the chapter in the full-length novel. Indeed, there *were* revisions, including both the deletion and addition of material for its appearance in *The Dark Tower V: Wolves of the Calla*. These changes were clearly made to avoid giving away plotlines in the novel ahead of its publication. The short story is therefore more of a variation to, than a version of, the tale. Further detail is provided in the later chapter, *Stories Swallowed By Monsters*.

That Feeling, You Can Only Say What It Is In French was first published in *The New Yorker* for 22 and 29 June 1998. King made minor changes for *Everything's Eventual* collection (2002).

They're Creeping Up On You appears in the 1982 graphic novel, *Creepshow* and, in a slightly different version, as part of the screenplay for the movie of the same name.

Trucks was originally published in *Cavalier* for June 1973 and appeared, with very minor changes in *Night Shift* (1978). A theatre adaptation published as *Stephen King's 'Trucks'*, appeared in *Scholastic Voice* for September 6, 1991. *Maximum Overdrive* is a wholly different story, inspired by *Trucks* but not an adaptation of that tale.

A Castle Rock story, *Uncle Otto's Truck* originally appeared in *Yankee* magazine for October 1983. It was substantially rewritten for *Skeleton Crew* two years later. An error was also corrected - in the earlier version the price of land Schenck and McCutcheon bought was said to be at a rate of $23 per acre. They bought 4000 acres and this would total $92,000, not the $10,000 mentioned.

Another crime caper, *The Wedding Gig* was originally published in *Ellery Queen's Mystery Magazine* for December 1980 and the same version was reprinted in that magazine's June 2004 edition. The tale was substantially revised for *Skeleton Crew* (1985).

The story known in the King community as *Weeds* was originally published in *Cavalier* for May 1976 and reprinted in *Nugget* for April 1979. In both *Cavalier* and *Nugget* it is listed on the Contents page as *Weeds* but the headline of the story, spread over two pages, reads: 'More Than a Green Thumb ... Will Be Necessary to Stop the Weeds: A chilling new story by the author of *Carrie* and *'Salem's Lot'*. When King updated this story for the two *Creepshow* versions (screenplay and graphic novel) the story was retitled *The Lonesome Death of Jordy Verrill* and became a Castle Rock tale. As a result, there are effectively three versions of this tale.

Why We're in Vietnam, one of the stories in the *Hearts in Atlantis* collection, is effectively a new version of *The New Lieutenant's Rap*, as mentioned earlier.

There are two versions of the tale of the Word Processor. The story was originally published in *Playboy* for January 1983 as *The Word Processor*. A substantially revised version was included in *Skeleton Crew* (1985) under the new title, *Word Processor of the Gods*.

You Know They Got a Hell of a Band, set in the town of Rock and Roll Heaven, Oregon, was first published in the 1992 anthology, *Shock Rock*. King substantially rewrote it for *Nightmares and Dreamscapes* the following year.

THE UNCOLLECTED, AND THE UNPUBLISHED

Each of King's uncollected and unpublished works is reviewed in this section.

Before we begin, a note about a screenplay titled *They Bite*. In the first two editions of this book I had this to say:

The screenplay for *They Bite* is held in Box 1010 at the Special Collections Unit of the Raymond H Fogler Library at the University of Maine, Orono. Written permission from King is required to access this work. The 115-page screenplay may have been written about 1976 (this conclusion is drawn from the timeline of the story) and it appears to be incomplete, although it is clear the story is nearly told as at the last page.

The Third Edition (Cemetery Dance e-book) carried this further note: *Further research since this piece first came to light has been unable to clarify whether or not the screenplay* is *by Stephen King, so it may be deleted from King's canon at some future point.* In July 2011 I was able to confirm directly with King that he did not write *They Bite*[54]. It is likely someone had sent it to him to read and it somehow got caught up in his Papers.

The Aftermath (1963)

According to King *The Aftermath* is the first novel he completed. The manuscript is held in Box 1010 of the Special Collections Department of the Raymond H Fogler Library at the University of Maine, Orono. Written permission from King is required to access this work. A handwritten note on the first page of manuscript states, 'The 1st novel written, aged 16. The Aftermath. Unpublished.' It is made up of 76 single spaced manual typewritten pages and totals on the order of 50,000 words.

In this New Worlds tale a young man survives a nuclear war that devastates parts of America. After the trials of attempting to survive as a loner Larry Talman joins Sun Corps, a group that is trying to use military and bureaucratic means to re-establish order. However, he and his partner, Ian Vannerman, secretly plan to bring the Corps down.

In Sun Corps Talman is recognized as a brilliant mathematician and is promoted to work with the Corps' supercomputer, DRAC. Becoming ever more disillusioned he destroys the supercomputer and discovers that the Corps is a front for an alien race, the Denebians, that is planning to take over the Earth. The Denebians had been systematically eliminating anyone with ESP abilities, as those individuals could kill the aliens with mind power alone. Sun Corps will collapse without DRAC, and the Esper organization (those with ESP) determines to move in and fill the power vacuum. Disillusioned with any form of power Talman again wanders alone before finally realizing that civilization must arise again.

As few readers will ever have the opportunity to read this first of King's novels let's take this opportunity to present a brief summary of each Chapter. The novel is split into three parts, each with numbered Chapters.

Part One, Chapter One: Larry Talman and Kelly are attacked by looters in Graybill and Kelly is killed. Chapter Two: Talman remembers the nuclear attack on Manchester some fourteen months before, on 14 August 1967. This date was later known as 'A-Day'. He'd been in Woolworths at the time and afterwards had wandered with other survivors. In a rare piece of overwriting, which is quite excusable from any 16 year old, King writes, 'He cried because man was naked.' In present time Talman meets Reina Durrel who immediately attacks and nearly kills him. He knocks her out. Chapter Three: Reina explains that her sister, Iris, had been raped and murdered the day before. They reconcile and make love. Talman remembers a friend, Jimmy Tomlinson and how they had joined up after the War. A week later Tomlinson had been killed by looters in Marl's Quarry. In present time, Talman awakens the next morning to find Reina has stolen his car.

Part Two, Chapter One: Three months later. Talman has been wandering all this time alone. Ian Vannerman wanders into Talman's camp and rants against the Sun Corps, a militaristic group, which is building up strength in the Aftermath. Chapter Two: Vannerman reveals he had once been a member of the Sun Corps. He and Talman decide to travel to Nashville with a plan of joining Sun Corps and destroying it from the inside. They arrive at Nashville and are allowed to join. Chapter Three: Talman and Vannerman are given ESP tests and afterwards meet another Sun Corps member, Arnie Stowe, who tells them about Sun Corps' 'town patrols', by which they take over a town and provide it with defense against 'looters', which effectively includes anyone who opposes the Corps.

Part Two, Chapter Four: The next morning the other Sun Corps troops leave for Eustus, the next town to be 'patrolled'. Talman and Vannerman are told they are ESP-negative and will be sent to Los Angeles for training. In the meantime they will serve the Corps in Eustus. Chapter Five: They leave for Eustus by truck and are ambushed but survive. In Eustus they are put at work on fortifications. A month passes with no sign of trouble but Talman and Vannerman have not yet been posted to LA. Suddenly, a huge group of 'looters' appears. Chapter Six: March 1969. The looter army attacks the Sun Corps garrison at Eustus, Tennessee. There is a massive battle with large numbers of casualties on both sides but the Sun Corps troops finally prevail. Talman receives minor wounds; Vannerman's are more serious. At the end of that day Talman remembers a quote: 'It is colder now … there are dark stars near Arcturus.' That night Talman and Vannerman are finally posted to Los Angeles, Vannerman to be trained in Mechanics and Weaponry; Talman in Statistics and Logistics.

Part Two: Chapter Seven: Three days after the battle, Talman and Vannerman leave Eustus and fly to Los Angeles on a cargo plane from Nashville. They are inducted to LA Co-Center training. Chapter Eight: Talman actually enjoys learning statistics. His trainer, James Carvel, tells him he is the most promising logistics (extrapolating logic from statistics) student he has taught in forty years. Talman starts to consider whether he should actually destroy Sun Corps or work for it. He discovers Reina Durrel is the daytime keeper of the Corps' supercomputer, DRAC, is introduced to the computer's amazing powers of deduction but realizes that the Corps is planning to use DRAC's predictive ability to control the world.

Part Two, Chapter Nine: Vannerman asks Talman to destroy DRAC. Talman is undecided and meets Reina that evening. He is now in a moral dilemma over how to destroy DRAC without killing Reina. Chapter Ten: Talman and Reina grow closer as Talman works daily on DRAC. Talman now questions how Sun Corps could have built such a supercomputer in the post-War environment. Vannerman and Talman plot to place a bomb to destroy DRAC. Chapter Eleven: April 1969, Talman prepares to bomb DRAC and places the explosives. Reina attacks him and an Esper who works for Sun Corps reveals the plot. Using an Ear-Hum device Talman kills Reina, the Esper and Sun Corps Lt. Kritzman. Chapter Twelve: Talman escapes and gets to his teacher, Carvel. The bomb goes off and DRAC is destroyed. Carvel reveals to Talman that Sun Corps is a front for the Denebians, an alien race who plan to take over the world. Only Espers can stop them and, with the assistance of DRAC, the Denebians would have built a machine to detect them all. Carvel kills the only Denebian on Earth. Talman and Vannerman leave on a heli but Talman becomes upset when Vannerman reveals he too is an Esper and that the Esper group is planning to reconstruct society. Talman insists on being dropped off in the countryside.

Part Three, Chapter One: Fall. Gray streaks Talman's hair. He remembers Jason, a boy he'd found in a small Oregon town. Looters had killed the boy's mother and Jason himself died a week later. Talman finally realizes the foolishness of his anti-society views and decides to go to Esper headquarters near Chicago. 'Good to finally be a man … Someone would show him the way.'

In reading the manuscript much more detail is available about various characters and events. Larry Talman, the protagonist, was 17 at the time of the nuclear war. His father was in the Army and both he and Larry's mother were killed in the initial nuclear attack on 14 August 1967. While Larry survived, he was badly burned and thin and pallid for some time thereafter. He lived in Manchester until the War and was a loner after it until January 1969 when he joined the Sun Corps, now weighing 170 lbs. Sun Corps declared him ESP negative and sent him to Eustus for training before moving him on to Los Angeles to be a statistician and logistician. He met Reina Durrel there for a second time and fell in love. He was convinced by Vannerman to plant the bomb that destroyed the Sun Corps supercomputer. Remaining disillusioned by organized society, he returned to wandering alone (this style of hero in American entertainment has been aptly dubbed 'The Lone Ranger syndrome'). He finally realized the value of society to individuals and at the end of the story set off for Esper headquarters near Chicago.

Talman's love interest, Reina Durrel attacked and nearly killed him the first time they met, apparently as a reaction to the rape and murder of her sister Iris the day before. However, they later made love (a strange reaction from the young girl to her recent past) and afterward she stole his car. She was about 16 in 1968, with brown hair and blonde highlights. She joined Sun Corps and became the daytime keeper of the Denebian/Sun Corp supercomputer, DRAC in Los Angeles. Talman was forced to kill her during his successful attempt to destroy the computer.

The two men who convinced Talman to commit the bombing were Ian Vannerman and James Carvel. Vannerman, a big man who said he was opposed to the Sun Corps, had joined and deserted it once before rejoining in January 1969. Sun Corps also declared him ESP negative but he'd deliberately flunked the test. In fact he was an Esper, a member of the secretive organization opposing the Sun Corps. He encouraged Talman to bomb DRAC and provided the actual bomb. He then assisted Talman to escape but could not convince him to join the Espers.

Carvel, a former Cornell teacher, taught Statistics and Logistics at Sun Corps' Los Angeles Co-Center. He shot and killed the only Denebian still on earth in April 1969. It was Carvel who revealed to Talman that the Sun Corps was but a front for the Denebian conspiracy to control the Earth.

The alien Denebians came from Deneb IV. They moved in on Earth after the nuclear war in August 1967, having had their eyes on the planet for three to four hundred years prior (this reminds one of the Martians from *The War of The Worlds*, which probably served as an inspiration for this tale). The sole Denebian left on earth was a very tall, huge tentacled horror. It had bulbous cone-shaped eyes and a strange voice. When Carvel shot and killed it with a sonic gun purple ichor was blown onto the floor.

The Denebians' front organization was the Sun Corps (in King's presentation one cannot help but think of a fascist, paramilitary group such as the German S.S.). After the nuclear war they reorganized the US along military and bureaucratic lines. Their symbol was a golden sunburst on a green field. They had various garrisons around America by January 1969 but collapsed after Talman destroyed the computer.

The DRAC itself was the biggest computer ever built. Fourteen stories high, it had tremendous predictive powers and was apparently built by the Denebians to help Sun Corps take over the Earth. It could only be activated by the palm print of the keeper of that shift. It was operated by a sophisticated keypunch, known as the Fountain Head, and would print out coded results which were verbalized by the computer's simulated voice.

King introduces some other interesting technology in this tale. This includes the Gunnar-Hellman Bolt Pistol, sonic guns and a 'Laser Plate', which is used for both cooking and setting off nuclear devices! A Sonic Ear-Hum is a weapon used to rupture every brain, except the user's, within twenty feet, which Talman killed Reina Durrel and Kritzman. In a very interesting reference King mentions Talman learnt Asimov-Seldon theorems at the LA Co-Center Statistics school. This is clear homage to Isaac Asimov's groundbreaking science fiction *Foundation* series of novels. Seldon was a key character in that series, having created the First Foundation as a response to the imminent collapse of the Galactic Empire.

Like any good science fiction writer King set the story in the future, although in this case only four to six years from the time of writing. One could argue this was the first of King's apocalyptic stories, eventually leading to *Night Surf*, *Trucks*, his classic *The Stand* and *The End of the Whole Mess*. Much of King's literary career has addressed the vexed issue of technology spinning out of control to form the basis of a horror tale. In this way, King was one of the first writers to successfully meld the lure of the technology based tales that had traditionally been served up as science fiction with the horror genre. Even simple technology such as that used in a laundry serves as the basis for such a tale in *The Mangler*.

Interestingly, the novel contains the first recorded use by King of the term 'survivor type', which would later form a story title. Vannerman says this to Talman on page 23: '…you must be a pretty good survivor type to have made it as long as you have, on your own.' On page 27, Talman thought of a particular woman as being '…another survivor type.'

There are no direct links from this novel to other King works. King has made it very clear he considers this first attempt at a novel to be juvenilia and there is no possibility that it will ever be published. While epic in scope and an interesting story, it suffers from the expected lack of maturity of any sixteen-year old. However, it is very interesting to see the early stages of the development of the style that would become King's and reveals something of the writer who was to burst upon the world stage barely a decade later.

American Vampire (2010)

American Vampire is a comic book series launched by Vertigo (an imprint of DC Comics) in May 2010. It represents King's first original comic script. Each of the five issues in the first 'arc' (a comic book term for an extended or continuing storyline) carried one story by King and one by series creator, Scott Snyder. After the first arc King had no further involvement.

According to publicity material[55]: 'The series twists the well-trod vampire legend by allowing the creatures to evolve into a distinctly American creature and will follow the adventures of Skinner Sweet, a sociopathic outlaw in the Wild West who becomes the first American vampire. Unlike European vamps, Skinner is powered by the sun and, true to his native environment, has rattlesnake fangs. Each cycle, consisting of five individual comic issues, will take place in a different period of time in American history, tracing Skinner's descendants, with Skinner himself as a recurring character.'

Snyder originally sold his idea for 'a uniquely American take on vampires' to DC Comics then approached King for a blurb. The author enjoyed the tale so much he suggested he'd be willing to contribute to future issues. Naturally enough, this excited Snyder and the editors at Vertigo, who agreed. King then penned five stories relating to Skinner's origins in the American West. Again, according to publicity material: 'King's arc will trace the origins of the first American vampire, Skinner Sweet, as he goes fang-to-fang with even nastier vamps, a group out to get rich by damming up a river to create a new town. "It's really the vampire as American capitalist gone totally wild." (King said)'

Only the King stories in the first five issues are 'canon', or officially by King. King's story in Issue One is *Bad Blood*. Set in Sidewinder, Colorado in 1880, this first tale is narrated by Will Bunting, who 'only wrote one novel in my life – *Bad Blood*.' Sidewinder is an imaginary town from King's America Under Siege Reality – it first appeared in *The Shining* as the town closest to the Overlook Hotel, and has since appeared in *Before the Play*, *Misery* and *The Talisman*, along with both of King's adaptations of *The Shining*. It is notable that he chose to make this link.

Bunting says most of his 'novel' (later revealed as *Bad Blood, or The Monster Outlaw – A Terrifying Tale of the Old West* by William Bunting) is actually true. His story opens with Skinner Sweet, 'notorious murderer and bank-thief' in the custody of the Pinkerton Agency, operating on behalf of 'Percy', a wealthy banker. As the train carrying Sweet and his captors proceeds from Sidewinder towards New Mexico Sweet's crew prepare to derail the train, intent on freeing Sweet and killing all the passengers – 'No Witnesses!'

Meanwhile, Sweet regales a Pinkerton agent with the tale of his gang's robbery of a bank in Bakersville, Colorado six months earlier. While his men were raping the women (and one man!) a loan officer began a shoot-out, in which a number of people including a three year old child were killed. The gang retreated to a nearby mine to hole-up.

Just before the train is derailed Sweet unlocks his handcuffs, using a peppermint stick. Bunting watched the aftermath of the derailment: "What I saw next was surely colored by my imagination as well as by the dying hues of that terrible day's sunset ... but what I saw is more real than any *dream* or *memory*." Sweet and his gang are confronted by 'Old Man Percy' who amazingly says, "I think I've had enough of your shit, Mr. *Sweet*." The gang shoot Percy dead but he immediately rises and *bites* Sweet in the neck, baring lengthy fangs. Sweet shoots Percy again and again before being shot dead himself. His gang flees and Percy and the survivors leave Sweet's body by the side of the railroad. Percy (we now realize he is a vampire) is furious! Bunting closes this first tale, declaring, "I started writing that very night, and I think I knew two things even then: that what I wrote could only be published as fiction ... and Skinner Sweet's story wasn't over but *just beginning*."

Percy has 'very fair skin' and avoids direct sunlight as much as possible (he is seen carrying an unfurled umbrella), so unlike the traditional vampire he can go out in daylight (in fact he is suffering a mild sunburn). This begins our understanding that these peculiarly American vampires are actually powered by the sun.

King's contribution to Issue 2 was *Deep Water*. It is 1925, Los Angeles as Will Bunting addresses a few people who've turned up to 'celebrate' the reissue of *Bad Blood*, his 'one-of-a-kind' dime novel based on the life and death of Skinner Sweet. The book is said to combine the western thrills of Zane Grey and the horror thrills of Bram Stoker! Bunting tells his audience that most of the tale is true, even if he had to publish it as fiction. In Bunting's tale Percy and other European vampires discuss Sweet's death – Percy is certain Sweet is dead but two other vampires remind him Percy's blood had splashed on Sweet and he might yet rise. Ignoring this Percy discusses his plan to dam the Baya River in Colorado and make a fortune irrigating cheap land the vampires had picked up in the New Mexico territory. In 1883 the Baya River dam was completed and Sidewinder flooded – as a result water drained into the UnDead Sweet's grave on Boot Hill. Meanwhile, Bunting rode the West with the Pinkerton's Jim Book and Felix Camillo, dispensing justice. Felix married Benita Juarez, with Book as best man but four years later Benita died in childbirth, their daughter Abilena survived. By 1909, Lakeview, Colorado had replaced the flooded Sidewinder. Scavengers decided to dive on Sweet's grave – hoping to pick up artifacts of the famous outlaw they might sell – and the first diver found something entirely unexpected, a ravenous vampire from a new breed, one that could not burn in sunlight or drown in water. Newly fed, Sweet escaped his watery grave, heading into Lakeview, intent on taking revenge on Percy, "and the time of the *American Vampire* has come."

In Issue 3 King's tale is *Blood Vengeance*. Lakeview, Colorado – 1909. Sweet is back in town, confronted by the changes while he'd been underground – telephones, cinema, horseless carriages, and a Mexican mayor (Felix's father, Camillo), the last an affront to Sweet's racism. Sweet rampages in Lakeview, killing all in sight, feeding and growing stronger by the hour. Meanwhile the nest of vampires of which Percy was a member discover to their own horror that Sweet has risen, and that he can easily walk in full sunlight! A posse is formed to catch Sweet; even though Chief Finch denies claims the creature is the famous outlaw, 30 years in his grave. Sweet kills Finch after extracting from him that Book and Camillo now live in Cruces, New Mexico. Having killed Mayor Camillo, Sweet telegraphs ahead to Felix that he wants Felix and Book to meet him at the Old Bakersvilles Mines, claiming to have Felix's father – and signs it Skinner Sweet. Bunting recalls being with Book when the telegram arrived and they along with Felix and his daughter ride out to meet the man 'claiming' to be Skinner Sweet.

Issue 4 carries King's *One Drop of Blood*: Two days after the events in *Blood Vengeance* Felix and the others arrive in devastated Lakeview, rife with tales that Skinner Sweet had destroyed the town – bullets couldn't stop him, and the man had fangs! Bunting shares his suspicion that Sweet is a vampire, infected by Percy but he does not understand how these vampires can walk in full sunlight. When the group find Sweet in a mine outside town Felix enters and Sweet kills him. Felix's daughter tells Jim Book she loves him. As a result of a gunfight the mine collapses, apparently trapping Sweet and the surviving group members escape, although Book appears to have been infected. The European vampires observe all this and believe Sweet has been dealt with.

King's final contribution to *American Vampire* appears in Issue 5 as *If Thy Right Hand Offend Thee, Cut It Off*: Three years later in Cruces, New Mexico Book is still battling the infection as Sweet's legacy is alive and well in his own blood. Abilena Camillo is still with Book and expresses her love for him, despite their age difference. Some years later men sent by Percy dig Skinner Sweet up, he kills them and decides to make for Percy's ranch where Percy offers to let Sweet join them but is tricked. Sweet drags him into sunlight, burning Percy to death. Book asks Abilena to kill him, so as to escape his personal hell of vampirism and she agrees, if he makes love to her as she is in her 'fertile time'. They have sex and later that night she kills him as agreed; a year later she leaves town with their daughter, Will Bunting tagging along. In 1925 Bunting concludes his tale by explaining his motives – to reveal to the world that 'real monsters' are out on the roads and railways of America; and to explain Book's heroism. As he leaves the lecture hall he receives a note – from Skinner Sweet! Later, Abilena and her daughter Felicia observe Skinner as he walks down the street. Abilena promises Book's daughter they will deal with the man who'd destroyed her father, 'Not today, but soon.'

Copies of the comic books are easily purchased either new from specialist stores, or on the secondary market. The first five issues (covering King's tales) was published by Vertigo in a collection, *American Vampire Volume 1* in October 2010 and is currently in print. It is most unlikely King's material from the series will ever appear in one of his collections.

An Evening at God's (1990)

An Evening at God's is a 'one-minute play' that King wrote for a benefit evening. The manuscript was auctioned on 23 April 1990 at the American Repertory Theater's Institute for Advanced Theater Training. While it has never been published the text circulates freely in the King community.

According to Stephen Spignesi[56] other authors who contributed to the benefit included Art Buchwald, J K Galbraith, Larry Gelbart, David Mamet and John Updike. He reports an interview with Gail Caldwell of the *Boston Globe*[57] in which King summarizes the play as, 'God sitting at home and drinking a few beers and St Peter comes in with papers to pass, and God's watching a sitcom on TV. And the earth is sort of hanging in the way of the TV, and he keeps trying to look around it to see the television. So I sat down and wrote it. And it may have been a critical comment: The typewriter broke down while I was working on this, and I had to redo it.'

When God crushes the Earth St Peter is somewhat rueful, and points out that some of God's favorite comedians - Alan Alda, Robin Williams and Richard Pryor, all *used* to live on Earth. Initially disappointed, God remembers he has all the videotapes.

Typically of King a lot of fun and action are crammed into the 'one minute' in which this play should be performed. At the beginning there are signs that God has been drinking a lot of beer and, on finding he had destroyed the world on which his favorite comedians live he says, "Shit. Maybe I better cut down on my drinking." In addition to a drinking problem God also has a problem with certain foods, telling St Peter, "I should know better than to eat those chili peppers. They burn me at both ends."

This amusing little piece includes a line from God reminiscent of that uttered by Jake Chambers as Roland let him fall to his second death, "Go then. There are other worlds than these." St Peter says, "I actually sort of liked that one, God – Earth, I mean," and God replies, "It wasn't bad, but there's more where that came from."

A papier-mâché globe represents Earth, hanging between the TV and God. As it interferes with His viewing God smashes it out of the way, killing us all. In fact, God's housekeeper gets at least some of the blame. St Peter remarks before God lashes out at our planet, "So Earth's still there, Huh? After all these years", God replies, "Yes, the housekeeper is the most forgetful bitch in the universe."

Perhaps the most interesting exchange occurs when God mutters, "My son got back, didn't he?" St Peter: "Yessir, some time ago." At the beginning of the play God is described as 'a big guy with a white beard' reading a book – *When Bad Things Happen to Good People*. Concluding the script is an Author's Note: 'God's Voice should be as loud as possible.'

While no timeline for the events is given we know that Alan Alda, Richard Pryor and Robin Williams were all popular comedians. In Earth time the story is *probably* set in the 1980s. Due to this, and the Earth's demise, *An Evening at God's* is categorized as a New Worlds tale.

There are no links from this Work to any other King story.

Before the Play (1982, 1997)

Before the Play is the prologue to *The Shining*, cut from that novel in the editing process to help secure a lower cover price for the hardback! It is effectively a collection of five stories, loosely connected by the Overlook Hotel. Four are set at the Hotel and the remaining one during Jack Torrance's childhood. Not only do the 'scenes' provide fascinating background about the Overlook Torrance's motivations are more clearly explained, perhaps dictating his adult behavior.

The first appearance was in the magazine *Whispers* (Number 17/18) for August 1982. Copies can be purchased through the various King booksellers, although that particular edition is becoming scarcer as collectors permanently retain copies.

As part of the promotion for the mini-series version of *The Shining* King allowed an abridged version to be published in the 26 April to 2 May 1997 edition of *TV Guide*. The cuts were partly a matter of self-censorship to suit the sensibilities of that magazine. However, Spignesi cogently argues King felt there were weaknesses in the deleted scenes, stating as he does in his *TV Guide* introduction, 'I'm glad to see the best of it restored to print here.'[58]

Copies of the *TV Guide* version, which Bernie Wrightson illustrated, are relatively easy to secure through King booksellers and other sources.

King also wrote *After the Play* but that merged into the closing sections of the novel during the editing process and the author says that the original text has been lost.

In this loose set of stories, which King terms 'scenes', we learn something of the history of the Overlook Hotel and the Torrance family. Scene I is *The Third Floor of a Resort Hotel Fallen Upon Hard Times*. It deals with the construction of the Overlook, from 1907, by Bob T Watson. In 1908 his eldest son, Boyd, died on the grounds in a riding accident and the Grand Opening in 1909 was marred when a Congressman choked to death. After ploughing huge amounts of money into the Hotel Watson was forced to sell, receiving in return the promise of maintenance jobs for life for himself and his remaining son. In August 1922 the new owner, James Parris died of a heart attack – in the hotel's topiary, a fact that probably does not surprise readers of *The Shining*. Shortly after that death Bob T Watson imagined he heard his dead son riding on the grounds. (This entire scene was deleted from the *TV Guide* version).

In the second section, *A Bedroom in the Wee Hours of the Morning*, Lottie Kilgallon Pillsbury honeymooned at the Overlook in August of 1929 (Pillsbury was King's mother's maiden name). Lottie suffered a number of disturbing dreams, including one in which the hotel was on fire and, in another, she saw the topiary move.

Topping it all off, while Lottie smoked in bed: 'She reached down to get the ashtray and the thought burst on her like a revelation: *It does creep, the whole place – like it was alive!* And that was when the hand reached out unseen from under the bed and gripped her wrist firmly … almost lecherously.' Not surprisingly, Lottie insisted upon returning home immediately. After years of dwelling on the events at the Overlook she committed suicide in a Yonkers hotel room in 1949: 'It had been twenty years and the hand that had gripped her wrist when she reached down to get her cigarettes had never really let go.' This is perhaps the most memorable (and scariest) of any King scene in an uncollected short story.

In the third section, *On the Night of the Grand Masquerade*, Lewis Toner, head accountant and former lover of Overlook owner Horace Derwent, committed suicide by overdosing in a bathtub on the night of the 1946 Grand Masquerade Ball. Derwent bought off the coroner and other authorities to avoid a scandal. (This scene was deleted from the *TV Guide* version, almost certainly as a form of self-censorship due to its heavy sexual nature).

The fourth scene, *And Now this Word from New Hampshire*, reverts to the summer of 1953. When Jacky Torrance was six, his father came home drunk and broke the boy's arm in a rage. This, of course, presages Jack's breaking of *his* son Danny's arm twenty-two years later. One scene alone serves to show yet again how well King can position the reader in the mind of a child, in this case Jacky: 'His father was like God, like Nature, sometimes lovable, sometimes terrible. You never knew which it would be. Jacky's mother feared and served him. His brothers hated him. Only Jacky of all of them still loved him in spite of the fear and the hate, and sometimes the volatile mixture of emotions made him want to cry out at the sight of his father coming, to simply cry out: *I love you daddy! Go away! Hug me! I'll kill you! I'm so afraid of you! I need you!*' And, just before the senior Torrance kicked Jacky in the belly, sending him flying from his tree house to the ground, and a greenstick fracture, ' "Oh, Daddy," Jacky mourned for the both of them'. The scene ends as Jacky faints with: '*What you see is what you'll be, what you see is what you'll be, what you* – The break in his arm was cleanly healed in six months. The nightmares went on much longer. In a way, they never stopped.'

The story concludes with Scene V, *The Overlook Hotel, Third Floor, 1958*, in which there is a mob hit, when three men kill two guards and an underworld figure in the Presidential Suite. The piece closes, 'The Overlook Hotel was at home with the dead'.

As it was King's intention when writing *Before the Play* it would be the Prologue to *The Shining*, it is clear this small collection of scenes is part of that particular storyline of the America Under Siege reality. This being the case there are obviously a huge number of links to the novel and to King's other fiction, as well as some anomalies or errors between this piece and the novel itself.

Sidewinder, Colorado, 40 miles east of the Overlook and the nearest town also receives considerable mention in *Misery* and all versions of *The Shining*. It is also mentioned in *The Talisman*. The Overlook Hotel itself is, of course, the key location in all versions of *The Shining* and is mentioned in both *Misery* and *The Regulators*.

The following are some of the very extensive links to the novel version of *The Shining*. In both, Jack Torrance's father was an orderly at the Berlin Community Hospital.

In *Before the Play* Lottie Kilgallon, while staying at the Overlook Hotel in August 1929, dreamed that there had been a fire: 'Perhaps it had been the boiler. You had to keep an eye on the boiler, because if you didn't, she would creep on you.' In Chapter 12 of *The Shining* Watson says, "Just stuck around to remind Mr Torrance here about the boiler. Keep your good weather eye on her, fella, and she'll be fine. Knock the press down a couple of times a day. She creeps." Danny Torrance then thinks, 'She creeps'. Of course, the boiler exploded at midnight on 2 December 1977, destroying the Overlook. In *Before the Play*, Lottie Kilgallon dreamed a fire hose held her so that a fire could get to her. In *The Shining*, Danny Torrance thought he saw the fire hose move and was scared it would catch him.

In *Before the Play*, Jacky Torrance's father broke his arm in a drunken rage one summer night in 1953. In *The Shining*, Jack Torrance broke his son Danny's arm in 1975 while in a drunken temper. This critical piece of back-story is very useful to an understanding of how Jack Torrance came to be both an alcoholic and the cycle of violence he visited upon his son. The novel tempts us to believe the cycle has been broken and King pretty much confirms that with the graduation scene in the mini-series screenplay.

Among characters that appear in both this piece and the novel are: Horace Derwent, Jack ('Jacky') Torrance, his father Mark and Jacky's mother.

Grondin is the contractor who diddles Bob T Watson of $70,000 in 1911 in *Before the Play*. In *The Shining*, Charles Grondin headed the group of investors who purchased the Overlook from Derwent in 1952, then later also headed High Country Investments, which purchased the Overlook in 1963. As Charles was born in 1911 he could not be the same Grondin, but perhaps he was a descendant? King continually creates these sorts of connections and it does not seem likely that the use of this surname is a coincidence. Ironically, in this piece a company Horace Derwent controlled donated the Library in Sidewinder, Colorado. In the novel Jack Torrance used the very same Library to do research on the Overlook Hotel, and Derwent!

One of Bob T Watson's friends said the opening night of the Overlook Hotel on 1 June 1910 reminded him of Poe's story about the Red Death. In the Prelude to Chapter One of the novel there is a lengthy quote from Poe's *The Masque of Red Death* and in Chapter 18 Jack Torrance was reminded of a line from the same story.

In *Before the Play* in the summer of 1952 Jacky Torrance's father smoke-drugged a colony of wasps and burnt their nest. In the novel, Mark Torrance smoked out a colony of wasps in his back yard. This is presumably the same event. Of course, Jack Torrance's stinging by wasps while he is clearing the roof of the Overlook is a crucial event in the novel and carries more power in this context.

There is a possible inconsistency in the Presidential Suite Killings. In *Before the Play* in 1958 *three* men killed two guards and an underworld figure in the Presidential Suite. In the novel *two* men killed a mobster called Gienelli and two guards in the Presidential Suite in June 1966. Of course, it is also possible that these were separate killings. Either way if one's name is, say, Tony Soprano, one should *not* stay in the Presidential Suite of the Overlook Hotel!

There are some clear inconsistencies between the two stories. In *Before the Play*, the elevator at the Overlook Hotel was installed in 1927; in the novel and mini-series it was installed in 1926. In *Before the Play* Lewis Toner died in 1946 but in *The Shining* he died in 1945.

In another probable error we read that in 1922 Woodrow Wilson was the only President (prior to October 7, 1922) to stay in the Presidential Suite. 'When Wilson had come here he had been a sorry joke. There had been talk in the country that his wife was actually President of the United States.' In fact, Wilson finished his second and final Presidential term in March 1921. In 1922 Harding was President and it seems unlikely that people would have joked of the *previous* President's wife actually being President.

Frankly, it is surprising that King has not included this story (or more accurately, collection of scenes) in one of his collections. *Before the Play* is a tremendously valuable addition to the mythos of the Overlook Hotel and provides key motivation and background for one of the most towering and memorable characters in King's body of work. Hope should not be lost that King may at some point give this story a wider readership. After all, *TV Guide* had one of the biggest circulations of any US magazine, so it is unlikely that King does not want this story in broad circulation.

The other possibility would be its restoration in a future printing of the novel.

King restored *The Stand*; allowed excerpts from the original manuscript of *'Salem's Lot* to be published; revised *The Gunslinger*; and made minor alterations to *The Green Mile* when the six parts of that novel were collected in one volume. He has also updated a very large number of his short stories over the years. It may be that a 'Restored' version of *The Shining* is not out of the question.

THE HISTORY OF THE OVERLOOK HOTEL

Before the Play adds an enormous amount to the history of the Overlook Hotel, as provided in *The Shining*. From these sources, along with the mini-series screenplay, the unproduced movie screenplay, *Misery* and *The Regulators* it is possible to glean the following information about the Hotel, its history and owners.

It was built by Bob T Watson between 1907 and 1909 to be the grandest resort hotel in America and, at nearly 12,000ft above sea level, the highest. During the building Watson's son, Boyd was killed in a riding accident. The Hotel is forty miles west of Sidewinder. The first season was 1910, with the opening ceremony held on 1 June. A Congressman choked to death at the celebration dinner.

By September 1914 Watson was bankrupt and in 1915 the Overlook was sold to James T Parris, who died in 1922, after which it was sold to Clyde and Cecil Brandywine. In 1922 Woodrow Wilson stayed in the Presidential Suite. The Hotel was resold in 1929 and 1936; Horace Derwent purchased it in 1945. Derwent sold out in 1952 and the Hotel had a number of other owners before being bought in 1970 by Al Shockley and his associates, who refurbished it that year.

On 2 December 1977 the Overlook was destroyed when its boiler exploded while Jack Torrance was the caretaker (*note: according to the mini-series version this occurred in 1996 or 1997*). During the Overlook's history there were many violent deaths and murders and a number of suicides. It seems the Hotel was at least haunted, and possibly possessed.

The full list of owners: 1907-1915 Bob T Watson; 1915-1922 James T Parris; 1922-1929 Clyde and Cecil Brandywine; 1929-1936 Unknown; 1936-1945 Unknown; 1945-52 Horace M Derwent; 1952-1953/4 Charles Grondin and a group of investors; 1953/4-1957 Mountainview Resorts; 10 April 1963-1967 High Country Investments; 1967-68 Sylvia Hunter; 1970-77 Albert Shockley and Associates. (*Note: according to the mini-series version a company called the Sidewinder Corporation owned the Overlook at the time of its destruction in 1996 or 1997*).

The Blue Air Compressor (1971, 1981)

One of King's stranger stories and far from his best, *The Blue Air Compressor* was originally published in *Onan*, a student literary magazine published at the University of Maine at Orono (UMO), for January 1971, shortly after King graduated. He allowed republication in *Heavy Metal*, an 'adult illustrated fantasy magazine' in July 1981. King made numerous changes for that publication, although all were minor in nature, the removal or changing of words and the deletion of one sentence being the most severe.

It is virtually impossible to find an original *Onan* copy, except at very high price through a specialist King bookseller. *Heavy Metal* is generally available from the same sources. Those visiting the Special Collections Unit of the Raymond H Fogler Library of the University of Maine at Orono may request a photocopy of the *Onan* version. There are no links from this story to King's other fiction.

Early in the story King introduces *himself* as the author. It is a rarity for King to mention himself in his fiction and in this case it is very deliberate and self-conscious. It's interesting that he chose not to remove or rework these interjections when the story was republished. They have an air of pretension that is most unlike King and while in the original publication (which also carried a King poem, *In the Key Chords of Dawn* ...) this may have been appropriate; it fails completely in *Heavy Metal*. Other critics are kinder toward the story[59]. King's first interjection reads in part:

'My own name, of course, is Steve King, and you'll pardon my intrusion on your mind – or I hope you will. I could argue that drawing aside the curtain of presumption between reader and author is permissible because I am the writer; ie, since it's *my* story I'll do any goddam thing I please with it – but since that leaves the reader out of it completely, that is not valid. Rule One for all writers is that the teller is not worth a tin tinker's fart when compared to the listener. Let us drop the matter, if we may. I am intruding for the same reason that the Pope defecates; we both have to ... You should know Gerald Nately was never brought to the dock ... I invented him first during a moment of eight o'clock boredom in a class taught by Carroll F. Terrell of the University of Maine English faculty ... It is desperately important that the reader be made cognizant of these facts' (*this last was removed entirely from the* Heavy Metal *version*).

In a later and more interesting, if still heavy-handed, interjection:

'Most horror stories are sexual in nature. I'm sorry to break in with this information, but I feel I must in order to make the way clear for the grisly conclusion of this piece, which is (at least psychologically) a clear metaphor for fears of sexual impotence on my part ... In the works of Edgar A. Poe, Stephen King, Gerald Nately, and others who practice this particular literary form, we are apt to find locked rooms, dungeons, empty mansions (all symbols of the womb); scenes of living burial (sexual impotence); the dead returned from the grave (necrophilia); grotesque monsters or human beings (externalized fear of the sexual act itself); torture and/or murder (a viable alternative to the sexual act). These possibilities are not always valid, but the post-Freud reader and writer must take them into consideration when attempting the genre. Abnormal psychology has become part of the human experience.'

And, again:

'Part of the inspiration for this story came from an old E.C. horror comic book, which I bought in a Lisbon Falls drugstore. In one particular story, a husband and wife murdered each other simultaneously in mutually ironic (and brilliant) fashion ... He shoved the hose of an air compressor down her throat and blew her up to dirigible size ... In a horror story, it is imperative that the grotesque be elevated to the status of the abnormal.'

It seems very unlikely that this story will appear in a mainstream King collection. It is not of high quality, pretentious (even the tool-shed is described '...after the manner of Zola'), self-admittedly derivative and quite unrepresentative of King's style (even the time it was written).

In the actual story a writer rents a seaside cottage in Maine from a deceased friend's wife. When Gerald Nately arrived at Mrs. Leighton's nearby house, he found her to be a very large woman. He became obsessed with her weight and wrote a story about her, *The Hog*.

Nately showed signs of mental instability in the two or three months he lived in the cottage and debated with himself whether to let Mrs. Leighton read the story. He had actually decided to do so but found her reading it without his permission. He snapped when Mrs. Leighton laughed at him: ' "Oh Gerald ... This is such a bad story. I don't blame you for using a pen name, it's ... it's *abominable*! ... You haven't made me *big* enough, Gerald. That's the trouble. I'm too big for you. Perhaps Poe, or Dostoyevsky, or Melville ... but not you, Gerald. Not *you*. Not *you*."'

Nately hit her with a gun and then forced the hose of the blue air compressor down her throat and turned it on, causing her to explode. He then cut the body up, buried it under the floor (Poe's *The Tell-Tale Heart* is mentioned) and called the police to report her missing.

The majority of the story takes place in either Mrs. Leighton's home or in the cottage, with the murder taking place in the cottage's tool shed, where *The Hog* had been hidden. Conveniently for the plot, this is also where the blue air compressor was kept.

Leaving the scene of the murder, Nately rewrote *The Hog* in Bombay and gave it the new title, *The Blue Air Compressor*, then travelled to Kowloon some time before buying an ivory-figured guillotine, which he then used to cut off his own head! This last is perhaps the most interesting and apparently original part of the story.

No year is given for the story but Nately lived in the cottage from September to early December. It is unclear how much later Nately's death in Kowloon occurred but it was probably after quite some time, as Nately had time to write '...four twisted, monumental, misunderstood novels.' ('Misunderstood' was edited out of the *Heavy Metal* version, presumably on the basis the author realized the novels had most probably not been read by anyone else).

Interestingly King had this to say in a *Danse Macabre* footnote (first published the year the second version of this tale was released): 'My all time favorite [of 'bad end' tales]: A crazed husband stuffs the hose of an air compressor down his skinny wife's throat and blows her up like a balloon until she bursts. 'Fat at last,' he tells her happily just moments before the pop. But later on the husband, who is roughly the size of Jackie Gleason, trips a booby-trap she has set for him and is squashed to a shadow when a huge safe falls on him. This ingenious reworking of the old story of Jack Sprat and his wife is not only gruesomely funny; it offers us a delicious example of the Old Testament eye-for-an-eye theory.' Readers will note there is *no* mention of *King's* reworking of the tale.

But Only Darkness Loves Me and I Hate Mondays (Undated)

These stories were first rediscovered by the author of this book in King's papers at the Special Collections Unit of the Raymond H Fogler Library at the University of Maine in Orono, during a 17-day research trip in 2002.

A significant number of stories of which there was no record in published King research came to light. Research undertaken with the help of King's office determined which of the manuscripts were genuine and which had been written by others (the most likely 'suspects' being his wife, Tabitha and the King children). Among those manuscripts eliminated by King himself during this process are *Imaginary Places* (an intriguing poem), *Loon Call* (a bitter-sweet short story), *History Lesson* and *The Shepherd and His Flock* (suspiciously un-King in tone).

But Only Darkness Loves Me and *I Hate Mondays* were two of the ten stories rediscovered and announced to the world in early 2003. Each of these stories are collaborations with one of his sons and they form two of the few occasions King is known to have jointly written prose with another writer.

But Only Darkness Loves Me

This two page story fragment is headed 'By Stephen and Joseph King'. Part One is *The Most Beautiful Girl in the World* but only part of Chapter One, Section One survives. Of the two pages the first is typed and the second handwritten. The two pages are to be found in Box 1012 of the Special Collections Unit of the Raymond H Fogler Library at the University of Maine at Orono.

This story can be accessed by any member of the public attending the Library, as it is not held in a Restricted Box.

Joseph Hillstrom King is Tabitha and Stephen's oldest son and one of three children, the others being Naomi Rachel and their brother Owen Phillip. Joseph King is now a successful writer[60] using the pseudonym Joe Hill. King and Joe Hill co-authored *Throttle* (2009)[61], a riff on the Richard Matheson story *Duel*, adapted under the same title by Stephen Spielberg.

In the few words from this story left to us a boy is talking to a beautiful girl in a bar in Ledge Cove, Maine. She is too beautiful to look at directly, except in quick glances. She invites him back to her hotel but he only agrees to go to the lobby, not her room. To the reader the few words are mysterious and contain a *Nona*-like quality.

There is no indication when this piece was written and no dates for the action contained in it are provided. In such a short fragment there is little to report. The 'boogie band' at the The Ledge Cove Bar in Ledge Cove, Maine (this town is not mentioned in any other King story) play Mellencamp's *The Authority Song*. Due to its Maine setting it is classified as a Maine Street Horror tale. There are no direct links from this story to any other King fiction.

I Hate Mondays

This complete five page story is headed 'By Stephen and Owen King'. The manuscript is held in Box 1010 at the Special Collections Unit of the Raymond H Fogler Library at the University of Maine at Orono. Written permission from Stephen King is required to access this story. Owen Phillip King, now also published author[62], is Tabitha and Stephen's youngest son.

I Hate Mondays is written in a very immature manner and was probably no more than a bit of fun for Stephen and Owen. It is very unlikely that it will ever be published in any form. It is unclear when this piece was written and no dates for the action contained in it are provided.

In the story goons attack a man. Spike's wife has been kidnapped and is being held because she holds the combination to a bank's safe. The goons capture Spike by telling him they are holding her. Spike and Rita escape, killing most of the bad guys but in the process Rita is also killed. Finally, Spike kills the ringleader: 'And that was that.'

Readers learnt a little about the characters during the story. Spike was wounded while escaping (and seemed to have little real remorse over his wife's death, despite having originally gone to her rescue). Rita worked at the National City Bank and was captured by the goons, as she was one of only three people with the combination to the bank's big safe. She was shot in the head and killed while she and Spike were escaping the goons. Spike and Rita had kids and Spike wondered what would happen to them now Rita was dead.

Spike had some interesting habits, for instance he kept a razor blade under his shirt collar. Rita used it to free them. Later he used a pocket knife to deflect a bullet! Then again, one of Rita's earrings also deflected a bullet, which might otherwise have killed her! While attempting to escape Spike and Rita ducked into a barber shop, run by Tom. The goons shot up the shop, killing a customer.

The chief goon was nicknamed 'Dr. Mindbender' as he looked like the Dr. Mindbender of the cartoons. When Spike killed him he 'flew back and spiked himself against a cross. And that was that.' All the other goons were killed, mostly by gunfire, although Spike did for one by throwing a hand-carved knife into his eye.

The town or city in which the story is set is unclear, leaving it to be classified as an America Under Siege tale. There are no direct links from this story to any other King fiction.

The Cannibals (2009)

King originally attempted to write *The Cannibals* in 1978[63]. His second attempt was a novel of about 450 pages, composed as a rewrite of an earlier novel written while filming *Creepshow* in July to December 1981. King previously had this to say in a footnote to his *Full Disclosure* in *Blaze*: 'In my career I have managed to lose not one but two pretty good novels-in-progress. *Under the Dome* was only 50 pages long at the time it disappeared, but *The Cannibals* was over 200 pages long at the time it went MIA. No copies of either. That was before computers, and I never used carbons for first drafts - it felt *haughty*, somehow.' King's assistant, Marsha DeFilippo indicated in posts on his official message board in April 2008 that, 'We had sections, but not the complete draft, of The Cannibals in the office.' As part of promoting *Under the Dome* King released the first 61 pages of the second manuscript on his official website on 15 September 2009; and a further 63 pages on 4 October the same year.

In June of 2008, after the announcement King was rewriting *Under the Dome* Marsha DeFilippo reported on the official message board King had this to say: 'Those stories were two very different attempts to utilize the same idea, which concerns itself with how people behave when they are cut off from the society they've always belonged to. Also, my memory of THE CANNIBALS is that it, like NEEDFUL THINGS, was a kind of social comedy. The new UNDER THE DOME is played dead straight.'[64]

The two sections King released form part of an America Under Siege Tale. The first section, a scan of King's original typewritten manuscript, with handwritten corrections, is comprised of the first three chapters and the first two subsections of the fourth chapter from Part One of the novel.

Part One is titled *Yellow Morning* (actually in King's handwriting, crossing out three other words) and Chapter I is *The Tennis Club*. We are introduced to the Tennis Club Apartments, whose residents are immediately portrayed as isolated from society – upper middle-class, white collar people 'who lived mostly for themselves in the era of withdrawal from commitment' (the story is actually set at some point in the 1980s).

Chapter II is *Tom Hill in the Lobby* and features the first resident 'to encounter the problem which arose on July 19th.' A TV station executive on the way up, Hill is heading to work around 4.45am and proceeds to the apartment buildings' foyer and pulls on the outer door, which does not open, in fact when he pulls the door again it doesn't budge even slightly. Hill notices the approaching daylight is more suited to one hour later in the morning (a nice piece of foreshadowing). Only slightly irritated and investigating, Hill finds the building phone is not working and decides to head upstairs.

In Chapter III is *Pulaski* - another character is introduced, arriving in the lobby just as Hill headed back up in the elevator. We learn Dennis Pulaski is a twice-divorced Korean War veteran, a hunter and something of a 'man's man'. This section contains quite a bit of sexual content, mostly designed to establish the rigidity of Pulaski's world-view. He's also a racist. Pulaski discovers he too is unable to open the building's front door.

Meanwhile, Hill knocks on the door of the building office, looking for Ronnie Bamford, the night security guard. But there's no answer. Returning downstairs, he meets Pulaski, who informs him the back doors are also locked. They consider exiting through the alarmed fire door, which leads to the nearby sports complex but when they try, 'The square of metal did not move at all. It did not move an inch, a half-inch, not so much as a silly millimeter. The alarm did not sound. And the fire door did not open.' This disturbs the two men, who understand that locking a normal door is one thing, locking a fire escape is serious indeed.

When they return to the lobby quite a few more residents have appeared and are milling about. Pulaski rings the building superintendent, Rinaldi, briefly advises the situation and demands he come downstairs immediately. We learn that Rinaldi is a pompous control freak and not easily intimidated. As the residents wait for the superintendent to appear Pulaski also notes the daylight, he 'could not remember ever having seen a daylight quite like this one – thin, watery, almost *wavery*.' Rinaldi finally appears and also tries to leave the building. When he cannot it is revealed the external doors *cannot* be locked, as in fact they *have no locks*.

Chapter IV is *Jo's Bible; Rinaldi's Call; Pulaski's Bat* and begins with another in the growing cast of characters – a deeply religious Joanne Page. By the time she reaches the lobby, Rinaldi, Hill and Pulaski have left for Rinaldi's office. Rinaldi's jaundiced, perhaps realistic view of the building's occupants is revealed – they are each classified in his mind as Busybodies, Good Tenants, or Troublemakers. Careful to preserve his authority with the residents, and mindful of not looking incompetent to his employers, Rinaldi begins by calling the security guard's company on a dedicated line, but not before the first of what is likely to be many clashes with Pulaski. The security company answers and Rinaldi can hear the operator, Bo Franklin, but Franklin most certainly cannot hear Rinaldi. The three men begin to show concern, in Tom Hill's case, 'he felt something pierce his confusion and harried annoyance at being late. He found nothing welcome about the new emotion. It was fear.' And so ends the first manuscript segment.

The second section is also a scan of King's original typewritten manuscript, with handwritten corrections, continues directly from the first section, and is comprised of the remainder of the fourth chapter and part of chapter five.

As the story continues we learn more of Jo Page's peculiarly individual religious fervor – she is happy to study the Bible but won't attend church. She also notices the light which frightens her, 'She'd never seen daylight of that particular sick quality; had never, in fact, seen an artificial light which was quite like it.' Looking at it, 'she felt her insides go cold and numb. Her fingers and toes momentarily lost all sense of feeling, and for a horrifying space of time – perhaps only a second or two; however long it was, it seemed much longer in her mind – she was afraid she was going to wet herself.'

Pulaski insists Rinaldi recognize there is a real problem, while the superintendent seeks to maintain his dwindling authority. More people are gathering in the lobby and they are beginning to notice the strange nature of the light, through which 'the cars in the parking lot stood out like pop-ups in a child's activity book. They looked so real that they somehow went too far and seemed false.' The residents notice there is no traffic on the nearby Interstate highway, which at this commuting hour is impossible. When Jo looks that way she momentarily sees traffic, which disappears with next blink of her eyelids. After deliberately squeezing her eyes shut the traffic returns, and stays. Something is very wrong.

The superintendent and the two tenants move to Rinaldi's apartment, only to find the same problem with a normal telephone line – they can call out but no-one can hear them. When Hill calls the television station another weird event occurs – the sound of the receptionist's voice suddenly 'accelerated so rapidly that it became insectile, unintelligible … the hideous thing was somehow *organic*…'

Back in the foyer some of the residents are losing it – one man is chanting, 'The cars are there' over and over. As they watch the traffic appears and disappears, then reappears. Pulaski returns to his apartment, where he is revealed as something of a gun fanatic, but ignores the firearms and instead grabs a baseball bat. More of Pulaski's back story is revealed, including how he had survived what he thought was certain death in a robbery when he was driving a taxi. After that scare he started carrying the bat in his cab, and had used it when another robbery was attempted – 'the junkie didn't wake up for four days, and Pulaski heard he didn't walk right for six weeks. Pulaski didn't lose any sleep over it.'

Hill is already back in the foyer when Pulaski returns with his bat, and his appearance immediately inspires both fear and respect among the milling residents. Pulaski's intent is to smash the foyer glass but when he strikes it with full force it not only doesn't smash, it doesn't 'so much as shiver.' Real concern sweeps the crowd.

Chapter V is titled *The Tennis Club (II); First Weird Scenes inside the Goldmine*. It's now 8am and almost all the residents are both awake and realize a serious problem has developed. Another group of residents forms and converge upon Rinaldi's apartment, demanding answers and that he give them the keys to the doors that form the normal entryways to the Tennis Club.

As matters begin to spiral out of control Tom Hill observes 'scenes both comic and tragic' that he comes to think of as 'weird scenes inside the goldmine.' The term would come into common use by those trapped inside the building and had been coined by Jo Page, who'd remembered a line from *The End*, by The Doors. These 'scenes' introduce more characters and we learn the building has no television or radio reception (further isolating the residents), and that the world is receding further (now the leaves on nearby trees are sometimes visible, sometimes not). Some take to booze, others to drugs. The story starts to meander at this point and the segment ends.

It seems unlikely King will release more of the manuscript, as to do after nearly a quarter of the unpublished work was publicly available would be tantamount to full publication of an unedited and incomplete novel. We can presume many of the social issues of isolation in a limited society are dealt with in *Under the Dome* and will most likely never know what phenomenon is responsible for the isolation of the apartment building. The most compelling part of what we can read is the strangeness of the outside world and, while there are the beginnings of interesting characterizations, they do seem a little one-dimensional. Of course, we are left to contemplate the meaning of the novel's title.

At the time of writing both sections of *The Cannibals* were still available at www.stephenking.com[65]. If they are removed at some point it is likely copies will still circulate freely.

Cat's Eye (1984) and General (1997)

The screenplay of *Cat's Eye* is difficult to find but copies do circulate in the King community and are sometimes available from online King specialists. Often there is no final or authorized version of a movie screenplay, as they are constantly adjusted during filming and some alterations are never properly documented. This chapter was compiled from the version dated May 14, 1984. It has never been published and it seems unlikely that it will be as King allowed a different version of *part* of the script to be published, as *General* in Rich Chizmar's *Screamplays* (1997). That piece is reviewed at the end of this chapter. As the two other parts of *Cat's Eye* represent published King stories, there is no real justification for the full screenplay to be published as a single entity.

Cat's Eye

The main screenplay was released as the movie *Cat's Eye* in 1985, by Dino De Laurentiis and MGM/UA Entertainment Company - it is also known as *Stephen King's Cat's Eye*. According to Stephen Jones[66] De Laurentiis asked King to create another vehicle for Drew Barrymore during the mid-1983 shooting of *Firestarter*, in which the young actress starred. King's initial treatment, over fifteen pages, was titled *The Cat*. Delighted, De Laurentiis asked King to add another two stories.

The key actors were Drew Barrymore as Our Girl/Amanda; James Woods as Dick Morrison; Robert Hays as Johnny Norris; Alan King as Dr. Donatti; and Kenneth McMillan as Cressner. The DVD was released in 2002. Director Lewis Teague also helmed *Alligator*, a 1980 movie that, according to this screenplay, was showing on TVs at an Atlantic City store. A few scenes earlier 'Teague Pier' in Atlantic City is mentioned. Teague also directed *Cujo*, to which there is a humorous nod during this movie (see below).

The America Under Siege storyline presented in the screenplay involves a cat saving a little girl's life. Carrie blamed her nine-year-old daughter's cat, Darcy for the girl's death, not knowing she had actually been killed by an evil five-inch tall Creature that stole her breath. Carrie attempted to kill the cat with an Uzi sub-machine gun (!), shooting out her front window and allowing his escape.

For part of an evening the cat stayed with Cressner, who called him Sebastian. That night, Cressner forced Norris to traverse the entire 32nd Floor of his apartment on a five-inch wide ledge after he caught Norris having an affair with his wife. After successfully negotiating the ledge, and a very nasty pigeon, Norris managed to force Cressner himself out on to the ledge, from which he fell to his death after kicking out at the same annoying pigeon.

Next the cat was captured by Quitter's, Inc., an anti-smoking company with rather radical methods, and subjected to electric shocks. During the cat's confinement the company used its methods on Dick Morrison.

Escaping again the cat then made its way to eight year old Amanda's house in Westport, Connecticut where she named him General. Amanda's mother, Sally-Anne, also believed cats could steal a child's breath, having heard this myth from her mother, a Polish or Russian immigrant, and determined to see the cat out of the house. After the Creature re-appeared and killed Amanda's pet parakeet, the cat was once again unfairly blamed. Amanda's mother took him to an Animal Shelter to be destroyed, but he escaped, yet again! The Creature again tried to steal Amanda's breath but the returning General fought it and the Creature was thrown into a fan and killed.

It should be noted that the screenplays of *General* and the last part of *Cat's Eye* (Scenes 385 on) are the same story, although they have significant enough textual differences to be called versions, rather than variations. For instance, the last part of *Cat's Eye* has Amanda's town as Westport, Connecticut. No town name is given in *General*. Most characters recur in both *General* and its equivalent section in *Cat's Eye*. However, the Cat is known only as General in *General*; but as Darcy, Sebastian and General in *Cat's Eye*. In *Cat's Eye* neither of the attendants at the Animal Shelter are named, however in *General* one is called Billy.

The screenplay effectively has three parts – *General*, an original story; and versions of King's short stories, *The Ledge* and *Quitter's, Inc.*, both of which are significantly different from the original stories. In *The Ledge* and the screenplay Mr Cressner and Marcia Cressner are recurring characters; but Norris is known as Stan in the original short story and Johnny in the script. The Pigeon does not have a nickname in the story but is known, rather humorously, as 'Yassar Arafat' in the screenplay.

As to *Quitter's, Inc.* the characters recurring in both versions are Donatti – Vic in the story, but simply Donatti in the screenplay; Jimmy McCann; Sharon McCann (her first name is not given in the screenplay); Morrison – Richard in *Quitters, Inc.*, Dick in the screenplay; Morrison's wife – Lucinda or Cindy in the story, Cindy in the script; the Morrison's child – Alvin (a boy) in the story but Alicia (a girl) in the screenplay. The founder of Quitters, Inc. is not named in the screenplay but is Mort Minelli in the story.

One of the joys of reading any screenplay, but most particularly one penned by King, is the little side-notes and information provided for the actors or directors by the scriptwriter. In these cases the reader is afforded further information about characters or scenes. From these notes and the storyline it is possible to provide the following potted summaries of certain key characters.

The Creature that killed the little girl (Carrie's daughter) later stalked Amanda and tried to kill her, but General saved her. He was about 5 inches high, humanoid with yellow eyes, green blood, clawed fingers and fanged teeth. He wore a breachclout or loincloth, wore a cap of bells and made a chittering sound. During a fight with General he was thrown into a fan and killed.

The Cat was a male angora with green eyes. Carrie blamed the cat, known as Darcy, for stealing her daughter's breath and thereby killing her, although it seems the Creature actually killed the girl. Carrie attempted to shoot Darcy but he escaped and began roaming the streets. For part of an evening he stayed with Cressner, who called him Sebastian. He was then captured by Quitter's, Inc. and subjected to electric shocks but escaped after Morrison's fight with employees of the company. He then travelled to Amanda's house in Westport, Connecticut where Amanda gave him the name General. Unfortunately, Amanda's mother took him to the Animal Shelter to be put down after the Creature killed Amanda's pet parakeet, Paulie but he was able to escape, return home and save Amanda from the Creature.

The man who forced Norris onto the Ledge was Cressner (his first name is not given), a silvery haired crime boss aged about 60. His penthouse was on the 32nd Floor of Westlake Towers in Atlantic City. He caught his wife, Marcia, fooling around with Norris, a tennis-pro and former con, and had him kidnapped and brought to his apartment. He presented Marcia's severed head to Norris and then forced him at gunpoint to travel around the entire 32nd Floor of his apartment on a five-inch wide ledge. Norris managed to successfully negotiate the ledge, got Cressner's hired hand's gun and then forced Cressner himself out on to the ledge, from which he fell to his death.

The Quitter's Inc. company could best be described as original in their tactics. Its logo was a cigarette in a circle with a red line drawn through it. If smokers did not desist, or were caught sneaking cigarettes, the company would take retribution on them or their family, escalating at each breach until such time as they either gave up the habit or were killed. They even kept a disturbed man on their books to rape the wives of recalcitrant patients! Dick Morrison, a new client, learnt a bitter lesson when he was caught sneaking a cigarette. His wife Cindy was brought it to the office and given electric shocks. Morrison had been introduced to the company by Jimmy McCann, whose wife was missing a little finger, which she probably lost during her husband's time as a client of Quitter's, Inc.

There are a number of apparently deliberate homages to King's work in this screenplay:

- Scene 7: The girl's mother's name is Carrie (*Carrie*)
- Scenes 33-35: Darcy chased by a St Bernard dog (*Cujo*)
- Scene 34: Darcy nearly hit by a 1958 Plymouth with a red body and white top. Behind the wheel was a bespectacled kid. The car carried a bumper sticker reading, 'Rock and Roll Will Never Die' (*Christine*)
- Scene 36: A ten wheeler truck sped past Darcy, ruffling his fur (*Pet Sematary*)
- Scene 55: One character's father was a bookie from Terre Haute. Donald Merwin Elbert ('Trashie') spent time in an institution there in *The Stand*
- Scene 260: *The Dead Zone* movie was showing on TV in the Morrison living room, with scenes featuring Dr. Weizak

No timeline is given for the story, but it must occur well after *The Dead Zone* movie was released in 1983, as that was showing on the Morrison's television.

Cat's Eye is best described as fun. It was not intended to have the highbrow content of a movie like *The Shawshank Redemption* but was positioned in the comedy-horror genre. It did not fare well at the box office, taking only $8 million in the US, but for King fans it did provide one original tale and entertaining adaptations of two short stories.

General

King allowed a different version of part of the *Cat's Eye* script to be published as *General* in *Screamplays*, published in 1997. Edited by Richard Chizmar, the book carried an introduction by horror writer Dean Koontz. The other screenplays, all published for the first time were: *The Legend of Hell House* by Richard Matheson (based on his book *Hell House*); *Moonlighting* (adapted from his *Ormond Always Pays His Bills)* and *Killing Bernstein* (from his short story of the same name) by Harlan Ellison; *Dead in the West* by Joe R Lansdale (based on his novel); *Track Down* by Ed Gorman (also based on his own novel); and an original script, *The Hunted* by Richard Laymon.

The collection is the only form of publication for *General*. The book can be sourced via second hand booksellers and the usual online King sources.

As noted, while the screenplays of *General* and the last part of *Cat's Eye* are the same story they have significant enough textual differences to be called versions, rather than variations.

In short summary, in this America Under Siege story a cat saves a little girl's life. Amanda's parents, Hugh and Sally-Ann had blamed her cat, General, for the death of her pet parakeet Paulie, not knowing the cat had been fighting an evil five inch tall creature that had intended to steal the girl's breath and kill her. The mother took General to an animal shelter to be put down but he escaped and returned to the family home, where he jumped through Amanda's bedroom window and again saved her from the Creature, this time killing it.

In the movie *Cat's Eye* Candy Clark played Sally Ann and James Naughton appeared as Hugh. Other than its originality, the key interest in this piece for readers is the fact that it represents one of only four published King screenplays, along with *Storm of the Century*, *Silver Bullet* and *Sorry, Right Number*, which appeared in *Nightmares and Dreamscapes*.

Charlie (Undated)

The manuscript of *Charlie* is held in Box 1010 of the Special Collections Unit of the Raymond H Fogler Library at the University of Maine, Orono. Written permission from King is required to access this work. The manuscript shows King's address at the time as RFD#2, Kansas Road, Bridgton, Maine 04009. There are six pages of manuscript, and a total in King's own note of approximately 3900 words. Another note on the folder says 'Missing Pages' and the story most certainly ends in the middle of a paragraph.

King told Douglas Winter[67] about his sending science fiction stories to *The Magazine of Fantasy and Science Fiction*: 'One of the few good ones was about an asteroid miner who discovered a pink cube, and all this stuff started to come out of the cube and drive him back further and further into his little space hut, breaching the airlocks one after another. All the science fiction magazines sent it back, because they knew goddam well there was no science in it … There was just this big pink thing that was going to eat someone, and it ate him.' If this is the same story, King's memory seems a little faulty (see below) but at least he hints at the ending.

In this New Worlds tale, while wildcat mining for copper on Asteroid 419C (that is, 419C for 'Charlie') Carl Willys found some incredibly valuable pink cubes. Before he could leave the asteroid an alien creature attacked and trapped him in his Hut. He named the creature Charlie, presumably after the asteroid itself, and fought it for four months, including using an oxy-acetylene torch to burn it. Charlie finally broke the airlock door and readers last see Willys becoming ever more desperate as Charlie covers the entire Hut.

Carl Willys was an old man and a wildcatter so this find would appear to have been his last chance at riches, but he has apparently become inescapably trapped. Other miners had done well by selling the pink cubes - Ben Dauphine found good deposits of the pink cubes on Asteroid 1004D and made $4 million selling them and Frank Jamieson also found the cubes on Asteroid 731A and made $1 million.

All we know of Charlie is that it is very big and, while it looks like black jelly, red flashes are visible through its nerve system or synapses.

It is a real shame the manuscript ends in mid-paragraph. While it is far from King's most interesting story and science fiction is not his greatest strength, it would have been interesting to understand the direction the story would take next. Will Willys escape somehow? Will he be driven insane? Why does 'Charlie' want the pink cubes, for instance are they the 'eggs' of its species? Does Charlie want them at all, or is it just attacking an alien intruder? Will there be a supernatural or other horror intervention? Or did Charlie just eat Willys, as King told Winter?

It seems unlikely King will ever revitalize and publish this unfinished story.

King and Science Fiction

King has written only a small number of purely science fiction stories and most critics suggest these are not the best of his works. King may agree, as he has not allowed many of his shorter science fiction works to be published. Clearly influenced by the lurid tales he read as a boy and young man they often tend contain relatively unsophisticated science. In the case of one, *The Jaunt*, King agreed his original science was 'wonky'. However, there are many other stories with a science fiction angle or connection and these tend to be the more satisfying tales.

The following stories represent King's science fiction output, or stories with a significant science fiction component. It should be noted that some of these stories may actually represent a connection with the Dark Tower Cycle, which is generally recognized as fantasy. Such definitions are fluid and the list below represents the authors' opinion.

The Aftermath	*Battleground*
Beachworld	*Cell*
Charlie	*Code Name: Mousetrap*
Crouch End	*The Dead Zone*
Donovan's Brain	*Dreamcatcher*
11/22/63	*The End of the Whole Mess*
Everything's Eventual	*Firestarter*
From a Buick 8	*Golden Years*
Graduation Afternoon	*Home Delivery*
The Hotel at the End of the Road	*The House on Maple Street*
I am the Doorway	*I Know What You Need*
I've Got to Get Away/ The Killer	
I Was A Teenage Grave-Robber/ In A Half-World of Terror	
The Jaunt	*The Langoliers*
The Lonesome Death of Jordy Verrill/ Weeds	*The Mist*
Mobius	*Night Surf*
The Regulators/ The Shotgunners	*The Reploids*
The Revelations of 'Becka Paulson	*The Running Man*
The Stand	*The Sun Dog*
The Tommyknockers	*Trucks*
Under the Dome	*Ur*

Children of the Corn – Unproduced Screenplay (c.1978)

Children of the Corn was originally published in *Penthouse* for March 1977. King rewrote it for its appearance in the 1978 collection *Night Shift*, that rewrite mostly involved cosmetic wording changes although there are specific factual changes. In addition, King wrote a screenplay of the tale. In total, this means King has created three versions of this one tale.

One of his most original stories, *Children of the Corn* has twice been produced as a film and has spawned more 'adaptations' than any other of his works. Most, though, are barely connected and that only by the use of the title (*see feature panel*).

The first adaptation was the 1983 short film, *Disciples of the Crow*. It is best described as a very ordinary movie. It can be seen as one of two movies on the videocassette *Two Features from Stephen King's Night Shift Collection* (1991); or on *A Trilogy from Stephen King's Nightshift Collection*. The screenwriter and director for this version was John Woodward; Eleese Lester played Vicky and Gabriel Folse portrayed Burt.

The much better known film version is 1984's *Children of the Corn*, which is widely regarded as one of the worst King adaptations ever! It was the first feature movie made from a King short story. Fritz Kiersch directed, Peter Horton played Burt Stanton and *Terminator* co-star Linda Hamilton portrayed Vicky. John Franklin appeared as Isaac. Also known as *Stephen King's Children of the Corn*, it is available on DVD.

The screenplay for the movie was credited to George Goldsmith. In fact, King wrote a screenplay on which Goldsmith's was allegedly based. King was denied a writer's credit by The Writer's Guild of America and, after the movie flopped, was glad of it. He even told *Cinefantastique* magazine, 'The picture was a dog.' In the September 1985 issue of *Castle Rock* King gave his opinion in an article titled *Lists That Matter (Number 8)*. In this piece he lists his ten worst movies of all time. At number six is *Children of the Corn*:

'Here is another horror movie, and to me the most horrible thing about it is that it was based on one of my stories. Not very closely – just closely enough so the producers could call it *Stephen King's Children of the Corn*, which it really wasn't. In the movie version, the creature appears to be some sort of gopher from hell. There are some classic bad lines in this movie. "Outlander, we have your woman!" is one I like; later on the hero scooches down beside the little kid and says in a friendly voice, "Just what did this monster look like, Jobie?" I understand this gobbler made money, but so far I haven't seen any of it, and I'm not sure I want to. It might have corn-borers in it.'

King's second draft screenplay is summarized in this chapter. It appears to have been written about 1978 as, in an interview with David Chute (published in *Take One* for January 1979 and later reproduced in *Feast of Fear*[68]), King comments that he had written a screenplay of this story, "not because I thought a movie would come of it but because I needed some practice."

The basic storyline of this America Under Siege story is well known to King fans but in this version King makes a number of significant changes, which are summarized later.

In the tale two travellers are sacrificed to a savage god. In about September of 1968 a bizarre cult of children sprang up in the town of Gatlin, Nebraska. The children slaughtered the thousands of adults in the town and began to worship a creature they called He Who Walks Behind the Rows. This evil entity was old when Jesus was 'unborn', according to Isaac, one of the Children. It was huge, with a shifting manta shaped outline, huge green eyes and a hell-fire red mouth.

In 1980 one of the children tried to escape Gatlin. However, eleven year old Joseph was caught in the corn by the other Children, his throat was slit, and he was pushed into the road where he was run down by a Thunderbird. In shock, Burt Stanton, the car's driver and his wife Vicky stopped and picked up the body. Fatefully, they then decided to drive into Gatlin to report the accident.

Burt Stanton had served at least three years in the Special Forces of the US Marines in Vietnam, returning from 61 patrols, winning the Congressional Medal of Honor and holding the rank of Captain. He and Vicky, residents of Boston, had been married for six years but they were facing marital problems at the time they drove into Nebraska. Vicky was beautiful, with long hair and a 'dynamite' body and had been the Prom Queen.

The Stantons arrived in the apparently abandoned town but quickly realized something was wrong - for instance, there were skeletons on the roof of the Town Hall! In the Bureau of Registrations there was a gigantic portrait of a vulpine Christ-like being with corn hair.

Suddenly, vicious Children appeared and surrounded the couple. The Children quickly captured and killed Vicky and left her crucified body in the cornfields as a sacrifice to their 'god'. After initially escaping the mob, Burt headed into the cornfields where he found himself at dawn in a clearing in which his wife's body and the crucified skeleton of the town's police chief had been left. The Children called this place 'the clearing of the Blue Man', a reference to the dead cop's uniform.

He Who Walks Behind the Rows then killed Burt. Until this point all Children over the age of 18 (the so-called 'Age of Favor') had walked into the corn to their fate at the hands of the creature. To appease He Who Walks Behind the Rows after the incident with the Stantons the group's 'Seer', Isaac immediately reduced the Age of Favor to 17 and a group of more than twelve boys and girls were required to walk into the corn.

In updating the storyline from the two versions of the short story to the screenplay King made a number of very important changes. Burt and Vicky

Robeson become Burt and Vicky Stanton. The date of the initial killings and takeover of the town by the creature and its disciples moves from about August 1964 to about August 1968; and the arrival of the Stantons to July 1980 from the original July 1976 for the Robesons (maintaining the twelve year gap).

Norman Staunton, the 7-year-old preacher from Vicky Robeson's childhood becomes Norman Stanton, from Vicky Stanton's childhood. Very strange indeed! The population of Gatlin varies from *Penthouse* (5431) to *Night Shift* (4531) to the Screenplay (5438). The Police Chief also acquires an ironic name: Samuel Cross.

In the earlier versions the Children chased Burt into the corn, eventually driving him toward the sacrificial clearing. In the screenplay they were afraid to go into the corn and did not follow him until Isaac had given them clearance. He Who Walks Behind The Rows' eye color changes from red to green. Originally Isaac reduced the Age of Favor from 19 to 18; in the screenplay he reduced it from 18 to 17.

In the screenplay King also deliberately and specifically links *Children of the Corn* to a number of his other works. In Scene 16, Vicky tells Burt that the road forks ahead (the fork is at a point *after* Joseph was hit by their car). 'One fork goes to a place called Gatlin, the other one goes to a place called Hemingford Home.' Hemingford Home, described as just a wide place in the road, was not mentioned in either version of the original short story. It is the town near which Abagail Freemantle lived nearly her entire life in *The Stand*. In the Original version of that classic novel the superflu hit in June 1980; in the Uncut version it struck in June 1990. In this script the Stantons arrived in Gatlin in July 1980 so this version cannot be in the original timeline of *The Stand*.

Of particular interest is that in the *Complete and Uncut* version of *The Stand* (but not the original) Stu Redman dreamed of crucifixions along Highway 6 near Hemingford Home. Of course, there *were* crucifixions near Gatlin. King was clearly linking these stories when he updated *The Stand*.

Hemingford Home, Nebraska is also mentioned in *It* (Benjamin Hanscom lived there between confrontations with Pennywise) and *The Last Rung on the Ladder* (Larry and Kitty grew up there). Gatlin, Nebraska is also mentioned in *It*, where it is described as a small *deserted* town on the road to Hemingford Home.

While this script was not produced and it is most unlikely it will ever be published its importance lies in revealing King's intent for the film version (compared to the dreck that was actually produced); its renaming of characters; and its deliberate linking to other King stories and locales.

Children of the Corn – The 'Sequels'

A series of sequels to the 1984 movie *Children of the Corn* have been released. However, they have little more connection to the original short story than the name of the series. In the movie industry such sequels are known as a 'franchise' and it never ceases to amaze that these movies, some of which are execrable, ever reached production let alone release! Not one of these movies even makes a 5 rating out of 10 at the world's leading movie database, www.imdb.com. Key details of each production follow.

Children of the Corn II: The Final Sacrifice (1993). Follows on from the events of the first film and released direct to video. IMDB rating: 3.8. Screenplay – A L Katz, Gilbert Adler and Bill Froehlich; Director – David F Price. Actors – Terence Knox (John Garrett); Paul Scherrer (Danny Garrett); Ted Travelstead (Mordechai). DVD: 2000.

Children of the Corn III: Urban Harvest (1994). Released direct to video. IMDB rating: 3.4. Screenplay – Dode B Leveson; Director – James D R Hickox. Actors – Daniel Cerny (Eli); Ron Melendez (Joshua); John Clair (Malcolm). DVD: 2003.

Children of the Corn IV: The Gathering (1996). Made for video. IMDB rating: 3.8. Screenplay – Stephen Berger and Greg Spence; Director – Greg Spence. Actors – Naomi Watts – later an Academy Award nominee for *21 Grams* - (Grace Rhodes); Emmy award winner William Windom (Doc Larson); Karen Black – also an Oscar nominee - (Julie Rhodes). DVD: 2003.

Children of the Corn V: Fields of Terror (1998). Released direct to video. IMDB rating: 3.7. Director and Scriptwriter – Ethan Wiley. Actors – Stacey Galina (Alison); Alexis Arquette (Greg); Eva Mendes (Kir); Fred Williamson (Sheriff Skaggs); David Carradine (Luke Enright). DVD: 2001.

Children of the Corn 666: Isaac's Return (1999). Released direct to video and set back in Gatlin. IMDB rating: 3.3. Screenplay – Tim Sulka and John Franklin; Director – Kari Skogland. Actors – John Franklin (Isaac); Nancy Allen (Rachel Colby); Golden Globe winner Stacey Keach (Dr. Michaels); Natalie Ramsely (Hannah). DVD: 1999.

Children of the Corn: Revelation (2001). Released direct to video. IMDB rating: 3.1. Screenplay – S J Smith; Director – Guy Magar. Actors – Claudette Mink (Jamie Lowell); Kyle Cassie (Armbrister); Michael Ironside (Priest). DVD: 2001.

> *A new television adaptation was released in 2009, titled 'Children of the Corn' (or 'Stephen King's Children of the Corn'. Yet another flop, directed and written by Donald P Borchers, it starred David Anders (Burt Stanton), Kandyse McClure (Vicky), Daniel Newman (Malachai) and Preston Bailey (Isaac). A DVD was released in 2009. IMDB rating: 4.0.*
> *Children of the Corn; Genesis* (2011). Released direct to DVD. IMDB rating: 4.7. Screenplay – Joel Soisson. Director – Joel Soisson. Actors – Bill Drago (Preacher); J J Banicki (Young Cole); Dusty Burwell (The Child). DVD – 2011.

Chinga (1998) and Molly (1997)

King originally wrote a screenplay for an episode of the hit FOX television series, *The X-Files* titled *Molly*. Chris Carter, the creator of the series, added and significantly changed material and both writers were credited with the new teleplay, *Chinga*, making Carter one of King's few collaborators. The episode is also known as *Bunghoney* in the UK and some other markets (the change of title for non-North American markets was caused by the belief that Chinga can mean 'fuck' in Mexico in certain circumstances).

While the screenplay has not been published copies freely circulate in the King and X-Files communities. There is also the possibility that all *The X-Files* scripts will see publication at some point.

King originally approached Chris Carter to talk about writing an episode for *Millennium* but was convinced to write an episode of *The X-Files* instead, although at least one source has King becoming a fan of the program after meeting David Duchovny on *Jeopardy!*, later finding his kids were 'junkies' and then becoming one himself after Carter sent him the first season tapes.[69]

Research confirmed that the first teleplay (in two drafts) King did for *The X-Files* was titled *Molly*. King's office also confirmed that first teleplay was *not* an early version of *Chinga* but a totally different one, which will become obvious later in this chapter. After King and Chris Carter discussed the changes Carter would want made to *Molly*, King went in a different direction and wrote a completely new teleplay, later further changed by Carter and filmed as *Chinga*.

King super-collector Chris Cavalier kindly provided a copy of the *Molly* teleplay to assist with research for this chapter and a letter from Carter to King dated 8 December 1997 in which Carter sought King's agreement for King to take credit for the teleplay of *Chinga*. At some point in the next two months King and Carter obviously agreed to take joint credit for the script. In one part of the 8 December letter Carter writes, 'Believe it or not, yours is the first episode we're filming that's come from a writer completely outside the staff.'

And: 'To have you write Mulder and Scully, to put them through their paces, it's been a thrill and an honor. A giant honor.' Thanks go to Chris Cavalier for providing the teleplay to assist in the writing of this chapter.

Chinga

Chinga first aired on 8 February 1998 as an episode of *The X-Files* (Series Five). Among the credits are: Teleplay by Stephen King and Chris Carter; Director – Kim Manners; Actors – David Duchovny (Fox Mulder); Gillian Anderson (Dana Scully); Jenny-Lyn Hutcheson (Polly Turner); Larry Musser (Captain Jack Bonsaint); Susannah Hoffmann (Melissa Turner). The episode is available on DVD as part of *The X-Files - The Complete Fifth Season*.

The X-Files ran on the FOX network in the US from 1993 to 2002 and was a worldwide sensation, winning many awards, including a number of Emmys. The series followed FBI agents Mulder and Scully (Fox Mulder, played by David Duchovny, was replaced towards the end of the franchise's run by John Doggett, played by Robert Patrick) as they investigated the strange and paranormal while 'hidden forces' worked to impede their efforts. A huge ratings success at a critical time in the expansion of Rupert Murdoch's US network, it is also a major syndication success and a best seller in DVD format.

In this Maine Street Horror storyline an FBI agent visits an unnamed small Maine coastal town while on a weekend break. Polly Turner's fisherman father had found a Doll in a lobster pot and given it to his daughter. He was killed three days later in a freak boating accident involving a grappling hook.

Later, people began to act strangely around the Doll, clawing their eyes, suffering strange accidents, and killing themselves in odd and gruesome ways. Those who said no to little Polly also faced the wrath of the Doll. Polly is said to be autistic, an affliction also suffered by Annie Wheaton, the 'heroine' of King's screenplay, *Rose Red*.

In one incident the FBI agent, Dana Scully, entered the town Super Saver store just as Polly and her mother Melissa exited, leaving many people inside attempting to claw their eyes out. Intrigued, Scully discussed the incident with the town police chief, Captain Jack Bonsaint. She also called her partner, Agent Fox Mulder, who suggested that St. Vitus' Dance (or 'Dancing Sickness') might be a cause of the problems in the town. Scully responded that particular illness had not been diagnosed since the Middle Ages.

Among the Doll's victims was Jane Froelich. She had once been the proprietor of the day-care center Polly Turner attended but, after slapping Polly's face, lost her license. Inside the Super Saver she glared at Polly and her mother. Later that day she cut her own throat with a broken record. The butcher at the Super Saver, Dave, had an unrequited love for Melissa and, when the shoppers started clawing their eyes, he stabbed a knife into his own right eye, and died.

Another victim was a waitress at a fast food restaurant, who caught her very long ponytail in a milkshake mixer after upsetting Polly and, presumably, the Doll.

Under the Doll's direction Melissa Turner tried to kill herself with a hammer but survived thanks to the intervention of Bonsaint and Scully. Realizing something was not right with the Doll Melissa prepared to burn down her house with herself, her daughter and the Doll inside. Scully arrived in time in to prevent this, threw the Doll into the microwave, and turned it on.

In typical X-Files tradition, however, this was not the end of the Doll, and another fisherman later pulled it, still burnt, from another lobster trap.

Interestingly, Carter and King chose to center this episode on Dana Scully, the skeptic of the two FBI agents (Mulder was the 'true believer'), placing her in this small Maine town while it was briefly under siege from the apparently possessed Doll.

It seems the storyline is set about October 1997 on the basis that the expiry date on a bottle of orange juice in Mulder's refrigerator was for that month.

The basic storyline of an evil doll is not entirely original (in fact Chucky, from the *Child's Play* movie series which premiered in 1988, is even mentioned by Mulder) and it is possible this was a story concept King had previously considered but did not use until this opportunity arose.

Unlike some authors King has chosen to incorporate as much of the real world in his fiction as possible (trademarks, the cultural trends of the day and so on). He has also found it of interest on occasion to step into the 'realities' created by other writers or artists.

He has, for instance, stepped into the following fictional worlds – Arthur Conan Doyle's Sherlock Holmes (*The Doctor's Case*); H P Lovecraft's Cthulhu Mythos (*Crouch End* and *N*); Dorothy L Sayers' Lord Peter Wimsey (*Wimsey*); and the X-Men (*Heroes for Hope*). He has also paid homage to Poe, in *Dolan's Cadillac* and *The Old Dude's Ticker*, among other tales, and adapted Ray Bradbury's *Something Wicked This Way Comes*.

X-Files fans and critics do not rate this episode as one of the best from the franchise but King fans will find this small diversion into another mythology of interest. The teleplay forms the base of a reasonably interesting episode of a landmark science fiction series, adding to both the mythology of that 'reality' and linking its major characters, Mulder and Scully, into King's Maine Street Horror reality. *The X-Files* is also mentioned in another Maine Street Horror story, *Dreamcatcher*.

If readers cannot access a copy of the screenplay they can at least view the produced episode to appreciate this work.

Molly

As stated earlier, King's first original screenplay for *The X-Files* was actually *Molly* (the cover page reads *The X-Files* / "Molly" / written by / Stephen King). It seems clear that it was written in 1997, after discussions between King and Chris Carter about a possible episode for *Millennium* turned into an episode for *The X-Files*. The script is of 79 scenes over 57 pages.

King's cast list for *Molly* is Fox Mulder, Dana Scully, Melissa Turner, Polly/Molly Turner, Jack Bonsaint, Mr Bierce, Jane Froelich, Agent In Charge (Hal), Agent Two (Buddy), Agent Three (Jose), Agent Four (James), Rebecca Callahan, Supermarket Woman, Supermarket Man (Older Gent), Cop, Kid, Waitress, Man in Uniform, Prison Matron and Little Girl.

The story is set in Ammas Beach, Maine (this fictional town does not appear in any other King fiction). Dana Scully is staying with her college friend, Rebecca Callahan (could she be related to Father Callahan?). Scully visits the Ammas Beach Supr Savr, where Melissa Turner is shopping with her five-year-old daughter, Polly. Jane Froelich is also in the shop, 'about sixty, with stern, narrow face … The vibe is similar to the old lady who wanted to scrag Toto in *The Wizard of Oz*.' All this is being recorded by a security camera, timing from 2.14:09 PM. After Polly sees Froelich her eyes narrow and, shortly afterward, Froelich begins slapping herself across the face and smashing a box of cookies into her forehead. A woman who tries to help also begins uncontrollably slapping her own face! The 'epidemic' spreads to other shoppers, with many dancing or screaming uncontrollably. As she tries to help, Scully begins to slap herself and to dance – the market is in total pandemonium. Cut to Melissa, who orders Polly to "Stop it!" 'Polly says nothing, but her frightened eyes say it all: "I can't".' Her eyes cut left and we see 'The Polly Doppelganger' *inside* a frozen food case, 'peering out through the frost-etched glass with MALEVOLENT HATE.' Meanwhile, the chaos continues… Following this introductory scene, the Opening Credits were due to roll.

In Act One Mulder arrives at the Portland Jetport and joins Scully, who tells him there is video of the incident in the supermarket, "No flying saucers, Mulder. No little gray men. As for the rest, see for yourself." Scully, Mulder, Mr Bierce (the Supr Savr manager) and Ammas Beach Chief of Police Jack Bonsaint review the video from the four different security cameras. Mulder speculates what they are seeing is 'The Dancing Sickness', from the 14th century Rhineland. Starting about 1370, it spread across all of Europe within six months and burned itself out within two years, although thousands died. "One school of thought believes the Dancing Sickness was caused by a kind of contagious psychokinesis, and may have started with as few as half a dozen telekinetic senders. Maybe only one." Scully demurs that most people think it was caused by an organic hallucinogen in the wheat used in bread at the time.

Carefully reviewing the tapes Mulder notices that neither of the Turners is slapping, dancing or leaping and that Melissa is looking at one of the frozen food cabinets, 'her face caught in a look of surprise.' Bonsaint tells the FBI agents that Melissa's husband had 'died in an accident about three years ago' and that Polly is autistic (as was Seth Garin in *The Regulators*; Annie Wheaton in *Rose Red*; and, of course, the version of Polly Turner appearing in *Chinga*). There was also bad blood between Melissa Turner and Froelich, with Melissa having been involved in the closing down of Froelich's daycare, after Froelich continually lost her temper, and sometimes hit the kids. Finally, she broke little Todd Carter's nose. When Bonsaint interviewed the woman she admitted hitting the boy but claimed, "I never slapped any of the others … they slapped themselves."

Mulder decides to get an enlarged print of the frozen food cabinet's glass doors, 'On it we see what looks like a cloud-shadow … or a ghost image.' When the agents and Bonsaint visit Mrs. Froelich she refuses to talk to them, saying it would be "unwise" and that they are "not the right ones" for her to talk to, suggesting they visit Mrs Turner and, "that bad little girl of hers."

When Mulder and Scully receive the video enlargement that evening they see, 'It's not a shadow Melissa is looking at in the glass door of the freezer compartment; it's a Little Girl. She stands with her hands pressed against the glass, indistinct but really there. There is the SNARLING LOOK OF HATE on her face.'

Mulder claims it's the same girl, "Polly. Same striped top, see? The hair's the same. It's her." Scully suggests the image is a reflection but Mulder points out one of the girls is sitting in a supermarket cart, the "other is on her feet, chilling out with the Stouffer's frozen dinners and the Tombstone pizza." They decide to visit the Turners, not realizing there are four government agents in a house across the street, armed to the teeth with tranquillizers and child restraint devices! Just before knocking on the Turners' door, Mulder picks a Raggedy Ann doll up from the porch glider, looks at it and puts it down as the door opens.

Melissa refuses to let Mulder and Scully in. Meanwhile the agents across the road record the events on video as Polly comes downstairs chanting, "Chinga. Chinga. Chinga." Melissa tells Polly she hasn't seen Chinga and continues to talk to Mulder and Scully. After Mulder frightens Melissa with threats that she might end up "talking to some people who don't bother knocking" Polly reacts, pulling away, her eyes widening. Mulder suddenly loses control of his hand, smashing a wind-chime and cutting himself on the shells from which it is constructed. His arm starts to bring a sharp-edged shell toward his throat as Scully struggles to help. Mulder sees 'the same little girl' as the one now held by her mother 'standing in the shadows halfway up the stairs, dressed in the same white nightgown', hissing at him! Act One ends.

Act Two opens with the shell's sharp edge at Mulder's throat and Melissa yelling to Polly, "Make her go away! Make Molly go away." Scully now sees

Molly on the stairs and the strange little girl forces Scully to slap her own face. Mulder asks Polly, "Do you still want Chinga? ... Make her go away, then. Make Molly go away and I'll give you Chinga." Mulder regains control of his arm and hands the Raggedy Ann doll to Polly who cries out, "Chinga!"

Apologizing, Melissa takes them all inside while the Agent in Charge across the road tells his men that they will be taking the girl but "...maybe not right this minute ... That was Fox Mulder and Dana Scully. They are prophets without honor in their own country."

Melissa explains to Mulder and Scully that such incidents had occurred almost since Polly was born, mostly in the form of making her and her husband dance. The slapping had only begun after Polly went to daycare. Queried about Molly Melissa replies, "I don't really know. I don't think I *want* to know." Mulder warns Melissa that she needs to help them as, "Molly may have attracted attention from the wrong people." She replies that Molly is getting stronger, "and more violent." Mulder sends Scully to visit Froelich again to determine who else has been talking to her. He tells Scully that Molly is, "Polly's mirror-image. Her doppelganger. If there was ever an evil twin, it's Molly." As Scully leaves, the Agent in Charge of those watching remarks that, if she is going to see Froelich, she's wasting her time.

Sure enough, at the Froelich house Scully finds the woman hanging from an overhead beam, with a note on her body reading, 'I'm so ashamed.' Searching the house Scully finds a balled up note reading 'LITCHFIELD PROJECT' and 'WHITING INSTITUTE'. Back at the beach Mulder asks if Scully believes the death is suicide, particularly after finding the note, "The Whiting Institute for the Criminally Insane. Where the government keeps their failures, their genetic leftovers ... their Adams ... their Eves." He claims Polly will become part of the Litchfield Project, where "they'll study her. And reproduce her. If they can." Of course, it is not Polly they want but Molly, yet Mulder speculates 'they' do not yet know of Molly's existence. Mulder also claims, "the Bureau doesn't know us on this one – the people behind the Litchfield Project are very powerful, very high up. We've got Chief Bonsaint on our side, and that had better be enough." Mulder had already briefed Bonsaint and called "a guy in Ohio. He's in another Federal organization. He's also a friend." They begin to plan.

In Act Three Bonsaint and Mulder arrive at the Turner house the next morning, with Mulder claiming that Scully had been called back to Washington late the previous night. Bonsaint says his investigation had revealed "some fellas" in the house across the street. To Mulder's comment that they had been "remarkably careless" the Chief responds, "I'd say they think we're hicks. They might find out different. That'd be lovely."

Mulder briefs Melissa about the men across the street and his plan to help her and Polly escape. He joins Polly in a pretend picnic for Chinga and begins to talk to her about Molly. After he asks her if she wants Molly to go away, she nods and tells him, "Molly-bad. Molly-slap." Mulder convinces her to try and bring Molly outside, "so she can't ... can't run back inside." Mulder gives Bonsaint a pre-arranged signal and he drives off, siren howling, drawing the attention of the agents across the road.

Immediately, they don Federal Marshal jackets and grab their equipment. The Agent in Charge tells his team if Mulder gets in the way, "Nobody likes him anyway – he's a bowser. Kill him."

Mulder and the Turners make a run for Mulder's car just as the agents spill out of their house yelling but their targets climb into the car while one aims a gun at Mulder. Now we can see the ghostly image of a 'HATEFUL little girl' in the front passenger seat. Of course, the 'Marshals' begin to attack themselves, probably saving Mulder's life, and his car screeches away. Mulder catches a glimpse of what might be Molly in the front seat before the image disappears.

The 'Marshals' jump in their car for the chase, with Mulder careful *not* to lose them! They race down Maine Highway 114 through crowds of beachgoers. The angry reaction of a kid in a dune buggy they pass brings Molly back 'too soon' and Mulder begins to slap himself, but Polly calls "Chinga!" and Molly disappears again.

Act Four begins with Mulder's car roaring into the parking lot of the Lobsterland restaurant in Newshire, Maine (another fictional location not mentioned in other King works). They wait for the chasing 'agents' and then run into the restaurant. As the pursuers burst in Agent in Charge Hal, yelling that they are Federal agents, demands everyone hit the floor. 'They are waving guns and looking as crazy as an ATF posse out to roast 'em a bunch of Branch Davidians. People don't argue with that look; they grab for some tile.'

Hal has his gun trained on Mulder but the Turners have already made it into the ladies' room, where they meet the waiting Scully. Melissa now asks Polly to bring Molly "all the way" out. Mulder, disarmed, announces to those in the restaurant, "I'm Fox Mulder, Federal Bureau of Investigation. And although these men's jackets say they are federal marshals, I doubt very much they have convincing ID to back that ... Please note their descriptions ... and could someone take down the plate number of their car please?"

Molly appears in a bathroom stall, whispering in a creepy voice, "Give me Chinga. I want her ... Give her to me, you little brat." Polly cries, "Molly-bad! Molly-bad, mummy, can't have Chinga! Molly pulls Chinga's hair!" Meanwhile, the bad guys are demanding the Turners come out or they'll kill Mulder. Melissa convinces Polly that the chasers intend to "hurt mummy" and Polly gives in, making her 'sadder than anything in her whole unfortunate life, perhaps' and passes the doll under the stall wall to Scully, who gives it into the grasping hand of the nasty little doppelganger.

As Hal is about to order Mulder's death Polly comes out of the toilet with Chinga in hand, 'But it's *not* Polly, and Mulder knows it straight away.' The 'agents' again begin attacking themselves; one shooting most of his hand off and Mulder also begins slapping himself in something of a Three Stooges take-off. Meanwhile, Scully escapes with Melissa and Polly.

Inside the restaurant Molly watches the mayhem as patrons and workers join in the slap and dance-fest. She is 'hugging Chinga and smiling. She's having the time of her life …' but she has overlooked Hal, who shoots her in her now very real neck with a tranquillizer dart. She turns to him and tries to force him to gouge his eyes out with a broken water glass but succumbs to the drug before she can inflict this (well-deserved) damage. Hal and his men grab Molly's slumped body and Hal prepares to shoot Mulder before approaching sirens convince him that discretion is the better part of murder.

Scully drives her charges toward Boston's South Station, telling Melissa, "We've got to make at least one stop somewhere along the line. This little girl needs a new doll."

Back at FBI Headquarters Scully tells Mulder she'd handed the Turners over to a tall, blond man after being given the right password: 'Believe'. Mulder has arranged for them to be relocated under new names and tosses Scully a tee shirt. It reads, in big letters across the middle, 'You Don't Know Me' and, on the breast, carries a Federal seal with the words FEDERAL WITNESS PROTECTION PROGRAM.

The action cuts to a view of the Whiting Institute for the Criminally Insane (which had appeared in the *Eve* episode of *The X-Files*, first broadcast on 10 December 1993) while in voiceover Scully asks Mulder what will happen to Molly. He replies, "It may already have happened, Scully. Molly wasn't really a doppelganger; she was an extrusion. Extrusions don't have much of a future when they're cut off from the life-systems which have supported them."

In the same Cellblock Z as appeared in *Eve* we get a brief view of various steel doors, each stencilled with Eve and a number, 'Eve 6', 'Eve 8', and so on. 'At one of them, a hand that ends in three curved claws grips the mesh-covered slot in the door.' A burly prison matron explains to a uniformed man that she doesn't know what happened, "she was alright … at seven, when the orderly brought her breakfast." The man replies, "She's not all right now. There's going to be a complete investigation of this, I guarantee you." And Hal, looking furious, declaims, "Ask Mulder. He knows. That *I* guarantee *you*." The uniformed man simply comments, "Mulder is back in Washington. Among such friends as he has. You should have taken him out while you had the chance."

Looking into the cell we see Molly's clothes. 'Surrounding them is a vaguely humanoid shape made of gray fluff … looks like the stuff that comes out of a vacuum cleaner bag. At the end of one dusty "arm" is Chinga, lying on her back and peering up into the shadows.'

The final scene takes us to DeMeara Heights, Chapel Hill, North Carolina where Polly is having tea with her new doll. Polly is now Sally and Melissa is

'Mrs. Drake'. Polly/Sally holds the doll up, smiles radiantly at it and says, "Chinga!"

It is clear that *Molly* is very different to *Chinga*. Using the same characters and with the full participation of Mulder, it takes a totally different tack as to the basic storyline, with a nasty doppelganger/extrusion rather than a possessed doll.

Of the two, *Molly* is much the better and more interesting story. Carter, as Master of the X-Files Universe, of course had every right to seek a storyline more in tune with the 'reality' he created and the flow of his series. However, it is a shame that the imaginative, interesting and fast-paced story created by King in *Molly* was, as a result, lost to King fans and students alike. Investigation has confirmed that there is no possibility of King ever allowing publication or circulation of *Molly*.

King, as quoted in *Cinescape Presents The X-Files Yearbook* (1998), 'would happily repeat the experience', and had 'already concocted an idea for a future plot'. In an amusing aside he noted he would not do an *X-Files* novel, excepting one in which 'Mulder and Scully go to bed together.'

Comb Dump (Undated)

The author of this book 'rediscovered' this story in Box 1012 at the Special Collections Unit of the Raymond H Fogler Library of the University of Maine at Orono during a research trip in December 2002. As the box is unrestricted readers who attend the Library may read this partial story.

The 41 page double-spaced undated manuscript, headed 'by Stephen King', is incomplete and there is no indication that King ever continued writing it past the point at which it ends. It can be presumed he lost interest in the story, intriguing though the developments in it are.

In this story fragment a young cocaine addict decides to attend a rehabilitation clinic. Tommy Brigham, only twenty-one years old, had watched one of his young addict friends, Roy Duchien, suffer a stroke after taking cocaine. Brigham became the sole remaining of Duchien's so-called friends still helping him shortly after the stroke. As a result of observing the damage, and a conversation with a young doctor at Augusta General, Tommy decided to kick his habit.

Brigham then worked for seven months on a construction job and for a short time became a drug dealer to accrue half the money he needed to check in to the Cold Strap Psychiatric Hospital. The remaining half of the $18,000 fee for the 28 day course at Cold Strap was to be paid by Blue Cross. The Hospital, a stand-alone complex, set in the countryside, was 16 miles north of Augusta, Maine. The hospital was in a Y shape with the adult and juvenile dependency units in the left arm, administration in the down stroke and the psychiatric ward in the right arm. The adult dependency ward had 26 beds. Violent inmates were sent to the Quiet Room.

Brigham had an old black comb in his pocket when he checked into Cold Strap. It had three broken teeth in the middle and a little broken jagged bit at one end. He couldn't find it when he was leaving his apartment until he conducted a lengthy search. This gave the comb talismanic qualities in Brigham's mind. The comb started to replicate a week after he checked in, with absolutely exact replicas mysteriously continuing to appear until there were six in total.

Concerned for his sanity, Tommy approached George, an orderly. George confirmed the combs were real and exact duplicates. As a teenager and for most of his 20s George had also been a heroin addict but he'd been clean for nine years when Brigham came to the Hospital, and he was doing post-graduate work in substance abuse counseling. At this point the story fragment ends.

No timeline is given but the story is certainly set after 1984, as that was the year the Hospital began treating junkies, and probably in the mid to late 1980s. Due to the tale's setting at The Cold Strap Psychiatric Hospital, sixteen miles north of Augusta, Maine it is naturally enough classified as a Maine Street Horror story.

There are strong links with other King fictional tales through the fact the same corporation that owns the Cold Strap Psychiatric Hospital also owns the Juniper Hill Asylum for the Criminally Insane. Juniper Hill is also mentioned in *Bag of Bones, Cell, The Dark Half, Gerald's Game, Insomnia, Needful Things*, the *Nightmares & Dreamscapes* version of *Suffer the Little Children, The Tommyknockers, Cell* and *It* (*see feature panel*).

An even stronger link is the fact that the town of Derry is said to be upstate from Augusta. Derry is second only to Castle Rock as King's best-known fictional town. It is a key location in *Autopsy Room Four, Bag of Bones, The Bird and the Album, Insomnia, It, The Road Virus Heads North* and *Secret Window, Secret Garden*. It receives considerable mention in both *Dreamcatcher* and *The Tommyknockers* and is also mentioned in *The Body, The Dark Half, Dolores Claiborne, Gerald's Game, Hearts in Atlantis, Mrs. Todd's Shortcut, Pet Sematary, The Revelations of 'Becka Paulson, The Running Man, Storm of the Century, Under the Dome* and *Uncle Otto's Truck*.

As always, King had already introduced some other interesting characters by the point at which this manuscript ends. For instance, another patient who was probably called 'Ray' was an ancient drunk with thick bowed-glasses and hearing aids. He died the first night.

The wonderfully named Billy Boggs was Tommy Brigham's original roommate at Cold Strap. Employed by a private trash collection company in Derry he would take old medicines from the garbage. He'd checked in to kick the habit. One wonders if he had collected trash from the homes of any other King characters?

One other character with a spectacular name is Bongo Bill Bongarsarian, who ran the Bongarsarian Billiard Hall in Augusta. It was located between a barbershop and a dirty bookshop. When Bongo Bill sold Brigham cocaine to deal on the streets he advised him to get out of the game as soon as possible.

This is an unusual King story in that the early part is set in Augusta, the state capital of Maine, a city rarely visited in depth in King's fiction. A number of businesses are mentioned, including a drug store at which a young employee had developed a taste for his own product; the Augusta High School, to whose students Brigham sold cocaine; The Oven, a pizza place at which he also sold his drugs, but only for one day; and the University of Maine at Augusta (he sold his product there next to the cannons).

All in all, this story is hard to assess, as it is just getting interesting at the point where the manuscript ends. What was causing Brigham's comb to replicate perfectly? After the reader, along with Brigham, wonders about his sanity, George the orderly seems to close off that option. Why did King tentatively title the story *Comb Dump*? We can only presume the story moves to a psychiatric hospital for a very good reason, but what is it? Atmosphere? The reaction of other inmates/patients?

The answers to these questions will probably remain unrevealed; as it is most unlikely King will ever return to this tale.

> **The Juniper Hill Asylum for the Criminally Insane**
>
> Probably King's most famous mental asylum, and as well-known as Shawshank Prison to his Constant Readers, it is revealed in *Comb Dump* that Juniper Hill is owned by the same corporation as The Cold Strap Psychiatric Hospital. Importantly, the corporation bought Juniper Hill from the State in August 1983.
>
> In *The Dark Half* Dolly Arsenault claims Juniper Hill is not far from Castle Rock and from *It* we know that it is near the Sidney town line. In *Cell* we are told it is in Augusta. We also know from *Bag of Bones* and *It* that the asylum has a Blue Ward Wing and from *It* that it has a Red Ward. *Comb Dump* reveals that violent inmates were sent to the Rubber Room.
>
> Its residents over the years include the following characters. (*Note:* Cass Knowles was sent to *a place* in Augusta after she killed her son in 1939 in *Sword in the Darkness*, and it is quite possible that place was either Juniper Hill or Cold Strap).
>
> | Name | Story | Crime; Dates of Incarceration |
> | --- | --- | --- |
> | Benny Beaulieu | *It* | Pyromania; 1985 |
> | Henry Bowers | *It* | Murder; 1979 – 30 May 1985 |
> | Nettie Cobb | *Needful Things* | Murder; 1977 – 1982 |
> | Franklin D'Cruz | *It* | Rape |
> | George de Ville | *It* | Murder; 1962 - ? |
> | Jimmy Donlin | *It* | Murder/Cannibalism; 1965 - ? |
> | Raymond Joubert | *Gerald's Game* | Sex Crimes 1979 - 1984 |
> | Bill Keeton | *Needful Things* | Unknown; c. 1977 - 1982 |
> | Charles Pickering | *Insomnia* | Arson; 1982 - 1983 |
> | Emily Sidley | *Suffer the Little Children* | Murder |
> | Arlen Weston | *It* | Unknown |
>
> Among the known guards were Adler, Fogarty and the amusingly named John Koontz (*It*).

The Crate (1979)

The Crate is one of King's quirky horror tales in the tradition of E C Comics. It was first published in a men's magazine, *Gallery* for July 1979. Within months King had included a revised version of the story in his 1st Draft Screenplay of *Creepshow* and the story also appeared, again revised, in the graphic collection of the same name released in 1982. A separate chapter of this book reviews the *Creepshow* screenplay.

This chapter concentrates on the text version, to which too few King fans have had access. We presume that, after using the story for the *Creepshow* 'comic' book and film, King saw no need to allow its reproduction in one of his prose collections, as it had already 'appeared'.

Some hope remains that King will one day allow stories such as this and *Weeds* to appear in one of his short story collections. The easiest way to access the tale currently is to purchase the anthology *Shivers 6*, edited by Rich Chizmar (Cemetery Dance Publications, 2010).

Of course it also appears in *Gallery*, which resells for over $100 per copy, or one of the other anthologies that included the story. They are: *Fantasy Annual III*, edited by Terry Carr (Timescape Books, 1981); *Arbor House Treasury of Horror & The Supernatural*, edited by Bill Pronzini, Barry Malzberg and Martin Greenberg (Arbor House, 1981); *Great Tales of Horror and the Supernatural*, (Galahad Books, 1985); *Classic Tales of Horror and the Supernatural* (William Morrow/Avon Books, 1991); and *The Giant Book of Horror Stories* (Magpie Books, 1991). Those anthologies, with the exception of *Fantasy Annual III*, were edited by Pronzini, Malzberg and Greenberg and are basically the same volume published under different titles.

In this America Under Siege tale a dropped quarter leads to tragedy and release. When a janitor flipped a quarter but failed to catch it the coin rolled under the basement stairs of Amberson Hall, the Zoology Department building at Horlicks University. Looking for the quarter, he discovered an unusual crate carrying the date June 19, 1834 and bearing the inscription 'Arctic Expedition'. He contacted Dexter Stanley, who noted from the stencils on the box it had first come from Paella. He later told his friend Northrup, 'Paella is a very small island south of Tierra del Fuego ... Perhaps the smallest island ever inhabited by the race of man. A number of Easter Island monoliths were found there just after World War II. Not very interesting compared to their bigger brothers, but every bit as mysterious.' When Northrup later pointed out that Tierra del Fuego is near the *Antarctic*, not the Arctic, Stanley replied that in those days the terms sub-arctic, Antarctic and Antarctica had not been invented. 'In those days there was only the north arctic and the south arctic.'

Together, Stanley and the janitor opened the crate, Stanley telling Northrup later, ' "We opened the crate ... God help us, Henry, we opened the crate."' As the boards were removed a strange whistle began to emanate from within, '... no cheerful whistle this, but something like an ugly, hysterical shriek by a tantrumy child. And this suddenly dropped and thickened into a low, hoarse growling sound. It was not loud, but it had a primitive, savage sound that stood Dex Stanley's hair up on the slant.' A strange creature then grabbed and killed the janitor, '...something with huge claws. It tore at the janitor's straining, knotted throat and severed his jugular vein.' Stanley froze, watching the body being slowly dragged into the crate before finally running for help, right into graduate student Charlie Gereson who, when told what had happened was clearly disbelieving. Gereson insisted on investigating and was also killed. As it savaged Gereson '...the thing raised its head and those small green-gold eyes stared balefully into Dex's own. He had never seen or dreamed such savagery.'

Stanley ran again, this time to confide in his good friend Henry Northrup. Henry, conceiving a plan, drugged Dexter and left a note tricking his own shrewish wife Wilma into coming to Amberson Hall later that night. He then pushed Wilma to the creature and her death ('Just tell it to call you Billie, you bitch'). Northrup cleaned up and disposed of the crate, creature and victims intact, into the depths of Ryder's Quarry. Henry received some small payback for his deed when he peered into the crate, 'I saw Wilma's face, Dex. Her *face* ... I saw her eyes, looking up at me from that box. Her glazed eyes.'

The next morning Northrup calmly told Stanley what he'd done, 'I've killed Wilma. Ding-dong the wicked bitch is dead ... I've killed my wife, and now I've put myself into your hands.' After again considering Wilma's nature ('He thought of his friend, at last free of that other species of Tasmanian devil that killed more slowly but just as surely – by heart attack, by stroke, by ulcer, by high blood pressure, yammering and whistling in the ear all the while') Stanley agreed to keep their secret, 'Dex smiled slowly, "That's all right," he said. "After all, what are friends for?"'

Of course the story was adapted in King's own screenplay for a segment in the 1982 George Romero directed movie, *Creepshow*. In *The Crate* segment Hal Holbrook played Henry Northrup, Adrienne Barbeau appeared as Wilma Northrup and Fritz Weaver as Dexter Stanley.

Beahm states:[70] 'The original inspiration came from a real-life incident at the University of Maine at Orono, where an old crate dating back to the previous century had been discovered in the basement of one of the buildings on campus. What, King thought, *could* have been in that crate?' This story is set in August of 1974, while the *Creepshow* segment (the only one given a timeline) is set in August of 1980.

In the *Introduction* to the anthologies listed above edited by Pronzini, Malzberg and Greenberg, King acknowledges 'ripping off' a device from Poe's *The Tell-Tale Heart* when a cackling Henry Northrup pushes his wife to the creature, and death:

'In the Poe classic, "The Tell-Tale Heart", the murdering narrator tells his story in a kind of cackling frenzy, laughing as he explains how cleverly he got rid of the old man's body ... (and I quite consciously ripped the device off in my own story, "The Crate", where the narrator laughs uncontrollably as he pushes his bitch of a wife under the stairs where she is awaited by a monster of such ferocity that it is really a cartoon).'

There are a couple of very interesting links from this story to other King fiction. Stanley and Northrup teach at Horlicks University (although no town and state is given). This university also appears in *The Raft*, also first published in *Gallery*. The unfortunate victims of the creature in the lake in that tale were students. There is no timeline for that story, but we know it occurred after 1981, which also means after the events covered by *The Crate*.

In the clearest of links King toys with hard-core fans in his 1983 novel, *Christine*. There Jimmy Sykes' uncle said there was an opening for a janitor at the unnamed college where he worked, because the other janitor had disappeared! Regina and Michael Cunningham, the parents of Christine's owner Arnie, taught at Horlicks before their deaths at the hands of the demonic car on the same day as their son, 19 January 1979.

In *From a Buick 8*, Curtis Wilcox wanted to take some science courses at Horlicks and even wore one of their t-shirts. This was the first mention of Horlicks in a King story since *Christine* was published, nineteen years earlier. Of the various tales *The Crate* tells us the most about Horlicks, which was founded in 1672. Female students were first allowed to attend in 1888. Amberson Hall was also known as the 'Old Zoology' building and was being replaced by the new Cather Hall.

Ryder's Quarry, into which the Crate was dumped, has a tragic history. Twelve miles from Horlicks University some said it was over 400 feet deep. A dozen people had drowned there between 1944 and 1974. It is only in *The Raft* that readers discover Horlicks is located in Pittsburgh, Pennsylvania. The Pennsylvania connection remains in *Christine* and *From a Buick 8*, despite the location of Horlicks not being clearly identified in those novels.

There is one apparent error in the tale. The early part of the story, describing the creature's seizing of the janitor, reads: 'Something as dry and brown and scaly as a desert reptile came out of the crate – something with huge claws.' Later, when the creature caught Gereson, Stanley '…caught a glimpse of a furry, writhing shape spread-eagled on the young man's chest…' And, later again, when Northrup described what he saw of the creature to Stanley, '"I saw something else, too. Something white. A bone, I think. And a black something. Furry. Curled up. Whistling, too. A very low whistle. I think it was sleeping."' It seems unlikely the creature could be scaly *and* furry.

Unlike the film version this original story clearly underlines the depths of Henry Northrup's motivation in killing his atrocious wife, Wilma. 'Three years before, Northrup had made a run at the vacant English department chairmanship. He had lost, and one of the reasons had undoubtedly been his wife, Wilma, an abrasive and unpleasant woman … it seemed he could always recall the hard mule-bray of her voice, telling some new faculty wife to "call me Billie, dear, everyone does!"' At one point we learn '…when Wilma insisted on a thing, she did so savagely.'

Henry had tricked Wilma into coming to Amberson Hall using her own nature. The note Henry left said Stanley, his only real friend and the only part of his life Wilma could not control, had gotten into trouble through an indiscretion with one of his female grad students. When Wilma arrived she was 'excited and happy ... because she was finally going to get control over that last ... little ... bit' of Henry's life. By this point the reader is unlikely to have any sympathy for Billie as she suffers her demise.

We have more reason to dislike Wilma in this version compared to the film or comic book as King has the opportunity to delve more deeply into her character. We are normally only *satisfied* by death in a horror story when it is a villain who expires. The satisfaction readers derive from Wilma's fate comes from seeing her, rather than the monster in the crate, as the true villain of this tale.

In a classic piece of King prose we read toward the end of the tale, and just before Stanley agrees to go along with Northrup, he: '... thought of the janitor, casually flicking his quarter, and of the quarter coming down and rolling under the stairs, where a very old horror sat squat and mute, covered with dust and cobwebs, waiting ... biding its time ...'

The story is remarkably effective, well-paced with perfectly timed flashbacks, full of intrigue and motive. Most of those attributes were somehow lost in the *Creepshow* version and it is therefore to be hoped that King will one day relent and give the full text version of the tale a much wider circulation.

Creepshow Screenplay (1979)

The material in this chapter was compiled using a copy of King's 1st draft screenplay, dated 1979. While the screenplay has never been published copies of it circulate freely within the King community. Due to use of that version, the only draft publicly available, readers should note that the screenplay varies in places from the final film version.

The screenplay includes three original King stories as well as two which previously appeared in other versions. The stories from *Creepshow* were also published in a Graphic Novel. The five stories are:

Father's Day (the only versions of this story are the screenplay and the Graphic Novel);

The Lonesome Death of Jordy Verrill (previously published in two early men's magazines as *Will Be Necessary to Stop the Weeds*);

The Crate (originally published in *Gallery* magazine for July 1979);

Something to Tide You Over (the only versions of this story are the screenplay and the Graphic Novel); and

They're Creeping Up on You (the only versions of this story are the screenplay and the Graphic Novel).

The Graphic Novel was a movie tie-in, published by New American Library in 1982. The art is by Berni Wrightson and the cover art by Jack Kamen. Interestingly, King has not collected a single one of these stories in one of his mainstream text collections. King's screenplay was produced as the movie *Creepshow* and released in 1982.

Members of www.imdb.com give the movie the slightly high rating of 6.5 out of a possible 10. George A Romero was the director. The main actors were big screen veteran Hal Holbrook as Henry Northrup; Leslie Nielsen of *Naked Gun* fame as Richard Vickers; E G Marshall as Upson Pratt; Ed Harris as Hank Blaine; with *Cheers* and *Becker* star Ted Danson as Harry Wentworth.

Producer Richard P Rubinstein told a magazine King had written the screenplay in two months and Stephen Jones claims[71] that Romero shot virtually the exact script, as written, a very unusual event in the movie industry. Made on an $8 million budget, the movie grossed nearly $20 million in the US market, half of that on its opening weekend, Halloween. It was released on DVD in 1999.

As Beahm points out[72] King's participation in this project marked his first professional involvement in the film and television industry. In *Stephen King: The Art of Darkness*, Winter describes the film as '…a studied tribute to E.C. Comics …' – Winter's chapter on this work is highly recommended.

This was only the second visual adaptation of King's work in which he appeared, on this occasion wonderfully made up in the role of the hapless Jordy Verrill. King's son, Joe, also appeared as Billy, the original owner of the *Creepshow* comic book[73]. A full listing of King film and television projects, including his screen appearances, appears as a feature panel.

A sequel, *Creepshow 2*, was released in 1987. That movie included an adaptation of King's story *The Raft*, along with two new pieces, *Old Chief Wood'n-head* and *The Hitch-hiker*. King did *not* write these latter stories. George Romero wrote the overall screenplay. King played a cameo role as a Truck Driver in *The Hitch-hiker* segment. *Creepshow 2* was released on DVD in 2001.

The quick summary of the *Creepshow* script from *The Complete Guide to the Works of Stephen King* reads: 'In which a father returns from the dead in a foul mood; a man becomes infested by an alien growth and takes the only course of action open to him; a hen-pecked professor finds an ingenious way of riding himself of his wife; a man takes revenge on his wife and her lover, using the ways of nature to prolong the agony; and a man with a cleanliness fetish, and a disrespect for other humans is visited by his worst nightmares.' How about that for succinct?

No timelines are given for the action in the screenplay, other than *The Crate* segment, which is set in August 1980. In the following pages we summaries each story segment, providing considerably more detail.

Wrap-Around

The screenplay includes a 'wrap-around' segment. It is set in the wonderfully anonymous town of Centerville, USA, where a young boy named Billy had the First Issue Collector's Edition of the comic magazine, *Creepshow*. Even though his mother defended his right to it his father took the comic and threw it away. Later, a trash collector picked the book out of the garbage and pocketed it for his kids. Included among the stories shown in the actual comic book are all the segments we are to see in the movie.

The first issue advertised a 'Genuine Haitian Voodoo Doll'. The cover of the second issue advertised Billy with a voodoo doll, which he was apparently using to attack his father!

The 'character' introducing each segment is itself called Creepshow. This creature looks like an 'old witch, or maybe a rotting corpse'.

Father's Day

Father's Day is an original story, developed specifically for this screenplay. Its only other appearance is in the Graphic Novel, *Creepshow*. Apart from the Grantham home, described as a 'Victorian monstrosity' (shades of *The Glass Floor* there), no setting is given for this America Under Siege tale. Nathan Grantham was buried in a graveyard behind the house.

On Father's Day, seven years to the day after Bedelia Grantham killed her father with a glass ashtray; his reanimated corpse rose from the grave and strangled her to death. Nathan Grantham had made the Grantham clan's money in bootleg, smuggling, extortion and murder-for-hire back around 1910. In his nineties he had a stroke and sometime later Bedelia killed him, apparently as cold revenge for his arranging the murder of her handsome would-be lover, Peter Yarbro, in a hunting 'accident' many years before. Bedelia had not been indicted for her father's murder, apparently after her niece Sylvia helped cover up the evidence.

Nathan's corpse also killed the housekeeper, Mrs. Danvers (clear homage there), and the other members of the Grantham clan - Sylvia; Cassandra and her husband, Henry Blaine; and Cassandra's brother Richard.

The Lonesome Death of Jordy Verrill

The storyline of *The Lonesome Death of Jordy Verrill* had previously been published in two early men's magazines as the short story *Weeds*. This book contains a separate chapter about that story, which has never been included in a King collection. It was originally published in a men's magazine, *Cavalier* for May 1976 and republished in another so-called 'skin' magazine, *Nugget* for April 1979.

In the prose version Jordy Verrill lived near Cleaves Mills, New Hampshire but for *Creepshow* his farm has relocated close to Castle Rock, Maine. It is therefore classified as a Maine Street Horror story. As a side note King's editor at Viking from 1979 was Chuck Verrill, a relatively unusual surname and a probably homage, although this surname can be seen on certain mailboxes in western Maine on roads Stephen and Tabitha King ('Mrs. Todd') would have regularly driven.

The Verrill farmhouse was just off Route 26 and about five miles from Castle Rock. It had seen better times, 'probably around 1940'. It had junk in the yard, plastic on the windows and a lot of weeds grew around the house. The Bluebird Stream ran through the property. Jordy himself was a farmer aged about 45 and was not very bright.

One night he saw a meteor crash on his land. When Jordy investigated he found the meteor to be slightly bigger than a softball, regular and spherical. The poor farmer imagined he could sell the extraterrestrial object and pay off his bank loan with the proceeds. But, when he threw water on to the meteor to cool it, the object broke into two pieces. The center was hollow and a gray liquid seeped from it. Unfortunately, the curious Jordy touched this liquid.

A green, grass like material grew rapidly from the liquid after the meteor split, taking over the farm and also spreading over Jordy's body. It particularly benefited from access to liquid and when Jordy took a bath to alleviate the itch it brought on, the 'weeds' gained a new burst of growth. They finally spread over his entire body and, in extreme pain, Jordy committed suicide by gunshot. Meanwhile, the 'weeds' spread across the farmland, heading inexorably toward the nearby town.

The Crate

The Crate was originally published in the magazine *Gallery* for July 1979 and was reprinted in a number of anthologies. This book contains a separate chapter about that story, which has never been included in a King collection.

In this America Under Siege segment a janitor finds an old crate that had apparently been addressed to a Julia Carpenter in 1834. Mike, working at Amberson Hall of Horlicks University, reported the find to Dexter Stanley, the handsome professor emeritus of the Zoology Department, which was located in the building. When they returned to check out the crate a creature from inside it killed and ate the janitor. When Stanley called a 23-year-old grad student, Charlie Gereson to assist the young man was disbelieving. Insisting on investigating he too was killed by the creature.

In panic Stanley next called upon his chess partner buddy from the English Department, Henry Northrup. Seizing a once in a lifetime chance Northrup used sleeping pills to drug Stanley and conned his own shrewish wife Wilma into meeting him at Amberson Hall. He then lured Wilma into her demise at the claws of the creature. Covering up the evidence of the creature's killings, he was able to encase the crate in another large box, which he then dumped in the deep water at Ryder's Quarry. Northrup then happily moved on with his life, without Wilma!

The Creature itself had been sent to Horlicks University in June of 1834, following an Arctic Expedition. It made a chittering sound and had large, green eyes with slit pupils. With a body like a whippet, it was furred, had six spider-like arms with claws, and large teeth. It made a whistling sound just before attacking. Despite Northrup trapping and dumping it in the water at Ryder's Quarry it escaped. This contrasts with the original story, in which there was no indication of an escape.

This is the only story for which a timeline is given, that of August 1980.

Something to Tide You Over

Something to Tide You Over is an original story, developed specifically for this screenplay. Its only other appearance is in the Graphic Novel, *Creepshow*.

The main settings for this story are Comfort House, Richard Vickers' beach house at Comfort Point, almost certainly in the state of Massachusetts; and the nearby beach, of which Vickers owned 'almost 70%'. The house was a tall angular Victorian, with gables, gambrels and turrets, 'very much like Norman Bates' home'. This segment is classified as an America Under Siege tale.

In the segment Vickers discovers his wife, some sort of star, has been having an affair with a bank loan officer, Harry Wentworth. Vickers was a very successful TV producer, with three top rating shows on network TV but was more than a little jealous. Vickers kidnapped Wentworth and, holding him at gunpoint, buried him up to his neck on the beach. After revealing the gun had not been loaded he forced Wentworth to watch Rebecca, who had also been buried, drown on the incoming tide. Wentworth then suffered the same fate.

However, a surprise was in store for our Mr Vickers. That night the living corpses of Rebecca and Harry chased him. He shot the corpses to no effect and, in terror, he committed suicide by slashing his throat with a razor blade.

They're Creeping Up on You

They're Creeping Up on You is an original story, developed specifically for this screenplay. Its only other appearance is in the Graphic Novel, *Creepshow*.

This America Under Siege segment is set in the New York apartment of an elderly and very wealthy businessman, Upson Pratt, a man with a nasty disposition. Pratt also had an unnatural fear of bugs, presumably caused by the fact that rats, roaches, bedbugs and silverfish had infested his home when he was a boy.

The ruthless Pratt was in the process of taking over Pacific Aerodyne. After finding control of his company had passed to Pratt Corporation, CEO Norman Castonmeyer shot himself through the right eye. Mrs. Castonmeyer rang to berate Pratt over the suicide but Pratt showed no concern.

That night much of the city was blacked out and bugs began to invade Pratt's apartment. The first was a cockroach, which he sprayed to death and put in a matchbox. However, the body mysteriously disappeared. Among other bugs that now came into the apartment were some big, ugly ones with greenish carapaces; and 'spider-things'. When these bit Pratt they drew blood. Many other types of bugs followed and Pratt kept up a valiant fight using Black Flag and other bug sprays but he was ultimately overcome and killed. After his death one last cockroach climbed out of a nostril!

As the scriptwriter King was able to include numerous links in the screenplay to his other works of fiction and a number of homages. Castle Rock is mentioned as being five miles from Jordy Verrill's farmhouse. The town is a key location in *The Body*, *Cujo*, *Gramma*, the *Nightmares and Dreamscapes* version of *It Grows on You*, *The Man in the Black Suit*, *Mrs. Todd's Shortcut*, *Needful Things*, the *Skeleton Crew* version of *Nona*, *Premium Harmony*, *The Sun Dog* and *Uncle Otto's Truck*. It receives considerable mention in *Bag of Bones*, *The Dark Half*, *The Dead Zone*, *Squad D* and *The Huffman Story*; and it is also mentioned in *Dreamcatcher*, *Gerald's Game*, *The Girl Who Loved Tom Gordon*, *Riding the Bullet*, *Rita Hayworth and Shawshank Redemption*, *Under the Dome* and the *Complete and Uncut* version of *The Stand*.

In *Christine* Jimmy Sykes' uncle said there was an opening for a janitor at the college where he worked because the other janitor had disappeared! *The Crate* is set at Horlicks University (where Regina and Michael Cunningham of *Christine* were teachers) and, of course, one of the victims of the creature in the Crate was the janitor, Mike! The unfortunate students from *The Raft* attended Horlicks University and, in *From a Buick 8*, Curtis Wilcox wanted to take science courses at that college. Now, while it is true it's hard to get into a good college these days, this is one students who intend to graduate may wish to avoid!

The bumbling Jordy Verrill is also mentioned in the notes to King's unproduced screenplay of *Pet Sematary*. In that script the Baterman place 'looks like the home of Jordy Verrill'. Finally, the screenplay notes that there 'may' have been a Letter to the Editor in the *Creepshow* comic book that mentioned *'Salem's Lot*. The comic book did carry a full-page advertisement for *Dawn of the Dead* and also 'may' have carried a Letter to the Editor mentioning *Night of the Living Dead*. In a nod to the director of both those movies and *Creepshow*, there was also feature on George Romero in the comic book.

The Grantham's housekeeper in *Father's Day* is Mrs. Danvers. In *Bag of Bones* King reminds readers that Mrs. Danvers was Rebecca de Mornay's housekeeper in the Daphne du Maurier novel, *Rebecca*. The use of this name is an apparent homage.

Considering readers and viewers can access this screenplay in a number of ways, including viewing the DVD/video or reading the Graphic Novel, and the passage of years, it would seem most unlikely that this screenplay will ever be published. Readers wishing to more fully experience *The Lonesome Death of Jordy Verrill* will need to find a copy of *Weeds*; and those interested in *The Crate* will need to access *Gallery* magazine, its reprint in *Nugget* or one of the anthologies in which it appears. This book also contains separate chapters on these last two tales.

KING AT THE MOVIES

King's love affair with the silver screen began at a very early age. As a result of his great success as a best-selling author he has been able to pen a number of screenplays and meet and work with over a dozen significant directors. He has also taken the opportunity to show his acting skills, which are quite acceptable for the roles he has taken. Hardcore King fans delight in each of these roles. He was at his best as the inept Jordy Verrill in *Creepshow*. The movies and television episodes in which he has appeared are listed below.

Appearances
The movies and television episodes in which King has appeared are listed below.

- *Baseball* (1994) as Himself (documentary series)
- *Chappelle's Show* (2003) as Himself (comedy series)
- *Creepshow* (1982) as Jordy Verrill (segment, adaptation of *Weeds* and *The Lonesome Death of Jordy Verrill*; Joe King appears in the movie as Billy)
- *Creepshow 2* (1987) as Truck Driver (segment, *The Hitchhiker*)
- *Diary of the Dead* (2007) as Newsreader (uncredited, voice only)
- *Fever Pitch* aka *The Perfect Catch* (2005) as Himself (uncredited, he throws out a pitch)
- *Frasier* (2000) as the Voice of Brian (*Mary Christmas* episode)
- *Golden Years* (1991) as Bus Driver (original TV series written by King)
- *Gotham Café* (2005) as Mr. Ring
- *Kingdom Hospital* (2004) as Johnny B Good, lawyer on TV and as AA sponsor (TV series written by King)
- *Knightriders* (1981) as Hoagie Man (Tabitha King also appeared, as this character's wife)
- *The Langoliers* (1995) as Tom Holby (adaptation of the novella)
- *Maximum Overdrive* (1986) Man at the Cashpoint (original script inspired by *Trucks*)
- *Pet Sematary* (1989) as the Minister (adaptation of the novel)
- *Rose Red* (2002) as the Pizza Delivery Man (original mini-series written by King)

- *The Shining* (1997) as Gage Creed (mini-series adaptation of the novel, King's character is named after the unlucky child in *Pet Sematary*)
- *The Simpsons* (2000) as Himself (*Insane Clown Poppy* episode)
- *Sleepwalkers* (1992) as Cemetery Caretaker (original script)
- *Sons of Anarchy* (2010) as Bachman (*Caregiver* episode)
- *The Stand* (1994) as Teddy Weizak (mini-series adaptation of the novel)
- *Stephen King's Gotham Café* (2005) as Mr. Ring (off camera, dollar baby adaptation)
- *Storm of the Century* (1999) as TV Lawyer (original mini-series written by King)
- *Thinner* (1996) as Dr. Bangor (adaptation of the novel)

Director

King's sole directorial effort was 1986's *Maximum Overdrive*.

Executive Producer

King has been listed as the Producer or Executive Producer for the following TV productions. Of these King also wrote the screenplay of all but *Ellen Rimbauer*, which is based on characters he created for *Rose Red*; and *Riding the Bullet*.

Desperation, The Diary of Ellen Rimbauer, Golden Years, Kingdom Hospital, Riding the Bullet, Rose Red, The Shining (mini-series), *The Stand* (mini-series) and *Storm of the Century*.

Credited as the Writer

As of mid-2011 King's work was already credited with the creation of well over 100 film or TV projects that had actually been released. These range from the first, *Carrie* (1976) to *Secret Garden* and *The Mist*, from 'dollar babies' such as Frank Darabont's *Woman in the Room* to blockbusters by leading directors such as Darabont's *The Shawshank Redemption* and *The Green Mile* and Stanley Kubrick's *The Shining*. This last is but one of a number of stories that have been professionally adapted twice, the others include *Apt Pupil* (one production was not completed); *The Dead Zone*; *Children of the Corn*; *Sorry, Right Number*; *Carrie*; *Firestarter*; and *'Salem's Lot*.

Cujo – Unproduced Screenplay (Undated)

The material in this chapter was compiled with the assistance of a copy of King's 1st draft screenplay. While the screenplay has never been published copies of it do circulate within the King community and there is also a copy in Box 2316 of the Special Collections Unit of the Raymond H Fogler Library at the University of Maine, Orono. As this is a public box interested readers may access the screenplay there.

There is an interesting history to the *final* screenplay for the 1983 movie adaptation of King's early novel *Cujo*. After King wrote the first draft responsibility passed to Barbara Turner (credited as Lauren Currier), who wrote two revisions, and Don Carlos Dunaway, who rewrote it again. The Writer's Guild of America denied King a writer's credit after Turner lodged a protest. King told *Cinefantastique*, 'I was in England at the time and I just didn't have time to mess with it.' In the end, the movie version is only slightly different from this first draft screenplay.

Considering the dispute over the credit, the fact that novel is likely to be in print for decades to come and that the movie may be rented or purchased on DVD/video, there would appear to be no prospect of this screenplay ever being published.

As readers will be very familiar with the premise and storyline of *Cujo* the summary of King's screenplay may be kept to the minimum. In the script a bite presages a fight to the death. On 16 June the Camber's dog Cujo, a good, gentle St Bernard was bitten by a rabid bat while chasing a rabbit. As the disease took hold Cujo slowly lost his mind.

On 12 July, having won $10,000 in the Maine State Lottery five days earlier, Charity Camber and her son Brett left Castle Rock, Maine by bus to visit relatives in Connecticut, leaving husband Joe with Cujo on their isolated property. Vic Trenton also left Castle Rock, on a business trip, still angry over his wife Donna's recent affair with a local poet and furniture refinisher, Steve Kemp. Their son Tad had been suffering from night fears, including of a bat shaped monster in his closet, but his father had alleviated the terror by teaching Tad 'monster words' that would fend off anything lurking in the dark.

Cujo, now suffering from rabies, attacked and killed one of Camber's neighbors, Gary Pervier. Shortly after, he also killed Joe Camber. Unsuspecting, Donna Trenton drove her ailing blue Pinto to the garage on Joe Camber's property to be repaired. On a day where the thermometer hit 87°F, Cujo trapped Donna and Tad in the car after the Pinto failed to restart.

The next day, while Vic Trenton was in New York, Cujo kept Donna and Tad trapped, with the thermometer hitting 100°F. Tad's condition deteriorated and Donna also suffered from heat stress and sunburn. Steve Kemp trashed the Trenton's house and then left Maine for New Hampshire. That evening, after Donna left the car and ventured into the Camber's house, Cujo attacked her, savaging her leg and stomach. Concerned about his wife's failure to answer the home phone, Vic contacted the Castle Rock police.

Shortly after midnight, policeman Roscoe Fisher went to the Trenton home, which he found vandalized. At 1.02am Sheriff George Bannerman called Vic Trenton in New York to tell him what had been found and Vic immediately left for Castle Rock. At dawn on the 14th Donna and Tad were still trapped in their car. Cujo killed another neighbor, egg farmer Alva Thornton. Tad suffered a convulsion and Donna had to revive him with mouth-to-mouth resuscitation. At 6.50am Vic Trenton arrived in Castle Rock where it rapidly became another very hot day, with the temperature already 85°F at 8.15am. Tad was in a very bad way and it appeared he would not survive. Donna left the car and fought Cujo, he savaged her again and she severely injured him with her tire iron, puncturing his right eye. Bannerman and Vic Trenton arrived at the Camber place and Bannerman shot Cujo dead. Somehow, Donna and Tad had survived.

In adapting his novel for the screen King made particularly important changes to the entire final confrontation between the antagonists, along with a number of minor alterations. In the screenplay Tad Trenton survives (as he did in the actual movie) whereas in the book he dies. In the screenplay Bannerman kills Cujo but in the novel it is the other way around (as a result this 'second' Bannerman has an alternative life in King's fictional world). Cujo also killed Alva Thornton in the screenplay, a fate the farmer did not suffer in the original version.

This adaptation of King's Maine Street Horror novel is quite faithful to the original (however, King is quoted in Jones' *Creepshows* as saying, 'I thought my script was pretty good. It was not as faithful to the book as the final result was.') As a result it is not surprising to find there are many links to King's other fiction. Cujo himself is also mentioned in *Mrs. Todd's Shortcut, The Sun Dog, Pet Sematary, Needful Things, The Body* and *The Dark Half*, usually in the context of Castle Rock.

Of course, Castle Rock is the setting for *The Body, Cujo, Gramma*, the *Nightmares and Dreamscapes* version of *It Grows on You, The Man in the Black Suit, Mrs. Todd's Shortcut, Needful Things*, the *Skeleton Crew* version of *Nona, Premium Harmony, The Sun Dog* and *Uncle Otto's Truck*. The town receives considerable mention in *Bag of Bones, The Dark Half, The Dead Zone, Squad D* and *The Huffman Story*; and is also mentioned in the *Creepshow* screenplay, *Dreamcatcher, Gerald's Game, The Girl Who Loved Tom Gordon, The Lonesome Death of Jordy Verrill, Riding the Bullet, Rita Hayworth and Shawshank Redemption, Under the Dome* and the *Complete and Uncut* version of *The Stand*.

George Bannerman also appears in *The Body* (although it seems likely this is a different George Bannerman) and in *The Dead Zone*. Bannerman is also mentioned in *Needful Things, The Dark Half* and *The Sun Dog*.

Donna Trenton and Tad Trenton also appear in *The Monster in the Closet* (an excerpt from the novel published as a short story) and *Needful Things*; and are also referred to in *The Sun Dog*. Joe Camber is also mentioned in *Needful Things, The Sun Dog, The Body, Gramma* and *Mrs. Todd's Shortcut*. Charity Camber is also mentioned in *Needful Things* and Castle Rock police officer

Roscoe Fisher also appears in *The Dead Zone*. Gary Pervier is also mentioned in *Needful Things* and *The Sun Dog*.

Interestingly, the only other mention of Town Road #5, on which the Cambers and Gary Pervier live, is in *Needful Things*. For some reason King changed the name of the road from the novel's Town Road #3. In another interesting road reference Donna's erstwhile lover, Steve Kemp, lived and worked on Castle Rock's Back Harlow Road (this is the only King work where this road is mentioned), a name that echoes Castle Rock's neighboring town.

When King was originally approached to change the ending to make it more marketable to movie audiences by letting Tad Trenton live he agreed, despite having told the book's publisher that such a change was 'non-negotiable'.

The result was that King had to totally rewrite his original ending. In the novel Donna and Tad were trapped by Cujo until Bannerman visited the Camber property at Vic's request (Vic was still away on business) but was attacked by Cujo and killed. Donna was able to beat the dog to death with a baseball bat. However, the ordeal was too much for Tad and he died before help could arrive. In the screenplay Vic returned to Castle Rock and went out to the Camber property with Bannerman, who shot Cujo, saving Tad's life. This rewrite leaves George Bannerman alive. King also provides a new future for Bannerman (remembering there will soon be a new Sheriff to accommodate in the Maine Street Horror reality in the person of Alan Pangborn). That November, the script tells us, Bannerman was elected to the Maine State Senate and was expected to run for Governor in 1988.

However, little Tad does not get off lightly. The screenplay tells us that the following August he was diagnosed with leukemia but was later in remission. In other developments both Vic Trenton and the Municipality of Castle Rock sued Charity Camber but the suits were later dropped. Charity and her son Brett then moved to northwestern Maine. When Donna's lover, Steve Kemp, left Castle Rock he had posted a poison pen letter to Vic Trenton and trashed the Trenton's home. He was arrested for this crime in Twickenham, Massachusetts. The Trentons later dropped the charges and he moved to Santa Fe, New Mexico.

The novel is set in 1980 but no specific year is given for the events portrayed in the screenplay. It must be set before 1988, as Bannerman was elected to the State Senate the November following Cujo's rampage and was expected to run for Governor in 1988. As is often the case in King screenplays he takes the opportunity in this one to tip a nod to close associates. Charity Camber mentions Chris Chesley in the script as someone she could get to go up to her house to check on Cujo and Joe. Chris Chesley and Stephen King self-published *People, Places and Things* in 1960, a publication covered elsewhere in this book. Chesley was a childhood, teenage (in Durham, Maine) and early adulthood friend of King's.

In the script Vic Trenton asked his secretary to get Chris Spruce on the phone. Christopher Spruce is the brother of Tabitha King and Stephanie Leonard, King's sister-in-law. Spruce both assisted in editing and published the *Castle Rock* newsletter and, for a period, ran WZON, a Bangor radio station King owns.

All in all, any King fan would have been happy with King's screenplay for this movie. The actual movie, made on a budget of $5 million, took over $21 million at the box office, a substantial result in 1983. It starred *E.T.* actress Dee Wallace as Donna and www.imdb.com members rate it 5.8 out of a possible 10, which seems a little harsh. While it was a competent movie, and the final production is not enormously different from King's script, perhaps King's feel for the story and the characters would have ensured a more effective translation to the screen.

Dave's Rag: Jumper and Rush Call (1959-60)

Jumper and *Rush Call* were originally published in a neighborhood newspaper, *Dave's Rag*, put out by King's older brother David. The first of the two was apparently *Jumper*, published over three parts in the Winter of 1959-60, technically making it the earliest published of King's works (Part One was published in the December 29, 1959 issue).

The stories were re-published in the Book-of-the-Month Club's collection of miscellaneous King writings, *Secret Windows: Essays and Fiction On the Craft of Writing* in 2000. This book is fairly easy to obtain from specialist King booksellers or the usual internet sources. The stories were re-published as originally written, with only the spelling corrected.

While clearly juvenilia there are some sentences that are stunning when one considers a 12-year-old boy wrote them. Sophisticated thinking is evident and it is clear that King the best-selling author and quality writer was beginning to spread his wings.

Jumper

In the story a man threatens to jump off a building. Robert Steppes was a serial 'jumper' and had escaped after being committed. Jeff Davis was called to talk him down after he threatened to jump from the 15th Floor of the Chrysler Building. Steppes was knocked from the ledge by a cable holding a hook the police used to try and catch him, but he grabbed the ledge and pulled himself back up. Davis decided to use unusual methods and was able to stop Steppes from jumping.

This as an America Under Siege story. It is effectively set in (or outside!) the Chrysler Building in New York City and no timeline is given. There are no links to other King works of fiction.

The story is written in the first person, from the perspective of Davis: 'I'm a police counselor, or in simple terms, I try to determine what's wrong with people who try do somebody else – or themselves – in.' Steppes was a compulsive jumper, having tried to jump off a building six times, always 'escaping' (presumably from some institution to which he had been confined as well as, obviously, death). Steppes constantly calls Davis 'Dr. Castle'. This *may* be an error by King but it is more likely that Steppes, in his insanity, believes Davis to be one of his therapists.

At the beginning of part three Steppes withdraws his threat. Now, Davis jumps out onto the ledge and walks toward Steppes, '…I was sure that I was right. Although theoretically, any man can take his own life, few men could really commit suicide, and Robert was not one of these men.' It is worth remembering again that King was only 12 when he wrote that sentence! The story concludes with, 'It was one of the most harrowing cases I've handled – "The Case of the Jumper That Could Not Jump."'

Dave's Rag

Dave's Rag was a self-published local newspaper issued by King's adopted older brother, David in the Durham, Maine area from January 1959 through at least the winter of 1959-1960.

A number of original copies of the newspaper must exist. One page, dated December 29, 1959, is reproduced in *Secret Windows*. Dave King told the fascinating story of *Dave's Rag* to Stephen Spignesi, who reproduces the conversation in his *The Complete Stephen King Encyclopedia*. Following their interview, reproduced in the *Growing Up with the Boogeyman* chapter, Dave found a copy of one edition. Spignesi was given permission to reproduce this 'Summer Special 1959' issue in full in the *Encyclopedia*. As neither of these copies include *Jumper* or *Rush Call* it would be interesting to discover how these came to light for *Secret Windows*. One can only presume they came from Stephen King's personal collection.

Dave King told Spignesi the paper was published from January 1959. Spignesi reproduces an article from the April 23, 1959 issue of the Brunswick *Record*, titled *3 Durham Lads Publishing Bright Hometown Newspaper*. (The third was a cousin, Donald Flaws, at 15 four years older than Steve). By that time six issues had been published; Dave was a freshman at Brunswick High School and Steve 'attends the West Durham school.'

King also relates the story of *Dave's Rag* in sections 17 –19 of the *C.V.* section of *On Writing*. According to this, 'The *Rag* was an odd combination of family newsletter and small-town bi-weekly.' Initially the paper had a 'circulation' of five family members but reached fifty or sixty at its maximum, including neighbors and relatives of neighbors in the small town of Durham, Maine (King tells us it had a population of 900 in 1962). In the first year the newspaper was printed on a hectograph, producing purple print but was later printed using stencils and a small drum printing press. Steve typed the stencils, as he was less prone to typing errors than Dave!

Rush Call

In this America Under Siege story a young boy is trapped after a car accident. A grouchy, bitter old doctor volunteers to take out his appendix while the boy is still trapped in the car. Dr. Thorpe, 'one of the best in his day', climbs into the car on Christmas Eve and by Christmas morning he has saved the boy's life. After the commotion dies down he realizes he has recaptured the real meaning of Christmas – 'The Beginning'.

In trademark King style we have an old, bitter man walking the quiet hospital corridors and calling on a patient, Mrs. Simmons. ' "I can't sleep," she told him. "I keep thinking about my Carol marrying that tramp. The fortune hunter! I simply can't," she talked on, and although Dr. Thorpe smiled and nodded and agreed, her voice became only a background to him.' When the rush call emergency buzzer goes off Thorpe joins the other doctors in the hospital president's office and finds himself the only one volunteering to worm into a wrecked car and perform an appendectomy on a trapped and badly injured boy.

After succeeding in the operation, '…somehow, he wasn't the same man he had been four hours ago – something had happened in that car – something in the small hours of Christmas morning. Something had washed out of him. Call it bitterness. Call it irony.' Hearing 'Silent Night', really hearing it for the first time, Dr. Thorpe suddenly understood, 'God had sent his son for a million times the ordeal he had faced that morning … And as the sun blazed over the horizon in full glory, Dr. Thorpe knew the meaning of Christmas. THE BEGINNING.'

While no year is given for the story it occurs over the period of Christmas Eve and into Christmas morning. There are no links to other King works.

The Dead Zone – Unproduced Screenplay (c.1982)

King's screenplay of his classic 1979 novel *The Dead Zone* is held in Box 2317 of the Special Collections Unit of the Raymond H Fogler Library at the University of Maine, Orono. As Box 2317 is open to the public those interested in this version of the tale may read the screenplay at the Library.

Both this screenplay and the novel are part of both the Maine Street Horror and America Under Siege realities. One of the most interesting aspects of this screenplay is King's decision to move Frank Dodd's killings from his archetypal town, Castle Rock in Maine to the town of Cleaves Mills, also in Maine. By changing the town King was also obliged to change the media name for the killer from the 'Castle Rock Strangler' to 'The Destroyer'. Of course the question remains, why move this part of the action from Castle Rock at all?

In this screenplay, effectively an alternate version of the story, a young man enters a four and a half-year coma following a car accident. When Johnny Smith awoke he found that he had lost his fiancée, Sarah Bracknell, and gained psychic powers. These powers were generated by touching others and resulted in visions. At the request of Sheriff Bannerman of Cleaves Mills, he helped solve the baffling 'Destroyer' murders by revealing that the killer was actually a local deputy, Frank Dodd.

Later, at a political rally, Smith shook hands with Greg Stillson, a politician with presidential aspirations and through a vision realized that Stillson would lead the world to a total holocaust. Smith resolved that to avert this fate he must assassinate Stillson. During the attempt, Stillson held a small boy up as a shield, effectively ending his political career. Johnny was shot dead but his mission had been achieved. Stillson, voted out of the House of Representatives by disgusted voters, committed suicide.

Paul Monash wrote the first two drafts of a screenplay adaptation of *The Dead Zone* for Lorimar Productions. King told *Cinefantastique*, 'Neither of the drafts was particularly successful.' Jeffrey Boam completed his first draft in early November 1980. When Dino De Laurentiis purchased the production rights in 1982, he asked King to write a script but rejected the submission as 'too complex'[74]. It therefore seems likely King wrote the screenplay in 1982, as production on the movie began in January 1983. More drafts were written, including one by Andrei Konchalovsky. Finally, Director David Cronenberg decided to use the screenplay written by Boam. Boam, Cronenberg and Debra Hill reworked it in over a three-day period and that re-work was used for the movie.

The film, released in October 1983, is one of the better King adaptations and www.imdb.com members rate it a very respectable 7.3 out of a possible 10. It starred one of the most talented actors of his generation, Christopher Walken, who played Johnny Smith to perfection; Brooke Adams as Sarah; the great character actor Herbert Lom as Sam Weizak; *The West Wing's* Martin Sheen brilliantly portrayed Stillson; and *Picket Fence's* Tom Skerritt played Sheriff George Bannerman (Skerritt would later appear in *Desperation*). The movie was released on DVD in 2000. The character of Johnny Smith was also used as the basis for the USA Network television series *The Dead Zone* from 2002 through 2007.

As an adaptation of the novel there are many links from King's screenplay to his other fiction. King also revised details about certain characters and places in the script.

The hero, Johnny Smith is also mentioned in *Needful Things, The Tommyknockers* and *Cujo*. The villain, Greg Stillson is also mentioned in *The Tommyknockers* and *The Night Flier* (but only the *Prime Evil* version). George Bannerman also appears or is mentioned in *The Body* (although it is doubtful this is the same man), *Cujo, Needful Things, The Dark Half* and *The Sun Dog*.

In this script, Deputy Frank Dodd's mother Henrietta was shot dead by George Bannerman on 17 November 1975 after she tried to kill Smith. However, in *Cujo* she suffered a stroke and died shortly after Dodd killed himself (no information about her demise was provided in the novel of *The Dead Zone*, although this source did tell us she was ill with hypertension, thyroid problems and a semi-diabetic condition). She was also the busybody gossip who was on the same party line as the Bruckners in *Gramma*.

Annie Dussault was the sister of journalist Roger Dussault. In the novel she died of a heart attack aged 27 as a result of drugs. In this screenplay she jumped to her death.

Dodd's victims, Alma Frechette and Mary Kate Hendrasen, are also mentioned in *Cujo*. Dr. Sam Weizak is mentioned in passing in King's screenplay for *Cat's Eye*. Smith tutored Chuck Chatsworth and his father Roger agreed that Chuck could attend Stovington Prep. Jack Torrance was dismissed from his teaching position at that school in *The Shining*.

Although King moved the town in which Dodd committed his killings from Castle Rock to Cleaves Mills (both in the state of Maine), Castle Rock was mentioned, when two boys found one of Dodd's victims in 'a gravel pit near Castle Rock'. Castle Rock appears in many King works of fiction. It is the setting for *The Body, Cujo, Gramma,* the *Nightmares and Dreamscapes* version of *It Grows on You, The Man in the Black Suit, Mrs. Todd's Shortcut, Needful Things,* the *Skeleton Crew* version of *Nona, Premium Harmony, The Sun Dog* and *Uncle Otto's Truck*. It also receives considerable mention in *Bag of Bones, The Dark Half, Squad D* and *The Huffman Story*; and is mentioned in *Creepshow, Dreamcatcher, Gerald's Game, The Girl Who Loved Tom Gordon, The Lonesome Death of Jordy Verrill, Riding the Bullet, Rita Hayworth and Shawshank Redemption, Under the Dome* and the *Uncut* version of *The Stand*.

In the novel Johnny Smith was living in the town of Cleaves Mills, Maine at the time of his car accident. In the screenplay, as previously mentioned, Cleaves Mills is the location of Dodd's murders. The town is mentioned in passing in *It* and also appears in *The Tommyknockers* (Roberta Anderson started writing *Hangtown* there). The only other time King uses the town name of Cleaves Mills is in the short story *Weeds*, in which Cleaves Mills, New Hampshire is the nearest town to Jordy Verrill's farm. In the revised version of that story, *The Lonesome Death of Jordy Verrill*, King changes the nearby town to Castle Rock, Maine – confused yet?

By moving Dodd and the killings to Cleaves Mills, King also had to move Sheriff George Bannerman and Dodd to the Cleaves Mills Sheriff's Department. The bandstand, such a symbol of fear and death in the novel, is also part of this new town. King adds a twist in that not only did Dodd kill Alma Frechette there but he also later watched Walt and Sarah Hazlett's wedding from it! Delivered well, that scene would likely have chilled movie viewers to the core.

Another town that receives a name change is Trimbull, New Hampshire. In the novel Johnny Smith attended Stillson's rally in this town and shook his hand, receiving the vision that would lead him to attempt to the assassination attempt. In the screenplay this town is called Timmons, New Hampshire.

In the novel Sarah and Johnny visited the Esty fair but in the screenplay this becomes the Cleaves Mills carnival or County Fair. In an emotional closing scene to the script, Sarah Hazlett visited the midway at the Cleaves Mills County Fair, which was being dismantled. While there, she thought she heard John Smith's voice on the wind.

King broadly keeps to the timelines of the original novel. However, in the novel Johnny awoke on 17 May 1975 but in the screenplay on the 1st of that month. In the screenplay Johnny uncovered Dodd as the killer on 17 November 1975 and in the novel exactly a month later on 17 December. In the screenplay it was on 30 July 1976 that Johnny shook hands with Greg Stillson and received the apocalyptic vision. In the novel this event occurred on 19 August 1976. In the novel Cathy's Roadhouse burned on 23 June 1977 but King cut that particular event from the screenplay.

Finally, in the screenplay the assassination attempt took place on 12 November 1976 in the Timmons town hall. In the novel these events occur on 27 January 1979 in the town hall of Jackson, New Hampshire. King excluded the plot for the intervening two years from the screenplay. *The Dead Zone* is a relatively long novel and the excision of these portions to allow for a movie length script would seem to have been a sensible move on the author's part.

In other changes Greg Stillson's life takes a wildly different turn. In the screenplay he had been elected mayor of Ridgeway and a state senator in New Hampshire and, as the Founder of the Great American Hot Dog Party, was elected to Congress as an Independent candidate from New Hampshire's third district in 1976. After he disgraced himself by using a boy as a shield against Smith's gun the US House of Representatives voted 381-0 on 14 August 1977 to expel him. That day he committed suicide by carbon monoxide poisoning in his Lincoln. In the novel the party he formed was the America Now Party and there is no formal resolution to his political career, although it is clearly finished. No information is given as to his future and certainly not a suicide. Apparently, King took the opportunity of this screenplay to provide closure in the matter of Greg Stillson and may even have felt in retrospect that such a conclusion should have been included in the novel.

As to Frank Dodd, King simplified the list of his victims from those in the novel, namely Alma Frechette (12 November 1970), Pauline Toothaker (17 November 1971), Cheryl Moody (16 December 1971), Carol Dunbarger (November 1974), Etta Ringgold (about 29 October 1975), Mary Kate Hendrasen (17 December 1975) and probably Ann Simons (12 November 1972) in Colorado. The screenplay victims were Alma Frechette (29 October 1970), Mary Kate Hendrasen (mid-October 1975) and at least two unnamed women. In the screenplay version of their lives Alma and Mary Kate had even shorter lives!

While it is disappointing that De Laurentiis and Cronenberg chose to ignore King's script the actual movie was a box office and critical success even without the original author's script. Made on a budget of $7 million, it took nearly $21 million at the box office.

Fortunately, even though most King fans cannot read this screenplay, they do have both the novel, one of King's best, and an excellent movie with which to entertain themselves.

THE LIFE AND TIMES OF JOHN SMITH

The son of Herb and Vera, John was born sometime between January 1946 and December 1948 (probably in 1947). In January 1953 he fell on the ice at Runaround Pond in Durham, Maine (*note: the town in which King grew up and in which there is an actual Runaround Pond*) and blacked out. He graduated from high school as salutatorian and then from University of Maine at Orono in 1970 (*note: the same year King graduated that very institution*) and began a career as a teacher at Cleaves Mills High School in October that year. He was tall with dark hair that started graying in 1976. Originally from Pownal, he was living at 110 North Main Street at Cleaves Mills and went on a date with his girlfriend, Sarah Bracknell, to the Esty Fair on 29 October 1970 where he had a great run of luck on the Wheel of Fortune. Early the next morning he was critically injured in a car accident and was left in a coma. He woke on 17 May 1975 and had a number of operations on his legs and neck, these left scars. John had developed psychic powers involving touch while comatose and a number of public and private incidents demonstrated this after his recovery. After leaving hospital in August 1975 he moved back to his father's home in Pownal where he made love to Sarah Hazlett (now married) once that October. In December 1975, using his powers, he unmasked Frank Dodd as the 'Castle Rock Strangler'. In mid-February 1976 he moved to Kittery and took a job as a short order cook before taking another in May 1976 tutoring Chuck Chatsworth in New Hampshire. During the 1976 election campaign John formed the habit of meeting various candidates and visiting their rallies, including Greg Stillson's. After predicting a fire at Cathy's Roadhouse in June 1977, thereby saving many lives, John fled the resulting publicity and moved via Florida to Phoenix, Arizona. He worked for the Phoenix Public Works Department in 1977 and 1978 before leaving for New Hampshire just after Christmas 1978. In late January 1979 he attempted to assassinate Greg Stillson, the Congressman from whom he had received a doomsday vision when shaking his hand in 1976. John was killed in the unsuccessful attempt and was buried at 'The Birches' cemetery.

Source: *The Dead Zone* novel

> The son of Herb and Vera, a teacher, he was the boyfriend of Sarah Bracknell, whom he intended to marry. On the night of 29 October 1970 he was seriously injured in a car accident and left in a coma. He awoke in May 1975 to find Sarah married to another man. He appeared to have developed a psychic ability with which he could intermittently see things that were happening elsewhere or that would happen. In November 1975, using these powers, he unmasked Frank Dodd as the Cleaves Mills 'Destroyer'. In mid-1976 he tutored Chuck Chatsworth. He met Greg Stillson at a 1976 political rally and had a vision of Stillson causing a nuclear war. After grappling with the issue he determined to kill Stillson and attempted to do so in Timmons, New Hampshire on 12 December 1976 but was shot during the attempt. Stillson was unhurt but disgraced himself and his career was at end. Smith, lying mortally wounded, was able to hold Stillson's hand and confirm this new future.
>
> Source: *The Dead Zone* unproduced screenplay

Desperation – Screenplay (Undated)

King adapted his novel *Desperation* in a screenplay, a copy of which is held in Box 2289 of the Special Collections Unit of the Raymond H Fogler Library at the University of Maine, Orono. As this Box is available to the public those interested may read the 133-page script at the Library.

A later version of King's screenplay was produced for a 23 May 2006 premiere on the US ABC-TV network. King did three feature drafts before Mick Garris put the script into television format. Garris directed the mini-series versions of *The Stand* and *The Shining* and the films *Sleepwalkers, Quicksilver Highway* and *Riding the Bullet.* ABC has a long relationship with King, having delivered *The Stand, The Shining, Storm of the Century, Rose Red* and *Kingdom Hospital* to viewing audiences.

The telemovie starred Ron Perlman as Collie Entragian; Tom Skerritt as John Edward Marinville; Steven Weber[75] as Steve Ames; and Charles Durning as Tom Billingsley. It rates below this author's estimation with members of www.imdb.com giving it only 5.2 out of a possible 10. The DVD was released in 2006.

According to King *Desperation* addresses '...the question of why, if there is a God, such terrible things happen' (King also classifies *The Stand* and *The Green Mile* as other of his works on this theme).[76] Michael Collings states the novel reflects '...King at his best, with incremental horrors, children (and adults) in peril, monsters in human form, and a quintessential quasi-alien entity devoted to evil. It is significant that here King approaches making explicit the spiritual elements implicit in the conclusion to novels such as *Needful Things*;

overt horror gives way to an understated sense of restitution and restoration.'[77] Stephen Spignesi describes *Desperation* as '…a sprawling tale of a band of … pilgrims? … who come face to face with a minion of a possibly eternal evil and who must depend on the wisdom and God-centeredness of a young boy who just may have a direct line to the Big Guy himself.'[78]

The screenplay version of this story[79] concerns an ancient creature, which is released from its tomb. Desperation was a small mining town in the Nevada Desert and most of the inhabitants had been brutally murdered by the town policeman, whose body had been taken over by the evil entity. In the aftermath the cop, Collie Entragian, arrested and brought passing travellers into town. The victims soon realized that they were nothing more than future hosts for the entity, known as Tak, which had escaped from an old mine shaft accidentally re-opened at the China Pit, a nearby mining site. Tak had to keep new hosts available because it quickly wore out its victims' bodies.

In a flashback we learn that Chinese miners had uncovered Tak at the Rattlesnake # 2 mine in Desperation in the 1850s. Exposed to Tak the Chinese turned on and killed their white overseers and each other. A cave-in shortly thereafter trapped Tak once more.

David Carver, a devoutly religious schoolboy and one of Tak's modern-day captives escaped from his cell. Carver felt he had direct contact with God following a series of promises he had made after one of his friends was seriously injured in a car accident. David released the other prisoners and the group retrieved weapons, heading to the Chinese Theater to plan their next move. A local, Tom Billingsley, related the history of the mine to the others but was then savaged and mortally wounded by a cougar. Tak, it turned out, had the ability to control all manner of creatures.

David then led the survivors out to the mine. Meanwhile Tak, having exhausted the body of Entragian, entered the body of David's mother Ellen but found it quickly failed and next chased Mary Jackson. He failed to secure her body and was forced to enter a buzzard.

The group reached the China Pit and set explosives. The buzzard attacked and killed David's father. John Marinville, an author with a checkered past, went into the shaft on a suicide mission and set off the explosion, once again sealing Tak in its rocky tomb. King specifically notes that David Carver's faith was not destroyed by the deaths of his entire family and the events in Desperation.

No timelines are given for the modern day action in the screenplay but the 'flashback' section is set in the 1850s. In the novel the modern timeline is July of 1995 and the events with the Chinese miners occurred on 21 September 1859.

We are treated with a number of links to King's other fictional works. For instance, Collie Entragian had writer John Marinville sign an autograph for him as 'Your Number One Fan'. This is, of course, how Annie Wilkes described herself to *her* captive Paul Sheldon in *Misery*. And, when Steve Ames saw the dead bodies in the mining company lab he stopped, '...rubbing his mouth like Jack Torrance.' Of course this reference is to the lead character of *The Shining*. Torrance is also a character in *Before the Play*, the prequel to the classic haunted hotel novel.

Cynthia Smith, one of those terrorized by Tak in Desperation, also appears in *Rose Madder*, in which Norman Daniels attacked her at the Daughters and Sisters picnic. The screenplay also notes that Cynthia reads Dean Koontz. Koontz is a best-selling horror writer and is sometimes described as 'the poor man's Stephen King.'

Of course, both the novel and screenplay versions of *Desperation* link with the altered reality novel *The Regulators*, in which 40-50 Chinese miners were killed when the Rattlesnake Number One mine in Desperation, Nevada collapsed. The term, 'can tah', important in this story is repeated by the Manni in *The Dark Tower VI: Song of Susannah*.

One point of interest in both the novel and screenplay is that the writer, John Marinville (played by *The Dead Zone* star Tom Skerritt), was a great Harley fan and was travelling cross-country on one when Entragian captured him. King is known to be a Harley fan and owner. In 1997, shortly after *Desperation* was published, King travelled across Australia on a Harley. A picture of him with the Harley was once proudly displayed in the foyer of his office in Bangor. He followed up with a similar trip in 2006.

Overall the screenplay is faithful to the novel. There are few changes and most of those are minor. For instance, in the novel Peter Jackson was shot dead by Entragian but in the screenplay Entragian broke his neck.

It is unlikely that the screenplay will be published in book format, as was *Storm of the Century*, as the story itself exists in the form of the novel. In the meantime readers can enjoy that novel and also the audiobook version, read by *Misery* and *Dolores Claiborne* actress Kathy Bates.[80]

> **TAK: AN ETERNAL EVIL**
>
> An ancient Evil that lived in an ini* in the old China Pit near Desperation, Nevada. It could inhabit the bodies of people and animals and cause them to do its bidding. Its influence also caused people to grow and degenerate rapidly, causing death in a matter of hours or days. John Marinville may have killed it when he blew up the ini in July 1995.
> Source: *Desperation* (Novel)
> A creature that took over the bodies of an assay crew member, Entragian (using him to kill most of the inhabitants of Desperation), and Ellen Carver; intended to take over Mary Jackson but was foiled; and lastly took over a buzzard. It spoke the Language of the Unformed and controlled animals by using can tahs. Tom Billingsley speculated it was a 'waisin' or earth spirit that had nearly escaped 150 years earlier, during mining of the China Pit near Desperation, Nevada. At that time, when it sensed the outside world within its reach, it projected reddish smoke that drove those who came in contact crazy. John Marinville trapped it forever by blowing up the ini.
> Source: *Desperation* (Unproduced Screenplay)
> An evil entity, it took over an autistic boy, Seth Garin in the small town of Wentworth, Ohio. It fed on death and hurt of the people around it. Seth eventually outsmarted it and it died on 15 July 1996 because it had no host.
> Source: *The Regulators*
> ini: A cupped hole in the floor of an isolated part of the China Pit in front of the pirin moh ('a weird Lovecraftian building'), it is lined with hooks of protruding stone and can tahs (stone statues of animals) are littered around it. Tak lived there and David Carver thought it went through into another dimension. The hole at the bottom of it the ini is no more than an inch across.

Dolan's Cadillac – Unproduced Screenplay (Undated)

Box 1012 at the Special Collections Unit of the Raymond H Fogler Library at the University of Maine, Orono contains five pages of a screenplay by Stephen King, adapting his short story *Dolan's Cadillac*. It is unclear when this screenplay was written and there are only five pages, representing the initial action in the story, a montage marking the passage of seven years and the very beginning of the aftermath to that initial action. As Box 1012 is a public box those interested may read these few pages at the Library.

Dolan's Cadillac was originally serialized in the *Castle Rock* newsletter (edited initially by Stephanie Leonard and later by Christopher Spruce) over five issues, from February to June 1985. King revised it for publication in a Limited Edition by Lord John Press in 1989 and that revision appeared in the 1993 collection, *Nightmares and Dreamscapes*.

The following is a short summary of the partial screenplay. In this America Under Siege tale a woman starts her vehicle and is instantly killed by a car bomb. It is 1968 and Elizabeth Robinson, who had previously seen something (just what is not revealed), had been interviewed by the police. Shortly afterward a mobster, Jim Dolan, had her killed.

By 1975 Elizabeth's widower Dave had spent seven years focused on the man he rightly thought responsible for his wife's death. Although he lived in Las Vegas he had taken another apartment in Los Angeles for his frequent visits there researching Dolan and had also purchased a truck, which he left in that city. The script ends with Dave attending the 1975 Nevada Teachers' Convention with Dana, Dean and Steve.

Not surprisingly, as most of the five pages cover a rolling montage conveying the passage of the seven years, there is only limited information to present. The original story did not specify years for the events; but the gap between Elizabeth's death and Dolan's demise was nine years. For whatever reason King deliberately chose in the screenplay to set the killing in 1968 and there may well have been two more years of movie action before Dolan and his Cadillac reached their demise!

In the montage Dolan is shown with different women in 1968, 1970, 1972 and 1974, with the clear intent of comparing Dolan's continued life, and 'love' life, to Dave Robinson's life without Elizabeth. In 1968 Dolan had black hair but it had turned silvery-white by 1974. Dolan's cars in the montage also change with the years, from a 1968 Cadillac DeVille sedan to a 1970 Fleetwood Brougham, a 1972 Fleetwood limousine and finally to a 1974 silver-white short stretch limo.

Noted King expert Stephen Spignesi states *Dolan's Cadillac* is '…King's modern update of Poe's 1846 short story "The Cask of Amontillado".'[81] The leading King academic, Michael Collings also acknowledges King's debt to Edgar Allen Poe saying, 'King updates his story, amplifying his protagonist's motivation and suffering.'[82] Tyson Blue, another leading King critic, wrote a particularly incisive review of the story in his *The Unseen King*[83]. While readers will find this out-of-print book difficult to find that particular criticism alone would make the effort worthwhile.

For those whose memory of the original short story has dimmed the following is a summary of the *Nightmares and Dreamscapes* version.

In which a man takes revenge for the death of his wife. Elizabeth Robinson, a first grade teacher was in the wrong place at the wrong time and witnessed a crime committed by James Dolan. She agreed to testify against him but before she could was killed when her car was blown up. Her husband then began watching Dolan's movements in Las Vegas and California and planning his revenge. Nine years after Elizabeth's death he got the opportunity to deliver on a plan. He secured a summer job working with a highway repair gang. On a long weekend when the roadworks were halted for the holiday, Robinson dug a large hole and created a false detour. Dolan, on one of his regular trips to the West Coast in his Cadillac, crashed into the hole. Robinson then filled the hole, complete with Dolan and Cadillac, but not before taunting Dolan with the possibility that he might just let him out. Robinson returns to his normal life.

The key change from King's original story is the acquisition of a first name by Robinson. In both versions of the short story King does not provide it, although Harvey Blocker, his foreman at the Las Vegas Streets and Highway Department gave him the nickname 'Bubba'.

Elizabeth's car in the script was a 1965 Chevrolet, whereas in the stories it was a 1968 Chevrolet. This change is presumably because it was unlikely a teacher would have a brand new model car in the 1968 setting of the movie.

There are no links from this screenplay, or indeed the other versions of *Dolan's Cadillac* to any other King work of fiction. In many ways this is a relatively unusual piece of King fiction, a tale of cold revenge in the crime genre into which King delves but rarely (for instance, *The Fifth Quarter*, *The Wedding Gig* and *Man with a Belly*.) However, *Full Dark, No Stars* (2010) is said to be a collection of stories about retribution.

Dolan's Cadillac was finally adapted as a direct-to-DVD in 2009 (2010 in the United States), starring Christian Slater and produced from Richard Dooling's screenplay. Dooling also wrote *Kingdom Hospital*. It received poor reviews and a rating of 5.7 out of a possible 10 from members of www.imdb.com.

The Drum Stories (1965, 1966)

In researching *The Complete Guide to the Works of Stephen King* in Bangor, Maine in December 2002 I met Stu Tinker, the superb proprietor of the specialist King bookshop, Betts Bookstore[84]. Tinker mentioned he had heard from a collector that an unknown story from King's high school days had come onto the market. After some months of research I made contact with Kerry Johnson, who provided me with a copy and the provenance of *Code Name: Mousetrap*.

One of King's earliest published writings, *Code Name: Mousetrap* was printed in the Lisbon High school newspaper, *The Drum*, for 27 October 1965. King was a senior that year and had been on the newspaper staff for three years (*see feature panel*). That academic year Ms. Prudence Grant was in her first year of teaching and her extra-curricular assignment was to be advisor to *The Drum*. Ms. Grant retired in June 2002 and while cleaning her files ran across some original copies of the newspaper, including the one containing *Code Name: Mousetrap*. Kerry Johnson purchased it from her through eBay. Ms. Grant provided Johnson with excellent background information and he also corroborated the background with another teacher from the school.

In a letter to Johnson, dated 15 October 2002, Ms. Grant wrote: 'I have the copies after all these years because I'm something of a packrat and had not cleaned those things out of my file cabinet. I found them again when I cleaned out my papers because I retired in June 2002.'

In an interview with Ray Routhier of the Portland, Maine *Press-Herald* Ms. Grant said that while she never had King in class she remembered him working for the paper. She recalled him as "a goofy guy who went on to do far, far, far better than any of us."

When the story's existence was initially revealed I thought this '...was King's only piece of fiction in the paper.' I was surprised but delighted when shortly thereafter another collector, Bob Jackson, advised he had bought a different copy of *The Drum* from Ms. Grant, also over eBay. Jackson also provided a copy and the provenance of this story, *The 43rd Dream*. That edition of *The Drum* was dated 29 January 1966.

In total Grant sold four copies of the 27 October 1965 issue, containing *Code Name: Mousetrap* for between $400 and $500. The single copy of *The 43rd Dream* went for $800! In 2009 I had the joy of meeting Ms. Grant, when lecturing to the Lisbon (Maine) Historical Society, on the impacts of Lisbon and Durham on King's fiction. Along with Ms. Grant and another of King's teacher, Merton Ricker, I also got to meet and learn from many of those who attended school with the boy who would become one of the world's best-selling, and best loved authors. They, and the officials of the Society, were gracious in their hospitality.

Each story was published as written by 'Steve King'. The first full details of these stories were then released to the public in May 2003, in *The Complete Guide* in May 2003. I provided copies of the stories to King's office, as it was my understanding Steve no longer had a copy. Marsha DeFilippo, King's personal assistant, later reported King said, '...he had great fun writing them.' The author was 'news editor' of *The Drum* in 1963-64 (the first issue – Vol 1, No 1 is dated November 27, 1963); 'Editor-In-Chief' in 1964-65; and, as a senior, was credited for 'Copy' in 1965-66.

In 2009 King allowed reproduction of *The 43rd Dream*, from collector Bob Jackson's copy, in *The Stephen King Illustrated Companion* by Bev Vincent. *Code Name: Mousetrap* has not been published outside the original *The Drum*. Copies do not circulate. It is very unlikely that readers or researchers will be able to obtain a copy unless the original eBay purchaser resells their copy or further copies turn up in file cabinets or attics somewhere in Maine.

Code Name: Mousetrap

In this America Under Siege story a man breaks into a supermarket with a recently installed burglar alarm. The burglar, Kelly, becomes somewhat wary after reading 'B.J. Burgular Alarms' (*sic*) had installed a new burglar (also misspelt 'burgular') alarm. The bottom of the note read: 'Code Name: MOUSE-TRAP'. It was a very large store, 'Twenty cash-registers, full of Friday night receipts, faced him blankly.' Suddenly, a buzzer sounded and the lights came up, causing Kelly to run for it.

With that, '…the soup display began to move. It clattered toward him, spilling individual cans, and revealing the glitter of stainless steel beneath.' One can clearly see King in those last words! 'Now, he could clearly see the shape of the Mousetrap. Three limber-jointed steel tentacles snaked out at him. An insectivorous row of TV eyes stared at him. In the silence of the store, he could actually hear the clitter of the relays in its electronic brain.'

As he ran from this creature, he '…could not believe what he saw – and when he did, he let out a soft moan' - dozens of beefsteaks were rolling over the meat counter and coming after him along with a '…rump roast with two glittering antenna…' that '…crashed into his leg and clutched him with bright steel claws. 98 cents a pound, he thought widly (*sic*), my rump roast certainly isn't as cheap as it use (*sic*) to be.' Dodging a 'V-formation of sirloins' and a shopping cart, 'waving tentacles like a wild Medusa on wheels' Kelly crashed through a plate-glass window and onto the pavement.

'His arms dripped blood, and he picked jagged shards of glass out of them numbly. But I made it, he thought, getting up. I made it! And then the parking-meter grabbed him.' No timelines are given in this story but clearly the burglary occurred on a Friday night, as the cash registers were 'full of Friday night receipts'.

While not directly linked to any other King work this story has foreshadowing elements for such future stories as *Trucks*, *Maximum Overdrive* and *The Mangler*, where technology suddenly becomes animate, and dangerous. This is one of King's most original horror themes and, apparently, an old favorite!

King had just turned 18 when this story was published and it shows a growing level of maturity, compared to *People, Places and Things*, written two to five years earlier. It is similar in maturity to *The Aftermath* (see the separate chapter in this book), written in 1963.

The 43rd Dream

In this story a high school student relates his dream. The narrator was in his Batmobile when approached by a bum who said, '…you shoot your high school teachers and forbid your birds to fly.' Quickly, a cross-eyed cop accused the narrator of looking like John Wilkes Booth and a crowd formed, beating the narrator with hula-hoops. Running to a bar he was served by Jack the Ripper before stealing money from a blind, fat card dealer who then hit him with his cane.

The narrator then '…ran down the kitchen drain…' and came up in Lisbon High, '…where a friendly rat said I could,' and attended his favorite class, '…capitalistic Basket-Weaving', taught by Captain Hook.

After being sent to detention hall the narrator ran into a man in uniform, '…I think it was Captain Bligh', who wanted to swing him from the yardarm, '…we wanted Pontius Pilate, but you look enough like him.' Just then Brigette (*sic*) Bardot arrived and the narrator awoke, '…it was just going through my mind, I wouldn't knock another dream, but not quite the same kind.'

One of the more entertaining aspects of this story is its constant use of rhyme. ' "I'm goin' outta my head!" This girl began to scream. Her stockings were red and her makeup sky-blue green.' Or: 'I said, "I need a drink, I'm feeling rather sick." He poured it but wanted to know just where was my hockey stick.'

This use of rhyme has caused some experts to speculate *The 43rd Dream* is actually a poem, but the layout and tone militate against that view. It is classified as a New Worlds short story.

The narrator, who wakes from his/her dreams of various matters wishing for a different dream next time, is apparently a student at Lisbon High, and male (after all, the cop likened the person to John Wilkes Booth). It is not too much of a stretch to imagine 'him' as Steve King, Lisbon High School senior. No timelines are given.

While there are no links to other King works of fiction the theme of shooting high school teachers would reappear in one of King's more controversial works, the Bachman novel *Rage*. Of course, in today's society rather than being a throw-away line or a sign of some teenage angst a student might be arrested for writing '…you shoot your high school teachers.'

The reference to forbidding 'your birds' to fly very interesting indeed (see *The Dark Half*) and the use of drains as a method of travel recurs in *It*. It seems that in this short story, written in early 1966, some of King's later ideas already lay in his fertile imagination, waiting to be translated into print.

KING, *THE DRUM* AND *THE VILLAGE VOMIT*

King tells of his efforts as the editor of *The Drum* and his mis-adventure with a satirical equivalent in his non-fiction work, *On Writing*.

'…during my sophomore year at Lisbon High I became editor of our school newspaper, *The Drum*. I don't recall being given any choice in this matter; I think I was simply appointed. *The Drum* did not prosper under my editorship. Then as now, I tend to go through periods of idleness followed by periods of workaholic frenzy. In the school year 1963–1964, *The Drum* published just one issue, but that one was a monster thicker than the Lisbon Falls telephone book.'

'One night — sick to death of Class Reports, Cheerleading Updates, and some lamebrain's efforts to write a school poem — I created a satiric high school newspaper of my own when I should have been captioning photographs for *The Drum*. What resulted was a four-sheet which I called *The Village Vomit*. The boxed motto in the upper lefthand corner was not "All the News That's Fit to Print" but "All the Shit That Will Stick." That piece of dimwit humor got me into the only real trouble of my high school career. It also led me to the most useful writing lesson I ever got. In typical *Mad* magazine style ("What, me worry?"), I filled the *Vomit* with fictional tidbits about the LHS faculty, using teacher nicknames the student body would immediately recognize.'

Taking the *Vomit* to school for his friends to 'bust a collective gut' over King was caught when a copy was confiscated by one of the teachers lampooned in the paper, on which King had, '… either out of over-weening pride or almost unbelievable naiveté, put my name as Editor in Chief & Grand High Poobah, and at the close of school I was for the second time in my student career summoned to the office on account of something I had written.' One teacher ("Maggot" Margitan) took enormous offence at her description and demanded King be disciplined. 'In the end, Miss Margitan settled for a formal apology and two weeks of detention for the bad boy who had dared call her Maggot in print.'

If it makes any difference, my apology was heartfelt. Miss Margitan really had been hurt by what I wrote, and that much I could understand. I doubt that she hated me — she was probably too busy — but she was the National Honor Society advisor at LHS, and when my name showed up on the candidate list two years later, she vetoed me. The Honor Society did not need boys "of his type," she said. I have come to believe she was right. A boy who once wiped his ass with poison ivy probably doesn't belong in a smart people's club. I haven't trucked much with satire since then.' (Apart from *Slade*, which has a separate chapter in this book, King's

> most notable later attempts at satire are *A Possible Fairy Tale* in a UMO Campus newspaper in May 1970; and *America the Literate* in *Book* magazine for July 2003.)
> As a direct result of this incident the school principal secured King a role as sports reporter for the Lisbon *Enterprise*. That was the first time King was paid to write professionally.

The Dune (2011)

This America Under Siege story appears in the Fall/Winter 2011 issue of *Granta* magazine (an edition devoted to horror). Released on October 27 the issue also featured stories by Roberto Bolaño, Joy Williams and Don DeLillo. *Granta* is a British literary magazine, founded in 1889 and with a reputation for literary integrity. It has published such famous writers as A.A. Milne, Sylvia Plath, Ted Hughes, Bill Bryson, Peter Carey, Gabriel Garcia Marquez, Salman Rushdie and Mario Vargas Llosa. At the time of writing copies of the issue carrying King's story were available from the publisher. It is likely the story will be part of King's next collection, although that may be some years away.

In which Harvey Beecher, a retired Florida Supreme Court Judge tells his lawyer about 'The Dune', a mysterious sand dune on an unnamed island a short distance off the Gulf coastline of his family's property. He'd first visited the island in aged 10 in 1932, after his grandfather, a scoundrel and land speculator who'd created the family fortune, told him Blackbeard's treasure might be buried there. Later, Harvey speculated 'Grampy' had simply been trying to get him out of the way so he could investigate beneath the petticoats of a pretty housemaid.

On that first trip to the island Harvey found the words, 'Robie Ladoosh' written in the Dune, an apparent corruption of the nickname of his best friend Robert LaDoucette. A few days later the boy was killed in a horse-riding accident. As the years passed from time to time Beecher found other names written in the sand, often using the nickname he used for that person, and they invariably died within a short period. Beecher also noticed that even great storms did not destroy the Dune, despite its seaward facing nature and precarious hold on the rocky low lying island.

Travelling to the island became a daily addiction when Harvey was in residence at the family estate. In 1940, he saw the words 'Grampy Beecher' drawn in the sand – two days later his grandfather was dead of a heart attack.

Beecher qualified as a lawyer and was later appointed a County Circuit Judge and finally to the Florida State Supreme Court in Tallahassee – a town he hated, conceding that was possibly because it interfered with his addiction. In 1959 he saw large numbers of names written all over the Dune - shortly afterwards a plane crashed in the Everglades, killing 119 people. Beecher recognized many of the victims' names when they appeared in the newspaper as those he'd seen in the Dune's 'predictions'.

He retired from the Florida Supreme Court in 1993 and returned to full-time residence at the family home and the daily ritual of kayaking out to the island to check if any more names had appeared in the Dune.

One day, when Beecher was 90, he undertook his now very difficult daily trip to the island and saw something else written in the Dune. That evening he had his lawyer, Anthony Weyland, come to the house and update his will. Among the new bequests was $4,000,000 to the Sarasota County Beach and Wildlife Preservation Society on the condition they successfully petitioned the State Legislature to have the island "declared forever wild." He asked Weyland if he was interested to know why he would want to protect such an insignificant island and Weyland, as good lawyers will, considered the question carefully before answering in the affirmative.

So, for the first time in his long life, Beecher told another of his experiences with the Dune. Of course, Weyland was skeptical, but politely listened to the tale and made some pertinent interjections, including advising the Judge to be wary who else he related the story to, considering wills could be challenged on the criterion, "Being of sound mind and body."

When Weyland asked if Beecher had ever tried to warn any of those named in the Dune predicted the Judge explained, 'I felt – I still feel – as if there on that island, there's a hatch that's come ajar. On this side is what we're pleased to call "the real world". On the other is all the machinery of the universe, running at top speed. Only a fool would stick his hand into such machinery in an attempt to stop it.'

At the conclusion of the tale, during which Weyland had consumed a couple of glasses of very fine Scotch, the lawyer was of the view that Judge Beecher had updated his will after seeing his own name in the Dune. Indeed, the Judge has once final revelation to make.

Beecher's comment about the Dune perhaps being a hatch that's come ajar between our world and the 'machinery of the Universe' has undertones reminiscent of such tales as *The Dark Tower* cycle, *Mile 81* and *From a Buick 8*.

It is perhaps the unobtrusive way that King leads the reader to believe that Beecher has seen his own name written in the Dune – his age, his infirmities, the rewriting of his will and so on – that is the class act of this tale. It has the feel of a classic Shirley Jackson story and when the final two sentences are delivered King has the reader entirely in his hands – and therefore totally invested in the ultimate outcome. The conclusion is a small classic and the reader is likely to immediately go over the story again and perhaps again. Reading those final sentences over will lead to full consideration what they *really* mean.

For the Birds (1986)

This 'story' appeared in a collection of stories that all end with a malaproped quotation or popular phrase. The collection also features the writing of Roy Blount, Jr., John D. MacDonald, Peter Schickele, Elmore Leonard, Anna Quindlen, Tony Hillerman and King's partner in writing *The Talisman* and *Black House*, Peter Straub.

King's closing line, 'Bred Any Good Rooks Lately?' became the title of the collection and was the malapropism of 'read any good books lately?' *Bred Any Good Rooks Lately?* was published by Doubleday in 1986 and reprinted in 1990 and 1994. While now out of print the book can be purchased from second hand booksellers and online King resources.

The *very* short story begins with the line, 'Okay, this is a science fiction joke.' Only 235 words in length the tone is very casual, as befits a joke – for instance, when describing how two cases of rook eggs are sent via Concorde King writes, '…they keep the shipping compartment constantly heated and all that stuff.'

In this tale the rooks of London start to become extinct and a solution is sought. As they had been a popular tourist attraction the English decided to breed rooks in Bangor, Maine and re-populate London with them. Each day the English sent a telegram to North American Rook Farms containing the words: 'Bred any good rooks lately?'

King vaguely links this story to his other works by the use of his home town as the place chosen to build the repopulation of London's rooks, with the payment of a guy there, 'at the rate of $50,000 a year to raise rooks'. Despite this link, as King himself classifies the tale as 'science fiction' it is best placed in the New Worlds reality, rather than that of Maine Street Horror.

In a strangely redundant note for the science fiction date of 1995 (even though the story was written in 1986, just as fax machines were beginning to rollout) King has the London City Council send a daily telegram!

The Furnace (2005)

This America Under Siege piece consists of the first two paragraphs of a story, written by King and is headed 'By Stephen King and …' It was first published in a magazine for US school students, *Know Your World Extra* for September 2005 and simultaneously on the parent company's web site, www.weeklyreader.com .

Winning entries were posted weekly on *The Weekly Reader*'s web site. King's assistant, Marsha DeFilippo, confirmed King would not be completing the story; and that the author himself had not named provided the title.

According to the website of the publisher, the Weekly Reader Corporation, *Know Your World Extra* builds reading success and self-esteem by motivating students to read with high-interest, age-appropriate topics. Written for teens and near-teens in a mature tone (never patronizing or childish), at a second-to fourth-grade reading level, KYW Extra includes original plays and dynamic nonfiction content …'. The magazine is distributed 'For teens (and near-teens at a second- to fourth-grade reading level)' by subscription.

In the two paragraphs we learn that a ten-year-old boy, Tommy, has been sent to get firewood from a cellar that he hated. He believes there is something alive behind the furnace ('breathing back there', he 'knew it was watching him') and, as he is getting the wood, the door swings shut and the light goes out.

There are no links to King's other fiction. Copies of the magazine will be very difficult to find (one of King's previous items in a sister magazine, an abridged version of *Battleground* in *Read*, is one of the rarest King pieces). As the existence of *The Furnace* was brought to the attention of the King community during the month of publication some copies of *Know Your World Extra* may have been saved and, if so, are likely to appear for re-sale. A number of King websites published the entire text in September 2005 and, despite some possible copyright issues, they may still appear. Copies of the website post of the story circulate freely.

George D X McArdle (1980s)

George D X McArdle is a partial novel held in Box 2315 at the Special Collections Unit of the Raymond H Fogler Library of the University of Maine at Orono. As this box is unrestricted readers who attend the Library may read the work.

The 123 page single-spaced manuscript is undated, incomplete and there is no indication that King ever continued it. It is likely it was written in the 1980s.

McArdle is a delightful, humorous Western. King has only rarely attempted this genre, most notably in the satirical *Slade* and in one other busted novel (see the *Untitled* entry in *The Lost and Hidden Works* chapter earlier in this book). One suspects he has an underlying desire to dabble in the genre, having incorporated elements of it in other works such as *The Dark Tower*, *The Shotgunners*; and through characters such as Bobbi Anderson (*The Tommyknockers)*, who is a successful Western novelist.

In this America Under Siege tale a young man awakes on the side of a stream in the Old West. Peter Crager's erstwhile partner, Jake Box, had shot him in the head and killed the third member of their gang, which had robbed the Kingston Stage.

George D X McArdle and his 'girls' found Crager lying wounded. McArdle and Crager began to exchange their personal stories while considering robbing the payroll from a B S & M train that would be guarded by the famously vicious Bob Valery, a railroad private detective, along with one hundred soldiers.

McArdle grew up in Boston and attended Harvard, where he was involved in a cheating episode that lead to his being blackballed for employment at most Eastern schools. He did secure a position in Kingsport, Rhode Island and six years later began an affair with a fellow mathematics teacher's wife. The man discovered their love letters and committed suicide. As a result of the scandal McArdle was forced to resign, setting him on the road and a spiral of adventures, including being lost in a swamp, time as a gigolo and various business ventures. He was a gun dealer in Richmond, Virginia prior to the Civil War but a bank manager stole his savings after he dueled with the manager's friend over McArdle's getting the friend's middle-aged and unmarried daughter pregnant. Avoiding the Civil War by going to Canada he returned to America intending to become the world's first progressive Whoremaster. In 1868 he formed a travelling medicine show with Asa Burroughs and, after the death of Burroughs in September 1871, had collected a group of six girls as part of his prostitution plan. They were headed to San Francisco but the axle of their wagon (which also carried a tiger!) had broken and they were contemplating how to fund its replacement when they met Crager.

Peter Crager grew up in Pennsylvania but had to leave the family farm after punching his stepfather, Rev. Floyd Hastings, who was in the process of selling off parts of the property and giving the money to overseas religious missions. Crager went to Kansas before deciding to head South just before the Civil War. He served in the 215th Georgia, including at the Battles of the Wilderness and Gettysburg before being captured shortly before the War ended. He was sent to the brutal Shalagh prison camp where he was severely beaten by guards in March of 1865. After his release he became a petty criminal and robbed the Kingston Stage in 1873. When Jake Box shot him in the head the bullet entered just above an eye and travelled around the skull, exiting at his neck.

The story ends at this point but we can speculate that McArdle and Crager did rob the payroll train as Crager states he was 'nearly hung for the killing of Bob Valery'.

The 'present day' of the story is set in 1873, near Gordon's Stream in the state of Missouri. The back-stories of both McArdle and Crager are deep and full of detail. As most readers will never enjoy reading this partial story further detail follows.

George McArdle was very tall, at 6 foot 6 inches and fat, weighing 350 lbs. An atheist, he had thinning black hair and blue eyes. Born in 1820 in Boston, the third eldest of the nine children of a successful baker, he attended a Boston grammar school, where he was a good student and was accepted into Harvard in 1838. While there he regularly did magic tricks. In his sophomore year he was elected to the elite Harvard society, The Hellenists, even though he did poorly at Greek. He was involved in trying to steal a Greek exam, which resulted in the expulsion of a fellow student, John Reynolds, but he personally escaped punishment. Afterwards Reynolds' father set the son up in a first rate law firm where he did not progress and ran up debts, which the father had to pay off.

McArdle completed his four years at Harvard, graduating 23rd in his class and got his degree. However, he was blackballed for teaching positions across the East by one of the Greek teachers, Young and another student, Stewart, who had failed to have George thrown out after the exam scandal.

In August 1842 McArdle managed to secure a role as maths teacher at the Kingsport Preparatory School for Boys in Rhode Island. In the summer of 1848 he took as a mistress Jennifer Pettigrew, a wife of another teacher at the school. When her husband Norman discovered the affair in August 1849, he committed suicide by hanging, leaving the love letters from McArdle scattered about his body. McArdle collected and burnt them, but was still forced to resign.

He next got a job speechwriting for a US Senator, who died of a heart attack in 1853 while in a brothel with two women. McArdle then became a barker at an Atlanta carnival and medicine show and followed this up by working building a railroad in Georgia. In 1856 he survived being lost in the Okeefenokee swamp when he came across a mute man with no nose or teeth, three toes on his left foot missing and feet and legs covered with running sores. McArdle thought he was a leper. He successfully demanded McArdle have sex with him before he would guide him out of the swamp!

Travelling to Richmond in January 1857 he became a gun merchant and in the summer of that year got Cynthia Devereaux pregnant. As a result her father challenged him to a duel. His opponent had a heart attack just after the shots were fired and died a month later while tongue lashing a nurse!

George then drifted to Canada and became a rancher. In 1860 he went into logging but nearly went broke in 1861. That year he got a job as a bartender at The Velvet Garter in Curser's Mill in Canada, where he was initially exposed to the whoring business. After the Civil War he drifted back to the US intending to become the world's first 'progressive whoremaster'. He next became a pillow vendor on a New York railroad and in 1867 a gigolo to a matron in Port Stephen, New Jersey. In 1868 McArdle invested all his capital with Asa Burroughs and they formed a travelling medicine show. For the purposes of the show he claimed having been Professor of Economics at the University of Connecticut and a magician, with a Ph.D. He displayed the letters BA, LMS (for Legerdemanic Magical Specialties) and DM (Doctor of Magic) on his wagon. He wanted to be the greatest whoremaster the West had ever known and, from September 1871, collected a group of working girls. They then set out for San Francisco to set up shop in that city.

Peter ('Pete') Crager's background was nearly as exciting. Effectively the hero of the tale and its narrator, he was born 1838 in Pride's Corner, Pennsylvania, the youngest of four children. He was six foot one inch tall, with black hair and blue eyes. After his father, a blacksmith and farmer of some means, died of a stroke in 1854 his mother re-married. Peter had to leave town after punching her new husband, more of whom later.

After living for a period in Paterson, Kansas before the Civil War Crager headed South to Georgia in late 1859. He took a clerking job in Waycross and joined the local militia. Stars and Bars flags were everywhere in the South in 1861 and Peter had sex sixty odd times on account of his uniform. Fighting for the Confederacy (one of the rare notable King characters to fight on either side) he was at many battles, including the Wilderness, Chickamauga and Gettysburg, but made no higher than corporal. He was wounded at Stone Mountain, captured there (or in Virginia, the manuscript is a little confused on this point) and sent to the brutal prison camp at Shalagh, Pennsylvania, where he was severely beaten by Negro guards in March 1865.

During the Kingston Stage robbery in 1873 he used the fake name 'Ray' and he had used other names at various times, including 'Peter Kirk'. Immediately after that robbery Jake Box shot Crager and left him for dead.

Crager's stepfather was the Reverend Floyd Hastings (although he is also called Harkness on page five of this admittedly unedited manuscript). A tall thin preacher from Daniels County, Crager's mother took up with him after her husband died. Hastings had blue eyes and slicked back hair and they married in 1855 or 1856. He then began selling parts of the family farm and giving the money to Christian missions. In frustration Peter punched him and had to leave town ahead of the law. Hastings died in 1885. Mrs. Crager/Hastings died of consumption, probably in August 1863, while Peter was serving in the Rebel Army.

The woman who first taught McArdle about whoring was Annabelle Dupray, who had whored in Alberta and Saskatchewan and bore ten children! In 1861 she was a gray-haired, old and dirty whore at The Velvet Garter in Curser's Mills, where McArdle became her friend. Born and raised in a Baptist family in Ohio she had been brutally raped by the boy next door when she was 18. She did not report the rape and he attacked her more and more often, to her slow acceptance. When she fell pregnant he denied responsibility and her parents put her on the road.

As one would expect King produces tremendous back-story for each of McArdle's 'girls'. Crager was attracted to Marianne Franklin. She was shy, 5 foot 9 inches tall, with gray-green eyes. She was 18 and McArdle had recently aborted her unborn child. Another of the girls was Tabitha ('Tabby') Gordon (one wonders how Mrs. King reacted to this character's proposed profession). She had brown hair tied in horsetails and was four month's pregnant. She had decided to take her child to term and then give it up. Helen Grier had given birth to a stillborn child in the second half of 1871 and joined McArdle in early 1872 after working in a St Louis café. Victoria ('Vicky') Johns was middle-sized and had dark black hair. McArdle's group found her delirious at Canner's

Falls, Missouri in mid-1872. On recovering, she could not remember her past.

Amanda Lowell was blonde, with blue eyes. She met McArdle in December 1871 or January 1872 when she was two months pregnant and contemplating suicide. McArdle and Jane Stockholm talked her out of it, McArdle aborted her and she agreed to the offer to join in his prostitution plan. Jane ('Janey') Stockholm was born in 1855. She had milky skin, red hair and played the piano. She fell pregnant in about January 1871 and joined McArdle in September of that year as a servant, initially refusing to consider prostitution. Her son was born in October or November 1871 and was adopted out to a bank teller and his wife in the town of Doogan. At that point she decided to prostitute herself after all.

There are many other interesting characters in both McArdle and Crager's background. For instance, Henry Hyde was another student at Harvard in McArdle's time. He almost certainly raped and murdered a barmaid at The Storm Pig tavern near the college. The tavern was then severely damaged by a fire set in the employee's wing. His father, rich and influential in Boston, probably saved Henry from the consequences of these crimes.

McArdle's lover at Kingsport Preparatory School for Boys was the auburn haired Jennifer ('Jenny') Pettigrew. After a lengthy affair, including the exchange of love letters, her husband and McArdle's fellow maths teacher, Norman discovered the letters. In a deeply melodramatic turn he committed suicide by hanging. Tall, gangling and balding, with a bushy red beard, he was also an unsuccessful writer of short stories and religious verse.

McArdle's partner in the medicine show and tigers was Asa Burroughs. McArdle invested with him in 1868, when Burroughs was making his CorrectAll 'medicine' (McArdle himself had been making and peddling 'African Wonder Liniment and Cargo Elixir'). Their business was called Professor D X McArdle's Pandaemonium Magic Show. Burroughs died of a stroke on 8 September 1871, 20 miles from Westbound, Missouri and was buried the next day by the Warren River. The tigers (reminding the reader only slightly of *The Night of the Tiger*) were Sheenah, a female Bengal who died in the winter of 1870; and Yaphet, a male Bengal with deep emerald eyes. It seems certain King had plot development intentions in mind when he introduced such an exotic animal, caged in McArdle's wagon.

The man who shot Pete Crager and left him for dead was Jake Box. He claimed to have ridden with Quantrill's Raiders during the Civil War. Five foot seven, bow-legged and dirty, he had only six teeth left and most of those were black. He had a salt-and-pepper beard and long, clotted hair. Their partner in the robbery was Frank Carter. A country ploughboy from St Louis, he was six foot tall, blonde, with a walleye and a yuk-yuk laugh that showed he was a little slow. He couldn't 'shoot for shit'. During the Kingston Stage robbery he was shot in the elbow. Back at their hideout Jake Box shot him dead.

Frank Sybert and his wife Katherine were childless and farmed near Paterson, Kansas before the Civil War. He employed Peter Crager for just over a year and gave him many books to read, becoming a surrogate father. He was big and gangling, a fierce drinker but also a kind-hearted man. He was diagnosed with cirrhosis of the liver and died from it in 1858.

The manuscript does not bring us in direct contact with the apparent villain of the piece, Bob Valery. Valery was 'the meanest railroad dick west of the Mississippi'. Big, with red hair, he had lots of freckles and a scar on his neck. He had been head 'prod' on the B S & M railroad since it began in 1865. In 1868 he killed three of four would be train robbers. He beat tramps and others taking a free ride on the railroad. Once he threw a pregnant girl off a freight car causing her to give premature birth. He may have invented the 'frankfort' and was thought to have killed 36 people with one. He was killed during a robbery on the Benton, St Louis and Missouri Railroad ('B S & M') and Peter Crager nearly hung for the crime. This part of the story was not written or is no longer extant.

King provides a description of the 'frankfort', a cruel device used by railroad police in the 1880s and 1890s. It was a piece of pig iron about 6 inches long. A railroad policeman would drop it about six cars up when a train was speeding. It would bounce and slash and injure tramps riding on the rods below the cars, sometimes forcing them under the wheels to their deaths. In that case a railroad 'dick' would notch his frankfort.

Maine receives a mention in the story in that Bowdoin College initially offered McArdle a teacher's position but withdrew it when Young and Stewart blackballed him.

King's personal feelings may be reflected in the character of Sam Backinger. A Confederate, he was wounded and captured near Grand's Hollow, Virginia in late December 1864. He took a bullet in his left arm, which became gangrenous and had to be amputated. He was also shot in the left kneecap. Big and bluff, he laughed a lot but was dangerous. Crager saw him again in Atlanta in 1885, begging in his uniform (much as certain Vietnam vets would after another War).

There is one interesting link from this story to King's other fiction. Quoting Peter Crager in *McArdle*: 'When I was a boy, my poppa gave me a pet rabbit and after I'd gotten used to having it, I forgot to feed it for over a week. When I went into the barn, it was stiff and dead.' Pretty much exactly this happened to Lloyd Henreid as a boy in the *Uncut* version of *The Stand*.

In an amusing incident, one of McArdle's fellow Harvard students and member of The Hellenists read the group an essay disparaging Longfellow and praising Poe. Peabody was so castigated by the silence that followed that he never returned. As he left the room Stewart wittily murmured 'Nevermore'. McArdle's favorite story was Poe's *The Cask of Amontillado* (the inspiration for King's *Dolan's Cadillac*), although George's attempts at writing were poor compared to it.

Having read the manuscript as it exists one is left wondering where the tale was heading. Crager and McArdle's back-stories are amusing and interesting and there is certainly the robbery in which Valery was killed to come, the mystery of the tiger and other elements that may have resulted in an interesting conclusion. The undertone of the story is certainly one of humor, not quite satire, but close to it. One is left wondering if King was simply having fun and realized the end result was likely to be somewhat uncommercial and certainly not what the average King fan would have expected.

Perhaps one day King will complete a 'serious' Western, something which would be of great interest to Constant Readers. He has already acknowledged attempting a second such Western, in 1989 (see one of the *Untitled* tales in The Lost and Hidden Works chapter of this book for more information).

The Glass Floor (1967, 1990)

This America Under Siege story first appeared in *Startling Mystery Stories* for Fall 1967. It has the honor of being the first fiction for which King was paid ($35). He was but twenty when he received the first payment for his years of writing, and the five years of rejection slips he had collected perhaps seemed to shrink a little on its receipt. There is no doubt that King, like most writers, successful or not, had paid his dues. Barely six or seven years of selling short stories and writing novels later King would sell *Carrie* and the rest, as they say, is history.

Nearly a quarter century after its first publication King allowed *The Glass Floor* to be reprinted in the Fall 1990 issue of *Weird Tales*. As to that republication King says in an introduction, after acknowledging that the story was not as bad as he'd thought: 'Darrell Schweitzer, the editor of *Weird Tales®*, invited me to make changes if I wanted to, but I decided that would probably be a bad idea. Except for two or three word-changes and the addition of a paragraph break (which was probably a typographical error in the first place), I've left the tale just as it was. If I really *did* start making changes, the result would be an entirely new story.' (*See the feature panel for more detail of the story's history.*)

In fact the most significant change is toward the end of the story, in which the original read: 'The ladder was still there, stretching up into the darkness and down into the glimmering depths of the mirror'; and was changed to: 'The ladder was still there, stretching up into the glimmering depths of the mirror.' There are other minor changes, for instance the changing of the word 'accursed' to 'cursed'.

Securing either copy of the story is less difficult than it once was. The original publication runs in the hundreds of dollars, on the rare occasion it comes to market. The republication appears more often but has commanded prices near $100.

In the story Charles Wharton visited the home of his brother-in-law, Anthony Reynard, wanting to discover the circumstances of his sister's death. Initially, Reynard refused to give details but was browbeaten into telling Wharton that Janine had fallen from a ladder in a room that was now plastered shut.

Wharton insisted on breaking through the plaster and entering the room. He found it had a glass floor and ceiling and, losing his own perspective and balance while standing on the floor, died. Reynard used a pole to pull the body from the room and asked his housekeeper to bring more plaster.

The closing sentence is a small classic, 'Not for the first time he (Reynard) wondered if there was really a mirror there at all. In the room, a small pool of blood showed on the floor and ceiling, seeming to meet in the center, blood which hung there quietly and one could wait forever for it to drip.'

It is interesting to note that King also used the device of a mirrored floor library in his screenplay for the TV mini-series *Rose Red* over three decades later. In *Rose Red* Bollinger disappeared and apparently hung himself in the Mirror Library of the Rose Red house, which had bookcases lined with books and a mirrored floor. In *The Glass Floor* a library (empty of bookshelves) with a mirrored floor and ceilings was the location of at least two deaths.

Critiquing his own work in the Introduction to the *Weird Tales* version nearly a quarter century later King writes: '…there is at least a token effort to create characters which are more than paper-doll cutouts; Wharton and Reynard are antagonists, but neither is "the good guy" or "the bad guy". The *real* villain is behind that plastered-over door. And I also see an odd echo of "The Library Policeman". That work, a short novel, will be published as part of a collection of short novels called *Four Past Midnight* this fall, and if you read it, I think you'll see what I mean. It was fascinating to me to see the same image coming around again after all this time.'

King then writes: 'Mostly, I'm allowing the story to be republished to send a message to young writers who are out there right now, trying to be published, and collecting rejection slips … The message is simple: you *can* learn, you *can* get better, and you *can* get published. If that little spark is there, someone will probably see it sooner or later, gleaming faintly in the dark. And, if you tend the spark nestled in the kindling, it really can grow into a large, blazing fire. It happened to me, and it started here.'

The genesis of the story, according to King: 'I remember getting the idea for the story, and it just came as the ideas come now – casually, with no flourish of trumpets. I was walking down a dirt road to see a friend, and for no reason at all I began to wonder what it would be like to stand in a room whose floor was a mirror. The image was so intriguing that writing the story became a necessity. It wasn't written for money; it was written so I could *see better*. Of course I did not see it as well as I had hoped; there is still that shortfall between what I hope I will accomplish and what I actually manage. Still, I came away from it with two valuable experiences: a saleable story after five years of rejection slips, and a bit of experience.'

Of course, readers of this book will wonder just what the other stories were that resulted in those five years of rejection slips. Does King still have those stories, tucked away in a box or filing cabinet?

There are two likely errors in the tale, relating to historical periods. At the beginning Wharton approaches Reynard's house, '…craning his neck to get a better look at the Victorian monstrosity his sister had died in. It wasn't a house at all, he reflected, but a mausoleum …' In the next paragraph, 'There was a rose-tinted fanlight over the door, and Wharton could barely make out the date 1770 chiseled into the glass.' Queen Victoria did not ascend the throne until 1839. In 1770 George III was King of England (and still ruled over the Colonies) so the mansion should be described as Georgian or in American terms, Colonial. Later, the house is described as '…this Revolutionary War-vintage crypt.' The American Revolution or War of Independence took place from 1775-1783 but the use of the term 'vintage' mitigates or possibly eliminates an error.

Most King experts refer to the Poe-like nature of this story; also pointing out that it is some way from King's best. For the authors *The Glass Floor* is an entertaining tale, informing of King's development and well worth seeking out and reading. In fact, one of Poe's stories is recalled by Wharton as he first saw the freshly walled-off room: '…a straggling remnant of Poe's "Black Cat" clanged through his mind: "I had walled the monster up within the tomb…"'

While there are no direct links to other King works, the description of the Reynard house reminds the reader of other mysterious houses in the King canon, including Joe Newall's in *It Grows on You*. King wrote of the Reynard home, 'It seemed to grow out of the hill like an outsized, perverted toadstool, all gambrels and gables and jutting, blank-windowed cupolas.'

> **King Sells His First Story**
>
> King's introduction to the *Weird Tales* version relates something of the first time he sold a story – *The Glass Floor*. He says it was written, '…to the best of my recollection, in the summer of 1967, when I was about two months shy of my twentieth birthday. I had been trying for about two years to sell a story to Robert A. W. Lowndes, who edited two horror/fantasy magazines … (*The Magazine of Horror* and *Startling Mystery Stories*) … He had rejected several submissions kindly (one of them, marginally better than "The Glass Floor" was finally published in *The Magazine of Fantasy and Science Fiction* under the title "Night of the Tiger", then accepted this one when I finally got around to submitting it. That first check was for thirty-five dollars. I've cashed many bigger ones since then, but none gave me more satisfaction; someone had finally paid me some real money for something I had found in my head!'
>
> The story King mentions above, *Night of the Tiger*, has never been published in a King collection and is the subject of another chapter of this book.
>
> With 23 years of further writing experience to hand, King continues about *The Glass Floor*: 'The first few pages of the story are clumsy and badly written – clearly the product of an unformed story-teller's mind – but the last bit pays off better than I remembered; there is a genuine *frisson* in what Mr. Wharton finds waiting for him in the East Room. I suppose that's at least part of the reason I agreed to allow it to be reprinted after all these years.'

Golden Years (1991)

The screenplay for the first King television series, *Golden Years*, has never been published but copies circulate within the King community. A copy is also held in Box 2317 at the Special Collections Unit of the Raymond H Fogler Library at the University of Maine at Orono.

The review in this chapter is of King's screenplay for Episodes 1 and 2 from the Final Shooting Script, dated 17 January 1991; and Episodes 3 to 6 from Box 2317. Episode 7 and the Alternate Ending Scripts held in Box 2317 were written by Josef Anderson and as such are not summarized here.

As the series is now available on DVD in an abridged form and with a formalized ending it is important that readers who view that form understand that it varies from the TV series actually shown. For the purposes of this chapter the scripts have been deal with *exactly* as written in the drafts noted above. There are numerous changes from the script to the actual series produced. Also, it should be noted that the drafts in Box 2317 interchange Terrilyn Spann and her father, Otis Spann. Nevertheless, it is important to summarize only what King wrote, not what a director or others changed at a later time, as those variations are no longer 'King'.

The scripts were produced for television as the series *Golden Years* or, as it are sometimes known, *Stephen King's Golden Years*. The first two-hour episode was shown on the American CBS network on 16 July 1991. The remaining episodes screened on 18 and 25 July; and 1, 8, 15 and 22 August, after which the series was cancelled. According to the credits the produced screenplay was by Stephen King for episodes 1 to 5; and Josef Anderson for episodes 6 to 7; with the story by Stephen King for Episodes 6 and 7. The directors for the series were Kenneth Fink, Allen Coulter, Michael Gornick and Stephen Tolkin.

The lead actors were Keith Szarabajka as Harlan Williams; the wonderful character actress Frances Sternhagen (*Cheers*, *E.R.*, *Misery*) as Gina Williams; Felicity Huffman as Terry Spann; Ed Lauter as General Crewes; Stephen Root as Major Moreland; and R D Call as Jude Andrews. King delivered a delightful cameo as a grumpy bus driver. The DVD is available individually as *Golden Years*, released in 2002; and boxed with other titles as the *Stephen King Horror DVD Collection* (1999); or *Stephen King's Golden Years/The Langoliers* (2001).

The original 104-minute pilot and six 52-minute episodes (a total of 6 hours and 56 minutes) were edited down to 236 minutes (3 hours and 56 minutes), including added material for the video/DVD. The slow pace and the questionable acting from a number of the players will disappoint viewers. However, if one can bear these defects the actual storyline is quite interesting. It is clear the series suffered from trying to squeeze too many TV hours out of too little story action. As the series was cancelled midway through its first season it was necessary for the producers to compile an ending for the video/DVD and, to avoid the inevitable let down at the end of some four hours of viewing, it is important to understand this when viewing the final product. Overall, the result is disappointing, as evidenced by www.imdb.com members rating it a poor 5.0 out of a possible 10.

In the storyline a janitor is accidentally exposed to an explosion at a top secret Government facility. The Department of Scientific Affairs (DSA) ran the Gold Series experiments at the Falco Plains Testing Station in New York under the brilliant but erratic Dr. Richard Todhunter. During one of the experiments in October or November 1985 Todhunter ignored protocol. This resulted in an explosion, killing Dr. Charles (or 'Tommy') Jackson and fatally injuring Horace Redding, an intern.

Green dust from the explosion 'infected' Harlan Williams, a 70 year old janitor working at the plant and he started to become younger as a result. When the injured Redding was examined it was noted that about the age of 6 or 8 he had suffered a cut, scarring his left forearm. He'd also had an appendectomy aged about 14; a vasectomy and he had a large napalm burn scar on his lower right calf. Sometime between his death and the examination the later scars, from the burn and the vasectomy, mysteriously disappeared.

The day following the explosion investigators from a secretive government organization known as the Shop interrogated Dr. Todhunter. Jude Andrews was one of the Shop agents and he began to focus on Williams. Andrews began killing those who had witnessed the changes in Redding and Williams. Williams decided to flee with his wife, Gina and they were assisted in the escape by a DSA employee, Terrilyn ('Terry') Spann, who had recently begun a sexual relationship with the head of the Falco Plains facility, General Louis Crewes. Spann wished to expose Todhunter, protect Harlan Williams from capture and Gina Williams from most likely being murdered by Andrews.

Andrews and his men chased Spann and the elderly couple through New York, Pennsylvania and Ohio. They narrowly avoided capture before heading toward Chicago, the home town of the Williams' blind daughter, Francie. At this point King's script ends.

There are a number of interesting links to King's other fiction in this America Under Siege work. Harlan Williams told his wife Gina that the Virginia Shop installation had burned down 'a couple of years ago'. Andrews mentioned that he was aware of the pasting the Shop took over the McGee operation. Spann mentioned that people in the Shop thought John Rainbird was the best field operative ever but she thought Andrews was better. Crewes also mentioned Rainbird. These are all references to events and characters in *Firestarter*.

The Shop is also mentioned in *The Langoliers*, the *Uncut* version of *The Stand* and *The Tommyknockers*. It is interesting that King has not returned to this shadowy and unprincipled government agency since *Golden Years* was written in 1991. One new aspect of the Shop is King's revelation in the script that it has a facility in Maui, likened to a Club Med, where the residents can use beads to buy sex and drugs. The catches are that the place is surrounded by electrified barbed wire and the 'vacation' never ends!

In scene 123 Spann says to Andrews (having previously been told to stop calling him 'Popeye'), 'Really? You want to go for it, Stud City?' *Stud City* is the name of a story that forms part of the novella *The Body* and was originally published as a King short story in the University of Maine literary magazine *Ubris* for Fall 1969.

At one point the Williams and Spann came across an accident on Route 17 West near Zanesville, Ohio and stopped. They were recognized by a State Cop and ended up stealing his cruiser. Zanesville, Ohio is also mentioned as the town in which Chip Coombs and Red McFarland learnt barbering in the unpublished and incomplete King story, *Chip Coombs*.

Falco Plains Testing Station reminds one of The Arrowhead Project in the classic King novella *The Mist*. In that story the Project was on a small preserve near the town border with Stoneham, it was manned with sentries and surrounded by wire. It was only 30 or so miles from Bridgton. Bill Giosti claimed something atomic was going on there while Dick Muehler thought it was simply an agricultural station. It may have been responsible for the Mist's appearance.

Compare that description with the Falco Plains facility, which was a classified location, with signage indicating it was a US Department of Agriculture facility. It was surrounded by an electrified fence and could only be entered via a security station at the facility's road connection to the two-lane county blacktop road. There was a lot of security at the site. Clearly Arrowhead and Falco Plains are birds of a feather.

Golden Years is yet another example of a major theme in King's fiction, the disaster that may be wrought when science, often manipulated by government, spirals out of control. This thread weaves its way through King's writing career, from the early days of *I've Got to Get Away* and *I Was a Teenage Grave Robber* to its sophisticated expressions in *Firestarter* and *The Stand*, through *The Mist* and *Golden Years* to *The End of the Whole Mess* and *Everything's Eventual*.

King had never before mentioned the town of Falco Plains, New York and he has yet to revisit it. It is upstate, near Falco Lake. Among the businesses in town are the Falco Plains Drug Store and the Falco Plains Hotel, where Andrews stayed in Room 422. These and a bar opposite the hotel are all on Main Street. It is unclear where the other businesses mentioned are located. These include the town newspaper, the *Free Democrat*; Hayman's Funeral Home; the hairdresser, Suzy's Unisex Express; and Warren's Market, where the body of Eakins was kept in a meat locker, as the operators of the funeral home could not be contacted (a typical King touch!). Andrews had murdered Eakins, Harlan William's optometrist.

It is most unlikely at this late date that these scripts will ever be published, leaving readers with the choice of travelling to Orono to read the entire set, acquiring one of the copies that circulate in the King community, or viewing the heavily altered DVD version of the series.

As a footnote readers may be interested in King's article *How I Created Golden Years ... and Spooked Dozens of TV Executives* published in *Entertainment Weekly* for 2 August 1991. Spignesi reviews this article[85], noting King had originally intended to write the story of Harlan Williams and The Shop as a novel.

As King's first attempt at series television (the next, *Kingdom Hospital* would not screen for another 13 years) this disappointing production at least stands as an important historical note to King's career.

> **King in *The New Yorker***
>
> *The New Yorker* is a prestigious literary magazine. For a writer whose first short stories were published in pulp and men's magazines King's acceptance by the editors of this magazine must have provided some satisfaction. These are the King works of fiction (they have also carried his non-fiction) published there to date:
>
> | | |
> |---|---|
> | *The Man in the Black Suit (*)* | October 31, 1994 |
> | *That Feeling, You Can Only Say What It Is In French (*)* | June 22 and 29, 1998 |
> | *All That You Love Will Be Carried Away (*)* | January 29, 2001 |
> | *The Death of Jack Hamilton (*)* | December 24, 2001 |
> | *Harvey's Dream (**)* | June 30, 2003 |
> | *Premium Harmony* | November 9, 2009 |
>
> (*) These stories also appear in King's collection, *Everything's Eventual* (2002)
> (**) Appears in King's collection, *Just After Sunset* (2008)

Heroes for Hope Starring the X-Men (1985)

This story, partly by King, appeared in a Marvel Comic, *Heroes for Hope Starring the X-Men*, volume 1 number 1, 1985, published on 1 December. All proceeds from the comic book (cover price $1.50) went to Famine Relief and Recovery in Africa. The total story was written by 18 different authors over 48 pages.

King wrote only pages 10 to 12 inclusive. Berni Wrightson, who has illustrated a number of King projects including *The Dark Tower V: Wolves of the Calla* and *Cycle of the Werewolf* was the 'penciler' for King's section. The 'inker' was Jeff Jones, the 'letterer' Tom Orzechowski and the 'colorist' Christie Scheele.

Chris Claremont, Ann Nocenti, Bernie Wrightson, Jim Starlin and Jim Shooter wrote the overall story. Harlan Ellison wrote the section appearing on pages 22 to 24. Shooter, the Editor in Chief of the book, explained its genesis on the inside back cover:

'One night, a few months ago, artist Jim Starlin called me at home to propose an idea that his friend and fellow artist Bernie Wrightson had suggested to him – that Marvel Comics publish a special issue of The X-Men, a benefit book for famine relief in Africa. Jim and Berni wanted to do the book as a "jam", with many artists and writers contributing, which would enable us to bring a small army of outstanding talents together on the project, making it a real event. I thought it was a great idea. I pitched it to Publisher Mike Hobson and President Jim Galton. They liked it. They agreed that if the creators would donate their work, Marvel would donate all revenue from the book to an appropriate charity organization ... So we began. Jim and Berni recruited the artists. Chris Claremont, the highly-acclaimed regular writer of The X-Men, quickly volunteered to recruit writers ...'

The story is unique in that it is the only time prior to *American Vampire* King had contributed original material to a comic book/story other than his own complete work (*Creepshow*) and is yet another example of King's willingness to try different delivery methods and styles. However, as only a small part of a comic book and pretty not much more than an (effective) diatribe against hunger in the third world, this is perhaps the least interesting of all King's fiction and is often overlooked by both critics and fans.

The comic book is not difficult to find and is generally available from specialist comic book sellers, specialist King booksellers and various on-line sites for under $10.00 per copy.

Only King's part of the story is summarized in this chapter. There are no links to other King works of fiction and no timeline for the story is given. *Note: Kitty's surname was provided in a previous section of the comic and is therefore shown in italics.*

In King's part of the story Kitty *Pryde* leaves her X-Men friends for the kitchen, seeking food. A creature, dressed in a black cowl, grabs her when she gets there, '...the tendons in his thin hands feel as powerful as steel cables.' 'Dry hands settle over her face; its breath is rank with empty death. And yet she has never been so hungry.' Kitty quickly transforms into a ravenous, starving husk.

The creature then offered her a meal of medium rare steak and hot buttered corn, ' "I've spent most of the morning slaving over a hot stove, but *I* don't mind ... you might say I take great *pryde* in my work." Kitty reaches out with shaking hands that have become little more than bones wrapped in skin. Her head swims with the maddening aroma of juicy meat and buttered corn ...' When she accepts, the meal immediately turns into a '...sickening slush of putridity ... maggots squirm in the rotted remains of the sirloin...'

She asks the creature who he is, and he replies, ' "I am misery's maître d', the chef of starvation, waiter to the waifs of the world, hash-slinger to the homeless! I am, my dear, every hungry bloated belly, every dying eye, every picked bone drying in the desert. I'm pestilence and desolation, Kitty ... but my friends just call me *hungry!*"'

The creature then instructs Kitty to 'starve' and Nightcrawler, curious over the length of time Kitty has been away, finds her wasted, but still living, body on the kitchen floor.

Other writers and artists then continue the story, which is part of the New Worlds reality.

Herman Wouk is Still Alive (2011)

This short story was first published in *The Atlantic* magazine for May 2011. In an interview in the same magazine King said this of the tale's provenance, "Every year my son Owen and I have a bet on the NCAA March Madness Tournament, and last year the stakes were that the loser would have to write a story [with a title] the winner gave to him. And I lost. Except I really won, because I got this story that I really like. The title that he gave me for the story was 'Herman Wouk Is Still Alive,' because he'd just a read a piece saying that the guy *was* still alive and he's still writing even though he's 95 or 96 years old."

"So I thought about it a lot—believe me, I thought about it a lot. The tournament was over by the first of April that year, and I mulled that over in my mind until about July. So there was a period of about four months when I thought, "What am I gonna write, what am I gonna write?" Usually you get an idea yourself and then you write a story — you don't think of a title and then write a story to go with it. So it was kind of an ass-backwards kind of thing. And my first thought was to write a story about a guy in a mental asylum who believed that he was keeping certain writers alive by brainpower. And it was going to be kind of a funny story, and there was going to be a list of writers that he'd gotten tired of and that he had allowed to die. Like J. D. Salinger. When he finally decides J. D. Salinger's never going to publish another book, It's kind of like, "Fuck it! Move on!" So I had this idea, and then one day there was a terrible motorcycle crash about a mile from our house and a woman died and about two days later, you know how it is, the crosses started to appear and the flowers and that sort of thing, and I started to think about that, and this is the story that came out of it."

Brenda is part of America's underclass – a single mother with little income and three children. She wins $2,700 on the lottery, pays off her maxed out credit card and arranges a road trip to Mars Hill, Maine from the southern part of the state with her friend Jasmine and her four children. Jasmine is just is desperate and neither perceives a future that can be any different, for them or their children.

As the women and children drive north on I-95 two elderly poets and former lovers, spread a picnic at the Rest Area near Fairfield. As they read poetry to each other Brenda and Jasmine, tired of living in poverty and quiet desperation silently agree to drive their rented van at reckless speed. The vehicle careers off the road at the Rest Area. With no hope there will be survivors the two witnesses run toward the wreck.

In the magazine interview mentioned above King claimed the two women in the van had chosen suicide as a way out: "And then on the other hand you've got these women whose lives are the absolute opposite of poetry. Who are living below the margin, below the radar, this kind of desperate life, and it seems to me that when they look at each other, and take this unspoken decision to just end it, not only for themselves but for their children, who are going to have lives that are just the same – that's almost like a poetic epiphany. That moment. Their deaths are a kind of poem. It's an awful poem, it's an awful decision – nobody's saying that this suicide is the right thing to do — but if you read the story and respond to the story, you can say, 'Well maybe for them at the time it was the only thing to do' ..."

This is King showing once again what a clear eye he has for observing society. He clearly portrays the desperate lives the two women have drifted into and their quiet despair, without judgment. This is another mainstream story that illustrates the horror that lurks in real life.

Readers can purchase back copies of the magazine on the internet and it is very likely the story will appear in King's next collection.

I Was A Teenage Grave Robber (1965) / In A Half-World of Terror (1966)

I Was A Teenage Grave Robber was the first of King's stories to be independently published. It initially appeared in partial form in a mimeographed 'fanzine', *Comics Review*, serialized over three issues in 1965[86]. The fourth and concluding issue never appeared but the remaining text of King's story was posted to at least some subscribers as printed pages and not as part of a magazine. The material that appeared in the third issue (Chapters 5 & 6) was reproduced in *The Stephen King Illustrated Companion* in 2009[87].

The following year the entire story was published in another fanzine, *Stories of Suspense*, as *In A Half-World of Terror*. However, the text was so different as to have almost certainly been printed from a different manuscript. In one major change the lead character's surname is Gerard in the original version and Gerad in the *Stories of Suspense* form. Of course this could simply be an initial error by Wolfman when typing the second version that he had to continue throughout the tale, considering its form as a mimeograph. Both versions of the tale were credited to 'Steve King'.

King tells something of the story's background in *On Writing*: 'The first story I did actually publish was in a horror fanzine issued by Mike Garrett of Birmingham, Alabama (Mike is still around and still in the biz). He published this novella under the title, "In a Half-World of Terror," but I still like my title much better. Mine was "I was a Teen-Age Grave-robber." Super Duper! Pow!'

In fact, King has it wrong. The reprint, in Marvin Wolfman's fanzine, was retitled to *In A Half-World of Terror*. Garrett had actually published the story as *I Was A Teenage Grave Robber*.

Wolfman recalled receiving the manuscript from Jeff Gelb, later Garrett's partner in the *Hot Blood* erotic horror series.[88] In his editorial for that issue of the fanzine Wolfman wrote: 'The next tale of fright, written by Steven King (*sic*), is the third end to this issue. "In A Half-World of Terror" was originally published by Mike Garrett in his fangzine (possible *sic*, probable pun) "Comics Review" under a different title. The title: (gasp, I cringe when I hear this) "I Was A Teenage Grave Robber" certainly didn't do anything for the story, so when (eeech) Wolfman got permission to print the thing, the title was changed ... The story has an atmosphere of the horror movies you see on TV so we tried it."

King is also quoted in Collings' *The Shorter Works of Stephen King* as having said of this story, "One of the things I think has been good for me – really, really good – is that I stayed out, mostly by luck, of that circle of fanzines and fans that club together." To this point Beahm [89] writes, "Unlike H P Lovecraft whose life and writing career were handicapped by his involvement with fanzines – amateur publications done for fun and not profit – the young Stephen King, early in his career, wisely avoided organized fandom ... As King said 'I was never part of a fan network. I never had that kind of a support system.'"

In fact, it seems it was indeed luck that kept King out of fanzines. In material sent with the concluding part of *I Was A Teenage Grave Robber* Garrett told subscribers: 'Steve King and I are going ahead with a new fanzine, *Teen-Zine*. It will feature a variety of things and should be of interest to everyone. So, for further details write either to me or Steve at this address: Steve King / R.F.D. #1, Pownal Maine / Thank you very much for your co-operation.' Having checked with Garrett it can be confirmed this project never proceeded[90].

In Chapter One of the tale the narrator, later revealed as Danny Gerad/Gerard, is in a graveyard with a man called Rankin, digging up the freshly buried body of Daniel Wheatherby ('1899-1962 / He has joined his beloved wife in a better land' – all quotes are from *In A Half-World of Terror* version unless noted). The story starts ominously, 'It was like a nightmare, like some unreal dream that you wake up from the next morning. Only this nightmare was happening.' Danny had been asked to leave school, as he could no longer cover his fees. He and Rankin drove to Steffan Weinbaum's combined home/laboratory with the body. In a flash toward many of King's future scenes of horror, such as the Marsten House (*'Salem's Lot*), and in the great traditions of horror movies, we read: 'And then we came out into the open and I could see it, the huge rambling Victorian mansion that sat on the summit of the steep grade.' Weinbaum himself was in the mold of the archetypal mad scientist, 'tall, rigid... face much like a skull; his eyes were deep-set and the skin was stretched so taughtly over the cheekbones that his flesh was almost transparent.'

In Chapter Two readers learn Gerad/Gerard's parents died in a car crash when he was thirteen. 'It left me an orphan and should have landed me in an orphan's home. But my father's will disclosed the fact that he had left me a substantial sum of money and I was self-reliant ... I was left in the somewhat bizarre role as the sole tenant of my own house. I paid the mortgage ... and tried to stretch a dollar as far as possible.' By the age of eighteen there was little money left, and wanting to attend college, Gerad/Gerard sold the house for $10,000. He was then defrauded of all he had and, after bluffing his way through the first four months of college, was asked to leave for failing to pay his fees. That very day he met Rankin in a bar. 'It was my first experience in a tavern. I had a forged driver's license and I bought enough whiskys (*sic*) to get drunk.' Rankin took him to a secluded booth to discuss an employment proposal. After he offered Gerad/Gerard 'five hundred a job', suspicions were aroused. Against his better judgment, Gerad/Gerard agreed to meet Weinbaum.

In Chapter Three Weinbaum took Gerad/Gerard on a tour of '…the house, including the laboratory.' Weinbaum stared at the boy '…with fixed eyes and once again I felt a blast of icy coldness sweep over me. "I'll put it to you bluntly," he said, "my experiments are too complicated to explain in any detail, but they concern human flesh. Dead human flesh." … He looked like a spider ready to engulf a fly, and this whole house was his web. The sun was striking fire to the west and deep pools of shadows were spreading across the room, hiding his face, but leaving the glittering eyes as they shifted in the creeping darkness.' (Not a bad piece of writing for a teenager). After threatening to leave, Gerad/Gerard found that Weinbaum somehow knew of his college fee problem and finally agreed to working on a 'trial basis … I got the eerie feeling I was talking to the devil himself and I had been tricked into selling my soul.'

Reverting to the night of Wheatherby's disinterment Rankin and 'professor' Weinbaum began to work on the body. Gerad/Gerard left, driving past the cemetery, realizing the 'nightmare' was real.

In Chapter Four as Gerad/Gerard drove on, he came upon a startling scene, 'a panel truck crazily parked' in the middle of the road, 'a girl of about eighteen running toward my car, an older man running after her.' Slamming on the brakes, Gerad/Gerard rolled his car but immediately jumped out of it and ran to the girl, who was being yanked into the truck by the other man. In an awkward piece of dialogue he said to Gerad/Gerard, "You stay out of this, buddy. I'm her legal guardian." He then punched Gerad/Gerard and started to drive off, but not before the boy threw himself onto the van's roof (!) and 'clawed through about five layers of paint to hang on.' Reaching through the driver's window, Gerad/Gerard then caused the truck to crash over a cliff. 'I landed hard, but the rock I landed on was harder.' The driver was dead, but the girl miraculously untouched. After being interviewed by the police, Gerad/Gerard and the girl were taken away in an ambulance. She introduced herself as Vicki Pickford, and told Gerad/Gerard that her guardian was '… a drunkard and all-around crumb … I hated him and I'm glad he's dead.' They agreed to meet for a movie the following day, '…at 7.30'.

In Chapter Five Weinbaum, having read of the crash in the afternoon paper's, rang Gerad/Gerard to check that he had not revealed anything of his nocturnal work to the police, and booked his services again for two nights later. 'The next morning, at 7.30 sharp,' Gerad/Gerard collected Pickford at her motel. This certainly seems like a strange time to go to a movie! They kissed once or twice. 'All in all, a pleasant evening.' (It seems the young King and his 'publishers' could have done with some editorial assistance at this point). The plot takes an even less likely twist when an usher approached them and asked if he was 'Mr Gerad. Daniel Gerad' and stated he had a life or death phone call to take. It was Rankin (who presumably had some form of ESP) demanding Gerad/Gerard come to the Weinbaum house immediately. 'There were sounds of a scuffle, a muffled scream, then a click and the empty dial tone.' Grabbing Pickford, Gerad/Gerard headed immediately for the danger. As they arrived, 'Grim and gaunt against the overcast sky, I could see the house.' Telling his girl to wait in the car, Gerad/Gerard found the laboratory 'empty but ransacked' with bloodstains trailing into the 'darkened garage.' He also noted that several sheeted tanks had been broken and that a 'green liquid' flowed over the floor 'in sticky rivulets'.

Entering the garage, 'the light from the lab threw a golden shaft along the garage floor, but it was next to nothing in the Styngan (*sic*) blackness of the garage. All my childish fears of the dark returned. Once again I entered the realm of terror that only a child can know. I realized that the shadow that leered at me from out of the dark might not be dispelled by bright light.' This passage foreshadows the *Monster in the Closet* section of *Cujo*, *The Boogeyman* and any number of scenes in King's fiction. Realizing he was standing at the top of a stairway Gerad/Gerard retreats to his car.

In Chapter Six Pickford revealed that she had been to the house once before, and told Gerad/Gerard that 'Uncle David' had become her guardian after her parents were killed in a train-wreck four years earlier. He had worked for Weinbaum and she'd brought him his lunch, at midnight. At the time he was appointed guardian David was a kind man, but after losing his job as a night-watchman, he got the job with Weinbaum and became mean, regularly got drunk and she 'watched him decay before my very eyes.' One night he returned home and beat her, causing her to run away, leading to the truck crash, and David's death.

As Pickford told her tale Gerad/Gerard nearly determined to drive away, 'but then a faraway, thin scream …' reached them. After failing to convince Gerad/Gerard not to re-enter the house, Pickford demanded to go with him, a demand Gerad/Gerard rejected. He then went back into the house, down the stairway, and into a short passage. 'Suddenly, a scream, terrible and thick with fear sounded in the darkness ahead of me. It was the sound of terror, the sound of a man confronted with something out of the deepest pits of horror.' Gerad/Gerard stumbled over Rankin's body, 'his eyes staring in glazed horror at the ceiling.' Finding an armed Weinbaum, he and Gerad/Gerard began to argue about the length of time it had taken the boy to arrive. They were cut off '…by a sound that has hounded me through nightmares ever since, a hideous mewling sound, that of some gigantic rat in pain.' (This line reminds the reader of *Graveyard Shift*.) While craning to see what horror was making this sound from within a pit, they both heard a 'wail of terror' and Weinbaum realized Gerad/Gerard had brought a companion.

At the beginning of Chapter Seven the two men returned through the lab, 'the place now swimming in green liquid' as the remaining cases had been broken and were now empty. Gerad/Gerard found the girl's tracks outside and those of something else, 'it was more as if something huge had dragged itself into the woods.' Taking Weinbaum's gun, Gerad/Gerard headed out to rescue the girl, who escaped the shambling creature following her, which seemed to able to climb down a gully, but not back up it, much as Weinbaum had trapped the other creature in the pit. Still, Gerad/Gerard knew a third thing was still on the loose and now heard '…a scream from the lab. And … mewing.'

In Chapter Eight hero and heroine ran back to the lab. Gerad/Gerard alone kept running into the garage and has '…ever since have been glad that Vicki stayed in the lab and was spared the sight that has wakened me from a thousand awful nightmares.' This is what *he* saw: 'A huge, white maggot twisted on the garage floor, holding Weinbaum with its long suckers, raising him towards its dripping, pink mouth from which horrid mewing sounds came. Veins, red and pulsing, showed under its slimy flesh and millions of squirming tiny maggots in the blood vessels, in the skin, even forming a huge eye that stared out at me … In a half-world of terror I fired the revolver again and again.' In his desperation Weinbaum yelled for Gerad/Gerard to set the creature on fire and, using a box of matches, he set the green liquid aflame, '…just as Weinbaum screamed his last. I saw his body through the translucent skin of the creature, still twitching as thousands of maggots leached onto it.' Grabbing his girl, Gerad/Gerard ran for the car as the whole house went up in flames.

In Chapter Nine Gerad/Gerard says, 'There isn't too much left to say.' The fire swept into the woods, destroying fifteen square miles of forest and residential homes. 'I couldn't feel too badly about that fire; I realize that hundreds might have been killed by the gigantic maggot-things …' He drove out to the house after the fire and, with some unlikely good fortune, found Weinbaum's diary in a metal cabinet. This revealed that he had been exposing the dead flesh to 'gamma rays' (that great staple of science fiction) and these had caused the maggots to group. 'Perhaps the radioactive bomb had speeded up the revolution.'

The story ends, 'In a way, I suppose, I assisted in Rankin's death; the flesh of the body whose grave I had robbed had fed perhaps the very creature that had killed him. I live with that thought. But I believe there can be forgiveness. I'm working for it. Or, rather, *we're* working for it. Vicki and I. Together.'

We know the story is set in 1962 (the date of Wheatherby's death) and Weinbaum's lab was in the Belwood District in California. The Crestwood Cemetery, from which Wheatherby was disinterred, is the first cemetery mentioned in King fiction, but certainly not the last! There are no links to King's other fiction.

As King rightly considers the story to be juvenilia it is very unlikely it will ever be republished in any form. Photocopies of *In a Half-World of Terror* circulate within the King community and these would represent the best opportunity for readers to access this America Under Siege Tale.

A single complete set of *Comics Review* material is held in The Murray Collection at Duke University's Rare Book, Manuscript, and Special Collections Library. To the author's knowledge this is one of only two sets of the three issues that exist (another is held by a comics' collector). It seems Duke holds the only extant copy of the concluding material that was to have appeared in Issue #4. The Murray Collection is a huge archive of comics and fanzines collected over 40 years by Edwin and Terry Murray and donated to the Library in 2003.

Not surprisingly, the story is derivative of 1950s B-Grade science fiction/horror movies and has both structural and internal logic problems. However, Spignesi [91] says of it: "…it is an important step forward for the teenaged King. In retrospect, it illustrates just how developed King's storytelling abilities were by the age of eighteen …"

Jhonathan and the Witchs (1993)

King wrote this story in 1956 or 1957, at the age of nine. It was first published over three and a half decades later in *First Words: Earliest Writing from Favorite Contemporary Authors*, edited by Paul Mandelbaum and published by Algonquin Books of Chapel Hill. In the editor's introduction King states he wrote the story for his Aunt Gert, who paid him a quarter for every story he wrote. Unfortunately, there are no other known examples of these stories. Reading this, the earliest of King's writings to come to light, is tremendously interesting (the first page of the manuscript, in King's handwriting, is also reproduced).

The best way to access this story is to purchase *First Words* on the second hand market. Copies sometimes appear at specialist King booksellers or at other on line sellers. Among other authors whose 'First Words' are included in the book are Isaac Asimov and Joyce Carol Oates. It seems very unlikely that King will re-publish it in one of his short story collections.

Due to the fantasy content *Jhonathan and the Witchs* is classified as a New Worlds story. In it the King sets a young man the task of killing three witches (correctly spelt in the manuscript but not in the title), with the penalty for failure to be death. Jhonathan, a cobbler's son, had been sent out into the world by his father to seek his fortune and he intended to start by asking the King for work. But on the way to see the King he met '…a rabbit who was a fairy in disguise' and was being chased by hunters. After Jhonathan saved the rabbit/fairy it granted Jhonathan three wishes. When he could not think of anything the fairy agreed to give him the wishes when he needed them.

When Jhonathan reached the kingdom, '…as luck would have it, the king was in a very bad mood that day. So he vented his mood on Jhonathan.' The King set Jhonathan a reward of 5,000 crowns for killing three witches who lived on '…yonder Mountain…' but the alternative was dire – 'If you cannot do it I will have your head!'

As Jhonathan approached the first witch intending to kill her with a knife, he heard a voice in his ear. This voice explained that each witch could not be killed by certain methods.

The first witch could not be pierced, so he used his first wish: 'She was in a cave near the foot of the mountain, and was a mean looking hag … before the witch could do anything but give him an ugly look, he wished she should be smothered. And Lo! It was done.' The second witch could not be pierced or smothered, so he wished her crushed, 'And before the witch could do anything but give him an ugly look, he had wished her crushed. And Lo! It was done.'

The final witch could not be pierced or smothered and was invisible, yet he still had to kill her to receive his reward so '…he was plagued with thoughts of how? Then he hit upon a wonderful plan … He waited outside the entrance until he heard the witches (*sic*) footsteps. He picked up a couple of big rocks and wished the witch a normal woman and 'Lo! She became visible and then Jhonathan struck her head with the rocks he had.'

'Jhonathan collected his 5,000 crowns and he and his father lived happily ever after'.

The kingdom remained unnamed, the timeline is not given and there are no links to other King works, although the fantasy aspects of Kingdoms and witches make appearances in such later King works as *Eyes of the Dragon, The King Family and the Wicked Witch* and the Dark Tower Cycle.

Basically *Jhonathan and the Witchs* is a Grimm-like fairy tale, of the sort read and loved by young children. In his development as a writer, we see King attempting his own fairy tale at the tender age of nine, even using the time honored opening, 'Once upon a time…' While simplistic, clearly written by a juvenile and short at just over 500 words, there are signs of a sophisticated vocabulary and the ability to organize a fairly consistent story. One last interesting aspect is King's spelling of Jhonathan, one wonders if it was a spelling mistake at the time or an intentional device?

Keyholes (c.1984)

A spiral bound notebook donated by King was auctioned on 1 May 1988 to benefit the American Repertory Theater. The notebook contained the fragmentary story that has become known as *Keyholes*, as well as notes by King to himself and Tabitha King, a handwritten revision of *Silver Bullet* and a series of algebraic equations solved in King's handwriting!

Keyholes appears only as a story fragment in the notebook, handwritten by King over 2 ½ pages and totaling only 768 words. Copies of the pages circulate in the King community. The story was apparently written in early 1984, prior to the release of *Silver Bullet* in 1985.

According to Spignesi[92] the notebook has since changed hands 'several times' on the secondary market for large sums of money.

From only two and one half pages of notebook manuscript there is little to be said about this America Under Siege tale. In it a man visits a psychiatrist. Michael Briggs, a construction worker, was seeing Dr. Conklin about his 7-year old son, Jeremy at Conklin's New York City office. Jeremy's mother, Briggs' wife, is dead.

Briggs, apart from being the widowed father of at least the one child, was a 45 year old construction worker and lived in Lovinger, New York, 40 miles from New York City. ('Conklin's first, snap, judgment was that this man ... was not the sort of fellow who usually sought psychiatric help. He was dressed in dark courderoy (*sic*) pants, a neat blue shirt, and a sport-coat that matched – sort of – both. His hair was long, almost shoulder-length. His face was sunburned. His large hands were chapped, scabbed in a number of places, and when he reached over the desk to shake, he felt the rasp of rough calluses.')

Conklin had suggested Briggs consider seeing another psychiatrist, Milton Abrams, in Albany but his nurse, Nancy Adrian had convinced the doctor to see the new patient. Saying he had sounded 'distraught' and that he was 'a man who had control ... but by inches' she had replied to the idea of a referral with, 'Can I suggest you see him once before your decide that?' and he had agreed after some prompting, even though child psychology was not his specialty and his schedule was full.

Briggs had told the nurse, "I just want to know what's going on with my kid – if it's me or what." She told Conklin, "He sounded aggressive about it, but he also sounded very, very scared." And, "He sounded like a man who thinks there's something physically wrong with his son. Except he called the office of a New York psychiatrist. An expensive New York psychiatrist. And he sounded scared," she repeated.

The nurse finally convinced her doctor by telling him that Briggs had worked on '...a pool addition at Abrams' country house two years ago. He says he would go to him if you still recommend it after hearing what he has to say, but that he wanted to tell a stranger first and get an opinion. He said, "I'd tell a priest if I was a Catholic."'

Conklin himself has one interesting habit to do with his cigarette case. 'Each morning he filled it with exactly ten Winston 100s – when they were gone, he was done with smoking until the next day. It was not as good as quitting; he knew that. It was just a truce he had been able to reach.'

In this handwritten and unedited version Nancy Adrian, the 45-year-old receptionist and nurse, is twice referred to as 'Nurse Abrams' (a confusion with the doctor in Albany) in error. Conklin had a strong attachment to his employee. He thought '...when she grinned she looked twenty ... In his way he loved Nancy Abrams (*sic*) – once, over drinks, he had called her the Della Street of psychiatry, and she almost hit him.' Della Street was Perry Mason's secretary, more of a Girl Friday, in Erle Stanley Gardner's novels and the TV series *Perry Mason*, starring Raymond Burr as the defense attorney cum sleuth and Barbara Hale as Della.

Keyholes is at least tangentially reminiscent of King's short story *The Boogeyman*, originally published in *Cavalier* for March 1973 and slightly revised for its appearance in the *Night Shift* collection.

There is little else to say about this fragmentary story. Readers are given so little of the plot that many questions come to mind. Is the real reason Briggs wants to see a psychiatrist really a problem with his son, as he has claimed? Is there something of a sexual or sinful nature to what Briggs has to say, after all he said he would tell a priest if he was Catholic (sound like confession to you?) Is the problem of the boy's or the father's mind or is it physical, as nurse Abrams speculated? Why was Briggs scared? How did Mrs. Briggs die?

The likelihood is that we shall never know the answer to these questions. The fragment was probably written nearly thirty years ago and there is no indication King has ever returned to it, or ever will.

The Killer (1994)

The Killer is effectively a rewrite of *I've Got to Get Away*, one of the stories in King and Chesley's self-published collection, *People, Places and Things* (see separate chapter). It was obviously written in King's teenage years and the only publication was in *Famous Monsters Of Filmland*, issue #202, for Spring 1994. Readers wishing to access the story will have to purchase this publication from one of the specialist online King booksellers.

In *On Writing* King has this to say of a story he submitted to a magazine called *Spaceman*:

'In the late 1950s, a literary agent and compulsive science fiction memorabilia collector named Forrest J. Ackerman changed the lives of thousands of kids - I was one - when he began editing a magazine called *Famous Monsters of Filmland*. Ask anyone who has been associated with the fantasy-horror-science fiction genres in the last thirty years about this magazine, and you'll get a laugh, a flash of the eyes, and a stream of bright memories - I practically guarantee it.

Around 1960, Forry (who sometimes referred to himself as "the Ackermonster") spun off the short-lived but interesting *Spacemen,* a magazine which covered science fiction films. In 1960, I sent a story to *Spacemen.* It was, as well as I can remember, the first story I ever submitted for publication. I don't recall the title, but I was still in the Ro-Man phase of my development, and this particular tale undoubtedly owed a great deal to the killer ape with the goldfish bowl on his head.

My story was rejected, but Forry kept it. (Forry keeps *everything,* which anyone who has ever toured his house - the Ackermansion - will tell you.) About twenty years later, while I was signing autographs at a Los Angeles bookstore, Forry turned up in line . . . with my story, single-spaced and typed with the long-vanished Royal typewriter my mom gave me for Christmas the year I was eleven. He wanted me to sign it to him, and I guess I did, although the whole encounter was so surreal I can't be completely sure. Talk about your ghosts. Man oh man.'

It is quite possible this anecdote refers to *The Killer*, as the author is in possession of a photocopy of a one-page manually typewritten copy of *The Killer* by 'Steve King', which is signed by King, with the dedication, 'For FJA – With all best wishes.' If in fact this is the story, signed about 1980, it would seem to explain its subsequent publication in *Famous Monsters Of Filmland.*

However, Ackerman's introduction to *The Killer* in *Famous Monsters of Filmland* tells a different version. As Ackerman tells it:

'Stephen King was at my house sometime in the early 80s and I surreptitiously produced this manuscript. "Steve," I said, "I'd like to try a little experiment with you. I'd like to read a portion of a story and see if you can identify its author." ... I wish I'd had a vidicam to record the expression on his face when the dam finally broke and he realized it was *his own story* from ... two decades out of the past!" I asked him at the time I tested his memory if I could publish it, and he gave me his blessing.'

King's link with Ackerman does not stop there - he wrote an introduction for Ackerman's book, *Mr Monster's Movie Gold*. The introduction's title is *The Importance of Being Forry* - in it King lauds the influence of *Famous Monsters of Filmland* on the young Steve King, growing up in rural Maine. He says Ackerman '...stood up for a generation of kids who understand that if it was junk, it was magic *junk.*' It is clear that this influence and King's understanding that he was part of a wider circle of 'kids' in love with the genres of science fiction and horror lead directly to his continuing interest in the genres and almost directly to the best-selling author he is today[93].

The Killer begins, 'Suddenly, he snapped awake, and realized he didn't know who he was, or what he was doing here, in a munitions factory.' The subject could not remember his name or, indeed, 'anything'. Picking up a gun, on which he had apparently been working, he approached another man packing bullets, ' "Who am I?" he said slowly, hesitantly'. The other man did not answer and our protagonist screamed out, "Who am I? Who am I?" but all the other workers ignored him, not even looking up.

He then 'swung the gun at the bullet-packer's head', knocking him out. He then picked up some of the bullets, which 'happened to be the right caliber' and loaded his gun. Another man approached on an overhead catwalk. When the 'killer' yelled, "Who am I?" to the newcomer the man reacted by running away. Instantly, 'the killer' shot at the running man who, though hit, managed to press a red button, setting off a wailing siren.

"Killer! Killer! Killer!" a loudspeaker screamed, yet still the other workers did not look up, but simply 'toiled on'. The 'killer' ran but came across four uniformed men who 'fired at him with queer energy guns'. He managed to shoot one of them but now more were coming, from all sides. 'He had to get away' (effectively the title of the other version of this tale). ' "Please! Don't shoot! Can't you see I just want to know who I am?" They fired, and the energy beams slammed into him. Everything went black ...'

The twist of the tale is revealed in the last three paragraphs of this one-page story. As the body of the killer was loaded onto a truck one 'guard' said, ' "One of them turns killer every now and then ... "I just don't understand it," the second said ... "Take that one. That he'd say – "I just want to know who I am." That was it. Seemed almost human. I'm beginning to think they're making these robots too good." They watched the robot repair truck disappear around the curve.'

Other than *I've Got to Get Away*, this story is not linked to any other King fiction. There is no timeline setting other than the future. Derivative of pulp science fiction, this short tale is nevertheless fairly well written for a probable 13 or 14 year old, and King must have had some affection for the story to allow it to be published more than thirty years after it was written.

The King Family and the Wicked Witch (1977)

The King Family and the Wicked Witch has one of the more interesting histories of the stories that have been published but have never been included in a King collection. It was published in *Flint*, an obscure Kansas newspaper, no longer operating. It is effectively impossible to secure an original copy of the newspaper but photocopies of the story circulate within the King community.

Beahm stated the newspaper was based in Flint, Michigan in *The Stephen King Story*, (page 301) but Stephen Spignesi disputed the certainty of this, stating only that it is assumed *Flint* was a Michigan based publication. In 2004 researcher Justin Brooks was able to confirm that the newspaper was based in Manhattan, Kansas and that the publication date was 25 August 1977.

The editor, Roy D Krantz, prefaced the story with this note: 'Stephen King and I went to college together. No, we were not the best of friends but we did share a few brews together at the University Motor Inn. We did work for the school newspaper at the same time. No, Steve and I are not best friends. But I sure am glad he "made it". He worked hard and he believed in himself. After eight million book sales, it's hard to remember him as a typically broke student. We all new (*sic*) he'd make it though. Last January I wrote of a visit with Steve over the Holiday vacation. We talked about his books, *Carrie*, *'Salem's Lot*, *The Shining*, and the soon to be released, *The Stand*. We talked about how Stanley Kubrick wants to do the film versions of his new books. We didn't talk about the past much though. We talked of the future, his kids, FLINT ... He gave me a copy of a story he'd written for his children. We almost ran it then, but there was much concern on the staff as to how it would be received by our readers. We didn't run it. Well, we've debated long enough. It's too cute for you not to read it! We made the final decision after spending an evening watching TV last week. There were at least 57 more offensive things said, not to mention all the murders, rapes and wars ... we decided to let you be the judge. If some of you parents might be offended by the word 'fart', you'd better not read it - but don't stop your kids, they'll love it!'

As intimated by the editor, for reasons that shall become obvious, the story is also known as *The King Family and the Farting Cookie*. Spignesi states this was the original title of the story and says Douglas Winter had a copy of a manuscript with this title[94].

In this Maine Street Horror tale a Witch plots against a local family. Witch Hazel, who lived 'on the Secret Road in the town of Bridgton' did not like the King family because they were 'the happiest family' in Bridgton, Maine. She was so wicked that she turned '...a prince from the Kingdom of New Hampshire into a woodchuck. She turned a little kid's favorite kitty into whipped cream. And she liked to turn mommies' baby-carriages into big piles of horse-turds while the mommies and their babies were shopping. She was a mean old witch.'

Witch Hazel disguised herself as a fan of Stephen King, bought some of his books at the Bridgton Pharmacy, and drove out to the King house, pretending '...she wanted daddy to sign his books. She drove in a car. She could have ridden her broom, but she didn't want the Kings to know she was a witch.' After 'Daddy' signed her books, 'Mommy offered her tea' and, to thank the family for their kindness, Hazel gave them four magic cookies.

After the Witch left the Kings made the mistake of trying the cookies. The first evil, magic cookie turned Daddy's nose into a banana and '...when he went down to his office to work on his book much later on that terrible day, the only word he could write was banana.' The second cookie turned Mommy's hands into milk bottles, 'What an awful thing! Could she fix food with milk-bottles for hands? Could she type? No! She could not even pick her nose.'

The last two cookies made Naomi and Joe cry all the time, 'They cried and cried and could not stop! The tears streamed out of their eyes. There were puddles on the rug. Their clothes got all wet. They couldn't eat good meals because they were crying. They even cried in their sleep.'

After suffering this fate the '…Kings were not the happiest family in Bridgton any more. Now they were the saddest family in Bridgton … Daddy couldn't write books because all the words came out banana, and it was hard to see the typewriter anyway because his nose was a banana.' On the other hand, 'Witch Hazel was as happy as a wicked witch ever gets. It was her greatest spell.'

While out walking in the forest about a month later, Mommy found a woodchuck caught in a trap, '…Poor thing! It was almost dead from fright and pain. There was blood all over the trap.' The mother ran for the rest of the family, who banded together and released the animal, using 'six drops of banana oil' from Daddy's nose to loosen the trap's rusty hinge. Then we read, 'Have you guessed yet? Oh, I bet you have. He was the Prince of the Kingdom of New Hampshire who had also fallen under the spell of Wicked Witch Hazel.' With the woodchuck's release all the spells were broken and the Prince appeared before the Kings, 'in a Brooks Brothers suit'. 'Daddy's banana nose disappeared and was replaced with his own nose, which was not too handsome but certainly better than a slightly squeezed banana … The Prince … shook hands with daddy and said he had admired daddy's books before he had been turned into a woodchuck.'

'All five of them went back to the nice house by the lake…' and plotted to teach Witch Hazel a lesson. They made a cookie out of 300-year-old baked beans that daddy got from New Hampshire and took it to her home. They disguised themselves as poor people and when the witch opened the door, 'She was wearing a tall black hat. There was a wart on the end of her nose. She smelled of frog's blood and owls' hearts and ants' eyeballs, because she had been whipping up a horrible brew to make more black magic cookies.'

Witch Hazel did not recognize the Kings and the Prince in disguise, so they tried to sell her their cookie, with daddy claiming, 'It is the wickedest cookie in the world. If you eat it, it will make you the wickedest witch in the world, even wickeder than Witch Indira in India.' Greedily, Witch Hazel, saying she would not pay for something she could steal, '…snatched the cookie and gobbled it down.'

However, the old witch soon began to realize she had made a mistake – 'It was a Farting Cookie. Witch Hazel felt something funny. She felt it building in her tummy and her behind. It felt like a lot of gas. It felt like an explosion waiting to happen.' The Prince and the Kings revealed themselves and the evil old witch tried to cast a new spell, to turn them '…all into cheap antiques that not even tourists will buy … She felt a big fart coming on. She squeezed her butt to keep it in … but it was too late. WHONK! Went the fart. It blew all the fur off her cat ... Witch Hazel went up in the air like a rocket.' When she landed she let out another, blowing down her house and the Bridgton Trading Post, 'You could see Dom Cardozi sitting on the toilet where he had been pooping.' The Witch went even higher in the sky this time and, just before she landed, '...she cut another fart, the biggest one of all. The smell was like two million egg salad sandwiches.'

This time, 'Up and up went Witch Hazel until she was out of sight. During the news that night the Kings and the Prince of New Hampshire heard Barbara Walters report that a UFW had been seen ... over Bridgton, Maine – an unidentified flying witch. And that was the end of the wicked Witch Hazel. She is on the moon now, and probably still farting. And the Kings are the happiest family in Bridgton again ... Daddy writes books and never uses the word banana ... As for Witch Hazel, she was never seen again, and considering those terrible farts she was letting (*off*) when she left, that is probably a good thing.'

The article carried three line drawings 'by Naomi' (almost certainly Naomi King), which are childish in the extreme but suit the tone of the article. One is presumably the witch, another appears to be of two of the King children, and the last is of the witch with the 'windy' effects of the cookie spiraling from her rear end!

The King family lived in the town of Bridgton, Maine in 1977 and this is both the location and timing of the tale. It can also be determined from the Editor's Note that the story was written that year. Bridgton is mentioned in many King stories, the most important being *The Mist*, in which the supermarket central to that story is located. Witch Hazel bought some of Stephen King's books at The Bridgton Pharmacy, also mentioned in *Cujo*, *Dreamcatcher* and *The Mist*.

The other links to King's fiction are via the King family ('They were nice people'). Stephen King appears in this story; although his first name is not mentioned ('There was a daddy who wrote books'). He is also referred to but not named in *The Leprechaun*. King is a horror author mentioned by Ardelia Lortz in *The Library Policeman*; is mentioned as an author in *The Regulators*, *Thinner* and *Slade* and in the *Prime Evil* version of *The Night Flier*; and is mentioned as the narrator of *The Blue Air Compressor*. He appears in the last three books of the *Dark Tower* Cycle, with his family also being mentioned in *The Dark Tower VI: Song of Susannah*.

Tabitha King appears in this story as 'Mommy' (she 'wrote poems and cooked food') but her first name is not given. She is also referred to but not named in *The Leprechaun*. Joseph King is the four-year-old son of Stephen and Tabitha and the brother of Naomi in this story. He also appears as the older brother of Owen, although he is not named, in *The Leprechaun*. Naomi King is the six-year-old daughter of Stephen and Tabitha and sister of Joe in this story. She also appears as the older sister of Owen, but was not named, in *The Leprechaun*.

Of course, not only was this story something of a nightmare for the Kings, can you imagine the nightmare suffered by millions of King fans if 'Daddy' had indeed been unable to write any word other than banana from 1977 onwards?

The story shows King entertaining his young children with a little harmless toilet humor. It can best be described as a children's fairytale but, due in part to its subject matter and in part to the inclusion of the King family, it seems certain King will never allow it to be republished.

The Leprechaun (1983)

According to Spignesi's *The Lost Work of Stephen King*[95] the five pages that make up *The Leprechaun* were the beginning of a rewrite of some thirty pages King lost from the back of a motorcycle '…somewhere in New Hampshire during a Harley-Davidson trip from Boston to Bangor'. Apparently the original intention was for *The Leprechaun* to be a full-blown novel, although this seems unlikely, at least with the King family as characters.

The story was apparently never completed and has not been published. Copies of the fragment circulate in the King community and finding such a copy would be the reader's only opportunity to read and appreciate this partial tale.

In the story a little boy saves a little man. 'Once upon a time - which is how all the best stories start – a little boy named Owen was playing outside his big red house…' but was bored because '…his big brother and big sister, who could always think of things to do, were in school. His daddy was working, and his mommy was sleeping upstairs.'

At the front of the house Owen saw his sister's new cat, Springsteen, toying with something in the grass. Owen disliked Springsteen partly because he thought the cat was always trying to eat his pet guinea pig, Butler. Springsteen was big and black and had '…deep green eyes that seemed to see everything.' The reader will be excused if reminded of the cat Church from *Pet Sematary*. Owen knew that not only did Springsteen like to kill things; he also '…liked to play with them before he killed them. Sometimes Owen would open the door in the morning and there would be a dead bird on the doorstep … Owen would ask permission to bury the dead bird. Sometimes his mommy or daddy would help him.'

When Owen investigated he found Springsteen's latest victim, a '…*person*, a tiny little man wearing a green hat made out of a leaf. The little man looked back over his shoulder, and Owen saw how scared the little guy was. He was no bigger than the mice Springsteen sometimes killed in their big dark cellar.' Springsteen had injured his victim and challenged Owen for possession of the prize but the boy saved the little man by picking the cat up, even though Springsteen bit and clawed. Putting the feline down and '...trying to think of the very worst thing he could he added: "Leave him alone or I'll put you in the oven and bake you like a pizza!"' Springsteen continued to challenge Owen, who said, "I don't care if you *are* mad! ...You can't kill people on our lawn even if they *are* little!"

The cat then ran away and Owen found the little man, '...lying on his side ... Owen touched him gently with his finger. He was terribly afraid the little man was dead.' When Owen inquired if he was all right the '...fellow in the grass made a face and clapped his hands to his ears ...' and Owen realized his voice must '...sound like thunder to such a small person.' Owen now saw that the man's shirt '...was not just the color of grass; it *was* grass. Carefully woven blades of green grass. Owen wondered how come they didn't turn brown.' At this point the fragment ends.

Spignesi relates a further episode from the lost original in which Owen made the leprechaun a house from a Band-Aid box. The only other character mentioned in this fragment is Chris, Owen's friend, '...the big boy who sometimes came to play with him ... but Chris was in school...'

The description of Springsteen stalking the guinea pig is classic King: '...he would jump up on the shelf where Butler's big glass cage was and stare in through the screen on top with his hungry green eyes. Springsteen would sit there, all crouched down, and hardly move at all. Springsteen's tail would wag back and forth a little, and sometimes one of his ears would flick a bit, but that was all. *I'll get in there pretty soon, you cruddy little guinea pig*, Springsteen seemed to say. *And when I get you, I'll eat you! Better believe it! If guinea pigs say prayers, you better say yours!*' Considering King's love affair with rock music the choice of name for the cat is quite amusing.

We should also note that the struggle between a little man-like creature and a cat forms the basis of the screenplay *General* and a segment of the related movie script *Cat's Eye*, although the roles are reversed in that tale, with the cat being the hero. This is no coincidence, as both *Cat's Eye* and this piece were written in the two-year period of 1983-1984. It's possible that when King abandoned *The Leprechaun* he may have incorporated the concept in the screenplay.

This work is classified in the Maine Street Horror reality, as it was set at Owen's home. Although the author never comes out and states Owen is Owen *King* this is rather obvious and can be safely assumed. Of course, we know that the Kings lived in Maine! There is no timeline setting for this story but as Owen was below school age, we can again assume it is set about 1983.

The links to King's other fiction from this tale derive from the various Kings referred to in it.

Stephen King is referred to in this work as Owen's novelist father, '...Daddy said, and went off to work on a novel – that's what he did for work.' Stephen also appears in a similar context in *The King Family and the Wicked Witch*. He appears as a horror author mentioned by Ardelia Lortz in *The Library Policeman*; is mentioned as an author in *The Regulators, Thinner, Slade* and the *Prime Evil* version of *The Night Flier*; and as the narrator of *The Blue Air Compressor*. King appears in the last three books of the *Dark Tower* Cycle, with his family also being mentioned in *The Dark Tower VI: Song of Susannah*.

Tabitha King is referred to in this work as Owen's novelist mother, '… Mommy said, and went off to work on a novel – because that was what she did for work too.' Tabitha also appears in *The King Family and the Wicked Witch*. Joseph King is the four-year-old son of Stephen and Tabitha and brother of Naomi who ate the crying cookie Witch Hazel gave him in *The King Family and the Wicked Witch*. In this story he appears as the older brother of Owen, although he is not mentioned by name.

Naomi King is the six-year-old daughter of Stephen and Tabitha and sister of Joe who also ate the crying cookie Witch Hazel gave her in *The King Family and the Wicked Witch*. In this story she appears as the piano playing older sister of Owen but is not mentioned by name. Owen, the hero of this tale does not appear in the earlier King family tale. However, most King experts believe that the poem *For Owen* is dedicated to the Kings' youngest son.

This whole work is most unusual in that it appears to use the King family as characters. The only other tale in which this occurs is the aforementioned *The King Family and the Wicked Witch*. While that story has seen print, the publication was an obscure Kansas newspaper. King has not allowed that story to appear in any other publication, including his own collections. The decision not to widely publish either story would appear to be a wise one. Doing so would probably bring unnecessary ridicule upon King as restless critics might take such publication as an opportunity to attack one of the world's most popular writers for being egotistical or suffering from hubris.

The fact remains that both this story and *The King Family and the Wicked Witch* are actually delightful children's tales and King's usual empathy for children and his ability to write their characters as we remember ourselves at that time in our lives shines through yet again.

The Little Green God of Agony (2011)

This America Under Siege story first appeared in *A Book of Horrors* (Jo Fletcher Books, 2011), an anthology edited by Stephen Jones. At the time of writing this was the only appearance but it seems certain to appear in King's next collection.

A note at the end of the tale in *A Book of Horrors* includes this: 'Monsters are real,' says King, 'and ghosts are real too. They live inside us, and sometimes, they win.' The same note says the story 'is a tribute to the classic monster and old dark house stories.'

In the tale, billionaire Andrew Newsome summons Reverend Rideout to his Vermont home on a stormy November evening. Newsome is in agony two years after a plane crash from which he was the sole survivor. He'd suffered multiple fractures and serious burns but is refusing to follow the rehabilitation regime prescribed by his doctors out of fear of the pain the rehab would require. As he discusses what he describes as his 'agony' to Rideout his nurse, Kat MacDonald, considers the situation – she thinks Rideout a fraudulent faith healer and Newsome a lazy patient who believes he can buy his way back to health, rather than go through the required physical work and related pain.

Rideout claims a demon which he describes as a little green god of agony, is feeding on Newsome and that he can draw it out. His only fee will be $750,000 to rebuild his church, which had burned the previous summer in a wildfire; this after Newsome has offered $10,000,000 if his agony can be relieved. Rideout explains he can expel the demon but only at great risk to his own life, as he'd suffered a major heart attack five years earlier, after successfully performing just such a withdrawal from a young car accident victim.

Newsome and Rideout agree to proceed but MacDonald loses her temper, claiming Rideout to be a charlatan; and Newsome a lazy patient. Newsome fires her but Rideout calms the situation by saying the nurse can be educated in the ways of pain as she had become inured to her patients' suffering. Arming MacDonald with a broom, and Newsome's assistant Jensen with pepper spray Rideout begins the attempt to expel the demon; as Newsome's housekeeper Melissa and cook, Tonya look on. If Rideout is not a charlatan the plan is to stun the demon and secure it in a glass jar.

The pastor invokes God, Jesus, the saints and martyrs and a strange bulge appears in Newsome's throat. A green creature, bladder like and with 'stubby green spikelets' emerges from Newsome, who is instantly relieved of his agony as Rev. Rideout collapses. MacDonald tries to swat the creature but misses and all in the room are terrified by seeing it as the mains power fails and the generator kicks in. Jensen fires off the pepper spray but, in shock, manages to get it in his own eyes and is blinded. The creature latches onto Melissa's eye causing instant agony but the nurse manages to strike it from the housekeeper's head and then steps on the ghastly mass, sending 'green stuff' shooting from its body. MacDonald checks Rideout and finds no pulse, as Newsome begins to make demands and Jensen screams for his eyes to be washed out.

In the chaos the generator fails, the lights go out and in a totally darkened room Kat MacDonald feels the creature on the back of her hand.

This story is deeply informed by King's own rehabilitation from the accident that nearly took his life in 1999, as was also the case with *Kingdom Hospital*. It's a rollicking tale which picks up pace rapidly towards the end and has a satisfyingly creepy ending. King's 'Constant Readers', particularly fans of his early short fiction, will genuinely enjoy the ride.

Man With A Belly (1978)

Man With A Belly is one of King's relatively rare crime stories. First published in *Cavalier* for December 1978, it was reprinted in *Gent* for November/December 1979. Copies of these two issues are quite difficult to come by, with *Cavalier* coming to market much more often but even that sells for $100 or more. Those seeking a copy should contact specialist online King booksellers.

In this America Under Siege story an old man tries to control his young wife and reaps the consequences. A 78-year-old Mafia boss Vittorio Correzente offered hit man John Bracken $50,000 to rape his wife Norma. 'The story was simple, and yet there was a beautiful circularity to it which Bracken appreciated. Correzente had married Norma White because he had an itch. She had accepted his suit for the same reason. But while his itch was for her body, her bloodline, and the heat of her youth, hers was a much colder thing: money ... Norma White was a compulsive gambler.'

Don Vittorio's self-image was at stake, 'The matter could have been resolved simply and suddenly if he had been cuckolded by some young tony in tight pants, but to be cuckolded by his own wealth was more complex and contained a bitter irony which perhaps only a Sicilian could fully grasp ... (*he was*) never afraid to show the iron fist inside the glove. He was a man with a belly, in the Sicilian argot ... He had struck upon the solution because it was fitting. It was pure object lesson and vengeance all in one. He had chosen Bracken because he was independent and unlike many hit men, he was neither homosexual nor impotent.' King's representation of hit men here is rather interesting!

Bracken took the job, 'He reflected that it would be the first contract in his career where the weapon would need no getting rid of'. After Bracken raped Norma in a park he said expressionlessly, 'I am told to tell you that this is how your husband pays a debt to his honor. I am told to tell you that he is a man with a belly. I am told to tell you that all debts are paid and there is honor again.' Norma convinced Bracken to walk her to her second apartment, 'the one not even Benny Torreos (*Correzente's consigliore*) knew about', and on the way offered him twice what her husband had paid to do a job for her. Bracken demurred that such a thing would be bad for business but Norma told him it did not involve killing Vittorio. 'Bracken said sardonically: "Rape is out."''

On arriving at the apartment they made love, in Norma's words, '...in a civilized way' and '...she poured out her virulence toward the man she married ... he was a wop, a stinking spic, a lover of sheep, a crude bludgeoner who went to chic restaurants and ate pie with his fingers; a grabber and a twister, a blacker-and-bluer of flesh; a lover of junk shop gimcracks; an aficionado of Norman Rockwell; a pederast; a man who would not treat her as a diadem but rather as a brace for his sagging manhood; not as a proud woman but as a dirty ... joke to bolster the admiration of his pasta-eating, sweaty associates.'

The next morning, 'she made this proposition: "Make me pregnant. I will pay you do to this ... He wants a child. Could he make one? She shrugged. "Perhaps lasagna is good for potency. I, however, take pills. He knows I take them." Bracken sipped his coffee. "Stud service?"' Norma's plan was to go to Vittorio offering to be the good wife and to give him a son, ' "I'll get what I want, which is freedom of the tables. And he will get what he wants, which is an heir."'

Bracken agreed to the proposition, $100,000 his fee. 'Ten weeks after the contract with Don Vittorio had been fulfilled, she killed the rabbit ...' and Bracken left town.

Seven months later in Palm Springs, Bracken received a call from Torreos about the Don, ' "He wants to see you. He's dying." Bracken thought carefully, knowing his life almost certainly depended on his next words ... "Why does he want to see me?" "To ask a question." The connection was very bad, and Bracken knew that to simply replace the instrument in its cradle would likely mean death. The family has a long arm. It was either go to Vito, or run ... "How is Mrs. Correzente?" he asked politely. "Dead," Benny Torreos said flatly. "She died last month, in childbirth."'

With no other alternative Bracken went to the Don, only to find him on his deathbed and relatives congregating, 'The women ... were dressed in black, and shawled. Even the business suits of their men seemed old-fashioned, as if death had dragged Sicily back into the fabric of the clothes and the wearers by force.'

Calling Bracken to the bed the old man said, 'They told me you did a good job. You do. You have killed my wife and me.' He then claimed pride had made him continue to make love to Norma even after suffering a minor stroke, as he was determined to place a child in her belly. One night, after announcing the pregnancy to the world, the couple had argued, bringing on a massive stroke. Running for help Norma had fallen on the living room steps and also had to be hospitalized. After telling Bracken this, the Don whispered, "You see? The irony?" Bracken simply replied, "Benny said you had a question."

The Don responded by telling him the baby had survived but was in an incubator, '"They say the baby has pretty blue eyes." Bracken said nothing. "You made one of Norma's eyes black. But they were brown. And there is no blue-eyed Sicilian".' Bracken again pointed out there must be a question but the Don said he had asked it and his doctor had responded that it was only a matter of genes, "I do not know genes, I only know what a dying man lies in beds and thinks."

Bracken leaned forward and told the old man he was stupid, "Death has made you senile. I have my own belly. Do you think I would take my own leavings?" He said the baby's eyes would turn brown but that Vito would not see it. Bracken then rose, 'the room was white and full of death', and left for Palm Springs.

No timeline or city location is given in the story, nor is it linked to any other King fiction, making it very much a stand-alone tale.

As is often the case with these uncollected stories it is disappointing that King has not allowed *Man With A Belly* a wider audience. All three main characters are conceptually interesting and the storyline bold, even if the ending is somewhat unsatisfactory (compare it, for instance, with a similar scene in the movie *Braveheart*, when Princess Isabelle, daughter in law of the stroke-bound and mute King Edward whispers in his ear that the child she is carrying is not her husband's but that of the King's worst enemy, William Wallace). There are some inconsistencies – where did the Don think Norma was later the night he organized for her to be raped? If Norma was such a terrible gambler why did she still have the $100,000 she used to pay Bracken for his 'stud service'? King has her explain it is money from her wealthy Boston family but it seems unlikely a compulsive gambler could have kept such funds aside and this explanation rings hollow. Finally, one wonders if a woman, just brutally raped, would take the rapist home, make love to him and pay him to get her pregnant, even in these circumstances.

This tale shows King in his crime genre mode and that alone makes the story interesting for King students and hardcore fans alike. King's reasons for not including it in a collection are unknown but we speculate that, as the story was written very specifically for the men's magazine market and includes brutal sexual content, he may have felt it would not reflect well upon his overall work if included in one of his later short story collections. Quite possibly, he simply does not like the story. There does remain a slim possibility that King will allow its republication at some point, perhaps in a crime anthology, rather than one of his own collections.

Maximum Overdrive (1985)

The screenplay of *Maximum Overdrive* is difficult to find but copies do circulate in the King community and are sometimes available from online King specialists. Often there is no final or authorized version of a movie screenplay, as they are constantly adjusted during filming and some alterations are never properly documented. This chapter was compiled from the commonly circulating version dated May 22, 1985. King expert Tyson Blue[96] has reviewed an earlier draft, dated February 8, 1985 and titled *Trucks*. At other times the movie was simply to be known as *Overdrive*.

Maximum Overdrive represented King's directorial debut. King found the task enlightening and the fact that he has never attempted to helm another movie or television episode indicates that, in retrospect, he did not find the task to his liking. Beahm quotes King as saying, when asked if he did in fact enjoy being behind the camera, 'I didn't. I didn't care for it at all. I had to work. I wasn't used to working. I hadn't worked in 12 years.'[97] Jones makes this interesting comment [98]: ' "I'd like to direct once," Stephen King told *Starburst* magazine in the early 1980s, "because I have a feeling that I could probably make a movie that would scare a lot of people *very badly*. I *think* I have the capability, but I'm not sure. I might really screw it up." The King of Horror didn't know how prophetic he was.'

King fans and moviegoers alike probably do prefer that King continue to spend his time on prose and screenplays, delivering original product and allowing other directors to interpret his stories. While this sometimes leads to such unfortunate productions as *Dreamcatcher* the result can equally be superior product such as *The Green Mile*.

Maximum Overdrive is often said to be an adaptation of *Trucks* but in fact the stories have no real connection other than the base idea of trucks becoming sentient and attacking humans. Both stories illustrate King's thematic fascination with machines gone wild, which, while not entirely original to the writer from Maine, he has certainly made his own over the years. King's original stories in this category go back as far as 1960 with *I've Got to Get Away!* (rewritten as *The Killer*). Among other such King stories with this theme are his high school effort *Code Name: Mousetrap*; the semi-autobiographic *The Mangler*; *Christine*; *Uncle Otto's Truck*; *The Sun Dog* and *Word Processor of the Gods* (originally published as *The Word Processor*). A great many elements of *The Dark Tower* cycle also fit this theme, for example *The Bear*, a stand-alone story that appears in a revised version as a section of *The Dark Tower III: The Wastelands*.

Trucks was made into a television movie, which debuted on the USA Network on 29 October 1997 and was issued on DVD one year later. That production has one of the worst ratings at for any King adaptation at www.imdb.com of only 3.5 out of a possible 10!

In *Maximum Overdrive*, a New Worlds tale, the Earth passed into the tail of Rhea-M, a rogue comet, at 9.47am EST on 19 June 1987. At 9.48am a sign on the First Bank of Wilmington building suddenly flashed 'FUCK YOU', instead of '9:48' and '79' degrees. Machines became sentient all over the world and started attacking and killing humans. A drawbridge in Wilmington, North Carolina, acting of its own volition, opened with cars and trucks still on it, causing multiple crashes and many deaths. At a nearby Little League Field a pitching machine and a Pepsi dispenser attacked the players and coach. All over the city and suburbs machines such as lawn mowers and kitchen devices attacked their previous masters.

A group of people was trapped at the Dixie-Boy Truck Stop on Route 17 near Wilmington by sentient trucks. Just after dawn the next day a bulldozer attacked the building in which they were taking refuge and a battle ensued, with the humans using illegal weapons that had been stored at the Truck Stop by its owner. A number of customers and employees were killed by machine gun fire from an army truck and the survivors were then forced to refuel vehicles under threat of the machine gun. That evening Wilmington, North Carolina was on fire. The remaining survivors at the Dixie-Boy were able to escape via a sewer pipe. In apparent anger the remaining trucks demolished the now empty buildings.

The survivors made it four miles cross-country to a coastal marina and set off on a sailboat. They were immediately attacked by a Coast Guard boat, which fired on them. After Robertson blew the attacking boat up using a bazooka they sailed on toward Haven, an island about six miles off the coast. There were said to be no motor vehicles of any kind on the island. King sends a clear message with the choice of name for this island. Of course, the Haven in Maine appearing in *The Tommyknockers* is quite the opposite of the word's dictionary meaning!

Six days later, at 3.16pm on 27 June 1987, the Earth left the tail of the comet.

The movie *Maximum Overdrive* debuted in American movie theatres on 25 July 1986. Made on a budget of $10 million and largely shot in Wilmington, North Carolina in July and August of 1985 it took only $7.4 million at the box office and was largely regarded as a flop. The heavy metal soundtrack inserted by King, featuring the Australian band AC/DC, may not have assisted the appreciation of wider audiences, although King is largely unapologetic about that aspect of the movie. Members of www.imdb.com rate the movie a very poor 4.8 out of a possible 10, a little below our assessment of its worth.

Emilio Estevez played Bill Robinson; Pat Hingle appeared as the dislikeable Hendershot; Laura Harrington as Brett; Holter Graham as Deke; and King provided an entertaining cameo as 'Man at Cashpoint' (*see the feature panel for more detail*). Estevez is the son of Martin Sheen, who starred in *The Dead Zone* movie and *Firestarter*. The movie was released on video in 1988 and on DVD in 2001.

King wrote a related short non-fiction piece that may be of interest to readers. *A Postscript to 'Overdrive'* appeared in the February 1987 issue of *Castle Rock: The Stephen King Newsletter*. The article particularly focuses on the requirement to delete scenes from the movie to secure an R-rating in preference to the original and 'dreaded' X rating the production attracted.

Considering it has been two decades since *Maximum Overdrive* was released it seems certain the screenplay will never be published. However, King fans and readers who cannot access a copy of the script can always rent or buy the DVD to experience this unique King work.

MAXIMUM OVERDRIVE: THE KEY CHARACTERS

Bill ('Billy') Robertson: On parole, he was a cook working at the Dixie Boy Truck Stop Restaurant on 19 June 1987. He had been jailed after robbing a 7-11 when he was 23. During the siege at the Dixie-Boy he was something of a hero. Good looking, he and Brett Brooks quickly built a romantic relationship. He was one of the survivors who escaped the Truck Stop on 20 June and survived to sail off toward Haven.

Brett Brooks: Pretty and young, she was hitch-hiking when trapped at the Dixie-Boy on 19 June 1987. One of the survivors, she escaped the Truck Stop the following day. She and Bill Robertson quickly formed a romantic relationship. She received a minor gunfire wound on 21 June but sailed on to Haven with the other survivors.

Hendershot: Owner of the Dixie-Boy Truck Stop, he employed parolees to maximize his profits. A cigar smoker, he stored illegal arms at the Truck Stop, some of which he used in the fight against the sentient vehicles. He was shot and killed on 20 June 1987.

Duncan ('Dunc') Keller: Deke's father, another parolee and the Fuel Station Manager at the Dixie-Boy Truck Stop on 19 June 1987. Diesel shot into his eyes just after 9.50am as the machines started attacking humans. Later that day, he was run down and killed by a garbage truck. His son, **Deke Keller** was playing baseball when the machines started attacking humans and he later made his way to his father's workplace. He was one of the survivors who escaped on 20 June and survived to sail off toward Haven the next day.

Curtis ('Curt') Spaulding married **Connie** on or about 19 June 1987 (they were both only seventeen). After being chased by vehicles and crashing they were trapped at the Dixie-Boy Truck Stop on their wedding day. Both escaped on 20 June and survived to sail off toward Haven.

Reginald Speakes aka **'Asshole'**, while not a major character, was played in a cameo by King. Speakes was married and resided at 249 Cedar Street, Wilmington, North Carolina. On 19 June 1987, shortly after the Earth passed into the comet's tail, an ATM insulted him, using the highlighted nickname. Fans of King's acting should watch the movie simply to see King's reaction when the ATM sends its message!

Mile 81 (2011)

Mile 81, a lengthy story at nearly 17,000 words, was first published as a stand-alone electronic book electronic book on 1 September 2011. It is quite likely the story will appear in a future King collection although *UR*, published in 2009, did not appear in 2010's *Full Dark, No Stars*. Of course, readers can purchase the e-book at any time!

A Maine Street Horror tale, most of the action occurs at an I-95 Rest Area backing on to the outer suburbs of Auburn, a few miles from where King grew up and a place he must have passed hundreds of times on the interstate. The actual Rest Area, with gas pumps and fast food, is now closed and, of course, that is part of the set-up.

One cloudy Spring vacation morning 10 year old Pete Simmons is abandoned by his brother George and his friends and left to play on his own. He'd wanted to show them how he could burn things by focusing the sun through his new magnifying glass but his brother thought that 'a baby trick' his friends would not want to see. Pete remembers a nearby abandoned Rest Area close to the Mile 81 marked on I-95 and decides to see if a friend's tale of going there through cut fences and some nearby bush is true – in short, he's creating an adventure to fill the day. Sure enough, he finds his way to the abandoned site, finds some vodka left by 'Really Big Kids' and enters the building, observing the detritus of visits by the young adults – card tables, some mattresses, a dart board made from a Justin Bieber poster, and hanging centerfolds. He throws darts and tries a few sips of vodka. Feeling tipsy he lies down for a nap.

Meanwhile, 'a station wagon of indeterminate make and vintage' rolls off the interstate, crashes through barriers and comes to a halt in the Rest Area. The exterior, including the windscreen is covered with mud, even though there had been no rain in the area for a week and the highway itself is dry. The driver's door opens but no-one gets out and the door remains ajar, 'like an invitation'.

Doug Clayton, an insurance man from Bangor on his way to Portland, is driving past and notices the 'station wagon'. A Christian and a great believer in the parable of the Good Samaritan and living by that philosophy, he quickly signals and pulls into the Rest Area intending to help. He approaches the 'vehicle' but when he grabs the driver's door his hand is suddenly sucked into the surface of the vehicle and literally chewed on, slicing his wedding ring off. As Doug fights for his life the vehicle pulls his body into its maw and devours him.

Shortly after Julie Vernon, driving home towing a trailer holding her new horse, DeeDee, sees the stopped vehicles and decides to turn in and assist, carefully placing traffic cones to advise oncoming traffic. A large former mud-wrestler, she lives on a farm with her female partner and their menagerie of livestock; her rural Maine upbringing dictates she is always willing to help neighbors or strangers. Concerned by seeing a wedding ring and a cellphone lying near the mud covered station wagon she approaches cautiously, but not cautiously enough. Her skirt brushes the surface of the strange vehicle and it grabs her, shredding all flesh from her bones as her hands and body passed through the visible membrane. She dies quickly but in agony. The Rest Area is again quiet, as a few cars pass, and Pete Simmons sleeps on in the nearby building.

Worse is to come as the Lussier family are the next to pull over – six year Rachel, four year old Blake, and their parents – Johnny and Carla, all in their brand new Expedition. They'd met Julie Vernon and DeeDee at an earlier stop, so the sharp-eyed Rachel notices the horse-trailer and calls it out. Carla, irritated by her children's fighting and noticing the traffic cones, demands Johnny pull over to see if the 'horse-lady' needs assistance. Her husband gets out to investigate as the 'station wagon' driver's door slowly opens again – he approaches, looks inside and the door suddenly swings shut, striking his head and he's dragged struggling into the entity. In panic, Carla rushes over and grabs her husband's shaking body, noticing in a flash that his neck is broken. A thought races through her mind – 'It's the car, you have to stay away from the car!'

She releases Johnny's body a moment too late, as a sheaf of her hair touches the vehicle (entity? monster?) she's rudely pulled into its grasp and devoured. The entity's surface is made up of some sticky substance from which humans apparently cannot escape. Little Rachel and Blake are in full panic back in the Expedition and get out of their car. Rachel picks up Julie Vernon's dropped cellphone but Blake wanders close to the station wagon. Rachel orders him to stop with her most authoritative voice. The little girl dials 911 but struggles to convince the operator she isn't playing a game. She has to hang up and retreats with her brother when she spies the station wagon's tire forming a tentacle and reaching out for him.

Passing motorists also start calling 911 as they notice the two unaccompanied kids near the dangerous highway. The Maine State Police dispatch Trooper Jimmy Golding, who is a couple of miles away. He gathers up the crying children, who claim a 'bad car' has eaten their parents. As he watches, the driver's door of the station wagon swings open, seemingly by itself. He calls for anyone inside to come out with their empty hands in the air but there is no response. He can see the kids are badly traumatized so he puts them in the back suit of the cruiser and calls for backup, only to find the nearest unit is ten minutes away.

Little Rachel warns Trooper Golding that the car is dangerous and 'sticky' and he must not touch it. Not understanding what this really means will prove to be Golding's last mistake. He draws his Glock and approaches the wagon, still demanding any occupant come out. He remembers Rachel's admonition not to touch the sticky car just as he reaches for the door and pulls his hand back. And then he makes his fatal error – touching the door with his gun, the car instantly sticks to and begins to pull. Golding doesn't even think of letting go – his training has drilled into him never to surrender his weapon and within seconds the car has eaten not only his gun, but his hand and an instant later Golding too has disappeared into the maw of the monster. He screams but once. The sun breaks through the cloud, flooding the disturbingly peaceful scene with bright light.

Pete Simmons, suffering a light hangover, has woken to the screams of the children and has run outside just in time to see the State Trooper swallowed up by the station wagon. He considers running away to avoid getting in trouble but decides to stay and help the children he can see heading towards the dangerous highway. Pete remembers his magnifying glass and decides to try an experiment – he thinks the next policemen and maybe a few more will not believe three kids when they tell them the car is 'sticky' and 'eats' people, and therefore more will die. His plan is to focus the sun through his magnifying glass on the station wagon as, even though he thought the creature was from outer space, it probably hadn't seen that 'baby trick' before.

The station wagon was cunning and tries to draw him closer, first opening its door and then sending tendrils out from a tire. Pete tries to focus the sunlight through the magnifying glass but he has to move dangerously close to the monster. 'For a moment nothing happened. Then tendrils of smoke began to drift up. The muddy white surface beneath the dot turned black.' An 'inhuman growling sound' issues from the creature and rose in intensity as the first back up unit, driven by Trooper Al Andrews. Andrews has time to see a young boy holding something to the side of the 'station wagon' and to see the 'vehicle' catch fire, pull itself into a 'tight fiery ball', then shoot up into the afternoon sky before disappearing.

As more sirens can be heard approaching the scene the shocked surviving Trooper begins to wonder how he will write up a report of what he's just seen and runs towards the kids. Blake and Rachel thank Pete, who decides his day's efforts will be worth getting grounded for, and thinks, 'You know what? I fuckin rock.'

King dedicates the tale 'to Nye Willden and Doug Allen, who bought my first stories.' He acknowledges both gentlemen in the *Foreword* to *Night Shift*; Willden (editor of *Cavalier* magazine) is acknowledged individually in his *Introduction to The Old Dude's Ticker*; and also in the *Introduction: Practicing the (Almost) Lost Art* to *Everything's Eventual*.

This is another of King's classic tales in which he quickly and easily reminds us what it was like to be child – Pete Simmons' motivations, thoughts and emotions are clear and real to readers, most of whom left that part of their lives in the 'long ago'. The same applies to the portrayal of Rachel and Blake Lussier – six and four year olds, who react pretty much as we expect any children of that age would when confronted with a sudden shocks like seeing their parents devoured by what appears to be a station wagon!

Mobius (c. 1979)

The 17 double-spaced pages of the manuscript *Mobius* is held in Box 1212 of the Special Collections Unit of the Raymond H Fogler Library at the University of Maine, Orono. The manuscript is headed 'by Stephen King' and was written when Kirby McCauley was still his agent (from 1977 to 1988). Readers wishing to enjoy this story may do so at the Fogler as it is kept in a publicly accessible box.

This is both an America Under Siege and a New Worlds tale for reasons that will become clear. In this short story a student is called urgently to the Westhaven Physical Sciences laboratory. Wayne Parsons worked with Dr. Weaver on the Mobius, a futuristic machine, the capabilities of which had not yet been determined. Time-travel experiments using the machine were banned by 'the trustees' due to the dangers of unintended consequences. Indeed, theoreticians had been given ten years to consider the consequences of time travel using the Mobius, which was the biggest thing since the Moon landings a decade before. There were actually two nuclear powered Mobius machines, which run back-to-back.

As Parsons arrived a hugely fat man was trying to escape the building but Weaver shot him dead. Amazingly, a passing couple did not react to the sound of the four shots he fired. When Parsons examined the fat man's body he found his own features on the face of the corpse.

Weaver then forced Parsons to enter the Mobius at gunpoint, having set the return time for thirty minutes earlier and Parsons arrived in an idyllic land, which he called 'Limbo'. The women there were very attentive of him when he first arrived but as he grew fat the young girls began to laugh at him. Their men lived in the Hills. After Parsons finally became grossly fat and 47 years had passed he decided to return on the Mobius, knowing that Weaver was waiting to kill him.

He successfully avoided death on this second return, thirty minutes before he had left but, as he was about to meet himself arriving at the lab, he disappeared. As he did not meet and warn himself of the danger time would loop eternally. (*What is known of Parsons and Weaver is summarized in this chapter's feature panel*).

The story is rather derivative, there being any number of science fiction and time travel tales along the same lines. This may explain its lack of publication. It could be that King and McCauley were unable to sell it, or simply that King realized its lack of originality and held it back from the market.

The story is set in 1979. Considering King's penchant for setting stories in timelines just after the year in which he writes this may mean it was written in 1978 or 1979.

> **MOBIUS – THE LEAD CHARACTERS**
>
> **Wayne Parsons**
> Born in 1956, he was a 23 year old, 160lb student at the Westhaven Physical Sciences complex in 1979 when Dr. Weaver forced him to travel through time using the Mobius machine. He spent 47 years in an idyllic land but grew grossly fat and returned to 1979 where he successfully avoided being shot and killed by Weaver (as had happened to his older, fatter self the first instance he had time travelled). As a result he did not meet and warn himself and time would loop eternally. The first version of Parsons was 70 years old when he was shot dead in 1979.
>
> **Dr. Weaver**
> Born in 1920, he worked at the Westhaven Physical Sciences complex. In 1979 he forced Wayne Parsons to use the Mobius to travel through time, creating a permanent time loop paradox.

Morality (2009)

Morality first appeared in the July 2009 edition of *Esquire* magazine. It seemed to attract little attention, even in the King community but in 2010 it was nominated for a Shirley Jackson Award for Best Novelette (whatever that strange beast a novelette might be). Initial publicity surrounded the cover of the magazine, which showed words from the story printed in shoe polish on the naked body of female model Bar Refaeli!

In the tale a married couple is presented with a moral dilemma. Chad and Nora Callahan are struggling on his substitute teacher salary (when he has work) and her income from home nursing the Reverend George Winston. Meanwhile the bills are piling up and Chad has the opportunity to complete a book of stories that just might get them out from under their creditors and off to a new life in Vermont. As well as nursing Winston, a stroke victim, Nora also acts as his secretary, physical therapist and masseuse. Out of the blue the patient offers Nora $200,000 but of course this is not without strings.

The Reverend has led a good life, free of any major sin, and has now determined to "commit a major sin before I die. A sin not of thought or word but of deed … I could sin by proxy. In fact, I could double my sin quotient, as it were, by making you my accessory," he tells Nora.

Of course, the author strings out both the dilemma for our heroine and her would-be writer husband, and doesn't expose the Reverend's actual requirement until well into the story, building reader interest. However, it is perhaps fair to say there is something just a little lacking, at least compared to the usual King – the feeling is more of 'drift' than ratcheting up the tension.

What the Reverend requires is for Nora to go to a playground and punch a child, while Chad records the events on camera. After much debate the crime, or 'sin' as Winston would have it, is agreed by Nora; and she proceeds to act out the deed. Readers may expect her to be back out at the last minute, or be caught, or even confess to the police (as Chad thought might happen) but she gets away scot free. And after watching the video the two have sex, during which Nora demands Chad hit her. He does, spilling blood.

The next day Nora shows Winston the video, takes her money, and quits the job on the spot. Creepily, Winston tells Nora the second time they'd run the tape, he'd watched her and not the screen. He wonders, "...is feeling dirty always a bad thing?"

As time progresses the price to be paid, for there almost always is one, is an unraveling of the Callahan marriage – first through escalating but apparently mutually exciting violence during sex; then Nora makes love to another man, demanding he hit her during the act (he declines, "What king of crazy lady are you?"). They move to Vermont shortly after Winston apparently commits suicide but not before Chad declines any more violence in the bedroom. When Chad's book sells, but for a low advance, Nora taunts him and he breaks her nose; then tells her he's leaving the marriage, the whole sordid episode having tainted both their relationship and his writing. And there the tale largely ends.

It is mildly interesting to speculate why King chose the surname Callahan for Chad and Nora, considering the importance of the Reverend Donald Callahan (*Salem's Lot*, *The Dark Tower*) in his canon, but no clear conclusion can be drawn.

Rather obviously this is a tale of *morality*; but King also captures the feeling of 'ordinary' – how simple events might happen and how lives might unwind as a result of fateful decisions. King, of course, is a highly *moral* writer and this tale can be safely filed in that section of his work but perhaps without being dusted off and read too often.

Morality was also published in the mass market version of Blockade Billy, published in May 2010, and that may be the easiest form of access for readers ahead of the inevitable inclusion in the next King collection.

The New Lieutenant's Rap (1999)

The New Lieutenant's Rap has a unique history. Printed as a chapbook from King's own imprint, Philtrum Press, the entire text is in King's handwriting. It was provided to guests at the 6 April 1999 New York City party at the Tavern on the Green to celebrate King's 25th anniversary in book publishing. Marsha DeFilippo, King's assistant, confirmed that copies were left at the party by guests who clearly did not know what they were leaving behind! In total only 500 copies were printed, with up to 150 distributed at the party.

The front and rear covers simply show a hand drawn peace sign. King's introduction to the chapbook reads:

"The New Lieutenant's Rap" is from Hearts in Atlantis, to be published by Scribner's in the fall of 1999. This version, which differs considerably from the one which will appear in the book (it's longer, for one thing), is offered as a little keepsake – my way of marking twenty-five fruitful (a little too fruitful, some critics would say) years as a novelist and freelance writer. It is limited to no more than 500 copies, each of which has been signed by me and numbered or lettered by Michael Alpert, who has so brilliantly executed all the Philtrum Press books, from The Plant to The Ideal Genuine Man. The printing is my own. So are the mistakes and scratch-outs.

I hope what follows makes you as uncomfortable as it does me.

Stephen King

This America Under Siege story has never been published in the mass market and most likely will not be. As King states, it is effectively a version of *Why We're In Vietnam*, which appeared in *Hearts in Atlantis* later that year. It was substantially revised for that appearance and those with a strong interest in King's prose and its development should try to secure a copy of this story. It is as great a pleasure to read a story in King's handwriting as it is to listen to his audio readings. A certain amount of character is added to the story when reading the handwritten version and one is amazed by the neatness of King's penmanship.

Copies are rarely offered for sale. Photocopies also circulate in limited numbers in the King community.

As one of the *Hearts in Atlantis* stories it includes characters that appear in other stories from the group. These are John L ('Sully-John') Sullivan, who also appears in *Low Men in Yellow Coats*, *Blind Willie* (*Hearts in Atlantis* version only), *Heavenly Shades of Night Are Falling* and *Hearts in Atlantis*; and is the key character in *Why We're In Vietnam*; and Dieffenbaker, who also appears in *Why We're in Vietnam* and *Blind Willie* (*Hearts In Atlantis* version only).

In the story two Vietnam vets talk at another veteran's funeral. Dieffenbaker had been the new lieutenant when John Sullivan served in Vietnam. They met again for the first time in a couple of years and talked after attending Dick Pagano's funeral. They remembered and discussed many of the things that happened during the War but Dieffenbaker, now a bald computer salesman, appeared to be extremely negative. He reminded Sullivan of the things their generation had created, from video games to crack cocaine, but most were mentioned in a negative or sarcastic way. Dieffenbaker finally apologized to Sullivan for the way he had spoken, and they parted.

Once reading, we are quickly into the story. As Dieffenbaker and Sully stand outside the funeral parlor, smoking, Sully remembered the day in Dong Ha Province when '…old *mamasan* died. That day he had been shit scared. They had all been shit scared.' Sully recalled that Dieffenbaker, the 'new lieutenant', had stood tall that day and '…given the order that needed giving. Sully thought if it had come down to him, Clemson and Malenfant and those other fuckheads would have killed until their ammo ran out – wasn't that pretty much what the men under Calley and Medina had done? But Dieffenbaker was no William Calley, give him that. Dieffenbaker had given the nod. Slocum nodded back, then raised his rifle – goddam, I say goddam – and blew off the back of Ralph Clemson's head.'

For those old enough to remember the trauma of the Vietnam War era, one of the defining memories is the My Lai massacre and its aftermath. In just one paragraph King recalls the tragedy and the trauma while instantly making readers consider the impact one battlefield officer's choices can have. The instant shock of understanding that a US soldier had killed another gets the story moving at pace.

As they talk Dieffenbaker's cynicism emerges but it is Sully who asks the question that presages the title under which the story appears in *Hearts*: ' "Why were we in Vietnam to begin with?" Sully asked. "Not to get all philosophical or anything, but have you ever figured that out?"'

Then, shortly: ' "Fuckin yeah, it matters," Dieffenbaker said. "Because we never got out. We never got out of the green. Our generation died over there."' He then argues that their generation, '...those of us who ran north to Toronto, those of us who marched and protested ...' and even those who simply stayed home had achieved little of value since that time. What they had done was to become a generation of watchers, selling out their beliefs - a rather heavy slap on their generation's first President's sexual peccadilloes is also delivered – '...our generation is a joke.'

Deef (and he hates that nickname) reminds Sully that '...there was a time when it was all in our hands.' This sets Sully to remembering Carol Gerber, not the Carol of college or peace-marches; but the time they and Bobby (Garfield) had gone to Savin Rock Amusement Park in 1960. 'It *had* been in their hands then; he was quite sure of it. But kids lose everything, kids have slippery fingers and holes in their pockets and they lose everything.'

Dieffenbaker continues, postulating that they are still really in Vietnam, and that all that appeared to have occurred in their lives since was just part of a 'pot-bubble' and that Vietnam is/was in fact the better of the realities. Realizing his bitterness Dieffenbaker then apologizes (if apparently half-heartedly) to Sully as he prepares to leave and they now '...looked at each other across the years – it felt like years, not space' and Sully thought: '...It's still klicks instead of miles and Dieffenbaker is still the new lieutenant. We stay because it's better. He's right. We stay.'

The story, presumably King's partial take on his own generation's past and present dilemmas, is entirely set outside the funeral home in which Dick Pagano lay (dead of pancreatic cancer) but really the story is of Vietnam and the lasting impact on Sully, Deef and their entire generation. We know from *Heavenly Shades of Night Are Falling* that it is the summer of 1999, as in that story John Sullivan died of a heart attack while returning home from Pagano's funeral.

The *Hearts in Atlantis* stories

Hearts in Atlantis is a five-story collection, first published in 1999. There are autobiographical overtones (and undertones) in some of these stories. For instance, *Low Men in Yellow Coats* recalls a short period of King's childhood, when he and his family lived in Stratford, Connecticut (re-cast as Harwich for this story). The *Hearts in Atlantis* story draws directly from King's past, considering he was studying at the University of Maine at Orono during the same time setting.

The stories are loosely linked by certain characters and by the Vietnam War era. In order of their presentation in the collection they are: *Low Men in Yellow Coats, Hearts in Atlantis, Blind Willie, Why We're in Vietnam* and *Heavenly Shades of Night Are Falling*.

What is not well known to most fans is that a number of these stories also appear in differing versions.

Low Men in Yellow Coats is an original Dark Tower story, first appearing in the collection. However, an excerpt was published in *Family Circle* for 3 August 1999. There are very minor wording variations in that publication.

Blind Willie was first published in the literary magazine, *Antaeus* for Autumn 1994 and then republished in King's *Six Stories* collection with quite a number of minor changes. King then completely rewrote the story for its appearance in *Hearts in Atlantis* so as to fit the story line of the collection. Bill Teale became Bill Shearman (one of those who beat up Carol Gerber) and instead of Blind Willie Teale, Shearman posed as Blind Willie Garfield (he still had Bobby Garfield's glove, which he used when begging).

Why We're in Vietnam is a substantial revision of *The New Lieutenant's Rap*, given out as a chapbook earlier in 1999.

Only *Hearts in Atlantis* itself and *Heavenly Shades of Night Are Falling* have not been revised in any way.

The movie version of *Hearts in Atlantis*, a much under-rated and warm-hearted adaptation, is actually mainly of *Low Men in Yellow Coats* (the *Hearts in Atlantis* storyline does not appear in the movie) and of *Heavenly Shades of Night Are Falling*. The screenplay was by William Goldman (*Misery, Butch Cassidy and the Sundance Kid*) and the Director was Scott Hicks. Anthony Hopkins played Ted Brautigan, Anton Yelchin the Young Bobby Garfield, with David Morse (*The Green Mile*) the adult Bobby.

The Night of the Tiger (1978)

The lack of inclusion of *The Night of the Tiger* in a King collection is passing strange. The tale was first published in *The Magazine of Fantasy and Science Fiction* for February 1978 and appeared in various anthologies but has not been republished in English since 1992. Perhaps King is unhappy with the tale. If this is the case, fans would benefit from a rewrite to correct any inadequacies. In fact, King expert Tyson Blue says:[99] 'It may be that the ultimately unsatisfying nature of the story, with its plethora of unresolved loose ends and plot inconsistencies, are among the reasons why it has yet to be collected in a King anthology.'

Readers seeking the story should be able to find one of the anthologies at an online King bookseller or second hand bookseller of the traditional or Internet type. *The Magazine of Fantasy and Science Fiction* is collectable in its own right and copies may be available from specialist sources. These are the anthologies in which the story has appeared: *More Tales of Unknown Horror* edited by Peter Haining (New English Library, 1979); *The Year's Best Horror Stories* edited by Gerald Page (DAW Books, 1979); *The Third Book of Unknown Tales of Horror* edited by Peter Haining (Sidgwick & Jackson, 1980); *Chamber of Horrors* (Octopus Books, 1984); *The Best Horror Stories from the Magazine of Fantasy & Science Fiction* edited by Edward Ferman and Anne Jordan (St Martin's Press, 1988 and Viking, 1989 as *The Best of Modern Horror*); *Horrorstory, Volume Three* edited by Gerald Page and Karl Edward Wagner (Underwood-Miller, 1992); and *Tails of Wonder and Imagination* edited by Ellen Datlow (Night Shade Books, 2010).

King relates a little of the story's history in *On Writing*: 'By the time I was sixteen I'd begun to get rejection slips with hand-written notes a little more encouraging than the advice to stop using staples and start using paperclips. The first of these hopeful notes was from Algis Budrys, then the editor of *Fantasy and Science Fiction,* who read a story of mine called "The Night of the Tiger" (the inspiration was, I think, an episode of *The Fugitive* in which Dr. Richard Kimble worked as an attendant cleaning out cages in a zoo or a circus) and wrote: "This is good. Not for us, but good. You have talent. Submit again."

Those four brief sentences, scribbled by a fountain pen that left big ragged blotches in its wake, brightened the dismal winter of my sixteenth year. Ten years or so later, after I'd sold a couple of novels, I discovered "The Night of the Tiger" in a box of old manuscripts and thought it was still a perfectly respectable tale, albeit one obviously written by a guy who had only begun to learn his chops. I rewrote it and on a whim resubmitted it to *F&SF.* This time they bought it. One thing I've noticed is that when you've had a little success, magazines are a lot less apt to use that phrase, "Not for us."'

The reference to King's sixteenth year suggests the story was originally written about 1963.

In this America Under Siege tale two tigers fight during a storm. The story begins, 'I first saw Mr. Legere when the circus swung through Stuebenville, but I'd only been with the show for two weeks; he might have been making his irregular visits indefinitely. No one much wanted to talk about Mr. Legere, not even the last night when it seemed that the world was coming to an end – the night Mr. Indrasil disappeared.'

The narrator is Eddie Johnston, who had joined Farnum & William's All American 3-Ring Circus and Sideshow after becoming bored with small town life in Sauk City. As the circus toured Illinois and Indiana that hot summer the crowds were good and everyone was happy, 'Everyone except Mr Indrasil. Mr Indrasil was never happy. He was the lion-tamer, and he looked like old pictures I've seen of Rudolph Valentino.' Indrasil had a reputation, sullen and silent, it was said he had once nearly killed a roustabout for the crime of spilling coffee on his hands. 'And the only two things he was afraid of were Mr Legere and the circus's one tiger, a huge beast called Green Terror.' Indrasil had once used Green Terror in his act but had stopped after the cat 'almost ripped his head from his shoulders before he could get out of the cage. I noticed that Mr Indrasil always wore his hair long down the back of his neck.'

On that day in Steubenville Indrasil was about to assault Johnston for an imagined infraction when Legere intervened. From the exchange of words and body language between the two men Johnston realized, 'I was a pawn in what must have been a long combat between the two of them. I had been captured by Mr Legere rather than Mr Indrasil. He had stopped the lion-tamer not because he felt for me, but because it gained him an advantage, however slight, in their private war.' When Johnston asked Legere if he was with the circus he said, with a slight smile, 'No. You might call me a policeman,' before disappearing into the surging crowd.

As the Circus moved between towns Johnston saw Legere from time to time and finally asked the barker, Chips Baily and the red-headed wire walker, Sally O'Hara whether Legere and Indrasil knew each other. They told him that Legere had followed the circus in the Midwest almost every year of the twenty or so since Indrasil had joined the troupe from Ringling Brothers.' When Johnston tried to probe further they suddenly changed the subject and remembered tasks that needed immediate attention.

As the hot spell went on accidents began to happen, including O'Hara fracturing her shoulder falling from the wire; and tension built in all the circus performers, human and animal, most particularly in Indrasil. And, almost all the time, Legere was by Green Terror's cage, watching the tiger. One evening Johnston saw Indrasil, under 'a swollen Kansas moon', baiting Green Terror with a long, pointed pike. The cat refused to cry out in pain or anger no matter how hard Indrasil poked it. 'Then I saw something odd. It seemed a shadow moved in the darkness under one of the far wagons, and the moonlight seemed to glint on staring eyes - green eyes.' After Indrasil suddenly left and Johnston looked again at the far wagon, the shadow was gone. The roustabout formed this view, 'He was a rogue. That was the only way I can put it. Mr Indrasil was not only a human tiger, but a rogue tiger as well. The thought jelled inside me, disquieting and a little scary.'

The heat wave continued, 'Everyone was reaching the point of explosion.' Legere was now at every performance, 'always dressed in his nattily creased brown suit, despite the killing temperatures. He stood silently by Green Terror's cage, seeming to commune deeply with the tiger, who was always quiet when he was around.'

Finally, in the town of Wildwood Green, Oklahoma a storm began to brew on the horizon. That afternoon a lion tried to attack Indrasil, seemingly spooked by a timely ear-splitting roar from Green Terror. After Indrasil escaped the cage, 'Green Terror let out another roar – but this was one monstrously like a huge, disdainful chuckle.' A tornado warning was issued and the circus cancelled its evening performance, battening down in preparation for the storm. Green Terror refused to move into a larger cage and Indrasil was sent for but initially could not be found. As the storm rose, Johnston finally found Indrasil, drunk and raving about Legere, "He isn't here now is he? We're two of a kind, him and me. Maybe the only two left. My nemesis – and I'm his … Turned the cat against me, back in '58."

Green Terror roared through the noise of the storm and Indrasil realized the cat was still outside, exposed in his cage, and headed there. Johnston followed, 'And Mr Legere was standing by Green Terror's cage. It was like a tableau from Dante. The near-empty cage-clearing inside the circle of trailers; the two men facing each other silently, their clothes and hair rippled by the shrieking gale; the boiling sky above; the twisting wheatfields in the background, like damned souls bending to the whip of Lucifer.'

Legere challenged Indrasil, "It's time Jason," and opened the cat's cage! The tiger seemed to be caught between the will of the two men and stopped briefly. 'I think, in the end, it was Green Terror's own will – his hate of Mr Indrasil that tipped the scales.' Then, 'something strange happened to Mr Indrasil. He seemed to be folding in on himself, shriveling, accordioning. The silk shirt lost shape, the dark, whipping hair became a hideous toadstool around his collar. Mr Legere called something across to him, and, simultaneously, Green Terror leaped.' Johnston saw no more, as he was thrown to the ground, catching 'one crazily tilted glimpse of a huge, towering cyclone funnel, and then the darkness descended.'

When Johnston awoke he asked where Indrasil and Legere were and, reluctantly, Chips Baily began to tell him the rest of the story - not exactly what 'we told the cops … Anyhow, Indrasil's gone. I didn't even know that Legere guy was around.' When asked about Green Terror Baily replied, ' "He and the other tiger fought to death." "*Other* tiger? There's no other ..." "Yeah, but we found two of 'em, lying in each other's blood. Hell of a mess. Ripped each other's throats out."'

'And that's the end of my story – except for two little items. The words Mr Legere shouted just before the tornado hit: '*When a man and an animal live in the same shell, Indrasil, the instincts determine the mold.*' The other thing is what keeps me awake at nights. Chips told me later, offering it only for what it might be worth. What he told me was that the strange tiger had a long scar on the back of its neck.'

The story has the immediate feeling of King's response to Bradbury's classic circus visits small town horror novel, *Something Wicked This Way Comes*. King wrote a screenplay of that tale, which is the subject of another chapter in this book. King academic Michael Collings finds *The Night of the Tiger* lacking[100]: '...Johnston does not even succeed as a narrator. The difficulty is that the story is too allusive (if not illusive) ... too much is missing. Who is Legere and why does Indrasil hate and fear him? Legere says he is a kind of policeman; if so, where is his authority? Why does Green Terror destroy Indrasil? If one is willing to work hard, there may be answers – but the story does not seem sufficiently strong to warrant much work.'

In a mark of how unique this story is there are no links from it to King's other fiction. No timeline is given for the story, the only date provided being 1958, when Legere allegedly turned Green Terror against Jason Indrasil.

In the end this story is unsatisfying and inconclusive, yet it provides the casual reader and the student with another signpost in the development of Stephen King, the writer.

Night Shift – Unproduced Screenplay (Late 1970s)

The material in this chapter was compiled with the assistance of the 88-page typewritten screenplay held in Box 1010 of the Special Collections Unit of the Raymond H Fogler Library at the University of Maine, Orono. The script is marked 'First Draft' in Stephen King's handwriting. Written permission from King is required for access to this screenplay so most readers will never be able read it.

In *Danse Macabre* King says that NBC 'optioned three stories from my 1978 collection, *Night Shift*, and invited me to do the screen-play. One of these stories was a piece called 'Strawberry Spring', about a psychopathic Jack-the-Ripper-type killer ... About a month after turning the script in, I got a call from an NBC munchkin at Standards and Practices (read: The Department of Censorship). The knife my killer used ... had to go ... Knives were too phallic. I suggested we turn the killer into a strangler. The munchkin evinced great enthusiasm ... The script was finally coughed out of the network's large and voracious gullet by Standards and Practices, however, strangler and all. Too gruesome and intense was the final verdict.'

In an extensive interview with *Famous Monsters* magazine for April 1980 King had this to say about the script: 'I did that, and that was shot down by NBC. Basically, all the people that were involved with on the creative end, myself included, were very happy with what we had. It was presented to NBC, who had the deal, and their standards and practices thing just said, "No, too gory, too suspenseful, it's too intense." They axed it for those reasons and it's now gone over to the Martin Poll organization, who, the last I knew, were trying to develop it for theatricals. This is my script, and we'll see if anything happens. I don't think they're working on it with any degree of speed or real enthusiasm at this point.'

It seems likely it was written in 1978 or 1979.

King's screenplay has never been produced and includes adaptations of *Strawberry Spring*, *I Know What You Need* and *Battleground*, along with an original wrap-around tale set in the previously unknown town of Weathersfield, Maine. As a result this screenplay is part of the Maine Street Horror Reality.

Readers of the script are told that Weathersfield is but eight miles from Jerusalem's Lot and forty miles from the sea. Indeed, the far end of Main Street leads to Jerusalem's Lot. Richard Davis mentioned the 'Boogies' in that town and Harold Davis thought it 'a strange place'. Of course, Jerusalem's Lot, Maine is a very important town in the Maine Street Horror reality (*see the feature panel*). An invasion by vampires occurred in the town, which is better known as 'Salem's Lot, in 1975. In October 1976 Mark Petrie and Ben Mears set a fire intended to burn the town flat but, in 1977 (see *One for the Road*), vampires from the town were still preying on passers-by. So, in 1978, the year in which this screenplay is set, the Davis' comments would make sense.

Weathersfield was the only town that far north in the Massachusetts Colony to put supposed witches to death and this fact plays an important role in the storyline. A feature is the Town Common. Not only were the supposed witches burned there but the apartment building in which two major characters, Ed Hamner, Jr. and John Renshaw lived, was opposite it.

In the script two men observe the town of Weathersfield, Maine and discuss its past. Richard Davis was the grandson of Harold Davis and the editor of the town newspaper. We are taken back to 1968, when there had been a series of murders on the campus of the Weathersfield Community College. 'Springheel Jack', who left no tracks, killed four female students. At the time Richard was a student and roomed with Lonnie Rennaker. A fellow student, Carl Amalera was arrested but released after the killings continued while he was in custody. We also learn Harold Davis' grandfather had called a late winter thaw a 'strawberry spring'.

John Renshaw, a hired killer was living in an apartment building overlooking the Weathersfield Town Common at the time he was killed by an explosion in his apartment. 'Toy soldiers', made by the company whose owner was one of his victims, were activated by the victim's mother, a witch. She had achieved this feat after raising a Demon that told her the name of her son's killer. After Renshaw died during an attack by the soldiers the witch walked into the Demon and disappeared.

Edward Hamner, Jr. had begun dating a Weathersfield student, Liz Neely, following her boyfriend's tragic death in a road accident. Investigating Hamner's past Neely discovered he was using voodoo to influence her and was probably responsible for the deaths of his parents and her boyfriend. When she confronted him with this information Hamner killed himself.

In 1978 the Springheel Jack murders began again. Cindy Rennaker found a girl's body in her husband Lonnie's car. Lonnie then strangled his wife.

Finally, Richard Davis saw Renshaw, Lonnie Rennaker and Hamner in a vision over the graves of three supposed witches who had been burned at the stake in Weathersfield in 1717. This would indicate that Lonnie, too, was dead.

Although this screenplay has not been produced *Strawberry Spring* itself was adapted as a 'dollar baby' film in 2001 by Doveed Linder.

There are in fact two other versions of this tale. It was originally published in the University of Maine literary magazine, *Ubris* for Fall 1968. King substantially revised the story for its publication in *Cavalier* for November 1975 and *Gent* for February 1977. That version was collected in *Night Shift* in 1978. The two *Strawberry Spring* stories are versions of the same story but the setting is completely different, moving from Wiscasset College in Maine in the *Ubris* version to the New Sharon Teachers' College in an unnamed but probably New England state in the *Night Shift* version. It probably does not matter if King was adapting the earlier or latter version for this unproduced screenplay as he *again* moved the location, this time to Weathersfield Community College, back in Maine.

In the original *Ubris* version readers never discover who the 'Springheel Jack' killer really is but are left suspecting it may be the unnamed narrator, who does not appear to be married. In the *Night Shift* version the killer is clearly the narrator. During his second set of killings his wife suspected no more than that he was seeing another woman. In the screenplay the killer is clearly Lonnie Rennaker.

In another change in *Ubris* the murders occurred in 1968, with no subsequent killings. By *Cavalier/Night Shift* King had added the 1976 murder. In the screenplay King extended the rampage by having Rennaker kill another student and his own wife in 1978. Readers may be pleased to know that the original 1968 victims – Cerman, Bray, Parkins and Curran almost remain the victims in all three versions of this tale (Parkins becomes Perkins in the screenplay). The 1978 victim in the screenplay was Cynthia Baker, while the 1976 victim in *Cavalier/Night Shift* is never named. Finally, King loses the second student to be falsely accused of the 1968 murders, Hanson Gray, from the screenplay version.

All these changes effectively mean there are three distinct versions of *Strawberry Spring*, with each extending the killing spree and providing more detail as to the killer's and victims' identities.

King sold the 'dollar baby' rights to *I Know What You Need* and that film was first shown at the 2nd Annual Stephen King Dollar Baby Film Festival in Bangor on 1 October 2005. Frankly, it is a very poor adaptation. The short story was first published in *Cosmopolitan* magazine for September 1976 and was republished with minor changes and the correction of an error in *Night Shift*.

The original *I Know What You Need* was also set in Maine but neither the town nor the college Elizabeth Rogan attended are named. While in the screenplay Ed Hamner, Jr. killed himself after Elizabeth Neely (one wonders why King changed her surname?) confronted him, in the short story Elizabeth Rogan simply took his voodoo items and threw them away, breaking Ed's power and influence over her. There is no indication that Ed reacted in any other way in the short story than simply leaving. King also changed the name of Liz's unfortunate boyfriend Tony Lombard in the original story to Tony Lester in the screenplay. Unfortunately for the character, regardless of his surname, he dies in both versions. In the original story the timeline was 1971.

It is a little known fact that *Battleground* has been adapted as an animated feature. Titled *Srajenie* (this Russian title translates as 'The Battle') it was made in the Soviet Union in 1986 and is almost entirely without dialogue. The screenplay is by V Goryachev and Mikhail Titov directed the ten-minute film. Denis Gatiatullin brought this adaptation, previously unknown in the King community, to our attention.

It was also adapted as the first episode of the *Nightmares and Dreamscapes* TV series (2006), with a teleplay by Richard Christian Matheson and tremendous acting by John Hurt playing Renshaw.

Battleground was originally published in *Cavalier* for September 1972. For its publication in *Night Shift* in 1978 there were very minor wording revisions. In the original story it was Hans Morris' wife who set the soldiers upon Renshaw but in the screenplay King uses a powerful device in having Morris' mother, a witch aged about 80, arrange Renshaw's death. This fits nicely with the closing twist of the script, at the witches' graves. No dates were given for the events in the original story.

The entirely original wrap-around story features Harold Davis, and his grandson, Richard, editor of the town newspaper. They discuss recent and past events in Weathersfield and these recollections form the three stories. This storyline is set in 1978, the same year as the second 'Springheel Jack' murders. Harold had lived in Weathersfield all his life. He'd joined the Weathersfield Community College security department in 1930 and retired in 1973. About 70 in 1978, he had raised Richard. Harold suspected that Lonnie Rennaker was Springheel Jack. Richard Davis was about 28 in 1978 and had roomed with

Rennaker at Weathersfield Community College. After graduating he single-handedly ran the town's newspaper, the *Independent*.

At the end of the script Richard Davis saw three old crones who were almost certainly the three alleged witches (Abigail, Tamson and one unnamed) who had been burned at the stake in 1717 and buried on the Town Common. They appeared where their gravestones had been, had toothless mouths, heads giving off a green glow and white pupil-less eyes. They disappeared and were replaced by Lonnie Rennaker, Ed Hamner Jr. and John Renshaw. A hand from the earth then grabbed Davis' ankle. He ran, the three men faded and the gravestones reappeared. Of course, King used the device from Brian de Palma's film of his own work *Carrie* with the hand suddenly shooting up from the ground.

This screenplay contains a significant link to King's other fiction with the mention of the nearby town of Jerusalem's Lot, the setting for King's American vampire novel *'Salem's Lot*, its sequel short story *One for the Road* and the Lovecraftian short story *Jerusalem's Lot*. The town is also mentioned in *The Body*, *The Dead Zone*, *Dreamcatcher*, the *Prime Evil* version of *The Night Flier* (in that vampire story it is said to be 'mostly deserted') and *Pet Sematary*. Most importantly, King reintroduced the town in Pere Callahan's back-story in *The Dark Tower V: Wolves of the Calla*.

We also read in the screenplay that Mrs. Carmody was an old woman who ran an antique shop on Carbine Street, Weathersfield. Interestingly, and knowing King this can be no coincidence, in *The Mist* a Mrs. Carmody ran an antique shop in Bridgton. In that story she became the leader of a religious group inside the supermarket and tried to have her people kill Billy Drayton and Amanda Dumfries.

This anthology screenplay is in the style of *Creepshow* or *Cat's Eye*. It would make a great addition to that style of filmmaking and King adaptations in general. However, there seems little hope it will be produced and it is most unlikely the screenplay will ever be published, consigning Harold and Richard Davis and the town of Weathersfield, Maine to a twilight zone existence.

Considering the variety and quality of the stories in the *Night Shift* collection it is not surprising that most have been adapted to film. Many were produced as 'dollar babies', including: *The Boogeyman, The Last Rung on the Ladder, The Lawnmower Man, Night Surf, Strawberry Spring* and Darabont's *The Woman in the Room*. The wider release productions include *Children of the Corn, Graveyard Shift, The Lawnmower Man* (that production bears no resemblance to the story), *The Ledge* (as a segment of *Cat's Eye*), *The Mangler* and *Sometimes They Come Back*. *Trucks* was made into a TV special for the USA Network.

This leaves one wondering how long *Grey Matter, I Am the Doorway, I Know What You Need* (apart from the execrable dollar baby), *Jerusalem's Lot, The Man Who Loved Flowers* and *One For the Road* will escape adaptation.

Jerusalem's Lot – A 'Strange Place'

Jerusalem's Lot (widely known as 'Salem's Lot), having been the earlier site of devil-worship and the disappearance of its entire populace in 1789, was taken over by a colony of vampires and effectively abandoned again by the living in 1975. Despite the town's destruction by fire in 1976 vampires were known to be in the area as late as 1977. Jerusalem's Lot's history may be read and discovered in the following order: *Jerusalem's Lot*, *'Salem's Lot*, *One for the Road* and parts of *The Dark Tower V: Wolves of the Calla*. It is also mentioned in *The Dark Tower VI: Song of Susannah* and *The Dark Tower VII: The Dark Tower*.

It was founded by a splinter group of the Puritan faith, headed by James Boon, in 1710. On 31 October 1789 the entire population of town disappeared.

Source: Jerusalem's Lot (in the *Night Shift* collection)

A small town east of Cumberland and 20 miles north of Portland, it is in Cumberland County and can be accessed via Route 12 from Falmouth. It was incorporated in 1765 and named after one of Charles Belknap Tanner's pigs, Jerusalem, which escaped into the woods and went wild. Tanner would warn small children away from Jerusalem's wood lot. The township is nearly circular and two major roads, Brock Street and Jointner Avenue cross dead center at right angles. Central Maine Power pylons march across the town in a northwest to southeast diagonal, forming a 150ft wide gash in the timberland. The northwest quadrant is North Jerusalem and includes the high ground, including the Marsten House. The northeast is mostly open farmland and the Royal River flows through it to Drunk's Leap. In the southeast section are farms and the homes of white-collar commuters. In the southwest area known as The Bend are many shacks and trailer homes. Town government in the Lot was by town meeting. In 1960 it had 1252 inhabitants and in 1970 1319. The majority of these were of Scotch-English and French ancestry. In 1975 the town was abandoned after an infestation of vampires. On 6 October 1976 it was apparently largely destroyed by fire.

Source: 'Salem's Lot

Also known as 'The Lot', Richard Davis mentioned the 'Boogies' there. It is eight miles from Weathersfield. Harold Davis thought it 'a strange place'.

Source: Night Shift (Unproduced Screenplay)

> Father Donald Callahan moved there in the Spring of 1969. He became convinced that vampires had infested the town in 1975. He confronted one in October that year but, after losing his faith and being forced to drink the vampire's blood, fled the town in shame.
> *Source: The Dark Tower V: Wolves of the Calla*
> The town was apparently taken over by vampires in 1975 and burned flat in 1976. In 1977 there were still vampires in the area.
> *Source: One for the Road* (in the *Night Shift* collection)
> Donald Callahan was once the Catholic Priest in this 'little' town. By 1999 it no longer existed on any map.
> *Source: The Dark Tower VII: The Dark Tower*

The Old Dude's Ticker (2000)

The Old Dude's Ticker was first published in the *NECON XX Commemorative Volume* for 2000. That volume was limited to 333 copies. It was reprinted in *The Big Book of Necon* (Cemetery Dance, 2009), which is likely the only way readers might secure a copy of the tale.

King actually wrote the story nearly three decades earlier. He explained the story's genesis in an introduction to the tale:

'In the two years after I was married (1971-1972), I sold nearly two dozen stories to various men's magazines. Most were purchased by Nye Willden, the fiction editor at *Cavalier*. These stories were important supplements to the meager income I was earning in my two day jobs, one as a high school English teacher and the other as an employee of The New Franklin Laundry, where I washed motel sheets. These were not good times for short horror fiction ... but I sold an almost uninterrupted run of mine – no mean feat for an unknown, un-agented scribbler from Maine ...'

'Two of them, however, did not sell. Both were pastiches. The first was a modern day revision of Nikolai Gogol's story, "The Ring" (my version was called "The Spear", I think). That one is lost. The second was the one that follows, a crazed revisionist telling of Poe's "The Tell-Tale Heart". I thought the idea was a natural: crazed Vietnam vet kills elderly benefactor as a result of post-traumatic stress syndrome. I'm not sure what Nye's problem with it might have been; I loved it, but he shot it back at me with a terse "not for us" note. I gave it a final sad look, then put it in a desk drawer and went on to something else. It stayed in said drawer until rescued by Marsha DeFilippo, who found it in a pile of old manuscripts consigned to a collection of my stuff in the Raymond H Fogler Library at the University of Maine.'

'I was tempted to tinker with it – the seventies slang is pretty out of date – but resisted the impulse, deciding to let it be what it was then: partly satire and partly affectionate homage...'

The story is short, only six small pages in the Volume, and is headed *The Old Dude's Ticker* – Stephen King and Edgar Allan Poe. Typically of King in an environment where he feels very comfortable with the 'audience', he signs the introduction 'Steve King'.

It is unlikely King will include this tale in one of his short story collections. As he says, the slang is very dated and the story would have fitted much more comfortably in one of the early collections such as *Skeleton Crew*. It would be jarringly out of place with King's more modern style in a collection such as *Everything's Eventual*. This being the case, readers will need to purchase either the NECON XX Volume or the reprint in the much easier to find *Big Book of NECON*, edited by Bob Booth (Cemetery Dance, 2009).

King says in his introduction, 'If you have half as much fun reading it as I had writing it, we'll both be well off, I think. I hope some of Poe's feverish intensity comes through here ... and I hope the master isn't rolling in his grave too much.' In fact, Poe's style does come through in the story and it is certainly excellent homage to *The Tell-Tale Heart*. While the seventies slang is indeed dated, it serves the story well as it is supposed to be the killer's own words recorded shortly after the murder. All in all, this is a fun story, to be appreciated as much for its intent as its content.

In the tale an old man is murdered. Richard Drogan apparently lived with the Old Dude but even though he '...had no case against him ...' he became obsessed with one of his eyes - 'Pale blue, with a cataract on it. And it bulged. When he looked at me, my blood ran cold. That's how bad it freaked me. So little by little, I made up my mind to waste him and get rid of the eye forever.' Richard watched him sleep each night for a week, using a narrow penlight beam to search out the man's eye but it was always closed. On the eighth night the Old Dude woke up while Richard was watching. As he stood and waited for the Old Dude to go back to sleep Richard finally decided to shine the light on the eye, only to find it open ('This dull dusty blue with that gross-out white stuff all over it so it looked like the bulging yolk of a poached egg').

Richard claimed to have supersensitive hearing following service in Vietnam and could hear the old man's heart ('ticker') beating. Panicking and thinking the neighbors would hear it he smothered the old man. He then cut up the body in the shower and pushed the parts under the bedroom floorboards.

At four the next morning, alerted by a neighbor's call about a yell in the night, the police asked to look around the house. Richard invited them in but after talking for a while he began to suspect they knew his secret. He became agitated as time progressed and could now hear a beating noise growing steadily louder, presumably that of the old dude's ticker under the floorboards. Fearing the cops would hear it he then confessed to the murder and showed them the body. ' "Stop it!" I screamed at them. "Stop it! I admit it! – I did it! – rip up the boards! – here, here! its (*sic*) his heart! It's the beating of his hideous heart!"'

It turns out that Richard Drogan was actually Robert Deisenhoff, a Vietnam veteran who had scragged an officer there and been sent to the Quigly Veterans Hospital, from which he had escaped more than five years earlier. At the end of the story we find the whole thing is actually Deisenhoff's statement to the police. This is King's little twist at the end of the tale, even though we knew early on Richard/Robert was a killer, it is only at the last we realize he had been caught and come to fully understand his mental illness.

Working backwards we come to understand that Deisenhoff had been in Vietnam but had lost his mind and killed ('scragged' in the parlance of the time) his lieutenant and been shipped back to a Veteran's Hospital and placed under armed guard. Richard/Robert tells the police he heard a sound from the old dude as he held the light beam to his eye. 'Didn't I tell you how sharp my hearing has been since Nam? And what came to my ears was this low, quick noise. You know what that sound was like? Have you ever seen a squad of MPs on a parade ground? They all wear white gloves, and they all carry these little short sticks on their belts. And if one of them takes his stick out and starts tapping it into his palm, it makes a sound like that. I remember that … from that hospital where they put me after I came home. Sure, they had MPs there.' King's twist on Poe's tale is to have the killer compare the sound of the heart/ticker to his military background. 'I knew what that sound was, there in the dark. It wasn't any GI head-bopper. It was the old dude's ticker. It made me even madder, the way beating a drum will make a GI feel ballsier.'

The closing paragraph of the story reveals that the police statement was taken on August 14, 1976 and that investigations had confirmed that Richard Drogan was indeed Robert Deisenhoff, 'who escaped from the Quigly (Ohio) Veteran's Hospital on April 9, 1971.' This leaves one wondering what other deeds or misdeeds Richard/Robert may have got up to in the intervening five years. One also wonders if there is just a hint of General Anthony Hecksler, the insane killer in both versions of *The Plant*? Deisenhoff's name reminds one of Dieffenbaker, the new lieutenant and Vietnam veteran in *The New Lieutenant's Rap*, although the soldier 'scragged' in that story was Ralph Clemson, shot by Slocum under Dieffenbaker's orders to stop Clemson from massacring Vietnamese civilians. Dieffenbaker also appears as the lieutenant in the heavily revised version of *The New Lieutenant's Rap* published as *Why We're in Vietnam* in the *Hearts in Atlantis* collection.

King had not written a great deal relating to America's Vietnam trauma until the *Hearts in Atlantis* collection. Despite being at University during the heyday of the anti-war movement, or perhaps because of that, King seemed to almost studiously avoid both the War and its impact upon American society in his fiction until later in his career. *The Old Dude's Ticker* was apparently written about 1971-2 (but not published until 2000) and *Squad D* (which has never been published) was written in the late 1970s. The next significant Vietnam stories appeared decades after King's involvement with the anti-war movement.

Blind Willie, the next King story heavily influenced by Vietnam, was first published in 1994, before being heavily revised for its appearance in the *Hearts in Atlantis* collection. *The New Lieutenant's Rap*, *Hearts in Atlantis*, *Why We're in Vietnam* and *Heavenly Shades of Night Are Falling* were all first published in 1999. However, King had written of many characters who served in Vietnam or even died there (for instance, Peter St George from *Dolores Claiborne*) and referenced some of the events there from time to time.

The influence of Vietnam and the fact that King never reveals the geographical location of the murders makes this an America Under Siege story. There are no direct links to other King works from this story.

King in Men's Magazines

Before King was a best-selling novelist, and for some time afterward, he supplemented his income selling short stories to lurid men's magazines, which contrasted articles and fiction with spreads of naked women. In recent times he returned to the now venerable *Playboy* magazine. The following is a list of these stories (and two poems)

Graveyard Shift	*Cavalier*	October 1970
I Am the Doorway	*Cavalier*	March 1971
Suffer the Little Children	*Cavalier*	February 1972
The Fifth Quarter (*)	*Cavalier*	April 1972
Battleground	*Cavalier*	September 1972
The Mangler	*Cavalier*	December 1972
The Boogeyman	*Cavalier*	March 1973
Trucks	*Cavalier*	June 1973
Gray Matter	*Cavalier*	October 1973
Sometimes They Come Back	*Cavalier*	March 1974
Night Surf (^)	*Cavalier*	August 1974
Strawberry Spring (#)	*Cavalier*	November 1975
The Boogeyman (+)	*Gent*	December 1975
Weeds	*Cavalier*	May 1976
The Ledge	*Penthouse*	July 1976
Strawberry Spring (+)	*Gent*	February 1977
Children of the Corn	*Penthouse*	March 1977
The Cat from Hell	*Cavalier*	March and June 1977
The Man Who Loved Flowers	*Gallery*	August 1977
The Man with a Belly	*Cavalier*	December 1978
Weeds (+)	*Nugget*	April 1979
The Crate	*Gallery*	July 1979

The Man with a Belly (+)	*Gent*	December 1979
The Monkey	*Gallery*	November 1980
The Raft	*Gallery*	November 1982
The Word Processor	*Playboy*	January 1983
Willa	*Playboy*	December 2006
Mute	*Playboy*	December 2007
The Bone Church (%)	*Playboy*	November 2009
Tommy (%)	*Playboy*	March 2010

(*) under the pseudonym John Swithen
(^) in a revised version, it was originally published in *Ubris* for Spring 1969
(#) in a revised version, it was originally published in *Ubris* for Fall 1968
(+) effectively a reprint, as there were no changes from the earlier version
(%) poem

People, Places and Things (1960)

People, Places and Things is a collection of eighteen short stories self-published by King and his friend Chris Chesley under the name of the Triad Publishing Company. First published in 1960, it was reprinted in 1963. Chesley was one of King's close childhood friends growing up in Durham, Maine.[101] They apparently wrote many stories together, and singly, for their amusement and that of their family and friends and it is a small tragedy that most have been lost.

King owns the sole known copy of the collection, which he re-discovered in his papers in 1985. However, partial photocopies of the 'Second Printing, 1963' version circulate freely in the King community. It is thought that less than a dozen original copies were ever printed.[102]

The Table of Contents for *People, Places and Things* is as follows:

Forward (*sic*), 1
Hotel At the End of the Road, 2 — Steve King
Genius, 3 — Chris Chesley
Top Forty, News, Weather and Sports, 4 — Chris Chesley
Bloody Child, 5 — Chris Chesley
I've Got to Get Away!, 6 — Steve King
The Dimension Warp, 7 — Steve King
The Thing at the Bottom of the Well, 8 — Steve King
Reward, 9 — Chris Chesley
The Stranger, 10 — Steve King
A Most Unusual Thing, 11 — Chris Chesley

Gone, 12	Chris Chesley
They've Come, 13	Chris Chesley
I'm Falling, 14	Steve King
The Cursed Expedition, 15	Steve King
The Other Side of the Fog, 16	Steve King
Scared, 17	Chris Chesley
Curiousity (*sic*) Killed the Cat, 18	Chris Chesley
Never Look Behind You, 19	Steve King – Chris Chesley

The cover is headed 'People, Places and Things – Volume 1' and the authors are listed as Steve King and Chris Chesley. This version is listed as the 'Second Edition – Complete and Unabridged'. The Table of Contents page shows the booklet as being 'Produced in Association with the Triad Publishing Company', with 'Copyright 1963, by Steve King and Chris Chesley – First Printing, 1960 – Second Printing, 1963'. In simple terms, King and Chesley 'self-published' these stories.

Unfortunately, two of the King stories listed in the Table of Contents have been lost – no known copies of *The Dimension Warp* and *I'm Falling* exist.

All in all the stories are best described as what they are – 'juvenilia'. However, clear hints of the King to come appear in each story and it is in this that they perhaps retain their greatest value. Michael Collings writes in his *Horror Plum'd*[103]: 'In approach, content, theme, and treatment, however, they clearly suggest directions the mature King would explore in greater detail…'

Six King stories and one written with Chesley have survived the years and each is briefly reviewed below.

The Hotel at the End of the Road

Readers can access this story in *The Market Guide for Young Writers* (Fourth Edition onwards only) by Kathy Henderson[104]. To date, this is the only time the story has been republished. According to King bibliographer Justin Brooks King sent a copy of the story to Carol Fenner, the managing editor of a student literary magazine, *Flip*, but the magazine folded before the story could be republished!

In the story Tommy Riviera and Kelso Black are the target of a high speed police chase. They turned up a dirt road, saw an old hotel ahead and decided to stay for the night. After being initially ignored by an old man at reception he directed them to Room Five, but only after being threatened at gunpoint!

When Tommy woke up the following morning he was totally paralyzed. The old man he had seen the night before came into view and informed him that they were new additions to his living 'museum', but they would be well cared for and would not die.

This 365-word story is as derivative as one could expect from an early teenage writer.

This story is in King's America Under Siege reality but it is possible the criminals had driven into another reality, which would make it a very early New Worlds story. IN support of this view, as Riviera and Black were being chased by the police, they turned onto a gravel road then, 'The uniformed policeman scratched his head. "Where did they go?" His partner frowned. "I don't know. They just – disappeared."' When the fleeing pair arrived at the Hotel it 'looked just like a scene out of the early 1900s'.

The main characters are the two criminals – Riviera and Black, and the mysterious old man, who informs them they are 'the first additions to my museum in twenty-five years' and, 'You'll go well with the rest of my collection of living mummies.' The key setting is the Hotel, which is old and, in Black's words, '…a crummy joint. I'll bet there's enough cockroaches in here to fill a five-gallon can'. The old man had Kelso and Black stay (perhaps forever?) in Room Five, which was '…barren except for an iron double bed, a cracked mirror and soiled wallpaper.'

No timeline is given in the story. This early King work has one very interesting link – Kelso Black also appears in *The Stranger* but meets a very different end in that story.

It should be noted that the title shown on the story page is *The Hotel at the End of the Road*, even though the first 'The' is not shown on the Table of Contents page of the compendium.

I've Got to Get Away!

In this story Denny Phillips woke to find himself on an atomic factory assembly line but could remember nothing. Those around him looked like zombies or prisoners.

As he tried to escape guards shot him and he blacked out. One of the guards commented that the x-238A robots occasionally seemed to go haywire and try to run away. Two weeks later, after being repaired and returned to work, Denny Phillips again had the urge to get away.

The roots of the story appear to be in King's voluminous science fiction readings, with the 'conscious' robot wishing for humanity being a staple of the pulp SF market. An interesting development in King's early writing is changing from first person narrative in the first half of the story where the robot feels '…as if I had just awakened from a slumber' to third person as the guards comment on the problems with the 'x-238A … Denny Phillips, name' and Phillips' second re-awakening, two weeks later. King also uses repetition to bring the reader into Phillips' dilemma – 'I had to get away!'; 'I've got to get away'; and the final words of the story, now capitalized: 'I'VE GOT TO GET AWAY!!'

Due to science fiction theme of this story (robots working on 'an atomic factory assembly line') it is part of King's New Worlds reality.

The main character is, of course, an x-238A robot, Denny Phillips and the setting is the factory. King's device of having the factory guarded, '…and the guards had guns' is required to prevent the robot's escape after it becomes self-aware but also serves to provide a dark, almost concentration-camp like feel to the story. The ubiquitous 'Acme Robot Repairs' company took Phillips away for repair, although there is no sign of the Coyote! No timeline is given in the story.

This 308-word story has an interesting link, as it was apparently re-written as *The Killer* (see the separate chapter).

The Thing at the Bottom of the Well

In this story a mean little boy meets a meaner opponent. Oglethorpe Crater enjoyed hurting people and animals. From tying a rope across the stairs so the cook fell, to poking pins into his pet dog, nothing was beyond his wretched ways.

One day he heard a voice down a well inviting him into it. He went down and was found a month later, tortured, and dead.

This story is perhaps the least derivative of those in *People, Places and Things* and shows flashes of King's future themes. Oglethorpe Crater, '…an ugly, mean little wretch' was visited by the very same tortures he had inflicted on other creatures – '…his arms were pulled out … pins had been stuck in his eyes, and there were other tortures too horrible to mention.'

Oglethorpe had been dealt this ugly but deserving death (King quickly creates an intense dislike for the child in the reader) by something at the bottom of the well. 'But a soft voice called up, "Hello, Oglethorpe." Oglethorpe looked down, but could see nothing. "Who are you," Oglethorpe asked. "Come on down," said the voice. "And we'll have jolly fun." So Oglethorpe went down.' Any reader of *It* would recognize a prototype of Pennywise in this short passage. The last words of the story, as the searchers leave with the boy's body are '…it actually seemed that they heard laughter coming from the bottom of the well.'

This 355-word story falls into the America Under Siege reality. The main character, little Oglethorpe, is the sort of nasty child who might have grown into a Joe St. George, Sr. 'He dearly loved plaguing the dog and cat, pulling the wings from flies, and watching worms squirm as he slowly pulled them apart. (This lost its fun when he heard worms feel no pain).' We know nothing of the 'Thing' except it could clearly communicate and kill, somehow taking its tortures from its victim's own actions. No timeline is given in the story.

The Stranger

Kelso Black, a character in *The Hotel at the End of the Road*, has a reprise in this 235-word story. In each case he comes to a sticky end. In this tale, Black apparently meets the Devil, as does Gary in King's most critically awarded story, *The Man in the Black Suit*.

In the story Black killed a guard during a robbery. While toasting the $50,000 takings he heard footsteps coming up the stairs to the attic where he was hiding. A Stranger entered and Kelso Black began screaming after looking into the stranger's face. The two disappeared, leaving nothing but the smell of brimstone in the room.

In this America Under Siege tale, the main characters are Kelso Black, who had just committed the robbery, '...now he had fifty grand in his pockets. The guard was dead – but it was his fault! He got in the way'; and a 'stranger' the reader (and presumably, Black) assumes is the Devil. ' "It's time for you to come, Kelso," the stranger said softly. "After all we have a long way to go."' Then '...Black looked into that Face'. While Kelso screamed the 'stranger' simply laughed '...and in a moment, the room was silent. And empty. But it smelled strongly of brimstone'. Readers will know that King uses a similar artifice in *The Stand*, where looking into Randall Flagg's face at certain times could drive the viewer insane. No timeline is given in the story.

The Cursed Expedition

In this story James Keller and Hugh Bullford travel to Venus, where they find breathable air, perfect temperature and delicious fruit. Keller calls it the Garden of Eden but Bullford has his doubts. These doubts are confirmed the next morning when he finds Keller dead. He tries in vain to contact Earth even though there is nothing wrong with the radio.

After seeing the ground open up before his eyes he takes a soil sample, analyzes it and finds the planet is alive. Venus then swallows the spaceship, with Bullford inside.

This 324-word science fiction story falls into King's New Worlds reality. King returned to the story line of a living planet swallowing up visiting astronauts in *Beachworld*, published in *Weird Tales* for Fall of 1984 and a slightly revised version in *Skeleton Crew* the following year. Venus is also a key location in a King's *Night Shift* story, *I Am the Doorway*.

The main characters in the story are astronauts James Keller, who did not see the danger of Venus and ended up dead, with '...a look of horror on his face Bullford never hoped to see again'; and Bullford, the skeptic who sensed the danger in the idyllic landing spot – "I don't like this place Jimmy. It feels all wrong. There's something … evil about it." Before the planet reared up and ate the space ship, 'The landscape was the same, pleasant and happy. But Bullford could see the evil in it. "You killed him!" he cried.'

In a neat little phrase, after the planet's soil closes over the ship it '...almost seemed to lick its lips.' No timeline is given in this story.

The Other Side of the Fog

Pete Jacobs finds himself lost in time when he is surrounded by a fog outside his house. Stepping out of the fog, Jacobs found himself in a city in the future. Frightened, he re-entered the fog only to come out in at the time of the dinosaurs and again he ran into the fog. It seemed he was destined to be lost forever in the fog and time.

In such a short story King does a great job of bringing Jacobs' fear to us through the closing sentences, 'The next time the Fog closes in on you, and you hear hurried footsteps running through the whiteness... call out. That would be Pete Jacobs, trying to find his side of the Fog ... Help the poor guy.'

King later used the mist or fog element to tremendous effect in both *The Mist* and *Crouch End*. This 289-word science fiction story falls into King's New Worlds reality. Obviously, Jacobs is the main character. We do not know the timeline of Jacob's world but we do know the city is in the future: 'The cornerstone on a skyscraper read April 17, 2007'. To confirm the futuristic feel King wrote: 'People walked along on moving conveyor belts.' And: 'Strange cars that rode six inches or so off the ground narrowly missed hitting him.'

When the fog takes Jacobs to the past he is chased by '...a huge prehistoric brontosaurus ... The desire to kill was in his small, beady eyes.' We will of course allow a small error here to a writer of King's age at the time in that a 'brontosaurus' (from the mid-1970s this species has been called Apatosaurus) was in fact a plant eater, not a carnivore. The creature lived in the Jurassic Period, 157-146 million years ago.

Never Look Behind You

This 196-word story is King's collaboration with Chris Chesley. In the story a small-time criminal makes a mistake. George Jacobs had been a usurer for fifteen years but had never been 'hooked on a charge'. While counting his money one day an old woman entered the room. As he turned to her after she stated he would never be able to spend the money she raised a finger and he died. Two men who found Jacobs' body did not look behind them and were thereby saved from the same fate.

This America Under Siege story appears to be an-old fashioned case of revenge. Jacobs had so assiduously cleaned out his local community that '...people hated him.' His methods had been questionable but not enough to be prosecuted. This appears to have left an old lady to deliver justice, 'Her clothes were mostly filthy rags and other crude material.' When she held up her '…boney *(sic)* hand' there was '…a flash of fire in his throat; and a scream. Then, with a final gurgle, George Jacobs died.'

As in most of the *People, Places and Things* stories it is the punch line that makes the story: ' "I wonder what – or who – could have killed him?" said a young man. "I'm glad he's gone," said another. That one was lucky. He didn't look behind him.'

No timeline is given for this story and while it is not linked to any other, revenge is a powerful motive and appears in many King a story, including *Dolan's Cadillac* and *Dolores Claiborne*. As Spignesi has pointed out there is a hint of the future *Thinner* in the appearance of the old lady, although of course it is an old man who places the curse in that dark tale.

Pet Sematary Screenplay (1986)

Released on 21 April 1989, *Pet Sematary* was the first movie ever produced from a screenplay in which King adapted one of his own novel-length works. Also for the first time a King adaptation was filmed in Maine, a contractual requirement King insisted on when he sold the rights. It was made on a budget of $11.5 million and took $57.5 million at the US box office alone, making it a hit in the dollar terms of the time. *Pet Sematary* is a genuinely frightening film and many a moviegoer was caught literally on the edge of their seats at screenings. Its accuracy to the book and the realistic presentation lead viewers to think, 'Oh my god, they won't do that, will they?' and, sure enough, *they* do!

Actor Denise Crosby is quoted by Jones[105] as saying of King: 'I think the fact that he wrote the script made a big difference. He can really tell a story. That's his genius.' And the July 1989 edition of *Cinefantastique* commented, 'Thanks to the excellent script penned by Stephen King himself, this long-awaited film rendition of his scariest novel to date also proves to be the most faithful adaptation yet.'

Members of the world's leading movie website, www.imdb.com, give *Pet Sematary* a rating of 6.3 out of a possible 10, somewhat below a fair assessment of the movie and that of a number of leading critics. Mary Lambert directed. The main actors were Dale Midkiff as Louis Creed; Fred Gwynne (the original Herman Munster) stole the show as Jud Crandall; Denise Crosby played Rachel Creed; and Miko Hughes portrayed a suitably evil Gage Creed. Stephen King appeared in one of his cameos, this time as a Minister. The movie was released on DVD in 2000.

Copies of the First Draft of the screenplay freely circulate in the King and movie production communities. However, this chapter was compiled from the later Revised Draft dated February 1986. That draft consists of 120 pages and

303 scenes. A copy is held in Box 2318 at the Special Collections Unit of the Raymond H Fogler Library at the University of Maine, Orono and is available for public reading.

In the script a man's grief leads to even greater tragedy. The Creed family moved to Ludlow, Maine when Louis Creed took up his job as a doctor at the University of Maine. On his first day at work a sophomore, Victor Pascow died in the infirmary after being hit by a car. While dying Pascow warned Louis of the dangers of a Micmac burial ground but the doctor had no idea what he was talking about.

The family cat Church was then killed outside the Creed house on Route 15, which carried a constant flow of fast moving traffic. Concerned over his daughter's reaction Louis buried the cat in a nearby Micmac burial ground, which had the reputation of bringing back the dead, rather than in the local 'Pet Sematary', as a child's sign spelt the latter word. Church returned to life but was now a mean and unlovable animal and Louis was forced to kill it with morphine.

The worst happened when Louis and Rachel Creed's son Gage was hit by a truck on the road and killed. After the funeral Rachel and their daughter, Ellie, went to visit her parents, leaving Louis alone. Their neighbor, Jud Crandall tried to warn Louis against any thoughts he might have of reburying Gage in the Micmac burial ground by telling him the story of a local man who had buried his son there in 1944. Afterward Timmy Baterman came back to 'life' and wandered the town as a virtual zombie until the townspeople, including Crandall, beat and burned him to death.

Driven nearly insane by his grief Louis dug Gage's body up, ignored Jud's warning and reburied it in the Micmac burial ground. The boy returned as a vicious monster and killed Crandall with Louis' scalpel. Rachel, concerned for her husband's well-being, had returned home without his knowledge and Gage also killed her. The boy then attacked Louis, who killed him a second time with a lethal dose of morphine. Finding his wife's body Louis completely lost his mind and took the corpse to the Micmac burial ground, from which, to close the tale, it returned.

While the original novel was set in late 1983 and early 1984 no dates are given for the action in the screenplay. Interestingly, King changed the circumstances of Timmy Baterman's two deaths. In the novel Timmy was shot and killed fighting as a US soldier on the road to Rome on July 15, 1943. His father killed him a second time in late July or early August by shooting him in the chest. In the screenplay Timmy was run down and killed by a drunken driver in Georgia in 1944 while on his way back from the war and after his resurrection he was burnt to death by townsmen, including his father and a young Jud Crandall.

The novel *Pet Sematary* was published in 1983 and this script is indeed remarkably faithful to the original. King even resisted changing details of the major characters, which seems to provide him with great entertainment in other screenplays. Part of the novel was published in the *Satyricon II Program Book* that year, as *The Return of Timmy Baterman*. There were minor variations between the excerpt and the final book but these have no impact on the characters. The excerpted incident remained in the screenplay, with the variations noted above.

Many critics describe this tale as a variation of the horror theme of unholy resurrection first introduced by the W. W. Jacobs 1902 short story, *The Monkey's Paw*. In fact, as always with King, he took the theme contained in Jacobs' story, which ends with the father wishing his returned son away before being confronted by him and added the stark and real multiple returns Bill Baterman, Jud Crandall and Louis Creed suffer as his own powerful extension of the concept.

A dark tale in the Bachman tradition King finished writing the novel in 1979 but then put it away, refusing to offer it to his agent and publishers. He relented in 1983, partly to complete a Doubleday contract and refused to participate in publicity. Despite this the book became King's biggest hardback seller to that time with over 750,000 copies sold. He had apparently 'warmed' to the story enough by the late 1980s to write this screenplay and become deeply involved in the production when it was filmed in Ellsworth, Maine and surrounding areas.

Of course the subject matter, the death of one's child, is so horrific that it is rarely approached in fiction or at the movies. King was apparently inspired to write the story while living in a rented home right on the real Route 15 in Orrington (on the Brewer or east side of the Penobscot River) and commuting daily to the University of Maine at Orono, as writer-in-residence. The initial inspiration for the story was prosaic – Naomi King's cat Smucky was killed on Route 15, with Tabitha and Stephen deciding they must confront her with the truth, rather than pretend the cat had run away. King told Douglas Winter[106]: 'When ideas come they don't arrive with trumpets. They are quiet – there is no drama involved. I can remember crossing the road, and thinking that the cat had been killed in the road ... and (I thought) what if a kid died in that road? And we had had this experience with Owen running toward the road, where I had grabbed him and pulled him back. And the two things came together – on one side of this two-lane highway was the idea of what if the cat came back, and on the other side of the highway was what if the kid came back ...'

As is often the case with King screenplays he took the opportunity in this draft of the script to link this work with his other fiction. For instance, in the notes the Baterman place 'looks like the home of Jordy Verrill'. This is a reference to *Weeds*, its variant *The Lonesome Death of Jordy Verrill* and the *Creepshow* screenplay.

The little boy Gage Creed is a key character in both the novel and screenplay. After his death one of his sneakers was found in Atropos' lair, in the novel *Insomnia*. Also The Gage Creed orchestra played at the Masked Ball to re-open the Overlook Hotel in King's screenplay for the Mini-Series version of *The Shining*. In that production King played that Gage Creed on screen!

The town of Ludlow, Maine is also a key setting for *The Dark Half* and is mentioned in *Insomnia* and *The Tommyknockers*. Route 15 is also mentioned in *The Dark Half* and *Insomnia*.

A sequel movie, using Ludlow and the Sematary as its links and with Lambert again directing, was released as *Pet Sematary II* in 1992. Apart from an early appearance by *E.R.*'s Anthony Edwards it has few redeeming features.

As the first movie is available to the public on DVD and the novel will remain in print for many years there appears to be no likelihood that the screenplay itself will ever be published.

The Plant (1982, 1983, 1985, 2000)

The Plant is perhaps the best known of King stories that have not appeared in a collection. This is due to the incredible publicity that surrounded King's decision to sell downloadable chapters of the revised version on his website during the dot com boom. Worldwide publicity ensued, including such publications as *Time* magazine, newspapers and TV as well as the then relatively new medium of the Internet.

There are two versions of *The Plant*. The original was written, published by King's Philtrum Press as a signed, Limited Edition and provided as a Christmas gift from the Kings in 1982, 1983 and 1985 (in 1984 many received the Limited Edition of *Eyes of the Dragon*).

During a speech in 1989 King said he stopped work on the tale after seeing the movie, *The Little Shop of Horrors*, 'between the second and third installment and realized what I was writing and decided I'd better stop right away.'[107] If, as seems likely, King is referring to the remake, starring Rick Moranis, Vincent Gardenia and Steve Martin (and actually titled *Little Shop of Horrors*, no 'the') that movie was not released until 19 December 1986. This is, of course, *after* the third installment was released, and too late to stop even any 1986 segment being written, printed and mailed. In fact, the movie was a remake of Roger Corman's *The Little Shop of Horrors*, released in 1960 and which King references in *Danse Macabre*, as 'not even notable for what may have been Jack Nicholson's screen debut.'[108] *Danse Macabre* itself was first published in 1981.

Original copies of each part of this version are very difficult to find and run in the thousands of dollars. In fact, a complete set generally runs over $6000[109]. The best sources will be online King booksellers.

In 2000 King updated the story and released it on the Internet via his official website, www.stephenking.com. This followed the phenomenal success of his serial novel *The Green Mile* (at one point it held six places of the top ten on *The New York Times* bestseller list) and of *Riding the Bullet*. After the latter was released on the Internet on 14 March 2000 it was quickly downloaded more than half a million times! Both these successes prompted King to try *The Plant* as a subscription based offering on the 'Net.

After six parts *The Plant* folded its leaves again, with the story still unfinished. The first five parts, issued from July through November 2000, were charged on an 'honor' system, where the buyers downloaded the text and were expected to send in their payment. The last part was given away from 4 December by King as a Christmas gift to his readers and, presumably, as a small apology for stopping the story mid-stream, again! King also announced the six installments had formed the first part of the novel, with that part to be known as *Zenith Rising*.

Even though all six parts were once available for download for $7.00, they are no longer available from the website. Copies circulate in the King community but readers should note that the material is copyright and copies should not be offered for sale, or purchased.

The Plant is probably best described as a novel in progress, although that progress has been halted twice already, and it is possible the leaves of *The Plant* are permanently furled. As of mid-2004 the FAQ section of King's official website gives the answer, 'Time will tell' to the question, 'Are you going to finish The Plant?' Like many King novels the early parts can be a little unsatisfactory if read in isolation, as King often takes time to set characters, plot and tone in place (this was *not* the case with *The Green Mile*, which took off from the very first page). Even after six Parts readers may be a little disappointed with the story and we regard 'novel-in-progress' as the demon here.

Both versions are told in epistolary style, using letters, memos, newspaper articles and diary entries to provide the narrative. King also used this style for *Jerusalem's Lot* and *The End of the Whole Mess*, and *Carrie* delved into a similar style with various quotes from news articles and books. King has used the device of news article quotes throughout his career, as recently as the opening lines of *Dreamcatcher* and *The Dark Tower VI: The Song of Susannah*. Interestingly, King wrote the first three installments in longhand[110] and, at one point, projected the complete novel would be some 400 pages in length. King also told Tyson Blue that *The Plant* was 'social satire'.

The Original Version

In this America Under Siege story a failing publishing house is sent the gift of an ivy. Carlos Detweiller approached Zenith House in New York to publish his manuscript, *True Tales of Demon Infestations*. Zenith House editor John Kenton showed interest in the pitch and Detweiller sent the entire manuscript, including pictures of what appeared to be an actual human sacrifice.

Disturbed by the photographs Kenton reported Detweiller to the police. Their investigation revealed that the man 'sacrificed' in the photos was apparently alive and well and living in the same apartment building as Detweiller. Detweiller vowed revenge on Kenton. Soon after, the mysterious Roberta Solrac (we instantly understand this is 'Carlos' in reverse) sent Kenton an ivy named Zenith. He ordered it destroyed but the janitor and internal mailman, Riddley Walker decided instead to keep the plant.

Next, the insane General Hecksler escaped from a mental asylum, killing three people in the process. Reaching the Shady Rest mortuary he killed owner Hubert Leekstodder and his wife, then faked his own suicide, cremating the body of a bum instead. Hecksler had a grudge against a Zenith House employee and was intent on revenge. In the meantime, John Kenton's fiancée Ruth Tanaka broke off their engagement by letter from her home in Los Angeles.

The timeline of this version runs from 4 January 1981, when Carlos Detweiller wrote to Zenith House, offering *True Tales of Demon Infestations*, through to 29 March that year, when Hecksler recorded his faked suicide after the successful 'Operation Hot Foot'.

The Revised (or 'Electronic') Version

The summary of the story to the end of Part 3 is practically the same for both versions. The storyline continues in the revised version with Hecksler staking out the Zenith House office disguised as a female bum. Detweiller arranged the death of his employer, Tina Barfield, in a plane crash and also began stalking the Zenith office.

The team at the publisher, under pressure from their corporate owners, began to work on new concepts for best-selling books. They found one obvious bestseller sitting unread in the mailroom, and came up with ideas for more. It seems the ivy might have had some positive influence over their creative processes.

Detweiller and Hecksler both broke into the Zenith House offices on the same day, and killed each other. Hecksler's body was 'eaten' by Zenith the ivy and the employees disposed of Detweiller's body at a local waste disposal site.

The timeline in this version of the story had been extended to the body disposal on 5 April 1981; the day after the two maniacs killed each other.

Among the revisions King made between the versions are certain dates. For instance, in the original, Zenith arrived at Zenith House on 27 February 1981, but in the revision this has changed to 23 February.

Of course, readers are left mid-story by King's decision to halt the tale at this point. Part 6, the last to date, took the very surprising turn of eliminating two characters that most would have expected to continue to play a threatening role. The only obvious danger now is Zenith, the ivy. In *The Complete Guide to the Works of Stephen King* Zenith is described as, 'The plant sent to John Kenton by Roberta Solrac. The name 'Zenith' was on a small plastic tag on the plant. It is supposed to be 'common ivy' but there is no such plant and it is actually a rare

Tibetan Kendath Ivy. It has magical powers, was imported from 'another place' and appears to be able to think and recognize people! People who are not part of the Zenith House editorial staff only see it as a small, rather sick plant but the Zenith staff see it as a fast-growing plant that has spread into corridors and other rooms. It has small blue flowers and grows faster if fed blood.'

The central character of the story continues to be John Kenton, to whom Detweiller sent the ivy. Aged 26, he was an associate editor at Zenith House, which he joined in October 1979. Ruth Tanaka was his fiancée until she left him for Toby Anderson in March 1981. He was writing a novel, *Maymonth*, which he later trashed. He rejected Detweiller's manuscript and contacted the police about the photographs it contained. This set Detweiller against him.

Carlos Detweiller was born on March 24, 1958. A would be writer, he was trying to get his *True Tales of Demon Infestations* book published and sent the manuscript to Zenith House. Because it contained photos that appeared to be of a human sacrifice he was arrested but was released when the apparent victim was found 'alive'. He then began to write to Zenith House as Roberta Solrac and sent them a strange plant, Zenith the ivy. Employed at the Central Falls House of Flowers in Rhode Island, he killed his employer, Tina Barfield, her husband and his own mother, and turned Norville Keen, the apparent 'sacrifice victim' into a Zombie. He was attacked and killed at Zenith House by Anthony Hecksler on 4 April 1981, while he was waiting to attack the publisher's employees.

Hecksler, a complete lunatic, was born in 1909. A retired Major General, he served in Europe, leading partisans and commandos across France. The Germans briefly captured him in November 1944 and during interrogation they extracted two of his teeth. President Dwight Eisenhower personally decorated him in 1954. He was in Vietnam in 1970, where he was mostly uninjured by a bomb set off in Haiphong Charlies but as a result was left sensitive to loud noises. He wrote a manuscript titled *Twenty Psychic Garden Flowers* that Herb Porter of Zenith had rejected. After he stabbed a bus driver he was committed to Oak Cove Asylum in December 1978. He escaped, killing three asylum workers on 3 March 1981 and faked his death at the Shady Rest Mortuary Crematorium. He then stalked Zenith House while dressed as a female bum, entered their offices on 4 April 1981 and killed Carlos Detweiller. Zenith the ivy then killed him and ate the body!

Roger Wade, perhaps the least interesting of the major characters, was 45 in 1981. He attended Reading High School and Brown, graduating in 1968. He was Editor in Chief at Zenith House in early 1981. He had been a teacher for six years and married and divorced three times. He was trying to keep Zenith House afloat for as long as possible but was told that, unless they got some bestselling books, the corporate owner, Apex Corporation would close them down. He authorized work on *The Devil's General*, a sick joke book, *Alien Investing* and organized the hardcover/paperback release of *The Last Survivor*.

Riddley Walker seems destined to have a greater role in the story should it ever be revived. Aged 26, he lived in Dobbs Ferry, New York and had attended Cornell. An African American, despite his high level of intelligence, he delivered the mail and worked as a janitor at Zenith House. He was told to incinerate the ivy when it arrived but did not. He was having an affair with one of the female editors, Sandra Jackson and was *also* writing a book. He originally spoke with an accent but when he returned to Zenith House from his mother's funeral he dropped it and began to speak normally. On his return he was offered a full editor's job with Zenith.

Herb Porter's role is greatly expanded in the revised version. Born in 1933, he grew up in Danbury, Connecticut. An editor at Zenith House, he would sniff fellow editor Sandra Jackson's chair! Hecksler called him the 'Designated Jew'. He married Lisa in 1955 but they divorced in 1957 because of his impotence. He blamed this on having to deliver papers between the ages of 10 and 15 on a bike with a seat that was too narrow. Jackson confronted him about the seat sniffing by Jackson and had him follow her up to the 6th floor women's' toilets where they had sex. It was his idea to co-write a book on Anthony Hecksler (*The Devil's General*).

Sandra Georgette Jackson, an editor at Zenith House, was having an affair with Riddley Walker but this did not seem to affect her desire to teach Herb Porter a lesson by seducing him. While the killings were occurring at the office she was at Coney Island with her 11-year-old niece, Dina Andrews.

The last of the editors is Bill Gelb, described as an 'Ivy League Tie-Wearing devil' by Hecksler. He lived in Gates Falls, Maine as a child and attended Bates College, where he was known to smoke pot. He thought the ivy smelt like the seats in the Nordic theatre in Freeport and came up with the idea of producing the *Alien Investing* book for Zenith House. If the story is resurrected we might learn more of Gelb's childhood or of Gates Falls.

There are numerous links from *The Plant* to King's other fiction. The following links appear in both versions. The Beam is mentioned in a letter from John Kenton to Ruth Tanaka and appears to be a direct link to the Dark Tower Cycle.

In 1981 Carlos Detweiller lived and worked in the real town of Central Falls, Rhode Island. In 1975 Ben Mears and Mark Petrie briefly stayed there after leaving the vampire-infested *'Salem's Lot*.

Richard Ginelli ran the Four Fathers Bar, where Roger Wade often drank. This establishment also appears in *The Ballad of the Flexible Bullet* as a bar Henry Wilson visited (there is no reference to Ginelli); and appears in a similar guise as the Four Fathers pizza restaurant, run by a Ginelli (no first name), in *The Dark Tower II: The Drawing of the Three*. Richard Ginelli himself also appears in *Thinner*, where he was a silent partner in the Three Brothers (!) restaurant. In *Thinner*, he was murdered on 30 June 1983 and in both he has organized crime connections, so he could easily be the same Ginelli as in *The Plant*, which is set in early 1981.

Riddley Walker's Aunt Olympia lived in the fictional town of Babylon, Alabama. It is also mentioned in the *Six Stories / Everything's Eventual* version of *Lunch at the Gotham Café* (John Ring's mother lived there); and in *Dedication* (Martha Rosewall grew up there). There is certainly no coincidence in King's choosing to have these three women all live in Babylon at some point.

The following links appear only in the revised version. On Page 117 Kenton's journal refers to the movie *Carrie* – '... remembering that horror movie where the hand suddenly shoots out the grave and grabs one of the teenagers...'

Carlos Detweiller spoke the 'Language of the Dead' to Zenith to get it to attack Anthony Hecksler. The 'Language of the Dead' is also mentioned in both *Desperation* and *The Regulators*.

As mentioned earlier, Bill Gelb grew up in Gates Falls, Maine. One of King's earliest fictional towns, Gates Falls is a key location in *Graveyard Shift*, *It Grows on You*, *The Revenge of Lard Ass Hogan*, *Riding the Bullet* and *Sword in the Darkness*. It is also mentioned in *Blaze*, *The Body*, *The Dark Half*, *The Dead Zone*, *Gramma*, *Hearts in Atlantis*, *Movie Show*, *Mrs. Todd's Shortcut*, *Needful Things*, *Rage* and *'Salem's Lot*.

There are errors in the two versions of the story. In the original version the address of Zenith House is variously given as 5th Floor, 490 Park Avenue South or 9th Floor, 409 Park Avenue South. In the revised version the address errors from the original are not only left uncorrected but continue into the new Parts. Parts 1 to 3 give the address of Zenith House as 490 Park Avenue South, but Part 4 gives the address as 409 Park Avenue South on both pages 23 and 50. Part 3, page 38 has Zenith House on the 9th floor at 490 Park Avenue South, but page 23 of Part 4 has it on the 5th floor of 409 Park Avenue South.

The Synopsis at the beginning of Part 2 reads, 'On January 4th of 1981 Kenton receives a query letter from Carlos Detweiller...' As the letter was written on January 4 (see Part 1, Page 3) in Rhode Island it seems the earliest it would have arrived was January 5. Indeed, also in Part One (Page 4) Kenton describes the letter in his memo summarizing submissions of 'January 11-15th, 1981' (this error was *not* corrected in the revised version).

Herb Porter arranged a 25th Wedding Anniversary party for his parents in 1978, indicating they were married in 1953. The text indicates he was born in 1933 and states he married Lisa in 1955, divorcing in 1957. There is no indication that his parents are anything other than his natural parents, therefore it would appear this is an error. Page 130 states LaShonda's name is LaShonda McHue, but on page 141 she becomes LaShonda Evans. In Part 5 we read, 'I remember the narrative intro to that old TV show, *The Fugitive*. 'Richard Kimball looks out the window and sees only darkness..."' That character's surname was actually spelt Kimble.

In the early 1980s King included *The Last Survivor* as one of the submissions to Zenith House. The concept involved 24 people being put on an island where they had to survive for six months. One person was voted off each week and the last person got one million dollars! One wonders if the originators of *Survivor* had read *The Plant*?

Will King return to this novel-in-progress? The first hiatus was fifteen years and it has already been over a decade since we last heard from Zenith, John Kenton and his colleagues. It appears King had lost direction at the time of the second hiatus and completion of the tale is unlikely. As King's website says, time will tell.

The Poems

Most of King's published or known poetry was written in his college years or shortly thereafter. Poetry is an art that continues its slow death in the written form but remains vibrant in its oft-unrecognized incarnation as popular music lyrics. Rap artists, for instance, are but modern members of the Poet's Guild. King has retained an enormous appreciation for modern music throughout his life and one wonders at the lyrics he might write for one of the great solo performers or rock bands.

In total there are fifteen known King poems but only three have been published in his collections. *Brooklyn August*, a wistful and elegiac homage to the Brooklyn Dodgers' last season in New York, appears in *Nightmares and Dreamscapes*. That poem was first published in *Io* (Number 10) in 1971 and was not republished until Tyson Blue's *The Unseen King* in 1989, in which he tells the remarkable story of its rediscovery.

For Owen (1985), written for King's younger son, has a hilarious fantasy quality, and appears in *Skeleton Crew*. Its only other published appearance is in *Rosebud* magazine, #27, for Summer 2003. The third, *Paranoid: A Chant* (1985), a harrowing testimony to madness, also appears in *Skeleton Crew*.

The following poems were mostly published during or just after King's college years, yet to date King has not included any of them in his collections. Perhaps he has been concerned with the unevenness of the work or considers them too strong a juxtaposition to his prose.

However, there have recently been signs of King's softening in this matter, with his agreement allowing six to be republished in Cemetery Dance's spectacular dark horror poetry collection, *The Devil's Wine* (2004), edited by the fine writer, Tom Piccirilli. Although Piccirilli requested all eight poems known at the time (*Dino* was not 'discovered' until March 2004) it is unclear why King chose not to allow the republication of the two from *Contraband*, *Woman with Child* and an untitled poem beginning with the line, 'She has gone to sleep while …'

In 2009 King again began to publish poetry- *Mostly Old Men* and *The Bone Church* (2009), and *Tommy* (2010). And, as discussed later, King also kindly agreed to allow *Dino* to be reproduced in this book.

Harrison State Park '68 (1968)

In this America Under Siege poem the narrator describes a mixed bag of images, including a little girl dead on a hopscotch grid and a cow's skeleton in Death Valley. *Harrison State Park '68* first appeared in the University of Maine literary magazine, *Ubris*, for Fall 1968. Its only subsequent publication is in *The Devil's Wine*, which is the easiest access point for readers. It is also possible to photocopy the original *Ubris* at the Raymond H Fogler Library of the University of Maine at Orono.

The poem, the first of King's to be published, is headed by two quotes. 'All mental disorders are simply detective strategies for handling difficult life situations' (Thomas Szasz); 'And I feel like homemade shit' (Ed Sanders). Harrison State Park itself is also mentioned in *Rage*. In that Bachman novel, Charles Decker took a girl called Annmarie there.

The verse about the dead little girl (a recurring theme in King's prose in such works as *The Dead Zone*, *The Huffman Story* and *The Green Mile*) reads: 'We have not spilt the blood/ They have spilt the blood/ A little girl lies dead/ On the hopscotch grid/ No matter/ - Can you do it?/ She asked shrewdly/ With her Playtex living bra/ cuddling breasts/ softer than a handful of wet Fig Newtons./ Old enough to bleed/ Old enough to slaughter/ The old farmer said/ And grinned at the white/ Haystack sky/ With sweaty teeth'.

A possible portent of *The Stand* appears in one verse: 'and someone said/ - Someday there will be skeletons/ on the median strip of the Hollywood Freeway'.

There are strong sexual overtones in this poem, perhaps not surprising for a poet around his 21st birthday. It opens, '- Can you do it?/ She asked shrewdly/ from the grass where her nylon legs/ in gartered splendor/ made motions.' Later there is mention of 'Over a dozen condoms/ in a quiet box' and 'call me Ishmael/ I am semen'.

This work bears re-reading and is complex in its themes and tone, taking us for the first, but far from the last, time into the realm of murderous insanity. In retrospect it is one of his best poems, clearly part of the King canon and another signpost in the early development of the best-selling writer.

The Dark Man (1969)

This poem was first published in the University of Maine literary publication *Ubris* for Fall 1969 and was reprinted without changes in a small magazine, *Moth*, in 1970 (in both publications the poem is credited as 'Steve King'), along with two other King poems. Its next publication was not until *The Devil's Wine*, nearly three and a half decades later, in 2004. This may be explained by the fact that this poem serves as the basis for one of King's most significant characters, Randall Flagg, the anti-hero of *The Stand* and a key opponent for Roland in *The Dark Tower* Cycle. As King reached the end of that Cycle and began to consider future directions in his writing might he have reached a decision to 'release' this poem from its close confinement?

The figure of a/the Dark Man has consumed King and his writings from the time this poem was penned (and possibly even earlier); and the whole concept of the Dark versus the White lies at the moral core of all King's work. It is therefore impossible to overstate its importance. Any reader serious about King and understanding his motivations, and that of his characters, has an obligation to read and study this poem. Its easiest access point is now *The Devil's Wine* but the original *Ubris* may be photocopied at the Raymond H Fogler Library at the University of Maine in Orono. Alternately, copies of *Ubris* come to market rarely, commanding prices of up to $1000.

In an interview with Waldenbooks in July 2003 King had this to say, 'Actually, Flagg came to me when I wrote a poem called "The Dark Man" when I was a junior or senior in college. It came to me out of nowhere, this guy in cowboy boots who moved around on the roads, mostly hitchhiking at night, always wore jeans and a denim jacket. I wrote this poem, and it was basically a page long. I was in the college restaurant .... I wrote the poem on the back of a placemat. It was published, as a matter of fact, but that guy never left my mind.'

With this confirmation, the poem is linked directly to Flagg's appearances in all versions of *The Stand*, both versions of *Eyes of the Dragon* and the Dark Tower Cycle. Appropriately, no timelines are given for in the poem, which is an America Under Siege work.

Both in its original reading and in retrospect *The Dark Man* is stunning. In only five verses King manages to deliver a horrific spectral being, fully formed to prey on our subconscious. The poem is headed by a quote from T S Eliot: 'Let us go, then, you and I ...' It is filled with lines of great beauty and horror: '...and over it all a savage sickle moon that bummed my eyes with bones of light ...' and '...where witch fire clung in sunken psycho spheres of baptism...'

The poem ends coldly, with a verse fit for a Flagg: '...and in the sudden flash of hate and lonely/ cold as the center of a sun/ i forced a girl in a field of wheat/ and left her sprawled with the virgin bread/ a savage sacrifice/ and a sign to those who creep in/ fixed ways:/ i am a dark man.' (Note that the 'i' *is* in lower case in the poem. Indeed, there is no capitalization whatsoever in the body of the work.)

Donovan's Brain (1970)

The original appearance of this 12-line King poem was in *Moth* magazine in 1970. Its next publication was not until *The Devil's Wine*, the easiest access point for readers. It as an America Under Siege work.

In this 104 word, 24-line poem the reader receives mixed images of Shratt, his woman and an electric tank, more of which below.

Frankly, this is not one of King's better or more accessible poems, at least at first reading. Michael Collings says this[111]: 'Based on Curt Siodmak's novel and the subsequent film of the same name, the poem focuses on Shratt, the victim of a pseudo-science that transmutes into horror.' That novel, also titled *Donovan's Brain*, was published in 1942. It spawned two successful movies, *The Lady and the Monster* (1944), starring Erich von Stroheim and *Donovan's Brain* (1953).

King writes extensively about both the novel and the films in *Danse Macabre*[112]. There he tells us (in part), 'Horror fiction doesn't necessarily have to be nonscientific. Curt Siodmak's novel *Donovan's Brain* moves from a scientific basis to outright horror (as did *Alien*). Both the novel and the films focus on a scientist who, if not quite mad, is certainly operating at the far borders of rationality. This scientist has been experimenting with a technique designed to keep the brain alive after the body has died – specifically, in a tank filled with an electrically charged saline solution. In the course of the novel, the plane of W D Donovan, a rich and domineering millionaire, crashes near the scientist's desert lab. Recognizing the knock of opportunity, the scientist removes the dying millionaire's skull and pops Donovan's brain into his tank.'

'The operation is a success. The brain is alive and possibly even thinking in its tank. The scientist begins to try to contact the brain by means of telepathy … and succeeds. In a half-trance, he writes the name *W D Donovan* three or four times on a scrap of paper, and comparison shows that his signature is interchangeable with that of the millionaire.' (*'he signed checks with Donovan's name'*, *the poem tells us*).

'In its tank, Donovan's brain begins to change and mutate. It grows stronger, more able to dominate our young hero. He begins to do Donovan's bidding, revolving around Donovan's psychopathic determination to make sure the right person inherits his fortune. The scientist begins to experience the frailties of Donovan's physical body … low back pain, a decided limp (the poem again: 'Shratt came on limping' and '…there was a drag of pain/ in his left/ kidney'). As the story builds to its climax, Donovan tries to use the scientist to run down a little girl who stands in the way of his implacable, monstrous will (*the poem tells us: 'he tried to run down a little girl'*).

King concludes his dissertation in *Danse Macabre* by saying, 'Siodmak is a fine thinker and an okay writer. The flow of his speculative ideas in *Donovan's Brain* is as exciting as the flow of ideas in a novel by Isaac Asimov or Arthur C Clarke, or my personal favorite in the field, the late John Wyndham. But none of these esteemed gentlemen has ever written a novel quite like *Donovan's Brain* … in fact, no one has. For all its scientific trappings, *Donovan's Brain* is as much a horror story as M R James' 'Casting the Runes' or H P Lovecraft's nominal science fiction tale, 'The Color Out of Space'.'

Clearly this novel, and most likely the 1953 film, had a strong impact on King – strong enough to deliver a poem at the end of his college career, and a loving analysis of the book and films in his non-fiction work about horror. For this reason, this fairly inaccessible poem must be considered of import to the King canon.

Silence (1970)

The original appearance of this 12-line King poem was in also *Moth* magazine in 1970. Its next publication was not until *The Devil's Wine*, again the easiest access point for readers. It is an America Under Siege work. In it the narrator hears nothing except the fridge and stands waiting, with 'book in hand', for the furnace to kick on.

Typically of King, horror is close at hand with the two single word lines, 'murder/ lurks' and the line, 'the feary silence of fury'. Tyson Blue[113] says the poem '…is not as accessible as some of the other King poems, and has more in common with haiku, which tries to evoke within its rigidly-structured form the feeling of an event rather than a narrative of something which happened.'

Woman with Child (1971)

Woman with Child was first published in a magazine, *Contraband*, #1 for 31 October 1971 (Halloween). The 17-line poem has never been republished. The best chance for readers to access it is to acquire a photocopy at the Raymond H Fogler Library of the University of Maine at Orono, from the original magazine. Interestingly, King did not allow this poem to be reprinted along with six other poems from the 1960s and 1970s he *did* allow to be included in *The Devil's Wine*.

This poem, the most mainstream of his works in this form, is impossible to define as part of a particular 'reality'.

In it a pregnant woman gets out of the bath and feels her unborn child moving. The imagery in this poem is vivid: '…her groping/ fingers find the yellow bathsoap beneath one/ elephantine thigh …' and concludes, 'In the dark depths of her the creature turns silently,/ as if toward the surface,/ or the sun'.

This is a poem without horror or undertones, simply a mainstream reflection of a moment in time in a pregnant woman's daily life. There were actually two King poems in this publication, as discussed in the following section.

Untitled (She Has Gone to Sleep While …) (1971)

King had a second poem in *Contraband*, #1 for 31 October 1971. Untitled, it begins with the line, 'She has gone to sleep while …'

The 28-line poem has never been republished. Again, the best chance for readers to access it is to acquire a photocopy at the Raymond H Fogler Library of the University of Maine at Orono, from the original magazine. This is the second of the poems known to exist at the time that King did not allow to be reprinted with the six other poems from the 1960s and 1970s that he *did* allow to be re-published in *The Devil's Wine*.

In the poem, which is part of the America Under Siege reality, the narrator drives his car while a female we assume is his wife, sleeps. He thinks about what his life will become, as he grows older. In one interesting point the narrator thinks of his inner thoughts as 'the Library of Me'. This could just as easily describe Gary Jones' mind in *Dreamcatcher*.

This is another poem without horror or undertones, simply a mainstream reflection.

The Hardcase Speaks (1971)

The Hardcase Speaks was first published in a magazine, *Contraband*, #2 for 1 December 1971, with the credit erroneously given as 'Stephan King'. The magazine also carried a poem about vampires by King's wife, Tabitha and another by mentor Burton Hatlen. Only 66 lines long, it is written in the slightly delirious style of the late 1960s hippie generation, of which King was, of course, a part (see *Tommy* later in this chapter). It is an America Under Siege work.

Its next publication was not until *The Devil's Wine*, nearly three and a half decades later in 2004 and this is now its easiest access point for readers. The original *Contraband* may also be photocopied at the Raymond H Fogler Library at the University of Maine in Orono.

There are a number of interesting signposts in this poem. For instance, King uses a terminology that also appeared in *The Dark Man*. Here we read, 'punctuated by the sodium lightness glare of freights/ rising past hobo cinder gantries and pitiless bramble hollows:' In the earlier poem he wrote, 'i have ridden rails/ and burned sterno in the/ gantry silence of hobo jungles;'

Early in the poem 'Harlow' is mentioned. Harlow is a key location in a number of King stories: *It Grows On You* (the *Marshroots* / *Weird Tales* and *Whispers* versions), *Movie Show* and *Riding the Bullet*. It has a considerable role in both *Blaze* and *The Body* and is mentioned in *Bag of Bones*, *The Dark Half*, *Gerald's Game*, *Nona* (the *Skeleton Crew* version), *Rage*, *Under the Dome* and *Uncle Otto's Truck* (the *Skeleton Crew* version).

King refers to a serial murderer (a favorite in his prose): 'in 1954 in a back alley behind a bar they/ found a lady cut in four pieces and written in her juice on the bricks above/ he had scrawled PLEASE STOP ME BEFORE I KILL AGAIN in letters that leaned and/ draggled so they called him The Cleveland Torso Murderer and never caught him,'

And this: 'Real life is in the back row of a 2nd run movie house in Utica, have you been there'. King has famously declared to the inane repeat questioning of lazy reporters and interviewers wanting to know where he gets his ideas that he buys them in a small shop in Utica. King's fascination for Charles Starkweather, who killed ten people in 1958, recurs with: 'bore a little hole in your head sez I insert a candle/ light a light for Charlie Starkweather and let/ your little light shine shine shine'. This line also reminds readers of the pencil-probing exercise in *The Revelations of 'Becka Paulson* section of *The Tommyknockers*. Flagg also refers to his relationship with Starkweather in *The Stand*.

One spectacular two line verse reads with King's visceral power, 'in huge and ancient Buicks sperm grows on seatcovers/ and flows upstream toward the sound of Chuck Berry'.

After a series of strange observations ('The liberals have shit themselves and produced a satchel-load of smelly numbers') and instructions ('eat snocones and read Lois Lane') the poem ends with this: 'Go now. I think you are ready.' Manic, yet slightly disappointing, this poem is however clearly King – using trademarks, famous people and gruesome themes.

In the key-chords of dawn (1971)

This 18-line poem was published without a title in a literary magazine, *Onan*, in 1971 and would be King's last published poem for fourteen years. Here it is referred to in the manner it is often described in the King community, *In the key-chords of dawn*, for the convenience of readers. Piccirilli also lists it under the title *In the key-chords of dawn*... This work, which was almost impossible to access before the publication of *The Devil's Wine* in 2004, cannot be classified in a particular reality.

In it two people fishing realize that the pastime involves more than just eating the fish and it, like life, contains other responsibilities and complexities.

The poem opens with, 'In the key-chords of dawn/ all waters are depthless'. Philosophical in tone, we read in the second of the three verses that, 'when we say "love is responsibility";/ our poles are adrift in a sea of compliments.' And in the third: '...so we are/ forced to say "fishing is responsibility"/ and put away our poles.'

In his *The Annotated Guide to Stephen King*, Michael Collings interprets the fishing as a metaphor for love.

Dino (1994)

Dino was discovered by the King community in March 2004 as the result of an auction at the world's greatest flea market, eBay. C.S. O'Brien of Bowery Books in New York City offered for sale a copy of an obscure literary magazine, *The Salt Hill Journal*. The magazine happened to contain a poem by a Stephen King and, more importantly, carried a signature apparently from *the* Stephen

King. O'Brien was selling the magazine on behalf of one of the magazine's original student editors (this person does not wish to be named). His teacher at the time was Stephen Dobyns (more of whom below). It is thought that King signed only five copies. O'Brien kindly provided the author with scanned copies of the poem, magazine cover and signature.

After King expert Bev Vincent brought the auction to general attention its authenticity was quickly confirmed by King's office. Wendy Bousfield, the now retired Reference Librarian at the E.S. Bird Library of Syracuse University in Syracuse, New York[114] kindly provided your author withy not only a copy of the poem but the following interesting information describing how such an obscure magazine came to carry a poem by one of the world's best-selling authors; including a series of news articles relating to King's appearance at the University. Wendy Bousfield[115] and C.S. O'Brien are to be thanked for their assistance.

On 26 April 1991, King gave a reading in Syracuse University's Landmark Theatre to help raise funds for the Raymond Carver Reading Series (Carver also taught in Syracuse University's creative program, from 1980 to 1983). King refused to take any reimbursement for travel funds. The Theatre was completely full and, at between $7.50 and $35 per ticket, the evening netted $35,000, putting the reading series in the black.

According to the Syracuse *Herald-Journal* for December 12, 1995, 'The king of horror fiction novels autographed several copies of the journal for a silent auction Wednesday at Barnes & Noble bookstore.' This places the auction on 13 December 1995. According to the article, ' "He (King) has donated a considerable amount of money to the Raymond Carver Reading series and also has an interest in the creative writing program at Syracuse." Thomas said that he came to know King through a mutual friend, Stephen Dobyns, who wrote the book "Cemetery Nights" and also has a poem in the magazine. "He said he (King) was inspired to begin writing poems after reading Dobyns' book," Thomas said.' Thomas or the reporter must have been misinformed for, as we know, King had been writing and publishing poems a quarter century earlier. Of interest is that in *Insomnia* Dorrance Marstellar gave Ralph Roberts a copy of one of Dobyns' collections of poems, *Cemetery Nights*!

In *The* (Syracuse) *Post-Standard* for 21 April 1991 King told a reporter, ' "I like Dobyns. I admire him as a writer. My wife's a fan, too," the 44-year-old King says in a phone interview from his home in Bangor, Maine. "Besides, I like the idea that schools have you come and the people listen to a reading, as well as learn to write."'

The Salt Hill Journal is a literary magazine, publishing poetry, fiction and book reviews. It is still published irregularly by a group of writers affiliated with the Creative Writing Program at Syracuse University and is funded in part by the College of Arts and Sciences and the Graduate Student Organization of Syracuse University.

Dino appeared in the first issue of *The Salt Hill Journal*, for Autumn 1994, on pages 19 to 21. Stephen King kindly gave his permission to reproduce *Dino* here. It appears directly after this chapter and represents its first and only appearance in book form.

The twelve-verse poem, homage to Dean Martin, is very readable but not exactly what one might be expecting. It starts with the bald statement, 'Dino is dying/ "Tragic last days!" say the tabloids/ and when the tabloids speak of death/ they always speak the truth.'

It continues to describe Dino's failing body and mind ('Dino is getting a little soft upstairs'), he even forgot the words to " 'at's Amore" on stage in Atlantic City! King then mentions other members of the Rat Pack, referring by first name to the already deceased Peter Lawford, Sammy Davis, Jr. and the still living (at least in 1994) Frank Sinatra ('an afterlife where these hepcat scouts/ have already set out the/ cigarettes and whiskey,/ not for him but for Frank.') The poem goes on to mention Dino's erstwhile partner, Jerry (Lewis), 'Dino's dying/ Jerry's old pal'. We are reminded of the great hits, *Everybody Loves Somebody Sometime, Me and My Shadow*[116], *That Old Black Magic, I've Got You Under My Skin* and *Mack the Knife*, which Dino sings 'so cool and nonchalant at the Palladium.'

But now 'Dino's tux has been packed away', 'Dino's screwed his last starlet', 'Dino's in bed/ and almost dead/ "Tragic last days!" say the tabloids, and when the tabloids speak of death/ they always speak the truth.' And so the poem ends.

Martin actually died on Christmas morning 1995, a little more than a year after this poem was published, of acute respiratory failure, probably brought on by his years of smoking.

Previous to the poem's discovery there was little in King's body of work to indicate any fascination with, or any real interest in, Martin or the 'Rat Pack'[117].

Mostly Old Men (2009)

This poem appeared in *Tin House* magazine, #40 (the 10th anniversary issue, released in August 2009) and was the first King poem published for a decade and a half. It appears King may be returning to the form, with two more appearing in less than twelve months. The author had previously published *Memory*, an early release segment of *Duma Key*, in that literary magazine.

In only 30 lines King builds a picture of largely elderly men ('1000 old men') traversing America's highways, stopping at rest stops to allow their dogs a chance to relieve themselves and thereby forming a loose but anonymous coast-to-coast fellowship. In this poignant piece King shows yet again how he can draw the reader instantly into a scene. The poem ends, '…so many of them totter as they do/ their duty, tugged along by 1000 dogs/ (mostly old) sniffing the yellow tattoos/ on the grass – scents of other old dogs/ and old men, here where nobody knows anybody/ and the traffic never ends'.

Back copies of this issue of *Tin House* were available at the time of writing; and should also appear at eBay and other online sellers.

The Bone Church (2009)

This lengthy poem appeared in the November 2009 issue of *Playboy* magazine.

Here, a man describes an expedition to an elephant graveyard. The jungle they must traverse is so difficult, and the expedition faces such tragedy, that the geography itself (the jungle is nicknamed 'greensore') becomes a character.

Of the thirty two who entered the jungle only three survived to reach 'the bone church' (the elephant graveyard) and King's narrator lovingly describes many of the untimely departures; and the ghostly images of passing pachyderms, which ultimately lead to yet more tragedy for the survivors.

Copies of the magazine containing this highly evocative piece are easily found at online sellers.

Tommy (2010)

This one-page poem appeared in the March 2010 issue of *Playboy* magazine.

In it, the narrator reminisces about the day in 1969 when his friend Tommy's funeral and a subsequent reception were held. Tommy was a gay hippie, and was buried in his favorite clothes, wearing a gay pride button (which his mother had discretely placed under his vest). It is forty years later as the events flood back and the narrator wonders how many hippies died in 'those few sunshine years' and were buried in their iconic clothing, hair-styles intact: 'Sometimes, at night, I think of hippies asleep under the earth'.

Clearly reflecting on King's youth, the younger attendees of the funeral return to the narrator's apartment at 110 North Main (it is later revealed as being in Orono). King once lived at 110 North Main Street in Orono, the same address. It was there he began to write 'The Dark Tower'. As an aside there are a number of errors in timelines around music King refers to (each having been released after the events portrayed in the poem).

Copies of the magazine containing this elegiac piece are easily found at online sellers.

So, this is King in the poetic art form. Of course, there are also examples of poetry by characters in King's books (which, *presumably*, he wrote) to be examined by students of the form.

DINO

By Stephen King

For Stephen Dobyns

Dino is dying.
"Tragic last days!" say the tabloids,
and when the tabloids speak of death
they always speak the truth.
Dino Martini, we called him when we were kids,
as if even at ten we understood he was a soldier of booze,
the point-man of the highball generation.
Dino is dying,
bladder's bad
eyes're bad,
kidneys failing,
prolapsed here,
fused over there.
Dino is getting a little soft upstairs:
got on stage in Atlantic City,
dark Italian eyes glowing,
forgot the words to " 'at's Amore"
and went hobbling from place to place
in the pink cage of the spotlight,
confused, seeming to look for something,
and finally began to weep.
A man helped him from the stage.
> *Whenna da moon hitsa yew eye*
> *Like-a da big pizza pie*
> *'at's Amore:*

Remember?
Dino's headed after Peter,
after Sammy,
and will probably discover
an afterlife where these hepcat scouts
have already set out the
cigarettes and whiskey,
not for him but for Frank.
They'll have "You Make Me Feel So Young"
cued up on heaven's starry stereo –
that Nina Simone version, which is the one
Frank mostly likes.

In the meantime, however, there's this
little job to get out of the way,
these final dues to pay.
Dino is dying,
Jerry's old pal,
the host of Hollywood Palace;
him who looked so good in black and white
in a helmet with net and camouflage on it,
fighting a movie war he never saw at
first hand, any more than The Duke,
with whom he rode horses in
Rio Bravo.
Dino is dying,
him who used to be able to make people
laugh just by hoisting his martini glass
and making a sound like *Buh-buh-buh*,
Dino has finished singing
"Everybody Loves Somebody Sometime"
      "Me and My Shadow"
            "That Old Black Magic"
                  and "I've Got You Under My Skin".
Dino has finished snapping the fingers of one hand
with a cigarette smoldering between the first two fingers
of the other hand
while he sings "Mack the Knife"
so cool and nonchalant at the Palladium.
Dino's tux has been packed away.
Dino's passport has expired.
Dino's eaten his last steak in Lutece.
Dino's screwed his last starlet,
given his last concert,
made his last movie,
done his last TV special.
Dino's in bed
and almost dead.
"Tragic last days!" say the tabloids,
and when the tabloids speak of death
they always speak the truth.

Premium Harmony (2009)

Premium Harmony first appeared in *The New Yorker* for 9 November 2009, King's sixth piece of fiction for this prestigious magazine.

In this tale a couple arrive at Castle Rock's Quik-Pik on a hot summer day. Married ten years, Ray and Mary Burkett now argue constantly. Ray thought the deterioration in their relationship was connected to Mary's inability to have children, although 'a year so after that, he bought her a dog, a Jack Russell she named Biznezz. She'd spell it for people who asked.' The harsh economy has forced them to consider selling their house, and they're driving to a Wal-Mart to buy supplies. As they drive through Castle Rock we find, 'It's pretty dead. What Ray calls "the economy" has disappeared from this part of Maine.' They stop at the Quik-Pik and argue about money, including Mary's proclivity for sugary snacks. She leaves Ray and the dog in the car as she heads inside to buy her niece a ball, and a pack of the cheap cigarettes he's requested, the Premium Harmony brand.

Mary takes some time and Ray sits impatiently in the air-conditioned car, waiting. A large woman rushes out to tell Ray his wife has collapsed in the store and the manager has called 911. 'Ray locks the car and follows her into the store'. Mary is not just collapsed, but dead, having fallen without uttering a sound. This is confirmed when the Castle County Rescue E.M.T.s arrive, having been delayed at car accident in nearby Oxford. They prepare to take the body away, telling Ray he can contact the mortuary: 'Mortuary? An hour ago they were in the car, arguing.' Ray stays in the store, chatting inanely with the manager, and those who'd been there when Mary collapsed.

Finally, he goes outside. Perceptive readers, or at least those who own dogs, will have been on edge since Ray left the car. Sure enough, he's forgotten Biznezz. It is this smaller blow that releases Ray's emotions, '...this is so sad that he begins to cry. It's a hard storm.'

Premium Harmony is a simple and understated tale of tragedy – the isolation that exacerbates failing marriages; and of sudden death - again illustrating King's skill in relating simple slices of life. After Mary's death onlookers chat to Ray, as they might in the real world. An old man says, ' "My wife went in her sleep ... She just laid down on the sofa and never woke up."'

Many readers know King and his wife Tabitha are dog-owners and dog-lovers, which adds extra poignancy to Biznezz's ignoble death. As is often the case, King taps here into the American Zeitgeist - describing the Main Street of Castle Rock as 'dead'; and the fact the couple are being forced to sell their home; are both a reflection of the American economy at the time of writing.

The story seems to reflect earlier incidents in King's fiction. In *Cujo*, for instance a dog traps a woman and her son in a hot car (the boy dies in the book, but not the movie) – here another hot summer day in Maine results in a dog's death. More poignantly, Mary's sudden death seems eerily similar to Jo Noonan's in the heat of Derry in *Bag of Bones*. Perhaps this is one of the author's deep fears – that his wife may never return from performing one of life's mundane tasks? In real life, loved ones do die unexpectedly, and the survivors are left to carry on regardless – perhaps that is the lesson of this tale.

As a core Castle Rock story *Premium Harmony* is linked to all other King stories mentioning the iconic town. Castle Rock is the main setting for *The Body, Cujo, Gramma, It Grows on You* (but only the *Nightmares and Dreamscapes* version), *The Man in the Black Suit, Mrs. Todd's Shortcut, Needful Things, 'Nona'* (but only the *Skeleton Crew* version), *Squad D, The Sun Dog* and *Uncle Otto's Truck*. It is a key location in *Bag of Bones, The Dark Half, The Dead Zone* and *The Huffman Story*. It is also mentioned in *Creepshow, Dreamcatcher, Gerald's Game, The Girl Who Loved Tom Gordon, The Lonesome Death of Jordy Verrill, Riding the Bullet, Rita Hayworth and Shawshank Redemption, Under the Dome* and *The Stand* (*Complete and Uncut* version only).

In more specific links the Castle Rock Wal-Mart also appears in *Bag of Bones*; the Castle County Fair is mentioned and had previously also appeared in *Bag of Bones* – in that novel Dickie Brooks' father claimed to have kissed Sara Tidwell there. A high school in Castle Rock is mentioned – high schools in Castle Rock appear in the following stories: *Bag of Bones, Needful Things, Cujo, The Body, The Dead Zone* and *Uncle Otto's Truck*.

All King's previous stories in *The New Yorker* have appeared in later collections and there can be little doubt his next fiction collection will include this Castle Rock tale. In the meantime the magazine is held by many libraries and copies can easily be purchased on the internet.

The Reploids (1988)

The Reploids is one of King's least satisfying short stories, mostly due to an unsatisfactory and inconclusive ending that is explained by the fact it was part of a busted novel[118]. King has only allowed publication in one anthology (although that has appeared in three different guises) and a magazine. A decade and a half later, fans are yet to see the story in a King collection and will most likely will wait in vain.

In 1988 horror expert and King biographer Douglas E Winter[119] edited an anthology, *Night Visions 5*, which was released in a Limited Edition and a trade hardback. The anthology included three King stories, the most ever released in one volume outside one of King's own collections. They were *The Reploids, Dedication* and *Sneakers*. *Dedication* and *Sneakers* were completely rewritten for their appearance in 1993's *Nightmare and Dreamscapes*. In this context it is telling that King apparently chose not even to rewrite *The Reploids* for *Nightmare and Dreamscapes*.

Gollancz of the United Kingdom published the anthology in 1989 under the title, *Dark Visions: All Original Stories*. Berkley Books finally released the anthology in the US as a mass-market paperback in 1990 under yet another title, *The Skin Trade*. Readers wishing to access one of these books would be best to start with online King booksellers. Copies of *Night Visions 5* sell for over $40 but the other two, particularly *The Skin Trade*, often trade for under $20. The story also appeared in a short-lived British magazine, *Skeleton Crew* for July 1990.

In this America Under Siege tale the normal world takes a strange and very visible twist. On 29 November 1989, the filming of *The Tonight Show* was disrupted when Johnny Carson disappeared and was mysteriously replaced by Edward Paladin. Paladin seemed to think that he was the star of the show and that everyone should know him and treat him as such.

As the story begins we understand that something strange, in the tradition of *The Twilight Zone* and the later series *The X-Files*, has been going on. 'No one knew exactly how long it had been going on. Not long. Two days, two weeks, it couldn't have been much longer than that ... Not that it mattered. It was just that people got to watch a little more of the show with the added thrill of knowing the show was real. When the United States – the whole world – found out about the Reploids, it was pretty spectacular ... These days, unless it's spectacular, a thing can go on damned near forever. It is neither believed nor disbelieved. It is simply part of the weird Godhead mantra that made up the accelerating flow of events and experience as the century neared its end.' This comment could serve as proxy for the events in many a King story. How often do strange events escape the unknowing world in the King-dom? Think of the demise of *'Salem's Lot*; or the out-of-the way town, Rock and Roll Heaven, Oregon in *You Know They've Got a Hell of a Band*; or the strange events in *Rainy Season*; or the fact that only *The Ten O'Clock People* can see a species that lives unseen among us. Readers will have their own favorites but this concept certainly reflects a major theme of King's fiction.

The night Paladin appeared on *The Tonight Show* the guests were due to be Cybill Shepherd ('of *Moonlighting*'), magician Doug Henning, Pee Wee Herman and the Flying Schnauzers, the world's only canine acrobats! When Ed McMahon, as usual, announced, "And now heeeeere's JOHNNY!", there Johnny wasn't! Instead the man who later identified himself as Edward Paladin stepped on stage and acted as if he belonged in Johnny's shoes. However, 'the man who was not Johnny Carson was taken, bellowing loudly not about his lawyer but his team of lawyers, to the Burbank Police Station.' The Station had a wing known simply as 'special security functions', where the rich and powerful were taken. They could be dealt with there, quietly and discreetly.

Detective 1st Grade Richard Cheyney, only half-jokingly known as the 'Detective to the Stars', interviewed Paladin in a luxurious interrogation room, filled with magazines, cigarettes and even Cable TV for the use of the 'guests'. Paladin immediately denied knowing who Johnny Carson was and Cheyney's partner, Pete Jacoby, began making jokes. What Cheyney realized and Jacoby did not, was that the case had all the hallmarks of a major problem – media attention from both the Los Angeles *Times Mirror* and *The National Enquirer*, not to mention being taken over by the Feds if not solved within a day or so.

When Paladin demanded his lawyer and announced that gentleman's name to be Albert K Dellums neither of the cops recognized it. 'For the first time an expression of perplexity – it was not fear, not yet – crossed Mr. Edward Paladin's face.' Paladin now threatened the two detectives with walking a 'beat out in Watts' and was shocked when Jacoby said, "Shut your mouth, jag-off!' Cheyney could immediately see it had been years since Paladin had been spoken to that way and now he looked both stunned and frightened by the turn of events.

When Jacoby tried to contact Paladin's lawyer's home number all he got was a cleaning woman and the office number was not a legal firm but a stockbroker. There was no Albert K Dellums listed in the phone directory. The Mayor now arrived at the Station, joining a still stunned Ed McMahon and other cops observing the interrogation.

Trying to unravel the mystery Cheyney took Paladin's NBC Performer's Pass, which was perfect in every way *except* that the pass was salmon pink, as compared with genuine passes, which were bright red. He requested Paladin take a dollar bill from his wallet and place it on the table and then placed one of his own next to it. 'On the right was Cheyney's one, gray-green, not brand new by any means, but new enough so that it did not yet have that rumpled, limp shopworn look of a bill which has changed hands many times. Big number 1's at the top corners, smaller 1's at the bottom corners. FEDERAL RESERVE NOTE in small caps between the top 1's and THE UNITED STATES OF AMERICA in larger ones. The letter A in a seal to the left of Washington, along with the assurance THIS NOTE IS LEGAL TENDER, FOR ALL DEBTS, PUBLIC AND PRIVATE. It was a series 1985 bill, the signature that of James A. Baker III.'

'Paladin's one was not the same at all. The 1's in the four corners were the same; THE UNITED STATES OF AMERICA was the same; the assurance the bill could be used to pay all public and private debts was the same. But Paladin's was a bright blue. Instead of FEDERAL RESERVE NOTE it said CURRENCY OF GOVERNMENT. Instead of the letter A was the letter F. But most of all it was the picture of the man on the bill that drew Cheyney's attention, just as the picture of the man on Cheyney's bill drew Paladin's. Cheyney's gray-green one showed George Washington. Paladin's blue one showed James Madison.'

And there the story ends!

Just before the end of the story Cheyney thought: 'Walk softly, stranger, for here there be tygers'. *Here There Be Tygers* is the title of one of King's earliest stories. There is one other possible link, with King mentioning different 'politicians on the currency' with relation to alternate worlds in *The Dark Tower VI: Song of Susannah.*

There is one error in this story. Fairly early on we read, 'After repeated viewings of the videotape, Dave Cheyney ...' But, later, 'Detective 1st Grade Richard Cheyney looked at him calmly ...' Interestingly, this error had not been corrected by the time *The Reploids* was last published.

Reading the tale one is left with the distinct impression that King was intending a longer, more interesting story and we now know that is indeed the case. It seems very unlikely King will return to the novel.

King's Characters as Writers

King has provided us with a long and interesting list of characters who are writers, presumably reflecting parts of his own life to us through his fiction. He kindly updates us on many of them in later works (for instance in *The Dark Tower V: Wolves of the Calla* we find that Ben Mears of *'Salem's Lot* has died). Some of the more prominent and interesting are listed below. (Readers will note that an unhealthy proportion of King's major writer characters are now dead!)

Major Characters as Writers

Roberta ('Bobbi') Anderson	*The Tommyknockers* (also *The Stand*)
Thad Beaumont	*The Dark Half* (also *Bag of Bones*)
(...and George Stark)	*The Dark Half* (also *Bag of Bones* and *Needful Things*)
Richard Dees	*The Dead Zone* and *The Night Flier*
William Denbrough	*It* (also *Bag of Bones*, *Dreamcatcher*)
Carlos Detweiller	*The Plant*
Richard Hagstrom	*Word Processor of the Gods*
Peter Jefferies	*Dedication*
Howard Fornoy	*The End of the Whole Mess*
James ('Jim' or 'Gard') Gardener	*The Tommyknockers*
Richard Kinnell	*The Road Virus Heads North*
Stephen King	*The Dark Tower V, VI and VII*
Gordon ('Gordie') Lachance	*The Body* (also *Needful Things*)
Samuel Landry	*Umney's Last Case*
John Marinville	*Desperation*

Benjaman Mears	*'Salem's Lot* (and *The Dark Tower V*)
Gerald Nately	*The Blue Air Compressor*
Michael Noonan	*Bag of Bones*
Morton Rainey	*Secret Window, Secret Garden*
Paul Sheldon	*Misery* (also *The Library Policeman* and *Rose Madder*)
Reg Thorpe	*The Ballad of the Flexible Bullet*
John ('Jack') Torrance	*The Shining* (also *Before the Play, Misery*)
William ('Bill') Weiderman	*Sorry, Right Number*

Other Characters of Interest

Claudia y Inez Bachman	*The Dark Tower V*
Beryl Evans	*The Dark Tower III, IV and V*
David Bright	*The Dead Zone* and *The Tommyknockers*
Michael Cunningham	*Christine*
Susan Day	*Insomnia* (also *Rose Madder*)
Elizabeth Pillsbury Drogan	*Untitled (The Huffman Story)*
Jake Epping	*11/22/63*
Fletcher	*In the Deathroom*
Robert Jenkins	*The Langoliers*
Steve Kemp	*Cujo*
John Kenton	*The Plant*
Stephen King *	*The Blue Air Compressor, The King Family and the Wicked Witch, The Leprechaun*
Harold Lauder	*The Stand*
John Marinville	*The Regulators*
Peter Rosewall	*Dedication*
Selena St George	*Dolores Claiborne*
Julia Shumway	*Under the Dome*

* King is also mentioned in *Blockade Billy, The Library Policeman, The Night Flier, The Regulators, Slade, Sleepwalkers* and *Thinner*. We should perhaps regard these 'appearances' as similar to a cameo in a movie or TV show.

Rose Red Screenplay (2000)

Rose Red was carefully staged as a major media event with both television and book connections. When the prequel novel, *The Diary of Ellen Rimbauer* was released prior to the mini-series, using major characters from *Rose Red* and with a $200,000 marketing campaign there was much speculation as to whether Stephen King or even Tabitha King had written the book. The original paperback itself was purported to be by Joyce Reardon, herself a character in the upcoming mini-series. Sometime after the mini-series screened it was revealed that novelist Ridley Pearson had actually written the novel. Pearson is a member of The Rock Bottom Remainders band of which King is a founding member and a sometime player.

The *Rose Red* project had been in development for a number of years (in a post to his official web site on 2 November 1999 titled *Stephen King Comments on Fears That He's Unable to Write* King notes he'd recently begun work on *Rose Red*, which 'is an expansion of a screenplay I wrote some years ago') with King and Steven Spielberg attempting to put a project together. When King submitted the haunted house story script Spielberg kept asking for changes and after three drafts King felt the project was no longer his. According to Jones[120] King pitched the concept to producer Mark Carliner and Carliner loved the story. King was due to begin writing a new script on the following Monday. Jones continues, 'However, the following day King was hit by a mini-van while out walking …' King was nearly killed by Brian Smith's van on Saturday 19 June 1999.

Stephen King's Rose Red debuted on the US ABC-TV network on the nights of 27, 28 and 31 January 2002. Frankly, it suffered somewhat from poor casting, some strange editing, questionable special effects and outrageous overacting by Nancy Travis (later seen in *Becker*), playing Dr. Joyce Reardon. However, www.imdb.com members rate it a respectable 6.4 out of a possible 10. Craig R Baxley directed. The other main actors were Kimberly J Brown as Annie Wheaton; David Dukes as Carl Miller; Matt Ross as Emery Waterman; Matt Keeslar as Steven Rimbauer; Judith Ivey as Cathy Kramer; Melanie Lynskey as Rachel Wheaton; Tsidii Leloka as Sukeena; and Julian Sands played Nick Hardaway.

Unfortunately Dukes, aged only 55, died on 9 October 2000 while filming *Rose Red*. Most of his scenes had already been shot, with the ironic exception of his character's death scenes.

In another cameo Stephen King played a Pizza Delivery Guy, doing his job at Rose Red. The mini-series was released on DVD in 2002 and includes the 'Featurettes' *The Making of Rose Red* and *The Diary of Ellen Rimbauer*.

ABC was encouraged enough by the ratings *Rose Red* garnered to make the prequel as a one-off movie. *The Diary of Ellen Rimbauer* debuted on 12 May 2003 and was a ratings and artistic disappointment. Ridley Pearson and Craig R Baxley again helmed the screenplay. Lisa Brenner played Ellen Rimbauer; Steven Brand appeared as John Rimbauer; and Tsidii Leloka reprised Sukeena. It was released on DVD in 2003.

The actual screenplay has not been published. However, there are a very few copies of the official screenplay in circulation. Some of those, signed by King, were sold to benefit the Wavedancer Foundation, set up to assist Frank Muller, the most popular reader of King audio books. Muller was seriously injured in a motorcycle accident in November 2001.

This chapter was compiled with the assistance of a copy of the screenplay kindly provided by King's office, for which Mr. King and Ms. Marsha DeFilippo are thanked, and is dated June 1, 2000. There is officially no intention to publish the screenplay as, for instance, was the case with *Storm of the Century*. This is a shame, as it is a witty and entertaining script and reads better than the mini-series views. Of course, readers may view the DVD of the production to experience the story.

In this America Under Siege tale a professor recruits for an expedition aimed at awakening a house in Seattle she believes is possessed. The original owner of Rose Red, Ellen Rimbauer, had believed that as long as her house was under construction she would not die. She continually made additions to the house following its construction early in the 20th century and, after she disappeared in 1950, the house continued to build itself!

Professor Joyce Reardon of the University of Washington was obsessed with the psychic happenings at Rose Red. In the almost 100 year history to May 2001 many people had died there or simply vanished (*a list of known victims appears in the feature panel*). The house had grown quiet but Joyce believed that the right people could bring it to life and provide her with hard evidence of psychic phenomena.

Reardon gathered a group of people with different psychic abilities, headed by a 15 year old autistic girl Annie Wheaton, who was also telekinetic. The others were Annie's sister, Rachel Wheaton, Emery Waterman, the house's owner Steven Rimbauer, Victor Kandinsky, Nick Hardaway, Pam Ashbury and Cathy Kramer.

They entered Rose Red on 25 May and four of them, along with Kevin Bollinger, Kay Waterman and Carl Miller died the following day, after successfully 'awakening' the house. Bollinger, from the campus newspaper, went to Rose Red to take photos of Joyce Reardon's expedition but the house took him while he was in the solarium. He was later 'seen', having hung himself in the mirror library. Emery Waterman's mother Kay went to the house in search of her son and was 'taken' by Sukeena. Carl Miller was Head of the Psych Department and came to Rose Red after receiving a false message. He was led into the side yard by Sukeena, and was killed there.

In fact the only outsider to come to the house during the expedition and survive was the Belissimo Pizza Man, who never actually entered the building.

(As this delivery man bore an uncanny resemblance to master horror writer Stephen King, perhaps some muse warned him against proceeding too far?)

The remaining members of the expedition escaped the house alive, although Emery Waterman lost four fingers in a door. Joyce Reardon refused to leave and was also taken. In October 2001 the survivors laid roses at the house as demolition of Rose Red was set to begin the following Monday.

In back-story we learn that John Rimbauer built Rose Red from 1906 until 1909 for his new wife, the former Ellen Gilchrist. Between the end of World War One and 2001 twenty-three people had died or disappeared on the premises. Twenty years older than Ellen, John made his money in oil and they had married on 12 November 1907. He died when Ellen and her servant Sukeena pushed him from the Rose Tower of Rose Red in 1923. In 2001 Cathy Kramer found a dust covered wedding photo showing Ellen and John. She went into a trance and in the dust wrote 'NO SUICIDE MURDER ELLEN SUKEENA'.

At a séance in August 1914 Ellen Rimbauer was told she would live as long as Rose Red was under construction, so she kept making additions to it, both conventional and unconventional. However, she disappeared in the house on 15 January 1950 after last being seen in the Perspective Hallway.

The Rimbauers had two children. April was born in *April* 1911 with a withered arm. She disappeared in the house in 1917. Her brother Adam, born in 1909, had been sent to boarding school the same year. It was presumably because Adam was sent away that he survived the house and it was his grandson Steven who accompanied Reardon into the house in 2001. Steven was then about 25 and Joyce Reardon's lover. He let her attempt to awaken the forces in Rose Red. When he was eight his mother took him to Rose Red while she looked for valuables, he got lost in the house and 'met' Ellen in the attic. Ellen then asked him to help her continue to build Rose Red. Steven survived the 2001 expedition.

Sukeena was Ellen Rimbauer's servant. She came to America with the Rimbauers from Africa, where they met her while honeymooning. Ellen never called her a servant but rather a friend, and later a sister. She was severely treated by the authorities after April Rimbauer disappeared in 1917 and helped Ellen push John Rimbauer to his death in 1923. In May 2001 she 'took' both Carl Miller and Kay Waterman.

The members of Reardon's disastrous expedition were chosen for a variety of psychic skills. The concept will remind horror fans of Shirley Jackson's classic 1959 novel, *The Haunting of Hill House*, made into an excellent black-and-white movie, *The Haunting* in 1963 but poorly remade in 1999, with Catherine Zeta-Jones and Liam Neeson starring. As King has often acknowledged Jackson's influence on his writing there is little doubt that *Rose Red* is both homage and King's take on the 'wake-up the haunted house expedition' sub-genre. Indeed, the opening words of Jackson's novel might well describe Rose Red:

'No live organism can continue for long to exist sanely under conditions of absolute reality; even larks and katydids are supposed, by some, to dream. Hill House, not sane, stood by itself against its hills, holding darkness within; it had stood so for eighty years and might stand for eighty more. Within, walls continued upright, bricks met neatly, floors were firm, and doors were sensibly shut; silence lay steadily against the wood and stone of Hill House, and whatever walked there, walked alone.'

Apart from Joyce Reardon and Steve Rimbauer there were another seven members of the 'official' expedition, not including the photographer, Bollinger. The key to awakening the house was Annie Wheaton. A 15 year old autistic girl, Annie was also telekinetic, telepathic and psychokinetic. As a result, Reardon believed she would have the power to wake Rose Red. At the age of five she'd made stones rain on her neighbor's house after their dog bit her. Annie survived the expedition.

Her older sister Rachel wanted Annie to go to the Gatt school in Tacoma because she thought someone would understand her there, unlike her parents. The father, George did not like Annie and her mother was afraid of her. Rachel therefore saw the $12,000 offered by Reardon for Annie to attend Rose Red as means to an end. She also escaped the house.

Emery Waterman, about 28 and plump, was post cognitive. He lost four fingers on one hand when Rose Red slammed the door he was holding but otherwise survived the expedition intact. Victor Kandinsky, a precognitive, followed someone or something he thought was Pam Ashbury in the house and died of a heart attack. Nick Hardaway disappeared in the perspective hallway (for some reason this character and actor always remind your author of the British operative and hero of *The Langoliers*, Nick Hopewell). Viewers of the mini-series often comment on the lack of set up of an explanation for Hardaway's disappearance. In fact the other characters don't seem to notice his absence at any point!

Pam Ashbury was a 'touch-know'. She drowned in the little pond in Rose Red's back yard after following someone or something she thought was Cathy Kramer. Kramer was an automatic writer and was one of the survivors.

As ever in his screenplays King takes the opportunity to link the script with his other fiction in a number of ways (*Rose Red* is also mentioned in the later *The Dark Tower VI: Song of Susannah*). Andre Linoge of *Storm of the Century* is mentioned in the screenplay as a note for Emery Waterman's dialogue – 'Emery does Andre Linoge and says, "Tell the truth and shame the devil"'. Sukeena heard April Rimbauer singing *I'm a Little Teapot* after she disappeared. This was an important tune in *Storm of the Century*.

Bollinger disappeared and apparently hung himself in the Mirror Library of Rose Red, which had bookcases lined with books and a mirrored floor. In King's early short story *The Glass Floor*, a library (empty of bookshelves) with a mirrored floor and ceilings was also the location of a number of deaths.

Carrie White made it rain stones on a house. At the end of *Carrie* there is a letter from Amelia Jenks to her sister Sandra Jenks. In it she discusses her 2 year old daughter Annie (!) who is able to move things around without touching them, so obviously she is telekinetic. The letter is dated 3 May 1988, meaning that Annie Jenks was born in 1986, the same year as Annie Wheaton, who also made stones rain on a house after the neighbor's dog bit her.

The whole concept of a house building itself long after its owner has died was originally proposed by King in one of his more under-rated tales, *It Grows On You*. That story was first published in *Marshroots* for Fall 1973 and is therefore one of his earliest original storylines. It was significantly revised for its appearance in *Whispers* for July 1982. Another major revision for its appearance in *Nightmares and Dreamscapes* in 1993, in which it became a Castle Rock Story, represents a third version of the story. Another variation of *It Grows On You* appeared when the *Marshroots* version was published with minor textual variations in *Weird Tales* for Summer 1991. It certainly seems King has an attachment to this tale, and storyline!

In summary *Rose Red* is likely to be seen as a valiant attempt at network mini-series television of the haunted house sub-genre. The characters have great potential but do not seem to deliver on screen. While the haunted house sub-genre is certainly not original the storyline created around it (Ellen, Sukeena and the events surrounding them) most certainly is. King students and fans alike may enjoy the viewing experience but *Rose Red* will most likely not make the favorite lists of King tales for most.

ROSE RED AND ITS VICTIMS

John Rimbauer built Rose Red, a grand house in Seattle, for his wife Ellen from 1906 to 1909. Between the end of World War One and 2001 five men and eighteen women died or disappeared on the premises. After Ellen Rimbauer's disappearance in 1950 the house apparently continued to build itself. Dr. Joyce Reardon led an expedition to it in late May 2001, with disastrous results.

The known victims of the house are as follows.

1906	A foreman – shot by Harry Corbin on the building site
1906	Harry Corbin – possibly driven to murder by something at the site
c. 1906-1909	Three workmen died – one decapitated by a sheet of falling glass; another fell off scaffolding and broke his neck; and one choked to death on a piece of apple

1915	Douglas Posey, John Rimbauer's partner, hung himself at Rose Red in front of Adam and April Rimbauer
1917	April Rimbauer - disappeared
c. 1919	George Meader - died in the solarium of Rose Red after being stung by a bee
1923	John Rimbauer – pushed from the Rose Tower by Ellen Rimbauer and Sukeena
15 January 1946	Deanna Petrie - disappeared while at Rose Red
15 January 1950	Ellen Rimbauer - disappeared in the perspective hallway
1972	Liza Albert - went missing while touring Rose Red
26 May 2001	Pam Ashbury - drowned in the little pond in Rose Red's back yard
26 May 2001	Victor Kandinsky - died of a heart attack
c. 26 May 2001	Kevin Bollinger - Rose Red took him while he was in the solarium. Later he was 'seen' hanging in the mirror library
c. 26 May 2001	Nick Hardaway - disappeared in the perspective hallway
c. 26 May 2001	Carl Miller - led into the side yard by Sukeena and killed
c. 26 May 2001	Kay Waterman - taken by Sukeena
c. 26 May 2001	Joyce Reardon – disappeared after refusing to leave Rose Red

The Shining Screenplays (Late 1970s, 1997)

King has effectively created three versions of the tale many non-King fans associate him with, *The Shining*. Most fans would immediately identify both the novel and the mini-series screenplay but many fewer would know that King also wrote a movie length screenplay that, of course, was never produced.

One of King's most searing psychological pieces, *The Shining* was first published in 1977. He wrote *Before the Play* as a deliberate prelude to *The Shining* - that story is covered in a separate chapter. King also penned *After the Play*, an epilogue to *The Shining* but this was merged into the novel. King has said that the full version of that story has been lost.

The novel was inspired by Ray Bradbury's *The Veldt* and was originally to be titled *Darkshine*. The draft of that story was on the backburner when the Kings went to visit the Hotel Stanley in Estes Park, Colorado on 30 October 1974, where they are said to have stayed in Room 217. Inspired by the eerie atmosphere of the end-of-season hotel King began working again on the manuscript, now known as *The Shine*. At publication the book was given its final title.

Stanley Kubrick's classic movie adaptation, starring Jack Nicholson as Jack Torrance, was released in 1980. Kubrick and his movies are the subject of endless debate in artistic and movie industry circles. The director of the brilliant *2001: A Space Odyssey*, *Dr. Strangelove*, *Full Metal Jacket*, *Lolita* and the execrable *Eyes Wide Shut* arouses strong emotions among movie critics and fans alike and *The Shining* was no exception.

Kubrick's adaptation is also the subject of much controversy within the King community. Despite its obvious brilliance as a movie and the outstanding acting of Jack Nicholson, many King fans cannot bring themselves to fully appreciate the movie as a result of the many changes Kubrick made to the storyline and the way he presented Jack Torrance's character. Instead of the slow decline into insanity portrayed in the novel moviegoers understood that Jack was quite mad to begin with (this was perhaps further influenced by Nicholson's Academy Award winning role as an asylum inmate in *One Flew Over the Cuckoo's Nest*, released only five years earlier).

King himself did not particularly enjoy the adaptation. King's childhood friend, Chris Chesley told George Beahm: 'I went with Steve to see *The Shining*. I could tell ... that he liked what the director had done, but the supernatural side of it had been excised – it wasn't his vision at all. That's what he said when we left the theater. It wasn't his book – it was Kubrick's movie.'[121]

Regardless of the feelings of many King fans, used as they were to the written format of storytelling, there is no doubt the high-profile and the cinematic, critical and box office success of the movie added greatly to King's early career, bringing ever more readers to his novels. Considering King's appreciation of the silver screen, it still surprises somewhat that he appears to dislike the movie so intensely. One wonders if it was the actual film, or the effects of dealing with the notoriously difficult Kubrick, that created that dislike.

King always harbored a strong desire to remake the movie in the manner in which he would have preferred and got his chance with the 1997 mini-series, appropriately named *Stephen King's The Shining* (as compared to Stanley Kubrick's!) While that adaptation is faithful to the core storyline and motivations of the novel (with some changes, as noted later) it lacked the dramatic punch of the movie.

The debate over which version is the better will rage on for decades but each should be viewed on its own terms – Kubrick's as a brilliant piece of movie making, with superb imagery and never to be forgotten scenes ("Here's Johnny!") that have entered movie lore, along with outstanding acting by Nicholson; King's as a superb piece of television, genuinely frightening and a faithful adaptation of the material, along with an element of fun lacking in both the book and the movie.

All versions of *The Shining* are America Under Siege stories and link to other King fiction (*see the feature panel*).

Unproduced Movie Screenplay

King wrote a 132 page, 369 scene screenplay for a movie length production of *The Shining*. It has never been published and it is clear that for any number of reasons, not the least of which is King's writing of the later mini-series screenplay, it never will be. A copy is held in Box 2318 at the Special Collections Unit of the Raymond H Fogler Library at the University of Maine, Orono and readers can access it there. It is enlightening that, despite the controversy over the Kubrick and King screen versions, King has *not* placed this earlier screenplay in a restricted box, but one that allows public access. Readers may therefore peruse the script at UMO if they wish.

The screenplay was written *before* Stanley Kubrick and novelist Diane Johnson developed their version, which *was* used in Kubrick's film. In fact, Jones points out that Kubrick declined the script, '...because he did not want to be influenced by anyone else's view of the book (not even the author's!).'[122] A copy of King's rejected screenplay was displayed at a Kubrick exhibition in Melbourne, Australia in January 2006. King aficionado Denis Gatiatullin noted the date on it as 7 October 1977.

King speaks of the difficulty of writing this script, under contract, in an interview with David Chute, first published in *Take One* for January 1979 and reproduced in Underwood and Miller's *Feast of Fear*[123].

Although the novel is set in late 1977, no date is given for the action in this screenplay. However, we know it occurs after 1975, as that was the year we are told the Overlook Hotel first made money.

The screenplay will not be summarized here, as it is very faithful to the novel. There is a summary in the next section of the mini-series screenplay, which does include subtle changes from the novel. Among the minor changes in this script is that the Woman in Room 217 is not named (few but the most fanatical of King's reader base will know her actual name, given in the novel as Mrs. Massey). After trying to strangle Danny Torrance she was seen in the Colorado Lounge images, very drunk and '...not looking much more alive than when Danny saw her in the bath.'

In another change, Danny's imaginary playmate, Tony (actually a projected older version of himself) is not included in this script. Al Shockley, Jack's recovering alcoholic friend who got him the job at the Overlook is also deleted (it seems King's *Word Processor* is as powerful as Richard Hagstrom's).

Although this script would have adequately served a movie adaptation it lacks the power and passion of Kubrick's interpretation and we should be thankful that the King screenplay actually produced was that for the mini-series, written nearly two decades later, allowing more maturity to his scriptwriting and the valuable extra length allowed in that television format. All in all, the second script is the richer and more expressive of the two.

Mini-Series Screenplay

King's screenplay for the mini-series version of *The Shining* has never been published and it is most unlikely that it ever will be, as readers have the novel and viewers the DVD/video to enjoy. Copies of the telescript do however circulate freely in the King community and readers should have no great difficulty in finding one.

The screenplay was produced on a budget of $25 million and shown as a mini-series in the United States, not surprisingly under the title *Stephen King's The Shining*. To be allowed to produce the mini-series Warner Brothers had to make a payment described as 'rather enormous' to Kubrick, who held the sequel and remake rights from the original movie[124]. The mini-series debuted on the ABC-TV network on the nights of 27 April, 28 April and 1 May 1997. IMDB members give the production a surprisingly low 6.0 rating out of a possible 10. Mick Garris directed, having earlier helmed *Sleepwalkers*, the mini-series of *The Stand* and *Quicksilver Highway*; and King was credited as Executive Producer. The production won two Emmys and the DVD was released in 2003.

The actors included Steven Weber as Jack Torrance[125]; Rebecca De Mornay as Wendy Torrance; Courtland Mead as Danny Torrance; Melvin Van Peebles as Dick Hallorann; Elliott Gould as Stuart Ullman; Pat Hingle as Pete Watson; and Cynthia Garris (the wife of the Director, in fantastic makeup) as the Woman in Room 217. Stephen King played Gage Creed, more of which later. Of the lead actors, perhaps only Gould was a truly satisfying casting choice.

As there are subtle changes in this screenplay from the novel a short summary of the storyline follows. Jack Torrance, a failed teacher and struggling writer with a drinking problem, took a caretaking job for the winter at the haunted Overlook Hotel in Colorado. Jack's wife Wendy and son Danny also settled into the Hotel, hoping for a better turn in their lives after Jack's alcoholism had led to his both sacking from a teaching job in Vermont and to the breaking of Danny's arm in a drunken rage. Danny had a strange ability to feel and see things no one else could, which hotel employee Dick Hallorann told him was called 'the shine' or 'shining'. Hallorann left for the winter, subtly warning Danny against the forces of the Hotel.

Torrance became fascinated with the sordid history of the Overlook Hotel and spent more time looking into its history than working on his caretaking or the play he had promised himself and his wife he would write. Snow finally cut the family off from the nearby town of Sidewinder. Both Danny and Jack saw strange things in the Hotel - a Masked Ball at which the Gage Creed orchestra played; topiary creatures that moved; and Delbert Grady, the bartender in an empty and alcohol free hotel. Danny even saw a dead woman in the bath in Room 217 and the word 'MURDER' reflected in a mirror to read 'RE-DRUM'.

Jack suffered a slow descent into insanity, urged on by Grady, who suggested he kill his family. Jack attacked Wendy with a croquet mallet and injured her but she managed to knock him out and lock him in the pantry, from which he escaped with the help of the Hotel and its denizens.

In fear, Danny had earlier called Hallorann in Florida, using the 'shine'. Hallorann arrived during a snowstorm at the Overlook, where Jack also attacked him. As Jack was considering killing his son, Danny reminded him that he had forgotten his caretaking job, and had not dumped the boiler, which slowly 'crept' upward in pressure. Danny, Wendy and Hallorann escaped the hotel shortly before the boiler exploded, destroying the Hotel and killing Jack.

Eleven years later Danny Torrance graduated from Stovington High School in the presence of his mother and their friend, Dick Hallorann.

The inclusion of Danny's graduation, from a school in the same town (but *not* the same school) in which his father had taught before being fired, is an addition to the mythology of this particular storyline, and a satisfying one at that. In the produced mini-series the *ghost* of Jack Torrance also appears, and this is one of the better emotional moments King has wrung from the screen in his role as scriptwriter.

For the purposes of this visual adaptation King escalated the presence of Danny's 'invisible playmate', Tony. Tony showed Danny things that would happen, both good and bad. Of course, he is really an older version of Danny himself, the name Tony is simply a shortening of Danny's middle name, Anthony. He is portrayed as a handsome, blond teenager who wears round spectacles.

The Delbert Grady who appeared in the novel had killed his wife by shotgun and his daughters with a hatchet, while caretaking the Overlook one winter. Presumably, these two girls (aged 6 and 8) were the models for the twins Kubrick portrayed in his film. Perhaps as a deliberate snub to Kubrick, Watson tells Torrance in this version that Grady killed himself with a shotgun, and was alone at the time.

King also moved the Masked Ball from the novel's date of 29 August 1945 (also used in the unproduced moviescript) to 15 May that same year.

A further addition to the original storyline is the Gage Creed Band and its bandleader, the definitely *not* one and only Gage Creed, played by Big Steve himself, wonderfully camping the role. Of course, Gage Creed is the name of the little boy killed on Route 15 in *Pet Sematary* and whose sneaker was found in Atropos' lair in *Insomnia*. This is a nice little in-joke for King's faithful fans, to go with his enjoyable acting cameo.

There are, of course, many other links from this script to King's other fiction and these are summarized in this chapter's feature panel. King again does not name the unfortunate bathtub suicide, but she is no less menacing to young Danny Torrance in this version.

It is unclear if the screenplay is set in 1996 or 1997, a deliberate update from the 1977 of the original novel. This change in dates was apparently to satisfy the viewing audience (the mini-series was originally screened in 1997) by providing a current timeline.

There is one error in the script - while at one point it is stated that on Route 50 it was 23 miles from the Overlook Hotel to Sidewinder, when Dick Hallorann hired a Sno-Cat in Sidewinder to drive to the Overlook he went past a sign that read, 'Overlook Hotel 37 miles'.

Certainly this is the better of King's two scripts but all three visualizations (including Kubrick's) somehow fail to capture the psychological power of the novel. *The Shining* is one of King's greatest novels and will certainly be on the reading list for students of the American Novel for decades to come.

LINKS FROM *THE SHINING* TO OTHER KING FICTION

The Shining is one of King's major works, existing in three forms – the novel, the mini-series screenplay and the unproduced movie screenplay. *Before the Play* was published separately in two different versions and these relate some of the early history of both the Overlook Hotel and Jack Torrance (as that story is a virtual prequel the extensive links from it are not summarized here). The links from the various versions of *The Shining* to King's other fiction are summarized below.

John 'Jack' Torrance	*Misery*[126], *Desperation* (Telescript)[127], *The Dark Tower VI*
Daniel 'Danny' Torrance	*The Dark Tower II, Storm of the Century*
Dick Hallorann	*It* [128]
Gage Creed	*Pet Sematary, Insomnia* [129]
The Overlook Hotel	*Misery, The Regulators*
Overlooked	*The Stand* [130]
Sidewinder, Colorado	*Misery, The Talisman*
Stovington, Vermont	*The Stand, Everything's Eventual*
Stovington Prep	*The Dead Zone*
The Shine	*The Stand* (*Complete and Uncut* version)

The Shotgunners (Undated)

The screenplay for an unproduced movie, *The Shotgunners* is held in Box 2318 of the Special Collections Unit of the Raymond H Fogler Library at the University of Maine, Orono. The good news for potential readers is that this screenplay can be accessed by attending the Library, as it is not held in a Restricted Box. There are 113 pages in the screenplay, covering 423 scenes.

According to various sources the legendary film director Sam Peckinpah died while pre-producing this script. Peckinpah made *Straw Dogs*, *The Wild Bunch* and was famed for the violence portrayed in his later films, long before the emergence of Quentin Tarantino in the 1990s.

The Shotgunners is clearly the forerunner of *The Regulators*; the Richard Bachman credited companion volume to King's *Desperation*. While the premise is the same, the characters are completely different. It appears this screenplay actually developed into *The Regulators* novel. If Peckinpah was indeed working on pre-production for this screenplay when he died in 1984, it was over a decade until it appeared reworked as *The Regulators* in 1996. Bachman's dedication in the book, 'Thinking of Jim Thompson and Sam Peckinpah: legendary shadows' would seem to confirm the story.

Further, in a non-fiction piece, *Digging The Boogens*,[131] published *Twilight Zone Magazine* for July 1982, King has this to say about the plot of Taft International's 1982 film *The Boogens*, directed by James L. Conway: 'A Colorado silver mine is closed by a series of explosions and cave-ins in 1912; miners are trapped, and most of them die (all of this background is elegantly presented over the credits in a series of frontier-style newspaper headlines and gorgeous sepia photographs). Seventy years later, a mining company reopens the mine. What else do you need?' Sound familiar? Perhaps this movie partly inspired *Desperation*, *The Regulators* and *The Shotgunners*?

The location of Maple Street for the shootings also links *The Shotgunners* to *The Regulators*, although it should be noted that the house numbers are separated by two blocks from each other. In *The Shotgunners* the house numbers range from 1 to 12 and Maple Street is in an unnamed Ohio suburb or town near what was, in 1874, Marionsville, Ohio. In *The Regulators* the house numbers range from 240 to 251 and Maple Street is in Wentworth, Ohio.

In this America Under Siege tale the shootings begin late one afternoon. While the timeline is clearly modern day an exact year or decade is not provided. Cars start to cruise onto Maple Street and shotguns protrude from them, randomly shooting at people and houses. Various survivors gather together as one by one the victims mount. The group soon realize that something is very wrong - no police are attending, there is no reaction from the outside world. Bill Hoffman, Georgia Kellogg and Lou Stein determine to escape and make it across the intersecting Hyacinth Street.

They find themselves in the Ohio of about 1874, the year six radicals, known as The Shotgunners, were hanged for their crimes. The leader of the group that executed the Shotgunners was a Hoffman and we therefore assume the modern day attack is some form of revenge from beyond the grave by the Shotgunners on Hoffman's descendant and his neighbors. The modern day group see seven mounted men, which turn out to be straw men on wooden horses. The Shotgunners cruising Maple are also straw men, but very much active and firing their shotguns. After one final massive attack on the street, dawn arrives and Maple Street returns to our reality.

The police arrive and find Bill Hoffman wired to a stake, with his eyes sewn shut, just like the scarecrow that had stood near the 1874 hangings.

The key characters in the screenplay are the Shotgunners; Bill Hoffman; the Ashley family; Andy and John Bellingham; Alicia and Tom Brewton; Mike and Angie Connaught; Georgia Kellogg; the Parker family; the Stein family; Susan Stuben; Alan and Marlene Wilson; and Hannibal, the Connaught's Irish Setter (this is the only character name King retained for *The Regulators*, where Hannibal was the Reed's German Shepherd, unfortunately the poor dog was killed in both versions). Of course, the main characters in *The Regulators* are a sort of alternate reality use of the character names from *Desperation*.

The unfortunate Bill Hoffman was a divorced father of two who lived at 9 Maple Street and worked as a bank officer. His wife had left him and taken their two daughters to California. Georgia Kellogg, the pretty 7-11 clerk who ventured to the 1874 reality with Hoffman and Stein, was one very lucky young lady. For some reason the Shotgunners chose not to shoot her outside the store. Later she made it to the Ashley house. She was wounded while returning from the altered reality but survived. Lou Stein, the 14 year old, son of Al and Kathy, lived at 11 Maple Street. He survived the shootings, unlike his mother, who broke her neck trying to climb a fence and his father, shot dead.

The Ashley family lived at 1 Maple. The father, Roger (also called Richard in the screenplay) was not at home at the time of the shootings. His wife, Priss and their two children, eleven year old Stacey and six year old Anne, also survived. The Bellinghams lived at number 5. While the parents were not at home, the handsome fifteen year old twin boys, Andy and John were, and both were able to survive the massacre. (In *The Regulators* the twins were the 17 year old Reed boys, David and Jim. Jim died under the influence of Tak.)

Alicia and Tom Brewton lived at 7 Maple and both were shot dead. Mike and Angie Connaught were the residents of number 3. Mike, handsome and in his mid-40s and Angie, pretty but a little overweight, were luckier and both survived.

The Parker family lived at 4 Maple. Rob was the father of Herbie and Carl and husband of Darla. The street's resident bore and a big gun collector and shooter, he was a writer for magazines on hunting and related matters, often working from home. He attacked the Shotgunners' Dodge with his Uzi but was quickly shot and wounded. He then looked into the Dodge and saw, to his horror, two scarecrows just before he threw a grenade. He died, along with Darla who fired at the Shotgunners' LTD, six year old Herbie, and twelve year old Carl, shot and killed while struggling for a gun with his brother.

The Stubens resided at 11 Maple. Susan survived the shootings and her husband Steve (also called Hank), was not on the street during the incident. Alan and the unpleasant Marlene Wilson lived at number 5. Drunk, Marlene approached one of the cars and was shot dead. Alan, about 50 and an alcoholic, survived. 10 Maple was vacant, as the Plummers had moved away before the shootings.

The Shotgunners drove standard road vehicles, including a Chevrolet, a Dodge, a Ford LTD, an Oldsmobile, a Plymouth, a Ford Country Squire Wagon, a Pontiac Bonneville and a mid-seventies model Thunderbird. The problem for the residents was that there were hundreds of these vehicles, lined up in the alternate reality at each end of Maple, waiting to enter the street, all bristling with shotguns.

In the screenplay the Shotgunners themselves were all stuffed dummies but were animated and used shotguns to kill their victims. In the later novelized version the killers were characters from Seth Garin's favorite movie, *The Regulators*. A creature called Tak used the autistic Garin's mind to attack and murder many Wentworth locals. The strange weapons and vehicles the Regulators used looked as if they had come from the mind of a child and, of course, they had. We are told the original Shotgunners were a radical offshoot of the Ku Klux Klan. They were basically nothing more than robbers and terrorists. Six of them were hanged outside of Marionsville, Ohio on 18 August 1874.

Readers of *The Regulators* will recall that Cynthia Smith worked at the E-Z Store 24 on the corner of Poplar and Hyacinth. *The Shotgunners* version has Rudy Halpern and Georgia Kellogg as clerks at the 7-11 on the corner of Maple and Hyacinth. Cynthia and Georgia survived, Rudy was shot dead.

While the action in *The Shotgunners* is undated that in *The Regulators* occurs on 15 July 1996. Of course, while the theme and storyline of the two are similar, in the screenplay it is supernatural revenge that causes the murders; while in the novelized version it is the power of a strange creature, Tak, operating through an autistic boy that is the basis of the killings.

This screenplay should make a better movie than the rather crazed altered reality storyline of *The Regulators*. Filming that story would require either full animation; or a mix of live action and animation. *The Shotgunners* could be filmed fairly cheaply as a standard violent horror movie of the type that Sam Peckinpah would undoubtedly have made a good fist of directing.

Perhaps King will choose to sell or revise this Screenplay for production at some point in the future, now that he has allowed the production of a mini-series version of *Desperation*, directed by Mick Garris. Indeed, might we one-day see Garris or even Quentin Tarantino helm the film of *The Shotgunners*? We should indeed be so lucky.

Skybar (1982)

In 1982 the Doubleday & Company imprint, Dolphin Books, published a cheap paperback workbook for budding writers titled *The Do-It-Yourself Bestseller – A Workbook*. A number of well-known authors were convinced to contribute the opening paragraphs and closing paragraph of a story. Empty lined pages were provided between the opening and closing sections and the reader was to 'complete' the story.

The contributing authors were Isaac Asimov, Belva Plain, Stephen King, Erskine Caldwell, Marilyn Harris, Arthur Herzog, Ken Follett, William F Buckley Jr., Robin Cook, Georges Simenon, Alfred Kazin, Richard Llewellyn, Barbara Taylor Bradford, Steve Allen, Leslie Waller, Colin Wilson, Irving Wallace, John Jakes, Michael Blankfort and Alvin Toffler. King is quoted on the rear cover as saying, '…sounds like fun … God knows what goes on in the middle; perhaps one of your readers will.'

Photocopies and text copies of the sections circulate in the King community and copies of the *Workbook* appear on the second-hand market from time to time.

This was actually the second time King had contributed a partial story for writers to complete. The March 1977 issue of *Cavalier* magazine contained the first five hundred words of *The Cat From Hell*. In June of that year King's completed story, along with that written by the winner of the readers' competition were published in the same magazine. The third occurrence was *The Furnace* (see separate chapter).

The two sections of *Skybar* King contributed total 579 words. The opening section begins with, 'There were twelve of us when we went in that night, but only two of us came out – my friend Kirby and me. And Kirby was insane.' The closing paragraph of the story ends with, 'I see these things in my dreams, yes, but when I visit Kirby in that place where he still lives, that place where all the windows are crosshatched with heavy mesh, I see them in his eyes. I take his hand and his hand is cold, but I sit with him and sometimes think: *These things happened to me when I was young.*'

As it is unclear where the Skybar Amusement Park is (other than close to the coast) this is an America Under Siege story. In it the narrator recalls how he and eleven other people went to the Skybar Amusement Park when they were young. Ten of them did not come out alive and of the two survivors, only the narrator was sane. We never discover the narrator's name but he was eleven and in sixth grade when he and his friends went to the exciting local amusement park, which contained such great attractions as Pop Dupree's Dead-Eye Shooting Gallery, the Whip, a Mirror Labyrinth and an Adults Only freak tent. The youngsters had to wonder what was in there, '… you especially wondered when the people came out, white-faced, some of the women crying or hysterical. Brant Callahan said it was all just fake, whatever it was, but sometimes I saw the doubt even in Brant's tough gray eyes.'

King abruptly changes gears in the last paragraph before the fill-in writers were due to begin, 'Then, of course, the murders started, and eventually Skybar was shut down.' Of course, we do not know exactly what happened but King quickly creates a foreboding atmosphere, '…the only sound the mechanical clown's mouth produced was lunatic hooting of the sea breeze.' We find that the 'murders started' when Randy Stayner, a seventh-grader, 'was thrown from the highest point of the SkyCoaster'. By writing 'thrown' King leaves us in doubt as to whether Randy was thrown by a person, or a mechanical fault caused by sabotage. The narrator and Kirby '...both heard his scream as he came down.'

The closing paragraph King provides begins with, '…I feel Kirby taking my hand and telling me it was okay; we were safe, we were home free.' But the horrors have not ended and an animated corpse begins to chase the boys and Kirby loses his mind, beginning to scream. 'Behind me I can see Randy's corpse pushing the safety bar back and he begins to stumble toward me, his dead, shredded fingers hooked into seeking claws'. The narrator awakes from his dream, in his wife's arms (he is now 12 years older).

The main characters appear to be the narrator and Kirby, with Randy Stayner a definite victim of the 'murders' and Brant Callahan likely to have been another. The storyline takes place in the Skybar Amusement Park, five miles toward the coast from the narrator's childhood home. Although we do not know the timeline of the story we do know that hi-test fuel sold at Dewey's Sunoco for 31.9 cents per gallon in those days. Twelve years later it sold for $1.40 per gallon, so perhaps it is safe to assume it occurred before the Oil Crisis of the early 1970s.

There are no links from the story to other King works. However, the story does contain King's trademark style, quickly establishing the atmosphere and reminding the reader of the carnival segment of *The Dead Zone*, portions of *It* (*this* scary clown is mechanical) and even of *The Body*.

Who knows what tremendous story King may have chosen to write between these enticing paragraphs? As it seems very unlikely he will do so perhaps the reader should fill in the blanks to his or her satisfaction.

Slade (1970)

Slade, one of King's earliest public works, is best described as western satire. It was published as a serial (King would later use this publishing technique for *The Plant* and *The Green Mile*) in *The Maine Summer Campus* (the summer edition of *The Maine Campus*) issues for June 11, June 18, June 25, July 2, July 9, July 23, July 30 and August 6, 1970. King had just graduated (on June 5) and had earlier written a series of 47 non-fiction columns, *King's Garbage Truck*, for the newspaper. That column ran from February 20, 1969 to May 21, 1970.[132]

It is effectively impossible to secure a copy of these publications. It seems the original copies held by the Raymond H Fogler Library of the University of Maine at Orono were stolen in the late 1980s. Apart from text copies that circulate in the King community the only way to secure a copy is from the Library's microfiche.

As a serial, the story was spread over eight chapters, most ending in typical cliff-hangers. In Chapter One we read, 'It was almost dark when Slade rode into Dead Steer Springs.' We are regaled with his description, '...tall in the saddle, a grim faced man dressed all in black. Even the handles of his two sinister .45s, which rode low on his hips, were black.' There had been whispered legends about his dress '...since the early 1870s, when the name of Slade began to strike fear into the stoutest of Western hearts.' In one version the black was mourning dress for his 'Illinois sweetheart, Miss Polly Peachtree of Paduka', killed when a Montgolfier balloon crashed into her barn while she milked the cows. Others had it that he was 'the Grim Reaper's agent in the American southwest – the devil's handyman. And there were some who thought he was queerer than a three-dollar bill. No one, however, advanced this last idea to his face.'

Lighting one of 'his famous Mexican cigars' Slade entered the Brass Cuspidor Saloon in which a honky-tonk piano was beating out *Oh, Them Golden Slippers*. An 'old sourdough' brings us into the story by questioning Jack Slade as to whether he was in town to work for Miss Sandra 'of the Bar-T' or 'mebbe' Sam Columbine, who was hiring hard cases to run the lady off her ranch. After Slade winged the old geezer 'for luck' the saloon went quiet, even 'the fancy dan gambler at the back table dropped three aces out of his sleeves – two of them were clubs.' In a wonderful cliché the piano player fell off his stool, regained his feet and ran out the back door (oh, for an Elton John album when you need one). Slade now confronted 'John "The Backshooter" Parkman, one of Sam Columbine's top guns.' Slade revealed he was indeed working for Sandra Dawson and this elicited a response from Parkman, "They also say yore queerer'n a three dollar bill". Slade demanded he draw.

In Chapter Two (the excited readers of *The Maine Campus*, like good moviegoers in the lost and lamented days of the serials, had to wait a week for the next installment) Slade filled Parkman with lead. 'Slade was a peace-loving man at heart, and what was more peace-loving than a dead body. The thought filled him with quiet joy and a sad yearning for his childhood sweetheart, Miss

Polly Peachtree…' Sending the bartender to get an undertaker Slade poured himself a whiskey, considering the lonely life of a gun for hire, always expecting a bullet in the back, or gall bladder, 'It sure was hard to do your business with a bullet in the gall bladder.' A shapely, beautiful blonde then threw the batwing doors open, awakening Slade's desire ('Hubba-hubba') but this quickly subsided before the memory of Polly Peachtree, 'his one true love.' Revealing herself as Sandra Dawson the girl claimed that Parkman was one of those who killed her father, and thanked Slade for dispatching the killer by kissing him, full on the lips. She was just 'melting into his arms' when the bartender returned, yelling that the Bar-T's bunkhouse was on fire. Immediately Slade mounted 'his huge black stallion, Stokely' and rode for the ranch.

Chapter Three opens with Slade arriving at the Bar-T to find Sunrise Jackson, Shifty Jack Mulloy and Doc Logan, three of Columbine's hired gunmen, 'laughing evilly' in front of the burning bunkhouse. Slade was 'cold steel and hot blood – not to mention his silk underwear with the pretty blue flowers.' Shooting a cowpoke running from the bunkhouse Logan claimed he'd, 'Thought he looked hot from all that fire … so I ventilated him.' When challenging Slade to draw, Shifty Jack said, 'Pull leather, you Republican skunk!' This was something of a mistake as Slade now shot Mulloy and Jackson but missed the escaping Logan, 'as the light was tricky.' Proceeding to the wounded Mulloy, Slade told him, 'You never should have called me a Republican … He showed him his Gene McCarthy button and then blasted him.' Just then, Sing-Loo, the Chinese cook, ran from the bunkhouse and Slade bagged him, realizing his mistake too late. Holstering his gun 'and feeling a great wave of longing for his one true love, Miss Polly Peachtree of Paduka', Slade said sadly, 'I guess you can't win them all.' Returning to town our hero discovered that Miss Dawson had been kidnapped by the dastardly Columbine, 'Ain't you gonna go after her … Columbine may try to rape her – or even rob her!' his informant asked.

But, in Chapter Four, we learn that Slade is tired from blasting the 'three gunslingers and one Chinese Cook'. He decided to head for the Dead Steer Springs Hotel, 'his spurs jingling below the heels of his Bonanza boots (they had elevator lifts inside the heels, Slade was very sensitive about his height).' When a young boy asked for his autograph Slade, 'who didn't want to encourage that sort of thing, shot him in the leg and walked on.' After undressing and putting his boots back on, he fell asleep. Around one in the morning Hunchback Fred Agnew, 'the most detested killer' in the American Southwest crept into the hotel room through the window, armed with a three foot Arabian skinning knife (he had once used it on an old lady from Boston, on her way to Arizona to recuperate from Parkinson's disease, but never once on an Arab). Agnew set his twelve-foot python (Sadie Hawkins) to attack Slade.

'In that instant, the faint hiss of scales on the sheet came to Slade's ears. A woman was in bed with him! That was his first thought …' In disappointment

Agnew threw his knife, which only nicked one of Slade's earlobes and Slade shot him dead, 'his sinister career was at an end.' The python, meanwhile, curled up on the bed and went to sleep! Dressing, Slade 'grimly' set off to find Columbine 'and put a crimp in his style once and for all.'

Chapter Five has Slade arriving back at the Brass Cuspidor, stunning Dawson's drunken foreman with the news of Agnew's demise. Awed, the man whispered, ' "There was talk he might be the next Vice President of the American Southwest"'. Inexplicably for a man who was set on finding Columbine, the gunslinger now demanded a drink from the bartender that he'd never had before or the unfortunate man would 'be pushing up daisies' before dawn. Slade drank three zombies while finding out more about Columbine, including the location of his Rotten Vulture Ranch. Totally drunk and trying to leave the saloon, Slade was arrested by Deputy Marshall Hoagy Carmichael, on a charge of public intoxication!

In Chapter Six King the author rails against the staff of *The Maine Campus* for refusing to publish 'a pretty damn good love scene' between Slade and Dawson, managing to pretty much tell all he had intended anyway, and advising he had provided an alternative scene (the fact that there were two weeks between chapters in this case may be related to the dispute). After being sprung from jail Slade shot the foreman and Deputy Marshall ('blame it on his terrible hangover') and headed to the Rotten Vulture where he dropped three of Columbine's henchmen in their 'slimy tracks' and freed Dawson. The henchmen were Big Frank Nixon, 'Quick Draw' John Mitchell and Shifty Ron Ziegfeld. Delighted to be saved Dawson yelled, "You came just in time". ' "Damn right," he replied. "I always do. Steve King sees to that."' Dawson pushed her 'firm, supple, silken-fleshed body' into Slade's arms and tried to kiss him, so he 'promptly clubbed her over the head with one sinister .45...' "Watch it ... my mom told me about girls like you!" One presumes the editors were much happier with the violence of this scene than the presumably salacious prose King originally had in store for his breathless readers!

Over in Chapter Seven Slade headed for the border, 'where Sam Columbine was torturing Mexican customs men' with his sidekick, 'Pinky' Lee. Pinky got the nickname in the Civil War when riding with Quantrill and 'his Regulators'. A Union officer bombed him while he was passed out in a fancy bordello in Bleeding Heart, Kansas. As a result he '...lost all his hair, his eyebrows, and all the fingers on his left hand, except for the fourth, and smallest. His hair and eyebrows grew back. His fingers did not.' Approaching the border, Slade dismounted and tied Stokely to a parking meter (!) before trying to sneak up on Lee and Columbine. When the shootout began Slade realized he had forgotten to reload after the Rotten Vulture shootout. Lee rolled behind a barrel of corn chips and Columbine crouched behind a 'giant bottle of mayonnaise that had been air-dropped the month before after the worst flood disaster in American

Southwest history (why drop mayonnaise after a flood disaster: none of your damn business).' Guns reloaded, Slade calmly shot Pinky in the head after tricking him out of his cover and started for Columbine ...

In the closing episode of this epic Western Columbine challenged Slade to a man on man draw. As is always the case in any B-grade Western the girl now ran into the picture. Dawson suddenly declared she had something to tell Slade, "I'm Polly Peachtree". She claimed to have escaped the burning balloon but ' "...had amnesia! It's all just come back to me tonight!"' Pulling off her blond wig Slade could now see she was indeed 'the beautiful Polly Peachtree of Paduka, returned from the dead!' Like all good villains, Columbine now took this opportunity to shoot Slade in the back, three times! In another twist Sandra/Polly now thanked her 'darling' Sam, ' "You don't know how terrible it's been ... Not only was he killing everybody, but he was queerer than a three-dollar bill."'

Suddenly, Slade 'sat up and blasted them both.' It was a good thing he was wearing his bulletproof underwear he said, as he lit a new Mexican cigar. Staring at the bodies, '...a great wave of sadness swept over him. He threw away his cigar and lit a joint. Then he walked over to where he had tethered Stokely, his black stallion. He wrapped his arms around Stokely's neck and held him close. "At last, darling," Slade whispered. "We're alone." After a long while, Slade and Stokely rode off into the sunset in search of new adventures.'

This rare foray by King into satirical comedy references a number of prominent figures of the day, including President Nixon, Vice President Agnew and Attorney-General John Mitchell. The Nixon administration was the subject of considerable satirical review, even before the Watergate affair. Even today, the 1971 satire by *Portnoy's Complaint* author Philip Roth, *Our Gang (Starring Tricky and His Friends)*[133] is both readable and *funny*. Roth won the Medal for Distinguished Contribution to American Letters from the National Book Foundation in 2002, the year before King.

There are a couple of possible links to King's later fiction. Captain Quantrill and his men, 'The Regulators' are mentioned. The Regulators are, of course, characters in the Bachman alternative reality novel, *The Regulators*. Slade's huge, black stallion horse was Stokely, a very unusual name. Stokely Jones is a significant and amusing character in *Hearts in Atlantis*, set at the University of Maine. Tyson Blue speculates the name is actually homage to a prominent black activist of the time, Stokeley Carmichael.[134]

Of course, 'Steve' King (to whom Slade refers) is also referred to but not named in *The King Family and the Wicked Witch* and *The Leprechaun*. He is also the horror author mentioned by Ardelia Lortz in *The Library Policeman*; mentioned as an author in *Prime Evil* version of *Night Flier*, *The Regulators* and *Thinner*; mentioned as the narrator of *The Blue Air Compressor*; and is a character in the Dark Tower Cycle.

King expert and academic Michael Collings has this to say about *Slade*, '(*It*) is in many ways the most revealing of King's uncollected early works, especially as it shows King reveling in the sheer joy of words, puns, and outrageous storytelling. It is an engaging explosion of off-the-wall humor, literary pastiche, and cultural criticism masquerading as a Western.'[135] And, in *The Shorter Works of Stephen King*, ' "Slade" is as derivative as King's early extant tales; the difference is that he is now aware of the fact … Everything – every movement, every line of dialogue, every locale and every character – functions strictly according to stereotypes, yet King gives them new life by blending them with both parody and burlesque.'[136]

In *The Unseen King* Tyson Blue summarizes the story by saying, '(*It*) shows King's eye for choosing just the right elements of the Western genre to poke fun at, and he uses anachronisms – the air-dropped giant mayonnaise jar, the political jokes and references, the authorial intrusions – here in much the same fashion as Mel Brooks did in his filmic genre spoof "Blazing Saddles", and to similar effect. If nothing else, "Slade" shows that King's ability to tell a good story serves him just as well in a comic framework as it does in his more serious tales.'

In the end though, this obscure 6500-word tale is actually little more than an exercise in satire by a 22-year-old recent graduate writing for his college newspaper. It is most unlikely King will allow republication, as it certainly does not reflect the Stephen King most readers know. In fact, according to Beahm, '…when UMO's *The Maine Campus* was planning on incorporating it as part of a student anthology years after the fact, SK put an immediate stop to it, stating it was clearly juvenilia and that he would not allow its reprinting.'[137]

There is no doubt King is fascinated with the Western form. He often refers to Westerns in his fiction (for instance, Bobbi Anderson of *The Tommyknockers* wrote novels, mostly with a Western feel) and his central fictional character Roland Deschain *is* a gunslinger. In fact, King began *The Dark Tower* the same summer he wrote *Slade*. Also, *George D X McArdle*, subject of another chapter of this book, is an incomplete novel based in the Old West.

Hardcore fans and students of King's development will both gain from reading *Slade*. If nothing else, it is still funny today, three and a half decades after it was written, and we can all do with a good laugh.

Sleepwalkers (1991)

Sleepwalkers was the first wholly original King movie screenplay ever produced. It was made on a budget of $16 million and was released on 10 April 1992, taking over $30 million at the box office. The screenplay has not been published but copies circulate in the King community and readers would best access it in that manner. Considering its originality it would be a prime candidate to be published should King consider allowing one or more of his screenplays to be published in some format.

Sleepwalkers, also known as *Stephen King's Sleepwalkers*, attracts only a 4.6 rating out of a possible 10 from the members of www.imdb.com but deserves better. Mick Garris directed, the first time he had done so for a King production. He would go on to helm the mini-series of *The Stand* and of *The Shining*, as well as *Quicksilver Highway*, *Riding the Bullet* and *Desperation*.

The actors were Brian Krause as Charles Brady; Madchen Amick (who also appeared in the cult show *Twin Peaks*) as Tanya Robertson; and Alice Krige (who played the Borg Queen to perfection in *Star Trek: First Contact*) as Mary Brady. There were a number of cameos, including that of the director's wife Cynthia Garris as Laurie Travis; *Animal House* director John Landis as a Lab Tech; *Gremlins* director Joe Dante as a Lab Assistant; Stephen King as a Cemetery Caretaker; and horror writer Clive Barker and *The Texas Chain Saw Massacre* director Tobe Hooper as Forensic Techs. The movie was first released on DVD in 2000.

This chapter was compiled from the Sixth Draft of the original screenplay, dated 20 March 1991. That draft is 107 pages in length. An earlier draft appears in a Journal originally held in Box 2702 at the Special Collections Unit of the Raymond H Fogler Library at the University of Maine, Orono but since moved to a Restricted Box, 1010. That draft appears under the title, *Tania's Suitor*.

In this America Under Siege script incestuous and ancient creatures face their mortal enemies. Sleepwalkers had evolved from cats and in their true form had reptilian *and* feline features. They fed upon the life force of humans and modern cats were their mortal enemies.

Carl and Martha Brodie had lived in Bodega Bay, California (apparently the same town in which Alfred Hitchcock's classic *The Birds* was set) before being attacked by local cats, which had discovered that Sleepwalkers were in their midst. The mother and son barely escaped with their lives and moved to Travis, Indiana. Settling into this new town as the Bradys, Charles enrolled at the local high school and set his sights on the attractive 17-year-old Tanya Robertson, an all-round American girl, who also worked part time at the town's only movie theatre.

Seducing Tanya, Charles attacked her in Homeland Cemetery but she fought back and Clovis, a local cat, seriously wounded him. While fleeing, Charles passed a speed trap and was pursued by a local Deputy Sheriff, who saw him transforming into his true shape. Charles then shot and killed the police officer and returned home, critically injured.

Clovis and a gang of cats from Travis and nearby Castle Rock now targeted the Brady house as the police, alerted by Tanya, also moved in. Mary Brady fought back, killing a number of police and kidnapping Tanya to provide Charles the life force he needed to recover.

However, the cats outsmarted her and gained entry to the house, saving Tanya's life. The script tells us, 'Charles battles on until he reaches Mary and one by one throws off the marauding cats. And at last he takes Mary in his arms, the two of them ancient destroyed creatures, burning alive on the pyre of their own bodies. Slowly, like tallow, they begin to melt and fuse together. And together they HOWL their final note. A LONG, ULULATING CRY that is as old as their race on earth. It echoes and fades with the only dignity this cursed kind knows.'

Sleepwalkers is a genuinely original tale in which King introduces creatures never before seen in horror fiction. In their true form Sleepwalkers have reptilian and feline features. They evolved from cats and were an ancient race, feeding upon the life force of humans. Modern cats were their mortal enemies and would seek out Sleepwalkers and, if possible, kill them. Although Mary Brady believed there were others of their kind still alive Charles doubted her. King has not returned to these creatures since, so Mary and Charles may indeed have been the last. Sleepwalkers have an ability to make themselves 'dim', in fact Mary Brady used this exact word to describe the act. This is a skill Randall Flagg and certain other characters in King stories display (particularly those with the initials 'R.F.').

The dimming ability is another example of King enjoying the linking of his screenplays to his other fiction and the making of small in-jokes for the benefit of Constant Readers and long-time fans. In this case there are a number of other examples. For instance, one of Tanya Robertson's classmates was a girl named Carrie!

For some reason this screenplay/movie was set in Indiana. The town of Castle Rock, Indiana is close to Travis, as Sheriff Ira of Travis called for help from Castle Rock; and cats were even able to get from it to Travis for the final confrontation with the Bradys. Castle Rock, Indiana is strangely similar to Castle Rock, Maine. For instance, in the script someone called Pangborn was the Sheriff of Castle Rock, Indiana. In *The Sun Dog, The Dark Half, Gerald's Game* and *Needful Things*, Alan Pangborn was Sheriff of Castle Rock, Maine. He is also mentioned in *Bag of Bones*. There is a Mellow Tiger bar in Castle Rock, Indiana. There was also a Mellow Tiger bar in Castle Rock, Maine in *The Body, Needful Things, Bag of Bones, Cujo* and *The Sun Dog*; and a Mellow Tiger bar in Castle County, Maine in *The Dark Half*. None of this is coincidental and the only question is why King felt obligated to move a town so closely associated with his work to another state for this tale?

Travis is described as having a '…certain Norman Rockwellesque charm.' The Bradys lived at 66 Wicker Street, which Charles Brady claimed sounded like the address in an 'old horror movie'. The cemetery in which Charles attacked Tanya was the Homeland Cemetery, almost the archetypal location for a writer so skilled at describing these places of the dead and using them in his fiction. The word 'Homeland' appeared in rusted ornamental ironwork arches over the front gate. It was surrounded by rock walls that had crumbled and broken and the surrounding woods had overgrown the back wall. Inside the walls it was old and overgrown and consequently served as a local make-out spot.

While no timelines are given in the script the events in Travis must occur after the release of the movie, *Misery* in the United States on 30 November 1990 as the Aero movie theater in Travis, Indiana was showing that movie when the Bradys tried to abduct Tanya Robertson. The script mentions that the movie is 'Stephen King's *Misery*'. This is a relatively rare mention by King of himself in his fiction. King also appears in *The King Family and the Wicked Witch* and is referred to but not named in *The Leprechaun*. He is a horror author mentioned by Ardelia Lortz in *The Library Policeman*; and is also mentioned as an author in the *Prime Evil* version of *The Night Flier*, *Thinner* and *Slade*; mentioned as the narrator of *The Blue Air Compressor*; and notably as a character in the Dark Tower Cycle.

George Beahm[138] relates King's inspiration for the story. Apparently Stephen and Tabitha King's son, Joe[139] had a crush on the popcorn girl at the Bangor Hoyt's Cinema, '…one night when we were at the movies, he was talking to her and I could see why he was attracted to her. She was just this beautiful, vital girl who played a lot of sports and had this kind of healthy, wholesome glow about her … And it made me think of a guy wanting to ask the popcorn girl out for all the wrong reasons, and the story just followed that burst of inspiration.'

In retrospect this is an interesting tale, introducing a new species native to our planet, which preys on humans much as vampires are said to do, in this case sucking out our life force rather than our blood. There are strong sexual overtones in the script – the Bradys are physically incestuous and both Charles and Tanya display teenage physical lust toward each other. Somehow, the power of the tale and the interaction fail to come across on screen. Perhaps the budget simply wasn't there to allow the sort of movie the script would have allowed.

The screenplay pretty much ends with Tanya saying, 'Let *them* sleep together. Forever.' And: 'Is she relieved of the horror or does she remember the pilgrim soul she loved for a moment? Suddenly she pulls out of Ira's arms and rushes forward. Is she going to Charles? Hell no, just to pick up Clovis who watches solemnly from the sidewalk.'

THE *LAST* OF THE SLEEPWALKERS

In their true form Sleepwalkers have reptilian and feline features. They evolved from cats and were an ancient race upon the earth, feeding upon the life force of humans. Modern cats were their mortal enemies and would seek out Sleepwalkers and, if possible, kill them. Although Mary Brady believed there were others of their kind still alive, Charles Brady doubted her. King has not returned to these creatures since, so Mary and Charles may indeed have been the last. Sleepwalkers have an ability to make themselves 'dim', in fact Mary Brady used this exact word to describe the act.

MARY BRADY (MARTHA BRODIE)

Mary was the mother of Charles. They are Sleepwalkers and incestuous. She had lived in Bodega Bay, California under the name Martha Brodie before moving to Travis, Indiana. She was slim, pretty and young looking. After Charles was seriously hurt by a cat, Clovis she kidnapped Tanya Robertson, intending to give her to Charles to feed upon her life force. An army of cats, led by Clovis, entered the house and tore Mary and Charles apart, causing them to catch fire and die.

CHARLES BRADY (CARL BRODIE)

Mary's son and possibly the last male of his race, when in Sleepwalker form his eyes are green. He had lived in Bodega Bay, California under the name Carl Brodie. He was very good looking and appeared to be about 18. He registered as a student of Travis High School and attracted Tanya Robertson with the aim of feeding on her life force. When he attacked Tanya she fought back and injured him. When Deputy Sheriff Simpson chased him after the attack he saw Charles metamorphosing but Charles shot him dead. Simpson's cat, Clovis then seriously wounded Charles, forcing him to leave Tanya. He made it home but his wounds caused a reversion to his Sleepwalker form. He again tried to feed on Tanya when Mary brought her home but Tanya attacked him once more, and an army of cats, led by Clovis, tore Charles and his mother apart.

CLOVIS THE ATTACK CAT

Clovis belonged to Travis Deputy Sheriff Andy Simpson. He was a large, sleek, green-eyed tomcat, with a green velvet collar to which was attached a silver tag reading, 'Clovis the Attack Cat'. After Charles Brady killed Simpson, Clovis attacked Charles and seriously wounded him. Clovis later led an army of cats to the Brady House where they attacked and killed both Bradys and saved Tanya Robertson's life.

Something Wicked This Way Comes (1970s)

The screenplay of *Something Wicked This Way Comes* is held in Box 1010 at the Special Collections Unit of the Raymond H Fogler Library at the University of Maine, Orono. Written permission from King is required to access this work. There is no indication when the screenplay was written but a film adaptation of the book was released in 1983.

In an interview with David Chute (published in *Take One* for January 1979 and reproduced in *Feast of Fear*[140]) King talks of having written this script, saying: "...I felt more divorced from the source material. I loved the book, and I think that of all the screenplays I've done, that was the best. But in spite of loving it I was a little divorced from it, where I wasn't with my own book." The date of this interview indicates the script was completed no later than 1978.

A note on the Folder holding the screenplay at the Library states 'Incomplete - Pages Missing'. Of the 81 pages those missing are pages 5, 9-13, 16, 33-36 and 39-40, for a total of 13 missing, leaving 68 extant.

The screenplay is of Ray Bradbury's novel of the same title. Published in 1962, it is regarded as a classic in both the fantasy and horror genres. Noted King expert Stanley Wiater describes it as a '...masterpiece of modern Gothic literature.' Bradbury is also the author of the magnificent anti-censorship novel, *Fahrenheit 451*, *The Martian Chronicles* and that collection's short story, *Mars Is Heaven* (more of which later), among over five hundred works of fiction. Both Bradbury and King are recipients of the National Book Foundation's Medal for Distinguished Contribution to American Letters.

Due to the release of the 1983 film with Bradbury himself as the scriptwriter it would seem most unlikely that King's screenplay will ever be produced. It is also certain that it will never be published or be made available for public reading, as King has chosen to place it in a Restricted Box at the Fogler Library. The best solution for readers who have not had the pleasure of being exposed to this story is to read Bradbury's novel or to rent the video/DVD of the film.

King writes extensively of the novel in Chapter 9, section 6 of *Danse Macabre*. The amount of space King used to comment on the tale is a clear indication of how important he considers its impact to be in the horror genre. He says, '...I believe that *Something Wicked This Way Comes*, a darkly poetic tale set in the half-real, half-mythical community of Green Town, Illinois, is probably Bradbury's best work ...' King quotes Bradbury's re-telling of the story's inspirations saying it, '...began as a short story in *Weird Tales* called "Black Ferris" in May 1948 ...' Bradbury then turned that short story into a movie outline called *Dark Carnival* that he pitched to Gene Kelly, who loved it but could not raise the finance. Bradbury said, '...to hell with it and sat down and spent two years, on and off, finishing *Something Wicked* ...' as a novel.

King's analysis of Bradbury's writing and the novel itself is superb and readers should take the time to read this section of 1981's *Danse Macabre*, in which King makes no mention of his own screenplay. If you have read the novel, it will enhance your understanding. If not, you will be unable to resist by the time Big Steve is finished.

In this screenplay, which is part of the America Under Siege reality, a carnival comes to Green Town, Illinois. Cooger and Dark's Pandemonium Shadow Show suddenly appeared in the small mid-Western town on 23 October 1962 and set up in Rolfe's Meadow. Shortly after the Show's arrival a hunched old man with wild gray hair (known in the script only as 'The Drummer') gave a local boy, Jim Nightshade, a lightning rod to place on his house. Apparently the carnival denizens had done something evil to this old man but we do not discover what it was.

When Nightshade visited the carnival with his friend Will Halloway they realized something was very wrong. Their reaction somehow alerted Cooger, Dark and their cohorts, including the 'Dust-Witch'. The carnival had strange attractions, including a Mirror-Maze reflecting different ages of the viewer, and a carousel that could increase or decrease the rider's age.

Cooger used the carousel to take himself back to twelve years of age. He then went to the house of a local teacher, Miss Foley and confused her by introducing himself as Robert, her nephew. However, Nightshade and Halloway interrupted his plan to rob her. Cooger then tried to set the boys up as the ones who had stolen her jewelry.

That night Dark and the Dust-Witch sought the boys, presumably to kill them. The Dust-Witch was an ancient, withered crone in gypsy clothes. She was blind and her eyes were sewn up but she could somehow sense using her fingers. She floated over the town in a balloon, using the fingers to seek the boys, and threw a bucket of silvery-stuff onto the shingled roof of the Nightshade house to mark it. Nightshade and Will Halloway washed the slimy stuff off with a garden hose. Later, Halloway shot the balloon down from the roof of an abandoned house, the Redman place, using a bow and arrow.

The next day the Cooger and Dark carnival paraded down Main Street, where Nightshade and Halloway were hiding from Dark and his followers. After being alerted to the danger by the boys Bill Halloway, Will's librarian father, researched the history of the carnival's visits to Green Town. Speculating it could be hundreds of years old, he also came to the realization that the evil could be laughed away.

About 9pm that night Dark, the Dust-Witch and the carnival's Dwarf succeeded in capturing the two boys at the Town Library. When Bill Halloway (*strangely King changes the father's name from the original Charles*) challenged Dark using a Bible, Dark claimed that it could not hurt him '...nor could silver bullets or dawn's early light.' Bill Halloway then followed the kidnappers to the carnival, intending to rescue the boys. However, Jim Nightshade was tempted by the chance to grow a little older and took a ride on the carousel as it turned forwards. Will Halloway jumped on to the infernal device to remove him, aging a year in the process. Jim had aged two years and appeared to be dead when taken off the carousel. However, the two Halloways were able to laugh and dance him back to life.

Bill Halloway then laughed the Dust-Witch to death. Although Dark had used the carousel to disguise himself as a nine year old boy Bill saw through the ruse, seized this version of Dark, as he would not have been able to hold the man, and 'lovingly laughed him to death'. The carousel and carnival then both self-destructed.

The carnival moved on, leaving a poster advertising Cooger and Dark's Pandemonium Shadow Show's visit to Dallas, Texas for 'one day only' on November 22, 1963. That is, of course, the date of John F Kennedy's assassination in that very city.

Among the things we learn of the Cooger and Dark Show is that it had visited Green Town in the Octobers of 1846 and 1860, on 12 October 1888 and in October of 1910, the year Bill Halloway was born.

The two boys are our heroes in the piece (although it is Bill Halloway who turns out to be the real hero, rescuing the boys and killing Dark and the Dust Witch). The boys were born only minutes apart, Will Halloway at 11.59pm on 30 October 1948 (All Hallow's Eve); and Jim Nightshade at 12.01am the following day. It is obvious that Bradbury took great care in naming the boys, who would turn fourteen a week after the carnival's visit.

Dark was also known as 'The Illustrated Man'. Tattoos covered his face, neck, chest and arms. He had tattooed photos of Will Halloway and Jim Nightshade on his palms and he had probably run the carnival for hundreds of years.

We know less of Dark's partner, Mr Cooger, also known as 'Mr Electro, the Man of Lightning'. He was tall with oiled, dark hair, dressed like a riverboat gambler and had a pocked face that was very pale. He somehow became trapped in the carnival's electric chair (*these are some of the pages that are missing from the screenplay*) and this was probably the boys' fault. As a result, he died and disintegrated into dust.

Among the Carnival's attractions were The Hall of Freaks and the Egyptian Mirror Maze. When the carousel spun backwards its calliope would play *The Funeral March* in reverse. The carnivals 'freaks' included Vesuvio, the fire-eater; The Crusher, who was the strongman; the Dwarf; and the Skeleton.

In this screenplay Miss Foley was the only 'innocent' victim of all this mayhem. An elderly schoolteacher with gray hair, Halloway and Nightshade initially saved her from the carnival's Mirror-Maze, where she could see visions of herself aged about 80, hunched and with snow white hair. Later, Cooger tricked her into believing the boys had stolen her jewelry. Later again, Dark and his cohorts tricked her onto the carousel and turned her into a nine-year old. Halloway and Nightshade found this young girl crying under a huge old elm tree on Brackman's Lot.

In the only link to King's other fiction Green Town, Illinois is also mentioned in *Bag of Bones*. In that novel it appears in the context of the first space travellers to Mars discovering they had apparently arrived in this town (or was it Heaven?) in Ray Bradbury's story *Mars Is Heaven* (originally published as *The Third Expedition* in the 1950 short story collection, *The Martian Chronicles*). That story is known to be one of King's earliest influences and favorite horror/science fiction tales. In fact, in *Danse Macabre* King writes, 'My first experience with real horror came at the hands of Ray Bradbury – it was an adaptation of his story 'Mars is Heaven!' on *Dimension X*. This would have been broadcast about 1951, which would have made me four at the time. I asked to listen, and was denied permission by my mother … I crept down to the door to listen anyway, and she was right it was plenty upsetting …'

We should note that it is Bradbury, not King, who chose to use Green Town, Illinois in both *Mars Is Heaven* and *Something Wicked This Way Comes* and this is therefore not a 'Link' in the sense of one created by King himself.

In King's screenplay Green Town has a population of 4063. There are three or four streets, which run at right angles to and intersect Main Street. Miss Foley lived on Culpepper Street, four houses up from Main. Both the Nightshade and Halloway families lived on Oak, the Nightshades at number 97.

All in all, this is a relatively unique King piece. Including this script, he is thought to have adapted only two works of other writers for the screen. The other is a screenplay of Patrick McGrath's novel, *Asylum*. That screenplay has not come to light, although one purported review of it has been seen on the Internet. The original claim was made in an article in the entertainment industry magazine *Variety* for 6 February 2001.

To the casual reader's eye this is a very competent movie script and it would have made an interesting note to King's career had there been a production of his screenplay of any other author's work, particularly one of such note. Ultimately, as we mentioned earlier, Bradbury himself wrote a script that was produced and, as we have argued elsewhere, this is generally preferable to scripting by another writer.

Sorry, Right Number – The Shooting Script (1986)

A version of the screenplay for a series episode on the horror anthology series, *Tales From the Darkside* appears in King's 1993 collection *Nightmares and Dreamscapes*. Most fans would be forgiven for believing this was the telescript actually used for the program. However, it varies significantly from the actual shooting script.

That script is held in Box 1012 at the Special Collections Unit of the Raymond H Fogler Library at the University of Maine, Orono. It is marked as the 'Final Shooting Script', dated July 11, 1986, 'Story and Teleplay by Stephen King'. As King chose to publish his first draft of *Nightmares and Dreamscapes* we can safely assume this shooting script will never be published. Box 1012 is open to the public so readers may access this version at the Fogler.

As the basic storyline can be enjoyed in *Nightmares and Dreamscapes* or watched on video we will satisfy ourselves here with a short summary of this shooting script and the key changes.

In this America Under Siege tale a woman briefly hears from an anguished caller. She and her husband tried to discover the source of the call, as she was sure she recognized the voice. That very night Kate Weiderman's husband Bill, a successful horror novelist, died of a heart attack.

Ten years later, on the anniversary of Bill's death, his daughter was about to marry at the family home. Katie absent-mindedly dialed her old phone number and was momentarily connected with her earlier self. She realized she had been trying to send a warning of the heart attack from the future and tried to blurt out that warning but was cut off. When redialed she discovered the number was not connected.

The script was produced as the episode *Sorry, Right Number* for *Tales From the Darkside* and was first televised on 22 November 1987. John Sutherland directed and the key actors were Deborah Harmon as Katie Weiderman; Rhonda Dotson as Dawn; Arthur Taxier as Bill Weiderman; and Catherine Battistone as the 'Voice on the Phone'. The episode is available on video as part of Volume 4 of a compilation set from the series. Mysteriously, it has yet to be released on DVD.

King gives the background to the screenplay in the *Notes* to *Nightmares and Dreamscapes*[141]. He says he wrote it, '…pretty much as it appears here, in two sittings.' After writing the telescript King relates, 'My West Coast agent – the one who does film deals – had it by the end of the week. Early the following week, Steven Spielberg read it for *Amazing Stories*, a TV series which he then had in production … Spielberg rejected it – they were looking for *Amazing Stories* that were a little more upbeat he said – and so I took it to my longtime collaborator and good friend, Richard Rubinstein, who then had a series called *Tales from the Darkside* in syndication. I won't say Richard blows his nose on happy endings – he likes happily-ever-after as well as anyone, I think – but he's never shied away from a downer; he was the guy who got *Pet Sematary* made after all … Richard bought 'Sorry' the day he read it and had it in production a week or two later.'

King continues, 'This version, by the way, is my first draft, which is longer and a little more textured than the final shooting script, which for budgetary reasons specified just two sets. It is included here as an example of another kind of story-telling … different, but as valid as any other.'

There are, in fact, key differences between the two scripts. The time lapse between Bill's death and Polly's wedding (that is, between the call being received and later being made) is ten years in the case of the shooting script, but only five years in the published version. Bill Weiderman's age at his death changes from 44 in this script to 45 in *Nightmares and Dreamscapes*. He and Katie have an extra child and he is credited with an additional novel in the published version, and the movie made from his work is of a different novel in each version (*see the feature panel for details*). In the published version, but not the shooting script, Katie had remarried (to an architect, Hank). In the opposite direction, in the published version Polly's husband-to-be remains unnamed but we know him as Jack in the shooting script. In another interesting twist there had been murders in Colville the month before Bill Weiderman died but these did not appear in the earlier, published version.

For those interested the number dialed in the shooting script was 555-4408 but no number is given in the *Nightmares and Dreamscapes* version. In yet another amusing in-joke from King, when Katie Weiderman called her daughter Polly at her dorm the person answering mentioned that, if the caller was Arnie, Christine was not in (this is a reference, however obscure, to *Christine* and its key characters).

This is not one of King's key works of fiction. It is derivative and the production itself suffered from a lack of real suspense.

BILL WEIDERMAN – NOT SAVED BY THE BELL

A successful horror writer, he was about 44 when he died of a heart attack. He was the husband of Katie and father of Polly, Connie and Jeff. Among his books were his first, *Spider's Kiss* (a best-seller, which had been made into a movie) and *Night of the Beast*.
Source: *Sorry, Right Number* (The Shooting Script)

A writer aged about 45 when he died of a heart attack. He was the husband of Katie and father of Connie, Dennis, Jeff and Polly. He wrote *Ghost Kiss* (also made into a movie), *Spider Doom* and *Night of the Beast*.
Source: *Sorry, Right Number* (*Nightmares and Dreamscapes*)

Squad D (Undated)

Squad D was written in the late 1970s for a Harlan Ellison edited anthology, *Last Dangerous Visions*. Ellison told George Beahm for *The Stephen King Companion*: 'Stephen sent me a story for *Last Dangerous Visions* that needs to be rewritten ... I was sent this short story, and I think there's a lot more in it than Stephen had time to develop. The story deserves better, the work deserves better, and Stephen's reputation deserves better.'

As part of research for the latest edition of this book Stephen King was asked what had happened to this tale. His response: 'What I remember most clearly about "Squad D" is the reaction of Kirby McCauley, my then agent, when I told him I'd given the story to Harlan. We were in a Checker cab, and Kirby punched the roof hard enough to make his knuckles swell (the cabbie never said a word—probably wasn't his personal cab). It was the only time Kirby was ever angry with me. "Why did you do that?" he shouted. "Harlan will never publish that book, and that story will rot in his files!" He was talking about *The Last Dangerous Visions*. And while Kirby was wrong about many things, he was right about that book. It never has been published.[142]'

As it now three decades later and the anthology has still to appear the only chance readers have to experience this tale is through the photocopies of *Squad D* that circulate quite freely in the King community. It is quite short at 'approximately 2000 words', according to a typed header on the eleven page manuscript.

Interestingly, there are apparently two versions of the manuscript circulating. The manuscript reviewed in this chapter sets the suicide three years to the day after the death of the rest of Squad D (see below). However, Spignesi refers to the deaths as occurring eleven years later. In Michael Collings' *The Shorter Works of Stephen King*, he also refers to the suicide occurring on the eleventh anniversary of the original deaths. Collings describes the tale as one '…of guilt and forgiveness, of peace growing out of turmoil.' As both these King experts have read the manuscript, one can only presume there are indeed at least two versions in existence.

The final victim of this tale, Josh Bortman, was a resident of Castle Rock and, as a result, it is classified as a Maine Street Horror story. As a Castle Rock story *Squad D* is linked to all other King stories mentioning 'The Rock'. Castle Rock is the main setting for *The Body*, *Cujo*, *Gramma*, *It Grows on You* (but only the *Nightmares and Dreamscapes* version), *The Man in the Black Suit*, *Mrs. Todd's Shortcut*, *Needful Things*, *Nona* (but only the *Skeleton Crew* version), *Premium Harmony*, *The Sun Dog* and *Uncle Otto's Truck*. It is a key location in *Bag of Bones*, *The Dark Half*, *The Dead Zone* and *The Huffman Story*. It is also mentioned in *Creepshow*, *Dreamcatcher*, *Gerald's Game*, *The Girl Who Loved Tom Gordon*, *The Lonesome Death of Jordy Verrill*, *Riding the Bullet*, *Rita Hayworth and Shawshank Redemption*, *Under the Dome* and *The Stand* (*Complete and Uncut* version only). Unfortunately, nothing more of Castle Rock is revealed in this story other than the fact that the Bortman family lived there, at least during the 1974 – 1977 period.

In this tale a soldier is the only survivor of his army squad, ('D'). On 8 April 1974, the Viet Cong had killed nine members of Squad D while they crossed a bridge over the Ky River at Ky Doc in Vietnam. The squad had been on '…a flank sweep of a jungle quadrant of which Ky Doc was the only village.' Josh Bortman was not with his Squad as he was in hospital, suffering bleeding hemorrhoids. Later, as some form of atonement for his survival, the survivor sent a framed photograph showing the nine dead members of Squad D to the relatives of each man killed.

On 9 April 1977 various relatives of Squad D members called the Bortman household after noticing another soldier appear in their photos. Bortman, still only 24, had committed suicide by hanging at his parents' home in Castle Rock the previous day, the third anniversary of the attack, and his image had now joined those of his comrades.

As most readers will not have the opportunity to read this classic tale let's take this opportunity to present further detail.

One of the key characters is, of course, Josh Bortman. Apparently overcome by remorse over the fact that he was the sole survivor of his Squad, and probably embarrassed by having been in hospital with bleeding hemorrhoids at the time, he killed himself on the third anniversary of his comrades' death. Bortman had sent a framed photograph of the nine deceased members of the Squad to each of their grieving parents or relatives from Vietnam. His letter to the Clewsons '…was anguished. He called the other nine "the best friends I ever had in my life. I loved them all like they was my brothers."'

'Rites of atonement with a soft-lead pencil …', Dale Clewson thought of Bortman's letter while re-reading it after he noticed the extra 'boy' in the photo. Dale thought he could read into the letter and photo a deep anguish, 'Please don't think I killed your son – all of your sons - by taking their picture. Please don't hate me because I was in the Homan base hospital with bleeding haemorrhoids (*sic*) instead of on the Ky Doc bridge with the best friends I ever had in my life. Please don't hate me, because I finally caught up, it took me ten years of trying, but I finally caught up.' This quote, claiming ten years since the original deaths, is from the manuscript your author has seen. As noted earlier there is apparently also a manuscript showing eleven years, rather than three between the deaths on the bridge and Bortman's suicide noted elsewhere in the manuscript in my possession.

After his suicide, many of the dead soldier's relatives noticed another person in their copies of the photograph. We can presume poor Josh is now at peace, joining his comrades in the death he had but temporarily cheated. One interesting question remains: where was Josh buried? If in Castle Rock, his name might reappear in some future King story, as a character wanders through one of the town's cemeteries, or mentioned as another character is interred there.

The other members of the Squad were Jack Bradley from Omaha, Nebraska; Billy Clewson from Binghamton, New York; Rider Dotson from Oneonta, New York; Charlie Gibson, a guitar player from Payson, North Dakota; Bobby Kale from Henderson, Iowa; Jack Kimberley, who liked to tell dirty jokes, from Truth or Consequences, New Mexico; Andy Moulton, the squad's Staff Sergeant, from Faraday, Louisiana; Jimmy Oliphant from Beson, Delaware; and Asley St Thomas from Anderson, Indiana. This simple roll call reflects the true horror of the Vietnam War, a group of young men from throughout the United States, dying in a foreign land, quickly forgotten by all but their loved ones and close friends.

The men who died on the bridge in Vietnam and Bortman were not the only victims of the tragedy. The story is from the viewpoint of Billy Clewson's father, Dale. He was one of those who called Josh Bortman's father, after noticing a tenth soldier appear in his photograph. At first, Dale thought he had simply mistaken the number of soldiers originally in the photograph but then began to question his own sanity. He was already under enough pressure following the death of both Billy and his wife.

Billy's mother, Andrea became a heavy drinker after her son's death and two years later died of the liver dysfunction and renal failure caused by her drinking. Quoting from the story: 'The Viet Cong had killed their son in a place called Ky Doc, and Billy's death had killed his mother.'

Considering Bortman's letter, the condolence letter from the Squad's lieutenant and the photo itself, Clewson found himself looking at the list of names on the rear of the photo, where all the dead boys were listed, along with the name Josh Bortman, Castle Rock, Me. and an asterisk next to his name: 'The asterisk means "still alive". The asterisk means "don't hate me."' Now pondering the unthinkable, Clewson was tempted to call the Bortmans. 'I never hated you, son, he thought. Nor did Andrea, for all her grief. Maybe I should have picked up a pen and dropped you a note saying so, but honest to Christ, the thought never crossed my mind.'

Clewson could stand no more and called the Bortman home (there was only one Bortman family in Castle Rock) only to get a busy line. When Mr. Bortman did answer later he immediately demanded, to Clewson's surprise, ' "Which one are you?" "My name is Dale Clewson, Mr Bortman. My son …" "Clewson, Billy Clewson's father … And has your picture of Squad D changed, too?"' Unfortunately, Bortman senior had assumed the concerned calls from other relatives were some sort of sick joke. Clewson quickly brought him to his senses, whispering: "You know this isn't a joke." Bortman told Clewson Josh had died the night before, hanging himself in the garage. Mr Bortman also revealed Josh had been concerned that people might discover the reason he was not with the Squad on the fateful day, but of course the story got out.

Now positions are reversed and Bortman is comforting Clewson. ' "Joshua didn't have many friends when he was growing up, Mr Clewson. I don't think he had any real friends until he got to Nam. He loved your son, and the others."'

' "Is he smiling, Mr Clewson. The others … they said he was smiling." Dale looked toward the picture beside the ticking clock. "He's smiling." "Of course he is. Josh finally caught up with them."'

Squad D is a very powerful and compelling story, one of those the reader's mind drifts back to and it deserves to be published. The opening sentences are a case in point: 'Billy Clewson died all at once, with nine of the ten other members of D Squad on April 8, 1974. It took his mother two years, but she got started right away on the afternoon the telegram came announcing her son's death, in fact.'

We can only hope that this story might somehow be recovered from the no-man's land in which it is currently trapped.

The Stand Screenplays (Undated, 1992)

> 'Be strong in the strength of the Lord ... and *stand.* Stand like the men you are.'
>
> *Abagail Freemantle to Stu Redman, Ralph Brentner and Larry Underwood as she sent them West to confront Randall Flagg.* From the unproduced screenplay of *The Stand.*

King has effectively created five versions of his seminal work, *The Stand*. This will surprise most readers, who would immediately identify two or three versions but would struggle to identify the remainder.

Regarded by many as King's masterpiece, *The Stand* was first published in 1978. Subsequent paperback editions used the original hardcover text for a period. The timeline of the events in this first version is 1980.

US paperback editions moved to a new timeline of 1985. The Signet edition of January 1980 was the first of these editions. King's *Author's Note* concludes 'minor revisions have been made for the Signet edition of this novel'. Books carrying this timeline form the second version. Most, if not all, overseas paperback editions stayed with the 1980 timeline.

In 1990 King famously republished the book as he had originally intended, in a *Complete and Uncut* edition. In the second part of the preface to that third version of this tale King stated, '... I am republishing 'The Stand' as it was originally written...', although he also comments that certain parts originally cut stayed on the cutting room floor. That first version, as noted, was published in 1978. However, Freddy Krueger is referred to at the end of the 'Uncut' Chapter 11. The first *Nightmare on the Elm Street* movie was produced in 1984. There is also a reference (without naming her) to Bobbi Anderson, a character who appeared first in *The Tommyknockers* in 1987. In both those cases we can see that more was added to the manuscript, rather than a simple restoration. There are dozens of examples of this 'updating'. In fact, indications are that some 150,000 words were added, whereas it appears 100,000 had originally been removed. King clarified this matter in his *Foreword* to the Revised and Expanded Edition of *The Gunslinger*: 'What I reinstated in the late eighties were revised sections of the pre-existing manuscript. I also revised the work as a whole, mostly to acknowledge the AIDS epidemic ...'. Therefore, the true Uncut version (or Original Uncut, if you will) has never been published.

King also wrote a movie script of *The Stand*, set in 1985, which has never been produced and is discussed in this Chapter. This forms the fourth version. Finally, in 1992, King wrote the screenplay for the ABC mini-series and that forms the fifth and, to date, final version! All versions, of course, are part of The Stand reality.

As readers and viewers we are fortunate that *The Stand* ever saw the light of day. In section 10 of the 'On Writing' section of *On Writing* King tells us that he suffered writer's block on the direction of the story after five hundred or so pages and was nearly incapable of completing it. In fact, it was the only book length work from that time until *On Writing* itself to suffer being laid away in a drawer, perhaps never to be completed. King's explosive solution to the problem is detailed in section 10. He also declares, of the fan base's high opinion of *The Stand*, that '... there's something a little depressing about such a united opinion that you did your best work twenty years ago, but we won't go into that just now, thanks.'

Unproduced Movie Screenplay

King wrote this screenplay for a movie length production. It has never been published. A copy is held in Box 2318A at the Special Collections Unit of the Raymond H Fogler Library at the University of Maine, Orono and readers can access it there. This summary is compiled from the 4th Draft.

Considering the varying timelines for the different versions of *The Stand* it is interesting that King chose to set this particular script in 1985 (the superflu outbreak begins in Arnette on 16 June 1985 and the nuclear explosion in Las Vegas occurs on 5 November 1985). This may indicate that the version of the script held at UMO was written about 1984, considering King's penchant for setting storylines one or two years in the future. Various sources note that King began writing scripts for a movie version of *The Stand* as early as 1979.

King was very true to the storyline in 1978 book version in this screenplay and readers will recognize this from the summary. However, there are a number of changes from the book, which are reviewed later.

In this script a superflu virus is released from a government facility and devastates the world, leading to an apocalyptic confrontation between good and evil. The virus escaped into the general populace when Campion and his family ran from the Project Blue Base in California shortly after an accident infected everyone there. A few days later Campion crashed into a gas station in Arnette, Texas where Stu Redman and his cronies were drinking and shooting the breeze.

The flu, quickly dubbed Captain Trips, had 99.4% communicability and 99.4% excess mortality and quickly engulfed the world. Within two weeks America lay devastated, with the few survivors in shock. As they slowly began to regroup most suffered vivid dreams of an old black woman or of a Dark Man.

Soon, almost everyone chose to take one side or the other in what appeared to be an upcoming clash between good and evil. A small group, led by deaf-mute Nick Andros, including Ralph Brentner and the intellectually handicapped Tom Cullen made it to the old woman's homestead in the cornfields of Hemingford Home, Nebraska. Abagail Freemantle, who quickly became known as Mother Abagail, made it clear that God had set her to the hard task of facing the enemy. She and her followers then moved to Boulder, Colorado and the apparent task of rebuilding civilized society.

They were joined in the Boulder Free Zone, as it had been dubbed, by Redman, who had narrowly escaped execution by the authorities after failing to contract the disease; and his new lover, Fran Goldsmith. Travelling with them was Harold Lauder, who had turned vengeful after his romantic designs toward Fran had gone unrequited. Also joining the Zone were Larry Underwood, a singer who was just enjoying the success of his first hit record when the superflu hit and Nadine Cross, a woman who was more attracted to the dark forces than she was willing to admit.

Meanwhile, the Dark Man, Randall Flagg, had discovered he could do magic and began forming an empire based in Las Vegas. He recruited a petty criminal, Lloyd Henreid as his right-hand man and began gathering the military might to smash his opponents. They were joined by a demented pyromaniac with a gift for weaponry, who was known only as the Trashcan Man.

The Zone sent spies west, one of them a hypnotized Cullen. Another, Judge Farris, was intercepted and killed but Flagg was unable to locate Cullen, even after he arrived in Las Vegas.

Lauder and Cross, now determined to cross over to Flagg, bombed the Free Zone Committee, killing Andros and a number of others. The killers escaped and headed toward Flagg but he arranged for Lauder to crash his motorcycle, breaking his leg. Cross went on and met Flagg in the desert, having sex with him and falling both pregnant and catatonic. Realizing his situation could not be redeemed Lauder committed suicide.

Freemantle ordered Underwood, Brentner and Redman to leave and walk to Las Vegas. Then, she died. Despite their misgivings and those of Goldsmith, the three men set off that afternoon with a dog, Kojak. As they walked the highway Redman fell and broke his leg at a washout and the others reluctantly left him to his fate. Kojak chose to stay with Redman and brought him small animals to cook and eat.

In Las Vegas there were signs that Flagg's iron-rule was cracking, including Cross killing herself. Cullen headed back east as instructed by his hypnotic suggestion.

Underwood and Brentner were captured as they approached Las Vegas and jailed. The next morning Flagg called all his supporters into the city to witness the proposed execution of the prisoners. As the execution proceeded toward its climax the Trashcan Man arrived with a nuclear weapon as homage to Flagg; and one of Flagg's supporters called for the crowd to stand up against him. Flagg attacked this last man with a blue ball of fire but it rapidly grew and formed into the shape of a hand before setting off the nuclear weapon, destroying his empire and dreams. Just before the explosion Flagg disappeared.

Back at the washout Cullen found Redman and took him to a nearby town to recuperate. Along with Kojak they made their way back to Boulder, arriving just after Goldsmith gave birth to her son, Peter Goldsmith-Redman. By 1989 Redman, Goldsmith and the boy were living in Maine.

King made a number of changes from the first book version in this script. In this version Kojak is Judge Glen Farris' dog. In the books, the Judge's name is Richard Farris. The reason for this first name change is King's elimination of the delightful character, Glen Bateman from this version. It is perhaps lucky it was not produced, as this character deletion would have been very unpopular with fans of *The Stand*!

In another interesting change from the books King does not give 'The Trashcan Man' a name. Of course, in the books his real name is Donald Merwin Elbert. Joe-Bob, the Texas Highway Patrolman who died of the superflu early in the piece, does not have a surname in this version. In the book his surname is Brentwood. In another change, Peter Goldsmith-Redman's natural father was an instructor at his mother's graduate school, while in the books the father was a fellow student, Jess Rider. The character known only as 'Poke' in this version is Andrew 'Poke' Freeman, Henreid's erstwhile partner in crime in the books.

The facility in which Redman was held by the authorities examining him changes from being the Stovington Plague Control Center in the books to the Stovington Experimental Center in this script.

All versions of *The Stand* link to other King fiction (*see the feature panel*).

Mini-Series Screenplay

This section was compiled from the Second Draft Screenplay, dated 16 October 1992. That screenplay has not been published and there would appear to be little point considering not only the two book versions of this classic tale but also the fact that readers/viewers may watch the mini-series produced from the script on TV or on DVD. Readers should note that copies of this screenplay do circulate within the King community but are very difficult to secure.

The screenplay was produced and shown as an ABC-TV mini-series in the United States as *Stephen King's The Stand*.

There was at least one questionable casting decision, with most fans of *The Stand* decrying the atrocious choice of Molly Ringwald as Fran Goldsmith. Indeed, her portrayal was as far from the strong young woman described in King's books as seems possible. The mini-series debuted on ABC-TV on the nights of 8, 9, 11 and 12 May 1994. The four parts were sub-titled *The Plague*, *The Dreams*, *The Betrayal* and *The Stand*. IMDB members give the production a very solid 7.2 rating out of a possible 10. The director was Mick Garris, who also helmed *Sleepwalkers*, the mini-series of *The Shining*, *Quicksilver Highway*, *Riding the Bullet* and *Desperation*. King was credited as co-Executive Producer. The production won an Emmy, for Best Achievement in Make-Up.

The actors included Gary Sinise as Stu Redman; Molly Ringwald as Fran Goldsmith; Jamey Sheridan as Randall Flagg; Laura San Giacomo as Nadine Cross; Ruby Dee as Abagail Freemantle; Miguel Ferrer as Lloyd Henreid; Ray Walston as Glen Bateman; Rob Lowe as Nick Andros; Kathy Bates as Rae Flowers; Ed Harris as Starkey; and Cynthia Garris (the wife of the director) as Susan Stern.

Stephen King played the role of Teddy Weizak. It is interesting to note that this character lived the whole way through this version, whereas he died as a result of the Lauder/Cross bombing of the Free Zone Committee in both the books and the unproduced screenplay. It seems the power of the author to give life or death can come into stark focus when that same author is given the role of acting out the character's existence!

Bates, Harris and King appeared in cameo roles. In his *Creepshows* Stephen Jones says director Garris has a 'predilection for guest appearances'. Others to appear were King's favorite drive-in movie critic, Joe Bob Briggs; basketballer Kareem Adbul-Jabbar as the Monster Shouter; and directors Tom Holland (Carl Hough), John Landis (Russ Dorr) and Sam Raimi (Bob Terry), as well as Garris himself. The Russ Dorr character played by Landis appears to be King's nod to Russell Dorr (P.A.) of the Bridgton Family Medical Center, one of two clinicians King credits in the *Author's Note* to *The Stand* with answering his questions about the flu and '…its peculiar way of mutating every two years or so.' King also credits Dorr in *Pet Sematary* and *Misery*.

Readers will have noted that this cast has an outstanding resume in other film and television work and it is therefore no surprise that the overall acting in this mini-series is some of the best seen in a television adaptation of a King work. With a cast this fine and a screenplay by King of one of his most outstanding tales it is no surprise the resulting production is so highly regarded.

Gary Sinise was Oscar nominated for *Forrest Gump* and won an Emmy for *George Wallace*, a Golden Globe for *Truman* and a Screen Actors Guild Award for *Apollo 13*. Laura San Giacomo appeared in the long-running *Just Shoot Me* as well as in the ground-breaking *Sex, Lies and Videotape*; Ruby Dee is an Emmy Award winning actress; Miguel Ferrer also appeared in *Night Flier* and the cult series *Twin Peaks*; Ray Walston was loved by the audiences of *My Favorite Martian* and *Picket Fences*, for which he won two Emmys; the controversial Rob Lowe has also won two Emmys, for *The West Wing*; Kathy Bates won both the Golden Globe and the Academy Award for her portrayal of Annie Wilkes in *Misery* and took the title role in *Dolores Claiborne*; and Golden Globe winner Ed Harris won the Best Actor Award from the Screen Actors Guild for *Apollo 13* and has already garnered four Academy Award nominations.

The mini-series was issued on DVD in 1999, with audio commentary by King and selected actors; and includes a 'making of' featurette. It was also boxed with other titles as the *Stephen King Horror DVD Collection* that same year.

We are not given a year in which the mini-series is set but it must be no earlier than 1990 as the schematic used by Harold Lauder to create his bomb won 3rd prize in the 1990 National Science Fair. In this version the superflu outbreak begins in Arnette on 17 June and the nuclear explosion in Las Vegas occurs at the relatively early date of 21 September 1985.

King was also very true in this screenplay to the storyline in the book versions. As the story is substantially the same as the unproduced screenplay, so there is no need to summarize it again. However, there are a number of changes from the books.

In one interesting change King again does not give 'The Trashcan Man' a real name. He also changes the sex of Fran Goldsmith's baby from a boy, Peter, in each of the earlier versions, to the very sentimental choice of a girl named Abagail in this offering. In the books the child's father is Jess Rider but in this version we do not learn Jess' surname. There is no mention of Goldsmith and Redman returning to Maine with their child.

The character known only as 'Poke' in this version is Andrew 'Poke' Freeman. The man who took the superflu to the world, Charles Campion, is an Army officer in this script but was only a 'government employee' in the books.

To allow for Kathy Bates' appearance as the DJ murdered by the Army at KLFT during the epidemic, the final screenplay included a sex change for the character and a change of the name from Ray Flowers to Rae Flowers.

The facility in which Redman was held for examination and from which he escaped execution changes from being the Stovington Plague Control Center in the books to the Vermont Disease Centre in this script.

In addition to the standard links from *The Stand* to other King fiction (*see the feature panel*) King took the opportunity in this script to make a few other subtle references. In the screenplay Tom Cullen was sent west from the Stanley Hotel in Estes Park, Colorado. This is, of course, the hotel at which King conceived *The Shining* and at which the mini-series of *The Shining* was filmed.

While in Mother Abagail Freemantle's cornfield, Randall Flagg is described as being 'dim'. This is a skill Raymond Fiegler (most serious King students believe this is but a pseudonym for Randall Flagg) taught Carol Gerber in the *Hearts in Atlantis* version of *Blind Willie*.

Serious King students and fans will find great interest in the minor changes King made to his own mythology in these scripts. But their greatest value lies in King's determination to see the story produced under his own terms. He initially wrote at least four drafts of the movie screenplay and followed it up with the mini-series screenplay for ABC-TV. By writing his own screenplay he avoided the pitfalls of allowing another writer to be introduced. It is amazing how often these writers are tempted to 'improve' on King's already superb tales.

The mini-series of *The Stand* ranks as one of the best TV and one of the superior visual adaptations of a King work and this should be credited directly to King's teleplay.

LINKS FROM *THE STAND* TO OTHER KING FICTION

As one of King's major works, in which the history of our world takes a rather radical turn, an entire 'Reality' is allocated to *The Stand*'s varying storylines. Many of the characters and places link to other King works of fiction, and the Dark Tower, Maine Street Horror, New Worlds and America Under Siege 'Realities'. The links are summarized here.

Randall Flagg	*Eyes of the Dragon, The Dark Tower* Cycle, *The Dark Man*
Abagail Freemantle	*The Dark Tower IV, The Dark Tower VI*
The Trashcan Man	*The Dark Tower III*
Bobbi Anderson[143]	*The Tommyknockers*
Arnette, Texas	*Desperation, The Monkey*
Castle Rock, Maine[144]	*Bag of Bones, The Body, Creepshow, Cujo, The Dark Half, The Dead Zone, Dreamcatcher, Gerald's Game, The Girl Who Loved Tom Gordon, Gramma, It Grows on You* (*Nightmares and Dreamscapes* version only), *The Lonesome Death of Jordy Verrill, The Man in the Black Suit, Mrs. Todd's Shortcut, Needful Things, Nona* (*Skeleton Crew* version only), *Premium Harmony, Riding the Bullet, Rita Hayworth and Shawshank Redemption, Squad D, The Sun Dog, Uncle Otto's Truck, Under the Dome* and *Untitled (The Huffman Story)*

Hemingford Home, Nebraska	*Children of the Corn* (Screenplay only), *It, The Last Rung on the Ladder*
Stovington, Vermont	*The Shining, Everything's Eventual*
Captain Trips	*Night Surf, The Dark Tower IV, Golden Years, The Dark Tower VI*[145]
The Shine[146]	*The Shining*
Overlooked[147]	*The Shining*
Legion[148]	*Black House, The Dark Tower: The Gunslinger* (Revised), *It Storm of the Century*
Ka[149]	*The Dark Tower* Cycle
The Shop[96]	*Firestarter, Golden Years, The Langoliers, The Tommyknockers*

The Star Invaders (1964)

King expert Tyson Blue kindly provided a copy of this story to the author, allowing the following detailed description and analysis. King apparently owns the only printed copy of this 17 page, slightly less than 3000 word chapbook. Two of the other very few King outsiders to have read it since King reached the best-seller lists are Blue and Dr. Michael R Collings.

The front cover reads, 'AA GAS-LIGHT BOOK 20¢ / The STAR INVADERS / By Steve King'. A handwritten 'Triad' with the 'T' appearing as a triangle and capital T superimposed appears in the bottom right corner of the cover. 'STAR INVADERS' appears as in a cross-word puzzle, with the word 'STAR' running down the page to meet the 'R' of 'INVADERS' running across the page. A stylized and hand-drawn star appears to the left of the word 'Star'. The inside front cover reads, 'The Star Invaders, Copyright 1964 by Triad, Inc., and Gaslight Books / FIRST PRINTING / June, 1964 / To Johnny, Who wanted one like this / All characters herein are fictitious'. The chapbook which measures 8 ½ inches by 5 ½ inches was self-published by King.

The tale is clearly under the heavy, and heady, influence of King's beloved 1950s science-fiction films and television episodes, radio drama and graphic comic books, most particularly the classic 1956 movie *Earth vs. the Flying Saucers* (as he confirmed in a 2011 Turner Classic Movies documentary).

In 2011 King confirmed, in personal correspondence with Rocky Wood, that *The Star Invaders* is the story he sometimes refers to *The Invasion of the Star-Creatures* (in section 18 of the *C.V.* part of *On Writing*); and as *The Invasion of the Star Monsters* (in the documentary, *A Night at the Movies: The Horrors of Stephen King*, first shown on the Turner Classic Movies channel in late 2011.)

The first two King experts to reveal parts of this story were Blue and Collings. Blue presents a detailed survey of this New Worlds story in his *The Unseen King*[150]. There he revealed that the aliens, who have clawed hands, dressed in 'iridescent uniforms that made them look like robots.' Collings revealed[151] that each alien's hand comprises 'three curved claws'.

Collings, writing in *Castle Rock* for August 1989[152], says *The Star Invaders* '…is an account of human encounters with hostile aliens intent on taking over the Earth, a dastardly plan foiled only by the strength of character and purpose of the hero, Jed Pierce.' He delivers two quotes from the story in his article. In the first Hiken is 'subjected to the ultimate torture, to that which he fears more than anything else … 'Lord they had locked him in a small room! It seemed even smaller than before. Jerry felt a cold sweat break out on his brow. He remembered back thirty years. He had been a kid then, a really small kid. His father had been a bear on discipline, and every time he'd done something wrong, he was locked in a closet to meditate … He had gotten to hate that closet. It was small and stuffed with clothes. The acrid smell of moth-balls made him cough, and to his terrified four-year-old mind, it always seemed that a tiger crouched in the corner.' Now, the room grows smaller and smaller, until the walls touch Hiken and he promises to tell the aliens all. After the walls are withdrawn Hiken again refuses to speak.

Quoting Collings, 'In the face of this new evidence of human defiance, the alien says ("implacably," as King specifies in the text): (*the next quote is from the story*) 'We can lock you in again … Only this time the walls will squeeze until the blood runs from your ears and your nose and even from the little black holes in the center of your eyes. It can squeeze you into just a blob of shrieking protoplasm, if we so desire.' After revealing the location of Jed Pierce to avoid his ultimate torture Hiken killed himself by beating 'his head in on the bulkhead of the floor'.

Blue tells us more of this incident, revealing this quote from an alien as Hiken is locked in the small room, ' "You see, earth creature, each being has his own devils … things that have horrified him always. We shall find yours, never fear … And then Jed Pierce will be ours!' Apart from the clunky and contradictory dialogue (we'll find your innermost fears, never fear?) this one line reveals much about King and his entire body of work. In the forty odd years since a teenage boy typed that line Stephen King has dedicated an entire career to finding our innermost fears and feeding them relentlessly into the myth pool.

Collings' assessment in *Castle Rock* is that the story itself is not particularly noteworthy. 'The characterization is flat, the aliens stereotypic, the story itself derivative – nothing unexpected in the writings of a 16-year-old storyteller. But, if one looks closely at the episode, especially in the light of King's subsequent productions, something more than a story-as-story unfolds. Through the clarity of hindsight, the torture-room becomes recognizable as a prototype of

Margaret White's punishment closet in *Carrie* ...' Of course, another terrifying closet, albeit from the view of a little boy *outside* it, appears in *The Monster in the Closet* section of *Cujo*, and a similar concept is the basis for *The Boogeyman*; and, in our assessment, is a closer match to those closets (reflecting as they do Jerry Hiken's childhood fears – and, perhaps, King's).

In *The Shorter Works of Stephen King* Collings stated, 'The story is not a culmination, but a beginning, showing King struggling with the form and structure of the short story. He succeeds in places but fails elsewhere, as when he devotes half the story to Hiken's treachery, then barely refers to the episode in the second part. The writing is serviceable, his style based on hackneyed expressions and trite phrasing ... The errors one might expect in a neophyte work appear: misspellings, faulty modification, subject-verb agreement problems, word choice. In 'The Star Invaders' he attempts to write science fiction. What he produces – what rises above the stereotypic and the conventional – is horror.'

Spignesi states[153] the story 'is rough and ends abruptly, but it clearly manifests the storytelling abilities King would soon perfect.' Collings wrote in Spignesi's masterwork[154], ' "The Star Invaders" is highly abstracted; there are few specific references to people, places or things – certainly nothing to suggest King's later "brand name" approach to creating verisimilitude. References to the nuclear reactor are equally vague, and the resolution to the story ... is abrupt and unconvincing. The great strength of this story is its nascent characterization, coupled with an occasional image that would resonate through much of King's fiction.'

Tyson Blue, in a kinder review, says the story, '...although overwritten and derivative, nevertheless makes interesting and entertaining reading, and offers a few clues to the developing talent of King ... a tale with lots of fast-paced action, thrills, dangers and the blood-and-thunder that so appeals to young adolescent boys ... King was giving his young audience what it wanted – lots of action and a fast-paced yarn bursting with excitement, and this was enough to overcome any shortcomings in style, plot, grammar or originality.'

King has guarded the story from release for so long that there can be no other belief than that it will *never* be published or released in any form. Even though it is extremely unlikely readers will ever be able to examine this tale, Blue points out '...it remains a fascinating study for those who are interested in tracing the evolution of his writing and the themes with which he has worked throughout his career.' This is certainly the case – an early attempt by a young man, who in only a decade would strike out on a highly successful career, to do what he would prove to do best – tell a story.

Stories from Journals (c.1989-1991)

In November 2002 your current author travelled to Maine and spent seventeen days working through King's papers at the Special Collections Unit of the Raymond H Fogler Library of the University of Maine at Orono. I'd taken the decision to check *every* page in each folder in every Box of King's papers, on the chance that interesting materials might be found. There was also a (slim) hope of finding one original item.

In fact I discovered, or perhaps rediscovered is the better term, ten stories that were previously unknown to the King community. The most interesting aspect of these discoveries was that the manuscripts had been lurking in dark boxes at the Fogler for years (like a certain creature in a 'Crate') waiting for daylight to expose them to the world. While a few were in the 'Restricted' boxes that cannot be accessed without King's written permission, others were in public access boxes.

It is well known that King keeps individual Journals in which he writes thoughts and stories, some containing up to ten different pieces to a book. Four incomplete stories were found in King's handwriting in just such a Journal. By strange coincidence it was in the very last Box I checked, and on my last possible research day. This public access box was number 2702 but, for security reasons, the Journal has since moved to a Restricted Box, 1010.

After reconfirming the authenticity of the Journal with King's office I was able to announce the existence of the stories to the world early in 2003. Using King's titles in the Journal they have been dubbed *Muffe*, *The Evaluation*, *Movie Show* and *Chip Coombs*.

One of the more interesting aspects of this Journal is how clean and clear King's writing is in his first handwritten draft. Not only is the handwriting neat and legible but the story seems to flow off King's pen and on to the page. There are virtually no corrections or scratching outs and yet it would be easy to see these first drafts published as they stand. Obviously King goes through various drafts, rewrites and editing before publishing short stories or novels but one wonders how many other modern authors could deliver such quality work in a first, handwritten draft?

Other story snippets in the Journal include *Library Policeman*, *Langoliers*, *Head Down*, *Sleepwalkers*, *The Waste Lands* (and its *Introduction*), *Needful Things* (and notes for it), *Chattery Teeth* and *Insomnia*. This dates the writing to the years 1989, 1990 and 1991 at the latest.

In 2009 King allowed the publication of a different two page snippet of *Muffe*, in Bev Vincent's book *The Stephen King Illustrated Companion*. The snippet comes from a different journal, although that journal also includes snippets from *Needful Things* and *Insomnia*, so is likely to have been written during the same 1989-1991 time period.

Muffe

This is a part manuscript only. There is one section of nine single pages which remains unpublished, the notation in King's handwriting reads 'More Muffe', as this was apparently a continuation of the story. A second section, published in *The Stephen King Illustrated Companion*, covers a slightly later period in the same tale.

In the first fragment a man is trapped in a cage. Children were pelting Muffe of the Finger Kingdoms with clods of earth and rocks. His crime had apparently been one of laughing at the Palace of the Great One, Lord Vaggar. Vaggar's right hand man approached and stopped the children from pelting the prisoner and at that point the fragment ends.

In the second section Muffe is no longer caged and is talking to Vaggar's right-hand man, now named as Mustus, initially about Clarissa. Muffe and the 'barbarian' begin to feel each other out in conversation. Mustus tells him that very evening Vaggar would visit with him to learn more about his lands but if he wanted to stay alive he should give Vaggar what he wants.

It seems these fragment were to be part of a fantasy. The town in which Muffe was trapped is called T'Kett and was apparently the capital of the Northern World, as it contained the Palace of the Great One, which is described as 'crude and multi-colored'. We discover that the 'Great One' is Lord Vaggar, who is also known as the 'Ruler of the Northern World and Absolute Emperor of the Far Places' and 'Master Vaggar'.

We are told little else about T'Kett, other than that Muffe's cage was in the Central Square and that the Marketplace was closed, as 'this was the day the barbarians worshipped their pagan gods'.

We are led to presume that Muffe is from another 'country' in that he is also known as 'Muffe of the Finger Kingdoms' and was a member of the Northern Expeditionary Force. Young, he had apparently been imprisoned for laughing at the imperiously named Palace of the Great One after being accused of doing so by Lord Vaggar's daughter. While imprisoned he was nicknamed 'The Laughing Man'.

Lord Vaggar's daughter Clarissa was fourteen, tall and ugly. She and her friends pelted Muffe. Vaggar's right-hand man, who stopped the pelting and appears fond of Clarissa, was also his heir apparent. He was very tall, clean-shaven, had long hair, a battle-scarred face and ice-blue eyes.

There are no indications of a timeline to this story or a location but the reader gets the immediate impression of lonely wind-blown steppes and the sort of fairly temporary towns occupied by the Mongol hordes during their long Westward expansion from Asia into Europe. Equally, certain scenes from the epic movie trilogy *Lord of the Rings* would not be out of place in the reader's mind. In Vincent's book it is claimed the story has 'the feel of the *Dark Tower*', although that was not my impression when reading either of the pieces.

This partial story is a New Worlds tale and it is not linked to any other King fiction. Other than the Dark Tower Cycle and *Eyes of the Dragon* King has published relatively little in the 'Fantasy' genre. There is too little of the storyline to make much of an assessment. Is Muffe the agent of Vaggar's enemy? What information does Vaggar seek that might threaten Muffe's life if he does not reveal it? We will probably never know!

The Evaluation

This is a part manuscript only. There are twelve single pages. The notation heading it in King's handwriting reads 'The Evaluation'.

In this America Under Siege tale a psychologist, Dr. Peter Judkins, prepared to evaluate Edgar Roos at the Crown County Mental Hospital in New York. Roos had been arrested after killing nine people that day, two with a butcher's knife and seven with a shotgun. The murderer had left his will in a locker.

Initially uncommunicative and sitting strait-jacketed and chained to an oak chair that was bolted to the floor, Roos told Judkins he might talk if Judkins took off a band-aid covering a shaving cut! The fragment ends at this point.

Edgar Roos was a slender young man, weighing about 150 pounds. He had a narrow face, glossy black hair and wore glasses. The killings had earned him the nickname 'The Commuter Killer'. All we really know of Dr. Judkins was that he had been married for eleven years. There is only one other character of note, a technician wearing an orderly's uniform, Hector Alonzo. He was to video and audiotape the interview and had also provided Dr. Judkins with the key to the locker in which Roos had left his will.

Judkins was assigned to evaluate Roos because the psychologist on call that week, Livermore, had just had his gall bladder removed (we are left with the uneasy impression that this might turn out to be bad luck for Judkins, and good luck for Livermore). Seven other psychologists were affiliated with the Crown County Mental Hospital.

The Crown County Mental Hospital is in 'the smallest county in the State of New York'. There is also a Crown City in the County (confused yet?) and the Crown City High School and Crown City YMCA are mentioned.

The story is not linked to any other King fiction. However, King does appear to have a fascination for stories involving psychologists or psychiatrists. In *Chip Coombs*, another story fragment from this journal the title character visits a psychiatrist and tells her his life story; and, in *The Boogeyman*, Lester Billing's psychiatrist turned out to be the title character. *Comb Dump*, another unpublished partial story is set in a Maine psychiatric hospital; and, in yet another incomplete piece titled *Keyholes*, Michael Briggs visited a psychiatrist to discuss his son.

The fact that King attempted two such stories in this one Journal and at least another two that we know of without publishing the result of any may indicate his desire to find another viable storyline from this potentially deep well. Typical of King, the story is already fascinating by the time it stops abruptly after only a few pages. Any multiple killer in a King story is likely to be of interest and Roos' refusal to talk to Dr. Judkins unless he took off the band-aid covering a shaving cut has ominous undertones. It seems unlikely that King will again pick up this particular storyline, but it would seem certain that the reader would be in for not a few chills, spills and twists if he did!

Movie Show

This is a part manuscript only. There are 25 single pages. The notation in King's handwriting reads 'Movie Show more', as it this was apparently a continuation of the story. Despite its fragmentary nature it is a very important work, due to its autobiographical nature, explained in detail below.

In this Maine Street Horror piece a boy heads to the movies. Jacky had been prepared to go strawberry picking in Harlow, Maine one morning in June 1959 but the work was called off due to rain. The boys picked for H.A. 'Frosty' Snowman, who owned a strawberry farm on Larkspur Road, on which Jacky and his mother lived. 'Frosty' had very bad arthritis, resulting in swollen, misshapen hands and leaving him in constant pain. After the work was called off Jacky hitched a ride to Lewiston with a fairly old man driving an old farm truck. The man wore bib overalls, had bright eyes and chewed tobacco.

Arriving on Lisbon Street in Lewiston Jacky headed to a movie theatre, the Ritz, and purchased a ticket for the advertised double bill, *She Beast* (starring Barbara Steele) and *The Black Scorpion* (starring Mara Corday and Kenneth Tobey). The ticket-seller was the magnificently named Delphinia ('Lillin') Ouelette. Jacky observed the other patrons, of whom there were few, and at this point the story fragment ends.

Jacky wrote the story when he was 45 (it is unclear exactly how old he was at the time he lived in Harlow and hitchhiked to the movies in Lewiston). He says he was attending Gates Falls High five years later, in 1964, and that when he grew up he lived at 131 Elm Avenue, Utica (a town King mentions ironically from time to time) in a second floor apartment. He had also dropped acid and almost died of an amphetamine overdose there.

We are told Jacky's mother was employed in June of 1959, quite an unusual circumstance for a mother in rural America in those days. We are left with the distinct impression that she was a single mother (much as was King's mother, Ruth; and Liz Garfield, mother of Bobby in the semi-autobiographical *Low Men in Yellow Coats*).

Among the other boys who lived in Harlow were Arthur; Alvin Andrews;

Bill Brown; the twin brothers, Myron and Steve Doucette (the latter described as a stool-pigeon for Snowman); and Tom Haverford.

King's favorite baseball team, the Red Sox, was mentioned, they had lost a double-header in June 1959, presumably because Williams was sidelined with a strained ligament. A single business in Harlow is mentioned, Downy's Store.

We are given a quick tour of Lisbon Street, Lower Lisbon Street and Maple Street in Lewiston. The businesses mentioned are Ben Wisden's Men's Shop; Kowloon Express, a Chinese restaurant that would later appear on the site of the Ritz movie theatre; a restaurant, Manoir; a pawn shop, Penchan's House of Loans; and two movie theatres – the Ritz, which would close in 1968, and the Met. Double bill admission tickets to the Ritz cost eighty cents in 1959.

King lovingly describes the advertisements published in the Lewiston *Sun* for the two movies. The *She Beast* ad showed a picture of a woman dressed as an alien coming out of the surf. Another girl screamed while a lobster-like creature tried to kill her boyfriend. The promotion for *The Black Scorpion* showed a picture of a young woman in a black bathing suit screaming while a gigantic scorpion demolished the Colosseum.

She Beast is an actual B-movie classic and did, indeed, star Barbara Steele. It was released in 1966 and so could not have been showing in mid-1959. *The Black Scorpion*, starring Mara Corday (but not Kenneth Tobey), has a storyline of mutant Mexican scorpions on attack and was released in the US in October of 1957.

There are three clear links to King's other fictional works in this fragment. Larkspur Road in Harlow, on which Jacky and his mother lived, leads from Harlow to Pownal, which is a real town. Johnny Smith's father lived in Pownal in *The Dead Zone* and Johnny was residing in that home when he and Sarah Hazlett (nee Bracknell) made love for the first, and only, time.

Harlow, Maine is the town in which Jacky and his mother, Arthur, Snowman, the Doucettes and the other boys lived. Between Lewiston and Augusta, the town '…sprawled in a tract of woods and seemed to have more graveyards than people'. When I visited Durham, Maine – the town in which King spent much of his latter childhood and his teenage years – this would have been a perfect description, even at the late point of 2002, more than forty years after *Movie Show* is set. Additionally this version of Harlow has a Shiloh Hill and to this day the spectacular Shiloh Church is set on a Durham hill. This Harlow is eighteen miles from Lewiston.

Harlow is also a key location in two of the three versions of *It Grows On You* (*Marshroots* / *Weird Tales* and *Whispers*) as well as *Riding the Bullet*. It receives considerable mention in both *Blaze* and *The Body* and is also mentioned in each of *Bag of Bones*, *The Dark Half*, *Gerald's Game*, *The Hardcase Speaks*, *Rage* and in the *Skeleton Crew* versions of *Nona*, *Under the Dome* and *Uncle Otto's Truck*.

King relates something of Larkspur Road, Harlow in this story (it is not mentioned in any other King tale). Arthur and Jacky lived at the west end of it in 1959. It was not paved in those days, but was later. Snowman's property was on the east end, as was the Doucette home. Later, a housing development was built on Snowman's farmland. The road makes it way to Pownal and New Gloucester and intersects with Route 9.

Jacky's mother had gone to Gates Falls to get her hair done the morning the strawberry picking was cancelled. Gates Falls, Maine is one of King's oldest fictional towns (it is almost certainly inspired by Lisbon Falls, Maine) and is a key location in *Graveyard Shift*, *It Grows on You*, *The Revenge of Lard Ass Hogan*, *Riding the Bullet* and *Sword in the Darkness*. It is also mentioned in *Blaze*, *The Body* (as the location for Gordie LaChance's Lard Ass Hogan tale), *The Dark Half*, *The Dead Zone*, *Gramma*, *Hearts in Atlantis*, *Mrs. Todd's Shortcut*, *Needful Things*, *The Plant* (but only the electronic version), *Rage* and *'Salem's Lot*.

Both these towns are clearly dear to King's heart, having been created early in his career and receiving constant encores, including replacing other town names in the revision of certain works. Their introduction in this aborted story must be regarded as noteworthy.

There are clear autobiographical overtones in this piece. King provided the following insights in part 18 of the 'C.V.' section of *On Writing* and it is clear from them that *Movie Show* derives directly from King's early teenage years in Durham.

'What I cared about most between 1958 and 1966 was movies.

As the fifties gave way to the sixties, there were only two movie theaters in the area, both in Lewiston. The Empire was the first-run house ... (but) when I lay in bed at night under my eave, listening to the wind in the trees or the rats in the attic, it was not Debbie Reynolds as Tammy or Sandra Dee as Gidget that I dreamed of, but Yvette Vickers from *Attack of the Giant Leeches* or Luana Anders from *Dementia 13*. Never mind sweet; never mind uplifting; never mind Snow White and the Seven Goddam Dwarfs. At thirteen I wanted monsters that ate whole cities, radioactive corpses that came out of the ocean and ate surfers, and girls in black bras who looked like trailer trash.

Horror movies, science fiction movies, movies about teenage gangs on the prowl, movies about losers on motor-cycles — this was the stuff that turned my dials up to ten. The place to get all of this was not at the Empire, on the upper end of Lisbon Street, but at the Ritz, down at the lower end, amid the pawnshops and not far from Louie's Clothing, where in 1964 I bought my first pair of Beatle boots. The distance from my house to the Ritz was fourteen miles, and I hitchhiked there almost every weekend during the eight years between 1958 and 1966, when I finally got my driver's license. Sometimes I went with my friend Chris Chesley, sometimes I went alone, but unless I was sick or something, I always went. It was at the Ritz that I saw *I Married a Monster from Outer Space,* with Tom Tryon; *The Haunting,* with Claire Bloom and Julie Harris; *The Wild Angels,* with Peter Fonda and Nancy Sinatra. I saw Olivia de Havilland put out James Caan's eyes with makeshift knives in *Lady in a Cage,* saw Joseph Cotten come back from the dead in *Hush... Hush, Sweet Charlotte,* and watched with held breath (and not a little prurient interest) to see if Allison Hayes would grow all the way out of her clothes in *Attack of the 50 Ft. Woman.* At the Ritz, all the finer things in life were available ... or *might be* available, if you only sat in the third row, paid close attention, and did not blink at the wrong moment.

Chris and I liked just about any horror movie, but our faves were the string of American-International films, most directed by Roger Corman, with titles cribbed from Edgar Allan Poe. I wouldn't say *based upon* the works of Edgar Allan Poe, because there is little in any of them which has anything to do with Poe's actual stories and poems *(The Raven* was filmed as a comedy - no kidding). And yet the best of them - *The Haunted Palace, The Conqueror Worm, The Masque of the Red Death* - achieved a hallucinatory eeriness that made them special. Chris and I had our own name for these films, one that made them into a separate genre. There were westerns, there were love stories, there were war stories ... and there were Poepictures.

"Wanna hitch to the show Saturday afternoon?" Chris would ask. "Go to the Ritz?"

"What's on?" I'd ask.

"A motorcycle picture and a Poepicture," he'd say. I, of course, was on that combo like white on rice. Bruce Dern going batshit on a Harley and Vincent Price going batshit in a haunted castle overlooking a restless ocean: who could ask for more? You might even get Hazel Court wandering around in a lacy low-cut nightgown, if you were lucky.'

So, there you have it. The answer to the question of how autobiographical is *Movie Show?* Very! It is clear that this fragmentary story is King's love letter to that part of his youth.

Readers will also recall that in story Billy Harper was a fellow student of Jacky's at Gates Falls High and they got into a fight there in 1964 over Jacky's wearing of Beatle boots (sound familiar?).

As a final note we are reminded yet again in this tale of King's very strong record of creating twins as characters. Perhaps the Doucettes were based on real twin boys King knew in Durham when growing up, Dean and Doug Hall?

Chip Coombs

The last new piece in the Journal is untitled but I sub-titled it *Chip Coombs* in honor of its lead character. This is a part manuscript only and there are 36 single pages in King's handwriting, making it the longest piece in the Journal.

In this America Under Siege story Chip Coombs attends his first appointment with a psychiatrist, Dr. Monica Good at her office in downtown Cleveland. He had unspecified concerns and had requested more and more frequent electro-cardiograms from his family physician, Dr. Amos Light, who had finally referred him to Good. Coombs had also begun to lose weight.

Coombs told Dr. Good about his background. He claimed to have a 'dangerous friend' and said they would call him Red McFarland. He and Red had attended school in Paradise Falls, Ohio together, played basketball on a Championship team and then decided to learn barbering together in Zanesville, Ohio. During their six-months at the barbering school they shared an apartment and a car (by this stage the reader is already wondering if Chips and Red are in fact the same person).

McFarland was very successful with women but started drinking heavily and then hitting the girls he brought home to the apartment. On graduation Mc-Farland moved to the town of Blood, Ohio in the hills above Paradise Falls, and opened his own barber shop in the Paradise Mall. Coombs, on the other hand, headed for Boston, got a job in a barber shop there and stayed for seven years. Coombs had then returned to Paradise Falls, eleven years before his appointment with Dr. Good.

Doctor and patient scheduled a second appointment for the next day. Coombs now mentioned A Cut Above, a barber's shop in the Paradise Mall in Blood, which had been owned by Roger McFerry but had now gone out of business. McFerry had been running the business into the ground for four years but had suddenly 'returned' with a nest egg. Presumably, the reader is to suspect that Red McFarland had morphed into Roger McFerry. Unfortunately, the story fragment ends at this point.

The first appointment took place about 16 June 1989 and the second the next day (Dr. Good cancelled her attendance at a cocktail party for the Mayor of Cleveland to make that appointment).

Chip Coombs' actual first name was Chester. He was born in 1951 or 1952, and was raised in Paradise Falls, Ohio. He attended Paradise County Consolidated school and was part of the team that won the Ohio State High School basketball championship in 1969. He graduated in 1970. In September that year he enrolled at the barbering school in Zanesville, Ohio and graduated in February 1971. He was not drafted for Vietnam due to flat feet and a perforated eardrum, which resulted from a childhood infection. After graduation from the barbering school he moved to Boston and worked at The Boston Clipper barber's shop. He returned to Paradise Falls in 1978 and gave up drinking in 1983, sometimes attending AA meetings (Chips did not like attending because of the 'drunks' there). Still a barber, he owned and operated his own shop in Paradise Falls at that time.

What we know of Red McFarland is no more than the information Coombs imparted to Dr. Good. In summary this was that Coombs had a 'dangerous friend' who was often drunk and might harm him if he remembered a night they'd had together in March of 1989. Coombs told Good they would call him Red McFarland. Red was born in Blood, Ohio and attended Paradise County Consolidated school. He was part of the same team that won the Ohio State High School basketball championship in 1969 and graduated in 1970. In September 1970 he also enrolled at the barbering school in Zanesville, Ohio from which he graduated in February 1971. He opened a barber's shop at The Paradise Mall in Blood, Ohio shortly thereafter. He was not drafted. By 1971 he was already a drunk. Good looking, he was also a successful ladies' man but had descended to violence towards his girlfriends.

On the other hand Roger McFerry apparently owned A Cut Above, a barber shop in The Paradise Mall. It had closed by mid-June 1989.

During Chip's time in Boston he worked for Al Carlson. Carlson had served in the United States Navy, was short, broad-shouldered and had tattooed forearms. He retired from the Navy in 1968 after 30 years' service. He owned The Boston Clipper barber shop, was a smoker and employed Coombs for seven years from about March 1971 (but only after a two week unpaid trial). He preferred to call Coombs 'Chet'.

We are told little of Dr. Monica Good. A smoker, she gave up in 1984 and had been a psychiatrist since 1977. Stella, her secretary, had at least one son, Timmy, who had named the office pet rabbit 'Mortimer the Good' before *her* sex had been known.

The barbering college Coombs and McFarland attended in Zanesville, Ohio was formally known by the rather grand title of the Zanesville College of Barbering and Tonsorial Design. A 45 chair barber shop, most of Zanesville's working class had its hair done there. Interestingly, Zanesville is also mentioned in *Golden Years*. In that screenplay Harlan and Gina Williams and Terry Spann came across an accident on Route 17 West near Zanesville, Ohio.

There are no other links from this story to King's other fictional works. The piece has the standard King trademarks of interesting character back-story, an imminent sense of doom early in the tale, and the creation of empathy with lead character. It is therefore disappointing we do not have access to more of the work, let alone a completed story.

We are left with many questions. Is Coombs also McFarland *and* McFerry? If so, was Coombs' time in Boston the fantasy, or is it the McF's time in Blood that is imaginary? Does the 'nest egg' exist and if so what will be its significance? What happened on the night in March 1989 that Coombs was so worried McFarland would remember? While again it is most unlikely King would ever complete this story there seems little doubt it would be fascinating if he did.

Overall, this Journal provides wonderful insights into King's writing. His clear and loving use of his own past in *Movie Show*, the relatively unusual detour into fantasy in *Muffe*, the continuing fascination with psychiatric assessment in both *The Evaluation* and *Chip Coombs* and the sense of deep, underlying secrets in the latter all remind us that King has a wonderfully fertile mind. Each of these stories, if completed, would add great value to King's published body of work. We are reminded, yet again, that there must be dozens or even hundreds of other story ideas, either partly developed or just sitting in the great writer's mind. As the years go by we can only hope that some of these ideas and storylines will escape onto the page and hopefully see the published light of day.

Stories Swallowed by Monsters

Throughout his career King has published short stories that later appeared in rewritten form in a novel or novella. One could argue the hidden monsters of the future had swallowed up these minnows.

This chapter reviews the eleven stories that appeared in substantially different form in later novels or novellas.

There appear to a variety of reasons as to why these stories appeared later in revised form. *The Bear*, *Calla Bryn Sturgis* and *The Tale of Gray Dick* were virtual teasers for upcoming Dark Tower novels and the changes appear to be a combination of editing and intentionally avoiding giving away important plot points of the novels.

The Bird and the Album was an early version of an incident later used in *It*, while *The Monster in the Closet* was a true excerpt from *Cujo* but had been edited for its particular publication. *The Revelations of 'Becka Paulson*, *The Revenge of Lardass Hogan* and *Stud City* were all genuine stand-alone short stories that King later rewrote for inclusion in *The Tommyknockers* and *The Body*, the latter two under the pseudonym of Gordon Lachance.

These stories deserve review, as it is certain they will never be published in these original forms in a King collection as they already appear in an amended form in the novels.

The Bear (1990)

The Bear forms part of the 1991 novel *The Dark Tower III: The Wastelands* but was originally published in *The Magazine of Fantasy and Science Fiction* for December 1990 (a 'Special Stephen King issue'). That magazine also included the first appearance of King's short story *The Moving Finger*, a King bibliography by his assistant Marsha DeFilippo, and a criticism of King's works by Algis Budrys.

Despite King's author's note in the magazine stating, 'What follows is the first section of *The Dark Tower III: The Wastelands* ...' the version of *The Bear* included in *The Wastelands* is significantly different from the magazine version. Those wishing to read the short story, particularly Dark Tower completists and fans, will be able to purchase a copy from King online booksellers or specialist magazine traders, as *The Magazine of Fantasy and Science Fiction* is collectable in its own right.

It is interesting to note that Eddie (Edward) Dean's middle name is given as Alan in *The Bear* and as Cantor in *The Wastelands*.

In this Dark Tower tale Roland and Susannah Dean are out shooting with live ammunition for only the third time. Roland upset and taunted Susannah to get her in the right mind to fire accurately at small target rocks. She hit five of the six and nicked the last. As they talked after the practice they heard a huge roar and the sound of trees falling in the forest near where they had left Eddie Dean, and ran to investigate.

A 70-foot tall bear, known by those who once lived in the area as Mir, had sensed the humans and was intent on destroying them. Eddie had been carving a slingshot from a piece of wood when Mir approached and he'd climbed the tallest tree to seek refuge. Safe from the bear's reach he waited for help and watched as it sneezed diseased, worm-filled snot from its nose and mouth.

As the bear was trying to break the tree and kill Eddie, Roland and Susannah arrived. Susannah shot the bear to get its attention and, as it charged, shot the radar dish on the top of its head, killing the creature (of course, the shooting or disabling of radar dishes would play a highly significant role in *The Dark Tower V: Wolves of the Calla*). The three looked at the corpse of the fallen bear and discovered it was actually a robot named Shardik.

The Bird and the Album (1981)

This story was published in *A Fantasy Reader: The Seventh World Fantasy Convention Program Book* on 30 October 1981. Thanks to the editor's introduction some sources state this tale is an 'excerpt' from Chapter 13 of the magnificent novel *It*. The story was actually published five years before the novel (the editor described it as '…from the opening of chapter 13 of a work in progress, a novel the author calls IT') but King substantially rewrote the piece for its appearance in the novel, where it actually appears as the beginning of Chapter 14. Among the changes is that from past to present tense.

In this Maine Street Horror tale friends meet in Derry after twenty-five years apart. Eddie Kaspbrak, Beverly, Richie, Ben Hanscom, Mike Hanlon and Bill Denbrough discuss the things they were starting to remember from their childhood. One of the former friends, 'a guy named Stan Uris … couldn't make it.' *(Note: Beverly and Richie's surnames are not given).*

Among the childhood incidents they could remember was Mike bringing his father's photograph album to the clubhouse where the pictures performed the '…same trick as in Georgie's room. Only that time we all saw it.' Ben remembered that they had turned a silver dollar into silver bullet.

When Mike left the room to get a beer from the lounge refrigerator he '...felt the shock sink into him, bone deep and ice-white, the way February cold sank into you when February was here and it seemed that April never would be. Blue and orange balloons drifted out in a flood, dozens of them ...' and then he saw what '...It had popped into the refrigerator ... Stan Uris's head was ... there in the refrigerator beside Mike's sixpack of Bud, the head of a ten year old boy. The mouth was open in a soundless scream but Mike could see neither teeth nor tongue because the mouth had been stuffed full of feathers.' Mike was in no doubt that these huge, brown feathers were from 'the Bird' he had seen in May 1958 and the whole group had seen that August. Mike remembered his dying father telling him he had also '...seen something like it once, too, during the fire at the Black Spot.' The head's eyes opened 'and they were the silver-bright eyes of Pennywise the Clown' and the mouth tried to speak around the feathers.

Something was trying to scare Mike and his friends out of town and away from their plan, even hurling racial epithets at Mike. The head popped out of existence but Mike could still see the balloons, some reading, 'DERRY NIGGERS GET THE BIRD' and others, 'THE LOSERS ARE STILL LOSING, BUT STANLEY URIS IS AHEAD'. Mike then remembered going down to the Barrens 'two days after he had seen Pennywise the Clown in person for the first time', the day the group began planning to kill It. He called the whole group into the lounge, as he continued to remember the warm welcome his future friends had given him that first day. The story ends at this point.

Just one example of the changes and deletions should serve to whet the reader's appetite to seek out the original version of the story. Early in section one of Chapter 14 of *It* (*The Album*), we find this line: '*They all look at Bill then, as they had in the gravel-pit, and Mike thinks:* They look at Bill when they need a leader, at Eddie when they need a navigator. Get down to business, what a hell of a phrase that is. Do I tell them that the bodies of the children that were found back then and now weren't sexually molested, not even precisely mutilated, but partially eaten?'

The Bird and the Album version reads: 'They all look at Mike then, as they had in the gravel pit, and Mike thought: They look at Bill when they need a leader, and me when they need a navigator. I wonder how they'd like it if I told them that in the movies the hero's never bald and, as for me, I lost my compass and rudder while I was working in my damned journal, trying to make sense of killing fires and giant birds, an explosion in an ironworks where the boilers had been shut down, a mass murder in a bar in Hell's Half-Acre, a mass murder seems to have happened while the customers went right on drinking; and if I told them all of those things, would I really be telling them anything they don't already know? Get down to business, what a hell of a phrase that is. Do I tell them that the bodies of the children that were found back then and now weren't sexually molested, not even precisely mutilated, but partially eaten?'

Readers at the time the original was published were intrigued by the tale but had to wait another five years for the context in which to place this slightly less than 3000 word piece. As an historical note this was the first published mention of Derry.

Those wishing to read this original version of the story today will find their task somewhat difficult. The convention book sometimes appears for sale at specialist King booksellers and that would be the best option for those seeking a copy.

Calla Bryn Sturgis (2001)

Calla Bryn Sturgis was first released on King's official website, www.stephenking.com on 21 August 2001, just three weeks before September 11. King provided the story free of charge as a thank you to long-suffering fans of the Dark Tower Cycle, who were awaiting the next installment, *The Dark Tower V: Wolves of the Calla*.

Readers were told this was the Prologue to the new novel but hints were provided that this would not be its final form in the book. In fact, so as not to give away certain events in the novel, there had been some careful editing and changes. The story was delivered in a substantially different form as the Prologue, *Roont* when *The Dark Tower V: Wolves of the Calla* was published more than two years later, in November 2003.

Both versions featured the return of King's benighted character, Father Callahan of *'Salem's Lot*, known in the Calla as Pere Callahan. King had said that, despite the Catholic priest having last been seen on a bus out of the Lot, he had not finished with the Father and he would reappear in some future story. *'Salem's Lot* was published in 1975, so there was in fact more than a quarter century between published novels featuring this character. This is the longest period between appearances by a significant King character!

In this Dark Tower tale a village in End-World considers a coming threat. Tian Jaffords tended his fields with the plough being pulled not by animals but by his twin sister! She, like many others in Calla Bryn Sturgis, was 'roont'.

Every generation or so 'Wolves' would come and take one child from each set of twins, returning them sometime later, large and strong but slow in the mind. In a village where almost all births were of twins the raids were far from welcome, but a robot named Andy now told Jaffords that the Wolves would return in a month.

That night forty men, mostly farmers from the area, met to discuss the upcoming raid. Various suggestions were offered and discussed, including killing the children, leaving town, accepting the loss of their children, and *even* standing and fighting. As it had been about 23 years since the Wolves had last appeared there was much speculation about the weaponry the kidnappers carried, which apparently included Light Sticks, Sneetches and Stealthies. Pere Callahan, who ran a Christian church in the village, then told the meeting three gunslingers and their apprentice were heading toward Calla Bryn Sturgis, along the path of the Beam.

It was time to stand and be true.

It was immediately obvious to fans of the Dark Tower series that the three gunslingers (one of whom was a woman) and their apprentice were Roland Deschain, Eddie Dean and Susannah Dean, along with Jake Chambers. In a nod to the later stages of *The Dark Tower IV: Wizard and Glass* Andy the robot spoke of a Palace of Green Glass that had appeared and then disappeared near the Big River in Out-World.

There is one error in the story. We are told that Tian's last name is Jaffords, but when Andy is standing in Tian's Son of a Bitch field, he thinks of: '…that thankless tract of Jaffrey land…' The error was corrected when the novel was released.

The story no longer appears on King's website and, as it was never published in a paper form, readers wishing to access a copy will need to contact a King collector or fan who has retained it in electronic format and may wish to provide a copy. It should be noted that the story is King's copyright and should not be purchased or sold.

King's serious fan base was delighted and intrigued by both the story and Callahan's appearance. Perhaps as a result of this positive reaction King also allowed another section of the novel, *The Tale of Gray Dick*, to appear in an altered version ahead of the novel's release (covered later in this chapter).

Lisey and the Madman (2004)

A chapter of the *Lisey's Story* was first published in an anthology, *McSweeney's Enchanted Chamber of Astonishing Stories*, edited by Michael Chabon and released in November 2004, as *Lisey and the Madman*. This section was heavily revised for the final novel. This was the second time King had been published in a Chabon edited anthology from the *McSweeney* series. The earlier story was the previous year's *The Tale of Gray Dick* in *McSweeney's Mammoth Treasury of Thrilling Tales*.

The co-author of *The Talisman* and *Black House*, Peter Straub also has a story in the anthology, *Mr. Aickman's Air Rifle*. King's contribution is dedicated to Nan Graham. The 'About the Contributors' section notes of King, 'He has promised to retire, but "Lisey and the Madman" is from what may eventually be a novel called *Lisey's Story*. In his defense, King points out that all novelists lie – sometimes to others, almost constantly to themselves." Of course, the novel was published, in October 2006.

The story was also reprinted in an anthology, *New Beginnings: A Tsunami Benefit Book*, released by Bloomsbury on World Book Day, 3 March 2005. Among other authors to contribute to this book, intended to raise funds to benefit victims of the 26 December 2004 Asian Tsunami, were Maeve Binchy, Margaret Atwood, Paulo Coelho, Scott Turow and Vikram Seth.

This America Under Siege story begins with Lisey Landon, wife of a famous novelist, recalling events eighteen years earlier. She is reminded of them by a now famous photograph, in which she appears, although no one else is aware of that fact. The photo shows a young man holding a small silver shovel, looking somewhat dazed, while a cop shakes his hand. Lisey's contribution to the photo is half a brown loafer in the far right-hand side of the photo a she left the scene for something much more important.

It had been a hot, muggy day at the University of Tennessee in August of 1986, when Scott Landon (Pulitzer and National Book Award winning novelist) was due to turn the first earth at the commencement ceremonies for the Shipman Library. From the first thing that morning, back at their Maine home, Lisey Landon had been suffering from a sense of foreboding. She had accidentally smashed a tooth glass in their bathroom and had not felt right since. After the accident Lisey cursed and remembered her grandmother, 'that old Irish highpockets', who had quite a store of sayings and curses and who had most certainly believed in omens, even if Lisey did not.

A large crowd had turned out to see the famous author say a few words. This, combined with the heat, only added to Lisey's concerns as she recalled the 'deep-space' fans that come with fame – one had hitchhiked from Texas to Maine to discuss Bigfoot with Scott (of course, this type of individual is a regular problem for both the King family and his office). She even noted one of the breed ('Blondie') standing in the crowd but, strangely, was not concerned by him, despite her foreboding.

Attended by the reluctant and pompous representative of the University, a student reporter and local newspaper photographer the official party proceeded to a point behind velvet-rope barriers where Scott Landon was presented with a small silver shovel. Landon proceeded to give a quick speech for the crowd and a small showy display for the photographer. In his speech he spoke briefly of current events, concluding, 'The world grows dark. Discordia rises.' Turning the sod he called the names of favored authors and asked the crowd to check out both their books and those of their own personal favorites when the Library opened. "'But if every book is a little light in that darkness – and so I believe, so I believe, so I must believe, for I write the goddamn things, don't I? – then every library is a grand bonfire around which ten thousand people come to stand and warm themselves each cold day and night.'"

After turning the last sod Scott handed the ceremonial shovel to his wife and the crowd began to break up, the official party heading for the air-conditioned haven of the English department, Nelson Hall. Lisey again noticed 'Blondie', walking against the flow of the crowd and muttering inanely; and *then* the gun tucked into the belt below his untucked shirt.

Lisey became entrenched in that dream-like quality of a crisis, unable to move quickly enough or draw attention to the danger only she could she. Before anyone could react, 'Blondie', actually Gerd Allen Cole, a grad student, shot Scott in the right chest. As Cole prepared the coup-de-grace shot to Scott's heart Lisey swung the silver shovel, striking his gun hand and causing the shot to fly harmlessly skyward. The swing continued, smashing into Cole's face and bringing the attack to an end.

Concerned about her wounded husband, who was walking off in shock, Lisey handed the shovel to the student reporter, Tony Eddington. As the campus security chief came up he mistakenly thought Eddington had been the hero (something the young man would never correct) and shook him by the hand. At that very moment the photographer, Stefan Queensland (UTenn class of '83) took the award-winning photograph that would, with time, become nearly as famous as that of the mortally wounded Lee Harvey Oswald clutching his stomach.

As Scott collapsed on the hot blacktop Lisey reached and began to comfort him. Seriously wounded, with blood flowing from his chest and mouth, Scott reverted to an apparently natural depressive mode, '"It's very close, honey. I can't see it but I ... I hear it taking its meal and grunting."' Although Lisey denied knowing what he was talking about Scott insisted she did. 'Yes, she knows. *It*. The long boy, he calls it. Or just the thing. Or sometimes the thing with the endless piebald side ... And actually, it's more than just a few times he's spoken of that thing. Especially just lately. He says you can see it if you look through dirty water glasses. If you look through them just the right way, and in the hours after midnight.'

Landon then made the sound he claimed the monster makes 'when it looks around'. Turning to Lisey he said, '"I ... could ... call it that way ... It would come. You'd ... be ... rid of me." She understands he means it, and for a moment ... she believes it's true. He will make the sound again, only a little louder this time, and somewhere the long boy – that lord of sleepless nights – will turn its unspeakable hungry head. A moment later, in this world, Scott Landon will simply shiver on the pavement and die. The death certificate will show something sane, but she will know. His dark thing finally saw him and came for him and ate him alive.'

'So now come the things they will never speak of later, not to others nor between themselves. Too awful. Each long marriage has two hearts, one light and one dark. This is the dark heart of theirs, the one mad true secret.' Scott asked Lisey again if he should call but she insisted he be quiet, '"*Leave that fucking thing alone and it will go away*."' Just before the paramedics took him away Scott insisted the monster may have seen Lisey and said the first thing she must do when she checked into a motel was deal with the water glasses. And, when she did check into the Greenview Motel and found the bathroom glasses to be actual glass and not the usual plastic, she 'puts both of them in her purse, careful not to look at either one as she does so' and then smashed them in the gutter outside. 'The sound of them breaking comforts her even more than the sound of that little shovel's scoop, connecting first with the pistol and then with Blondie's face.'

Once again King introduces us to a famous writer based in Maine although the story, both here and in the novel, is from the point of view of the spouse. Among other prominent Maine writers in King's canon are Mike Noonan (*Bag of Bones*), Bill Denbrough (*It*), Jim Gardener (*The Tommyknockers*), Gordie Lachance (*The Body*), Thad Beaumont (*The Dark Half*), Ben Mears (*'Salem's Lot*), Richard Kinnell (*The Road Virus Heads North*), Morton Rainey (*Secret Window, Secret Garden*) and, of course, the Stephen King of the latter Dark Tower novels. King has used such characters since at least 1971, starting with Gerald Nately of *The Blue Air Compressor*.

There is one particularly interesting link into King's other fiction. In his speech at the groundbreaking ceremony, Scott Landon reviews 1986's current events; including the 'Challenger' shuttle explosion, chaos in the Philippines, the nuclear reactor accident at Chernobyl and the AIDS epidemic. He then says, 'The world grows dark. Discordia rises.' Discordia is crucial in the last two Dark Tower novels, *Song of Susannah* and *The Dark Tower*. Dark Tower expert Bev Vincent defines the term as, 'The great chaos. All that will remain if the Tower falls.'[155]

In both the latter Dark Tower novels the great castle near Fedic is known as Castle Discordia or the Castle on the Abyss. At one point the Crimson King is described as the Lord of Discordia. King even had himself use the term in his fictional journals to indicate the day of his accident. There can be little doubt that, as King wrote *Lisey and the Madman* in 2004, he deliberately dropped the term 'Discordia' into the story.

Typically of King, what appears initially to be the simple description of crazed fan attacking famous artist (Mark David Chapman and John Lennon are referenced), or the great American tradition of gun wielded by crazy man (Bremmer and George Wallace is King's way of reminding us of this) turns into something much deeper and more sinister. The subtle ways in which King works in both Scott Landon's 'long boy' and the foreshadowing of events yet to be described show once again the depth of King's mastery of both the novel and short story forms.

Again King provides a number of memorable lines. One, 'No one loves a clown at midnight' is attributed to Lon Chaney and is said to be the epigram of Landon's third novel, *Empty Devils*, a sort of a riff on Romero's *Living Dead* movies. George Romero was, of course, the director of *The Dark Half* and *Creepshow*, as well as adapting *The Cat From Hell* for *Tales From the Darkside: The Movie* and writing the screenplays for *The Dark Half* and *Creepshow 2*.

As always with King even the minor characters are painted whole. The University's representative, Roger Dashmiel is made wholly unlikeable in just a few sentences. Gerd Allen Cole, 'the madman', is totally believable, fitting the profile of so many 'deep space' fans and muttering his inanities, "'If it closes the lips of the bells, it will have done the job. I'm sorry, Papa'". The campus cop, Heffernan, realized 'he may just get out of this mess with his skin on and his job intact' and will always doubt that Tony Eddington 'laid the gun-toting nutjob low' but will never voice those doubts. Eddington himself, thrust into the role of hero, is quickly caught up by events and never declares the truth.

Memory (2006)

Memory first came to public notice when King read it at the Seven Days of Opening Nights arts festival at Florida State University in Tallahassee on 26 February 2006 (he received a standing ovation). It was first published in *Tin House* magazine for Summer 2006 and by September of that year it became clear the episode would form part of an upcoming King novel, *Duma Key*. It was also included in the 2007 first edition of *Blaze*. The piece is revised in the novel.

This America Under Siege story is set in Minneapolis-St. Paul, Minnesota (an unusual location for King), although the main events of the novel would move to Florida (the first King novel to be set in that location, although short stories from that region started to appear some years after the Kings first bought a home there).

In the tale, Edgar Freemantle, the owner of a sizeable construction firm, recalls the pain of his initial recovery from a nearly fatal accident and begins to come to terms with the past. Freemantle had lost his right arm and suffered other severe injuries when a crane backed over his pickup truck at a construction site.

As well as his physical recovery stresses, he suffered rage attacks during his convalescence and tried to strangle his wife Pam (but did not realize this for many months). Shortly after he moved from the convalescent home to their suburban house she asked for a divorce. We learn a little of Freemantle's life and meet his two young adult daughters – Ilse, a student at Brown and apparently the weaker of the two; and Melissa ('Lissa'), a teacher on a foreign exchange program in France, apparently stronger.

He moved to their lake house in suburban St. Paul after Pam requested the divorce and, while walking one day, saw a dog struck and mortally injured by a yellow Hummer. Distracting a young neighboring girl, Monica Goldstein, who owned the Jack Russell, he was able to put poor Gandalf out of his misery, but the act finally released the memory of attacking Pam.

Freemantle had been secretly planning to commit suicide but his physical therapist, Kathi Green and his hugely fat psychologist, Xander Kamen were able to see the warning signs. Dr. Kamen asked him to wait a year before killing himself, so as not to lay guilt upon his soon-to-be ex-wife and daughters.

The tale is told from a distance of four or so years from the accident and with initial publication seemed unfinished (this was clarified with the announcement of the novel). It is rather obvious to even a casual King fan that at least this part of the tale is another working out of King's own accident and recovery. He writes specifically of the pain of physical rehabilitation but we also observe some possible emotional scars.

A powerful stand-alone piece, the short description of the accident from Freemantle's viewpoint as he found himself trapped in his pick-up cabin with a crane slowly crushing it, inexorably moving toward him and then slowly crushing his body from the right, is a tour-de-force of prose. For dog-lovers the short scene in which the dying Gandalf's 'eyes turned up to me and in them I saw a horrible expression of hope', is harrowing and deeply truthful.

Copies of the magazine are generally available from such sources as eBay and specialist King resellers.

The Monster in the Closet (1981)

An 'excerpt' from King's novel *Cujo* appeared as a stand-alone story, *The Monster in the Closet*, in the *Ladies Home Journal* for October 1981. The story is not in fact a direct excerpt, and spans a number of sections of *Cujo*. There are some minor changes to the novel's text and even some material added.

Although Maine is not mentioned, we know *Cujo* is a Castle Rock story and it is therefore classified as a Maine Street Horror tale.

In the story a young boy sees a monster in his closet. Four year old Tad Trenton awakened his parents with his screams. As Vic and Donna Trenton thought the monster was just a pile of blankets they moved them to the rear of the closet and closed the door. The following morning the blankets had returned to their previous position and Tad claimed that the monster had moved them back.

Vic was due to leave on a business trip two weeks later and created 'Monster Words' for Tad, which they could recite together each night to frighten the monster away. The 'Monster Words' were:

Monsters, stay out of this room!
You have no business here.
No Monsters under Tad's bed!
You can't fit under there.
No monsters hiding in Tad's closet!
It's too small in there.
No monsters outside of Tad's window!
You can't hold on out there.

No vampires, no werewolves, no things that bite.
You have no business here.
Nothing will touch Tad, or hurt Tad, all this night.
You have no business here.

Despite these brave words it seems the monster never left and, before the summer was over, it really did come out of the closet.

Readers will find it difficult to secure a copy of this issue of the *Ladies Home Journal*, the best source will be online King booksellers.

The Pulse (2005)

On 7 July 2005 the web site, www.amazon.com released *The Pulse*, boosting it as "the chilling first chapter of a work in progress", as part of their 10th Anniversary 'Hall of Fame Exclusive Content'. With revisions, the piece became part of *Cell*, published in 2006. As the novel is about zombies, at this point it can be classified as both an America Under Siege and a New Worlds story.

There are two sub-sections. In the first readers discover 'the event which came to be known as The Pulse occurred in the Eastern time zone of the United States at 3:03pm on the afternoon of October 1st.' By the second sentence King has the story racing, 'The term was a misnomer, of course, but within ten hours of the event, most of the scientists capable of pointing this out were either dead or insane.' Readers then meet Clayton Riddell, a young man 'of no particular importance to history' walking near the Boston Common.

The second sub-section features the typical King scene of normality suddenly being torn apart. Riddell was in a great mood, having 'just sold his first graphic novel – and its sequel, both for an amazing, totally unexpected amount of money …' Observing people buying ice cream from a Mr. Softee truck Clay starts to hear some unsettling screams, sees a businessman suddenly attack a dog ('… *surely I'm not seeing what I think I'm* seeing, Clay thought *not man bites dog*) and notices that a woman who had just hung up her cell phone attack the ice-cream vendor. The piece ends at this point.

The Revelations of 'Becka Paulson (1984)

The Revelations of 'Becka Paulson was first published in *Rolling Stone* magazine for 19 July and 2 August 1984. The story was substantially revised for inclusion as part of the novel *The Tommyknockers* in 1987. It also appeared in the Limited Edition of *Skeleton Crew*, published in 1985, but none of the mass-market editions. The last time it appeared in print in this form was in the 1991 anthology, *I Shudder at Your Touch*, edited by Michele Slung and published by New American Library.

Readers wishing to obtain a copy should start with online King booksellers and second hand bookshops. As *Rolling Stone* is quite collectable copies of the magazine can also be sourced from specialist traders. For those who cannot find a text copy Penguin Highbridge Books issued an audio book of *I Shudder at Your Touch* in 1992, which included this version of the story.

In this Maine Street Horror tale strange events follow a gunshot wound. While spring-cleaning, Rebecca ('Becka') Paulson found her husband's .22 caliber target pistol. Falling while holding the gun, Becka accidentally shot herself in the head, just above the left eye. When she awoke she was shocked to find a hole in her head that turned out to be five inches deep when she measured it with an eyebrow pencil inserted *into* the wound. By that night she could not remember anything that had happened to her earlier in the day, including the shooting.

A few days later a picture of Jesus atop her television began 'telling' Becka secret things. These included that her husband Joe was cheating on her with Nancy Voss, a fellow postal worker. Also that Moss Harlingen had murdered his father in revenge for being raped as a child but had successfully passed it off as a hunting accident; that Alice Kimball was a lesbian; that 17 year old Darla Gaines took drugs and made love to her boyfriend while her parents were out; and that Hank Buck had placed Ex-Lax in his boss' milkshake!

The picture of 'Jesus' then helped Becka make a modification to the television set that would kill her husband when he turned it on. As Joe turned the TV on Becka realized that it was she, and not 'Jesus', who had been responsible for the modification. When she tried to save Joe she was also killed by the electrical shock.

In this original version of the tale the events occurred in July of 1973, with Rebecca suffering the gunshot wound about 3pm on the 7th and the couple dying on the 10th. When included in *The Tommyknockers* the story had migrated to the 1988 timeline of that tale, with the picture of Jesus beginning to speak to Rebecca on July 7 and the two dying of electrocution on the July 10.

Even at the time this stand-alone incarnation was published the story linked to other King works of fiction. Among these links are the mention of the town of Derry being near Haven (by 1984 Derry had already appeared in *The Bird and the Album, The Body, Mrs. Todd's Shortcut, Pet Sematary, The Running Man* and the *Yankee* version of *Uncle Otto's Truck*); and Haven itself being mentioned in *Mrs. Todd's Shortcut*, published the same year. Apart from *The Tommyknockers* Rebecca and Joe Paulson and Haven would later be mentioned in *It*; and Derry would, of course, appear in many King stories, becoming the second most featured fictional town in Maine outside of Castle Rock.

The story was adapted for television as a series episode for the revival of *The Outer Limits*, with the title *The Revelations of 'Becka Paulson*. It was first screened on 6 June 1997. Brad Wright wrote the Teleplay and Steven Weber, who only weeks earlier had appeared as Jack Torrance in the mini-series of *The Shining*[156], both directed and played the Guy in the Photo (a normal Joe had replaced Jesus in this version, presumably to avoid offending certain viewers' sensibilities). Catherine O'Hara played Becka Paulson and John Diehl appeared as Joe Paulson.

The Revenge of Lard Ass Hogan (1975)

The Revenge of Lard Ass Hogan was originally published in *Maine Review* magazine for July 1975. King updated the story and included it in his novella *The Body*, published in 1982. The scenario was so irresistible that Rob Reiner retained it in the widely loved movie version of the novella, *Stand By Me*. It is very likely that the scene was adapted from *The Body*, rather than this version of the story.

As an aside, while most experts regard *The Body* as a novella, King described it in his *Entertainment Weekly* column for 22/29 August 2003 as 'my short novel'.

In this Maine Street Horror tale a fat boy plots a spectacular revenge on his tormentors. David 'Lardass' Hogan had a glandular problem and was picked on for his size by children and adults alike. Ace Carmody, Eyeball Chambers and Billy Norcross chased him down and forced him to enter the annual pie-eating contest in Gates Falls. But Hogan developed a plan.

On the day of the contest he climbed the stage after drinking three-quarters of a bottle of castor oil. Pitted against the previous year's champion, Bill Travis and three other contestants, Hogan ate like a madman. On his third pie he intentionally began to tell himself he was not actually eating pie but in fact other, disgusting, things.

During his fifth pie, he raised his head and vomited on Bill Travis, causing a chain reaction of vomiting from the contestants and spectators. This, of course, had been his plan all along.

Among the changes King made for *The Body* was the conversion of the character 'Ace' Carmody into the infamous John 'Ace' Merrill (played by Kiefer Sutherland in the movie). Ace would later appear in the *Skeleton Crew* version of *Nona* and *The Sun Dog* before meeting an inglorious end in *Needful Things*. The origin of Ace's nickname is revealed by this change. We know from King's fiction that pretty much the whole Merrill clan were trouble. Ace's uncle Reginald ('Pop'), a moneylender and a conman, died a result of his greed in *The Sun Dog*; Royce Merrill was one of the old farts who ganged up on Mike Noonan and Mattie Devore in *Bag of Bones*; and Roy Merrill was turned out by town meeting from his job as Road Commissioner in *The Huffman Story*, an unpublished partial manuscript. Roy had employed his wife as secretary and three brothers, four nephews and two cousins on the road crew!

One of Ace Carmody's friends in the short story, Billy Norcross becomes Billy Tessio, Vern's brother in the novella. This version of the story is set in late August of 1960. When Gordie Lachance tells the story as his own in *The Body* he does not give it a particular timeline.

In *The Body* Gordie Lachance set the contest in the 'fictional' town of Gretna, Maine rather than Gates Mills. King also cut out characters for the novella, including the entire balance of the Hogan family. In the short story Lardass' parents, Robert and Sheila and his sister Bobbi all threw up. There were also references to the mass murderer with whom King had a fascination in his youth, Charles Starkweather and that killer's girlfriend, Caril Ann Fugate (David Hogan was infatuated with her) but these also disappeared from the novella. Considering King's interest in Starkweather his appearance in this story is an important historical footnote to King's body of work.

The principal of David Hogan's school has a number of different incarnations. In the original short story he appears as Hubert Hansen, principal of Gates Falls High School. In the novella Gordie Lachance names the principal as Hubert Gretna III in the oral version but by the time Gordie had the story 'published' he was now John Wiggins, principal of Gretna Elementary School!

We are told in the novella that Gordon Lachance's story, *The Revenge of Lard Ass Hogan* (note the subtle difference from *Lardass* in King's version to *Lard Ass* in Lachance's) was published in *Cavalier* magazine for March 1975. This is another little in-joke from King, who published many stories in the 1970s in *Cavalier*, a men's magazine. *The Revenge of Lard Ass Hogan* by Stephen King *was* published in 1975, but as mentioned earlier, in *Maine Review* – perhaps *Cavalier* rejected it? It is also something of a shame that there was no actual story by Stephen King in the March 1975 edition of *Cavalier*!

Even at this early date in King's publishing history the story linked to other King fiction through its setting in the town of Gates Falls, Maine. The town had already appeared in *Graveyard Shift* (first published in *Cavalier* for October 1970); *It Grows on You* (first published in *Marshroots* for Fall, 1973) and that same year was mentioned in *'Salem's Lot*. It would go on to appear in *The Body*, *The Dark Half*, *The Dead Zone*, *Gramma*, *Hearts in Atlantis*, *Mrs. Todd's Shortcut*, *Needful Things*, *The Plant* (but only the electronic version), *Rage*, *Riding the Bullet* and also appeared in the unpublished works *Blaze*, *Movie Show* and *Sword in the Darkness*.

The Revenge of Lard Ass Hogan is one of the more difficult King stories to find. The particular edition of *Maine Review* rarely appears for sale and then almost exclusively through specialist online King booksellers. However, for serious King fans the search is well worth the effort. This is a tremendously entertaining story in King's gross-out mode and will remain a signpost for those who wish to study the development of King's career.

Stud City (1969)

In addition to *The Revenge of Lard Ass Hogan* King converted another short story from earlier in his career to a Gordie Lachance story appearing in *The Body*. *Stud City* was one of King's earliest published stories, appearing in the University of Maine literary magazine *Ubris* for Fall, 1969. King (or perhaps it was actually Lachance?) heavily revised it for its appearance in *The Body*. In that novella we are told that the story was first published in a college literary magazine (sound familiar?), *Greenspun Quarterly*.

In this Maine Street Horror tale a boy begins his journey toward manhood. Edward 'Chico' May made love to his 16 year old girlfriend Jane for the first time and then drove her home to Auburn. Later, he infuriated his father Sam by telling him he intended to join the Marines. Chico then told Sam of the intense dislike he had for his stepmother, Virginia, whom he believed had 'broken' his father's spirit.

Later, Virginia confronted Chico and asked if he'd had his girlfriend around while they were out. He told her he had and that the sheets on his bed needed changing. He then left the house and drove off, remembering his real mother and the birth of his brother Billy, which had taken her life. He also recalled having once had sex with Virginia! Chico drove on toward his friend Danny Carter's home, where he would stay for the night. He would decide his future in the morning.

This story, not at all in the classic King horror mold of much of his early published stories, is in fact more in line with *The New Yorker* stories of his later career. This piece goes to prove that King had the ability to write powerful mainstream fiction from an early age (he was only 22 when it was published).

When rewriting the story for *The Body* King made numerous changes. For instance, in the short story Chico's older brother Johnny had joined the Marines but in the novella he had been killed when a runaway car hit him while he was changing a tire at the Oxford Plains Speedway. He could have worked at the Gates Mills, but chose the speedway so he wouldn't have to be at home with his stepmother while his father was at work! In other changes the sexual encounter between Chico and his stepmother, Virginia is deleted; and Chico's natural mother Cathy is no longer mentioned, nor is her death in childbirth.

Another character deleted from the novella is Duane Conant, a friend of Chico's who was killed when his Mustang hit a pole on Stackpole Road (no town name is given). There are a number of Stackpole Roads in King's fiction, including the one in Blainesville, Maine where Nona lead 'the prisoner' to a cemetery in the *Shadows* version of *Nona*; the same road in Castle Rock in the *Skeleton Crew* version of *Nona*; in *The Dark Half*, where the Castle Rock cemetery is named as the Stackpole Cemetery on the road of the same name; another in Harlow, Maine in *Rage* and three of the four versions of *It Grows On You* (the Newall house is on it); and in Ludlow, Maine in *Pet Sematary*. The 'real' Stackpole Road is in Durham, Maine. Even today anyone visiting the location will see how King, growing up in this isolated rural township, would have found the Stackpole Road, close to the real Runaround Pond, so capable of tragedy.

Copies of *Ubris* are almost impossible to find, although the story can be photocopied from an original copy of the magazine held at the Fogler Library of the University of Maine at Orono. For those seeking an original copy of their own we can only recommend the normal online King booksellers but one should expect a long wait and a hefty price tag!

The Tale of Gray Dick (2003)

The Tale of Gray Dick is a version of the chapter of the same name in *The Dark Tower V: Wolves of the Calla*, published in November 2003. The stand-alone short story was first published in the magazine, *Timothy McSweeney's Quarterly Concern* on 25 February 2003; and in anthology, *McSweeney's Mammoth Treasury of Thrilling Tales*, published by Vintage Books in a large paperback format the following month. King fiction would again appear in a *McSweeney's* anthology, with *Lisey and the Madman*, in *McSweeney's Mammoth Treasury of Thrilling Tales*, released in November 2004.

There are revisions, including both the deletion and addition of material for its appearance in *The Dark Tower V: Wolves of the Calla*. These changes were clearly made to avoid giving away plotlines in the novel ahead of its publication. The short story is more of a variation to, than a version of, the tale.

In this Dark Tower story a woman takes revenge on her father's killer while using an innovative weapon. Roland Deschain and Jake Chambers talked to Vaughn Eisenhart and his wife Margaret at their Lazy B ranch near Calla Bryn Sturgis. Roland examined Vaughn's three guns, finding that only one rifle was of any value.

In the ensuing discussion Roland was told the story of Lady Oriza and her weapon. Gray Dick, an outlaw prince, had killed Lady Oriza's father Lord Grenfall and she sought revenge. Expertly learning how to throw a sharpened plate she took dinner with Gray Dick, who was suspicious of her motives but could not resist the offer to dine with her naked. During the meal she threw one of her plates, decapitating her victim.

Roland was also told that the plates were still made in a town far to the north, Calla Sen Chre. Most of the women in Calla Bryn Sturgis could throw the plates and Margaret Eisenhart reluctantly demonstrated her amazing accuracy with the weapon for Roland's benefit.

Copies of *McSweeney's Mammoth Treasury of Thrilling Tales* are available at second-hand bookshops, specialist King booksellers and such sources as eBay. An unabridged version of this story is also available as a Random House Audible download as part of *McSweeney's Mammoth Treasury of Thrilling Tales*, read by Kevin Gray.

Sword in the Darkness (1970)

The manuscript for *Sword in the Darkness* is held in Box 1010 at the Special Collections Unit of the Raymond H Fogler Library at the University of Maine, Orono. Written permission from King is required to access this work. Dated April 30, 1970 it contains 485 double-spaced typed pages and is on the order of 150,000 words.

King recalls writing *Sword in the Darkness* during his senior year at the University of Maine, in Section 14 of the second part of *On Writing*: '…back in my dorm room was my dirty little secret: the half-completed manuscript of a novel about a teenage gang's plan to start a race riot. They would use this for cover while ripping off two dozen loan-sharking operations and illegal drug-rings in the city of Harding, my fictional version of Detroit (I had never been within six hundred miles of Detroit, but I didn't let that stop or even slow me down). This novel, *Sword in the Darkness,* seemed very tawdry to me when compared to what my fellow students were trying to achieve; which is why, I suppose, I never brought any of it to class for a critique. The fact that it was also better and somehow truer than all my poems about sexual yearning and post-adolescent angst only made things worse. The result was a four-month period in which I could write almost nothing at all.'

Sword in the Darkness us both an America Under Siege story and a Maine Street Horror tale, this last due to a significant Maine back-story, more of which later.

In the novel a gang of crooks is planning a race riot in the mid-Western city of Harding, whose residents are unsuspecting of the upcoming mayhem. The death of Rita from a brain tumor and the subsequent suicide of her daughter Miriam, who was unwed and pregnant, shatter the Kalowski family. The son and brother, Arnie, tries to deal with the losses as well as organize his love life with girlfriend, Janet Cross and sometime lover, Kit Longtin. Meanwhile, Longtin and a gang friend blackmail the Harding High School principal, her uncle Henry Coolidge, who is something of a sex fiend.

Two teachers at Harding High, Edie Rowsmith and John Edgars, are slowly building a relationship despite the fact that Edie is at least two decades older. Rowsmith and Edgars also try to help Arnie Kalowski.

Marcus Slade, a radical African American, is to speak in Harding on 29 June 1969. Webs McCullough, a psychopathic criminal, plans to start a race riot during Slade's visit and use it as a cover for a series of robberies.

Slade arrives and McCullough's men start the riot through a series of violent acts. A massive fire breaks out as blacks and whites fight across the city. Cross is raped by an African American and seriously injured. McCullough's men undertake a number of robberies and proceed to stash their loot at the High School. Coolidge is in his office and shoots one of the gang before being killed himself. Finally realizing the psychopathic nature of their leader one of the gang shoots McCullough and the survivors escape the city.

In the aftermath of the riot Kalowski discovers Cross has died from injuries sustained during the rape and runs into the night. The next morning he agrees to meet with Rowsmith and Edgars who now appear to have formed a more permanent relationship.

Douglas Winter states[157] that *Sword in the Darkness* was rejected for publication 'an even dozen times'. King told Winter: 'I had lost my girlfriend of four years, and this book seemed to be constantly pawing over that relationship and trying to make sense of it. And that doesn't make for good fiction.' One presumes this explains the complicated love triangle between Arnie Kalowski, Janet Cross and Kit Longtin.

In an apparent reference to this manuscript King told David Bright, in an interview published in *Portland Monthly* and reprinted in the *Castle Rock* newsletter, 'I wrote one big-city book when I was in college. I looked at it two years later and was amazed at how bad it was. It was a big-city book written by a kid from the country.'

As few readers will ever have the opportunity to read the novel let's take this opportunity to present a brief summary of each Chapter. The novel is split into four parts, containing a total of 93 numbered Chapters. One can see that the average chapter length is only 5 pages. In fact only Chapter 71 is lengthy. As a result the story has an overly frenetic quality. Within a few years of writing *Sword in the Darkness* King had clearly learned to manage his overall pace and only lend speed to the story as required.

Part One is the Prologue and Chapter One, titled *Good Day, Sunshine*. Early morning takes the reader on a tour of the city of Harding.

Part Two is titled *Late Afternoon*. In Chapter Two Miss Edie Rowsmith heads detention hall at Harding High School. In Three Earl Neiman gets himself into trouble and is thrown out of the detention hall. In Four Earl Neiman and Pete Venness report to Webs McCullough at 'The Club', the headquarters of McCullough's gang, previously known as the Turner Street Oligarchs. Webs tells Earl that if he is suspended from school he will be kicked out of The Club. In Five Arnie Kalowski arrives home and finds his mother with a migraine and his sister, Miriam, in a foul mood. In Six Rowsmith and another teacher, John Edgars speak about Neiman and the upcoming Civic Board meeting. In Seven Rowsmith remembers her lost love, Don, now dead and buried.

In Chapter Eight Neiman remembers that another student, Kit Longtin had once told him that the school headmaster Henry Coolidge had molested her.

We are told that Coolidge is also her uncle. In Nine the Kalowski family argue over dinner in their apartment. Rita, the mother, has a migraine and Frank, the father has had a bad day. In Ten Neiman calls Longtin and asks for her assistance putting the screws on Coolidge. They agree to meet at Mike's Pizza.

In Chapter Eleven, set in San Francisco, radical African American leader Marcus Slade and his elderly assistant, Roy talk of their upcoming visit to Harding. In Twelve Neiman and Longtin meet at Mike's Pizza and plan to blackmail Coolidge by catching him in compromising photographs with Kit. In Thirteen Neiman and Arnie Kalowski fight outside Mike's but Neiman stops when he realizes that Arnie had talked Rowsmith out of suspending him from school. In Fourteen Coolidge is revealed as something of a pervert who constantly fantasizes about sex, even with his female students. His father had also been a womanizer.

In Chapter Fifteen Rita Kalowski considers her life and wonders why she is getting migraines. She feels her family is drifting away from her. Her daughter, Miriam, rings from The Arcade on an amusement park pier, and tells her that she has allowed two strangers to have sex with her for money. Rita collapses and strikes her head. In Sixteen Miriam Kalowski remembers telling Bill Danning, her boss, that she was pregnant with his child. He suggested an abortion and subsequently fired her. Miriam considered suicide but could not go through with it. In Seventeen Arnie Kalowski finds his mother and calls the doctor, who immediately leaves for their apartment.

In Chapter Eighteen McCullough and two associates, Jigs and Bull-Run, burgle the Chase and Allen Western Auto, stealing a shotgun and ammunition. In Nineteen Rita Kalowski is admitted to the Harding Memorial Hospital. She is immediately diagnosed with a brain tumor and operated upon. Arnie rings home and finally gets on to his father, who is drunk. Dr. Cassidy tells Arnie his mother died at 1.17am. In Twenty, at about 2 am, and while considering suicide, Miriam Kalowski falls off the pier into the lake and drowns. In Twenty One the Harding High School teachers discuss the impact of his mother's death on Arnie, who does not yet know of Miriam's demise.

In Chapter Twenty Two Slade meets an NAACP lawyer, Stanley Frobisher, who tries to talk him out of going to Harding. In Twenty Three McCullough's history is revealed. Aged only 14 he had killed a boy with a piece of rusty pipe and he'd killed twice more before arriving in Harding. In Twenty Four Arnie and Frank Kalowski discuss Rita's funeral arrangements. They believe that Miriam has run off but the police arrive and tell them that she has drowned. Arnie goes with them to the morgue to identify the body. In Twenty Five Arnie wanders South Harding and, in rage, smashes a shop window.

In Chapter Twenty Six Mayor Cox addresses the Civic Board and denies that the city has a race problem. Edgars, a member of the Board, also speaks, declaring the extent of the gang and race problem in Harding and advising that

Marcus Slade will be speaking in the South City part of Harding on June 29. In Twenty Seven Neiman and Longtin make love in a motel room and work out their plan to get compromising photographs of Coolidge. In Twenty Eight, at the joint funeral of Rita and Miriam Kalowski, Frank jumps into his wife's open grave.

In Chapter Twenty Nine, on 30 April, Meg DeClancy, a student at Harding, tries to seduce Edgars in the classroom. As he pushes her off, Janet Cross enters the room, briefly sees what is happening and runs off. In Thirty Janet Cross runs from Edgars' classroom and remembers being caught spying on her prostitute mother, as she turned tricks. She runs into the arms of Arnie Kalowski and cries. In Thirty One Meg DeClancy refuses Edgars' instruction to go with him to the headmaster's office. She yells 'Rape' and Edgars slaps her. He then forcibly takes her to Coolidge's office. Coolidge interviews both while enjoying the salacious aspects of the drama. Edgars leaves DeClancy with Coolidge and goes in search of Cross. In Thirty Two, Kalowski drives Cross home. She tells him of her dream to become an obstetrician. In Thirty Three Coolidge fires Edgars, by telling him his contract will not be renewed in June. Edgars then goes to Rowsmith's apartment to discuss the decision with her.

In Chapter Thirty Four Longtin arrives at Coolidge's home. As she and Coolidge undress Neiman is perched outside a window with a camera. He proceeds to take four shots, catching Coolidge in compromising positions. In Thirty Five, after realizing he has been photographed, Coolidge attacks Longtin with a lamp but soon desists and she escapes. In Thirty Six Arnie Kalowski visits the police to discuss his sister's death. Detective Lt. Proby mentions that he is investigating what he calls the 'Hardware Gang' (actually McCullough and his associates) who have been stealing guns and ammunition. Proby tells Arnie that Miriam had quit her job before her death.

In Chapter Thirty Seven Slade dreams of the night he was beaten by three rednecks for refusing to leave a white's only bar. His spine was broken and he was left wheelchair-bound (this scene reminds the reader of Odetta Holmes/Detta Walker/Susannah Dean of the *Dark Tower* Cycle). In Thirty Eight Neiman, who assists the school janitor, has a copy of the Harding High School keys made. In Thirty Nine it is now the first Friday in June and summer has arrived in Harding. Arnie Kalowski calls Janet Cross and asks for a date. She reluctantly agrees, stating it will be her first real date. The night before Arnie had driven to Bill Danning's house. In Forty Rowsmith goes to Meg DeClancy's house and convinces her to tell the truth about the Edgars incident.

In Chapter Forty One, during a meeting at the Club, McCullough outlines his plan for June 29 to his associates – Jigs, Neiman, Venness, Bull-Run, Hash, Marty and Spooner. The basic plan is to start a race riot during Slade's visit and, while the police are dealing with it, rob various banks and stores in the city, stashing the loot at Harding High School. In Forty Two Arnie Kalowski and Janet Cross leave on their date. In Forty Three Neiman gives copies of the blackmail photos and two of the negatives to Longtin. They discuss how to extract money from Coolidge. In Forty Four summer builds in Harding. On 13 June the Harding High School Senior class graduates, Arnie Kalowski and Janet Cross among them.

Part Three is titled *Full Dark*. In Chapter Forty Five Cross cancels her date with Arnie for that Saturday but asks to meet him at the Library the next day. Frank Kalowski is grieving and slowly losing his connection with reality. In Forty Six Edgars and Arnie speak on Edgars' last day at the school and Edgars is surprised that Arnie has decided not to apply to MIT. Arnie tells Edgars of his suspicions about his sister's death and they debate Arnie's future. In Forty Seven Edgars visits Edie Rowsmith's home and tells her that even though Meg DeClancy had changed her story the School Board will not renew his contract. Then they make love. In Forty Eight Arnie Kalowski is sitting in a go-go joint when Longtin comes in and offers to have sex with him. He loses his virginity to her in his car.

In Chapter Forty Nine McCullough visits The Arcade, plays various games and seriously beats a boy. In Fifty Arnie and Janet meet at the Library. Janet tells him that her real mother was a prostitute; and that she and a pimp had tried to kill Janet for spying on the mother turning a trick. The pimp tried to force Janet into an oven and she suffered burns. As a result the City Welfare Department had taken Janet away and a year later Dean Cross and his wife had adopted her. In Fifty One Longtin rings Coolidge and demands $10,000 for the incriminating photos. In Fifty Two Frank Kalowski finally suffers a mental breakdown. Dr. Scott talks to Arnie and recommends that Frank be committed. Arnie becomes angry and demands his father be sent home. In Fifty Three Arnie determines to get drunk and meets a wino, Samuel Delaney. They drink together before Arnie wanders drunk and alone into the South City.

In Chapter Fifty Four a photographer, Galey Womack who had developed the photos of Longtin and Coolidge went to the Club and demanded money for copies of the photos. Neiman had told McCullough that the flash on the camera had not worked and there were no photos. McCullough paid Womack $30 but told Marty to follow him to Womack's shop, beat him and trash the shop. In Fifty Five Slade meditates and remembers the power of the crowd – which he had first learnt at a baseball game at Shea Stadium.

In Chapter Fifty Six it is Sunday 24 June. Arnie Kalowski takes Frank Kalowski home from hospital. Arnie rings Bill Danning's house but hangs up after the phone rang for sixty seconds. In Fifty Seven Edie Rowsmith remembers that Edgars had apologized for having sex with her. She had replied, 'I love you, John.' His last words to her had been, 'Don't, Edie, don't'. She visits Paradise Park and finds Janet Cross at the Beach. They talk briefly. In Fifty Eight, Arnie Kalowski goes to Danning's home, where Danning admits that he and Miriam Kalowski had had an affair. Arnie hits him and leaves, then calls Janet Cross and tells her what he has done.

In Chapter Fifty Nine it is now Monday 25 June. Henry Coolidge puts the blackmail money into in a gym bag at his office at Harding High. In Sixty Spooner, staking out Coolidge's house follows him to Paradise Beach where Coolidge arrives to pay Neiman off. Jigs, Bull-Run, Marty and McCullough had followed Neiman and Longtin to the same location. In Sixty One Neiman and Longtin take the blackmail money from Coolidge. McCullough and his men then jump them. Neiman tries to stab McCullough but Bull-Run breaks his wrist. Neiman is severely beaten but Longtin escapes in Marty's Pontiac. In Sixty Two McCullough's men throw Neiman's body off the pier. Elsewhere, Coolidge remembers being in the Army in Germany, where a girl had jacked him off in a Berlin club.

In Chapter Sixty Three it is 26 June. Arnie Kalowski and Janet Cross make love in his apartment. He had told her everything the night before. In the afternoon they clean the apartment. In Sixty Four it is now Friday 29 June. Slade meets White at his San Francisco gym and gets a treatment in the steam room. He then flies out of San Francisco at 1pm Pacific time, headed for Harding. In Sixty Five, at 1pm that same day, Kenny Roth calls and invites Meg DeClancy to the dog races. In Sixty Six, still at 1pm, John Edgars rings to invite Edie Rowsmith to lunch but she decides they should go to dinner instead. In Sixty Seven, at 1pm, Webs McCullough calls a meeting of his men at The Club. He briefs everyone on the final plan for that night. In Sixty Eight, at 1pm, Kit Longtin rings Arnie Kalowski but the phone is not answered. In Sixty Nine and still at 1pm, Arnie Kalowski tells Janet Cross he wants to marry her but she replies that they are too young. They argue and she leaves. Kit Longtin gets through to Arnie by phone and they agree to meet at Uncle Pete's that evening.

In Chapter Seventy Slade arrives in Harding. In Seventy One it is the evening of 29 June. Rowsmith and Edgars meet for dinner at Uncle Pete's in Harding. She tells him something of her past, including the story of her dead boyfriend, Donald Knowles. Don's mother had murdered him after he decided to marry Edie while she lived with the Knowles family in Gates Falls, Maine. They also see Arnie Kalowski having dinner at the restaurant with Kit Longtin. As the chapter ends the riot is beginning in Harding.

In Chapter Seventy Two Janet Cross had wandered Harding that afternoon. She went to the movies, fell asleep and woke at 9.30pm. She went to Mike's Place but walked in on a confrontation between gangs. A Negro boy took her out the back of the restaurant and raped her. In Seventy Three Kenny Roth and Meg DeClancy return to the downtown from the dog races and head for a floating craps game behind Uncle Pete's. They are attacked and Roth is beaten and stabbed. Meg runs. Nearby, oil tanks explode. In Seventy Four the Slade rally begins at 8.25pm. Slade whips the African Americans in the audience into a frenzy. Suddenly, Webs McCullough yells racial abuse and throws a smoke bomb, causing a panic. In Seventy Five McCullough and his men escape Slade's rally. The rioting spreads in Harding. Webs' group arm themselves. Slade tours the streets of the South City in the back of a pickup truck, urging people to go home.

In Chapter Seventy Six an oil tank explosion finds Kit Longtin and Arnie Kalowski in a cheap fleabag hotel room on Dock Street, where they had just had sex. They leave the Hotel but one of Arnie's car tires is flat and he has to change it. Fire-trucks head toward the oil tank and docks fire. Four African Americans shoot at Arnie and Kit as they drive off. Arnie swerves to avoid hitting a woman, crashing the car into a light pole and stalling it. They run from the car into the crowd. In Seventy Seven, Coolidge sits at home, reading childhood books. His wife, Ann had gone to the Slade rally. He drives to his office where he falls asleep.

In Chapter Seventy Eight the Riot is described. Three separate 'rumbles' occur between the Dock Street Socializers (white) and Memorial Circle Traders (black) gangs and there are many deaths. It is interesting to note that during a gang fight between the Socializers and the Turner Street Oligarchs in 1962 a boy was turned into a vegetable after a brick was dropped on his head, reminding us Jack Mort from the Dark Tower Cycle. The firemen at the Docks fire are nearly helpless and the fire spreads to nearby tenements. The National Guard is called out. Thirty two people have been killed by midnight. In Seventy Nine Slade continues to try to get people off the streets but a white man shoots him. In Eighty McCullough's group robs the South City Savings and Loan, using plastic explosives bought with some of the blackmail money. They take the haul and head toward Harding High School. In Eighty One Rowsmith, who had served as a nurse during the Second World War, helps at the temporary infirmary in a police station and is there when a shocked Janet Cross is brought in.

In Chapter Eighty Two Kit Longtin is put on a police-protected city bus, leaving Arnie Kalowski to be put to work fighting the fires. He comes across Edgars who is also helping the firemen. After calling Rowsmith at the police station they set out to meet her there. In Eighty Three Coolidge awakes in his office and realizes there are people in the school. Coolidge shoots Pete Venness with a BB pistol. McCullough returns fire with a shotgun, killing Coolidge. In Eighty Four Coolidge is dead; Pete Venness wounded in the eye. McCullough locks Venness, the money and Coolidge's body in his office. Jigs, now realizing the danger McCullough presents, shoots him. Bull-Run then throws Jigs down the stairs, seriously injuring him. In the mayhem, McCullough accidentally shoots Bull-Run in the head. Marty, Spooner and Hash run, taking the unconscious Jigs with them; and in Eighty Five McCullough dies as he crawls back toward the money.

In Chapter Eighty Six, Slade wakes up in hospital and sees Roy at his bedside. He is then taken into surgery. In Eighty Seven the National Guard arrives in Harding and the fire is contained. A doctor tells Rowsmith that Cross had been raped. In Eighty Eight Arnie Kalowski and Edgars arrive at the infirmary. Edie Rowsmith tells them that Janet Cross had died at 2.50am that morning (30 June). Arnie screams and runs from the infirmary as dawn is just beginning to show.

Part Four is titled *Good Mornin', Blues*. In Chapter Eighty Nine Meg DeClancy awakens, having survived the riot. In Ninety Slade comes to after surgery. He will live and the attempted assassin has given himself up. In Ninety One the remaining gang members' car blows a tire 100 miles from Harding. Jigs had died during the trip. In Ninety Two Edgars drives Rowsmith to her apartment and they discuss both Arnie Kalowski's situation and the causes of the riot. They go inside, together. In the concluding Chapter, Ninety Three, Arnie Kalowski arrives home. Edie Rowsmith rings him and they agree to meet at 3pm. Arnie then tells his still catatonic father that he loves him and gets him ready for bed.

Although it has not been published *Sword and the Darkness* represents the debut of a famous King town – Gates Falls, Maine. Edie Rowsmith lived there with John and Cass Knowles before his mother murdered John and Edie moved to Harding. Gates Falls is one of King's earliest towns and he has continued to mention it throughout his career. It is a key location in *Graveyard Shift*, *It Grows on You*, *The Revenge of Lard Ass Hogan* and *Riding the Bullet*. It is also mentioned in *Blaze*, *The Body*, *The Dark Half*, *The Dead Zone*, *Gramma*, *Hearts in Atlantis*, *Movie Show*, *Mrs. Todd's Shortcut*, *Needful Things*, *The Plant* (the electronic version only), *Rage* and *'Salem's Lot*. The town of Gates Center is mentioned and it also appears in *It Grows on You*.

Harding, based on Detroit as noted earlier, itself appears to be the same city in which Richards lived in *The Running Man*.

Chapter Seventy One is the most powerful section of the entire novel and would make a superb stand-alone story, subject to some rewriting and editing by King. This Chapter tells Edie Rowsmith's back-story in Gates Falls, Maine before the War. In reading this Chapter I formed the view that as a stand-alone effort it would represent one of the top ten or so of King's short stories. In my opinion, if a reader did not know this was King's writing from 1970 most would assume it was from a later King period, most likely the early 1980s. This makes it some of the most exciting of the material at the Fogler, a clear if slightly unpolished view of Stephen King the professional writer. Indeed, this discovery makes it clear that King was destined to be a writer of the horrors humanity inflicts upon itself as much as mainstream horror, and most certainly not the standard run-of-the-mill writer of race riot and 'contemporary' novels.

As publication of this book neared King kindly agreed to allow this Chapter to be published, as originally written. It follows this review (readers should tackle the Chapter *before* reading the next paragraph).

Edie Rowsmith's story is a poignant as any King has ever produced. She related it to her school teacher friend and lover, John Edgars, the night of the Harding riots. Edie was one of twelve children, only four of whom lived beyond the age of five. Her only surviving brother died of peritonitis aged fifteen. She attended Gorham Normal School before moving to Gates Falls, Maine in 1938, where she began teaching at a two-room school. She boarded with the Knowles family. She and the son, Donald, fell in love. Don was college educated, worked at a bank in Brunswick and in addition to being the apple of his mother's eye was also the focus of her ambitions. On 31 January 1939 Don returned to Gates Falls with an engagement ring for Edie. When Don told his mother he wanted to marry Edie she killed him with a kindling hatchet and cut off his genitals. Edie found the body later that morning, along with a catatonic Cass Knowles. Cass ended up in a 'place' in Augusta. Her dreams lost, Edie moved to Harding and Edgars was the first chance she'd had for real love in the intervening thirty years.

One of the more interesting characters is 'Webs' (short for 'Cobwebs') Mc-Cullough, a psychopath in the tradition of *The Dead Zone*'s Greg Stillson. A white man born and raised in Wilmot, Pennsylvania, at an early age he began to kill cats and dogs. Aged fourteen, he killed a nine year old boy with a piece of rusty pipe. He left Wilmot at the age of 15 and five years later turned up in Harding, where he revamped a local gang, the Oligarchs. In between he had killed an itinerant laborer in south Texas and an old woman in Reno. He always wore dark glasses. He planned and started the riot in Harding in June 1969 as a cover for a series of robberies. One of the gang members shot him on the night of the riots after his psychopathic streak became too much even for them and he died shortly afterwards.

As one of King's earliest attempts at a novel *Sword in the Darkness* has numerous weaknesses, not the least of which is its overcomplicated, schizophrenic nature. There are simply too many storylines competing for the reader's attention, many of which add nothing to the overall impact. On the other hand it is exciting to see King literally bursting from the cocoon of his youth and college career, only three years before *Carrie* would be accepted for publication. Many of King's trademarks are clearly evident and future researchers will perhaps use this manuscript as a benchmark in King's career – one of the last transitional works before he became a fully-fledged brand-name author.

The story has a Bachman flavor to it, with its dark, unrelenting spin deeper and deeper into disaster. This Bachman feel is not unexpected, considering a number of the novels later published as Bachman paperback originals were written very early in King's career.

Another major flaw in the novel is the multitude of characters, which tend to overwhelm the reader and make it hard to keep all in focus. The gang members in particular go by a series of complicated nicknames and their gangs are hard to keep apart. The reader may also find it unclear which groups and characters are white and which black, something of a problem in a race riot novel. On the positive side King does a great job of showing the motivations of almost every character, a skill he would quickly refine, and presents Harding as a fully-fledged, living city through skillful and observant description.

King has made it quite clear that this novel will never be published, even in a revised form. The subject matter, a race riot, is highly dated and would perhaps even lead to accusations about King's motives in choosing such subject matter. At one point in his career there were ridiculous implications that King was somehow racist in his portrayal of African-American characters. These accusations did not stand even the simplest scrutiny.

In the author's opinion King's decision never to publish this novel is the correct one. While epic in scope and a compelling story it suffers from a certain lack of literary maturity. It *is* immensely interesting to observe the early developmental stages of the style that would become King's and shows us something of the writer who was to take the publishing world by storm.

CHAPTER 71 – SWORD IN THE DARKNESS BY STEPHEN KING

Editor's Note: For more detail of King's unpublished novel, Sword in the Darkness, *see the previous chapter. We thank Stephen King for allowing the publication of the Chapter below.*

As the Chapter opens on June 29 of 1969 disaster is about to visit the midwestern city of Harding. A criminal gang, led by the psychopathic Webs McCullough, is about to set off a race riot by creating a disturbance at a speech by black activist Marcus Slade. During the riot they plan to commit a series of robberies while the police are otherwise engaged.

As these events are about to unfold two teachers from Harding High School, Edie Rowsmith and John Edgars meet at Rowsmith's apartment before heading to dinner. Edgars had recently been dismissed from the school after being falsely accused of sexual harassment by a student and intended to leave town to remake his life. He and Rowsmith, some twenty years older than Edgars, had formed a casual romantic attachment.

He was five minutes early and sat in the living-room leafing idly through a copy of *Newsweek* while she carefully applied her lipstick. It had taken her almost a half-hour to make up; maybe she wasn't old (no maybe about it), but habits and fears were hard to reverse. She had a horror of making herself look garish, had been subconsciously afraid all afternoon that she would end up looking like Bette Davis in *Whatever Happened to Baby Jane*—that she would see herself in a sudden pained wince of his eyes.

"Well, this is the big night," John called in to her.

"It is?" She blotted the lipstick and looked at it anxiously; it was really too red. And yet anything pinker *would* be too young, perhaps make him think she was trying to be kittenish.

"Marcus Slade," Edgars said. "He speaks at South City Manual Trades tonight."

"I'd forgotten," she said, unhappily slipping her lipstick back into its holder. "Do you think he'll get a big crowd?" She ventured timidly through the door. She had worn the green dress with the low back—worn it almost defiantly. She had studied her neck and shoulders in the mirror. It looked good. Dammit, it looked good. The skin was smooth, unmarked. The skin of a girl, still.

He got up. "Yes, I think they'll turn them away at the doors. You look fine, Edie."

She felt the weight slip from her shoulders. "I look like what I am," she said dryly. "A lady French teacher on a hot night. But I'll take the compliment—I worked for it."

John grinned. He was wearing a light gray suit of some shiny fabric and a pale blue tie and he looked very fine indeed. She said so.

"Yah," he said. "Suit takes off ten pounds. But let's go."

He had parked his car in front of her building, and he drove through the heavy downtown traffic casually but well. The streets seemed oddly deserted, and the sun hung halfway over the horizon like a drop of blood.

"Red sun at night, sailor's delight," John said.

She nodded, but her thoughts were far off. Partly on Don and the evening in Gates Falls, Maine (the sun had been red that evening too, but it had been winter, a cold sun), and partly somewhere else, in a casual kind of limbo.

"John?"

"Yes."

"I think you're the nicest person I've met in Harding. And I've been here a long time."

"You're New England, aren't you?"

She was startled, then amused. "It still shows?"

"Only a little." They had skirted The Circle and were now approaching the docks; she could smell the salt, the fish odor, could see the dusty pigeons that flapped and wheeled against the darkening sky. "The way you go light on your r's. The way you drop your g's on some of your -ing words."

She smiled. "I was born in Scarborough, Maine. My mother was a schoolteacher and my father was a carpenter. They were quite a couple. Quite a couple." She looked down at her hands, plain, rather long-fingered, unringed. "I was the fifth of thirteen children. Eight of them died before they were five. My only brother, John, died of peritonitis when he was fifteen. He kept a journal. I have it. It's remarkable. I think he might have been quite a writer one day."

"And your sisters?"

"One died of breast cancer two years ago. Cal and Lois are both married. Pennsylvania and California."

"Why did you never marry, Edie?"

"I almost did. His name was Donald Knowles. He—" she hesitated only fractionally—"he was a great deal like you, John. Very nice. Gentle."

"What happened?"

"He died."

"I'm sorry," John said. He put on his blinker and she looked up to see they were turning into the parking-lot of Uncle Pete's. She blinked, a little surprised. She had all but forgotten where they were going.

"At times I am too," she said. "Sorry, that is. Sometimes not. I've had a reasonably good life. Not an exciting one, but good. I am satisfied." She told the lie with a calm ease.

"You're a remarkable woman, Edie." He stopped, and the car-park boy came over.

"You've said that before," she said, suddenly grinning. It wasn't an easy grin. The memory of Don, unquiet in its grave for so long, seemed to be stirring with a disquieting life of its own. Things better left covered were shifting. It frightened her.

John gave the car-park boy a dollar and they went inside. Uncle Pete's was all done in blue—blue tables, blue chairs, blue lights. An unobtrusive band dressed in midnight-blue tuxedos was playing an unobtrusive tune which also sounded blue. No one was dancing.

The headwaiter, also tricked out in blue, seated them, produced menus, then retired. "My God, the prices are unbelievable!" she said. "John, you can't—"

He put a finger across her lips.

"No more," he said. "This is my night, Edie. Give me what I want."

She smiled. "All right, Mr. Edgars. You asked for it." John beckoned the waiter, and she proceeded to order a huge steak (Maine or no Maine, she had always detested seafood), shoestring potatoes, peas, a small salad, and ice cream to follow. John ordered lobster.

"And to drink?"

Edie hesitated for a moment, at a loss, and John said promptly: "Martinis. Wine with the meal, which I leave to your discretion." The waiter nodded and melted away.

She was about to say something about martinis making her giddy when she stopped, hesitated, and said: "Isn't that Arnie Kalowski over there?"

"Where?"

"To your right."

He turned a little and looked. It was Arnie. He was with a stunning blonde girl who was wearing a low-cut blue minidress that had half the men in the room watching every twitch of her nyloned legs. And Arnie was looking at her with a kind of low-key lust that she could feel from where she sat. It was as if she had put her face perhaps two feet from an open fireplace.

"It's him, all right," John said. "I wasn't sure at first. He's aged five years since his people died. The girl's a knockout, isn't she? I've seen her around school, I think."

"She's Kitty Longtin," Miss Rowsmith said. "Mr. Coolidge's niece. She has a reputation."

"Oh?"

"Yes." She was about to say more but just then the waiter appeared with the drinks and she decided not to. She remembered Janet Cross, sitting beside her on the green bench, and how they had talked and looked at the bronzed people on the littered beach.

"He looks strung out," John said thoughtfully. "He wouldn't be taking drugs, would he?"

"Arnie?" The question surprised her, and she was upset to realize that she didn't know. "I don't think so. It's…everything, I think. Everything that's happened to him. It's too bad."

They tried to pick up the threads of conversation, but something had gone out of it. She felt Arnie's presence behind them like a dull pressure on her back, and could see it in John's eyes, too—that baffled, frustrated look that comes when you had to face something indecipherable, off the tracks, wrong. Failure. *Too bad.* The words echoed in her mind, and she thought of the day Earl Neiman had called Arnie a hunky in class.

The food came, and they ate. The band played old standards, and not many people danced. The steak was excellent, but she only tasted it in an absent way. The dessert was slow in coming and nowhere near excellent.

After, John lit a cigarette and said, "Well, it was a bust, wasn't it?"

"It was fine, John Edgars, and you know it."

"It was a bust. I wanted us to have a good meal and a good time and Arnie Kalowski and his girl with a reputation spoiled it."

"Not your fault, John."

"It is," he said softly. "It is. He came to me, Edie. For help. He wanted somebody to get him off dead center…somebody to make him move again. In any direction. And that was a bust, too. He walked out just like he walked in."

"I doubt that," she said softly.

He put his hand over hers and she shivered a little. "I'm going to miss you, Edie. Very much."

She felt her eyes sting, and suddenly she was crying. She dabbled at her eyes with a napkin. "You shouldn't go, John. You're running away. Stay here and fight their lousy system. That's what young men are for. Fighting lousy systems."

He avoided her eyes. "I'm not all that young, Edie. Maybe that's one thing that Arnie taught me. I want a clean slate and a fresh start. Harding has gone sour in my mouth."

"That's what we were going to have," she said softly. "Don and I. A fresh start. A new place. We even talked about this place, although we talked about lots of others, too."

"And he died."

"He was murdered," she said. The band was playing *Stardust*. "His mother killed him."

"Lord God—you don't mean literally—"

"Literally. Quite literally. There's nothing more literal than a kindling hatchet, is there?"

And suddenly it came back to her, the thing that had been stirring, that awful Gothic thing that had been buried for years. And here it came at her, covered with the rot and slime of years, lurching through this amazingly blue restaurant like a horrifically absurd Frankenstein's monster. It came back to her, home to roost. It came rushing back through all the vacuum barriers of the intervening years (the dry, closed years) with an ease that terrified her—as if it had been waiting, crouched directly under the trapdoor of her conscious mind, alive and well, thank you. The blood, the smell of burning apple pies, the icicles hanging from the eaves beyond the kitchen windows, and the woman, the horrible, drooling woman crouched in the corner with Don's genitals wrapped in her apron.

"I'm going to be sick," she said. "Get me out."

They rose quickly and he guided her across the room (the orchestra was playing *As Time Goes By*—it made her want to cackle) and she was vaguely aware that they had passed Arnie's table, but neither Arnie nor the girl had looked up, lost in their own thoughts.

She didn't throw up. The air of the parking lot was warmer than inside, but it was fresh. Even the lingering odor of fish seemed to make her feel better. It was, after all, here and now.

"Do you feel better?"

"Yes." She smiled a little shakily. "It happened a long time ago. Too long ago to throw up over."

"Can you talk about it?"

She looked up at him. "I don't know. I never have. I never did."

"Come on." He took her arm and led her back to the car. The car-park boy came over (he was black, Edie saw, and she was reminded of Luke) and John gave him another dollar. "The lady isn't feeling well. We thought we'd just sit in the car for awhile."

The boy nodded and went away. Even his shadow looked blue, a dark blue cutout against the arc-lamped cement.

John helped her in, got in himself, and lit a cigarette. He said nothing. He simply smoked and said nothing. Edie tried to think of how he had felt inside her, that strange feeling of pressure and *parting*. She could not recapture it. She opened her mouth twice and nothing came out. The third time she said, "Perhaps we'd better go."

"I don't think so," he said, and his voice was as crisp and blue as the car-park boy's shadow. It brought her mixed feelings of reassurance and fear. "Edie, I've wanted to do something for you...apart from the other thing. We did that together, and that was good, but I want there to be more. For both of us. It's necessary. For you and I both. It's the last thing. A hard way to go, but a good way."

She began to protest, but he held up a hand. "We love each other, Edie. We do. It has to be this way."

Edie stared at him, all her feelings frozen.

"You loved Don and you love me. Maybe they're both mixed up. But I only love you. I want to see you whole before I go away. Tell me. Tell me."

She touched his hand and he gripped it. She uttered a very small, unhappy laugh. "My system finds the act of vomiting very distasteful, John. The last time I threw up was twelve years ago at my older sister's wedding anniversary. There was a plate of bad shrimp. And even then - - "

"Make yourself," he said harshly. "Stick your finger down your throat, if you have to."

"Hold me, then. Hold me, John."

He put an arm around her and drew her against him. She pressed against his shoulder. She felt better. She put a hand to her forehead, nervously, and collected her thoughts.

Somewhere out on the lake a boat tooted, and that was a blue sound, too. John sat and smoked. He was very quiet.

"I was born in Scarborough," she said suddenly. "I went to Gorham Normal School, which was not far from there, and I graduated fifth in my class. I was a good student. I was dedicated to the idea of teaching. I wanted to teach. It wasn't a case of those who can't do something end up teaching it. I was like a missionary.

"Most of my class—the men at least—went out of state. My mother wanted me to teach in Scarborough or Portland. I didn't want to do that, and I didn't want to go to New York where the money was good. I got a position out in the piney woods, a place called Gates Falls. I'd sent out a number of inquiries, and that was the second lowest-paying place. I picked it over the first lowest because the conditions sounded worse at Gates Falls. An idealist, do you see?

"I was hired—by mail and with hardly any questions asked. My mother wept and my father took me aside and said: Don't you get caught alone with boys bigger than yourself, Edie. Do you understand what I am talking about?

"I had two suitcases and a toilet box and a copy of *The Ladies' Magazine* to read on the train. I got onboard at the old Union Station in Portland—there's a shopping center there now, I understand—and the train pulled out at 11:15 am sharp. That was the last time I ever saw my father—he died of a stroke a month later. I can remember him so well...even better than the rest of them, my mother and sisters. He was standing on the station platform in his dungarees, wearing a flannel shirt and suspenders. He had a walrus mustache and he was going bald. He and my mother and two of my sisters saw me off. They were still waving when the train went around the first bend. And when they were out of sight I sat up very straight with my toilet box behind my feet and my magazine in my lap. I didn't even cry. Do you see how idealistic I was?"

She drew a deep breath in the darkness and let it out, hoping he would say something, break the spell, somehow dam the memories that were boiling in on her, a river run over its banks.

"I was to board with a family named Knowles. Mister and Mrs. Knowles met me at the Gates Fall station and we drove back to the house in their buggy. It was a ten-mile drive, and you could smell the sea. Sometimes you could hear it, when the woods thinned.

"They were lobstering people. There was John and his wife Cass, and the children—Donald and Julia. Donald worked in Brunswick, at a bank. He was college educated, and John was very proud of him. Cass didn't let on if she was proud or not. She was thin—scrawny, really—and there were pouches under her eyes. The little girl, Julia, was a change-of-life baby, seven years old. She was solemn as the Pope.

"Don didn't come home that first night—he had business in Portland. But Cass fixed a huge roast and…and an apple pie for dessert. She made simply lovely apple pies. They won blue ribbons every Fourth at the town fair. We sat and ate and afterwards John had a cigar while Cass put the child to bed. And there I sat, watching the dark come in, listening to the sea, my toilet box safely stowed away in the bathroom, wanting my mother, wanting to be able to smell the special smell of the sachet she used, feeling lonesome and sad.

"Do you know the feeling?"

But John didn't speak. He had lighted another cigarette.

"I started the Monday following. I wrote my name on the blackboard in fine round letters—*Miss Rowsmith.* I wore a dark blue skirt and a white shirtwaist. I had put a comb in my hair.

"The rustic country school. The red Currier & Ives building peeking serenely through the elms. Gingham girls and happy little boys rolling hoops. Yes, yes, oh yes. Only this one was a yellow-gray, pitted and flaked with salt from the ocean. And there was an outhouse tacked on to the back of the building and it smelled of shit. Yes, that is the correct word. Shit. Not excrement. Much too juicy for such an academic word. Shit. It hung on the air until you hardly knew it was there. I used to sprinkle lime by the pound, but there was no drainage to speak of and the smell was always there. And the gingham girls and the bright-eyed boys turned out to be great hulking brutes and vapid sows, most of them. There was Alvah Campbell, who ran bootleg down to New Hampshire on the weekends, and there was Tom Guinn, who was supporting his mother on short lobsters. There was a boy named Joey Hall who was retarded—if you gave him a penny he would catch hopping things from under the shed stoop and eat them. Six-five if he was an inch. He used to pee himself, too. And cry about it. He might've been fifteen or he might've been thirty. It was impossible to tell. There were six girls in the whole eight grades. One was Julia Knowles. She was in the first grade. Two of them were twin sisters from Gates Center, cute and almost dear. They always dressed alike and held hands. One of them was a slut named Karen Genack. Fast? She was a streak. I caught her in the shed one recess with Alvah. She wasn't wearing any underwear. She was leaning up against the birch stovelengths and she had his money in one of her hands. She had him in the other.

"But all this wasn't the first day. The first day was just enough to start getting the smell of shit and to find the old books with rat-turds stuck to the covers and to sit and hear the woodchuck running under the floor. I had forty pupils and when I came home with Julia I nodded and smiled at Cass (she didn't even ask how things had gone) and then I went up to my room and cried. I decided to go home. I was homesick and disheartened and all the ideals in the world couldn't stand up higher than that smell. To the smell of shit and the vacant way Joey Hall stared at me.

"I was going to tell them at supper, but I never did. Don came back late that afternoon, fresh back from Portland and a day late, and I fell in love. I fell all at once, and there was never any question about it. He looked something like you—I said that once, didn't I?-only not quite as tall. He had blue eyes and he was wearing a tweed suit with a vest. He came just while we were sitting down to the table. Cass had the Bible to read from and she was just opening it. Julia scrambled up and threw herself at him. He laughed—a big, roaring laugh—and grabbed her up and swung her until she squealed and her underpants showed.

"John grinned and told him to come on and get his supper, and when he came to the table his father introduced us. He looked right at me, directly at me. Later on he told me he fell in love just as quick, and I think perhaps he was telling the truth. We shook hands and he sat down. He grabbed a chop and was starting to tell about his trip when Cass said: I was going to read from the Book, Donald. Course, unless you *mind*. She looked sour and put out.

"Don just smiled and said she should read the prodigal son story. Cass said: Don't you be *flip*, and she read from Job. By the time she was done, the chops had stopped steaming. We were all quiet for a minute. Cass closed the Bible and looked around at us, almost like a queen. But she looked like a chicken, too—an old hen whose laying days are done but who still rules the roost. It sounds funny, saying she looked like a queen and a chicken at the same time, but she did and it wasn't—funny, I mean. I think I started being afraid of Cassandra Knowles right then.

"But John asked his son something about the chances of getting a railroad loan for town roads, and that broke it. Everybody ate and Don talked about loans and banking and what was new in the city. He was a wonderful talker, witty, but not a bit filled with his own importance. I don't think he had any idea what a fine conversationalist he was. After supper we went into the sitting room and Cass knitted and Mr. Knowles read from a collection of stories by Arthur Conan Doyle. There was a little fire, and Julia sat between Don and I. I forgot all about going back, and I never thought seriously about it again.

"There was Don to think about, and Julia who was bright and perky enough when Cass wasn't around, and there was Peter van Nook. Peter was in the fifth grade. He was the son of factory people, and he came to school in the most horrible scarecrow pants and shirt. But his hair was always brushed and his fingernails were clean. He'd already read his way through most of H.G. Wells' science-fiction novels and there was always one of those pulp magazines hidden in the back of his Spiral notebook—God knows where he got the money for them. Sometimes in the winter I'd catch him dreaming out the windows as if he could see way past the snow and the slush. He wrote beautiful papers about countries he made up in his mind. Sometimes he drew pictures to go with them.

"The rest was pretty bad. It was the smell of shit and the blank wall of stalled minds. The ideals couldn't get past those things, but I held onto the ideals some way—Don had something to do with that. So I kept them. Their horizons had shrunk a good deal, but I kept them. And they seemed to center more and more around Don and that little boy with the pulp magazines. Peter. The other boys used to call him Nooky. I guess that word meant the same then that it does now. But he was strong enough, that was the fine thing. He wouldn't back off from them. He played ball and once he got hit by a pitch and his nose bled. I wanted him to go inside but he just sniffed it back and went on batting. He looked so little, waving the one big old splintery bat we had, blood on his nose and the front of his shirt.

"Then I got word that my father was gone."

"I went home for the funeral and to mourn with my family, and it would have been easy to stay home, but I didn't. I brought back a copy of *The Thousand and One Nights* for Peter. He was entranced. He asked me to write my name in it. A few weeks later, he came up to me after school. He wanted me to help him think of a way to earn the money for a library card in town. I offered to give him the money and he wouldn't take it and I was glad. I sat him to chopping kindling for the school stove, half an hour after school every night, twenty cents a week. By the end of the first week I had kindling enough for the rest of the winter and Peter was starting on stove-lengths.

"And it seemed I was staying on because I'd found somebody worth staying on for, but there was more than one. There was two. There was Don.

"When I came back after the funeral he began courting me. I didn't want to be courted; I wanted to grieve. There was a hole where my father had been. I kept seeing him on the Union Station platform, his arm around mother, in his overalls, in his walrus mustache. And I hadn't cried when I left home. It almost seemed as if his death was God's way of punishing me for not crying.

"Don didn't ask me to go riding until Thanksgiving. It snowed—just a powdering, like confectioner's sugar, and Cass laid out a tremendous spread, all of it with a sour face, like something in her stomach was bad and hurting her. She sometimes mumbled to herself in the kitchen when she must have thought she was alone, strange little half-prayers that made me uneasy. It was as if God walked with her, like He walked with Esau. Except that Cass's God wasn't Esau's. Sometimes she made faces. I don't think she had any idea she was doing it. As if there were ropes and pulleys inside her head, and her God was yanking on them every now and again, just to remind her. I tried to ignore it. It was her affair. That's the way people are in New England—or maybe everywhere.

"When he asked me to go out riding in the snow I said I was too tired. He said: That's not it, you know that's not it. With no school how'd you get so tired? I said: My mind is tired, Don. My father died, don't you remember? He said: If you brood over it, it will just hurt the longer. I'll take you into Gates and buy you a sundae at Roth's. I said: I'd rather not, Don, thanks. I'm full anyway. He said: Please? And I said all right, almost as if I were doing it to be polite, but I wasn't, I wanted it to be just politeness because my father was dead and I hadn't even cried the last time I saw him alive, but it wasn't that way. I wanted to go. I wanted him to love me because I already loved him.

"So we went riding that first time, and I can remember looking back just as we left the dooryard and seeing Cass looking out of the kitchen window at us. And the ropes and pulleys were making her muscles work with the faces she didn't know she was making and I almost screamed because she looked like a gargoyle.

"There was a lot of snow that early winter. I was out of school almost as much as I was in it. The sky was the color of lead and the smell of salt was always in the air, and the gulls would come right up to your feet for a scrap of bread or a piece of suet. Peter van Nook got his library card and asked me what he should get first. I recommended *The Count of Monte Cristo*. That same day I caught Alvah and Karen Genack in the shed. She screamed at me and tried to claw my face. I had to slap her. She slapped me back and ran out. She left her bloomers on the floor. Alvah stood there with his…his penis still in…a state of excitement. He grinned and said: She wanted too much anyway. He took a step toward me and I said: Kindly tuck yourself in, Alvah. And he looked down at himself and then looked at me and then took another step. I shut him in the woodshed and locked the door. He started pounding on it. He pounded and cursed and kicked, and I went on with my third grade geography lesson.

My heart was going like a crazy clock. Fifteen minutes or so later I saw him tramping down over the hill, plowing through snow up to his knees. He must have let himself out through the shed window. He came back the next day looking embarrassed and mumbled a little apology at the floor. I accepted it. Karen Genack never came back.

"When the snow was hard enough on the roads, Don took me out in the sleigh, both of us all wrapped up in robes, and when it got near Christmas he put bells on the horse, which was named Jason, and it was so gay! It was all very gay and sweet, like a fine wine that makes your mind warm.

"On Christmas eve, when we were coming home from town, he kissed me for the first time—he was very proper, you see. Very sweet and proper. It was snowing and almost dark and everything was white and gray and violet. His nose was cold on my cheek but his lips were very warm. He said: I'm afraid I love you, Edie. I said: Afraid? He laughed and said: No. No, not afraid. I said: I love you. Kiss me again. So he did and Jason found his way home by himself.

"When the traveling was passable, I went home for a week. It was the longest week of my life. Mother cried on the last day, but she didn't ask me to stay home. She wanted to, but she was very strong. When I got back, Don asked me to marry him. I said yes, and he almost squeezed the life out of me. We were in the entry and my bags were on the floor and we kissed each other until I saw stars. I said: Have you told your mother and father yet? He said: Not yet. Stay in the parlor this evening. We have to talk.

"So we talked in the parlor after Mr. and Mrs. Knowles had gone up to bed. I was knitting a sweater and he sat beside me on the divan in front of the fire. The wind groaned outside around the eaves while we talked. Or rather, while Don talked.

"He said: My father will be a happy man because of this, Edie. He's made that clear. He thinks you're a fine woman. But mother is apt to take on. You know her—or at least, you've seen her. She's strange. She wasn't, not always. Or not nearly so bad—I can't remember her when there wasn't at least a touch of the oddness. But it's gotten worse, especially in the last two or three years. My father blinds himself to it. He does not like to see what he can't cope with, and I am not sure I can blame him. Once a friend of his mentioned some kind of shaking disease and I asked him: Do you mean epilepsy? He said: Yes, that's it. Epilepsy. Father wanted her to go see a doctor in Mechanic Falls. She screamed at him. She actually *screamed* at him. That was three years after Julia was born. Father hasn't said anything since.

"He said: She may have it—epilepsy, I mean. But there's more, I think. Something in her mind itself, or her spirit. Have you sensed it? I said: Yes.

"He said: I want us to go away, Edie. Not like thieves in the night, no. That wouldn't be good or right. We'll tell them both, be married, and let the pieces fall. But after that I want to go far away.

"I said: Where? He said: Mr. Calligan at the bank recommends a town called Harding. He has a brother who works in a new bank there. Mr. Calligan says the town has a future. And Mr. Calligan will recommend me to his brother—I'm sure of it.

"I asked: Where is Harding? He told me, and I said: Why, that's halfway across the country (but the prospect rather thrilled me, and I imagine he could see that). He said: I told you I wanted to get away from here. How does it sound to you? I said: I love you. It's all right with me.

"After that we necked. It was very delicious, very satisfying. I felt him against me—hard—and it was the most amazing thing I had even felt in my life. It made me laugh and that made him laugh. He said: I'm going to bed now. While I can still go alone. I asked him when we were going to tell them and he asked me what I thought about the following night. I said that sounded fine. Then he kissed me on the base of the neck and said: Good night, Edie. I love you.

"I don't know how long it was before she came in. I sat on the divan in front of the fire, curled up like a pussycat. I felt like a pussycat, all warmness and content. There was the warmth and the love of a very definite singing in my brain. I think I dozed. Anyway, the next thing I knew, she was sitting across from me in Mr. Knowles' wing chair, with the last of the fire playing across her face in orange lights and shadows. Her face was working, bunching, twisting. She scared me and I jumped and that made her smile, just a little twitch of the lips. She was holding a book on her knees. At first I thought it was her Bible, but it wasn't. It was green. A bilious green. It reminded me of a copy of Hardy's *Tess of D'Urbervilles* I had once. Your mind associates things: Whenever I see a book that color I think of Cass, sitting across from me and making her poor unconscious faces.

"She said: He was touching you.

"I couldn't say anything. I was literally tongue-tied.

"She said: He was touching your breasts. I saw. It's coming out in him. Unto the third and fourth generations. I do not blame you. I blame myself. I blame him.

"I was sleepy and confused and it was such a turnabout from the happiness. I said the first thing that came on my tongue, and of course that was: We're going to be married.

"She didn't say anything. For a moment she just sat there with her face twisting and mugging at me (she didn't know—I'm almost sure she didn't know), and then she started to laugh. It was a dry, tittering sound, like leaves in autumn at the fall of night. She looked like a gargoyle. She said: You daren't.

"I said: What are you talking about?

"She said: It would be monstrous. Your children would be monstrous. Unto the third and fourth generations.

"I said: I'm sorry, Mrs. Knowles.

"She began to scratch her arms. Her arms were brown and tough-looking, like the branches on old trees, and she made great white marks on them that turned red. Her face worked. A log in the fireplace popped and sparks went up the chimney. I said: Do you feel all right, Mrs. Knowles?

"She said: He is a bastard.

"I said: Bast—

"She said: He was gotten in me by a railroad conductor on the Bangor & Aroostook Railroad. He was a harsh man, a big man, and we did it while my husband was working for our daily bread. We did it for the carnal pleasure of the thing. He bit me. I asked him to bite me. John and I hadn't been married two years. I took his thing in my mouth, and he put his filth in my mouth. Filth, filth. It was monstrous and filthy and I wallowed in it. He would come in with his tie pulled down and his vest open and I would reach for his fly. And he got my son Donald in me. Donald is monstrous. He is the devil's bastard.

"I stared at her. If I could have made a noise, I think it would have been somewhere between a laugh and a howl.

"She said: I have repented my sin. I have scourged myself. I have begun my atonement. Do you understand? Do you understand? Unto the third and fourth generations. I will not allow you and Donald to spawn the devil. Do you understand?

"I said: I'm going to bed. I stood up and she must have thought I was going to hit her because she shrank back in the chair. And I felt sorry for her. I never doubted that what she said had happened those years ago was true. She was literally eaten up with guilt. I felt sorry for her; she looked so little and demented. I thought she was harmless. That was where I made my mistake, John. Oh, how I wish I could go back and redo it, change it. She was like a cornered ferret, and ferrets bite, don't they, when their backs are against the wall?

"I got to the door and she whispered: Unto the third and fourth generations. I never looked back at her.

"The next afternoon I asked Don to take me out riding. We went into town and got hot fudge sundaes, and I told him the whole story. He took it very well. I can remember that he repeated the word over two or three times, tasting it, rolling it in his mouth: Bastard. Bastard. Then he asked: Did she say what his name was? I said: No. He took my hand and held it between his. He said: Does it feel any different? I said: Not a bit. He said: I love you.

"On the way back we talked about his father—his foster-father, Cass's husband. Don said: I don't think she could ever actually tell him. It's been hidden too long. I don't think she could even bring herself to tell me. I said: I hope you are right.

"He was. After supper that night Don stood up and announced that he had asked me to marry him and that the lady had said yes. Julia clapped her hands and said: *Yayyyyy!* She ran around the table and kissed me. For a moment John just looked at us, and then he dropped his napkin into his plate, smiled, and said: I could not be more pleased.

"Cass made an odd hissing noise. Her face had gone dead white. It began to twist. She knocked over her water glass getting up, seemed on the verge of saying something, and then ran out of the room. Julia had pressed herself against me. Outside it had begun to snow again.

"John said: You mustn't mind. You know how she has been, Don.

"Don nodded and his father said: Now perhaps you had better tell me your plans and how I can help.

"I said: Except for my father, you're the finest man I've ever known, Mr. Knowles.

"He got out his pipe and said: Then perhaps you ought to marry me.

"Then we all laughed, and things were a little easier. When Don told him that we planned to move here, he nodded and said that would probably be best. He said: I suppose this does not sound just right, but I think perhaps it will do your mother some good, Donald.

"Don said: I think that might be. We both looked at him, but his face was as unreadable as the back of a playing card. I still wonder how much he did know about Cass. Perhaps she talked in her sleep.

"I went to bed early. I was walking in a rose mist. April seemed an eternity away. I didn't even like to think what Cass would be like to live with for the next four months. As it turned out, I didn't have to live with her that long. Nowhere near.

"The next two weeks were heaven. I bought things. Two dresses, a set of dishes. I bought a nightie. A silk one. I felt very sinful, buying a silk nightie. I felt downright Babylonian. John went around smiling. He tried to make Cass smile too, but Cass didn't want to smile. She was beyond smiling. She cooked and she fetched the wood when Don wasn't there to do it (I offered; she only glared at me), and she read the Bible. For a while she went on reading it at the table, but John must have told her to stop. The last night she did it she read from one of the Books of Moses, something about wholesome and kingdoms of wholesome and fire and judgments.

"On the last day of January, Don came back from Brunswick with an engagement ring. It was very small—you could have put it in your eye and it wouldn't have hurt your eyesight any—but it was beautiful. Beautiful. I wept and he kissed me, and we lay down on the divan in the living room. He touched me all over and I touched him. I wanted to. He could have had me, right then. But he did not want it just then. He said: In the spring. In the spring. And we will have the windows open and we will be able to smell the earth starting to make.

"He got up and said: Good night, Edie. I love you. He was wearing his brown banker's suit, and how he *bulged*! I said: I love you too, Don. Goodnight. He said: Will you remember to take the milk out of the ice-box before you go up? I said: Yes, dear. Goodnight.

"Those were the last words he ever said to me. I loved him more than the world. He was mine and I was his and it seemed like it was us together that made the whole universe. And the last words he ever said to me were: Will you remember to take the milk out of the ice-box before you go up? How can there be a God? How can there, unless He's on an eternal LSD trip?"

John Edgars shifted his legs in the darkness. A fresh cigarette glowed. "Maybe He's just a lousy playwright. How's that for pseudo-philosophy?"

She put her hands on his. They were cold and he held them tightly, enfolding them.

"When I came home from school the next day I was really euphoric. Peter van Nook had gotten into a fight with one of his classmates, a boy named Arthur Hapgood who had been calling him a bookworm pansy. Peter thrashed him and made him take it back. Arthur finally did, after Peter almost broke his arm. Then he let Arthur go and said: I learned that hold out of a book, you stupid bastard. And Arthur said: Show me. Peter said: I'll bring the book tomorrow. And they went away with their arms around each other's shoulders. There was that, and there was Don. Don would be home when I got there—for the whole blessed and wonderful week.

"The sky was overcast, but we were having a thaw and the snow was melting. The roads were slushy but clear. All the icicles on the house were dripping, and the smell of the sea was as sharp as a slap. I took off my boots in the entry and came into the living room. I could smell apple pies. They smelled cinnamony and fresh. They smelled lovely.

"And right then, feeling as wonderful as I did, I decided to make friends with Cass. There wasn't the slightest doubt in my mind that I could do it. I could have done anything. That's how I felt.

"I pushed through the door into the kitchen—"

She was taken with a fit of shuddering and tried to draw her hands away from him. He held them and pulled her against him. He wrapped an arm around her and she pressed against his shirt, smelling the warm smell of him.

"I saw him right away. His head was in the wood box and at first I thought he had been sick. Then I saw the blood. There was blood underneath him and blood on the walls. I could smell it underneath the smell of the pies. A sharp smell, like heated metal. It smelled like a hog had been slaughtered.

"I screamed. I ran to him and tried to turn him over. I couldn't. He was too heavy. He was all…loose. God knows how many times she had hit him with that hatchet. I got blood all over the front of my dress. It was warm and gooey, like fudge-sauce. I rocked back on my heels and looked at the ceiling. I thought I was going to faint.

"That was when I heard her. I looked around and she was crouched in the corner between the stove and the wall. She was rocking back and forth and keening. There was blood on her ankles. Her eyes were closed. She didn't even know I was there. She was just rocking back and forth and clutching her apron. There was something in her apron. The hatchet was between her feet. I took two steps toward her, and I saw what was in her apron.

"She looked at me and I began wailing. I couldn't move. All I could do was stand there and wail, smelling the pies as they started to burn and hearing the icicles drip.

"She held it out to me. She said: Unto the third and fourth generations. Then I ran out. I ran straight down to the docks. It must have been a mile. I fell in the slush and screamed going down and getting up. I screamed all the time I ran. People came out and looked at me. I could smell the salt and the water but there was still the smell of apple pies. I found John and then I fainted."

There was a long, long silence in the car. She could feel something in her belly loosening, freeing itself. She began to breathe in long, shuddering sighs. He held her against him, fingers tangled carelessly in her hair.

"I went home. I had to go to the inquest, but not to the committal hearing. They put her in a place in Augusta very quietly. John Knowles wrote me a long and incoherent letter in late April. They had told him she was in something called a catatonic state and probably would be for the rest of her life. Completely withdrawn. There was, I understand, some kind of brain damage in addition to her mental obsession and feelings of guilt."

"And you?" John asked.

"I went home for a year. I didn't talk much. I did a lot of knitting and learned how to do crewl work. I went for walks. I slept a great deal. And over some space of time I decided to come here.

"My mother was fiercely against it. I was nothing but a sack of skin and bones, and she was convinced that I had consumption. She wouldn't lose me for good, that was what she said. Not after my father. It wasn't right and it wasn't fair and she wouldn't have it and that was an end to it.

"Except it wasn't the end. I applied for and got a job at the Canal Street Grammar School. I taught fourth grade. At first that meant nothing, either—my days were nothing but blurs—but I began to take an interest, little by little. There was another Peter van Nook, then another. The principal, a nice fat man named Grayson Henry, got me interested in more schooling. I began to take language courses at the University. After the war I went back full time and got my second degree. I started to teach French at Harding High School in September of 1949."

She was quiet for a long time. Finally, in a small voice, she said: "I think I'm through, John. Thank you."

"Feel better?"

"Much."

"I'm glad."

"You're not him," she said. "I started off thinking you were, and that has been part of the trouble. Do you think I've made an awful botch of my life?"

"No," he said, holding her hand. "Do you? Really?"

She smiled. "No. It's a temptation, but it's too easy. My life hasn't been a gothic novel, no matter how impossibly insane the introduction was. It's been sunny and for the most part, happy. I put romance out of it, but that seemed to be a decision above right and wrong—it seemed practical. I never realized the hole until you came along, maybe not until the afternoon that you left my bed. Then I realized the hole. I missed a whole dimension of love. Just let it slip away."

He started to speak, but she raised her head and stopped him. "No, don't say it, John. It isn't true. There may be another man—I think there could be at least that much now—but there isn't going to be another moon-June. No afternoon sleigh-rides. I'm not a late-bloomer and I don't want to be. I don't want to marry the postman and move to St. Petersburg. It's enough to know I've grown a little more."

"You're a lovely lady," he said simply. He kissed her.

She sat up and moved away from him a little, feeling a strange new lightness in her body. Her muscles felt stretchy, elastic. Her mind felt hosed down. She looked at her wristwatch.

"My Lord, John. It's almost ten o'clock. We ought to—"

A police siren started up, startling both of them. She suddenly realized that a tattered stream of people were hurrying out of the restaurant and going around the back of the building. The car-park boy walked by, going the other way, and John unrolled the window. "Excitement?"

"Aw, some boy got himself sliced."

"Bad?"

The car-park boy's face was a bland and savage mask. "Not for him no more. He daid."

Edie heard herself say "Oh dear God!"

Uptown, another siren began to wail, and they all three turned toward it. And it seemed to her that the boy's smooth brown face held something enigmatic and beyond her reach, a sense of expectancy, and perhaps of blind promise.

"John—" she began.

And then the huge explosions ripped through the night.

KING'S SCREENPLAYS

King seems to enjoy writing screenplays, either adapting his own work or, in two cases, that of another writer and writing original works for the screen. The following is a list of screenplays King is known to have written.

Asylum	Unproduced adaptation of Patrick McGrath's novel
Carrion Comfort	Unproduced original screenplay
Cat's Eye	Original movie script, released in 1985, including a wrap-around and three segments, *Cat's Eye, Quitter's Inc.* and *The Ledge*
Children of the Corn	Unproduced adaptation of his short story
Chinga	*The X-Files* episode written by King, with material added and changed by series creator, Chris Carter
Creepshow	Original movie script, released in 1982, including a wrap around and five segments, *Father's Day, The Lonesome Death of Jordy Verrill, The Crate, Something to Tide You Over* and *They're Creeping Up on You*
Cujo	Unproduced adaptation of his novel
The Dead Zone	Unproduced adaptation of his novel
Desperation	2006 TV adaptation of his novel
Dolan's Cadillac	Unproduced adaptation of his short story
General	Unproduced form of the wrap-around segment of *Cat's Eye*
Golden Years	Original TV series script, released in 1991
Kingdom Hospital	TV series, based on a Danish series, released in 2004
Maximum Overdrive	Original movie script, directed by King, released in 1986
Molly	Unproduced screenplay written for *The X-Files*
Night Shift	Unproduced adaptation of his short stories *Strawberry Spring, I Know What You Need* and *Battleground.* Also includes an original wrap-around segment
Pet Sematary	Movie adaptation of his novel, released 1989
Rose Red	Original mini-series script, debuted in 2002

The Shining	Mini-series adaptation of his novel, debuted in 1997
The Shining	Unproduced adaptation of his novel
The Shotgunners	Unproduced original movie script
Silver Bullet	Movie adaptation of *Cycle of the Werewolf*, released 1985
Sleepwalkers	Original movie script, released in 1992
Something Wicked This Way Comes	Unproduced adaptation of Ray Bradbury's novel
Sorry, Right Number	TV episode adaptation of his short story, debuted 1987
The Stand	Mini-series adaptation of his novel, debuted in 1994
The Stand	Unproduced movie adaptation of his novel
Storm of the Century	Original mini-series script, debuted in 1999
Training Exercises	Unproduced film treatment
Untitled	Unproduced telescript about a haunted radio station

Throttle (2009)

Throttle is the first published collaboration between King and his author son, Joe Hill. Hill is the Bram Stoker Award winning author of *20th Century Ghosts* (a collection), *Heart-Shaped Box: A Novel*, the *Locke & Key* graphic novel series and *Horns*.

The story is inspired by Richard Matheson's short story *Duel*[158] and has so far only appeared in print in *He Is Legend: An Anthology Celebrating Richard Matheson*, edited by Christopher Conlon (Gauntlet Publications, 2009). The book, which won the Bram Stoker Award for Superior Achievement in an Anthology for 2009, includes many fine stories riffing Matheson's outstanding canon, including *I Am Legend Too* by Mick Garris, director of many King films and TV adaptations.

It also appears on the audio book, *Road Rage* (Harper Audio), which includes both *Throttle* and *Duel*. It is unclear when, or if, the tale will be included in either a King or a Joe Hill collection.

King and Hill start this story with punch, 'They rode west from the slaughter, through the painted desert, and did not stop until they were a hundred miles away.' The reader is immediately thrown into a biker gang ('The Tribe – Live on the Road, Die on the Road') milieu. Race Adamson is a recently returned vet ('after two years in the sand') but other members, including Race's father Vince are Vietnam vets (King's understanding of these men instantly flows in this story, leavened as it must be, by Hill's influence). The slaughter occurred when the gang arrived to relieve Race's friend and Fallujah veteran and medic, Dean Clarke of $60,000 he'd borrowed to set up a meth lab (twenty grand of which had come from Race). The lab burned down the first day of operation and the bikers were determined this was not to be their financial loss. Of course, King comes back to the meth lab story line in *Under the Dome*, which is not surprising, as both stories were written about the same time.

When the gang cornered Clarke at his cabin in the hills they were surprised by his 17 year old girlfriend ('soaring on meth and clutching a little .22 in one hand). Wearing a sweatshirt that read Corman High Varsity[159], she opened fire but Roy Klowes immediately cut her down with his machete, then 'it was all sliding down the red hole, away from reality and into the territory of a bad dream.' As Clarke fled Race had killed him with one blow of a shovel. The money was gone but Race suspected Clarke might have left some with his sister, a prostitute in Show Low. While stopped at a truck stop after leaving the cabin Race and Vince discussed the killing, argued about whether to pay the sister a visit, or to return to Vegas. In anger, Race threw a glass whisky flask that smashed against the parked oil tanker they'd be standing next to during their discussion. 'Vince would've laughed if not for what he saw next. / The trucker was sitting in the cab. His hand hung out the driver's side window ... Midway up his forearm was a faded tattoo, Death Before Dishonor, which made him a vet ..' Of course, this is the set up for the King/Hill riff on *Duel*. Vince expects trouble, and is concerned about what the man might have overheard, but the vet (Laughlin, according to the name stenciled on the side of the tanker) simply started up the semi and drove off, as Vince and his men headed for the diner – 'It was almost an hour before he saw the truck again.'

Some members of the gang considered splitting to avoid getting caught up in the aftermath of the murders, even Vince's closest sidekick, Lemmy wondered if he might go and see Lon Refus out in Denver, for instance.

'The truck with LAUGHLIN on the side was laboring uphill when they caught up to it around three in the afternoon.' So the fun began. As the bikes passed the truck Vince 'cast a look up toward the driver on their way by, but could see nothing except that dark hand hanging out against the door', another direct reference to the trucker in *Duel*, who viewers and the car driver he pursues (played by Dennis Weaver) never see.

In classic King style some of Vince and Race's background is revealed when Race challenged Vince's leadership of the group as they stop at crossroads to decide whether to drive onto Show Low via a narrow two-lane road, or through 20 miles of road works. The father-son relationship had slowly broken over the years – Vince remembered telling a ten year old Race, "You know just because I'm your father doesn't mean I got to like you." He wonders, 'if he had known some other way to talk to Race, there would've been no Fallujah and no dishonorable discharge for ditching his squad, taking off in a Humvee while mortars fell; there would've been no Dean Clarke and no meth lab ...' The group decided to drive toward Show Low, and the truck followed.

The road turns out as a virtual trap for vehicles due to its narrow confines – 'To the left was a battered guardrail, and to the right was an almost sheer face of rock.' Suddenly, the truck accelerated and slammed through the rear three back bikes of the formation (King and Hill's description is at once gruesome, beautiful and, in the case of Vietnam Vet 'Doc', elegiac). 'Vince looked back again and saw the remnants of the The Tribe coming around the bend. Just seven now. The truck howled after ...'

Two more riders were run down and the truck seemed to almost supernaturally work its way through the carnage while actually speeding up, 'Vince knew Macks were fast – the new ones had a 485 power-plant under the hood – but *this* thing ... / Supercharged? Could you supercharge a goddam *semi*?' Vince desperately tried to think of a plan – he knew the road well but had not been there for some years and knew that, for the moment at least, they were trapped in a virtual canyon – with the monster truck bearing down.

They flew past a sign marking the 'played-out little mining town on the side of a hill' – Cumba, two miles ahead. As they reached the access road Vince used Morse code with his brake-light and signaled his crew to stay on the main road when the truck would expect them to exit, but Race apparently did not understand Morse, or had not seen the signal, and he swept onto Cumba's access road, with the truck in hot pursuit – and miles of dangerous hardpan dirt road ahead before Vince and his two remaining compatriots could rejoin the chase. The four men stopped to discuss the situation but Roy Klowes (the murderer of Clarke's girlfriend) simply turned tail and fled back East – leaving Vince with only his long-time tail man, Lemmy and another survivor, 'Peaches'.

Lemmy dragged out a weapon – 'The Tribe did not ride with guns. Outlaw motorheads like them never did. They all had records, and any cop in Nevada would be delighted to put one of them away for thirty years on a gun charge.' The weapon was 'Little Boy', an M84 stun grenade, which conveniently looked nothing like one, so that if searched most cops would have no idea what they were looking at. The three bikers shot off down the access road, hoping to beat the truck, and Race; and then use the grenade to save Vince's son, or at least take revenge for their losses. Vince was desperately hoping the trucker still had his cab window open, and that that Little Boy might still work after five years in Lemmy's saddlebag.

Vince raced ahead even as Peaches fell back after the head-gasket on his bike blew, considering his son and the others already lost, 'those bodies back there had, until this afternoon, been his running buddies, the only thing he had of value in the world. They had been Vince's brothers in a way, and Race was his son, and you couldn't drive a man's family to earth and expect to live. You couldn't leave them butchered and expect to ride away. If LAUGHLIN didn't know that, he would. / Soon.'

To Vince's relief, when he and Lemmy reached the place where the two roads again merged, they could hear *two* approaching engines – for the moment at least Race was still alive. Vince began to roll, trying to determine the right speed of approach, in the hope his attack might succeed. As he came up from behind the tanker, he contemplated the apparent madness of the trucker's actions and, on 'the truck's ass-end just ahead on his right, he saw something that seemed not only to sum up this terrible day, but to explain it, in simple, perfectly lucid terms. It was a bumper sticker … / PROUD PARENT OF A CORMAN HIGH HONOR ROLL STUDENT!' (Remember, Clarke's girlfriend had been wearing a Corman High sweatshirt).

Vince is able to get his shot away, lobbing the grenade through the cab window just as the trucker was about to swat him into oblivion. The grenade went off and the truck veered away, crashing through the guardrail and over a twenty foot embankment, the tanker going up in a fireball and the cab rolling past it, stopping 'with the driver's window up to sky.' Vince 'saw the figure that tried to pull itself through the misshapen window. The face turned toward him, except there was no face, only a mask of blood.' Then the body collapsed back inside the wreck. Race roared up in triumph and hugged Vince in celebration, actually calling him 'Dad'. Vince allowed this for a second before pushing his son away demanding, "What was her name?" After arguing Race allowed he knew Clarke's girlfriend's name, as Vince speculated the trucker must have overheard their conversation about the killings back in the parking lot ('Laughlin had settled on death before dishonor.') Meanwhile, Lemmy checked the cab, finding Laughlin dead and a snapshot of the very girl Klowes had chopped to pieces with his machete, sealing Vince's argument. Even now Race simply did not care – "Her name was Jackie Laughlin … And she's dead, too, so fuck her.'

Then Vince made his final choice – telling his son, "Ride on, son … Keep the shiny side up." He explained he intended to tell the police everything and Race's only chance was to hightail it. As Race rode away, he and Lemmy sat by the road, waiting for the State Police to arrive.

In the King tradition this is ultimately a tale of morality. Outside normal society he may be, but Vince does have values and respects the honorable choice Laughlin made to avenge his daughter. He finally sees through his son's lack of humanity. The juxtaposition of Vince's thought that 'you couldn't drive a man's family to earth and expect to live. You couldn't leave them butchered and expect to ride away. If LAUGHLIN didn't know that, he would,' with the reality of Laughlin's response to what *he'd* learned is worth the price of admission in itself.

This is one of the better short tales in King's canon (or, in this case, the King and Hill canon) so it is to be hoped it will receive wider circulation through inclusion in a forthcoming collection from either of these two important writers.

Untitled (The Huffman Story) (c.1976)

This story was first 'rediscovered' by the author of this book, in King's papers at the Special Collections Unit of the Raymond H Fogler Library at the University of Maine in Orono. During research for *The Complete Guide to the Works of Stephen King* I spent 17 days in November 2002 going through each page of every box in King's papers at the Library. This was one of the ten stories rediscovered and announced to the world in early 2003. While the story is untitled in King's manuscript it has been given the sub-title, *The Huffman Story* for ease of reference.

The part manuscript for this story is held in Box 2702 at Fogler and is incomplete. Although the pages are numbered to 72, there are in fact only 71 pages. There is no page 20 but it is not missing, as the text is continuous.

The tone and events of the story are hauntingly reminiscent of the Castle Rock murders in King's classic, *The Dead Zone*. Previous editions of this book indicated it might an early attempt at that novel and King has since confirmed that supposition: 'Yes, that was the book that eventually became *The Dead Zone*. The two things are entirely different in plot, but very similar in tone.'[160] As *The Dead Zone* was written in 1976 and 1977 it is likely this manuscript was written in 1976. The story itself is set from mid-January to early February 1976.

Well laid out, the manuscript is just reaching an interesting turning point at the last preserved page. It is a typical King tale in which we become deeply engrossed in the people, history and ambience (good and bad) of small town Maine within a few short pages. The characters leap off the page and the town itself seems fully realized as we rush forward with the storyline.

At the time of writing *The Huffman Story* is held in a public access box at the Fogler Library, meaning that readers who visit UMO can actually read these 71 pages.

In the story we read that on a Friday in mid to late January Tansy Dolgun arrives at her mother's shop, Pretty Penny in Huffman, Maine. A man on a park bench offers five year old Frances Tho candy. Later, Louise Bouchard, Frances' adoptive mother, reports her missing. Louise had been baby-sitting Sandy McCracken's daughter, Loretta, at the time of the disappearance. Bill Ouelette, a Huffman police officer finds Tho's body in a pond on the Town Green.

The Bouchards are given the bad news and Bob Bouchard faints. The town doctor, George Peters is called in. The County Medical Examiner is called to the murder scene and reports that Frances Tho had been stabbed and raped post mortem. The press arrives but Huffman Police Chief Andy Stone avoids them.

Harry Deems from the office of the Maine Attorney-General begins his investigation into the killing. We learn the history of the Thatcher family, headed by Morton, Senior, a local car dealer. Morton Thatcher, Junior determines to make a simple-minded town boy, 'Crazy Joe' (Joe Drogan) confess to Tho's murder. He and a friend beat Joe and leave him by the roadside suffering an epileptic seizure and with a broken nose, three cracked ribs and a mild concussion.

Bill Ouelette reminds Chief Stone Tho's killer has left no tracks. Elizabeth Drogan, Joe's mother and the local newspaper owner, reports the assault on Joe to the police. George Peters asks Janet Dolgun to dinner. We learn Elizabeth Drogan's history as something of a crusader and of her fear of telling Chief Stone what Joe had told her of being forced to 'confess'.

Elizabeth Drogan editorializes in the Huffman *Gazette-Intelligencer*. She offers rewards of $5000 in relation to the assault on Joe and $25,000 in relation to Tho's murder. We learn the sordid Chasswick family history. Tho's killer lures five-year-old Michael Chasswick into the woods behind his parent's house.

Unfortunately the story ends at this point. This is a Maine Street Horror - Huffman is in Maine and actually appears to be located in the same county as Castle Rock (interestingly, King never mentions Huffman in any other story), which is no surprise considering it is the prototype for *The Dead Zone*! This location in Castle County can be deduced from the fact that the med van boys were told to take Frances Tho's body to Castle Rock, combined with the fact that the body then fell under the control of the County Medical Examiner. (*See the feature panel for a summary of the information King provides about Huffman in the story*).

We know the killer is male, although he mysteriously left no tracks at Frances Tho's murder scene. He used comic books to lure Michael Chasswick to what we fear will be his death and also dropped a clue, the wrapper from the Tootsie Roll with which he lured Tho. Local school kids immediately nicknamed him 'The Slasher'. We can also presume the killer was a Huffman local as he knew the Chasswick's vicious dog by its name, Bopper.

Frances Tho was a five year old Vietnamese girl, adopted by Bob and Louise Bouchard as a sister for their natural children, eight year old Marilys (who was so traumatized by her sister's death that she attempted suicide with sleeping pills) and Rob. Poor Frances was stabbed as she attempted to cross the Town Green and raped post-mortem.

Confusingly, two major characters have similar surnames – Elizabeth Pillsbury Drogan (Pillsbury was King's mother's maiden name) and Janet Dolgun. Drogan was the richest person in Huffman, a power in the town, the owner of the local newspaper and a crusader on various issues, including development and the environment. Her son, Joseph, a small and constantly smiling boy was known as 'Crazy Joe'. Severely retarded and epileptic, he was viciously beaten by Morton Thatcher, Junior and his sidekick, Richie Evans in their attempt to make him 'confess' to the Tho murder.

Janet Dolgun, a widow who it seems may form an attachment with Dr. George Peters was also the mother of Tansy Dolgun, another five year old. Reading the story one cannot help but feel Tansy may become another victim (attempted, at least) of the killer. One also senses the prototype of Polly Chalmers (*Needful Things*) in Janet Dolgun. Peters was a shy 29 year old, addicted to obscure paperback Westerns (perhaps he would later read the works of Bobbi Anderson, protagonist of *The Tommyknockers*, whose first western, *Hangtown* was published in September 1975).

King sets us deeply in sympathy with Michael Chasswick, the next likely victim. Michael's mother, Charlotte, came to the aid of her five year old son, the last of her eighteen children, when she caught the boy's father, George, torturing him by burning his toes. She held a gun to George's head and threatened to kill him if he hurt the boy again. This reminds us of Dolores Claiborne's courage in defending her daughter against the sexual molestations of her equally brutal husband, Joe St George, Senior in *Dolores Claiborne*. Michael was an early developer, bright and a good reader, and King draws him as the exact opposite of the rest of his family, no-hopers who were all 'on the town'. One sister was so promiscuous she'd actually had sex with three of her older brothers, but in some sort of twisted morality, none of the younger boys! It is the very comparison between Michael and his loser family that brings the foreboding surrounding his being lured into the brush by the killer into sharp focus for the reader. Already the killer had taken an adopted Vietnamese girl, loved by all and now the one last hope of a dissolute family was at mortal risk.

The local police chief was Andy Stone, a Vietnam veteran who had uncovered a hot car ring protected by another policeman while serving as an officer in Clifton Notch, Maine. Another power in the town was the local Ford-Honda dealer, whose business was near the Bridgton town line, Morton Thatcher, Senior. A nasty man, he blamed his wife for the death of one their sons from leukemia. He doted on the surviving Morton Thatcher, Junior helping him avoid criminal charges and also represented a form of corrupt opposition to Elizabeth Drogan's campaigning. The junior Thatcher was a thug, small time criminal and habitual speeder and it was he who organized and participated in the severe beating of 'Crazy' Joe Drogan. (The Thatchers seem like early prototypes of the Rennies in *Under the Dome*).

Fans of King's mythical Castle Rock, Maine will be interested to know that Huffman is apparently in the same county as Castle Rock, which would place it in Castle County. The District Attorney covering Huffman is based in Castle Rock; and a judge there, having bought cars from Morton Thatcher, Senior's dealership in Huffman for twenty years, subsequently exonerated Morton Thatcher, Junior on one charge. However, another judge serving in the Castle Rock District Court fined the Junior Thatcher and took nine points from his license in a separate case.

From *The Huffman Story* we find that there is a State Mental Hospital located in Castle Rock and the Castle Rock District Court, as well as WODM, an FM radio station partly owned by Elizabeth Drogan (these are not mentioned in any other King story). The radio station is described as 'The Big Rock of Western Maine'. Joe Drogan was taken to Castle Rock Hospital (Royce Merrill was also taken there, in *Bag of Bones*).

Castle Rock appears in many King stories and this is one of two unpublished stories that add to the legend of that unfortunate town (the other is *Squad D*). It is also mentioned in the unproduced screenplays of *Cujo* and *The Dead Zone*.

Castle Rock is also the setting for *The Body, Cujo, Gramma, It Grows on You* (but only the *Nightmares and Dreamscapes* version), *The Man in the Black Suit, Mrs. Todd's Shortcut, Needful Things, Premium Harmony, The Sun Dog* and *Uncle Otto's Truck*. It is also a key setting in *Bag of Bones, The Dark Half, Nona* (but only the *Skeleton Crew* version) and *The Dead Zone*. It is mentioned in *Creepshow, Dreamcatcher, Gerald's Game, The Girl Who Loved Tom Gordon, The Lonesome Death of Jordy Verrill, Riding the Bullet, Rita Hayworth and Shawshank Redemption, Under the Dome* and *The Stand* (*Complete and Uncut* version).

Elizabeth Drogan had been involved in a successful campaign to stop development on the western end of Castle Lake and also to stop the drainage of sewage into it. Castle Lake is mentioned in *Cujo* (where we learn it is near Larch Street, the Trenton home in Castle Rock); *The Dark Half* (the Beaumonts had a lake home there – before the sparrows and fire destroyed it - it was said to be part of the town of Castle Rock, near Route 5); *Mrs. Todd's Shortcut* (the Todds had a lake home there, in the town of Castle Rock); and *Needful Things* (Andy Clutterbuck plunged to his death through the ice on it).

The old Huffman Mill is on Castle River, which is also mentioned in *The Body*. In that story the Castle River runs '…under the bridge between Castle Rock and Harlow …' The GW&SM trestle that Gordie Lachance and his friends crossed so dangerously also crossed the Castle River, which runs across all of New Hampshire and half of Maine.

Huffman borders Bridgton, a real Maine town and the setting for *The Mist* and a key location in *The Dark Tower VI: Song of Susannah*. Bridgton is virtually on Long Lake, on which the Kings had a home in the 1970s. In another King link the Bouchards adopted Frances Tho with the assistance of a placement agency in Boulder, Colorado. The Kings lived in Boulder in the summer and fall of 1974 and King largely wrote *The Shining* there.

THE TOWN OF HUFFMAN

Huffman is a small town at the far end of the Lakes district in Western Maine. Incorporated in 1840, its main industry in 1976 was a furniture factory. In January 1976 an apparent serial killer of young children began to stalk the town.

The Town Green is bordered by Main, Trafford, Shire, River, Chestnut and Maple Streets and was donated to the town by the Hosea Family in 1880. Two stone posts 6 foot high in a brick wall frame the entrance. Brass plates are set in each post, one reading 'Huffman Town Green', the other acknowledging the donation. Playground equipment is on the Main Street side of the Green. The War Memorial is on it, there is a small band shell, and a small pond in the middle, where Ouelette found Frances Tho's body.

Main Street is also Route 17, which runs parallel to the GS&WM freight tracks (now disused and presumably running in an easterly direction to Castle Rock and further, to the location many years before of the dead boy sought by Gordie Lachance and his friends in *The Body*).

While Huffman is close to Castle Rock, Fryeburg is the town over Huffman's town line in one direction and Bridgton neighbors it on another. As Harlow is the town neighboring Castle Rock it must also be close to Huffman, although it is not mentioned. Drivers stop in Huffman on their way to the nearby ski fields, such as Black Mountain, Pleasant Mountain and Sunday River.

Among other places King mentions is Hunington Road (location of the Chasswick place, before it the Sirois place and also known as 'Windy Acres'); Back Stage Road; Carbine Street (so named for the factory that had stood there in post-Civil War times); the Old Farm on Devonshire Road; the Huffman Stream, crossed by the Margaret Chase Smith–Lyndon Baines Johnson Bridge, built in 1965; Shire Street; Sirois Creek; Trafford Lane (those who live on it are not well-off) and its extension, Trafford Road, which crosses the Huffman Road via a wooden bridge built in 1932 but which was much run-down four decades later. In early 1976 the town had at least one kindergarten, a grammar school, a junior high and a high school, a library and the Huffman Country Club.

> Huffman's businesses in 1976 included a bank; Thatcher's Ford-Honda dealership; the furniture factory, at which Bob Bouchard was a foreman; two motels (one called 40 Winks); a pool hall and bowling alley; a drug store; the Brass Rail restaurant and the Home Folks Café; Carl Dusfrene's legal office; Dr. George Peters' surgery; an Exxon gas station; the Huffman Barber Shop; and retail outlets, including First National, the Huffman Federal Supermarket, Huffman Field & Stream Sporting Goods, Huffman Giftwize, the Leather Bar and Henry's Busy Corner. Janet Dolgun ran a half junk shop, half antique shop spread over four buildings on Main and called The Pretty Penny. The Huffman Mill was defunct and 'decaying' beside the Castle River by this time.
>
> Drogan's husband founded her newspaper, the Huffman Gazette-Intelligencer, in the early 1950s. She took control in 1964 and by 1976 had a circulation of 2000 in winter, doubling in summer. Its so-called competition was *The Wise Shopper*, put out as an attempt by Drogan's enemies to damage her economically. The Huffman Police Department fell under Chief Stone following Andy Ellerton's retirement in 1975. Local sports teams included the Lake Region Lakers and the Huffman Wildcats.

Untitled Screenplay (Radio Station) (c1977)

An untitled partial screenplay is held in Box 1011 at the Special Collections Unit of the Raymond H Fogler Library at the University of Maine, Orono. It has never been produced.

This 20 page, 24-scene telescript was apparently penned in Bridgton, Maine. There is no other indication of the year in which the action is set. It is unclear when the script was written, although the Kings lived in Bridgton from the Summer of 1975 to the Fall of 1977. King talked about the screenplay in an interview with David Chute (published in *Take One* for January 1979 and reproduced in *Feast of Fear*[161]), saying he was working on it 'now, off and on'.

In this Maine Street Horror story a local radio station is to be converted from manned to automated operation, with the changeover taking place one January evening at midnight. That night the owner, Roger Lathrop went to the station to confront his last DJ, the drunken Bob Randall.

The two debated the merits of automation, a service of the Century-2000 Corporation. Randall returned to his apartment and hanged himself. An angry Randall fan slapped Lathrop at his funeral. As it was January, Randall's body was placed in a vault, to await burial in the spring. At this point the script ends.

The station is WOKY, based in the countryside of Western Maine and which could be found at 1530 on the AM dial. Bridgton is also in Western Maine. We know that the script was not inspired by King's experiences with his own radio station, WZON in Bangor, as he did not buy that until October 1983.

Randall, about 35 at the time of his sacking and suicide, was a hippie type with a lot of gray in his long hair and a smoker. Also something of a drinker, he had worked at WOKY for five years.

The owner and station manager, Roger Lathrop, was married, to Maddy. He was about 40, a smoker, and 'good looking'.

The other sacked DJs were Tommy Lake; Chip Ripley, who weighed 306 lbs. and whose real name was Chester Robichaud (he is somehow reminiscent of Henry Leyden, the DJ of many characters in *Black House*); and Greg Starr. After automation Tyler Bracken, a 22 year-old college dropout, was to manage the radio station. Thin, with thick horn-rimmed glasses, he had been around the station since he was 16.

A number of the media outlets mentioned in this script appear elsewhere in King's fiction. WJBQ, the radio station Bob Randall was to join after leaving WOKY, is also mentioned in *The Mist*, where it was briefly on the air after the storm and Steffy Drayton managed to tune into it. WIGY, the radio station to which Chip Ripley was moving, is also mentioned in *The Mist*, as it was also on the air shortly after the storm. WLAM, the radio station in Lewiston, Maine Greg Starr was to join is mentioned in *The Body*. Bob Cormier, a DJ there, was a contestant at the pie-eating contest in the Lard Ass Hogan part of the novella. WCSH, the TV station on which Tommy Lake got an announcer's job, is the station in Portland, Maine on which executions were televised live in *The Stand* (*Complete and Uncut* edition only).

King gave away some of the storyline in his interview with Chute: "It's a story about the owner of a radio station in western Maine. He fires all his disk jockeys and imports this computer radio thing. It's one of those automated radio voices, with this syrupy, totally mechanical voice, totally divorced from any real human being. One of the deejays commits suicide, and after that the machine starts to take over. It's saying things like, "And now the latest from, and *blah, blah, blah* and fuck you, you're going to die; I'm going to kill you." I'm having a good time writing it." This clearly indicates more was written than the short piece held in Box 1011 at UMO. Hopefully, the extra scenes will one day come to light. Asked in 2011 during research for this book about the screenplay King said, 'I remember it well. What I can't remember is why it never got finished. Probably because something else came along. In those days, the ideas were popping like corn in a microwave.[162]'

We can presume Randall has come back to haunt the radio station (the automated voice would have allowed for plenty of potentially hilarious mayhem, particularly with regard to the tracks playing at any given point in time, and for the threats noted by King). The fact that his body was not buried, but lay in a vault, would also have allowed for a plot development such as the corpse's disappearance, but that is entirely speculative. Where King was actually going with this script we will probably never know but should he ever choose to return to the concept (having delivered haunted houses, hotels, hotel rooms, bathtubs and hospitals, among other places) his fans could well be in for a treat.

Ur (2009)

Ur was first published as a download for Amazon's Kindle 2 e-reader, on 12 February 2009. While it has yet to see a print publication the audio book was released on 16 February 2010 (King hand-picked the narrator, Holter Graham). It can be safely assumed the story will see a mass-market print version at some point, although it was not included in King's 2010 collection, *Full Dark, No Stars*, possibly due to contractual obligations with Amazon.

King's agent, Ralph Vicinanza[163], had originally approached King to write a story for e-book release to 'create some excitement' (as King's *Riding the Bullet* had done in 2000), at a time when the publishing industry was in the doldrums. Available as a download for $2.99, many King fans were critical or the tactic, claiming it was no more than an infomercial for Amazon and their Kindle. However, on reading the story, it is clear this was no quick knock-off. *Ur* is a full-blooded King tale and has very important Dark Tower links (the first notable Dark Tower information since the final novel in that series, published five years earlier).

The 21,000 plus word America Under Siege and Dark Tower story has seven sections – *Experimenting with New Technology*; *Ur Functions*; *Wesley Refuses to Go Mad*; *News Archive*; *Ur Local (Under Construction)*; *Candy Rymer*; *The Paradox Police*; and *Ellen*.

Wesley Smith, an English Department instructor at Moore College in Moore, Kentucky has purchased a Kindle 'out of spite' for Ellen Silverman, his ex-girlfriend and coach of the college's highly successful women's basketball team, the Lady Meerkats. King has long followed women's basketball (originally inspired through support of the University of Maine's Black Bears)[164]. Strangely, Wesley's Kindle is pink, even though Amazon only sells them in white – the idea of buying it to spite Ellen came after he'd called her illiterate when she threw one of his precious books across a room, demanding he learn to read from a computer screen, "like the rest of us." This has apparently ended their relationship.

Soon after the Kindle purchase Ellen leaves a message on Wesley's answering machine, saying she'd heard he had an e-reader and that this may be a sign they should try again, but not until after an important upcoming tournament in Lexington, to which she and the team would travel by bus. He was not to call her in the meantime.

Intrigued by the unique pink color of his Kindle and accessing the menu, Wesley finds an option called 'EXPERIMENTAL', under which there is a series of 'experimental prototypes', including 'UR FUNCTIONS'. Under this, he could access 'UR BOOKS', 'UR NEWS ARCHIVE' and 'UR LOCAL (UNDER CONSTRUCTION)'.

Clicking on 'UR BOOKS' Wesley is confronted with a picture of a large black tower (our first hint of a Dark Tower connection), and when he chooses to search for Ernest Hemingway books he is presented with unknown stories by that literary giant and information claiming different birth and death dates for 'Papa'. Wesley buys one of the stories he's never heard of, *Cortland's Dogs* and is delivered of a novel clearly in Hemingway's style – but one he never wrote, at least not in *our* reality. Worse, he discovers that if he searches for Hemingway in different 'Urs' each provides different novels and even different lives for Hemingway (in one he was a dime novel crime writer). The same applied to other famous, and obscure, authors. Poe had lived a quarter century longer in one 'Ur' than in our reality and had written six novels, one of which Wesley purchased and read overnight. The Kindle becomes an all-consuming drug, as he felt compelled to search out more and more 'new' tales by his favorite writers.

Is he deluded? When he shows it to a student and a colleague they both find strange new publications on the device, including new plays by Shakespeare. And the downloaded books are not being charged to Smith's MasterCard – something is *very* wrong.

The next 'EXPERIMENTAL' option to be investigated is the 'UR NEWS ARCHIVE', which contains only material from *The New York Times*. Different 'Urs' exist in this function as well, with one noting Hilary Clinton was sworn in as 44th President of the United States on 21 January 2009 (replacing President Gore)! In another reality the *Times* had not published after the Cuban Missile Crisis and subsequent nuclear war! Next, Wesley makes the mistake of accessing the 'UR LOCAL (UNDER CONSTRUCTION)' function, which offers nothing more than the local newspaper for the college town, the Moore *Echo*. When accessed it will only allow *future* dates to be entered and the download cost is *much* more expensive than past copies of *The New York Times*. Wesley enters the date of the following Monday, the day after his ex-girlfriend's team would have played in their tournament – only to discover big, black headlines of tragedy – the coach and seven students would be killed in an horrific bush crash on the way back to town. The crash would be caused by a Candy Rymer, who struck it at speed driving her SUV.

Wesley and his student are convinced the accident will happen but struggle to work out how to prevent it, and finally strike upon diverting the killer driver. Tracking down Candy Rymer, they stalk the woman as she tracks drunk from bar to bar, finally slashing her tires before Wesley slaps her nearly senseless. The accident is avoided but now, despite their relief, the two men are concerned they may have broken the 'Paradox Laws', which the Kindle had said protected the 'Ur Local'.

Back in town and alone Wesley parks across the street from 'a Cadillac ... in the glow of the arc sodium beneath which it was parked, it seemed too bright.' (This is a clear reference to the vehicles in *Low Men in Yellow Coats*). Suddenly he is filled with fear and begins to believe the 'Paradox Police' have come for him. And, when he enters his apartment, there they are, speaking in 'a not-quite-human voice' and calling him 'Wesley of Kentucky.'

They wear long mustard-colored coats ('dusters') and Wesley feels the coats were alive. Worse, the faces of the creatures kept changing and what lies beneath their skin appears reptilian, bird-like or both. 'On their lapels, where lawmen in a Western movie would have worn badges, both wore buttons bearing a red eye. Wesley thought these too were alive.' The creatures claim Wesley's actions have caused 'The Tower' to tremble and 'The rose feels a chill, as of winter.' Of course, even though the human has no idea what they are talking about, they demand a credible explanation for his actions, otherwise he will die. With Wes trying to justify saving a few lives, the creatures point out the Paradox Laws are there for a reason, and the consequences of avoiding the crash may well far exceed having allowed it to occur, including possibly that, 'one of these young women might give birth to the next Hitler or Stalin, a human monster who could go on to kill millions of your fellow humans on this level of the Tower.'

The creatures tell Wesley the consequences of his actions are unknown, the experimental program he'd accessed could only see clearly six months into the future. Remembering the tower from the 'UR BOOKS' interface Wesley asks about it. ' "All things serve the Tower," the man-thing in the yellow duster said, and touched the hideous button on its coat with a kind of reverence.' The Paradox Police demand Wesley return the Kindle, which he does, and he is able to convince them that Fate may have *chosen* him to receive the strange Kindle and even make the choices he did. Convinced, the creatures leave, choosing to let Wesley live.

The next day's local newspaper headlines the Lady Meerkat's winning the tourney and shows a photo of Ellen holding a sign reading, 'I LOVE YOU WESLEY'. For the moment, at least, the universe is back on its axis.

It seems this special Kindle allowed access to the million plus multiple realities of the Dark Tower and King makes this very clear to Dark Tower fans, with clear descriptions of the 'Low Men' – they are soldiers of the Crimson King or 'Regulators' from the Dark Tower, and feature in *Low Men in Yellow Coats* (where they are chasing Ted Brautigan), *Heavenly Shades of Night are Falling* and the last three volumes of *The Dark Tower* Cycle.

This information makes *Ur* a vitally important part of the Dark Tower mythos, and for this reason, fans will want a mass-market circulation of tale at the earliest possible time. In the meantime, readers will need to download a copy to Amazon's Kindle (avoiding the pink model with 'UR' applications); or purchase the audio book.

Weeds (1976)

Weeds was originally published in *Cavalier* (a men's magazine) for May 1976 and reprinted in *Nugget* (another men's magazine) for April 1979. In *Cavalier* the story is listed in the Index as *Weeds* but the headline to the story, spread over two pages, reads: 'More Than a Green Thumb ... Will Be Necessary to Stop the Weeds: A chilling new story by the author of *Carrie* and *'Salem's Lot.'*

It has never been reproduced in text format in a King collection and it is far from clear why. It is certainly a far better story than some of the 'pulp' fiction stories that King did allow into his collections, such as *Night Shift*, published in 1978. King clearly has a fond spot for the story itself but perhaps as the years passed found the text version less and less capable of meeting the tone set for each of his short story collections? Alternately, perhaps after *Creepshow* was released in 1982 King no longer felt a need to republish?

In *The Stephen King Story* George Beahm revealed that *Weeds* is part of an aborted novel. Apparently King had written 20,000 words at one stage. King told an interviewer: '...once the weeds started to grow beyond that closed world and toward the town, I couldn't find any more to say. It seemed to me that that was all I really cared about, and I ran out of caring about it.'

For the segment in the *Creepshow* screenplay/film it was retitled as *The Lonesome Death of Jordy Verrill*. King himself plays a wonderfully hammed Jordy in the film.

As a result there are three King versions of this story – the *Cavalier/Nugget* version; the *Creepshow* screenplay (unpublished and subject of a separate chapter in this book); and *The Lonesome Death of Jordy Verrill* segment of the *Creepshow* movie tie-in graphic album/comic book.

Readers can access the basic story by renting a video/DVD of *Creepshow*. The text versions are not difficult to find with photocopies circulating freely in the King community. Original copies of the magazines are harder to secure and sell via specialist sellers such as Betts Bookshop, although it is very difficult to find a copy of *Nugget*.

In the story a meteor falls on Jordy Verrill's farm. He was not a smart man but on the evening of July 4, when he saw the meteor falling to earth near his house, he decided to collect it and sell it to the local college. He put out the grassfire around the impact site and then dowsed the meteor with water, causing it to split and release a white flaky substance.

After touching the substance Jordy found himself with a strange infection that caused a green vegetation to grow all over his body and at various points around the house and property. Unable to stop its advance, and in terrible agony, Jordy shot and killed himself on July 6. Heedless to Jordy's death, the strange green vegetation continued to move towards the nearby town of Cleaves Mills, New Hampshire.

While this is an America Under Siege story, for *Creepshow* King moved Jordy's farm to a location near Castle Rock, relocating the tale into the Maine Street Horror reality.

King does a tremendous job of describing the run-down hardscrabble rural life Jordy leads, including the property (which reminds the reader of the Camber place in *Cujo*). 'A faucet jutted out from the side of the shed at the end of a rusty pipe; the ground underneath was the only place grass would grow in Jordy's dooryard, which was otherwise bald and littered with old auto parts.' Using Jordy's very limited mental capacities as a tool to his eventual demise King tells the reader, '…you can't predict what a man will do in a certain situation after he reaches a certain degree of dumbness.' As the weeds slowly infest Jordy's body he is trapped by his own inability to react logically (much as teenagers in slasher movies never go straight to the nearest police station but instead re-enter darkened houses).

Once it is established that Jordy is doomed King reveals the true horror – the weeds are spreading and have a rudimentary form of intelligence. When the weeds on his body point at the weeds rapidly growing on his farmland, 'Jordy, his thoughts dimming with the tide of greenness that now grew from the very meat of his brain, understood that a kind of telepathy was going on. *Is the food good? Yes, very good. Rich. Is he the only food? No, much food. His thoughts say so. Does the food have a name? Two names. Sometimes it is called Jordy-food. Sometimes it is called Cleaves Mills-food.*' At the end of the story, as in any good pulp horror classic, the weeds are growing toward town thinking Earth 'a fine planet, a wet planet. A ripe planet.'

Jordy Verrill '…wasn't bright; he had a potato face, large, blocky hands … and he got along as best he could.' He tends to speak and think in a very down-to-earth, rural manner. "There, you done it now, Jordy, you lunkhead," he says out loud after breaking the meteor. After burning his fingers he thinks, 'He was going to have a crop of blisters, sure as shit grows under a privy.' 'Thinking was hard work for him. Thinking hurt, because there was a dead short somewhere inside, and keeping at it for long made him want to take a nap or beat his meat and forget the whole thing.' Jordy felt that '…Verrill luck was Verrill luck, and you spelled that B-A-D' but hoped it had changed with the meteor, for which he might get $25 from the college. Little did he know how BAD his luck was about to become! The reader quickly develops sympathy for Jordy, who is in fact a likeable character, not one of the miserable, harsh rural characters King writes of so often and so honestly.

The story takes place exclusively on Jordy's farm, set on Bluebird Creek and near the town of Cleaves Mills, New Hampshire. The year in which the story occurs is not provided but the meteor struck at twilight one 4th of July. By the next day the 'weeds' were growing on Jordy and by the 6th, in despair, he had committed suicide. At dawn on that day the weeds had reached the highway, only two miles from the town.

There are just a few links to other King stories. Interestingly, in the *Creepshow* version the only other character from the small cast in the original who reappears is Jordy's father. Cleaves Mills is in New Hampshire. In the King universe there is a Cleaves Mills, Maine and this is the town where John Smith lived at the time of his accident in *The Dead Zone*. Jordy is also mentioned in passing in King's *Pet Sematary* screenplay. In that script the Baterman place is said to look like the home of Jordy Verrill.

This is one of the few King stories that have not been published in a mainstream King collection but have been adapted. It forms the basis of *The Lonesome Death of Jordy Verrill* segment in the 1982 movie *Creepshow*, for which King himself wrote the screenplay and which was directed by George A Romero. King played Verrill. The movie was released on DVD in 1999.

The Life and Hard Times of Jordy Verrill

The son of a farmer, he lived on Bluebird Creek, near Cleaves Mills, New Hampshire, was a subsistence farmer and odd jobs man who fixed cars, sold wood and drove Christmas trees to Boston at Christmas. He had faded blue eyes and had to wear glasses to read his Louis L'amour westerns and dirty books. He was not very smart. When he was 46 a meteor crashed onto his land and after it broke open he was infected by the 'meteorshit' inside it. The infection caused green stuff to grow all over his body. Two days later, on July 6, he killed himself by gunshot.

(Source: *Weeds*)

Son of Anita, his father was also a farmer who died three years before the meteor landed. An unfortunate simple-minded man, he touched a strange meteor that landed on his farm, which was on Route 26 near Castle Rock, Maine. The contents of the meteor slowly turned him into a walking weed. He killed himself with a shotgun when, in intense pain, he realized that there was no hope of surviving.

(Source: *The Lonesome Death of Jordy Verrill*)

He was about 45 when the meteor hit.

(Source: *Creepshow* screenplay)

Note: Stephen King played Jordy Verrill in the only adaptation of this character, the 1982 film *Creepshow*.

Wimsey (1977)

Wimsey is a story fragment from the Lord Peter Wimsey novel King worked on in late 1977. The piece is a double-spaced, typewritten manuscript, containing the first chapter of fourteen pages, and only the first page of a second chapter. Although it has never been published copies of this fragment circulate in the King community. A copy (typed on green paper) was offered for resale via Betts Bookshop in 2006.

The attempted novel was the result of both the King family's abortive move to England and a discussion between King and his editor of the time, Bill Thompson. The discussion revolved around the writing of a novel using the detective character, Lord Peter Wimsey, created by Dorothy L Sayers. More of Wimsey and Sayers later.

The King family moved to England in the Fall of 1977. King was reported in the *Fleet News* as saying he wanted to write a book "…with an English setting."[165] The house they settled on was Mourlands, at 87 Aldershot Road, Fleet in Hampshire. Beahm claimed the Kings had advertised for a home, reading: 'Wanted, a draughty Victorian house in the country with dark attic and creaking floorboards, preferable haunted.' King's US paperback publisher, NAL, issued a press release stating King had moved to England to write "…a novel even more bloodcurdling than the previous ones …" Although this does not sound at all like a genteel British detective novel, we can perhaps forgive the publisher's enthusiasm for its best-selling writer.

Once in England King did not find the inspiration required for an English novel, perhaps explaining the fragmentary nature of *Wimsey*, but he did begin one of his most famous novels, *Cujo* during the three months the family remained in the country. One story based in England did result from the trip, however. In mid-October 1977 the King family had dinner with Peter Straub and his wife in the London suburb of Crouch End. This resulted in King's Lovecraftian story, *Crouch End*, originally published in the 1980 collection *New Tales of the Cthulhu Mythos* and in a heavily revised version in 1993's *Nightmare and Dreamscapes*.

Of course, the best result of the England trip may have been the beginning of King's long and fruitful relationship with fellow author Straub, which has so far resulted in both *The Talisman* and *Black House*, with a reasonable likelihood that a third Jack Sawyer novel will be written.

Apparently King sent the fragment of *Wimsey* to Bill Thompson for review but Thompson's reaction is unknown. We can only presume it was either not positive or King himself had lost interest in the concept. In retrospect this is likely to have been a good thing. Despite King's typecasting as a horror novelist, which resulted from *Night Shift*, *The Stand*, *The Dead Zone* and *Cujo* being the books to follow *Carrie*, *'Salem's Lot* and *The Shining*, it is likely King's career has been all the more fruitful as a so-called horror novelist than as a so-called detective or mystery writer, along the lines of Sayers or Agatha Christie (although King's take on *Death on the Nile* would be interesting, to say the least).

In what we can read of this aborted novel Lord Peter Wimsey and his servant Bunter are on their way, through 'beastly rain' to a party at Sir Patrick Wayne's estate in the country. Wimsey had last met Sir Patrick in 1934. Wimsey and Bunter discuss the foul weather and the death of Salcomb Hardy, which has put Wimsey in a funk. During the trip the two men's dry sense of humor becomes apparent.

After they cross '…an alarmingly rickety plank bridge which spanned a swollen stream…' Wimsey calls for a toilet stop and, alerted by the contrast to its more solid nature the previous time he had crossed it, looks at the bridge, only to find that the supports had been cut almost through. Somehow this dangerous discovery seems to have enlivened Wimsey, who calls with '…more excitement in his voice than Bunter had heard in a long time … he could not remember how long.' However, Bunter thinks this flash will pass, '… gleams of what Wimsey had been and could not even yet deny utterly. It would pass, and he would become the Wimsey that was in this dull aftermath of the war that had made their war seem like child's play – a dreary ghost-Wimsey, distracted and vague, a Wimsey who did too much solitary drinking, a Wimsey whose wit had soured.'

Returning to the car Wimsey states that if the heavy weather continues the bridge will collapse. When they return to the road Wimsey even wonders if 'Sir Pat' was not himself responsible for trying to isolate his home from the world, considering in particular his '…invitation, renewed so tiresomely over the last month and a half, until we quite ran out of excuses. It began to take on a … a flavor, did it not?' Wimsey and Bunter begin to consider that Sir Patrick might have a problem '…requiring certain detective talents…' Then, 'Wimsey said quietly, "I don't detect. I shall never detect again." Bunter did not reply. "If I hadn't been off detecting for the British Secret Service, I … what rot."' Apparently Wimsey blamed himself for his wife's death in the Blitz.

Now their thoughts turn to Miss Katherine Climpson, another of Wimsey's employees. Wimsey tentatively asks how 'she' was and Bunter does '… not affect to know of whom Lord Peter spoke'. We discover that Climpson is mortally ill with cancer in a hospital near Wimsey's Picadilly flat and that he had '…gone to visit her himself in the first nine weeks of her stay, but at last he had been able to face it no more. He cursed himself for a coward, reviled himself, called himself a slacker and a yellow-livered slug … but he did not go.' The slow decline of Climpson was, 'Too much. Harriet was dead; his brother was dead; even Salcomb Hardy was dead; Miss Climpson was dying and Sir Patrick Wayne, a rich old bore who had been knighted for making himself richer at the expense of thousands of lives, was alive and apparently doing fine. "Is tomorrow Halloween, Bunter?" "I believe it is, my lord." "It should be," Wimsey said, and helped himself to a cigarette. "It bloody well should be.'"

As Sir Patrick's house approaches the brakes fail and their Bentley crashes (Bunter, still in character, laconically comments, "We appear to have lost all braking power, my lord"). Chapter One ends at this point.

In the aftermath of the crash and the beginning of Chapter Two Wimsey wakes and calls for Bunter. At this point what we have of the story ends.

Although *Wimsey* is relatively short there are a number of interesting facts to report. Sir Patrick Wayne's estate is seven miles from Little Shapley, England. If the bridge collapsed there was only one other road, barely a cart track, out of the estate. Wimsey and Bunter were driving to the estate on 30 October 1945 ("is tomorrow Halloween?"), less than six months after the end of the Second World War in Europe.

The only details of note that King provides us with about Wimsey himself are that he was formerly a detective with the British Secret Service, that his wife Harriet Vane Wimsey had died during the German blitz and the reader's presumption that the elder Duke of Denver was Wimsey's brother.

Wimsey's nephew, the current Duke of Denver ('Jerry') had visited Sir Patrick Wayne's daughter until she had become engaged to another man. Jerry had served in the RAF during the Battle of Britain and was one of the relatively few survivors of that action.

Katherine Climpson seems set to be an important character in the novel. She ran Wimsey's typing bureau, was unmarried, and was dying of cancer in a hospital on Great Ormond Street, London. Salcomb Hardy, who had recently died of a stroke, was a crime reporter and heavy drinker. Wimsey read his obituary in *The Times*.

King adopted a style for *Wimsey* that is indeed very English in tone, including a rather dry tone of exchange between Bunter and the title character. It is clear that King was quite capable of delivering in this style, as one might expect from a premier novelist. In one passage, as Bunter pulls the car over for a comfort stop, he reminds his employer, "If you would not take it amiss, my lord, your heavy overcoat is on the hook directly behind you. I'm afraid of the effects of the rain might be on that worsted." In another Wimsey says, "Let's go back to the car, Bunter, before we take a chill," in the best of British aristocratic tones of the 1940s.

Wimsey is mentioned as a literary character in both *Bag of Bones* and *Apt Pupil*. Adding this to the fact that King attempted a Wimsey novel leads us to speculate that King is probably a fan of the Wimsey series. King listed Wimsey's creator, Dorothy L Sayers, as one of the authors he most admired during an interview for *The Waldenbook Report* in late 1997.

Sayers' character, Lord Peter Wimsey was immensely popular in the 1920s and 1930s and the books are still read avidly today. The BBC made two successful television series based on the character, starring Ian Carmichael and Peter Haddon in the lead roles, and there were also 1935 and 1940 movies based on two of the novels.

The fourteen novels and additional short stories were all published from the 1920s through the early 1940s and feature Lord Peter Death Bredon Wimsey, the younger brother of the Duke of Denver and a World War I veteran. Bunter is his manservant. An avid rare book collector, Wimsey develops a penchant for investigating crime, often assisting Detective Inspector Charles Parker, his brother in law. Sayers' imaginary life of Lord Peter ends in 1942, with Wimsey married to Harriet Vane and the father of three sons. From the *Author's Note* in *Thrones, Dominations* we know that he served in Military Intelligence in World War II.

It seems that King has been faithful to the Wimsey mythology, as we would expect. He has Wimsey married to Harriet, although he extends the mythos by having her die in the Blitz. He also has Wimsey serving in the British Secret Service during the War, linking the note of his serving in Military Intelligence. Readers will conclude from the text that he is the uncle of the current Duke of Denver, which is the way Sayers had it.

Sayers herself was acquainted with a number of the literary circles of her time, being a friend of T S Eliot and C S Lewis. She was a figure of some controversy, having had a child out of wedlock in 1924 and being accused of anti-Semitism in her writing. Apart from the Wimsey and Vane stories (Harriet Vane was also an amateur detective), which set her up financially and which she then retired from writing, she also wrote religious essays and plays in an orthodox Anglican manner; and translated some of Dante's writings. Interestingly enough, she also translated the *Song of Roland* from the Old French. That work is an anonymous Old French epic, dating to the 11th Century and is regarded as the first of the great French heroic poems known as *chansons de geste*. Born in 1893, Sayers died in 1957.

King has continued to show an interest in crime and detective stories and has presented his Constant Readers with a limited but quality selection, including *The Fifth Quarter, Man with a Belly, The Wedding Gig, The Doctor's Case, Umney's Last Case* and *The Colorado Kid*.

END NOTES

[1] In making these calculations the seven stories from *People, Places and Things* are classified as 'unpublished', as they were produced in a self-published chapbook by King and Chris Chesley, rather than by an independent publisher
[2] Inclusive of *The Wind Through The Keyhole* (2012)
[3] Inclusive of *Full Dark, No Stars*
[4] Such as *Ur*, exclusively for Kindle; and *Mile 81*.
[5] See the *Appendix*
[6] In an Q&A session for young readers at www.weeklyreader.com
[7] In *Secret Windows: Essays and Fiction of the Craft of Writing*, New York, NY: Book-of-the-Month Club, 2000, page 400
[8] King has used this term for many years to describe his loyal reader base. In *The Dark Tower VI: Song of Susannah* he went so far as to describe them in his imaginary Journal as 'CRs'!
[9] *The Complete Guide to the Works of Stephen King*, Rocky Wood, David Rawsthorne and Norma Blackburn (1st Edition May 2003, Revised Edition November 2004). Now out of print.
[10] The five parts were: *The Gunslinger* (October 1978); *The Way Station* (April 1980); *The Oracle and the Mountains* (February 1981); *The Slow Mutants* (July 1981); and *The Gunslinger and the Dark Man* (November 1981)
[11] In *The Magazine of Fantasy and Science Fiction*, December 1990
[12] *Stephen King's The Dark Tower: A Concordance (Volume One)*, Robin Furth, p.177-178
[13] *Foreword* to *The Dark Tower: The Gunslinger (Revised Edition)*, Stephen King, page xx
[14] *The Lost Work of Stephen King*, Stephen Spignesi, p.277-284
[15] *H.P. Lovecraft: Against the World, Against Life*, Michel Houellebecq, p.10-13
[16] See http://video.mpbn.net/video/1357861895/# . Although the website says this interview was broadcast in December 2009, references in the actual interview indicate it was recorded in late 2003 or early 2004
[17] *Stephen King: The Art of Darkness*, Douglas E Winter, page xvi
[18] A store in Lisbon Falls, Maine that features prominently in 11/22/63
[19] Personal correspondence with Rocky Wood, 5 August 2011
[20] Personal correspondence with Rocky Wood, 22 July 2011
[21] Personal correspondence with Rocky Wood, 24 June 2008
[22] *Stephen King: The Art of Darkness*, Douglas E Winter, p.76

[23] Personal correspondence with Rocky Wood, 30 July 2011
[24] Personal correspondence with Rocky Wood, 1 October 2011
[25] *Danse Macabre*, section 16 of 'The Last Waltz – Horror and Morality, Horror and Magic'
[26] Personal correspondence with Rocky Wood, 29 September 2011
[27] Personal correspondence with Rocky Wood, 24 July 2011
[28] Personal correspondence with Rocky Wood, 24 July 2011
[29] In November 2011 King confirmed to Rocky Wood in personal correspondence that this is actually the same story as *The Star Invaders*. That story is subject of a separate chapter in this book.
[30] *Stephen King: The Art of Darkness,* Douglas E Winter, p.19
[31] Ethelyn Flaws, husband of Oren (both are referred to in *Song of Susannah*), sister of Ruth Pillsbury King
[32] *The Stephen King Story*, George Beahm, p.26
[33] A pastiche is defined as, 'A dramatic, literary, or musical piece openly imitating the previous works of other artists, often with satirical intent' (*The American Heritage Dictionary of the English Language*)
[34] *A Man with a Child's Embrace of the Questions*. 30 May 2005 edition
[35] Personal correspondence with Rocky Wood, 16 August 2011
[36] *Stephen King Collectibles: An Illustrated Price Guide*, George Beahm, p. 17
[37] *Stephen King: The Art of Darkness*, Douglas E Winter, p.17
[38] Personal correspondence with Rocky Wood, 1 August 2011
[39] Part of an online only article, *Stephen King on His 10 Longest Novels* by Gilbert Cruz, published 9 November 2009. The printed article included slightly edited material from a telephone interview with King
[40] Personal correspondence with Rocky Wood, 4 August 2011
[41] Associated Press article by Phil Thomas, published in a number of newspapers, including as *His Imagination Can Scare Anyone* in (Eugene, Oregon) *Register-Guard*, 5 April 1979
[42] Personal correspondence with Rocky Wood, 31 July 2011
[43] *The Stephen King Story* by George Beahm (Little, Brown and Company, 1993), p297
[44] Personal correspondence with Rocky Wood, 17 August 2011
[45] *Stephen King: The Art of Darkness*, Douglas E Winter, p.166
[46] Personal correspondence with Rocky Wood, 22 July 2011
[47] *Screem Chats With Stephen King, Screem* magazine #22 (2011), p.6
[48] Personal correspondence with Rocky Wood, 31 July 2011
[49] Personal correspondence with Rocky Wood, 24 July 2011
[50] Readers will note there is *no* F13 key on an IBM PC keyboard
[51] *On The Shining and Other Perpetrations*, in *Whispers* #17/18, August 1982, page 16
[52] *The Seventeenth Fontana Book of Great Ghost Stories*, edited by R. Chetwynd-Hayes. London: Fontana/Collins, 1981; *Great Ghost Stories: Tales of Madness and Mystery*, edited by R. Chetwynd-Hayes and Stephen Jones. Baltimore: Cemetery Dance Publications, 2004; and *Great Ghost Stories*, selected by R. Chetwynd-Hayes and Stephen Jones. New York, NY: Carroll & Graf Publishers, 2004

[53] The first independent reprint of the original text appears in *Zombies: Encounters with the Hungry Dead*, edited by John Skipp. New York, NY: Black Dog & Leventhal Publishers, 2009.
[54] Personal correspondence, 19 July 2011
[55] www.thedailybeast.com 25 October 2009 and 14 March 2010
[56] *The Lost Work of Stephen King*, Stephen Spignesi, p.242-244
[57] *Stephen King: Bogeyman as Family Man*, 15 April 1990
[58] *The Lost Work of Stephen King*, Stephen Spignesi, p.163-165
[59] See, for instance, *The Shorter Works of Stephen King*, Michael Collings and David Engebretson, Starmont.
[60] His first collection, *20th Century Ghosts* (William Morrow, 2007) won the Horror Writers Association Bram Stoker Award for Superior Achievement in a Collection; and his first novel, *Heart-Shaped Box* (William Morrow, 2007) appeared on *The New York Times* best-seller list and won the Bram Stoker Award for Superior Achievement in a First Novel. He also writes the *Locke & Key* graphic novel series.
[61] First published in *He Is Legend: An Anthology Celebrating Richard Matheson*, edited by Christopher Conlon (Gauntlet Press)
[62] *We're All in this Together: A Novella and Stories* (Bloomsbury, 2005)
[63] *The Cannibals*, www.stephenking.com, 15 September 2009
[64] http://www.stephenking.com/forums/showthread.php?t=7008&page=6#60
[65] http://www.stephenking.com/library/unpublished/cannibals_the.html
[66] *Creepshows: The Illustrated Stephen King Movie Guide*, Stephen Jones, p42-43
[67] *Stephen King: The Art of Darkness*, Douglas E Winter, p.18
[68] *Feast of Fear: Conversations with Stephen King*, Tim Underwood and Chuck Miller (editors), page 79
[69] *Cinescape Presents The X-Files Yearbook* (ISSN: 1077-3363, 1998), p.15
[70] *The Stephen King Story*, George Beahm, p.299
[71] *Creepshows: The Illustrated Stephen King Movie Guide*, p.25
[72] *The Stephen King Story*, Chapter 12
[73] Joseph Hillstrom King, writing as Joe Hill, is now an Award-winning novelist, short story and comic book/graphic novel horror author
[74] *Creepshows: The Illustrated Stephen King Movie Guide*, Stephen Jones, p.30
[75] Weber has made quite a career in King adaptations, also appearing as Clark Rivingham (in the *You Know They Got a Hell of a Band* episode of *Nightmares & Dreamscapes: From the Stories of Stephen King*); 8x10 Man (in the *Revelations of Becka Paulson* episode of *The Outer Limits*); and Jack Torrance (in the mini-series of *The Shining*)
[76] *On Writing*, Stephen King, in part 10 of the 'On Writing' section
[77] *Horror Plum'd*, Michael Collings, p.378
[78] *The Essential Stephen King: The Complete and Uncut Edition*. Stephen Spignesi, p.92
[79] All detail in this section is from the screenplay held at the Fogler Library
[80] *Desperation*, Penguin Audiobooks, 1996
[81] *The Essential Stephen King: The Complete and Uncut Edition*, Stephen Spignesi, p.189-191
[82] *Horror Plum'd*, Michael Collings, p.211

[83] *The Unseen King*, Tyson Blue, p.120-123
[84] Tinker has since sold the business but it still operates as a specialist King bookshop.
[85] *The Lost Work of Stephen King*, Stephen Spignesi, p.245-247
[86] Bob Jackson, a King collector, owns both Issue 3 of *Comics Review* and the *Stories of Suspense* version. *Comics Review* was small in size, measuring only 8.5" by 5.5".
[87] *The Stephen King Illustrated Companion* by Bev Vincent. It was reproduced from Bob Jackson's personal copy
[88] From personal correspondence between Rocky Wood and Marv Wolfman
[89] *The Stephen King Story*, George Beahm, p.41
[90] Personal correspondence with Rocky Wood 19 July 2008
[91] *The Lost Work of Stephen King*, Stephen Spignesi, p.23-25
[92] *The Lost Work of Stephen King*, Stephen Spignesi, p.177-179
[93] Ackerman died in 2008, aged 92
[94] *The Lost Work of Stephen King*, Stephen Spignesi, p.107-110
[95] *The Lost Work of Stephen King*, Stephen Spignesi, p.146-147
[96] *The Unseen King*, Tyson Blue, p.130-136
[97] *The Stephen King Story*, George Beahm, p.154
[98] *Creepshows: The Illustrated Stephen King Movie Guide*, Stephen Jones, p.44-46
[99] *The Unseen King*, Tyson Blue, p.49-50
[100] *The Shorter Works of Stephen King*, Michael Collings and David Engebretson, p.35-36
[101] See *A Talk With Stephen King's True First Collaborator* in Stephen Spignesi's *The Complete Stephen King Encyclopedia*. Chesley's story *Genius* from *People, Places and Things* is also reprinted there
[102] According to Chesley, in George Beahm's *The Stephen King Story*
[103] *Horror Plum'd*, Michael Collings, Overlook Connection Press 2002
[104] *Market Guide for Young Writers*, edited by Kathy Henderson, Writer's Digest Books 1993 (Fourth Edition), 1996 (Fifth Edition), 2001 (Sixth Edition)
[105] *Creepshows: The Illustrated Stephen King Movie Guide*, Stephen Jones, p.59
[106] *Stephen King: The Art of Darkness*, Douglas Winter, p.130
[107] Quoted in *The Lost Work of Stephen King*, Stephen Spignesi, p.151
[108] *Danse Macabre*, Stephen King, Chapter Six, Section 10. Nicholson's actual movie debut was in *The Cry Baby Killer* earlier the same year.
[109] See *Stephen King Collectibles: An Illustrated Price Guide*, George Beahm, p.85-87. The first three parts were limited to only 226 copies.
[110] *The Unseen King*, Tyson Blue, p.92
[111] *Horror Plum'd*, Michael Collings
[112] *Danse Macabre*, Stephen King, Chapter 11 – *Tales of the Hook*
[113] *The Unseen King*, Tyson Blue, p.105
[114] One of Syracuse University's campuses is Utica College in Utica, New York. King often tells reporters lazy enough to ask where he gets his ideas, 'from a small shop in Utica'!
[115] Wendy Bousfield is something of a King aficionado, having provided articles on three King novels to *Beacham's Encyclopedia of Popular Fiction*, and another on *The Shining* for the *Themaic Encyclopedia of Fantasy and Science Fiction*.

[116] Sung with Frank Sinatra and Sammy Davis, Jr.
[117] Martin is mentioned in *Black House, Hearts in Atlantis, Insomnia, The Monkey, Movie Show, The Dark Tower* and the *Cat's Eye* screenplay
[118] In personal correspondence with the author (24 July 2011) King revealed for the first time that he retains 40 pages of this failed attempt at a novel
[119] *Stephen King: The Art of Darkness*, Douglas E Winter
[120] *Creepshows: The Illustrated Stephen King Movie Guide*, Stephen Jones, p.131
[121] *The Stephen King Story*, George Beahm, p.106
[122] *Creepshows: The Illustrated Stephen King Movie Guide*, Stephen Jones, p.19-23
[123] *Feast of Fear: Conversations with Stephen King*, Tim Underwood and Chuck Miller (editors), p. 79-80
[124] *Creepshows: The Illustrated Stephen King Movie Guide*, Stephen Jones, p.109-111
[125] Weber has also appeared as Steve Ames in *Desperation*, as Clark Rivingham (in the *You Know They Got a Hell of a Band* episode of *Nightmares & Dreamscapes: From the Stories of Stephen King*); and 8x10 Man (in the *Revelations of Becka Paulson* episode of *The Outer Limits*)
[126] He is referred to, but not named
[127] He is named in the note for a character's actions
[128] Hallorann's appearance in *It* was as an army cook in Derry in 1930, but in *The Shining* he was born in 1918, making him rather young to be a soldier. It seems clear King intends this is the same character but there is a timing error between the stories.
[129] Different Gage Creeds – a small boy in the two linked stories; a band leader in the Mini-Series screenplay of *The Shining* only
[130] In the Uncut book version only. Brad Kitchner is addressing the Free Zone Committee in Chapter 58, Section 3: 'We had two of the generators going yesterday, and as you know, one of them overloaded and blew its cookies. So to speak. What I mean is that it overlooked. Overloaded rather. Well ... you know what I mean.'
[131] See *Stephen King: The Non-Fiction* by Rocky Wood and Justin Brooks. Abingdon, Maryland: Cemetery Dance Publications, 2009
[132] For a review of each column see *Stephen King: The Non-Fiction* by Rocky Wood and Justin Brooks (Cemetery Dance, 2010)
[133] *Newsweek* described it as, 'Perhaps the funniest and most complex exercise in sustained political satire since *Animal Farm*'
[134] *The Unseen King*, Tyson Blue, p.34-38
[135] *Horror Plum'd*, Michael Collings, p.428
[136] *The Shorter Works of Stephen King*, Michael Collings and David Engebretson, p.17-22
[137] *Stephen King Collectibles: An Illustrated Price Guide*, George Beahm, p.261
[138] *The Stephen King Story*, George Beahm, p.223-224
[139] Joseph Hillstrom King, now the Award-winning and best-selling horror writer, Joe Hill
[140] *Feast of Fear: Conversations with Stephen King*, Tim Underwood and Chuck Miller (editors), page 79
[141] *Nightmares and Dreamscapes*, Stephen King
[142] Personal correspondence with Rocky Wood, 20 August 2011

[143] She is referred to but not named in the Uncut book version only. The exact quote is '*Rimfire Christmas* …written by a woman who lived up north in Haven.'

[144] In the Uncut book version only

[145] Mentioned only as the superflu

[146] Mentioned only in the book versions. In the original Mother Abagail says: 'I've always dreamed, and sometimes my dreams have come true. Prophecy is the gift of God and everyone has a smidge of it. My own grandmother used to call it the shining lamp of God, sometimes just the shine.'

[147] In the Uncut book version only. Brad Kitchner is addressing the Free Zone Committee in Chapter 58, Section 3: 'We had two of the generators going yesterday, and as you know, one of them overloaded and blew its cookies. So to speak. What I mean is that it overlooked. Overloaded rather. Well … you know what I mean.'

[148] Mentioned only in the book versions

[149] In the Uncut book version only. When Judge Farris saw a crow tapping on his motel room window it came to him that this was '…the dark man, his soul, his ka, somehow projected into this rain-drenched grinning crow …'

[150] *The Unseen King*, Tyson Blue, p.13-17

[151] *The Shorter Works of Stephen King*, Michael Collings, p.10-12

[152] *Explorations of Theme, Image, and Character In the Early Works of Stephen King*, Michael Collings

[153] *The Lost Work of Stephen King*, Stephen Spignesi, p.20-22

[154] *The Complete Stephen King Encyclopedia*, Stephen Spignesi

[155] *The Road to the Dark Tower*, Bev Vincent, p.332

[156] He later appeared as Clark Rivingham (in the *You Know They Got a Hell of a Band* episode of *Nightmares & Dreamscapes: From the Stories of Stephen King*); and Steve Ames in *Desperation*

[157] *Stephen King: The Art of Darkness* p.21

[158] This harrowing 1971 TV movie, directed by Stephen Spielberg, is credited with bringing the great director to mainstream attention

[159] An almost certain homage to Roger Corman, 'King of the B-Movies', whose horror movies of the 1960s inspired a young Stephen King

[160] Personal correspondence with the author 2 August 2011

[161] *Feast of Fear: Conversations with Stephen King*, Tim Underwood and Chuck Miller (editors), page 79

[162] Personal correspondence with Rocky Wood, 19 August 2011

[163] Vicinanza died of cerebral aneurism in 2010, aged 60

[164] Tabitha King's *Playing Like a Girl* is a non-fiction account of Cindy Blodgett, basketball star of Lawrence High School (Blodgett later starred for the Black Bears, played professional basketball, and went on to be appointed head coach at the University of Maine)

[165] *The Stephen King Story*, George Beahm, p.98-100

APPENDIX: BIBLIOGRAPHY

Fiction

The following is a list of all known King fiction published or announced as at 14 September 2011. Where the author of this volume has assessed that the story appears in different versions or variations (*see Chapter 4 – Variations and Versions in King's Fiction for more detail*) these are listed individually. Otherwise, only the first point of publication and any inclusions in a King collection are listed.

The codes used below are: (a) = Abridgement; (e) = Excerpt
(n) = New Version; (r) = Reprint; (v) = Variation

The Aftermath	Unpublished Novel
All That You Love Will Be Carried Away	
	The New Yorker, 29 January 2001
	Everything's Eventual (v)
American Vampire	Graphic Novel
An Evening at God's	Unpublished Play
Apt Pupil	*Different Seasons*
Autopsy Room Four	*Six Stories*
	Everything's Eventual (r)
Ayana	*Paris Review*, Fall 2007
	Just After Sunset (r)
Bag of Bones	Novel
The Ballad of the Flexible Bullet	
	The Magazine of Fantasy and Science Fiction, June 1984
	Skeleton Crew (v)
Battleground	*Cavalier*, September 1972
	Night Shift (v)
	Night Shift Screenplay (n)

Beachworld	*Weird Tales*, Fall 1984
	Skeleton Crew (v)
The Bear	*The Magazine of Fantasy and Science Fiction*, December 1990
	The Dark Tower III: The Waste Lands (n)
Before the Play	*Whispers*, August 1982
	TV Guide, 26 April – 2 May 1997 (a)
The Beggar and the Diamond	*Nightmares and Dreamscapes*
Beneath the Demon Moon	Paperback Giveaway
	The Dark Tower IV: Wizard and Glass
Big Driver	*Full Dark, No Stars*
Big Wheels – A Tale of the Laundry Game (Milkman #2)	*New Terrors 2*
	Skeleton Crew (n)
The Bird and the Album	*A Fantasy Reader: The Seventh World Fantasy Convention Program Book*
	It (n)
Black House	Novel
Black Ribbons	*Black Ribbons* (album), 2010
Blaze	Novel
Blind Willie	*Antaeus*, Autumn 1994
	Six Stories (v)
	Hearts in Atlantis (n)
Blockade Billy	Novella
The Blue Air Compressor	*Onan*, January 1971
	Heavy Metal, July 1981 (v)
The Body	*Different Seasons*
The Bone Church	*Playboy*, November 2009
The Boogeyman	*Cavalier*, March 1973
	Night Shift (v)
The Breathing Method	*Different Seasons*
Brooklyn August	*Io*, 1971
	Nightmares and Dreamscapes (r)
But Only Darkness Loves Me	Unpublished Short Story
Cain Rose Up	*Ubris*, Spring 1968
	Skeleton Crew (n)
Calla Bryn Sturgis	www.stephenking.com
The Dark Tower V: Wolves of the Calla (n)	
The Cannibals	www.stephenking.com
Carrie	Novel
The Cat From Hell	*Cavalier*, June 1977

Cat's Eye	Unpublished Screenplay
Cell	Novel
Chapter 71 – Sword in the Darkness	*Stephen King: Uncollected, Unpublished*
Charlie	Unpublished Short Story
Chattery Teeth	*Cemetery Dance*, Fall 1992
	Nightmares and Dreamscapes (n)
Children of the Corn	*Penthouse*, March 1977
	Night Shift (n)
	Unpublished Screenplay (n)
Chinga	Unpublished Screenplay
Chip Coombs	Unpublished Story
Christine	Novel
Code Name: Mousetrap	*The Drum*, 27 October 1965
The Colorado Kid	Novel
Comb Dump	Unpublished Story
The Crate	*Gallery*, July 1979
	Creepshow Screenplay (n)
	Creepshow (n)
Creepshow	Unpublished Screenplay
Crouch End	*New Tales of the Cthulhu Mythos*
	Nightmares and Dreamscapes (n)
Cujo	Novel
	Unpublished Screenplay (n)
The Cursed Expedition	*People, Places and Things*
Cycle of the Werewolf	Novella
The Dark Half	Novel
The Dark Man	*Ubris*, Fall 1969
The Dark Tower: The Gunslinger	Original Novel
	Revised and Expanded Novel (n)
The Dark Tower II: The Drawing of the Three	Novel
The Dark Tower III: The Wastelands	Novel
The Dark Tower IV: Wizard and Glass	Novel
The Dark Tower V: Wolves of the Calla	Novel
The Dark Tower VI: Song of Susannah	Novel
The Dark Tower VII: The Dark Tower	Novel
The Dead Zone	Novel
	Unpublished Screenplay (n)
The Death of Jack Hamilton	*The New Yorker*, 24/31 December 2001
	Everything's Eventual (r)

Dedication	*Night Visions 5*
	Nightmares and Dreamscapes (n)
Desperation	Novel
	Unpublished Screenplay (n)
Dino	*The Salt Hill Journal*, Autumn 1994
The Doctor's Case	*The New Adventures of Sherlock Holmes*
	Nightmares and Dreamscapes (r)
Do the Dead Sing?	*Yankee*, November 1981
Dolan's Cadillac	*Castle Rock*, 1985
	Limited Edition Novella (n)
	Nightmares and Dreamscapes (r)
	Unpublished Screenplay (v)
Dolores Claiborne	Novel
Donovan's Brain	*Moth*, 1970
Dreamcatcher	Novel
Duma Key	Novel
The Dune	*Granta* magazine, Fall/Winter 2011
11/22/63	Novel
The End of the Whole Mess	*Omni*, October 1986
	Nightmares and Dreamscapes (n)
The Evaluation	Unpublished Story
Everything's Eventual	*The Magazine of Fantasy and Science Fiction*, October 1997
	F13 (v)
	Everything's Eventual (v)
Eyes of the Dragon	Limited Edition Novel
	Mass Market Novel (n)
Fair Extension	*Full Dark, No Stars*
The Falls of the Hounds	Paperback Giveaway
	The Dark Tower IV: Wizard and Glass
Father's Day	*Creepshow* Screenplay
	Creepshow (n)
The Fifth Quarter	*Cavalier*, April 1972
	The Twilight Zone Magazine, February 1986 (n)
	Nightmares and Dreamscapes (n)
Firestarter	Novel
For Owen	*Skeleton Crew*
For the Birds	*Bred Any Good Rooks Lately?*
The 43rd Dream	*The Drum*, 29 January 1966
	The Illustrated Stephen King Companion

1408	*Blood and Smoke*
	Everything's Eventual (v)
From a Buick 8	Novel
The Furnace	*Know Your World Extra*
General	*Screamplays*
George D X McArdle	Unpublished Novel
Gerald's Game	Novel
The Gingerbread Girl	*Esquire*, July 2007
The Girl Who Loved Tom Gordon	Novel
The Glass Floor	*Startling Mystery Stories*, Fall 1967
	Weird Tales, Fall 1990 (v)
Golden Years	Unpublished Screenplay
A Good Marriage	*Full Dark, No Stars*
Graduation Afternoon	*Postscripts*, Spring 2007
	Just After Sunset (r)
Gramma	*Weirdbook*, Spring 1984
	Skeleton Crew (n)
Graveyard Shift	*Cavalier*, October 1970
	Night Shift (r)
Gray Matter	*Cavalier*, October 1973
	Night Shift (r)
The Green Mile	Serialized Novel
	Omnibus Novel (v)
The Hardcase Speaks	*Contraband*, 1 December 1971
Harrison State Park '68	*Ubris*, Fall 1968
Harvey's Dream	*The New Yorker*, 30 June 2003
	Just After Sunset (r)
Hearts in Atlantis	*Hearts in Atlantis*
Heavenly Shades of Night Are Falling	*Hearts in Atlantis*
Here There Be Tygers	*Ubris*, Spring 1968
	Skeleton Crew (v)
Heroes for Hope Starring the X-Men	*Heroes for Hope Starring the X-Men*, #1
Home Delivery	*The Book of the Dead*
	Nightmares and Dreamscapes (n)
The Hotel at the End of the Road	*People, Places and Things*
The House on Maple Street	*Nightmares and Dreamscapes*
I Am the Doorway	*Cavalier*, March 1971
	Night Shift (r)
I Hate Mondays	Unpublished Short Story

I Know What You Need	*Cosmopolitan,* September 1976
	Night Shift (v)
	Night Shift Screenplay (n)
Insomnia	Novel
In the Deathroom	*Blood and Smoke*
	Secret Windows: Essays and Fiction on the Craft of Writing (v)
	Everything's Eventual (v)
In the key-chords of dawn	*Onan,* 1971
It	Novel
It Grows on You	*Marshroots,* Fall 1973
	Weird Tales, Summer 1991 (v)
	Whispers, July 1982 (n)
	Nightmares and Dreamscapes (n)
I've Got to Get Away	*People, Places and Things*
I Was a Teenage Grave Robber	*Comics Review,* 1965
As *In a Half-World of Terror*	*Stories of Suspense,* 1966 (n)
The Jaunt	*The Twilight Zone Magazine,* June 1981
	Skeleton Crew (n)
Jerusalem's Lot	*Night Shift*
Jhonathan and the Witchs	*First Words: Earliest Writing from Favorite Contemporary Authors*
Jumper	*Dave's Rag,* Winter 1959-1960
	Secret Windows: Essays and Fiction on the Craft of Writing (r)
Keyholes	Unpublished Short Story
The Killer	*Famous Monsters of Filmland,* Spring 1994
Kingdom Hospital	Unpublished Screenplay
The King Family and the Wicked Witch	*Flint,* 25 August 1977
The Langoliers	*Four Past Midnight*
The Last Rung on the Ladder	*Night Shift*
The Lawnmower Man	*Cavalier,* May 1975
	Night Shift (v)
	Bizarre Adventures, October 1981 (n)
The Ledge	*Penthouse,* July 1976
	Night Shift (v)
	Cat's Eye Screenplay (n)
The Leprechaun	Unpublished Novel
The Library Policeman	*Four Past Midnight*
The Little Green God of Agony	*A Book of Horrors*
The Little Sisters of Eluria	*Legends: Short Novels by the Masters of*

	Modern Fantasy
	Everything's Eventual (v)
Lisey and Amanda	
(Everything the Same)	*Cell*, 2006
	Lisey's Story, 2006 (v)
Lisey and the Madman	*McSweeney's Enchanting Chamber of Astonishing Stories*
	Lisey's Story, 2006 (v)
Lisey's Story	Novel
The Lonesome Death of Jordy Verrill	
	Creepshow Screenplay
	Creepshow (n)
The Long Walk	Novel
Low Men in Yellow Coats	*Hearts in Atlantis*
	Family Circle (v)
L T's Theory of Pets	*Six Stories*
	Everything's Eventual (v)
The Luckey Quarter	*USA Weekend*, 30 June – 2 July 1995
	Six Stories (n)
	Everything's Eventual (r)
Lunch at the Gotham Café	*Dark Love*
	Six Stories (n)
	Blood and Smoke (r)
	Everything's Eventual (v)
The Man in the Black Suit	*The New Yorker*, 31 October 1994
	Six Stories (v)
	Everything's Eventual (v)
The Man Who Loved Flowers	*Gallery*, August 1977
	Night Shift (v)
The Man Who Would	
Not Shake Hands	*Shadows 4*
	Skeleton Crew (n)
Man With A Belly	*Cavalier*, December 1978
The Mangler	*Cavalier*, December 1972
	Night Shift (v)
Maximum Overdrive	Unpublished Screenplay
Memory	*Tin House*, Summer 2006
	Duma Key (v)
Mile 81	e-book
Misery	Novel
The Mist	*Dark Forces*
	Skeleton Crew (n)

Mobius	Unpublished Short Story
Molly	Unpublished Screenplay
The Monkey	*Gallery*, November 1980
	Skeleton Crew (n)
The Monster in the Closet	*Ladies Home Journal*, October 1981 (v)
	Cujo
Morality	*Esquire*, July 2009
	Blockade Billy
Morning Deliveries (Milkman #1)	*Skeleton Crew*
Mostly Old Men	*Tin House*, Summer 2009
Movie Show	Unpublished Story
The Moving Finger	*The Magazine of Fantasy and Science Fiction*, December 1990
	Nightmares and Dreamscapes (n)
Mrs. Todd's Shortcut	*Redbook*
	Skeleton Crew (v)
Muffe	Unpublished Story
	The Stephen King Illustrated Companion
Mute	*Playboy*, December 2007
	Just After Sunset (r)
My Pretty Pony	Limited/Trade Novella
	Nightmares and Dreamscapes (n)
N	*Just After Sunset* (r)
Needful Things	Novel
Never Look Behind You	*People, Places and Things*
The New Lieutenant's Rap	Limited Edition Chapbook
The New York Times at Special Bargain Rates	*The Magazine of Fantasy & Science Fiction*, October/November 2008
	Just After Sunset (r)
The Night Flier	*Prime Evil: New Stories by the Masters of Modern Fiction*
	Nightmares and Dreamscapes (n)
The Night of the Tiger	*The Magazine of Fantasy and Science Fiction*, February 1978
Night Shift	Unpublished Screenplay
Night Surf	*Ubris*, Spring 1969
	Cavalier, August 1974 (n)
	Night Shift (v)
1922	*Full Dark, No Stars*
Nona	*Shadows*
	Skeleton Crew (n)

The Old Dude's Ticker	Necon XX Commemorative Volume
One for the Road	Maine, March/April 1977
	Night Shift (v)
As Return to 'Salem's Lot	Vampire Omnibus (v)
The Other Side of the Fog	People, Places and Things
Paranoid: A Chant	Skeleton Crew
Pet Sematary	Novel
	Unpublished Screenplay (n)
The Plant	Incomplete Novel in Three Parts
	Incomplete Novel in Six Parts (n)
Popsy	Masques II
	Nightmares and Dreamscapes (n)
The Pulse	www.amazon.com
	Cell (n)
Premium Harmony	The New Yorker, 9 November 2009
Quitters, Inc.	Night Shift
	Cat's Eye Screenplay (n)
The Raft	Gallery, November 1982
	Skeleton Crew (v)
Rage	Novel
Rainy Season	Midnight Graffiti, Spring 1989
	Nightmares and Dreamscapes (n)
The Reach	Skeleton Crew
The Reaper's Image	Startling Mystery Stories, Spring 1969
	Skeleton Crew (v)
The Regulators	Novel
The Reploids	Unpublished Novel
The Reploids	Night Visions 5
Rest Stop	Esquire, December 2003
	Just After Sunset (r)
The Return of Timmy Baterman	Satyricon II Program Book
	Pet Sematary (v)
The Revelations of 'Becka Paulson	Rolling Stone, 19 July/2 August 1984
	Skeleton Crew (Limited) (r)
	The Tommyknockers (n)
The Revenge of Lard Ass Hogan	Maine Review, July 1975
	The Body (n)
Riding the Bullet	Electronic Book
	Everything's Eventual (r)
Rita Hayworth and Shawshank Redemption	Different Seasons

The Road Virus Heads North	*999*
	Everything's Eventual (n)
Roadwork	Novel
Rose Madder	Novel
Rose Red	Unpublished Screenplay
The Running Man	Novel
Rush Call	*Dave's Rag*, Winter 1959-1960
	Secret Windows: Essays and Fiction on the Craft of Writing (r)
'Salem's Lot	Novel
	Novel (v) *Centipede Press edition*
Secret Window, Secret Garden	*Four Past Midnight*
The Shining	Novel
	Unpublished Movie Screenplay (n)
	Unpublished Mini-Series Screenplay (n)
The Shotgunners	Unpublished Screenplay
Silence	*Moth*, 1970
Silver Bullet	Screenplay
Skybar	*The Do-It-Yourself Bestseller – A Workbook*
Slade	*The Maine Summer Campus*, 1970
Sleepwalkers	Unpublished Screenplay
Sneakers	*Night Visions 5*
	Nightmares and Dreamscapes (n)
Something to Tide You Over	*Creepshow* Screenplay
	Creepshow (n)
Something Wicked This Way Comes	Unpublished Screenplay
Sometimes They Come Back	*Cavalier*, March 1974
	Night Shift (v)
Sorry, Right Number	Unpublished Shooting Script
	Nightmares and Dreamscapes (n)
Squad D	Unpublished Short Story
The Stand	Original Novel
	Original Novel (v)
	Complete and Uncut Novel (n)
	Unpublished Movie Screenplay (n)
	Unpublished Mini-Series Screenplay (n)
The Star Invaders	Unpublished Short Story
Stationary Bike	*Borderlands 5*
	Just After Sunset (r)
Storm of the Century	Screenplay
The Stranger	*People, Places and Things*

Strawberry Spring	*Ubris*, Fall 1968
	Cavalier, November 1975 (n)
	Night Shift (r)
Night Shift	Screenplay (n)
Stud City	*Ubris*, Fall 1969
	The Body (n)
Suffer the Little Children	*Cavalier*, February 1972
	Nightmares and Dreamscapes (n)
The Sun Dog	*Four Past Midnight*
Survivor Type	*Terrors*
	Skeleton Crew (v)
Sword in the Darkness	Unpublished Novel
The Tale of Gray Dick	*Timothy McSweeney's Quarterly Concern*, 25 February 2003
	The Dark Tower V: Wolves of the Calla (v)
The Talisman	Novel
The Ten O'Clock People	*Nightmares and Dreamscapes*
That Feeling, You Can Only Say What It Is In French	*The New Yorker*, 22/29 June 1998
	Everything's Eventual (v)
They're Creeping Up on You	*Creepshow* Screenplay
	Creepshow (n)
The Thing at the Bottom of the Well	*People, Places and Things*
The Things They Left Behind	*Transgressions*
	Just After Sunset (r)
Thinner	Novel
Throttle	*He Is Legend: An Anthology Celebrating Richard Matheson*
Tommy	*Playboy*, March 2010
The Tommyknockers	Novel
Trucks	*Cavalier*, June 1973
	Night Shift (v)
22/11/63	Novel
Umney's Last Case	*Nightmares and Dreamscapes*
Uncle Otto's Truck	*Yankee*, October 1983
	Skeleton Crew (n)
Under the Dome	Novel
Under the Weather	*Full Dark, No Stars* (paperback only)
Untitled (The Huffman Story)	Unpublished Novel
Untitled (She Has Gone to Sleep While)	*Contraband*, 31 October 1971

Untitled Screenplay (Radio Station)	Unpublished Screenplay
Ur	www.amazon.com, 12 February 2009
A Very Tight Place	McSweeney's Quarterly Concern, May 2008
The Wedding Gig	Ellery Queen's Mystery Magazine, December 1980
	Skeleton Crew (n)
Weeds	Cavalier, May 1976
What Tricks Your Eye	Unpublished Story
Why We're in Vietnam	Hearts in Atlantis
Willa	Playboy, December 2006
Wimsey	Unpublished Novel
The Wind Through the Keyhole	Novel
The Woman in the Room	Night Shift
Woman with Child	Contraband, 31 October 1971
The Word Processor	Playboy, January 1983
Word Processor of the Gods	Skeleton Crew
You Know They Got a Hell of a Band	Shock Rock
	Nightmares and Dreamscapes (n)

Non Fiction

King's contribution to non-fiction is often overlooked due to his huge output of fiction. However, he has actually been responsible for over 800 separate pieces of non-fiction, ranging from entire books to short articles, reviews and the like.

The most extensive review of these ever compiled (including even such minor items as letters to the editor) appears in *Stephen King: The Non-Fiction* by Rocky Wood and Justin Brooks (Cemetery Dance, 2009). The authors spent five years compiling this reference work, with the assistance of many of the leading King researchers, collectors and 'super-collectors'; and access to the Restricted Non-Fiction Works in King's papers at the Raymond H Fogler Library of the University of Maine, Orono.

Covering all King's published and known unpublished works from 1959 through late 2006, *Stephen King: The Non-Fiction* revealed *for the first time* dozens of pieces of non-fiction and their appearances that were previously unknown to King researchers.

Acknowledgements

The author wishes to thank the following for their assistance.

David Rawsthorne and Norma Blackburn, who worked with me on earlier editions of this book.

Marsha DeFilippo at Stephen King's office for her friendship, time, material provided and continuing gracious assistance.

Stephen King for his permission to read the Restricted materials at the Fogler Library; for his assistance in answering a raft of obscure questions during the compilation of the Fourth Edition of this book; and, of course, for his stories.

Betsy Beattie, Elaine Smith and Richard Hollinger at the Special Collections Unit of the Raymond H Fogler Library of the University of Maine at Orono for their assistance during my three week 'camping trip' at their wonderful resource.

Stu Tinker for his help, advice and hospitality.

The additional assistance in gathering materials and helping with corrections provided by Tyson Blue, Stephen Spignesi, Michael Collings, Bev Vincent, Kerry Johnson, Bob Jackson, Chris Cavalier, C.S. O'Brien, Justin Brooks, Wendy Bousfield and Matthias Belz is greatly appreciated.

Dave Hinchberger of the Overlook Connection for his friendship, and support in publishing the Fourth Edition of this book, bringing it back into physical print. Yo, Dave!

About The Author

Rocky Wood travelled to Bangor, Maine in November and December 2002 where he spent three weeks reading the Stephen King archives at the Special Collections Unit at the Fogler Library of the University of Maine at Orono. King personally gave written permission to view the 'Restricted' materials lodged at the Library.

As a result of that work, he compiled *The Complete Guide to the Works of Stephen King* with David Rawsthorne and Norma Blackburn. The first edition was released in May 2003; a second, revised edition in November 2003 and in a Third Edition in November 2004.

Rocky has been an avid King reader since 1977 and he has undertaken five research trips to Maine. He is the co-author of three other major King works – *The Complete Guide to the Works of Stephen King* (2003; 2004); *Stephen King: The Non-Fiction* (2009); and *Stephen King: A Literary Companion* (2011). He received the Horror Writers Association's Bram Stoker Award nomination for Superior Achievement in Non-Fiction for *Stephen King: Uncollected, Unpublished*; and for *Stephen King: The Non-Fiction*.

He has spoken at numerous conventions about King, including the SKEMER Con in Estes Park, Colorado (2003); Continuum 3 (2005) and Continuum 4 (2006) in Melbourne, Australia; Conflux 3 in Canberra, Australia (2006); the 2nd Annual Stephen King Dollar Baby Festival in Bangor, Maine (2005); the World Horror Convention in Salt Lake City (2008) and Austin, Texas (2011); the World Science Fiction Convention in Melbourne (2010) and the Horror Writers Association Bram Stoker Weekend in Long Island, New York (2011). He has published non-fiction worldwide for thirty years; and is recognized as one of the world's leading experts on King's work.

His first published fiction was the graphic novel, *Horrors! Great Stories of Fear and Their Creators* (McFarland, 2010), which was nominated for a Black Quill Award and the Aurealis Award, is illustrated by the Maine artist, Glenn Chadbourne. His second graphic novel, *Witch Hunts: A Graphic History of the Burning Times,* illustrated by Greg Chapman, is a collaboration with Bram Stoker Award winning horror writer Lisa Morton.

A New Zealander, Rocky lives in Melbourne, Australia. He is an avid Rugby Union, Cricket, Association Football (Soccer) and Boston Red Sox baseball fan. A proud member of the Horror Writers Association, he has served on their Board since 2008 and was elected President in 2010. He is also a Member of the Australian Horror Writers Association.

www.ingramcontent.com/pod-product-compliance
Lightning Source LLC
Chambersburg PA
CBHW060350190426
43201CB00044B/1927